STORY OF NATIONS

STORY OF NATIONS

BY

LESTER B. ROGERS

DEAN OF THE SCHOOL OF EDUCATION
UNIVERSITY OF SOUTHERN CALIFORNIA

FAY ADAMS

ASSOCIATE PROFESSOR OF EDUCATION
UNIVERSITY OF SOUTHERN CALIFORNIA

WALKER BROWN

PRINCIPAL, ALEXANDER HAMILTON
HIGH SCHOOL, LOS ANGELES

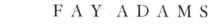

HENRY HOLT AND COMPANY · NEW YORK

PREFACE

First published in 1934, *Story of Nations* brought a new note into the
teaching of world history. It was rewarded by immense and widespread use.
Now, a decade later, the authors present *Story of Nations* as a completely
rewritten book. They have left nothing undone to make it a vivid and understandable interpretation of the modern world for high-school pupils. They
have not, however, surrendered any of the qualities which made the original
edition successful.

The teaching of world history in secondary schools has changed greatly in
the last quarter-century. The change consisted mainly in boiling down a two-
year course in ancient, medieval, and modern European history into a survey
of civilization suitable for a one-year course. In the last few years this course
itself has undergone great changes. These recent changes relate to content
and emphasis. World history is no longer concerned with Europe alone.
Lives in Europe, in Asia, in Africa, in Australia, and in all the Americas have
become inextricably interlaced. The interdependence of all peoples in all nations is now obvious. World history has had to become a history of the world.
Recognizing the profound truth that the roots of the present lie deep in the
past, emphasizing the contributions of unique cultural groups to the rise of
civilization, and more than ever stressing the importance of geographic controls upon the world's variegated life, the authors of *Story of Nations* have
recast their book in the realistic mold of the Nineteen Forties. This is the
world in which our students now live. Their future and the freedom of mankind must be based on their realistic understanding of this world — on their
understanding of how it came about, the condition it is in, and what it might
become.

A leading feature of this revision is its extensive use of geography — not
the casual mention of multitudinous place names or the cataloguing of geographic data, but the use of geography as an integral part of every major section
of the book to show the influence of terrain, climate, and neighbors upon the
development of any people. Each dominant culture is shown in its geographic
setting. The story of each nation opens with a picture of the " lay of the land,"
and a description of the ways in which geography has influenced the life of
the people.

Those who have used *Story of Nations* in some earlier edition will note
in this revision a new Part Seventeen describing the belt of Buffer States extending from Finland to Turkey. Some knowledge of these states, more than
a dozen of them, is necessary to an understanding of Europe's recurring conflicts. You will note, too, in the new Part Twenty-one, a much fuller treatment of the Americas than was given in earlier editions. Americans are inter-

ested as never before in their neighbors in all the Americas. It is right that this interest should be strong, and that the schools should foster it. Unlike the other Parts which deal with single nations, these two Parts, which deal with a number of nations and their complex stories, require the survey type of treatment.

Parts One through Nine, as in former editions, treat of major cultures and nations of the ancient and medieval world. Parts Ten through Twenty-one deal with modern nations. (This is one textbook, by the way, wherein a pupil may read the story of a modern nation without turning to the index, making notes of page references, and then reading bits of that nation's history scattered here and there throughout the book. In using many world history textbooks, the pupil must unscramble what the authors have so laboriously scrambled.) In Parts Ten to Twenty-one, the story of each modern nation has been brought down to the late Nineteen Thirties, with sufficient political, economic, and social detail to insure a clear understanding of each nation. Then in the final section of the book, Part Twenty-two, the threads of these separate national stories are woven together into one international story. Here is the story of the period from World War I to World War II. The authors have emphasized geographic controls, the growth of industrialism, the development of intense nationalism, and the extension of nationalistic viewpoints into imperialistic adventurings, the constant though uneven growth of democracy throughout the world, the quest for economic security by the control of resources and markets, and the incessant conflicts among various political ideologies. So, the world conflicts of our time are presented to the student as a unitary problem beginning before World War I, extending through that war and its inadequate peace, through a period of international depression, into ineffectual attempts at appeasement of aggressor nations, and eventually into World War II. The pathways to peace offer problems difficult to handle. The authors of *Story of Nations,* without indulging in undue pessimism or unwarranted optimism, have tried simply to be realistic in sketching such proposals as are likely to become part of any enduring program of peace among the nations. They have continually underscored the fact that whatever happens anywhere in the world, whether in our own country or in some other country, is important to everyone in the world. The interdependence of nations, in short, is a central theme of this revised edition of *Story of Nations.*

In selecting content materials, the authors have in this as in former editions been particularly careful not to be encyclopedic. That type of content and the kind of writing that goes with it have been the bane of confused students and overworked instructors in many history courses, especially in the course that must cover the vast field of the world's history. The principle of exclusion the authors have employed in this revision is the same as that employed in previous editions: to exclude everything which does not shed strong light on the story being told. It has taken courage to follow this principle, for all history teachers, the authors included, have their own sacred cows in the pastures of academic learning. Yet there is little doubt that the greatest help we can give to mid-adolescents, as they try to understand their world, is to present a limited number of major topics surrounded by a host of associative details. This practice in the organization of materials promotes learning and fixes recall as fragmentary mention of men and movements, in a sentence or even a few paragraphs, cannot do.

In style of writing, *Story of Nations* is direct, simple, and friendly. Long, involved sentences and paragraphs have been avoided. The content of world history is difficult enough without being encumbered with technical terminology. In vocabulary difficulty and diversity, *Story of Nations* is suited to the average pupil in the early years of high school. It is considerably less difficult than the average textbook in history at its level, rather more difficult, perhaps, than the average daily newspaper. *Story of Nations* offers ample opportunity for vocabulary growth and enrichment on the pupil's part without requiring much translation on the teacher's part.

In *Story of Nations* the authors have not attempted a critical analysis of political and social developments, nor have they discussed theories of civilization and moot issues still awaiting historical research. The grade level for which this book is intended, as well as the limitations of space and time, make that kind of treatment unreasonable. *Story of Nations* is a story of our world, written for high-school students. But there is plenty of opportunity in these several narratives for the students to see the play of historical cause and effect. And neither accuracy of fact nor reliability of interpretation has been sacrificed for the sake of simplicity.

The authors must acknowledge their indebtedness to many in making this revision. They are grateful to the teachers and students in various parts of the country who have used previous editions and have been kind enough not only to express their appreciation but also to suggest ways in which the book could be improved. They are also indebted to several specialists for invaluable aid in the rewriting of unusually difficult sections.

The maps and illustrations for this *Story of Nations* are the product of many artists. To these also the authors are indebted. Liam Dunne, map maker, whose work for *Fortune, Newsweek,* and the War Department has won him a reputation for vivid and accurate map making, deserves a special word of appreciation. His maps, which appear at the opening of each Part, are major aids to learning. The authors are grateful also to John C. Wonsetler, artist, and Adelaide H. Wonsetler. Mr. Wonsetler in his drawings has brought to life peoples of earlier civilizations. Mrs. Wonsetler has done vast research to assure accuracy in the details of these historical drawings.

L. B. R.
F. G. A.
W. B.

Los Angeles
November, 1944

Maps, Time Lines, and Charts

MAPS

TIME LINES

CHARTS

CONTENTS

ix

Part Four
THE HEBREWS AND THE PHOENICIANS MADE NEW CONTRIBUTIONS TO WORLD PROGRESS

Part Five
LEARNING, ART, AND CITIZENSHIP BROUGHT GLORY TO GREECE

Part Six
THE ROMANS ORGANIZED A VAST EMPIRE

CONTENTS

Part Twelve

THE NETHERLANDS AND BELGIUM WERE WRESTED FROM RUTHLESS FOES AND A HUNGRY SEA

Part Thirteen

SPAIN AND PORTUGAL BECAME GREAT POWERS, THEN GAVE WAY TO OTHER NATIONS

Part Fourteen

THE LEADERS OF ITALY SOUGHT THE GRANDEUR THAT WAS ROME

Part Eighteen

THE PEOPLES OF RUSSIA AWAKENED TO THE POSSIBILITIES OF THEIR VAST LAND

Part Nineteen

ANCIENT CHINA IS STRUGGLING TO BECOME A MODERN NATION

Part Twenty

JAPAN BECAME A WORLD POWER AND SET OUT TO DOMINATE THE ORIENT

Part Twenty-one

THE AMERICAN NATIONS, THEIR WELFARE, AND THEIR DESTINIES ARE CLOSELY INTERWOVEN

Part Twenty-two

DEVASTATING WARS HAVE MADE IT NECESSARY TO FACE WORLD PROBLEMS REALISTICALLY

INTRODUCTION

"The Roots of the Present Are Deep in the Past"

Considerable water has gone down the stream of time since your grand-parents were the same age that you are now. Automobiles were not common until after 1915. Electric lights and telephones were not common until well into the present century. Soap operas, name-band swing sessions, the news broadcasts were unknown to your parents and grandparents when they were of high-school age. There were no such things until about 1920. And thirty years ago anyone who said the time was coming when you could fly across the continent in seven hours would have been considered a wild-eyed dreamer. They called airplanes "flying machines" in those days.

Suppose instead of dropping back a mere thirty or fifty years we go back five hundred years, to the early 1400's. North and South America had not been discovered. Only the native American Indians were here. In Europe we would find no printed books, though there were some in China. We would find only a few cathedrals partly built in a few of Europe's larger cities such as Paris, Rome, and London. And five hundred years ago the population of such cities was far smaller than it is today.

But despite our science and inventions, life in the 1400's was in many ways much as it is today. People tilled fields and worked at trades. They fought with those they believed to be their enemies. People laughed, wept, danced, worked, and fell in love as people do today. Most of these statements would be as true for 1400 B.C. (before Christ) as they are for A.D. 1400 (from the Latin *Anno Domini,* "In the Year of Our Lord"), or as they are true today. One of the simple truths of history is that life goes on, though the *form* of living changes. This change is called *development.*

We must understand, however, that what happens depends upon what came before. No master hand lowers the curtain on one play and raises it in a new age on an entirely different drama. The drama of the story of mankind is one long play with many scenes and many acts. What happens in the last act depends on what happened in the first act. In other words, *the roots of the present are deep in the past.* Modern radio and television have grown out of earlier experience with the wireless and the telegraph. Modern democratic government has grown out of earlier experiences with self-government in England, and, far earlier, in ancient Greece. The long history of mankind is like the life of a tree whose trunk grows and throws out limbs that may live or die. Yet the tree grows, its annual rings marking its age. Far above, the smallest leaf bursts forth and grows. But it is a part of the tree and receives its life from the roots deep in the earth below. Therefore, to understand how complex life is in today's world and why it is so, we require a knowledge of the past.

Knowledge must be learned. Knowledge, unlike the shape of your nose or the color of your eyes, is not inherited. If one is to become intelligent about the world in which he lives, he must grow in knowledge. Such growth requires learning, and, in turn, learning requires effort. A person cannot become educated unless he is willing to apply his mind. Now at the beginning of a new year of high school, you are launched on a course in world history. No matter what you have heard about history, it does not need to be dull. In fact, if you like people and are interested in what people are doing, you should like this book. If you are interested in growing in knowledge and coming to understand the world in which you live, this book will be of value to you.

Story of Nations was written for *you* — with *you* in mind in every paragraph and line. It was not written for college students or for professors; it was not written for children or adults. *Story of Nations* has been written as a guidebook for high-school boys and girls who want to grow in knowledge and understanding about the world in which they live.

There are not many students today who would say, "The world and its people are nothing to me. I live at Crabapple Crossroads [or on Thirty-third Street] and that's all I'm interested in." No, indeed, there are not many such students now. Too much has happened recently, not only within the last few years but within the last twenty-five or fifty years. The world, its people, and its affairs have come to touch all of us. Your father or your uncle, for historical reasons, may wear the rainbow-colored service ribbon of World War I. Your brother or sister may have been in Europe or the Orient. The service flag of your school is probably studded with stars for boys, and for girls too, who have served in foreign countries. The world became very important to them. It took them away from Crabapple Crossroads and Thirty-third Street, and taught them that we live in one world where nations are neighbors, good or bad. These are excellent reasons why Americans should understand the world.

The historical approach is a basis for understanding. To understand a thing, one must really know how it came about. That is the historical approach. There is a good old expression that gives the idea: "How do you get that way?" It is the design of *Story of Nations* to answer that question: to answer it about peoples, about nations, and about ideas such as democracy and dictatorship.

In employing the historical approach, *Story of Nations* uses the method of the storyteller — the narrative style. To follow the trail of civilization from the dawn of intelligence in the mind of primitive man to the present accomplishments of mankind, is nothing less than high adventure. No fiction can compare with the truth of how man has built what we know as the modern world.

A new measure of distance makes our world smaller. Today, more than ever, it will pay us to understand our world. The air industry reminds us that it is but fifty hours from the nearest airport to any spot in the world. The constant improvement in planes and the development of better flying routes may shorten that schedule. Speed in the air has conquered distance. No longer does it take a week to travel from Mount Vernon to Philadelphia, as it did in the days of George Washington. Modern speed of travel and communication has, in a sense, made the world smaller. Whether in war or in peace, we must understand the significance of this new, smaller world in which distance must be measured in flying hours, not solely in miles. Unless we do understand it, we are unprepared to live in it.

More important than ever before are the *ideas* that men hold. From ideas come the actions of men and therefore of nations. At one time, perhaps, it was of not great concern to Crabapple Crossroads or Thirty-third Street what might be taking place in far-off China, or how Germany was being ruled. But today, whether we like it or not, we must understand world conditions, for they are bound to affect us. We must know how it happens that we believe in democracy, with its respect for the individual person, while in another country people believe that it is the state, not the individual, that counts. Thus if we are to live successfully in the United States, which is so much a part of the world, we must understand how conditions in the rest of the world have come about. The purpose of *Story of Nations* is to help you to find out how things have come about, and thus enable you to understand them.

A definite pattern of development begins with the geographic setting. As you study *Story of Nations,* you will notice that each story of a nation or culture follows a definite pattern of development. Always we begin with the land and the sea, with the natural geographic setting of the story. In this world people do not live in a vacuum. They live on land masses with mountains, valleys, lakes, rivers. Or they live on islands and sail the seas. The life of man is always affected by where he dwells. "The lay of the land" determines how he lives, and even what he thinks. Time and again, in *Story of Nations,* we shall see how geography has affected the development of mankind. Make good use of the many different kinds of maps which you will find in this book. They are as much a part of the text as the words you read. Some maps show how many of the main physical features of a region have helped to determine the boundaries of France, Spain, Italy, Great Britain, and other countries. You will also find some interesting illustrated or picture maps, such as the one of Great Britain on page 394, or that of Russia on page 640, on which the artist has made small drawings showing landmarks and the characteristic activities of a particular region. At the end of the book you will find colored maps of Africa, of Europe, and of the world in 1939. In reading *Story of Nations,* you should continually ask yourself, " Where did this part of the story take place, and what part did geography play ? " Look to both the written material and the maps for the answers.

" Story of Nations " is necessarily selective. Imagine a globe of the world, or if you have access to one, actually turn it slowly while scanning it. In rotation there are the Americas, Africa, Europe, Asia, Australia, and the myriad islands of the Pacific. Even though the world has been reduced by the decreasing of time-distance by flight, it still is a major problem to understand all the peoples of the earth. Within one book it would obviously not be possible to tell the stories of all the nations or groups, or even the complete story of any one great people.

Story of Nations employs the method of careful selection. Only large national groups are discussed in detail, and there are included only those events and names which are needed to show how our modern world came into being. But plenty of details are given about these major peoples and events, for that is how the picture becomes clear, so clear that you can remember it. In world history it has become necessary to pass over many events in order to remember the more important ones. That is why *Story of Nations* is highly selective.

After learning the strange story of early man and his remarkable discoveries, you will read of the contributions of the ancient peoples to civilization: how the contributions of the Egyptians, the peoples of the Tigris-Euphrates valley, the Hebrews, the Phoenicians, and the Greeks were drawn together by the Romans who passed them on to the peoples of Western Europe. You will read how life and learning slowed down in the Middle Ages only to awake again. Then you will read the story of the development of modern nations of Europe. Ancient China and ambitious Japan represent the Orient, while the story of India is treated as part of the British Empire. A complete Part on the Americas will help you to appreciate our neighbors, the other Americans. And finally, you will read of this changing modern world.

In the story of the modern world you will read less about separate nations and more about the problems of international relations. An exciting and sorry tale it is. Yet it is one that we must understand if our own democratic way of life is to continue for long. It is a record of jealousies and war, of clashes of ideas about human rights and kinds of government, and of the culmination of all these things in World War I and World War II. But the story is not all sordid. We shall see the constant light of democracy and the love of liberty in the heart of man; we shall observe the efforts of the peacemakers and their reasonable hopes for the future; and we shall mark the tremendous advances made by modern man in science, education, and the art of living.

That is the full bill of fare in *Story of Nations* — a year of education in the ways of the world for American high-school students who would like to understand the world in which they live.

Learning how to study is a part of your education. Many useful aids to study are included in *Story of Nations*. The good student knows the value of effective ways of study; the weak student needs them particularly. So every high-school student beginning this course should clearly understand how *Story of Nations* is planned to make his study effective.

1. *Introduction to each major Part.* At the beginning of each major Part of *Story of Nations* you will find (a) a symbolic picture or drawing; (b) the Part table of contents; (c) a map showing the particular region being discussed; and (d) an orientation globe to show you where the region is in the world, and what area it covers. For example, turn to page 321, on which the story of the British Empire begins, and you will see what we mean. Here is the way to use these study aids. First examine the drawing on page 321 to see if you can recognize anything in it, even without having read the story. Then scan the list of chapters. It will give you a quick impression of what this Part of the book is about. Now, on the next page, study the map for a moment. Finally, on the right-hand page, read the special introduction — a kind of map study. As you read on, pay particular attention to the paragraph headings which are printed in bold-face type. These tell in a few words what is being described in the paragraphs. They are so phrased that they are easy to remember, and serve especially well when you are looking back over the chapter for review.

2. *Illustrated Time Lines.* The illustrated or graphic time lines are a special feature of *Story of Nations*. They are included not merely as decoration, but as a part of the study material in the text. One of the most difficult things in the study of history is a sense of time — when certain things happened in relation to other things. This sense of time is sometimes called *historical perspective*. It is a hard thing to achieve because it depends so much on memory and imagination. Here is where time lines help.

A time line is not simply a list of dates, events, or names, but is something like a parade or procession. In this procession the thing you want to remember stands in line, with something coming before and after it. By looking at the whole time line, you can tell where the procession is headed and how long it has been going by. Time lines show the parade of events and characters in the story of a certain nation or people. Turn to pages 336–337 to see the time line for the British Commonwealth. Then turn to pages 412–413. Here, in Part Eleven, you see the time line in Part Ten repeated, and just above it, the new time line for Part Eleven. The succeeding Part repeats the time lines that you have already seen, and puts above them the time line for the new Part you are reading.

Then there is the master chart of time lines which you will find inserted at the back of the book. There are two of these time lines. One shows the long streams of world history, and the other shows five centuries in Europe and the Americas. These charts show historical time in cross section. When you are studying the life of one people, you should refer to these charts frequently to see what other peoples were doing at the same time. These Part and master time lines will help you gain that sense of time which is so necessary in the study of world history.

3. *The Shifting Pattern of Nations.* At the back of the book (pages 772–773) you will find a chart called *The Shifting Pattern of Nations.* It gives considerable information about the main modern nations or world powers. It can be used for a review of the conditions found in modern nations. But things in this age change rapidly. What was true just yesterday may not be true today or tomorrow. You will notice the date at the top of the chart. The whole class might make an enlarged chart (for the classroom), such as this one, and keep it up-to-date throughout the course.

4. *Part Summaries and Self-Tests.* At the end of each major Part of *Story of Nations* you will find a summary which will give you important points of the Part you have just read. It will help you to recall the highlights of the story. Following the summary is a self-test. The good student always checks his own learning.

5. *Interesting Things to Do.* Also at the end of each major Part you will find a suggested list of things to do with what you have learned. While studying a Part, select an activity which interests you. The list is merely suggestive; you, your classmates, and your teacher may think of many other good learning activities. But if you would learn to the point of mastery, do something with your knowledge.

6. *Interesting Books to Read.* Only when your new knowledge leads to new interest does it become significant. As we learned from the Bible, " Unto him that hath shall be given." Therefore, at the end of each Part, you will find a list of interesting books to read. Included in these lists are historical books, historical novels, books and magazines of travel and adventure, and biographical stories of interesting men and women. You can enrich your learning by reading one or two titles from each of these Part lists as you progress through your study of world history.

7. *What Maps Tell You.* At the back of this book, beginning on page 810, is a brief discussion of maps. It tells what each of several kinds of maps can show you about the world or a part of it. Although it is not an easy subject to learn about, if you want to study maps this section will help you.

8. *Index*. The index of a book is a valuable aid to efficient study. An index is so called for the same reason that the finger you point with is called the index finger. The index of a book points to what you want to find. The index in *Story of Nations* has been specially constructed for study purposes. The student who has acquired the index habit has reached the Sherlock Holmes stage of learning: he can track down almost any bit of information he wants to find. Whether it be in social studies or in other subjects, you should form the habit of using indexes.

The index of *Story of Nations* contains another useful feature — the pronunciation of difficult names and words. The first time a difficult word appears in the text, you will find a respelling, immediately following it, in brackets. If you see the word a second time and cannot remember how to pronounce it, you can easily turn to the index and look up the word. The respelling has been repeated there. The respelling is by syllables which will always have the same sound. Accent marks are used to show what syllables to stress. Light and heavy accent marks indicate light and heavy stress. For example: Istanbul [ee′stahn bool′].

The apostrophe is used in respelling syllables containing a vowel which is not sounded, as the second *a* in American [uh mer′i k'n]. The apostrophe is used also in respelling the consonant combination *sm* [z'm].

If at any time you are uncertain about a pronunciation of a vowel or a diphthong, you can refer to this key.

a	*a* as in m*a*n	N	nasalized sound of vowel preceding the *n* [1]
ah	*a* as in *a*rm		
ai	*i* as in *i*ce	o	*o* as in *o*dd
aw	{ *au* as in fr*au*d	œ	*u* as in *u*rn
	o as in s*o*ft	oh	*o* as in *o*pen, *o*bey
ay	{ *a* as in pl*a*y, ch*a*otic	ou	*ou* as in *ou*t
	ai as in f*ai*r	u (*or* uh)	*u* as in *u*p
	ei as in v*ei*n	uh	*a* as in *a*bout
e (*or* eh)	*e* as in f*e*ll	yoo	*u* as in *u*se, *u*nited
ee	*e* as in *e*ve		
i	*i* as in *i*ll		

Make good use of the many aids to study which are a part of this book. If you do so, your course in world history will be easier and more interesting. At the same time, you will be gaining valuable knowledge of how this modern world came to be, and you will be learning skills that can be put to good use in facing many of the problems of your life today and tomorrow.

---

[1] There is no equivalent English sound. For exact pronunciation, consult a foreign language teacher; or perhaps some student in your class who has studied French will show you the correct pronunciation.

PART ONE

THE STORY OF EARLY MEN

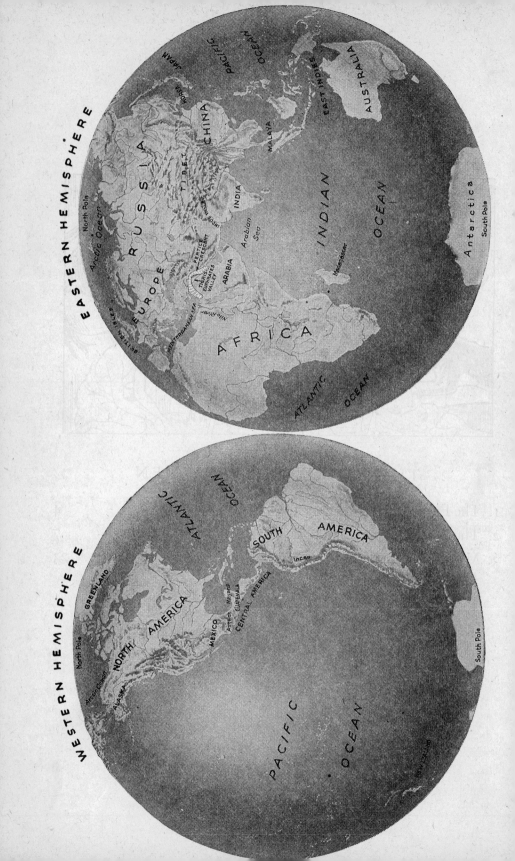

The Earth as the Home of Men

THE map on the opposite page shows the two hemispheres of the earth — the home of men. Have you ever wondered how long men have lived on earth, what the first people were like, and how they got along? In this first Part of *Story of Nations* you will read something about early men and how they worked and fought and made their homes. On the globe above, four pinpoints of light pick out the spots where the earliest remains of early men have been discovered. You will read more about these early men in the following pages.

Naturally, "The Story of Early Men" begins long before there were nations. On the map opposite, the artist has shown continents and oceans, and main rivers and mountain ranges. He has also labelled certain countries for you. You will read about early men in China, for example, though of course China as a modern nation did not exist then. As men gained skills and began to live in settled communities, the first great civilizations of the world came into being in certain favored locations. You can find these on the map too. Notice Mexico and Guatemala, the Nile Valley, the Fertile Crescent, and the Indus Valley, all homes of the first great civilizations built by men. Refer to this map often as you read "The Story of Early Men."

Chapter 1 ~ The Earth Before the Time of Man

The story of the earth extends deep into the past. No one really knows how old the earth is, but most scientists believe it may be about two billion years old. Some form of life, though not human life, has probably existed on earth for about one billion years, but again we cannot be sure. It is thought by some scientists that human beings have lived on earth about 1,000,000 years. Yet written records of man and his life go back only about five thousand years.

Turn to page 500 of this book and put your finger there to hold the place.

Let each one of the five hundred pages stand for two thousand years. Then, all the pages up to the place where you put your finger will stand for 1,000,000 years, or the length of time it is thought human beings have lived on earth. The last three of the five hundred pages will represent six thousand years. This is the length of time man has been civilized enough to write a record of his doings. Since it is now the 20th Century, the last page will stand for the time since the birth of Christ. You can figure for yourself what fraction of page 500 would

Courtesy Canadian Pacific Railway

A GLACIER IN THE CANADIAN ROCKIES

Glaciers lasted far beyond the glacial periods. This one is Athabasca Glacier, on the Columbia Icefields Highway, near Lake Louise, in the province of Alberta, Canada. You can see for yourself what these mysterious ancient fields of ice and snow were like.

represent the period in which the United States has been a nation.

There are historic and prehistoric times. In this story of mankind you should know the order in which things happened. To do this it will not be necessary to memorize a long list of dates. But when new peoples or new periods are studied, you will want to learn their proper place in the stream of history. Time lines such as the one across pages 38–39 will help you to picture the order in which things happened.

It is common for historians to divide the story of mankind into two parts. One is the *historic* period. The writers of history get their information about this period from the *written* records which have been left. Sometimes these evidences are in the form of books or scrolls; sometimes they are inscriptions on temple walls; and in some cases the writing has been done on little clay tab-

lets. These are but a few of the sources of information from which the facts of written history come. *Prehistoric* time is the name which the scientists and historians give to the long period before man set down his thoughts in writing, even though he may have built monuments, made drawings, and left other relics of his existence. Thus a written record is the beginning of historic times with any people.

The hand of time changes the surface of the earth. Millions of years ago the earth was a huge mass of liquid, gas, and flame. Gradually, over a period of many, many years, the earth cooled, and areas of land and sea appeared. It is likely that at one time all the land was a single mass, and that gradually the present continents were formed.

During these millions of years the earth has been in existence, many changes have occurred. Land masses

Photo by U. S. Forest Service

IMPRINTS OF A GLACIER

The grooves in this solid rock are the marks left by an ancient glacier in what is now Flathead National Forest, Montana. The marks have outlived the glacier that dug them as it planed and scraped its way to the south.

have been built up, torn apart, and weathered by nature. Scientists called *geologists* can tell us wonderful stories of the earth. They know, for example, that the earth has been made up of layers, called *strata* [stray'tuh]. If you have ever dug a deep hole you found that the topsoil came out easily. Beneath it, you found a layer of sand, clay, or other type of soil. And if you dug even deeper, you found still another kind of soil, or possibly rock. These layers of soil and rock extend far down into the earth. They have been deposited by nature over a period of many years. By digging into these strata, geologists find many things that tell us what the earth was like at the time each of the strata was being formed. The earth is thus a storybook for those who have learned to read its rocky pages.

Over a period of thousands of years, mighty forces have buckled the earth's strata and formed mountains and valleys. When such young mountains are formed they are rough and jagged in appearance — like our Rocky Mountains. Gradually the mountains get old, worn by nature's forces, like our Appalachian [ap'uh lay'chi'n] Mountains.

Land areas become old by the weathering of rain and wind and the wearing down of ever-flowing water. Sediment carried by water has built up vast plains of fertile soil. The water itself has flowed into the sea. The process is repeated when the water evaporates and is taken up into the clouds, only to fall again on the earth as rain.

Glaciers helped to mold the earth's surface. As the planer in the woodshop may cut off a fraction of an inch of wood each time the cutting tool passes over the board, huge masses of ice have planed off the surface of the earth. These great masses of ice, called *glaciers*

Three Lions

A YOUNG VOLCANO

In 1943 Parícutin [pah ree'koo teen] Volcano pushed its way up through a field in Mexico and came into active life. Sometimes its smoke has towered to a height of eight miles. Its lava covers the field in the foreground of this picture.

[glay'sherz], have flowed like rivers from the north. They have ground, scratched, dug out great valleys, and left a trail of polished boulders and gravel, or grooved rock like that pictured on page 5. Four times the ice covered most of North America and Europe. This period of glaciation is called the Glacial Age. The valleys and lakes of the British Isles, France, and Germany show many traces of the work of glaciers. Our Great Lakes were scooped out by the flow of ice. Perhaps you have seen evidences of the glaciers — deposits or valleys made by them — for at one time they covered much of the northern part of the United States.

No one knows why the ice appeared and disappeared four times. The climate changed; snow fell, and formed into ice.

From sheer weight it slid down from the north lands to engulf much of the land in the temperate zone. The Glacial Age lasted about a million years, and the last glacial period ended only about 25,000 years ago. Of course not all the glaciers melted away. We still have them in the polar regions; Greenland is largely covered by one; and we have small glaciers in the Alps, Andes, and Rockies, as shown in the picture on page 4. Will the great ice sheets come again? That, too, no one knows. But if the huge glaciers do return, it will not be in our time. Each one of these periods during which the ice came, the geologists call a glacial period. The times between, when the ice melted back and the weather became temperate again, are called interglacial periods.

The earth is still changing. We must not think that the earth has ceased changing. Most changes come about slowly, like the rising and falling of land masses. But we can still see some of them taking place. Islands rise and sink. New volcanoes still burst forth; the volcano shown in the illustration on page 6 erupted in a Mexican farmer's field. Earthquakes are not at all uncommon. There is a constant shifting and grinding of the earth's layers, sometimes violent and sometimes so gradual that man does not notice it. Tons of earth are moved by the wind, usually in almost invisible particles but sometimes in great dust storms. Gentle rains and destructive storms erode the land. The earth changes in many ways, and it is still changing all about us.

Chapter 2 ~ The Earth Became the Home of Man

Strange creatures lived in the Age of Reptiles. About five million years ago, before the Glacial Age, the greater land and sea masses were pretty much as they are now. (Remember that all time periods in prehistoric times are only rough approximations.) Many of the plants and animals were similar to some we see today. Man had not yet appeared. This was the Age of Reptiles, and the earth was inhabited by animals somewhat similar to, but larger than, our turtles, crocodiles, lizards, and snakes. Largest of all animals of that period were certain dinosaurs [dain'uh sawrz]. Some were about a hundred feet long and forty feet tall; others were short, heavy, and well armored.

The Age of Glaciers. Some scientists tell us that not long before the beginning of the Glacial Age the earliest forms of man had come into being. We do not know just what these men were like, because no actual remains of them have yet been found. But we do know they were present, because they left traces of their existence, sometimes shell mounds, sometimes simple tools, and even their bones.

Then came the time when the ocean currents which swept down from the north began to turn cold. It was the warning of the descending ice of the first glacial period. This was over a million years ago. Animal life was driven southward.

American Museum of Natural History

PREHISTORIC REPTILES

These creatures are one kind of dinosaur. Although one of them seems to be smiling, he would not have been a gentle reptile to meet.

The Piltdown Man made crude tools. By this time there were three kinds of prehistoric men who lived on the earth. The first of these is Piltdown [pilt′doun] Man, who probably lived a million years ago. The bone traces we have of him were found near Piltdown, in the county of Sussex, England. Workmen, digging for gravel on a river terrace, came upon the bones of a man. Not realizing the importance of their find, they carelessly scattered the bones. These men were not archæologists [ahr′kee ahl′uh jists], scientists who make a study of bones, tools, pottery, and other remains of early man. But later, archæologists did arrive on the scene. They found enough parts of the skull to be certain that traces of an early man had been found in Europe. We know very little about the Piltdown Man. It is thought that he probably did not live many years on earth.

The Piltdown Man knew how to make tools and use them. We find proof of this in the rough, chipped flints which were buried with his bones. Of course the tools were not very cleverly made, but it is quite certain that the flints had been chipped to fit the hand of man. These flints were used for scraping, boring, or possibly for throwing. Early man had to figure out how to make himself more powerful. He did this by inventing tools which could do more things than his bare hands could do. A fist hatchet such as you see on page 13 was really a milestone in the process of civilization.

Early man marked his progress by the tools he made. We could almost trace the development of man by the kind of tools that have been found. Scientists divide prehistoric men into periods or ages according to the tools which they used. The crudely shaped stones such as those made by the Piltdown Man give the name to the first of these periods. It is called the Old Stone Age. For thousands of years man made his implements by chipping them roughly into shapes which would fit his hand.

Another early man lived in Java. Far away in another part of the world lived another type of man of the first glacial period. This was Java [jah′vuh] Man. Java is a large island in the East Indies, which lies in the South Pacific between India and Australia. In 1891 a Dutch army doctor discovered there the top of a skull and a thigh bone in the gravels of an ancient river bed. These were the remains of the first Java Man. Just before the Japanese invaded the East Indies, in World War II, the skulls of three more Java Men were discovered. We now know a good deal about this kind of man. He had a small brain and a low forehead. He had a powerful body, but stood only about five feet tall. He did not stand as upright as we do, but was rather stooped. Java Man must have been capable of making stone tools, but none of his works have as yet been discovered.

Pekin Man also lived during the first glacial period. A third type of man who lived in the first glacial period was Pekin [pee′king′] Man. His remains were discovered in the late 1920's in a stone quarry near Peiping [pay′ping], or Pekin, China. The bones of well over a dozen Pekin Men have been found. This early man lived in caves. He looked very much like Java Man, except that he had a larger brain and was more upright in posture. Pekin Man made tools that were similar to those found with Piltdown Man.

The first interglacial period favored life. After a period of many years, the ice no longer came out of the north or

American Museum of Natural History

THE QUARRY OF THE "MONSTER"

The bones of the monster who died in this quarry show that he was something like a rhinoceros, with shoulders nearly thirty feet high. He lived probably from ten to fifteen million years ago.

Department of Interior Photo

NEVSKA GLACIER

This great glacier in Alaska, with its masses of snow and ice, has survived the glacial periods. Notice that its course is like that of a great sluggish stream.

gouged its way down the valleys of the Alps. This was about a million years ago. The days became warmer, even warmer than the climate in the United States today. The climate was about like that we now find in Mexico and on the coast of northern Africa. The first interglacial period, or the time between the disappearance of the first great ice sheets and the second coming of the ice, had begun. Plant and animal life flourished once again. This first interglacial period lasted only about 50,000 to 75,000 years.

Heidelberg Man lived during the first interglacial period. In 1907 the lower jaw and teeth of a man were found near Heidelberg [hai'd'l berg], Germany. He has been called the Heidelberg Man. His few remains were discovered in a deep pit which had been dug into the ancient river sands. Near these remains were the bones of many animals of the first interglacial period. Since none of his handiwork was buried with him, we know little about the Heidelberg Man. Perhaps other sites may be uncovered in the future which will give us new information.

The second ice age closed in. Then the ice descended again. A great ice field again covered much of the northern hemisphere. The second ice age, like the first, gave warning of its coming. The cold ocean currents swept down from the arctic. And like the first ice age, the second drove the animals southward.

The second interglacial period. Again the ice receded; the second interglacial period began. This was about 500,000 years ago. The climate was cool and moist. The forests, which had either been ground to splinters by the crushing ice or stunted by the cold, grew vigorously. Many of the animals which had been forced south returned. The stag, giant deer, bison, wild cattle, forest horse, boar, wolf, fox, lynx, wildcat, saber-tooth tiger, lion, bear, hippopotamus, rhinoceros, and certain kinds of elephants roamed the forests or splashed in the rivers of western Europe. There came a long period of warmth which caused the glaciers to melt back. Nor did the ice come again soon. This second interglacial period lasted for some 150,-000 years, much the longest of any of the interglacial periods.

The third glacial period. About 300,-000 years ago the ice fields again closed down upon Europe and North America. The third glacial period had arrived.

The ice fields were not so large nor the weather so severe as during the second glacial period. This third glacial period lasted 20,000 to 50,000 years.

Neanderthal Man lived in the third interglacial period. Then the warm sun and the soft winds ushered in the third interglacial age. Toward the end of this period another group of men appeared in Central Europe. These people of the Old Stone Age lived from about 30,000 to 50,000 years before our time. They are called Neanderthal [nee an′der tahl′] Men. The picture on page 13 shows how these early men are supposed to have looked.

The increasing cold, which was a sign that the fourth glacial period was approaching, drove Neanderthal Man to seek shelter in the mouths of caves and grottoes. In order to have a cave home,

Chicago Natural History Museum

THE ANCESTOR OF THE MODERN HORSE

The prehistoric ancestor of the modern horse, called orohippus, was about as large as a collie dog. As this painting shows, the orohippus had to be fleet-footed to escape the dangerous animals of early times.

Courtesy Los Angeles Museum of History, Science, and Art

THE SABER-TOOTH TIGER MADE HIS HOME IN PREHISTORIC AMERICA

This restoration shows the saber-tooth tiger and a larger animal caught in a tar pit at Rancho La Brea near Los Angeles.

he probably had to drive out the cave bear, lion, or hyena. The remains of all these animals have been found in the caves of the Neanderthals.

The use of fire. The charred wood and ashes which are found in the floors of the caves tell us that early man built bonfires. How he discovered fire is not known. Possibly the glowing embers of some forest fire started by a bolt of lightning were his first experience with it. Perhaps an accidental striking of flint produced sparks. Though we can only guess, it is likely that early man found fire in nature and with it lit his own bonfires. We do not know how early fire was discovered, but we know that Neanderthal Man found it a pleasant protection against the chilly days of the fourth glacial period which came upon Europe. Also, it may have been his most effective weapon in keeping the wild beasts out of his caves.

How Neanderthal Man looked. Many skeletal remains of the Neanderthal Man have been found throughout Europe. These remains show that he had a short, powerful body. His neck and arms were probably heavily muscled and his legs slightly bowed. His face was marked by heavy eyebrows, a large nose, and a powerful jaw. The women were about five feet tall and the men were seldom more than five and a half feet tall. Neanderthal Man constantly had to struggle against the odds of weather and wild animals. This will account in part for his physical development. In our own times we have wrestlers, woodsmen, and office workers whose bodies show the effects of the kinds of life they lead.

How Neanderthal Man got his food and clothing. Any modern hunter might well envy the kind of game which lived in the time of Neanderthal Man. There was not so much ice and cold weather in the fourth glacial period as in the three other glacial periods. But it was cold enough to drive many kinds of animals out of the northland. These animals, added to those which did not go

American Museum of Natural History

NEANDERTHAL MEN ON THE ALERT

Danger, from the animals in the river, has put these Neanderthal cave dwellers on guard. The man who looks like the best fighter has armed himself with a stone spear.

south from Europe during the fourth ice period, provided the Neanderthal with meat and clothing. In the meadows and on the plains he could find the woolly mammoth, the hairy rhinoceros, the Scandinavian reindeer, and the arctic fox and hare. In the higher lands he could find the marmot, the wild horse, and the moor hen. In the forests he met with the brown bear, giant deer, lynx, and wolf. In the caves he found hyenas, leopards, and cave bears.

The skins of the animals which were killed furnished the Neanderthal Man and his women and children with protection against the cold. The flesh gave them food. Around the campfires at the mouths of the caves and grottoes have been found hundreds of animal bones. Usually the larger bones are found split, and from this we know that early man used the soft marrow as a part of his food.

We must not get the idea that Neanderthal Man decided on the animal he wanted and went out and killed it. It may have been that early man was often the hunted and had to protect himself and family at all times from wild beasts.

Scientists believe that early men killed the animals which had become wounded and weakened in fight, or captured the beasts which had straggled behind the herd from sickness or old age. Providing there was something to eat, early man probably was not particular about the quality of his steaks and marrow. The mere struggle to keep alive must have been very hard indeed.

Metropolitan Museum of Art
American Museum of Natural History

TOOLS OF THE NEW STONE AGE

The larger implements at the top of the picture are a stone hammer, an ax or scraper of partly polished flint, a stone saw, and a flint dagger. Below are bronze spearheads.

CRO-MAGNON ARTISTS

This painting shows a group of Cro-Magnon artists painting bison on the wall of the Cavern of Font de Gaume in France. The light is probably from burning fat or oil.

Neanderthal Man improved his tools. Neanderthal Man also made progress as a toolmaker. It is true that his tools and weapons were crudely shaped, but the workmanship was a big improvement over the rough implements which were found with the Piltdown Man. During this time early men discovered that by applying pressure to the edge of flints small pieces could be flaked off. In this way weapons were given keen edges and sharp points. So we find the rounded, stone fist hatchets being displaced by choppers, drills, knives, scrapers, and spearheads. It is almost certain that some of these tools, such as the knife and the scraper, were used by the women as they worked near the fire at the mouth of the cave. The tools must have been of great assistance in preparing and scraping animal pelts. Even so, the implements of Neanderthal Man were rough enough so that they are necessarily classed with the Old Stone Age.

The idea of a future life developed. In 1908 the remains of a Neanderthal youth about sixteen years of age, were found buried in central France. The skeleton was in a sleeping position. The head rested on the right forearm and on a small pile of flints which made a sort of stone pillow. A fine fist hatchet was close by his hand. About him had been placed the charred and split bones of wild cattle. The presence of these implements and the supply of food would seem to show that Neanderthal Man had some sort of religious belief in a future life. Perhaps earlier people of the Old Stone Age also had some idea of a future life, but no evidence has been discovered to show that they buried their dead.

TIME CHART

NOTE: This chart is printed only to show the *approximate* sequence of events in prehistoric time, and the *approximate* relative time of events. Authorities differ on each of these dates. But the ones given here are rather generally accepted today.

	2,000,000,000 B.C.	Origin of the earth
	1,000,000,000 B.C.	Early forms of life appear
	5,000,000 B.C.	Age of Reptiles
Piltdown Man ⎱ Java Man ⎰ Pekin Man	1,000,000 B.C.	First Glacial Age
Heidelberg Man	500,000 B.C.	Second Glacial Age
	300,000 B.C.	Third Glacial Age
Neanderthal Man ⎰ Cro-Magnon Man	50,000 B.C. 25,000 B.C. 10,000 B.C.	Fourth Glacial Age

A new race of men took possession of Europe. In the latter part of the fourth glacial period, Neanderthal Man disappeared. Perhaps a stronger and more intelligent race of people conquered him. Perhaps he was eventually wiped out by the cold. Though he had lived thousands of years, Neanderthal Man became completely extinct. Only future discoveries can tell us why this happened.

When the fourth glacial period was at its height a new race of men called Cro-Magnons [kroh mag'nahnz] appeared on the scene. About 25,000 years ago these people arrived in Europe, spreading even as far as the British Isles. They may have come from Africa, or perhaps from lands that are now covered by the waters of the Mediterranean Sea.

The Cro-Magnons were the strong men of prehistoric times. Their splendid, erect bodies were well muscled, and they were quite tall. They had large heads, high brows, and broad faces. Like the Neanderthals, whose caves and grottoes they took over, this new race buried their dead. The Cro-Magnons placed not only food in the graves, but also colored shells and trinkets. They even covered the person to be buried with red paint.

Cro-Magnon Man was an artist. There was one thing which raised Cro-Magnon Man a step above savagery. He may have lived in caves and in the open. He may have gotten his food only by hunting. In many ways he may have been like the men who came before him. But he was an artist.

In parts of Spain and France evidences have been found of his artistic skill. Many statues and drawings made by Cro-Magnon Man have been found in caves. For materials he could not go to an art shop, but he had to use the things that were at hand. The earth furnished him with colors. The walls of

REINDEER IN EARLY ART

These reindeer were found drawn in colors on the wall of a cavern near Dordogne, France. They are examples of the work of early Cro-Magnon Man.

caverns became his drawing board. Bone, horn, and slabs of slate were the articles on which he placed his engravings. Out of clay, soapstone, and limestone he modeled his animal and human figures.

Though hunting scenes and animals, such as those in the picture on this page, were the chief subjects of his art, Cro-Magnon Man also sculptured the first statues of human beings. Most of the little stone statues which have been found are of women, who are round and plump. With Cro-Magnon Man, drawing, painting, engraving, and sculpture were born. His was a remarkable contribution to the progress of civilization.

Early man made rapid progress toward civilization in the New Stone Age. With the retreat of the last ice sheets from the continent of Europe a new era in the story of man began. Cro-Magnon Man moved north in the wake of the retreating ice. A flood of new peoples moved into Europe from the east.

As they came into contact with one another, each group learned from the others.

During this period men learned to polish their stone implements by rubbing them smooth with sandstone. This marks the New Stone Age, sometimes called the Age of Polished Stone Tools. Men found that a smooth, grooved stone could be fastened with a leather thong to a wooden handle to make a powerful ax or weapon. The careful shaping and polishing was not learned all at once. It took hundreds of years to make the change from the Old to the New Stone Age.

Another step in progress which came in the New Stone Age was the use of seeds and plants. As might be expected, men also invented simple implements for the planting and harvesting of crops. This was the beginning of agriculture, on which all civilizations rest. Still another new idea was the use of dishes. Pottery came to be used, first in the preparation of food.

RESTORATIONS OF PREHISTORIC MAN

A scientist has reconstructed these heads of prehistoric man. From left to right they are as follows: the earliest man of Asia, a Piltdown man, a Neanderthal man, and a Cro-Magnon man. They are probably reasonably accurate reproductions.

Prehistoric burial mounds tell us something about early man. From the time of Cro-Magnon Man to the beginnings of written history, more is known about early man. Our information comes from several sources. The graves of early men are one of the richest sources of information about life and living in bygone days. The burial mounds of England, Egypt, and America, for example, have furnished the scientist with the remains of human beings. From these remains he can tell us how tall and how strong prehistoric man was and can make reasonably accurate reconstructions like those which are shown in the above illustration.

From the face bones, skillful scientists have been able to reconstruct the features of early men in models, so that today we may have some idea of how early man looked. Of course these models may not show early men as they really were, for they are imaginary reconstructions. But since they have been designed from actual skull bones, they are more reliable than our unaided imaginations would be.

Prehistoric mines yield valuable relics. The places where prehistoric man fought, lived, and worked also give us interesting information about how he lived. In England an ancient flint mine has been found. With picks made of deer horns the first miners dug out chunks of flint from the chalky strata. In this mine eighty worn deerhorn picks were found in the underground tunnels. The skeleton of an ancient miner was discovered in a flint mine in Belgium. He had been crushed by the falling of rocks. Between his hands still lay the deerhorn pick which he held so many thousands of years ago.

Prehistoric village sites are rich in evidence. There was a very dry season in Switzerland in 1854 which caused the level of the Swiss lakes to go down. Many posts were discovered which had been driven into the lake bottoms. From the pottery, grain, bits of fishnet, dugouts, and other things found among the posts which had been preserved in the mud, it was realized that these wooden piles had supported the huts of a lake village. This dry season was of great

American Museum of Natural History

A SWISS LAKE VILLAGE

This model of a Swiss lake village was reconstructed from bits of evidence that the waters of the lake preserved through the ages. Notice the thatched roofs on the houses.

value to those who wanted to know something more about early man.

Sites of prehistoric villages on land also contribute to our story of early man. At one time in southern England the forests were full of wild animals. The Irish elk, wild ox, bear, wolf, and wild boar abounded. To protect themselves and their herds of cattle from these dangers, the prehistoric men sometimes made camps by throwing up earthworks. They built pit houses and constructed fortlike enclosures. In these places have been found shovels made from the shoulder blades of reindeer, hammers, many kinds of pottery, heaps of stones for sling shots, and wrist guards for use with bows.

Stone monuments of early man remain a mystery. Some of the most mysterious handiwork which early man has left are great stone monuments scattered through western Europe and southern England. One of these is Stonehenge [stohn'henj] in southern England. It is an enormous circle, about one hundred feet in diameter, made of upright stone shafts. Each of these stones is a slab about fourteen feet high,

half as wide, and three and a half feet thick. They were connected at the top by cross slabs. Within the circle there is a horseshoe formation of large stones. In the center of this is a large flat stone that gives the appearance of an altar. We can only guess what may have been the use of Stonehenge. It may have been a temple of the sun. Priests or medicine men may have made observations of the seasons and offered up sacrifices.

There are other examples of such monuments. In Brittany, which is in the northwestern part of France, are to be seen monuments or tombs made by huge, rough, flat stones supported by upright stone. And in the Easter Islands off the west coast of South America are great stone images which may have been a part of some early religion.

The end of the Stone Ages. About five thousand years ago, which would be near 3000 B.C. (before the birth of Christ), metal was introduced into Europe. Perhaps some trader from the land at the eastern end of the Mediterranean made his way into Europe. He may have gone from one village to another, bartering his metal knives, axes, needles, and trinkets for furs and other goods. The change from the stone axes and deerhorn picks to tools of bronze and iron was not rapid. It took a thousand years for the use of metal to spread from southeastern Europe, where it was first introduced, northward across Europe to the British Isles.

The use of metal made a great change in the life of prehistoric man. He now had more and better tools with which to work. With the introduction of metals the New Stone Age came definitely to an end. The Age of Metals had begun. When mankind learned to use metal, he took another stride toward the world of precision tools and machinery in which we live today.

Generally speaking, copper, bronze (an alloy of copper and tin), and iron came into use in that order. We use the terms Bronze Age and Iron Age to show the state of a civilization. We must remember, however, that these metals became known in different places at different times.

Modern man appeared on the scene. By 3000 B.C. all the earlier types of men, such as the Neanderthal and Cro-Magnon, had long since disappeared. Modern man had arrived on the scene. Scientists recognize that all living men belong to just one great race, called *Homo Sapiens* [hoh'moh say'pi'nz], meaning wise or thinking man. Within the great human family, from time to time, people have separated themselves into various groups. Each of these groups lived apart for a time and developed different customs and physical characteristics. When this occurred, these groups developed what we now call races. We should note, however, that today these races are, for the most part, so mixed that they overlap. And where they overlap it is impossible to know where one race ends and the next one begins.

Some scientists say that there are four great races of man. The white race is known as the *Caucasian* [kaw kay'zh'n]. The black race is known as the *Negro*. The race of yellow and red-skinned peo-

Culver Service

A VIEW OF STONEHENGE

Religious ceremonies are thought to have been held within this huge structure which was built by early man on the plains of Salisbury in southern England.

Ewing Galloway

TWO GENTLEMEN OF BOMBAY

The caste marks on the foreheads of these men show that they belong to India's rigid caste system. These men are of one of the higher castes.

ples is known as the *Mongolian* [mahng-goh′li′n]. And a fourth race sometimes included is the black, hairy *Australian* bushman. And there are many "in-between" peoples, like the Polynesians [pohl′i nee′zh′nz] of the South Pacific, North Africans, Hindus, and Siberians.

Many scientists believe that all of the races of man probably originated in Asia. In any case, we know that by 3000 B.C. the Caucasian race had spread to Europe, North Africa, and Southwestern Asia. The Mongolians lived in the central, northern, and southeastern parts of Asia. They had also migrated into North and South America and to many of the islands of the Pacific Ocean. The Negroes inhabited all of Africa south of the

Sahara desert. Some of them had traveled far out into the Pacific Ocean to live in the islands around Australia. The people of Guadalcanal [guah′dahl kah-nahl′], in the Solomon Islands, are a good example of such Negroes. You can see that each race tended to inhabit a particular part of the world.

The first civilized cities were built in India. The ancient peoples of northern India built the oldest civilized cities in the world. Long before 3000 B.C. there were three cities established in the valley of the Indus [in′duhs] River. Farther south in India the people were less highly civilized than the northern peoples. They were dark-skinned and had flat noses. They were called Dravidians

A Comparison of Words of Some Indo-European Languages

Sanskrit	Old Persian	Greek	Latin	French	Dutch	German	English
bhrata	bratar	phrater	frater	frère	broeder	bruder	brother
mata	matar	meter	mater	mère	moeder	mutter	mother
pita	pitar	pater	pater	père	vater	vater	father

[druh vid'i'nz] after the language they spoke. The highest castes [kastz] in India today are more Caucasian than the rest of the people. Most of the Hindus are descendants of a Caucasian and Dravidian mixture. Today various forms of the Dravidian languages are spoken by over fifty million people, mostly in the southern part of India.

The Caucasian race has three major divisions. In Europe and Asia, the Caucasians laid the foundations of their civilizations. By 3000 B.C. the three main divisions of the Caucasian race were already formed. These are the Mediterranean, Alpine, and Nordic peoples.

The new men who merged with Cro-Magnon Man in Europe during the New Stone Age, were mostly Mediterraneans. These people commonly have narrow heads with dark skin, eyes, and hair. The early Egyptians were mostly Mediterraneans.

The round-headed Alpines appeared in great numbers during the Iron Age. They, too, tend to be dark-colored. They lived mostly in central and eastern Europe.

The narrow-headed Nordics became numerous at the end of the Bronze Age. They are much like the Mediterraneans, but they have lighter skin, and tend to have blue eyes and fair hair. They grow much taller on the average. The Nordics seem to have developed in eastern Europe. They soon spread into many parts of Europe and Asia.

Indo-European and Semitic languages. Most of the many groups of Nordics spoke a single type of language known as Indo-European, because the main languages of India and Europe are descended from it. The Indo-European language developed just after 3000 B.C., probably in Persia. Sanskrit, the language of ancient Persia, is its oldest known form. One group of Nordics, called Aryas [air'yahz], conquered northwest India in 1400 B.C. They probably were the first ones to take the Indo-European language to India, so some people apply the name "Aryan" [air'-i'n] to this language. The roots of some words of the various Indo-European languages are quite similar, as can be seen from the table above.

In much the same manner, the ancient Semitic language contributed to the speech of the peoples in parts of the Near East, Ethiopia, and Northern Africa.

The Chinese and the Japanese are descended from Mongolians. China has long been a center of civilization; much of Japanese civilization was borrowed from China and Korea [kuh ree'uh]. In 3000 B.C. China was in its age of Bronze. The skills of the Age of Bronze were taken over in Japan many centuries after it was established in China. Writing began in China about 1500 B.C.; the Japanese, however, did not take over the art of writing until two thousand years later.

The modern Japanese migrated to Japan from northern China some time around 3000 B.C. Long before their arrival, a race of hairy white men, called

Burton Holmes from Ewing Galloway

AN AINU IN HIS VILLAGE

The Ainus live apart from the modern world in their villages of grass huts. The men wear beards and the women wear tattooed mustaches.

Ainus [ai′nooz], inhabited the islands. They were a New Stone Age people. They fought long wars with the Japanese for possession of the country. The Japanese triumphed, but a few thousand Ainus still live in the northern islands of Japan. An Ainu is shown in the illustration above.

Later on, a different type of people came by boat into Japan from the south. These people seem to have been a small, dark-skinned branch of the Caucasian race that had already mixed with Mongolians. Then in Japan they mixed with the Japanese. Thus they gave the Japanese the physical traits that make the Japanese look different from the Chinese.

Various groups of people migrated to the Pacific area. The people of the East Indies are also prehistoric migrants.

Their early ancestors moved from southern India eastward into the islands of the western Pacific Ocean. At first, they were very similar to the dark-skinned Caucasians who lived in Asia Minor. Later, Mongolians from China moved south and mixed with the people of the East Indies. Thus the people of the Indies also became somewhat Mongolian in type.

Other adventurers went by sea to the islands in the middle of the Pacific Ocean. These people were mostly Caucasians from India, mixed with Mongolians and some Negroes. They have brown skin, dark eyes, and dark, wavy hair. They are the Polynesians, of whom the natives of Hawaii [hah wai′ee] are a good example.

Ancestors of American Indians came from Asia. Scientists believe that as late as the end of the fourth glacial period there was a strip of land connecting Alaska and Siberia. When one studies the map of the Aleutian chain of islands, we find that is not hard to believe. The early Indians, who were Mongolians, must have migrated from Asia into this part of the world across this landbridge. Various waves of people came from Asia into Alaska, and traveled down through North America, Central America, and even down to the tip of South America. They may have first started coming around 20,000 B.C., when the Cro-Magnons were inhabiting Europe. Some evidence has been found of an early man, known as Fulsom Man, having lived in Alaska and North America about 10,000 B.C.

The Indians learned to improve their tools, and later emigrants from Asia kept bringing new ideas. Shortly after 3000 B.C. the Indians of Central America and northern South America began to develop their own centers of civilization.

Some writers think they were influenced by Egypt and India, but there is little scientific proof for such an idea and it is not generally accepted.

Courtesy of Grace Line

AN ECUADOR INDIAN

This Indian chief in Ecuador may be the descendant of peoples who lived in Asia.

Chapter 3 ~ Mankind at the Dawn of Civilization

The dawn of civilization. It is difficult to say just when man became civilized. Certainly it did not happen overnight. Historians differ greatly in the dates they give for this event — 6000 B.C., when writing was first developed; 4241 B.C., the first recorded date in history; 4000 B.C., 3000 B.C., 2500 B.C., and so on. But just as we have given you approximate dates for other events of the earth and man, we give you one for the dawn of civilization: 3000 B.C. But remember that this date is approximate; remember too that the milestones along man's path to civilization were different

in different places. Civilizations developed in many places, and they developed at different speeds and in different ways. But as you read this chapter you will see why we have selected that date.

Man learned to write. We have seen how early man became an artist, and drew pictures on the walls of his cave. Gradually he developed a kind of picture writing, and written history began. Much of civilization is based on written and spoken language, or communication. By this term "dawn of civilization," we do not refer to the first date in history. Rather we mean that approxi-

INDIAN PICTURE WRITING

This illustration of American Indian picture writing shows one of the earliest methods of written communication. The figure with empty hands means "nothing" or "no." The figure with one hand to the mouth means "eating" or "food." The whole message means "no food in tent."

mate time when man was fairly well started on the long, long road of civilization. By 3000 B.C. many peoples throughout the world had some form of writing, and the Egyptians and Babylonians had well-developed systems of writing. Both Egypt and Babylonia also had workable calendars by 3000 B.C. The illustration above shows a kind of early writing.

The world was well populated by 3000 B.C. As we have learned, about 25,000 B.C. various groups of men were scattered about Western and Central Europe, Southern Asia, and Northern Africa. Throughout the years, they spread about the several continents. At about the same time, the Western Hemisphere was also populated. By 3000 B.C. men were undoubtedly living on every continent.

The cradles of civilization. There are two regions of the world, one in each hemisphere, where the first great civilizations developed. In the Eastern Hemisphere it was where Europe, Asia, and Africa are connected: Egypt and the Nile valley, Mesopotamia [mes'uh puh-tay'mi uh] and the Tigris-Euphrates [tai'gris yoo fray'teez] valley, and Pales-

tine and Syria at the western end of the Fertile Crescent, on the Mediterranean. In the Western Hemisphere it was along the Isthmus of Panama — in southern Mexico and in Guatemala [gwah'tuh-mah'lah].

These two regions were similar in many ways, as we shall learn later in this *Story of Nations.* Certainly land and climate were favorable for the development of civilizations.

Man's basic needs. We know that man's basic needs are food, clothing, and shelter. Stone Age man had learned to provide these for himself. Caves were his home and the skins of animals his clothing. He not only brought in wild plants and animals for food; he had tamed a few plants and animals. Grains were probably his first cultivated plants, and dogs his first domesticated animals. By 3000 B.C., throughout most of the populated world, man had such plants as barley, wheat, millet, peas, lentils, beans, apples, and flax. Dogs, cattle, swine, sheep, goats, horses, cats, chickens, and ducks were more or less domesticated. Life was essentially agricultural.

The Age of Metals. By 3000 B.C. the Stone Age was over in some parts of the world, for man had learned to use metals. Copper and gold were the first metals to be used — copper for working utensils, and gold for ornamentation. Then tin came to be known, probably first in Persia, and spread from Babylonia [bab'-i loh'ni uh] to Egypt and throughout the Mediterranean region. (Later tin was found in Spain and England.) By about 1500 B.C. man had learned to add tin to copper to make bronze. With improved tools of bronze, which are harder than copper tools and keep a better cutting edge, man could work more efficiently and his civilization could develop more rapidly.

Early group life developed. Prehistoric men lived in small groups for their own protection. Gradually, out of family, clan, and tribal life, there evolved community life. Long before 3000 B.C. communities were established wherever men lived. There was a family and tribal division of labor; men were the hunters and warriors; women were the farmers and homemakers.

By 3000 B.C. moderately large cities flourished, and city-state civilizations were common. The term *city-state* means, in general, a self-ruling community, together with the surrounding territory which it influences and controls. The earliest city-states were merely confederations of tribes, who came together for protection and worship, and established a central meeting place. There were governors, courts of law, and police protection — and taxes to pay government expenses. Commerce and industry were being developed in 3000 B.C. The several centers of civilization of the Mediterranean, for example, affected one another as their peoples came into contact through trade and commerce. There were such centers as Egypt, Canaan [kay′nun], Phoenicia [fi nish′uh], Babylonia, and the Aegean [uh jee′′n] Islands. In America, Mayan [mah′i′n] civilizations in Guatemala and southern Mexico were flourishing.

Different peoples developed individual civilizations. By 3000 B.C., then, man had definitely established himself on earth. He was master of the land and had learned to work with nature. He had settled down in various fertile regions of the earth.

By 3000 B.C., in many parts of the world separate civilizations were being built. Although these civilizations had many effects on one another, many were quite unique. We shall therefore examine some of the early great cultures. In them we will find the backgrounds of modern nations. Later in this *Story of Nations* we will see how some of the great nations of the world developed. Within the covers of a single volume we cannot, of course, discuss every group, every nation; we can only look at a few outstanding ones. But as we take up the individual groups and nations, remember that from the time of the earliest civilizations, no people were completely isolated. Through travel, trade, and commerce, each group was in contact with others. And, of course, each group learned something from the others.

Contributions Early Men Made to Civilization

Many changes have occurred in the surface of the earth during the millions of years it has been in existence. Mighty forces have buckled the earth's strata. At four different times tremendous glaciers swept over much of North America and Europe, leaving deposits of boulders, grinding out valleys, planing away sharp ridges. Wind, rain, volcanoes, earthquakes, and other great forces have changed the face of the earth and are continuing to do so today.

Some anthropologists believe that even before the coming of the first glaciers, plants and animals lived on earth, and the earliest forms of man had come into being. The Piltdown, Java, and Pekin men lived during the first glacial period. Few traces have been found of the Heidelberg Man, who lived after the first glacial period. The Neanderthal Man lived after the third glacial period; and during the fourth glacial period, the most advanced of the prehistoric men, the Cro-Magnons, appeared in Europe.

Early man laid the foundations of civilization in its simplest form. Before man became definitely established on earth, he had to solve many problems. He struggled to protect himself from the wild beasts, to shelter himself from the weather, to increase his food supply. In meeting all these problems, early man made a number of significant discoveries. He began to use tools to help his hands. He discovered, perhaps accidentally, the use of fire. The use of fire and of tools laid the groundwork from which early man progressed.

Devices like the ax, the dugout canoe, and the bow and arrow all increased man's chances of survival. Prehistoric man learned to build dwellings and began to use clothing as a protective covering. He learned to cultivate seeds and plants to increase his food supply, and he domesticated cattle, horses, and dogs.

Of course, we know that early man learned to speak. Also, individuals learned to live with one another, in family and tribal groups. In feeding and protecting the family, they learned the value of the division of labor. The men hunted and fought while the women ran the home affairs.

Prehistoric man developed a religious and an artistic feeling. He often buried his dead and prepared them for a future life. His sense of the unknown expressed itself in his art. The animals he drew, carved, and molded seemed to have something to do with favoring his success in hunting. His attempts at art made him responsible for the first painting, sketching, engraving, and sculpture.

It is odd to think that whether a modern man goes fishing, makes a statue, or warms himself by a fire, he is doing things that were thought of thousands of years ago by early man. Even though the earliest people did all these things, we call them prehistoric simply because they could not write. Peoples of historic times have added accomplishments to those of early man. In many ways, however, they have in reality only been busy perfecting the original contributions which early man made to civilization.

By 3000 B.C. the earlier peoples such as the Neanderthal and Cro-Magnon men had long since disappeared, and modern man had arrived on the scene. All living men today belong to one great race called *Homo Sapiens*. But over a long period of time men have separated themselves into groups that have developed different characteristics. Today we have four different groups, although these groups have mingled so that there are many divisions within each one. It is believed that modern man originated in Asia. The Indo-European language, probably developed originally in Persia, was the mother language from which the main languages of Europe and India descended. The ancient Semitic language contributed to the speech of peoples in parts of the Near East, Ethiopia, and northern Africa.

There are two regions of the world where the first great civilizations developed: (1) the region of the Isthmus of Panama, and (2) the valleys of the Nile and Tigris-Euphrates rivers. As the first two great civilizations developed, other civilizations also grew up in other parts of the world. By 3000 B.C. the world was widely populated. A number of separate groups had developed individual cultures. These civilizations were essentially agricultural; some groups had also begun to use metals. Some of these different peoples were in contact with one another, and the knowledge and skills of one civilization affected those of another.

SELF-TEST

I. Copy and complete the following statements. Do not mark your book.

1. The story of mankind is divided into two parts, the —— period and the —— period. 2. Scientists who study the earth's history as shown in its surface and rock formations are called ——. 3. The earth is made up of layers called ——. 4. Changes in the character of the earth's surface have been caused by many forces, such as ——, ——, ——, and ——. 5. The three earliest kinds of men on earth about whom any evidence has been discovered are ——, ——, and ——.

II. Tell *why* each of the following statements is true or false:

1. The historic period of man's story goes back about five hundred thousand years. 2. Modern man's knowledge of prehistoric man is based upon actual evidence. 3. Early Man did not live during the Age of Reptiles. 4. The tools of the New Stone Age were roughly chipped.

III. Rearrange the following in the order in which they come in the story of early man: (*a*) Neanderthal Man, (*b*) Bronze Age, (*c*) third glacial period, (*d*) Heidelberg Man, (*e*) dinosaurs.

IV. We know that early man learned to meet his essential needs. Show how we know this, by listing on a sheet of paper, numbered to match the following items, a word or phrase which will give the evidence.

EXAMPLE: *Discovery:* Homes   *Evidence:* Swiss lake dwellers

(*a*) Weapons, (*b*) dishes, (*c*) cooking, (*d*) belief in after life, (*e*) painting and drawing, (*f*) clothing, (*g*) domestic animals, (*h*) seeds, (*i*) food, (*j*) sculpture, (*k*) tools.

INTERESTING THINGS TO DO

Here are some interesting things to do. You will find that if you put your new knowledge to use it will become more firmly fixed in mind. Choose one or more of these things to do, alone or with a committee of the class. Perhaps these activities will suggest an original idea which you will prefer to develop.

Topics for Talks

1. "My own region in prehistoric times." Make a thorough investigation of the prehistoric conditions of the part of the country in which you live. This report will lead to such topics as the local land formations, the geology of the earth layers, traces of the ice ages, and fossil remains of animal life. Your local librarian can probably direct you to good sources of information.

2. "Volcanoes and their work." Look up information about some of the active volcanoes that have made changes in the character of the earth's surface during the last hundred years. See *National Geographic Magazine,* February, 1944; the *New York Times* File, Oct. 8, 1943, or *Life,* April 17, 1944, for Parícutin in Mexico. For Mt. Pelée in Martinique, or Mauna Loa and Kilauea in Hawaii, consult any encyclopedia.

3. "Geology or archeology as a profession." Prepare a report on the work of geologists and archeologists in adding to our knowledge of the earth and mankind. Does either of these occupations appeal to you? What sort of person would make a success of this type of profession? Tell something of both the thrills and hardships of this work. See *Lost Worlds,* by Anne T. White, and *Digging in Yucatan,* by Ann Morris.

Projects for the Chart Maker and Artist

1. Make an illustrated time line showing the development of man and his tools from the time of the Piltdown Man to the present. Make sketches, or paste on clippings, showing the tools of various stages. Label approximate time periods and the names of the early men of each period.

2. Make a series of sketches that illustrate the chipped and smooth stone tools of primitive people who lived in historic times, such as the North American Indians, the Indians of Central and South America, and the peoples of the South Pacific regions.

3. Make a series of sketches or models of animals of the Age of Reptiles.

4. Make a large chart of the family tree of the horse that shows the changes that took place in the animal from the primitive horse of prehistoric times to the horse of today. Consult any good encyclopedia, the "Cumulative Index" of the *National Geographic Magazine,* or send to the American Museum of Natural History, New York City, for an inexpensive pamphlet on the story of the horse.

Ideas for Your Little Theater

1. Write a play or radio script dealing with aspects of the life of prehistoric man. Suggested titles: "Sunrise at Stonehenge," "How the Tiger Lost His Saber," "Man or Mammoth," "Early Man Makes Fire His Servant," "Prehistoric Murals."

2. Construct a miniature diorama or set, showing a scene of prehistoric times, as the Age of Reptiles, or the life of early men. Almost professional results can be achieved by the use of lighting effects.

INTERESTING READING ABOUT EARLY MAN

ANDREWS, ROY CHAPMAN. *Exploring with Andrews*. Selections taken from several of the author's absorbing books of exploration.

BURR, H. M. *Around the Fire*. Short stories of early man from primitive to barbarian life.

Compton's Pictured Encyclopedia. " Man: The Prologue to History — Early Man's Struggles and Triumphs "; and Index.

GORDON, CYRUS HERZL. *Living Past*. An entertaining and enlightening book on the work of the archaeologist in western Asia, illustrated with photographs of the places explored and the exciting discoveries made.

LIDE, ALICE A. *Princess of Yucatan*. A story of the early Mayas.

MILLS, D. *The Book of the Ancient World*. ". . . which must have been a terrifying experience for primitive man."

MORRIS, ANN. *Digging in Yucatan*. A lively, informal record of the work of an archeological expedition in the land of the Mayas.

National Geographic Magazine, Washington, D.C. June, 1933. " Explorations in the Gobi Desert," Roy Chapman Andrews. " Parade of Life Through the Ages," Charles R. Knight.

——, February, 1942. " Parícutin, the Cornfield That Grew a Volcano," James A. Green.

——, February, 1944. " Parícutin is the greatest show on earth."

OSBORN, HENRY FAIRFIELD. *The Pacific World*. " There is no doubt that natives did cross tremendous distances of open sea. . . ."

QUENNELL, MARJORIE, and QUENNELL, C. H. B. *Everyday Life in the New Stone, Bronze and Early Iron Ages*. A valuable and well-illustrated source of information.

VAN LOON, H. W. *The Story of Mankind*. " It is little enough we know and the rest is darkness."

WATERLOO, S. *The Story of Ab*. " She was as lithe as the panther. . . ."

WELLS, H. G. *The Outline of History*. " The savages sat huddled close together round their fire. . . ."

WHITE, ANNE T. *Lost Worlds*. This account of the finding of four lost civilizations is as thrilling as a detective story.

PART TWO

THE EGYPTIANS BUILT A GREAT CIVILI-ZATION ON THE BANKS OF THE NILE

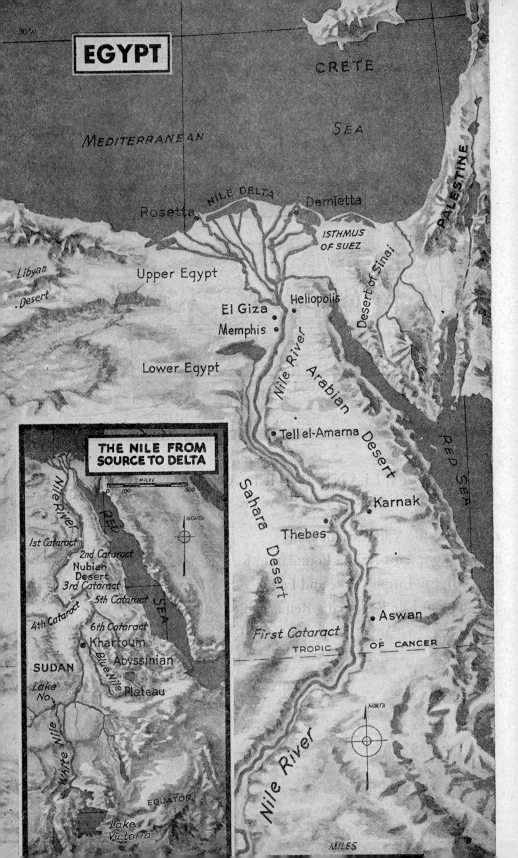

EGYPT

CRETE

MEDITERRANEAN

SEA

PALESTINE

Libyan Desert

NILE DELTA

Rosetta

Damietta

ISTHMUS OF SUEZ

Upper Egypt

Desert of Sinai

El Giza

Heliopolis

Memphis

Nile River

Lower Egypt

Arabian Desert

RED SEA

Tell el-Amarna

Sahara Desert

Karnak

Thebes

First Cataract

Aswan

TROPIC OF CANCER

Nile River

NORTH

MILES

THE NILE FROM SOURCE TO DELTA

MILES
0   100   500

NORTH

Nile River

RED

1st Cataract

2nd Cataract

Nubian Desert

3rd Cataract

5th Cataract

SINAI

4th Cataract

6th Cataract

Khartoum

Abyssinian

SUDAN

Blue Nile

Lake No

Plateau

White Nile

EQUATOR

Lake Victoria

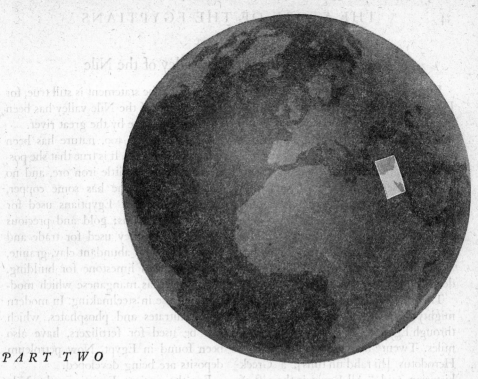

PART TWO

The Land of the Nile

THINK of this map of Egypt as being made up of endless stretches of burning white sand. Here and there are green oases. To these, wandering desert tribes bring their camels to drink. Sometimes they camp and rest in the cool shade of the date palms. Notice the great cliffs which border the Nile Valley. Between them, along each side of the Nile, is a narrow strip of land which is luxuriantly green and productive. Where fresh water touches Egypt there is a beautiful garden. The rest of Egypt is sand and barren rocky land.

Look at the map of Africa at the back of the book. See what part of that continent Egypt occupies. Now look again at the map on the page facing this one. Near Heliopolis, which you can find on the map, are the massive pyramids. Farther up the Nile is Karnak, where the ruins of a once-beautiful temple still stand. Karnak is not far from Thebes, an ancient capital of Egypt.

The small inset map in the lower left-hand corner traces the course of the Nile from its source to its mouth. In what great lake does the Nile begin? Do you find the spot where the Blue Nile joins the White Nile? This inset also shows the cataracts of the Nile. Count them. How many do you find? Can you explain why the early Egyptians found it difficult to travel up the Nile?

Chapter 1 ~ The Fertile Valley of the Nile

Egypt is the gift of the Nile. Egypt! Dazzling jewels, linen-wrapped mummies, hot desert sands, sailboats on the Nile — which picture flashes before your eye? Is it one of the massive pyramids built nearly five thousand years ago to preserve the body of an almost forgotten king? Is it the mighty Sphinx [sfingks] who for centuries has been a symbol of silence? Whatever comes to mind will be dramatic, for Egypt has always been thought of as a land of wonders.

The greatest Egyptian wonder is the mighty Nile which flows northward through Egypt for more than a thousand miles. Twenty-five hundred years ago Herodotus [hi rahd'uh tuhs], a Greek historian, said, " All Egypt is the gift of

the Nile." The statement is still true, for the very soil of the Nile valley has been carried into place by the great river.

In other ways, too, nature has been generous to Egypt. It is true that she possesses no forests, little iron ore, and no good coal. But she has some copper, which the ancient Egyptians used for tools and weapons; gold and precious jewels, which they used for trade and adornment; and abundant clay, granite, sandstone, and limestone for building. Egypt also has manganese which modern men use in steelmaking. In modern times, nitrates and phosphates, which can be used for fertilizers, have also been found in Egypt. Now petroleum deposits are being developed.

For the ancient Egyptians, the Nile was the most important feature in Egypt. By looking at the map on page 32 you can trace the great river back to its source — Lake Victoria, in central Africa, almost on the equator. This lake is approximately 250 miles long and 200 miles wide.

From the air we unroll the map of Egypt. Suppose you took an airplane from Lake Victoria to the place where the Nile empties into the Mediterranean. What would you see? First cruise about Lake Victoria, the largest of the many stream-fed lakes in this region. Notice the highlands in which these lakes are pocketed; they are about four thousand feet above sea level. Now turn northward, where the water of Lake Victoria pours through an opening in the cliffs. You see that the famous Nile begins as a swift mountain stream flowing from Lake Victoria.

Flying on northward, you see the Nile racing through rocky channels,

Strobel from Monkemeyer

A CALM STRETCH OF THE NILE
The powerful Nile River is placid here, near Edfu — but even in calmness the many-sided river shows its power.

and sometimes flowing around picturesque islands and over countless rapids.
At one place it rushes through a very
narrow channel and plunges into a
spray-covered abyss. Farther on it passes
through a rather level area, spreading
out so much that you can hardly follow
its course through the swamplands covered with papyrus and other reeds growing fifteen to twenty feet above the water. Farther along you see the river again
flowing in a normal course, as calm as it
appears in the picture on page 34. Then
come more rapids and swamps, each different from the others. After about two
hundred miles the Nile enters Lake No,
where it is joined by a smaller river of
white water. This water gives the name
White Nile to the river which leaves the
lake and continues northward.

Five hundred miles farther along you
come to the city of Khartoum [kahr-
toom'] where another river joins the
White Nile. This second branch, the
Blue Nile, comes down from the mountains of Abyssinia [ab'uh sin'i uh]. The
Blue Nile is wild and unsubdued like
the people of the Abyssinian Plateau.
The heavy rains in this region during
June and on through September cause
the river to rush down and overflow its
banks. As the Blue Nile surges into the
White Nile at Khartoum, it carries with
it a large amount of brown silt, drift-
wood of all sorts, and sometimes bodies
of dead animals. The White Nile has
kept the river flowing steadily from its
source to the sea; the Blue Nile has
brought down the flood waters and the
fertile soil that made Egypt the bread-

New York Public Library

THE FIRST CATARACT OF THE NILE

Here is a turbulent Nile — compressed in a narrow channel and churned into violence.
The Nile has as many moods as it has gifts for Egypt.

basket of the eastern Mediterranean world in ancient times.

Above the cataracts lies a land unknown to the ancient Egyptians. Continuing north from Khartoum your pilot gains altitude to avoid crashing into the great rocks on either side of the river. Here the Nile winds tortuously across the Nubian [noo′bi′n] tablelands, through sandstone cliffs, forming a series of six foaming cataracts, and on to the lowlands. These cataracts are not beautiful waterfalls like those of our Yosemite [yo sem′i ti] Valley or magnificent Niagara. They are more like rapids and are found in regions where the rock is so hard that the river has not been able to cut out a wide course. The water is forced into a narrow channel between the rocky banks and rushes over broken ledges and around jagged masses of stones in the turbulence shown in the picture on page 35.

Passing over the last of the six cataracts, which the Egyptians called the "First Cataract," as it was the first they came to in sailing south, you see the great dam built by the British to control the Nile floods and furnish water for irrigation. And just four miles below the dam is the town of Aswan [ahs wahn′].

The ancient Egyptians knew almost nothing of the land over which you have just traveled. Since they could not sail their ships past the six cataracts, the source of the Nile was a mystery to them. To explain where it came from they said its source was in Heaven, where it was guarded by the Nile-god who knelt, holding in each hand a sacred vessel out of which flowed the water of the Nile.

The Sphinx and the pyramids appear in the distance. Now the land flattens out. The river bed widens until the Nile winds along its course in a more leisurely way. For ten or fifteen miles on each side of the river there are green fields, but beyond these there is nothing but cliffs and rolling sand dunes. "Where water touches Egypt, there is a garden; where no water touches, a barren, desolate waste."

In time you are flying over the great pyramids and the mysterious Sphinx in the desert on the left bank of the Nile. A few miles beyond, is the city of Cairo [kai′roh], and fourteen miles farther north the Nile branches out to form what is called the Nile Delta. The Greeks called it that because it is the same shape as the Greek letter delta. In ancient days the river had several fingers reaching out to the sea. Now, the two channels, the Rosetta arm on the west and the Damietta [dam′i et′uh] arm on the east, carry to the Mediterranean all the water that has not been used for irrigation. On page 32 you will find an enlarged section map of this historic Delta of the Nile.

The Delta of the Nile is a garden land cut up into rectangular plots by irrigation ditches radiating from the two branches of the Nile, and by five canals that reach from branch to branch but do not extend to the Mediterranean. In addition to the usual garden and farm crops, much of the land is planted to cotton of the long-fibered type for which Egypt is famous.

Fresh water, sea, and land make Egypt secure. In your flight over Egypt you saw inspiring sights, but many of them were seen only from a distance. Had you landed to explore the country you might have seen many of the wild animals of Africa in their native haunts between Lake Victoria and the First Cataract. There would be the hippopotamus, then in different regions along the river the elephant, the giraffe, the buffalo, the white rhinoceros, and always the crocodile. Later we can stop and explore the pyramids and the ancient tombs, and the picture writing in which the early people left their first written records. But first let us look over the route you have just taken to see why the shape and surroundings of Egypt have had such a great influence upon her dramatic history.

Without a doubt one of the reasons why Egypt developed a civilization when other men were still following wandering herds of animals was because her land was very safe. Look at the map facing page 33 and you will see that

Egypt is hemmed in by deserts and seas. To the west we find the Libyan [lib'i'n] Desert. The Arabian and Nubian deserts lie to the east. The Mediterranean Sea to the north, and the Red Sea to the east, further protect the people of the Nile Valley from invading foreigners.

In ancient times there was only one easy way to come into the country from the east and that was across the Isthmus of Suez [soo ez']. We shall see later that invading conquerors from Asia Minor came by way of this arched neck of land that separates the Red Sea from the Mediterranean.

Ewing Galloway

SOMBER MAJESTY IN THE DESERT

The Sphinx, with claws reaching forward and back turned to the Pyramids, is a fateful brooding presence. Its creators built into it the massiveness and mystery that we associate with Egypt.

Chapter 2 ~ The Egyptians Built a Foundation for Greatness

Men of the Stone Age settled in the Nile valley. Archeologists have found Egypt a treasure house of information about the past. Crude flint tools found on the cliffs and deserts overlooking the Nile valley show that men of the Old Stone Age lived there. They did not live down in the valley or on the Delta, probably because the region was very swampy at that time.

The men of the New Stone Age, who were the forefathers of the ancient Egyptians, took possession of the Nile valley about twelve thousand to fifteen thousand years ago. These New Stone Age men were related to peoples of northern Africa, to peoples from the western coast of the Red Sea, and also to the Semitic nomads from what is now called the Near East. It happened that the Semitic language became the basis of the language of the Egyptians.

Egyptians of the New Stone Age laid the foundations of their civilization. Objects found in the deposits of the annual Nile floods and in the graves in the cliffs along the valley show that the Egyptians had made much progress before the beginning of recorded history. They had tools of polished flint fitted with carved or beautifully decorated handles. They raised grain and improved its quality. They made linen cloth, copper beads, needles, and chisels. They domesticated sheep, cattle, and donkeys, as well as dogs and cats. They learned to build boats and used them for fishing, hunting, and fighting. They learned to write by means of pictures and developed this picture writing to a high degree. In it they left accounts of their hunting, their fighting, their daily work, and their religious beliefs. This picture writing developed into a distinctive art among the Egyptians and was the basis of the writing in which the history of ancient Egypt was recorded.

The Egyptians learned to govern. The early Egyptians were tillers of the soil. They did not, however, live on the tracts of land that they cultivated as do American farmers today. They lived in villages along the banks of the Nile. So little communities were first developed with governments which were entirely independent of one another. After these local governments had been formed, the Egyptians of one locality began gradually to learn about those in other districts by rowing or sailing up and down the Nile. The Nile, as you see, became their highway of civilization.

The Nile made the Egyptians work together. Even as early as the New Stone Age, the Egyptians had begun controlling the Nile flood, draining the swamps,

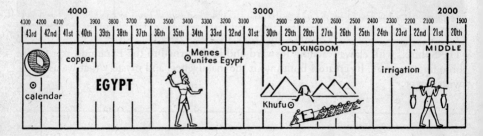

and using the river waters to irrigate the valley and the Delta region. The people of the different communities learned to co-operate with each other in order to build a good irrigation system, so necessary for farming. Thus the Nile taught the Egyptians the necessity of co-operating. The farmers held their land under petty chiefs or kings, some of whom became more powerful than others and controlled larger and larger areas. In time Egypt was organized into two kingdoms. One was for Upper Egypt, which included the southern part of the Nile valley, between the First Cataract and Memphis. The other was for Lower Egypt, which was formed by the Delta. The Egyptians themselves called their country the Two Lands.

Copper helped Egypt to flourish. The geography of Egypt was not the only reason that the Egyptians were among the first peoples to build a great civilization. The Egyptians were not content to live just as their forefathers had lived. They developed new ways of doing things. They were probably the first people to use copper. About seven thousand years ago they used copper in place of flint for making tools, and in place of clay for making bowls and ornaments. They soon discovered also that many new tools could be made from this soft metal. Craftsmen became skilled in working copper as well as gold. Centuries later Egyptian coppersmiths made the tools for building the pyramids.

As you will see in the next chapter, the Egyptians finally took possession of the copper mines on the near-by Sinai [sai' nai] Peninsula, shown on the map on page 32. For this reason they were able for a time to make greater progress than the surrounding peoples. But since the Egyptians did not have tin available for the making of bronze, and since the iron of the upper Nile was so hard to get, they continued to use copper long after other peoples were using bronze and iron.

The early Egyptians gave the world a calendar. The Egyptians were interested in astronomy even in prehistoric times. They were the first people to develop a calendar. Archeologists have figured out that the first calendar probably came into use in Egypt in 4241 B.C. This is the first fixed date of which we are reasonably certain in the history of the world. This first calendar was similar to the one we use today. The months were not exactly like ours, for the Egyptians had twelve months of thirty days each. Since there are 365 days in a year, the Egyptians had five days left over at the end of the year. They devoted these five days to a great feast and celebration.

The Egyptians also needed some way of counting the years. In early days, each year was named for some prominent event which occurred in it. The American Indians used this method, and we ourselves sometimes go back to this ancient practice. For instance, you may have heard someone who lives in San

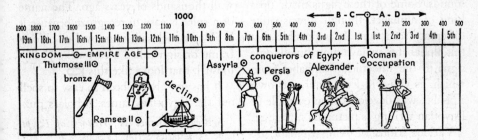

Culver Service

CUTTING STRAW IN EGYPT

Not all Egyptian scenes are somber. The laborers and their water buffaloes are going about their work simply, and doing it as well as their primitive straw-cutter will let them.

Francisco say, " It happened in the year of the great fire." This method of naming the years proved to be inconvenient, so the Egyptians began to number the years of each king's reign. Thereafter they spoke of the first, second, or third year of the reign of a certain ruler.

The Egyptians developed a means of writing. With the growth of trade and the increased activities of government, the Egyptians developed a new and simpler kind of writing. It probably came about in much the same manner that modern shorthand did. Clerks and scribes in their haste ceased to draw complete pictures and drew signs or symbols instead. Besides these signs which stood for objects, the Egyptians began to use signs that stood for certain syllables or sounds. Some of these signs made up a kind of alphabet, though it was quite different from ours. It is possible that this alphabet may have contributed some signs to the Phoenician alphabet from which, as you will learn later, our own alphabet was developed. An example of Egyptian writing is pictured on page 41.

Various kinds of symbols made up the hieroglyphics [hai′er oh glif′iks] in which the history of ancient Egypt was written. But in time the Egyptians used the sound signs more and the object signs less. One historian has written, " Had the Egyptian been less a creature of habit he might have discarded his syllabic signs 3500 years before Christ, and have written with an alphabet of twenty-four letters." [1]

Our first written records of Egypt date from about 3400 B.C., when the Two Lands were united under one ruler, as you will learn in the next chapter.

It is not hard to understand a few of the Egyptian hieroglyphics. In walking through an ancient Egyptian tomb one can soon learn to make out names of famous kings and queens written on the wall thousands of years ago. The name of a ruler is easy to recognize because it is always enclosed in an oval or oblong frame or sign called a cartouche [kahr-toosh′], that looks like this ▭.

It has not always been so easy to spell out the Egyptian names. Scholars puz-

[1] Breasted, James H., *History of Egypt*, page 45; Charles Scribner's Sons.

zled over the Egyptian writing for years before they could find a key to the mystery.

The key to Egyptian hieroglyphics was discovered. In the last year of the 18th Century Napoleon sent French soldiers to put down trouble along the Delta of the Nile. One day a young soldier who was walking near the Rosetta branch of the Nile found a stone which he thought would interest scholars. This stone (called the Rosetta Stone because of the place where it was found) is famous. It was inscribed in three kinds of writing: Greek, which the scholars could read very well; Egyptian hieroglyphic writing, which they had been trying to translate for a long time; and another unknown writing, which later proved to be a simplified and popular form of Egyptian writing. The Rosetta Stone is shown at the right.

THE ROSETTA STONE

Here was the key to Egyptian hieroglyphics — the same inscription in hieroglyphics, in ordinary Egyptian letters, and in Greek. The inscription itself is a decree drawn up by priests at Memphis in honor of Ptolemy V, almost 4000 years ago.

Scholars from many countries tried to untangle the Egyptian writing on the Rosetta Stone. Twenty years later, Champollion [shahɴ poh lee ohɴ'] made a discovery. The custom of putting rulers' names in cartouches gave him the clue which solved the puzzle. He found two cartouches that he had reason to believe contained the names of the Egyptian rulers Ptolemy [tahl'i mi] and Cleopatra [klee'oh pay'truh]. He found that these two names had some things in common. Notice, in the illustration at the foot of page 42, that both of these names contain the letter *L*. By means of these two names Champollion was able to decipher many symbols, and finally to translate the Rosetta Stone. The translation was difficult because, as you know, the Egyptians used several kinds of signs. For instance, in the draw-

Ewing Galloway

FRAGMENT OF A LEGAL DOCUMENT

This early Egyptian writing looks as if it might be a record of witchcraft, but it is believed to be part of a police-court record. The fraying of the papyrus must have left gaps in the story.

Courtesy Oriental Institute, University of Chicago

ILLUSTRATION FROM A PAPYRUS ROLL

This picture comes from a *Book of the Dead,* written by a royal Egyptian scribe. The roll contains charms for use after death. The upper scene shows Hunefer kneeling, with offerings to fourteen gods who are judging him. Below, the conscience of the dead man is being weighed. The ibis-headed figure is Thoth, the scribe of the gods.

ing here, the two little signs at the end of Cleopatra's name mean that it is a woman's and not a man's name.

The Egyptians found paper more convenient for writing than stone. Along the Nile grows a reedlike plant which the Egyptians found could be used as a writing material. If you remember the story of Moses being hidden in the rushes of the Nile, you will have an idea of how thickly such papyrus [puh pai′ruhs] reeds grow.

The Egyptians took the stem of this plant, cut it into long thin slices, and wove these strips into a mat which they placed on a board to dry. After this the surfaces were joined together by a kind of glue. Then the whole was pressed and dried to make the paper ready for use. The illustration above shows a piece of papyrus with hieroglyphics on it. The people of the Nile valley were

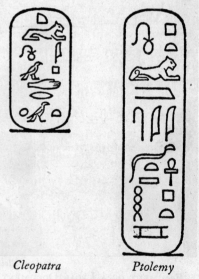

Cleopatra   *Ptolemy*

TWO ROYAL EGYPTIAN NAMES

The small cartouche contains the name of Cleopatra; the larger one, the name of Ptolemy. These cartouches helped to solve the mystery of Egyptian writing.

the first in the Mediterranean world to make paper.

With the invention of a writing material more convenient than stone, the Egyptians began to make books. These books, however, did not look much like the one you are reading. Instead of cutting the sheets of paper into pages, and binding the pages together as we do, the Egyptians fastened the sheets together at the ends and made them into long strips. These strips varied in width from six to fourteen inches and might be from a few inches to over a hundred feet long. It was not practical to leave the paper stretched out for its entire length, so it was rolled up and put into a jar. An Egyptian library was filled with many rows of jars containing such rolls of papyrus.

Chapter 3 ~ A Mighty Empire Rose and Fell

A pharaoh united all Egypt. The history of Egypt, as you have learned, has been preserved in writing from about 3400 B.C. At this date a powerful king from Upper Egypt named Menes [mee´neez] managed to unite the two Egyptian kingdoms and established his capital at Memphis. Until then the ruler of Upper Egypt had worn a red crown and the king of Lower Egypt had worn a white crown. But now the king of united Egypt wore a double crown, as pictured on page 44, to indicate that he was the ruler of both lands.

About this time the rulers of united Egypt came to be known as pharaohs [fair´ohz]. The word *pharaoh* means "Great House." The Egyptian people were in such awe of the pharaoh that they dared not call him by his real name, just as in Japan, the people were not to speak the emperor's name. Instead, the Egyptians spoke of the "Great House" in which their ruler lived.

It was believed that the pharaohs were descended from the gods. According to an old tradition Egypt was first ruled by gods who lived on earth with the common people. The last of these gods grew tired of the earth and longed to return to heaven. So he appointed his son, whose mother was an Egyptian woman, to rule after him. From then on the pharaohs were looked upon as half god and half man. The pharaoh was worshiped as the Divine Ruler, and his statue was placed beside those of the other gods.

There are three great periods in the story of United Egypt. Within four centuries after Menes had established the united kingdom of Egypt it had become both powerful and wealthy. From 3000 to 1000 B.C. Egypt was at its height. (Notice that one counts backwards the years before Christ, that is B.C.) Historians have divided this era into three ages — the Old Kingdom, the Middle Kingdom and the Empire Age. The Old Kingdom lasted from 3000 to 2500 B.C. By 2000 B.C. the civilization of the Middle Kingdom was at its height. The last and greatest age of progress came during the Empire period, from about 1580 to 1150 B.C. In each of these three periods Egypt rose to greater splendor.

THE DOUBLE CROWN OF AN EGYPTIAN
RULER

The double crown was worn by an Egyptian Pharaoh to show that he was king of Upper and Lower Egypt or lord of both lands.

Commerce was one source of Egypt's greatness during the Old Kingdom. The early Egyptians had discovered or invented many new tools and other conveniences, and new ways of doing things, before 3000 B.C. The Egyptians of the Old Kingdom developed and improved what had been handed down to them. Egypt made great advancement in her trade or commerce. Her caravans went far into the desert of Sinai to bring home copper from the mines and far up the Nile into the Sudan [soo dan'] region to bring back ivory, ebony, and fragrant gums. Her ships ventured out

into the Mediterranean Sea to trade with the inhabitants of coastal towns and islands.

The Egyptians of the Old Kingdom developed the sciences and arts. The Egyptians of the Old Kingdom advanced in their knowledge of science and mathematics. They particularly furthered the study of geometry, which was used in marking off the plots of land after each annual flood.

The knowledge of geometry proved a great help to the Egyptians in their building. They also learned the use of the lever and of the ramp, or inclined plane. Egyptian rulers and foremen were capable organizers and directed huge armies of workmen. The Nile dwellers of the Old Kingdom have left gigantic buildings which still stand as enduring monuments to the ability of their engineers.

The architecture of the Egyptians was remarkable for its great size and simple grandeur. Huge columns and great blocks made up their impressive but severe straight-lined temples. The arch was used but little, and never in important buildings, but these people knew its use long years before the Romans brought it to perfection.

The pyramids were built for the pharaohs of the Old Kingdom. One of the outstanding achievements during the Old Kingdom was the building of pyramids as tombs for the pharaohs. For this reason the Old Kingdom is sometimes called the Pyramid Age, though pyramids were built in the Middle Kingdom also.

Religion, and particularly the belief in life after death, were of first importance in ancient Egypt. The Egyptians of the Old Kingdom did not expect that most people would have a life after death. But they did believe that pharaoh was divine.

They thought that when pharaoh died he would join the gods and would continue to watch over the welfare of Egypt. But for this to be possible they believed that a pharaoh's body must be preserved, entombed with the proper rights, and surrounded with useful and precious things. They also believed that a pharaoh could grant immortality to a few chosen favorites and relatives by having their bodies similarly preserved.

Because of such religious beliefs the pharaoh could force all the people, from the chief engineers and architects to the serfs and slaves, to join in the building of his pyramid. The pyramid was the symbol of the passing of the king-god into the sacred realm of all gods. Each pharaoh wanted his pyramid to be as imposing and magnificent as possible. His chief engineers and architects strove to make it so. In return the " Divine Ruler " might see fit to let them join him in immortality.

The huge pyramids were built of large blocks of limestone. The religious beliefs of the Egyptians could not have found expression in the great historic pyramids had not the Egyptians learned how to make tools of copper and how to use stone in the place of sun-dried brick as a building material. The early Egyptians as well as later civilizations are indebted to the great Egyptian architect Imhotep [im'hoh tep], who is believed to have planned and built the first building of stone masonry. This man, who lived just before 3000 B.C., possessed great imagination and skill. The Egyptians of the Old Kingdom understood the use of the inclined plane in moving masonry, as well as the use of levers, skids, and rope-like cables.

To appreciate the achievement of the Egyptians during the Pyramid Age, one must see the great pyramids they built.

They are scattered in a north-and-south direction in the desert on the west side of the Nile, south of Cairo. Let us visit one of these ancient tombs.

Khufu built the Great Pyramid. The Great Pyramid of King Khufu [koo' foo], or Cheops [kee'ahps], lies six miles from the city of El Giza [el gee'zuh]. It is over five thousand years old and is one of the largest monuments in the world. Its base covers thirteen acres and it stands nearly five hundred feet high, or almost twice as high as our Capitol at Washington, D.C. Each of its four sides is 755 feet long — about equal to two city blocks. A diagram of the interior of this pyramid is shown on page 46.

The pyramid is made of solid blocks of stone, each carefully fitted to the ones next to it. At one time the pyramid had an outer surface which made it perfectly smooth and its top ended in a sharp point. This is no longer true, for much of the covering has worn away or been removed. Many of the buildings of modern Cairo have been built with stones taken from Khufu's tomb. The sides of the pyramid now look like a flight of stairs. The pyramid contains approximately 2,300,000 blocks of stone, each stone weighing two and a half tons, or about as much as an ordinary load of coal.

Slave labor built roads and quarried stone for the pyramids. It took thousands of men many years to build the Great Pyramid because the stone had to be brought over a road that had to be built across the desert. Many thousands of men worked on this roadway over a period of ten years. As the stones were dragged to the site of the pyramid, other thousands worked for more than twenty years putting the blocks in place.

When we think of the suffering and toil of the workmen who were forced

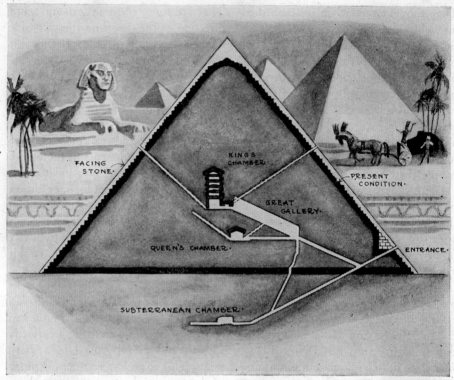

Drawing by John C. Wonsetler

DIAGRAM OF KHUFU'S PYRAMID

This cross section shows the interior of Khufu's grave. Long inclined passages lead to the different chambers. As you will see from this diagram, the Pharaoh had a distinguished burial place.

to labor so many years to put these pyramid stones in place, we can get some idea of the power of religious beliefs in ancient Egypt.

The pyramids were designed with secret doors. One can go inside Khufu's pyramid by means of an entrance on the north side, which is about fifty feet from the ground. This doorway is a movable stone that looks like all the others. It does not show when closed. When the secret of its position was lost, the door was concealed so perfectly that it was not found for centuries. About the Ninth Century an Arab, eager for wealth and treasure, hired workmen to drag away the stones on the north side. After many weary months they finally broke into the

main passage and opened the entrance to the tomb.

If you are not too stout, you can first slide and then push your way through the dark, narrow passages to the king's chamber. You will probably be a little disappointed when you get there, however, because all the treasures, which were buried with Khufu, have long since been stolen. Even the sarcophagus [sahr-kahf'uh guhs], or stone coffin in which the body of the pharaoh lay, no longer holds his mummy. One would think that the mountains of stone would keep the mummies of the dead rulers safe, but few of them still lie where they were placed. It is not certain what became of Khufu's body; perhaps the priests re-

OROC

PYRAMIDS ALONG THE NILE

On the shores of the Nile are massive pyramids. Although they vary in size, they are all of the same general shape. These huge structures, built as tombs, have given their name to a common geometric form.

moved it long ago to guard it from tomb robbers.[1]

Egyptian mummies were well preserved. This is how one writer described his visit to an Egyptian tomb:

We had to scramble down into the dark, where there were no stairs, to a lower level with only a candle for a light — like slipping and falling into a grave. At the bottom, in a small stone room, was a huge sarcophagus. The king lay, with the calm dignity of death upon his face, his shoulders and chest exposed, a single garment draped around his lower body in graceful folds. "Mummy" is not the word! There lay a man. The preservation was perfection itself, though he had been dead for some thousands of years.

[1] In later years pharaohs were buried in tombs hollowed out in the sides of cliffs. In 1923 some British explorers discovered a tomb which had been so well hidden that the robbers never found it. For a description of the treasure buried with the young Pharaoh Tutankhamen [toot'ahnk ah'mun] see the *National Geographic Magazine* of May 1923.

There are many pyramids on the sands of Egypt. The Great Pyramid of Cheops does not stand alone. If you have the physical endurance, you may climb up the hundreds of stones to the top of the Great Pyramid and see from there more evidence of the Egyptian belief in a life after death. About the pyramid on which you stand are clustered the lesser tombs of relatives and nobles. Near by are two other pyramids, and off in the distance over the desert, you will see many more of these massive geometrical structures. The Egyptian pharaohs built for all time! The photograph above shows the panorama that would be unrolled before you if you were there in person.

Dark days followed the Old Kingdom. The Old Kingdom was brought to an end by the outbreak of civil war within Egypt and by the invasion of a race of foreigners about whom we know little. A long, wretched period of disor-

A PHARAOH IN HIS WAR CHARIOT

This picture is one of the colorful scenes on the pillars of the Temple at Karnak. In these
scenes the Pharaohs are shown as skilled warriors who led their soldiers in battle.

der followed. More than one line of rulers claimed to be pharaohs. The country was in turmoil, and the records of these days are incomplete.

The Egyptians rose to greatness again in the Middle Kingdom. After a long time, we do not know how long, a strong line of princes made their capital at Thebes [theebz]. From there they finally ruled northern Egypt also. Once again there was a strong pharaoh over the Two Lands. The second age, or Middle Kingdom, had begun. But a change had come in the way people thought about things. They now knew of times when more than one man had claimed to be pharaoh. And they no longer believed that only pharaoh and his favorites could be immortal. They began to believe that all men might have life after death.

The Egyptians dug a canal at Suez. Under the pharaohs of the Middle Kingdom the Egyptians erected huge dikes

and made great reservoirs to store up the water of the Nile for irrigation. They cut through the rising ground between the Delta of the Nile and the Red Sea to join these waters. Look at the map on page 32 to see how the Damietta arm of the Nile could be made to flow into the Red Sea by cutting a canal. The Egyptians constructed their canal over three thousand years before the famous Suez Canal was built by a French engineer, de Lesseps, in 1869.

Egypt was invaded by Shepherd Kings. The second great age of Egypt, like the first, ended in confusion and invasion. The Egyptians were divided among themselves and defense of the kingdom was neglected. It fell easily, about 1800 B.C., before a wave of invaders called Hyksos [hik'sohs], or Shepherd Kings. These men came in from the western end of the Arabian desert, driving war chariots drawn by horses —

animals which the Egyptians had heard of but had never seen.

The Egyptians learned to use bronze. Egypt did not have tin, but during the Middle Kingdom tin was brought into the country by foreign trade. By about 1500 B.C., the Egyptians were using it with copper to make bronze weapons, which were much harder than their old copper weapons.

In the third age Egypt ruled the ancient world. After three or four hundred years under the rule of the Hyksos, the Egyptians rose in a spirit of national pride and drove the Hyksos out. This marked the beginning of a new period called the Empire. During these years Egypt rose to greater heights than ever before, as we shall see.

Iron had come into more common use, and from the Hyksos the Egyptians had learned the use of the horse and chariot. Egyptian charioteers were now famous. Strong generals organized powerful standing armies and conquered lands from the Euphrates Valley in western Asia to the Fourth Cataract of the Nile. For about four hundred years Egypt was the military power that ruled the ancient world.

Besides her great land armies, Egypt now boasted a navy. Powerful sailing vessels had been developed in Egypt since the Stone Age, when men first used square sails on their little rowboats. By the latter days of the Empire, Egyptian sailors were so capable that they were even hiring out to the king of Persia as mercenaries, or paid fighters.

Egypt conquered other lands because she had many strong and ruthless military leaders. One of these was Thutmose I [thut'mohz], whose armies went even into Syria. You can see how far the Empire was extended by looking at the map on page 50.

Metropolitan Museum of Art

AN EGYPTIAN OBELISK

This obelisk which now stands in Central Park, New York City, tells of the deeds of Thutmose III and Ramses II.

A woman became an Egyptian pharaoh. When Thutmose I was an old man he presented his young daughter Hatshepsut [hah chep'sut] to some of his great generals and told them that she was to be their pharaoh. Hatshepsut was accepted as their pharaoh, even though she was a woman. She married one of her younger half-brothers, Thutmose III, but during her lifetime he only helped her rule.

You will probably think it strange that Thutmose should marry his sister, but such marriages were common among the Egyptian rulers. Because it was beneath the dignity of a pharaoh to marry anyone who was not half god like himself, he usually solved the difficulty by marrying a woman of his own family.

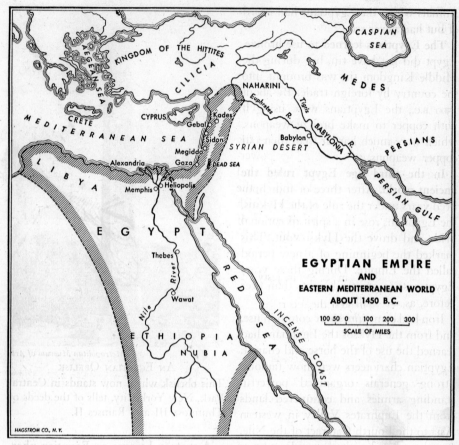

THE EGYPTIAN EMPIRE ABOUT 1450 B.C.

Hatshepsut, as a woman, was not expected to go to work. She spent much of her time and energy in having temples built to glorify the god Amen [ah′m′n] and in having obelisks [ahb′uh liskz] built to her own glory. It was the custom of the Egyptian pharaohs to erect these obelisks to celebrate their deeds and victories. Two of the greatest obelisks have been moved to other countries. One stands on the banks of the Thames [temz] in London and the other in Central Park, New York City. The latter one can be seen in the illustration at the top of page 49. Hatshepsut also directed expeditions to foreign lands which brought back luxuries for her temples. The efficiency with which Hatshepsut handled this work shows her success as a ruler.

We are told that the home life of the Egyptians was usually very happy, but that of Hatshepsut and Thutmose III seems to have been an exception to the rule. It may have been because the queen ruled. At least, after Hatshepsut was dead, Thutmose tried to cover up all the records that told of her accomplishments. He had the name of the queen cut from the tablets or hidden with masonry. These coverings, however, have fallen away so that tablets and obelisks still proclaim the achievements of Hatshepsut.

The triumphs of Thutmose III. After Hatshepsut's death Thutmose III became one of the greatest — and most ruthless — generals in history. He ruled Egypt for years, beginning about 1500 B.C., and more than twenty years of his reign were spent in active warfare. His armies crushed cities and kingdoms in western Asia. His war fleet subdued the islands of the Aegean Sea. This powerful man left a bloody record written and pictured on slender obelisks and on the walls of the Temple of Karnak, which you see on page 62. Here are parts of the "Hymn of Victory," which celebrates his deeds:

> I have made them see thy majesty
>   as a fierce-eyed lion,
> While thou makest them corpses
>   in their valleys. . . .
> I have made them see thy majesty
>   as a soaring hawk,
> Seizing that which he seeth, as
>   much as he desires.

Thutmose III was, however, a capable ruler and organizer, and established his large empire on a sound basis.

A new ruler introduced a new religion. About seventy years after the death of Thutmose III a pharaoh came to the throne who was neither a great general nor an able governor. Nevertheless his name is famous. Amenhotep IV [ah'm'n hoh'tep] was one of the first men to believe that there was only one god, the sun-god, Aten [ah't'n], who ruled over all men and all creatures. The king believed that his god was good and kind. He wrote a remarkably fine poem to him, two lines of which read:

The birds flutter in their marshes,
Their wings uplifted in adoration to thee.

The fact that Amenhotep IV believed in but one god is remarkable, for he had been taught to worship many gods.

The University Prints, Newton, Massachusetts
IKHNATON

Ikhnaton, shown in this statue, introduced the worship of a single god — the sun god — in Egypt. He was more interested in religion than in the preservation of his empire.

(Much later, as you will learn, the Hebrews interpreted for the world this idea of a single god, and on it is based the widely accepted idea of the Christian God.)

The pharaoh was so much interested in his new religion that he neglected governmental affairs. He commanded that the temples of the old Egyptian gods be closed and the wealthy priests be cast out. He ordered the people to worship only Aten. He had the names of the other gods, particularly Amen, taken off the temple walls and he changed his own name from Amenho-

Strobel from Monkemeyer

RAMSES II

This statue of Ramses II in the Temple at Luxor, shows him to be what we know he was — a vigorous, daring ruler, who fought and governed with determined purpose.

tep to Ikhnaton [ik nah't'n], which means "Aten is satisfied." He even moved the capital of his empire from the ancient city of Thebes to Tell el-Amarna.

Ikhnaton believed that he could make the Egyptians accept his new religion through force. But the Egyptians resisted the attempt to force them to change their religious beliefs, just as did our Pilgrim forefathers who left England partly because they were not allowed to worship God as they wished.

Ikhnaton's attempts to reform religion divided the Egyptian ruling class into two conflicting groups. As a result, the government was weakened. Moreover, Ikhnaton failed to send military support either to Egypt's allies or to outlying provinces of the Empire, which were threatened by invasion or revolt. Again, the result was the weakening of his rule.

After this pharaoh died, leaving no heir to rule Egypt, the Empire was torn by strife and bloodshed. The new pharaohs deserted Ikhnaton's capital at Tell el-Amarna and returned to the old capital and the old gods. Soon the desert sands drifted in and completely covered up the beautiful palace of Ikhnaton.

Letters to the pharaohs show Egypt's decline. Three thousand years later an old peasant woman was searching through the sand, hoping to find some relic of ancient times which she could sell to collectors of antiquities. She came across a large number of clay tablets written by the rulers of western Asia to Ikhnaton and to his father, who ruled before him. These three hundred letters make up the first diplomatic correspondence between rulers of different nations of which we have record. They are called the Tell el-Amarna letters, and are almost as famous as the Rosetta Stone. They tell the story of Ikhnaton's neglect of his Empire and the dissatisfaction everywhere, and they show that Egypt's empire in Asia was gradually falling to pieces. The Hittites and other invaders from the eastern desert were gradually invading Syria. Lesser kings in Syria, who were loyal subjects of Egypt, sent repeated requests to the pharaoh for aid; but their requests were largely unheeded. Then the outposts of the Empire fell apart.

Ramses II ruled Egypt with an iron hand. Warlike pharaohs who came after Ikhnaton restored the power of the Empire for a time. One of the most daring of these was Ramses II [ram'seez]. He fought against the Nubians, the Syrians, and the Libyans, and waged war against the Hittites in Asia Minor for fifteen or sixteen years. The map on page 50 will show you the location of these peoples. Ramses II ruled Egypt sternly for sixty-seven years and filled it with monuments to his power. He finished the great hall of the Temple of Amen at Karnak which had been begun many years before.

The long decline of the Empire was due to strife within and conflict without. The pharaohs after Ramses II also had to fight their neighbors who were trying to enter and break up the Empire. Sometimes it was a losing fight. Perhaps Egypt had seized more territory than she could handle. Many of the soldiers in the Egyptian army were now mercenaries from conquered lands. And some of Egypt's own soldiers, too, were now joining the army mainly for spoils and pay. Fighting for an empire was not like fighting for the homeland as the Egyptians had done in the days of the Old Kingdom. It is a story of downfall often to be repeated, as we shall see, with many nations. Weakness at home and attack from one's enemies became the formula for defeat and decline.

There was trouble within Egypt too. The leaders quarreled among themselves. Sometimes crops were poor and there was famine in the land. Another great pharaoh, Ramses III, had to drive out the Syrians who had seized Egypt itself for a time. The pharaohs after Ramses III lost power to the priesthood of Amen, and by the middle of the 12th Century B.C., the Empire had fallen before attacks, first by the Syrians, then by the Libyans.

For about four hundred years more Egypt remained a separate nation, though torn by warfare from within and without. At different times the ruling pharaohs were Egyptian, Libyan, or Ethiopian.

Finally, about 670 B.C. Egypt lost her separate existence as a nation and became a dependency of Assyria for a short time. Then about fifty years later the Persians conquered Egypt and made it a part of their empire.

The revival of Egyptian power under Cleopatra was short-lived. The long rule of the Persians ended in 332 B.C. when Alexander the Great, the Greek conqueror whom we shall meet later, took Egypt from Persia and established the capital of his world empire, Alexandria, at the edge of the Nile delta. It was after Alexander's death and the break-up of his empire that Egypt was ruled by the line of pharaohs called Ptolemies.

The last of these Ptolemy rulers was the famous woman, Cleopatra. Cleopatra threatened the rule of Rome and tried to make Egypt once again the center of a world empire by helping Mark Antony in a war against his Roman rival, Octavian. But the Egyptian fleet was destroyed by the Romans in 31 B.C. and the long story of ancient Egypt was ended. Egypt became a part of the Roman Empire.

Chapter 4 ~ Egyptian Life Reflected a Remarkable Culture

The Egyptians were distinguished in appearance. Up to this point we have told you about the geography of Egypt and the story of the development and downfall of the Egyptian Empire. But so far you have heard very little about the life of the Egyptian people.

In some ways life along the banks of the Nile was similar to life today in the United States. Today we are taught that a man's good character is his most important possession. So were the ancient Egyptians. As you read this chapter, watch for the origin of some of our modern beliefs and standards of conduct.

To get a picture of the Egyptian we will have to turn to the early Egyptian artists. There were no cameras five thousand years ago, but the Egyptians left pictures carved on the stone walls of the pyramids and temples.

No people in the ancient world were more proud and distinguished looking than the Egyptians. They were tall and slender, of good figure, with broad shoulders, and with finely molded hands and feet. Their faces were thin and their noses often aquiline, or highly bowed. Their eyes were large; their teeth small and white; their hair dark and wavy. Even the peasant had the characteristic broad shoulders and slender body. In many ways the Egyptians remind one of the tall, copper-hued, eagle-nosed Indians of some of the American tribes.

Egyptian dress reflected Egyptian life. From these same pictures we can get an idea of the way the Egyptians dressed to live in a country of hot winds, burning sun, and desert sands. Of course garments exactly like those shown in the pictures were not worn in every period

Metropolitan Museum of Art

EGYPTIAN PORTRAIT PANELS

In these stone carvings you can see the characteristic appearance of the Egyptians. The lithe, short-skirted figures have energy and spirit.

of Egyptian history. Styles changed in ancient Egypt even as they change to-day; but this clothing is typical. Frequently a beautiful jeweled girdle ·was worn at the waist. Heavy jeweled necklaces and wide bracelets were ·common ornaments for those who could afford them. The Egyptians in later days wore sandals of papyrus, the same reeds from which paper was made. The pharaoh's dress was like that of the other men except that it was embroidered with gold and a lion's-tail sash fell from the waist.

Much as a modern actress prepares for the glare of the footlights, an Egyptian woman prepared to face the dazzling sunlight reflected by the white sand of Egypt. A part of her extreme make-up was a black line painted under her eyes. Lips and face were rouged, and fingernails were stained a yellowish-red with the juice of the henna plant. Then the Egyptian lady looked into a highly polished copper mirror and pinned a lotus flower in her curled or braided hair.

Because the climate was so warm, the children rarely wore any clothes until they were three or four years old. As they grew older a cloth was placed about their waist, and later on they were clothed just like grown-ups.

The Egyptians could be cheerful and courteous. The Egyptians were light-hearted and full of laughter. Even the peasants were usually cheerful in spite of their life of hard work and poverty. The manners of the Egyptians were so charming that many ancient writers considered them the most courteous and courtly of the peoples of those times. The instructions below were translated from an ancient papyrus roll.

If thou art sitting in company hate the food which thou likest; restrain thy appetite, for greediness savoreth of the beasts.

A BEAUTIFUL EGYPTIAN

Nefertiti, Ikhnaton's queen, shows the perfection of the Egyptian type of beauty. Her face seems modern, perhaps because it is so flawless that any age would recognize its loveliness.

Young people were taught to respect their elders, much as they were in Colonial America in the 18th Century. Here is a rule given thousands of years ago which is still good today.

Sit not down when another is standing up if he be older than thou, even if thy rank in life be higher than his.

Egyptian women were respected and honored. An Egyptian child was taught to show the greatest courtesy and respect to his mother. Here is advice an Egyptian once gave to his son:

Thou shalt never forget what thy mother hath done for thee. She bare thee and nourished thee in all manner of ways. . . . She brought thee up, and when thou didst enter the school, and wast instructed in the writings, she came daily to thy master with bread from her house. If thou forgettest her, she might blame thee; she might lift up her hands to God, and He would hear her complaint.

Drawing by John C. Wonsetler

VILLA OF AN EGYPTIAN NOBLEMAN

In 1500 B.C. Egyptian nobles lived in lavishly decorated villas such as this, and enjoyed their jewels and pottery, their gardens, their animals, their wall paintings, and the music of their gifted servants. Notice the two pet dogs in the villa. Dogs were among the earliest animals to be domesticated and to become household pets.

Women had a higher place in Egypt than in almost any of the other ancient countries. It was the usual custom for Egyptian men to have but one wife, who shared the responsibilities of her husband whether they lived in a peasant's cottage or in the pharaoh's palace. All orders and laws were signed by the queen as well as the king. All land was owned by the women and it was passed down from the mother to the oldest daughter. Wives went with their husbands to the mountains on hunting expeditions, and to the river or the sea on fishing trips, just as women sometimes do today.

The wealthy Egyptians built beautiful homes. The people of Egypt loved beauty, and this feeling was fully expressed in the homes of the wealthier class. The well-to-do nobles built their houses with sun-dried brick or wood, and surrounded them with high walls and blooming gardens. The partitions between the rooms were merely gay-colored hangings which could be let down as a protection against sand and wind storms. On the floors were paintings that portrayed the shining water of the pools, banked by deep green marsh grasses in and out of which fish and waterfowl darted. The ceilings were sometimes made to represent the sky with stars shining out from the blue background. The interior of one of these homes of wealthy noblemen is shown above.

The Egyptians had much less furniture in their homes than we commonly have in ours. They did have low couches, beautifully inlaid tables, and chairs resting on the carved ivory body of a lion or an ox. They kept their clothing and jewels in chests and boxes.

Although the homes of the Egyptians were bright and cheerful, they were looked upon as only temporary dwellings, while the pyramids and tombs were constructed to last forever. This in itself illustrated the belief in ancient Egypt that life on earth was not as important as life after death.

The poor lived in mud huts and led a life of toil. The life of the rulers, the priests, and the wealthy does not present a complete picture of the ancient Egyptians.

There were various social classes among the Egyptians. An Egyptian's position in life was not absolutely fixed by the class into which he happened to be born, and it was possible for an ambitious man to rise from one class to another. There were marked differences in living conditions of the various classes. The groups who enjoyed the best of everything were only a small percent of the seven million people who lived in the valley of the Nile. The poor in the cities lived in thatch-roofed mud huts, so close together that the walls often were almost continuous. The furniture consisted of a stool or a box or two, and a few crude pottery jars. These people

did their cooking over an outdoor fire or in an outdoor oven. Little or no thought was given by the rulers to the health or morals of these people.

The farm workers, who made up the larger part of the population, had a little more room in their villages and slightly better living conditions. Both the serfs and the tenant farmers worked long hours and lived in fear of the tax collectors, who always collected at least the one-fifth of the crops that the law required, and sometimes more.

The three-year-old boy entered school. Very young children were left almost entirely to the care of their mothers, who often carried them about on their backs as an American Indian mother carried her papoose. These small children seem to have had a great many toys. Among those found in tombs were wooden dolls with real hair or hair made of beads; balls made of papyrus and leather; small, horrible crocodiles that moved their jaws from side to side with a crunching

THE COLLECTION OF TAXES

Egyptian farmers bring taxes to the collector. They are making their payments in farm products. The records of payment were made on the wall of the house in a crude manner. In the background at the far right you can see several homes of the farmers.

EGYPTIAN TOYS

The children who played with these toy animals, and may have had names for them, belong to Egypt's past. The toys are as alive as they ever were.

motion; and cats with crystal eyes, movable jaws, and metal teeth. A group of Egyptian toys is shown in the picture above.

Egyptian boys often were sent to school when they were three or four. So far as we know most girls were given little or no schooling. The boy learned to write by copying the sayings of famous men. Many of these copybooks have been found with corrections made in the margins by the masters, or with funny little pictures drawn by boys who were bored with their lessons.

For neglecting his work an Egyptian boy was punished severely. He was warned to "Spend no day in idleness, or thou wilt be flogged."

After a boy had learned something about writing, arithmetic, swimming, and the sacred songs and dances of his people, his elementary schooling was finished. Then he learned a trade from his father or was sent to the university to become a professional man. Perhaps his father taught him to be a farmer, a carpenter, a cabinetmaker, leather worker, goldsmith, potter, or shipbuilder. The boys who went on to the colleges of the priests learned about religion and astronomy.

Egypt established a great university. The greatest university of ancient Egypt was that at Heliopolis [hee'li op'uh-lis], the City of the Sun. This university was known particularly for its work in astronomy. The priests there were noted for their profound knowledge and were called the "mystery teachers of heaven." The high priest was known as the Royal Astronomer and wore over his robes a "sacred leopard skin spangled with stars." A few of the famous Greek graduates of this university were Solon [soh'lahn], the lawgiver; Plato [play'toh], one of the greatest philosophers; and Archimedes [ahr'ki mee'deez], who is considered one of the greatest mechanical geniuses of all times. You will learn more about some of these famous men in Part Five.

The work of the scribe was a steppingstone to success. The Egyptian's idea of an excellent profession was that of scribe, or secretary. A scribe might be one who kept accounts for a wealthy man or he might be the head of a great business. He could rise in the world; so the father who had an ambitious or clever son told him to —

. . . set to work to become a scribe, for then thou shalt be a leader of men . . . he who is industrious and does not neglect his books, he may become a prince, or perhaps attain to the Council of Thirty; and if there is a question of sending out an ambassador, his name is remembered at court.

Medical science began in Egypt. The Egyptians boasted that they were the healthiest of all mortals. Perhaps this was because they had a large number of doctors. Each doctor selected one particular subject in which he was to become a specialist. As a result, the Egyptian doc-

Metropolitan Museum of Art

AN EGYPTIAN SCRIBE

This statue shows a scribe reading a papyrus. His profession in Egypt was respected and had a good future.

tor had a good reputation among the ancient peoples. We are told by a writer of ancient times that " it was enough for a doctor to say that he had studied in Egypt to recommend him." Since the extreme heat of Egypt often seriously affected the eyes, there were many oculists. And the first dentistry in the world seems to have been done in Egypt, for mummies have been found at Thebes with gold foil neatly pounded into their teeth. Strangely enough, the scientific study and practice of Egyptian medical men existed side by side with old magic chants and charms which they continued to use. The Egyptians, nevertheless, were pioneers in many branches of medical science.

The Egyptians paid tribute to the god Amen. The Greek historian, Herodotus, said, " The Egyptians are very religious, surpassing all men in the honors they pay to the gods." The greatest of Egyptian gods was Amen, or Amen-Ra

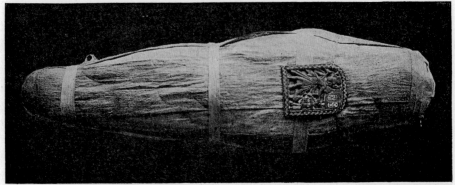

THE MUMMY OF A YOUNG PRINCE

A young prince of Thebes of the 18th Dynasty has been preserved for thousands of years in this mummy. The ornamental plate is called a " pectoral."

TWO " ANSWERERS "

These figures were found in an Egyptian tomb. They were called " Answerers " because they were intended to answer for, or do the work of, a nobleman in the next world. Commanding a number of men was a mark of prestige in Egypt. With these little " Answerers " the noblemen upheld their dignity in their future life.

[ah'm'n rah], who, like Ikhnaton's Aton, was a sun-god. He was believed to be the source of life and goodness as well as lord over all the other gods.

The " mother of the universe," who was the queen over the world and heaven, was called Isis [ai'sis]. Her husband, Osiris [oh sai'ris], the Egyptians probably loved more than other gods because they thought he gave them life after death. According to legend, Osiris himself had been brought back to life after death, and appointed King of the Underworld and Judge of the Dead.

The Egyptians believed in a life after death. It was this belief in the resurrection of Osiris that led the Egyptians to believe that men might go on living in another world after death. As we have seen, this belief led them to preserve the bodies of their dead. They did not believe that the spirit actually came back into the earthly body, but they thought the happiness of the spirit in heaven depended upon the preservation of the body in the tomb. Therefore they embalmed the body by the use of bitumen, natural gums, spices, honey, and other things of which we cannot be quite sure. The mummy was then wrapped carefully in white linen strips that had been soaked in resin and spices. In this form the Egyptian mummies, like the one pictured at the top of page 60, have been kept in a perfect state of preservation for thousands of years.

Next the mummy was placed, with many prayers and muttered charms, in a coffin which was decorated with figures and writings, and sometimes with beads or precious stones. As soon as the mummy was placed in the tomb the Egyptians believed the soul started on its long, perilous journey to heaven. In order that it might not be harmed by the serpents, dragons, and demons that haunted the path, a book of charms, which is known as the *Book of the Dead*, was also placed in the tomb. Part of one of these books is reproduced on page 42. If the charms in this papyrus roll were recited properly all terrors would be driven away.

The Egyptians called their heaven the " Fields of Content." They believed that one spent a great deal of his time there working in the fertile fields. To some of the nobles this idea of working in the fields was not pleasing. They were used to having someone else do the work in this world; so they decided that they would take along slaves to do their share in the next. These nobles placed little statues in their tombs to answer when the master called them to work. On page 60 is a picture of two " Answerers."

When the first part of the journey from the earth was over, the soul passed

Oriental Institute, University of Chicago

SENNUTEM AND HIS WIFE IN THE " FIELDS OF CONTENT "
This wall painting in the tomb of Sennutem shows the deceased and his wife working in the " Fields of Content," in a glorified agricultural life.

THE TEMPLE OF KARNAK

This reconstructed model of the Temple of Karnak shows the enormous pillars that support the roof. The tiny figure in the foreground will give you a general idea of the size of the decorated columns.

through the gates of the palace of Osiris, King of the Underworld, and entered the great Hall of Truth. In the center of this hall stood a pair of scales which was used to weigh the heart to see if it were true or false. All around the hall sat judges to whom the soul made a long plea, saying that he had not committed any of the sins that they would punish. Among his denials were these:

I have not committed murder.
I have not lied.
I have made no man weep.
I have not inflicted pain.
I have not brought my name
    forward for honors.
I have not made haughty my voice.

Then the heart was weighed with a feather, the Egyptian symbol for truth, on the other end of the scales. If the heart proved to be false it was thrown to a horrible monster called the "Eater of the Dead." If it were found to be true it was led into the presence of the sun-god.

The Egyptians were among the first people to believe that a man's character is very important and that he would be rewarded or punished in the next world in accordance with his life in this.

As we have seen, the religion of the Egyptians was probably the greatest single force in their lives.

Temples were built in honor of the Egyptian gods. People in many different periods of history have spent years constructing churches and cathedrals in which to worship, and the Egyptians were no exception. They built temples as the homes of their gods. Like the pyramids, the Egyptian temples were built to last forever. We find them still in the Nile Valley. Also like the pyramids, these buildings displayed dignity, grandeur, and simplicity. Although the temples were of many different sizes, they were all built on the same general plan.

Of all the ancient Egyptian temples the one at Karnak is probably the most famous. See the photograph of it reproduced on page 62. Approaching it, one walks the length of an imposing avenue of sphinxes which leads up to the temple gates. In front of the entrance, which is flanked by two high towers called pylons, stands the highest obelisk ever erected in Egypt. It is more than one hundred feet high and weighs nearly three hundred tons. Pliny [plin'i], a Roman author, tells us that Ramses II ordered the son of the chief engineer to be bound to the top of the obelisk he was erecting so that he would be more careful not to break it when putting it in place.

After passing through the gateway of the temple of Karnak you enter a large court surrounded by many pillars. Past that you see the great hall, the largest in any temple in the world. The high roof is supported by twelve enormous pillars, while smaller pillars form aisles and hold up the roof on each side. The great center pillars, which are decorated in glowing colors, are so large that a hundred and fifty men could stand on top of each one.

Twenty-one different kings had a hand in building the Karnak temple. It was not completed until eighteen hundred years after it was begun. For more than three thousand years it has stood as a monument to the greatness of Amen. Sands have drifted in, stones have cracked and crumbled. Still the temple of Karnak stands in its grandeur.

The Egyptians Changed Savagery into Civilization

In our story of Egypt we have seen a great nation spring from primitive life, attain great power and culture, decline, and almost disappear. Although Egypt ceased to be a power among nations centuries ago, the discoveries and ideas of ancient Egypt have lived on and have aided many later peoples.

Ancient Egypt's setting favored her unusual development. The Nile provided water and a fertile soil. The sands and the sea gave the Egyptians considerable protection from invasion and thus made it possible for them to develop one of the first of the ancient civilizations.

The Egyptians organized both local governments and a national government. They put copper to use. They learned from outsiders, probably the Hyksos, how to add tin to copper and make bronze. Iron was brought into Egypt by other nations.

The Egyptians invented the beginnings of our calendar. The Egyptians' hieroglyphic writings remained a mystery until the discovery of the Rosetta Stone in 1799 made it possible to translate them. The hieroglyphics of the Egyptians included some symbols which made up a kind of alphabet. The Egyptians made paper from the papyrus plant. They also began the study of the sciences, and gave us much of our geometry and a beginning of our astronomy.

The belief of the Egyptians that their rulers were descended from the gods gave the pharaohs unlimited power over the people. The Egyptians believed in life after death. To show their power and to provide a tomb for their bodies and for everything they might need in the future life, the pharaohs built great pyramids. The pyramids still stand as a symbol of Egyptian civilization.

As the Egyptians increased their knowledge of science they constructed more elaborate dikes and reservoirs for irrigation and flood control. They also cut a canal to connect the Nile with the Red Sea. Not content with their glory at home, the pharaohs of the Empire Age trained large armies and conquered neighboring peoples. Thutmose III, who extended and strengthened the Empire, and Ramses II, were two of the greatest military leaders. For more than four centuries Egypt was a great military nation. Finally, however, quarrels among the Egyptian leaders, revolts in outlying provinces and invasions by foreign foes brought about the downfall of the Egyptian Empire.

Egyptian homes of the upper classes were attractive and cheerfully decorated, and Egyptian home life was usually very happy. The position of women was secure. They held title to property. They were respected members of the family and community. The poorer classes lived in mud huts and led a life of toil.

Very young Egyptian children had many playthings. Many boys were sent to school when they were three years old to learn to read and write. When older, they were apprenticed to learn a trade. Universities were founded where boys studying for the professions could learn about astronomy, medicine, or the lore of the priests. The greatest of these was the university at Heliopolis.

The Egyptians produced skilled craftsmen who could spin fine linen thread and made skillfully wrought tools and jewelry. The scribe developed his work into a profession. There were doctors and dentists to serve the people.

With this story in mind we shall no longer think of Egypt merely as a country in northeastern Africa. The picture of the pyramids in a setting of waving palms will remind us of the long history and marvelous achievements of the Egyptians and of their contribution to the progress of civilization.

SELF-TEST

I. Jot down from memory a list of things of special interest which you would see in taking a trip down the Nile from its source to the delta.

II. Select the word or phrase which best completes the following statements:

1. The Greek historian Herodotus said, " All Egypt is the gift of the Nile," because (*a*) the Nile flows through the center of Egypt, (*b*) the Egyptians could use the Nile as a means of transportation, (*c*) the Nile overflows each spring, depositing fertile valley soil and providing water for irrigation, (*d*) the Nile connected the center of Egypt with the Mediterranean Sea.

2. The Egyptians were one of the first peoples in the world to develop a high degree of civilization because (*a*) the climate of Egypt was warm, (*b*) the Egyptians were more intelligent than other peoples, (*c*) the natural boundaries of sea and desert protected Egypt from invasions, (*d*) the Egyptians were naturally peaceful and did not waste their time and energy in fighting.

3. The first reasonably sure date in history is approximately (*a*) 10,000 B.C., (*b*) 4200 B.C., (*c*) 1000 B.C.

4. This date marks the first use of (*a*) copper, (*b*) chariots, (*c*) a calendar.

5. Egyptians advanced further in many ways than early man. Tell in a few sentences what progress and changes they made in (*a*) food, (*b*) clothing, (*c*) architecture, (*d*) writing, (*e*) recording of events, (*f*) art, (*g*) science, and (*h*) religion.

III. Under the headings Middle Kingdom and Hyksos Invasion, list the most important changes that characterized Egypt during each of those times.

IV. Match the following correctly by writing on a piece of paper the numbers and letters of the items which belong together or are most directly connected with each other. Do not mark your book.

(1)	source of the Nile	(*a*)	picture writing
(2)	papyrus	(*b*)	a woman pharaoh
(3)	Amen	(*c*)	a temple
(4)	Champollion	(*d*)	a pharaoh
(5)	Hatshepsut	(*e*)	Lake Victoria
(6)	hieroglyphics	(*f*)	Khufu
(7)	Ramses II	(*g*)	paper
(8)	obelisk	(*h*)	Rosetta Stone
(9)	Karnak	(*i*)	chief god
(10)	Great Pyramid	(*j*)	mummy
		(*k*)	stone shaft
		(*l*)	King of the Underworld

V. Tell in two or three sentences *why* each of the following statements is either true or false.

1. The Egyptian boy's education was limited to learning to read and write in school.

2. The women of Egypt were honored and had many privileges.

3. The Egyptians believed in a life after death.

INTERESTING THINGS TO DO

Topics for Talks

1. "Schools in ancient Egypt." What were the contributions or services given to the people by the universities? What were their limitations as compared to our modern universities? What do they reveal regarding the thoughts and attitudes of the ancient Egyptians?

2. "Egyptian manners and customs." What rules of manners and morals followed by the Egyptians do we still follow today? Why are standards of manners and morals necessary for good citizenship in any community or state?

3. "The Egyptian home." What was the position of women in ancient Egypt? How did they prepare their food?

4. "The architecture and tools of the Egyptians." How did the climate and the choice of building materials influence Egyptian architecture? What devices or tools did the Egyptians use?

5. "The Egyptian farmer." How did the Egyptians raise their food? Why couldn't each city-state along the Nile develop its own irrigation system? In what ways was the Egyptians' problem of irrigation similar to our problems of keeping up good cross-country highways and of controlling the floods of the Mississippi River? Do you think that the lot of the farmer was more difficult in ancient Egypt than it is in the United States today?

For information on any of the five topics above, see "Daily Life in Ancient Egypt" in *National Geographic Magazine* Oct., 1941. See also *The Story of Mankind,* by H. W. Van Loon; *Conquest of Civilization,* by James Henry Breasted; "Egypt" in *The World Book Encyclopedia;* and A. B. Gosse, *The Civilization of the Ancient Egyptians.*

Projects for the Chart Maker and Artist

1. Enlarge the time line for Egypt. Add events and achievements that will give a more nearly complete story of the Egyptians. Use sketches and other illustrations wherever possible.

2. Make a series of sketches or cartoons that illustrate Egyptian sculpture, architecture, jewelry, furniture, toys, or clothing.

3. Draw a map of Egypt, and illustrate it with pictures, quotations, and original sketches. Your map should tell its own story so clearly that it is as informative as a travel talk.

4. Draw a picture of an owl. Explain to the class how our letter *M* was derived from such a drawing. See page 222 in *The Story of Human Progress,* by Leon C. Marshall.

Adventures for the Amateur Author

1. Pretend that you were present when the tomb of King Tutankhamen was opened. Write a colorful description of that occasion, and describe some of the many relics found in the tomb. See *National Geographic Magazine,* May, 1923; also *Current History,* June, 1924.

2. Write a "Book of Etiquette" for an Egyptian youth.

3. Write a brief essay on our calendar. Why did so many of the calendars developed in early times divide the year into twelve months? What are the advantages and disadvantages of a twelve-month year? Would you favor a

lunar-calendar year of thirteen months? Why? See "Calendar" in *The World Book Encyclopedia*. Consult also *Conquest of Civilization,* by James Henry Breasted.

Ideas for Your Little Theater

1. Choose recordings of selections from Verdi's opera *Aïda* to play for the class. You can make the music more interesting for those who have not read or heard it before, if you first tell the story of the opera.

2. Dramatize the story of a pharaoh's trusted messenger who carried secret tidings in the face of great danger. See *How They Carried the Mail,* by Joseph Walker.

Candidates for Your Album of Famous People

" People make history." That is just another way of saying that in studying history you are really studying people — where they lived, how they thought, what they did, and why they did what they did. You will find it easier to understand and remember historic events if you become more thoroughly acquainted with the people who brought them about and had a part in them. As you study each nation in this book, plan to write in a notebook one or two biographical portraits of people important to the story of that nation. If possible, illustrate your Album with pictures from magazines or original sketches and cartoons. When you finish reading this *Story of Nations,* your " Album of Famous People " will serve as a " Who's Who " for reference and review.

Choose one or more of the following, from the story of Egypt, for biographical portraits: Cleopatra, Hatshepsut, Ikhnaton, Imhotep, Ramses II, Thutmose III.

INTERESTING READING ABOUT EGYPT

BAIKIE, J. *Wonder Tales of the Ancient World.* " The Fates said, ' He will die either by crocodile, or by the serpent, or . . .' "

BREASTED, JAMES HENRY. *The Conquest of Civilization.* This absorbing and helpful book has been called " one of the best books of history ever written." You will find it a treasure house of information for your study of all the ancient peoples.

CLODD, E. *The Story of the Alphabet.* " Thirst was represented by a calf running towards . . ."

Compton's Pictured Encyclopedia. " Egypt: The Kingdom of Father Nile," and Index.

GOSSE, A. B. *The Civilization of the Ancient Egyptians.* " The Egyptians were adept at caricature and many absurd sketches, full of humor, have been found."

HOLMES, BURTON. *Egypt and the Suez Canal*. A travel story of Egypt that includes history, customs, and the " sights of the land of the Nile," made more vivid by many excellent photographs.

MARSHALL, LEON C. *The Story of Human Progress*. Pp. 218–227. " It is a hieroglyphic sign used about five thousand years ago."

MAYER, JOSEPHINE, and PRIDEAUX, TOM. *Never to Die*. The revelations of Egyptian art and literature.

MORRISON, LUCILE. *The Lost Queen of Egypt*. A story that pictures social life in the time of Tutankhamen.

National Geographic Magazine, May, 1923. " At The Tomb of Tutankhamen," by Maynard Owen Williams. " The scarab . . . was much venerated in ancient Egypt, being sacred to the sun-god."

——, October, 1941. " Daily Life in Ancient Egypt," by William C. Hayes, with illustrations by H. M. Herger. " Those who drink of the Nile are Egyptians."

SMITH, D. E. *Number Stories of Long Ago*. " The people along the Nile had found the fingers of one hand would help them. . . ."

VAN LOON, H. W. *The Story of Mankind*. " A kindly river did the work of a million men."

WALKER, JOSEPH. *How They Carried the Mail*. Chap. II. " In a few moments the slave returned and bade Kosru, by signs, to follow him and . . ."

The World Book Encyclopedia. " Egypt: the Story of Egypt "; and Index.

PART THREE

THE PEOPLES OF MESOPOTAMIA FOUNDED A GREAT CIVILIZATION IN THE LAND BETWEEN THE RIVERS

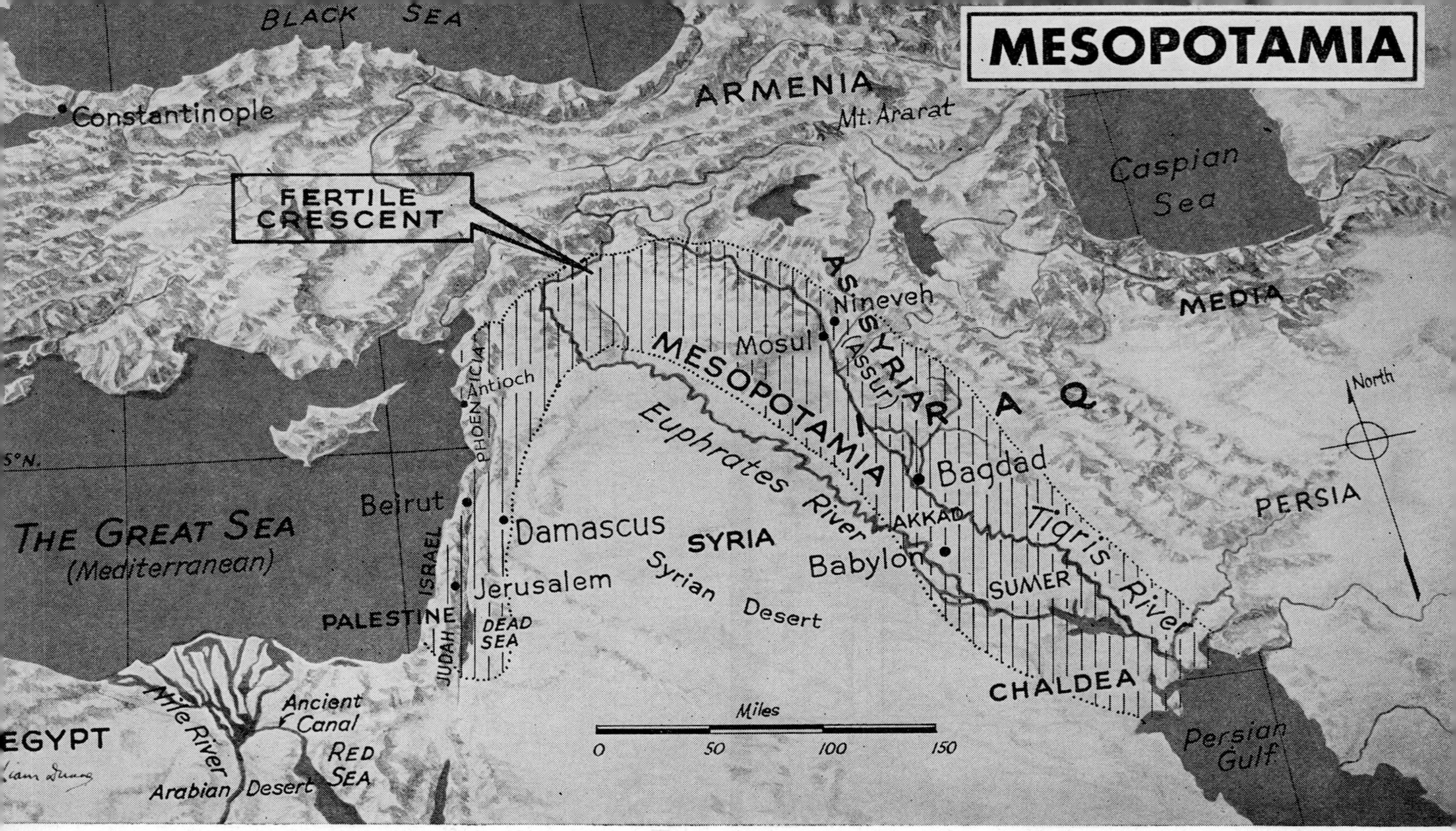

MESOPOTAMIA

North

PERSIA

Persian Gulf

Caspian Sea

MEDIA

ARMENIA

Mt. Ararat

BLACK SEA

Constantinople

Tigris River

CHALDEA

SUMER

AKKAD

Bagdad

Babylon

I R A Q

ASSYRIA (Assur)

AS...

Nineveh

Mosul

M E S O P O T A M I A

Euphrates River

SYRIA

Damascus

Syrian Desert

Jerusalem

DEAD SEA

JUDAH

ISRAEL

PALESTINE

Beirut

Antioch

PHOENICIA

FERTILE CRESCENT

THE GREAT SEA (Mediterranean)

Ancient Canal

Nile River

RED SEA

Arabian Desert

EGYPT

Miles

0   50   100   150

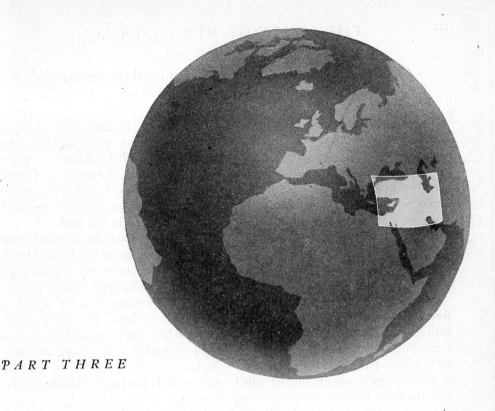

The Fertile Crescent

THE map on the opposite page will show you the "lay of the land" in Mesopotamia, the crossroad of the ancient world. There are important landmarks or features which you will want to recognize. Trace the sweep of the great Fertile Crescent as it stretches from the Mediterranean Sea to the Persian Gulf. Can you find the names of the two mighty rivers which have caused the land between them to be called Mesopotamia, or the land "between the rivers"? Why do you suppose that the desert folk and mountain tribes were attracted to the river valleys? Can you find Babylon, the city famous for its hanging gardens and temple towers? Do you see Nineveh, the capital of ancient Assyria? You will notice that just south of the Caspian Sea is Media. There the people called Medes built a kingdom. Persia, the land of the famous ruler, Cyrus the Great, lies north of the Persian Gulf. The Persians had made their earlier home to the north, near the Black Sea. As you read the story which follows, make a practice of finding on this map the places which are mentioned. Doing so will help you to picture more clearly the story of the different peoples of ancient Mesopotamia.

Chapter 1 ~ The Babylonians Conquered the Sumerians and Rose to Fame

The land between the rivers was the home of many peoples. Have you ever wondered where the garden of Eden was located? Of course, no one knows the exact location of this luxuriant garden which the Bible describes as the first home of man; but most people believe that it was in the region of the Euphrates River. The Bible records that this was one of the four great rivers that flowed from Eden.

At any rate, far back in the ages before recorded history began, the land between the Tigris and the Euphrates rivers must have cradled a part of the early human race. Here were born men of action — men who built and ruled over the great cities of antiquity whose names are still symbols of splendor.

Among these ancient cities of high-towered temples were Babylon, the great city of the Babylonians, and Nineveh [nin'uh vuh], the capital of Assyria. In this story you will read of five sturdy and fearless peoples, each of whom held sway for a while in this land.

The Fertile Crescent extended from the Mediterranean to the Persian Gulf. If you look again at the map on page 70 you will find a great crescent stretching across western Asia. It is like a new moon in shape. This sweep of fertile land lies with its arched back against high mountains at the north, and with its face toward a great sea of sand on the south. It has been called the Fertile Crescent.

Long ago, in the eastern end of the

FARMING IN MESOPOTAMIA

Like many of his ancestors, this present-day farmer in Mesopotamia uses dromedary and donkey power. Even the plow is very crude and old-fashioned.

A STREET IN MOSUL

This recent scene in the city of Mosul in Iraq still shows the traditional harem windows with their bars. Notice the projecting second stories of the houses.

crescent, the fertile lands were cultivated with care. (Later, in Part Four, you will learn about the land and peoples at the western end of this historic region.) Efficient rulers saw to it that the floods of the rivers were controlled and that canals were dug to supply water for the soil where needed. It became, indeed, a fruitful land.

Two mighty rivers give Mesopotamia its name. Far to the north of the Fertile Crescent, in the high tableland called Armenia [ahr mee'ni uh], rise the two mighty rivers which made possible another rich civilization much like that which developed in the valley of the Nile. The narrow strip of land between the Tigris and the Euphrates is fittingly named Mesopotamia, or the land "between the rivers." The great eastern river, the Tigris, flows rather directly toward the Persian Gulf, but the Euphrates bends to the west as it crosses the arch of the Fertile Crescent and takes a more leisurely course to the southeast. Through many centuries the two rivers piled up a great delta until the land extended farther and farther into the Persian Gulf. Today as the two rivers near the Gulf they pour their waters together and leave the land as one river. On the map on page 70 you can see that the coastline lies much farther south today than it did in ancient times. You of course know of the delta at the mouth of our Mississippi River and have just learned of the delta of the Nile. But each of these deltas was formed by a single river.

Egypt and Mesopotamia were alike in that they were fertile lands, but were very different in natural protection against enemies. Egypt was well protected from foreign invasion. Mesopotamia, on the contrary, could be easily entered from every side. Thus it is no

The Oriental Institute, The University of Chicago

WINGED BULL

The figure of a winged bull with a man's face was used often in Assyrian art. This one was carved in an alabaster-like stone, and was used as a decoration in the gateway of the palace of Sargon II at Khorsabad.

wonder that the story of the Fertile Crescent is one of continual strife, with invaders constantly seeking to take the land from the people who were fortunate enough to hold it.

An ancient garden spot is now wasteland. In the course of wars and invasions, many of the cities of ancient Mesopotamia have vanished. Only shapeless and unsightly mounds of debris now show where Nineveh once stood on the upper Tigris. The ruins of that once-great city are within sight of the modern town of Mosul [moh sool']. Babylon is gone, though a town of that name now exists near the old site. Bagdad [bag' dad] is now the important city of that region. The old canals were destroyed by the Mongols [mahng'g'lz] from Asia, who invaded the country in the 13th Century A.D. Since then much of the once-fertile land has become wasteland. But today the kingdom of Iraq [i rahk'], which covers most of the site of old Mesopotamia, is undertaking a new irrigation system. With proper irrigation it is likely that this ancient land will once again become productive.

The Sumerians built their civilization on the eastern end of the Fertile Crescent. Huge mounds of crumbled brick and human relics unearthed by archeologists are evidence of the fact that an ancient civilization developed on the eastern end of the valley between the two great rivers of Mesopotamia. The very early history of this region was not well known until comparatively recent times. It is now thought that a wandering people whose descendants came to be known as Sumerians [syoo mee′ri′nz] came in and took possession of the lower valley of the Tigris and Euphrates rivers soon after the close of the New Stone Age, perhaps about 6000 B.C. During the later part of the past century archeologists made discoveries, which, they believe, indicate that the first Sumerian dynasty began not later than 4200 B.C. Historians quite generally agree that the Sumerians had attained a well-developed civilization as early as 3500 B.C., at which time they had perfected a system of writing and had learned the use of metal. They were, therefore, somewhat in advance of the Egyptians.

The Sumerians did not gain possession of the whole of Mesopotamia. About 4000 B.C. tribes, whose descendants were to become the Babylonians and Assyrians, as well as enemies of the Sumerians, took over the northern part of this fertile valley. These invaders came from the Syrian Desert and spoke a form of Semitic language. There were also Arabian nomads or Bedouins [bed′ oo inz], of Semitic origin, who came from the plateau of Arabia. They took possession of the delta formed by the deposits of the two great rivers. The Sumerians were much more advanced than these Semitic tribes who lived to the north and the south of them. But in time these tribes became strong and conquered the Sumerians. With this outline of events in mind let us now turn back and learn more about the ancient Sumerians.

The civilization of the Sumerians was many-sided. Many of the Sumerians were skilled workmen in clay, fabrics, wood, and metals, but the chief occupation of these ancient people was farming. The Sumerian farmers raised wheat, barley, millet, flax, vegetables, and dates, which were very much the same crops as those grown in that region today. Like the Egyptians, they used a system of canals and dikes to control irrigation waters. Among their domestic animals were cattle, sheep, goats, and donkeys. The Sumerians invented and used a combination plow and planter which, after their civilization had disappeared, was not in use again until the 15th Century. They had small brick-domed ovens for baking bread; after building a fire inside one of these ovens they would plaster the dough on the oven's heated sides to bake it.

The Sumerians used the wheel at a very early time. You will no doubt agree that a knowledge of that useful device is good evidence of civilized progress. They harnessed their oxen to plows and their donkeys to wheeled carts. They also made practical use of the wheel on their chariots of war. For foot soldiers they developed a plan of fighting with a massed solid front of protecting shields which the Greeks and the Romans were to use centuries later as the basis for the famous phalanx [fay′langks].

One of the curious achievements of the Sumerians was the development of a system of numbers based on a unit of 60. It later resulted in the 360-degree circle, and led to the dividing of an hour into 60 minutes and the minute into 60 seconds. The roots of the present are surely deep in the past.

The Sumerians invented a kind of writing done on clay tablets, later adopted and improved by the Babylonians. It is called cuneiform [kyoo nee' uh fawrm] writing from a Latin word meaning *wedge*. Notice the picture on page 78 of a Babylonian clay tablet. The signs are made up of a number of small, wedge-shaped marks from which this form of writing got its name. The scribe, who was a professional writer, pressed a sharp triangular or square-pointed stylus [stai'luhs] into the soft clay. The tablets then were baked to make them more durable. You will read more about these tablets in a few pages.

Long before the famous city-states of Athens and Sparta in Greece, the Sumerians had well-organized city-states. In their system the priest was the ruler of the city-state as well as the religious leader.

The temple towers were centers of community life. In many cases the mounds of crumbled, sun-dried brick, which show where the ancient cities of the Sumerians were, are remains of temple towers. These were built to honor the gods of the people. (The Sumerians

generally built with sun-dried brick, because they had little stone. Because sun-dried brick crumbles easily, their buildings did not last as did the Egyptian pyramids and temples.) The people held their religious services and made sacrifices in the temples under the direction of the priests. But the temples were more than places of worship. They were also community centers where schools were maintained and other activities were carried on. Among these were the making of cloth, pottery, and implements for farming and for war.

The temples with their towers looked like six or seven huge blocks piled up, each one smaller than the one beneath it, reminding one strongly of the set-back type of skyscraper building in some of our great cities in America. In the picture on page 78 you can also see inclined walks winding up to a golden shrine; these were used by the priests. You may have seen inclined walks or ramps in the place of stairways in railroad depots and in large buildings. The next time you walk up these passageways, you can think that the ancient Sumerians employed this practice in architecture. (The Egyptians also used the ramp, to aid them in building.) In the course of building their temples the Sumerians

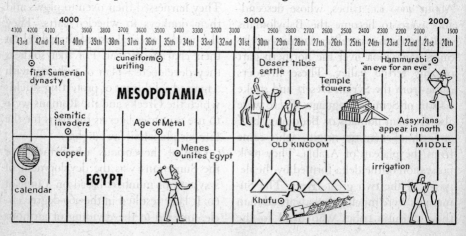

also developed the arch and the column, as well as the tower. Every story, or stage, of the temple tower was of a different color. The famous tower of Babel [bay' b'l], "whose top may reach unto heaven," had seven stages. The stages were painted black, orange, red, gold, pale yellow, dark blue, and silver. Each one was dedicated to such heavenly bodies as those we now know as Saturn, Jupiter, Mars, Mercury, the sun, and the moon. Many years later, when the Hebrews were carried into captivity and taken to Babylonia, they were so impressed by temples of this kind that they wrote descriptions of them which we can read today in the Old Testament of the Bible.

Naturally most of the things the Sumerians had learned came into the hands of the Babylonians and Assyrians. These two peoples were the next to rule in the Fertile Crescent. Later the contributions to civilization of the Sumerians, Babylonians, and Assyrians were passed on to the Phoenicians, Hebrews, and Persians, who, in turn, passed them on to the Greeks and thus to Western civilizations. As you must realize, it was a long process of development, each group making its own contributions to the progress of civilization.

The Sumerians failed to unite and the Babylonians conquered Sumer. Perhaps if the Sumerians had heard the slogan of our Revolutionary days, "Unite or die," they would have joined together in defense of their city-states. While they were developing their civilization, the Semitic tribes near by had been growing in power. This fact was especially true of the Babylonians, whose name was taken from their chief city, Babylon. You will see on the map on page 70 that Babylon was northwest of the land of Sumer [syoo'mer], which was in the southeastern part of Mesopotamia. The Sumerians had waged war more or less continuously with tribes who were trying to get control of their more favored land, but they did not realize what a great threat the Babylonians were to the security of their green lands. The Sumerians did not have much strength as separate city-states, and even at best, their land was small and their people relatively few. Therefore they were in a dangerous position.

About 2000 B.C. the Babylonians, under a strong leader named Hammurabi [ham'oo rah'bi], overpowered the Sumerians. This Babylonian ruler did not liquidate the Sumerians or destroy their civilization. Instead Sumer became a part

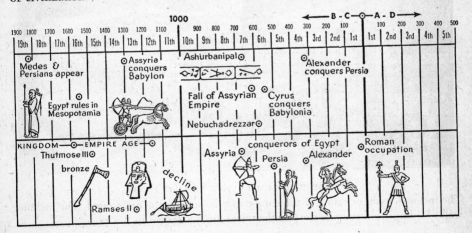

Metropolitan Museum of Art

A CUNEIFORM TABLET

The ancient Mesopotamians first wrote in pictures, much as did the American Indians, but they gradually changed and improved their pictures so that they became cuneiform signs.

of the kingdom of Babylon. Thus two civilizations merged. The customs, manners, and beliefs of the Sumerians really took the lead over the Babylonian culture. In this *Story of Nations* you will learn of many instances, such as in China and Greece, where military conquerors were themselves conquered by the learning of the people whom they had overthrown.

Hammurabi organized the first great code of laws. Hammurabi was a man strong enough to bind together all the city-states in his kingdom. He made Babylon famous throughout the known world, partly by the warfare which he carried on for more than thirty years and partly by his ability as a ruler.

Thus it is not chiefly as a warrior that Hammurabi is known. He was a remarkable organizer and lawgiver. A collection of letters that he wrote to his governors and officials shows how closely Hammurabi kept in touch with every part of his realm. He also wrote a code of laws, which were inscribed on a large slab of stone. The laws tell us much about the character of Hammurabi and the life of the Babylonian people. In the illustration on page 79, Hammurabi is shown with his code of laws.

Hammurabi was one of the first kings who believed that it was his duty to be a father to his people. He liked to be called

A SUMERIAN TEMPLE AND TEMPLE TOWER

The inclined walk, or ramp, of the temple may be seen in the foreground. The inclined walks leading from story to story of the tower are not shown in this picture.

"King of Righteousness" and "Builder of the Land." He began his famous Code of Laws by saying:

I am the pastor, the savior, whose scepter is a right one, the good protecting shadow over my city; in my breast I cherish the inhabitants of Sumer and Akkad [ahk'ahd]. By my genius in peace I have led them, that the strong might not injure the weak, to protect the widow and orphan. . . .

The code attempted to regulate almost every action in social and business life. It shows how the Babylonians believed in punishing an offense by inflicting the same injury on the guilty one. This old desert law of "an eye for an eye and a tooth for a tooth" sometimes resulted in injustice. But the Code of Hammurabi did much to impress upon men the need of respecting the rights of others.

The Babylonians worshiped many gods. When you look at the picture at the right you will see Hammurabi receiving the laws from the sun-god who is seated at the right. The Babylonians worshiped many different gods, as did practically all ancient peoples. Their supreme god, however, was Marduk [mahr'dook], originally the god who watched over the city of Babylon.

In every town throughout Babylonia were temple towers much like those of the Sumerians, which have already been described. Each temple was dedicated to a god. The Babylonians, like the Hebrews, believed in keeping the seventh day one of worship and rest from toil. It was on that day, particularly, that these people entered their temples for religious services. Interestingly enough, the services were conducted in the Sumerian, not in the Babylonian, language.

The Babylonians feared death and a future life. You will remember that the later Egyptians looked forward to a happy life in the next world if they had

Courtesy of the Syracuse University Library
THE UPPER PART OF THE TABLET
OF HAMMURABI

King Hammurabi is pictured receiving from the sun-god the code of laws inscribed on the lower part of the tablet.

been good on earth. This was not true of the Babylonians. They thought that the life after death was gloomy, miserable, and hopeless. They called the future home of the soul the "Land of No Return."

The Babylonians built their civilization with clay. As the papyrus plant did not grow in Mesopotamia, the Babylonians did not have the use of this reed which the Egyptians employed for their writing paper. It has been said that Mesopotamian civilization was built on clay. Certainly the Babylonians, like the Sumerians before them, had many uses for the clay found in abundance along the Tigris and Euphrates rivers. They used it to build houses and temples and, as was described, for the tablets on which they wrote. These writing tablets of clay were from a half-inch to an inch in thickness, and of almost any desired size. After they were inscribed with the wedge-shaped writing which the Babylonians had learned from the Sumerians, the tablets were baked, and thus could not be damaged easily by fire or water. If broken, they could be put together again.

Many Babylonian letters and business contracts have been found in ancient ruins in the Fertile Crescent. These clay tablets were usually enclosed in a thin outer layer of clay that served as an envelope. The document was usually duplicated on the envelope. If there was any question of change in the terms of the contract as they appeared on the outside, it was a simple matter to break off the clay envelope and find the unaltered document inside.

After reading the translations of some of the letters written in Babylonia almost four thousand years ago, one must conclude that these people thought and felt much as we do today. Take, for instance, the following letter which a young man sent inquiring about the health of his sweetheart.

To Bibea, thus says Gimil Marduk: may the gods Shamash [shah'mahsh] and Marduk permit thee to live forever for my sake. I write to inquire concerning thy health. Tell me how thou art. I went to Babylon, but did not see thee. I was greatly disappointed. Send the reason for thy leaving, that I may be happy. Do come in the month Marchesvan. Keep well always for my sake.

A Babylonian woman could have a career. Although the women in most ancient countries were little more than property or slaves, the Babylonian woman, like women in Egypt, had many privileges. She was permitted to control property. However, if she was so unlucky as to come to her husband without any " bride money " her position in the household was practically that of a slave.

A legal contract was required for every marriage, just as a license is required today. These marriage contracts varied. One of them might require that the bride wait upon her mother-in-law or even upon another wife. Or the contract might state that the husband should have only one wife, and that the woman was allowed to divorce him and take her wedding dowry with her if he broke his contract.

Women held positions in business and in the professions. During certain periods of Babylonian history, women are known to have been scribes or secretaries. There is an old payroll of the temple officials showing that certain men of the staff had been replaced by women, who received the same salary for the work as the men.

Babylonian students excelled in spelling. Both the Babylonian boy and girl were sent to school. About fifty years ago archaeologists uncovered the ruins of a schoolhouse, probably built when Hammurabi was alive. It was a one-story, dried-brick building, with several rooms enclosing a court which was open to the sky. Probably school began early in the morning because one of the old sayings in a Babylonian copybook reads: " He who would excel in the school of the scribes must rise like the dawn."

As each pupil entered the outer door of the school he gave his name to a doorkeeper, who was on the lookout for tardy pupils. The doorkeeper gave each student a small ball of soft clay which served as a slate or tablet. On this lump of clay the student practiced writing with his stylus the six hundred syllables that made up the Babylonian writing. The Babylonian schoolboy had to learn these six hundred syllables, a much harder task than we have today in learning the twenty-six letters of our alphabet. Great importance was attached to correct spelling. We find very few misspelled words in the letters that have been preserved.

Besides spelling, the children were taught reading, history, foreign languages, law, religion, astrology, map-making, and the study of signs and omens. The boys were also taught to shoot with the bow and to take part in other outdoor activities. The Babylonians laid great stress on the education of their children, and in this we do not differ from them.

Chapter 2 ~ The Assyrians, the Later Babylonians, and Finally the Persians Dominated Mesopotamia

Babylonia lost her supremacy to the Assyrians. It is difficult for a single nation to dominate forever all her neighboring nations. Certainly Babylonia did not keep her place of supremacy on the eastern end of the Fertile Crescent. Several hundred years after the time of Hammurabi, the Assyrians encroached further upon the verdant lands of the Fertile Crescent. They were another of those aggressor peoples whose ancestors had been uncivilized desert tribes in the time of the Sumerians. These Assyrian people settled in the region of the upper Tigris River. Assyria proved to be the great military nation of the ancient world. She defeated both Babylonia and Egypt. So fierce and warlike were the Assyrians that it seemed for a time that they would completely destroy Babylonian civilization.

Assyria was an aggressor nation of warriors. The story of the Assyrian kings is one of dreary conquest, for they did little to encourage their people to live a peaceful, prosperous life. They did not show much interest in improving crops. Even when Assyria spread into more fertile lands, she still neglected farming as well as industry and commerce. The chief interest of the kings

was to build up a strong army with which to subdue their neighbors. This army was composed of archers, supported by heavily armed spearmen and shield-bearers, and reinforced by chariots, horsemen, and infantry. The Assyrians had the first large armies in history to be equipped with weapons of iron. You will remember that the Egyptians had little iron, so they could not successfully meet the better weapons of the Assyrians. The approach of Assyrian soldiers with their spears and swords of iron struck terror into the hearts of a besieged people. Here we have the blitzkrieg of ancient times.

The Assyrian kings, like many conquerors, seemed to enjoy telling of their brutal military exploits. One might almost think these words are from a page of the account of modern aggressor nations. The warrior king wrote,

I shut up the king in his royal city. I raised monuments of bodies before his gates. All his villages I destroyed, desolated, and burned. I made the country a desert, I changed it into hills and mounds of debris.

Arrogant Nineveh was built with the spoils of war. The capital and greatest city of Assyria was Nineveh, whose mas-

A CORNER OF ASHURBANIPAL'S LIBRARY

Nearly 5000 years ago this library of clay tablets was a storehouse of knowledge and a pleasant place for study. Notice the winged bulls in the wall decoration.

sive double wall was called the "wall whose splendor overthrows the enemy." This wall, which was fifty feet thick and a hundred feet high, stretched for seven miles around the city, and was pierced by fifteen beautifully decorated gates. Eighteen mountain streams poured into the walled city and kept the city's water supply clean and fresh.

To the other people of the Fertile Crescent, Nineveh, the city built with tribute and spoils wrung from the oppressed, was a symbol of the pride and arrogance of the Assyrians, until its destruction several hundred years later.

Ashurbanipal built a great library. One of the last of the Assyrian monarchs, Ashurbanipal [ah'shoor bah'ni-pahl], was different from most of the rulers. He tried to promote education. Ashurbanipal had a remarkable library which he opened to the people. This library was famous in ancient times, and is still of great value today. It has told us much about the history of those times.

When the library rooms were uncovered by excavators they found a collection of 22,000 clay tablets. Ashurbanipal had employed scribes to gather and copy the religious, scientific, and literary works of Assyria and Babylonia. One interesting tablet tells the story of the Creation and the Flood in much the same manner as the Hebrews have told of these events in the Old Testament. Part of a room in the library is shown in the illustration above.

Babylonia rose to power a second time. The power of Assyria was not great enough to prevent another wave of desert people from sweeping into Babylonia. These were the Chaldeans [kal dee"nz] or Later Babylonians. With the help of the Medes they destroyed Nineveh in 612 B.C. and a wave of joy passed over the rest of the ancient world. This city, called "the lair of lions, the bloody city, the city gorged with prey," was never to rise again. Three centuries later, when Alexander the

Great took his army across the old site of Nineveh, little remained to show that there had once stood the proudest city in all the ancient world. The warfare which Assyria had carried on did not enable her to build an enduring civilization. Like Egypt, she tried to expand her empire too much, and did not have the strength to maintain it. But the roads Assyria built for her warriors helped to carry the learning of the Babylonians to other parts of the world.

The Later Babylonians guided Babylonia through her short but brilliant second career. This began late in the Seventh Century B.C., and continued only about seventy years. The ruler Nebuchadrezzar [neb'yoo kuhd rez'er], who established the new empire, is remembered for two very different things. He made Babylon the greatest city of antiquity, and he destroyed the capital of the Hebrews at Jerusalem, carrying the Hebrew people to Babylon to be sold as slaves.

Nebuchadrezzar beautified ancient Babylon. In spite of his wars, Nebuchadrezzar found time to make Babylon beautiful. Herodotus, the Greek historian, who visited the city in the Fifth Century B.C., describes it in detail.

Babylon extended over almost as much territory as a large modern city. It covered an area of 185 square miles, and was surrounded by a high wall and a deep ditch filled with water. Only a part of this area was covered with buildings, for the rest of the ground was given over to fruits, grains, and vegetables to feed the people in case Babylon was besieged.

Leading up to a temple or palace of the king was a long avenue which passed through an imposing gateway called the Ishtar [ish'tahr] Gate. Along the walls of the avenue about 120 lions were sculptured on blue glazed brick.

Alice Schalek from Three Lions

THE SITE OF NINEVEH

The famed city of Nineveh once stood here, in a place known in modern times as Mt. Koyunjik. Excavations in this place unearthed the Royal Library of Nineveh, composed of 22,000 clay tablets. The tablets contained the story of the Flood.

Brown Brothers

THE HANGING GARDENS

The hanging gardens of Babylon, one of the wonders of the ancient world, were built by Nebuchadrezzar for his wife who had lived among the hills.

On the roofs of the imperial palace were the hanging gardens for which Babylon was famous. These were made by building platforms upon tiers of arches and covering all with flowers, shrubs, and vines. According to the legend, Nebuchadrezzar's queen longed so much for the trees and verdant ferns of her mountain home that he built these gardens to remind her of them. The Greeks considered the hanging gardens one of the seven wonders of the ancient world. An artist's reconstruction of the hanging gardens is given above. The picture gives us a good idea of the lavishness of the palace.

Babylon fell a second time. Babylon's second rise to power was magnificent but brief. Nebuchadrezzar was the last great king of the Babylonians. When a new race began to drift in from the northern mountains, Babylon had neither the strength nor the energy to force them out of her territory. Let us see what the men were like who took the city of high walls and hanging gardens.

Persian tribes conquered the Babylonians. The men who next conquered the Babylonians were an Indo-European people, like the Sumerians of long years before. About 1800 B.C. several Indo-European tribes had begun to wander down from the northern European grasslands. Some tribes went as far as India, but two of the strongest peoples, the Medes and the Persians, settled in the mountains that border the northern edge of the Fertile Crescent. There they lived on the fringe of the crescent for a thousand years, gradually becoming stronger. They saw the early Babylonians subdued by the Assyrians. They remained secure in their mountain homes while Assyria plundered her neighbors. The Medes helped the Later Babylonians to burn Nineveh in 612 B.C. and, for a time, made upper Mesopotamia part of their own kingdom. At the same time Babylon was rising to her second period of power. Finally, about fifty years after the fall of Nineveh, the Persians were strong enough to overthrow Babylon herself. When this happened they also absorbed the kingdom of the Medes.

The Persians had been simple shepherds who wore animal skins for clothing. They had a religion with higher ideals than that of the Egyptians or of any of the other peoples of the eastern Fertile Crescent. It was founded by a great religious teacher, Zoroaster [zoh' roh as'ter), about 1000 B.C. It was said that a vision came to Zoroaster when he was living alone in the high, silent mountains. He went back to his people to tell them what he had learned. Life, said Zoroaster, is a constant struggle between the good and the evil in the world. Man must follow the Good and the Light or turn to Evil and Darkness. His choice brings upon him a judgment in the hereafter.

The religion of Zoroaster was reflected in the life of the shepherd tribes. The children were taught always to speak the truth. Herodotus, the Greek historian, said later that these people considered "nothing so shameful as lying, and after falsehood nothing so shameful as contracting debts, for he who has debts necessarily lies." It is interesting to note that even the Hebrew prophets respected the religion of Zoroaster. While they scorned the idol-worshiping of other foreign people surrounding Palestine, they did not condemn this religion.

Cyrus the Great led Persia to power. While Persia was still a small mountain kingdom, a king called Cyrus [sai'ruhs] came to the throne. Within five years he had made Persia the leading state of the Eastern world. He gathered his troops of peasants and marched on powerful Babylon. When the vast walls of Babylon opened to his conquering army in 539 B.C. the ancient world was astonished. A great king had risen among the Persians. It was not long before all the Semitic peoples who had come from the desert to settle in the Fertile Crescent were crushed before the new aggressors from the hills.

Cyrus was more than a courageous general and conqueror. He was a wise statesman and a noble king. He made many conquests to expand the Persian Empire, but his policy toward conquered peoples was kindness rather than oppression. It was Cyrus who released the Hebrews from their captivity in Babylon into which Nebuchadrezzar had carried them, and allowed them to return to their beloved land of Palestine.

When Cyrus fell in battle his people wept at the passing of a great king. His tomb can still be seen, though it was plundered and robbed long ago. This simple inscription tells who had been buried there: "O man, I am Cyrus, who founded the greatness of Persia and ruled Asia. Grudge me not this monument."

Darius organized the Persian Empire. Shortly after the time of Cyrus, a bold king by the name of Darius [duh rai´ uhs] acquired the Persian throne. He extended the boundaries of the empire until they stretched eastward to the Indus River in India, westward beyond the Nile and as far as the Aegean Sea along the north shore of the Mediterranean.

The greatest deeds of Darius, however, were not on the battlefield. He carried out the program of empire which Cyrus had only begun. He constructed roads, coined money to make trading easier, established a postal system, and built the greatest navy of the time. In Egypt Darius rebuilt the ancient canal which had once connected the Nile and the Red Sea. Persia was better organized than any earlier empire. As long as they paid tribute, the countries under Persia were allowed considerable independence. The rule of Darius was autocratic, but more just than that of most conquerors.

For the next two hundred years (until about 330 B.C.) Persian rule brought comparative peace and prosperity to the people of the Fertile Crescent. But the later Persian kings were not as good rulers as Cyrus and Darius. Too much luxury and ease in time brought weakness and decay to Persia.

Mesopotamia is now a part of Iraq. Perhaps some of the prosperity of ancient Mesopotamia will return to this land. It is now part of Iraq. See the map on page 70. When Iraq has finished putting into operation its plans for irrigation, the land " between the rivers " may again become a productive garden spot of the Near East. Crops, which even today are much like those of early times, will be improved. These include barley, rice, and dates.

Iraq is also of great interest today because of its oil fields which are among the richest in the world. During World War II, the Iraq government leased these fields to British, French, Dutch, and American companies, thereby greatly assisting the cause of the United Nations. Precautions were taken early in the war to safeguard this oil against use by Nazi Germany and by any other members of the Axis.

The Peoples of Mesopotamia Contributed Much to Later Civilizations

In this story of Mesopotamia we saw nations come into existence, rise to power, wane, and even disappear. Five different peoples each held sway for a time in this fertile land of the Tigris-Euphrates valley. A wandering people called Sumerians first took possession of a part of this land, perhaps as long ago as 6000 B.C. Many years later, peoples from the Syrian desert and the Arabian plateau took possession of other parts of Mesopotamia. The Sumerians, however, were at first more advanced than these other neighboring peoples. By 3500 B.C. they had learned the use of metal and had perfected a system of writing, today called cuneiform. This writing was done on tablets made of clay found along the Tigris and Euphrates rivers. The Sumerians also used this clay for building houses and temples. Their chief occupation was farming, and they invented and used a combination plow and planter. Like the Egyptians, they used canals and dikes to control irrigation. The Sumerians used the wheel at an early time, and they developed a system of numbers based on a unit of 60 that later led to the 360-degree circle, as we know it, and to the dividing of an hour into sixty minutes.

The Sumerians had well-organized city-states. They built great temple towers to honor their gods. The temples were also community centers where schools were maintained, and where weaving, pottery making, and toolmaking were carried on.

While the Sumerians were developing their civilization, the Babylonians, one of the neighboring peoples who held a part of Mesopotamia, were also growing stronger. About 2000 B.C., under a strong leader called Hammurabi, the Babylonians overpowered the Sumerians and the two civilizations merged. Hammurabi was a great warrior and an able ruler. He also organized the first great code of laws. The Babylonians, like the Sumerians, made use of the clay found in this region, both for building materials and for clay writing tablets. The Babylonians adopted the cuneiform writing of the Sumerians. Babylonian women, like Egyptian women, had many privileges, and held a respected position.

Another of the neighboring peoples of the early Sumerians, the Assyrians, also finally grew strong. They were aggressive warriors, and conquered not only the Babylonians, but the Egyptians as well. They built a great capital, the city of Nineveh, with the tribute and spoils they wrung from conquered peoples. The last great Assyrian ruler, Ashurbanipal, tried to promote education, and built a great library that is still famous today.

The Chaldeans, or Later Babylonians, destroyed Nineveh in 612 B.C. Their great ruler, Nebuchadrezzar, made Babylon the greatest city of antiquity. He also destroyed Jerusalem and brought some of the Hebrews to Babylon to be sold as slaves.

Finally the Persians, under Cyrus, conquered the Later Babylonians. Cyrus was a wise and noble king. He was kind to the conquered peoples and released the Hebrews from captivity. Another great Persian king, Darius, organized the Persian Empire. He constructed roads, coined money, established a postal system, and built a great navy. For two centuries Persian rule brought peace to Mesopotamia, but then Persia's power, too, began to weaken.

Today Mesopotamia is part of Iraq. A program of irrigation may make the land a fertile garden spot once again. The rich oil fields there are quite valuable.

SELF–TEST

Look back upon the story of Mesopotamia, and test yourself on these exercises:

I. Complete the following statements:

1. The curved section of fertile land lying along the eastern end of the Mediterranean and extending to the Persian Gulf is sometimes called ——.

2. The first great code of laws was organized by ——, a Babylonian ruler who lived about —— B.C.

3. The —— and the —— are the two rivers which gave this land the name Mesopotamia.

4. The peoples of Mesopotamia used a kind of writing which is called —— because the letters are —— shaped.

5. —— is the name of the religious leader who taught the Persians that life is a struggle between the good and the evil in the world.

6. The hanging gardens of ——, one of the —— —— of the ancient world, were built by ——.

II. Select the word which best completes each of the following statements:

1. The conquering Persians were (*a*) Semites, (*b*) Egyptians, (*c*) Indo-Europeans.

2. The Babylonians believed that life after death was (*a*) happy, (*b*) hopeless, (*c*) bright, (*d*) peaceful.

3. The Babylonian school child did his lessons on (*a*) paper, (*b*) papyrus, (*c*) clay.

III. Tell whether each of the following statements is true or false, and if false, give some reasons to support your answer.

1. The geography of Egypt protected her from invaders, but the geography of Mesopotamia afforded little protection.

2. The Persians were a race of peaceful, luxury-loving people.

3. Towers were a common form of architecture in Mesopotamia.

4. The laws of Hammurabi's time were designed to obtain revenge rather than justice.

5. The Babylonians did not consider education of great importance.

6. In Babylonia women were always treated like slaves.

7. The Assyrians are a splendid example of the saying that " might makes right."

8. Modern historians owe much of their knowledge of Mesopotamian history to an Assyrian monarch's interest in collecting writings.

9. The history of Mesopotamia is the story of one wave of people after another coming in from the deserts and mountains and conquering the people of the plains.

10. Ashurbanipal was Assyria's greatest military leader.

INTERESTING THINGS TO DO

Projects for the Chart Maker

1. Enlarge the comparative time line for Mesopotamia and Egypt. Add events and achievements that you think would give a more complete story of the Mesopotamians. Use sketches or other illustrations wherever possible.

2. Make a chart comparing the discoveries, achievements, and cultural contributions of the Egyptians and Sumerians. A simple method of making such a chart is to arrange three parallel columns headed as follows: "Things Distinctly Egyptian"; "Things Common to Both the Egyptians and Sumerians"; and "Things Distinctly Sumerian."

Topics for Talks

1. "What the pick-and-shovel historians have discovered in the Fertile Crescent." See *Living Past,* by Cyrus Gordon, or *Lost Worlds,* by Anne T. White. See also "Archeology" in *The World Book Encyclopedia.*

2. "Civilization spread on wheels." The Sumerians are thought to have been the first people to make use of the wheel. Discuss the part the wheel has played in the advancement of civilization since the time of the Sumerians. See "Chariot" and "Transportation" in *The World Book Encyclopedia.*

3. "The sundial was developed in Mesopotamia." Explain the principle of the sundial. A cardboard model will help make the explanation clearer. See "Dial" in *Encyclopædia Britannica* and "Sundial" in *The World Book Encyclopedia.*

4. "The justice of Hammurabi." Prepare a short talk on the kind of justice to be had under the code of Hammurabi as compared with that given under our laws today. If you are able to find a considerable number of Hammurabi's laws, perhaps different members of the class might each take one law to explain and compare with a similar law today. Three brief extracts from the Code of Hammurabi are given below. Your teacher may be able to help you find others.

"If a man has stolen an ox, or a sheep, or an ass, or a pig, or a ship from the priests or the king, let him pay thirtyfold. But if he have stolen from a poor man, he shall repay tenfold." "If a physician cure the shattered limb of a man of rank, the patient shall give him five shekels of silver. If the patient is the son of a poor man, he shall give three shekels of silver." "If a physician open a disease in the eye of man with a bronze knife, and if he destroy the man's eye, all his fingers shall be cut off."

Adventures for the Amateur Author

1. Imagine that you are a Babylonian schoolboy or girl and write a few pages of a diary telling of your experiences at school and at home. Include brief descriptions of some of the wonders of the great city in which you live.

2. Imagine you are one of the swift runners who carry messages for Cyrus, the Persian conqueror. Write a short narrative or a poem that tells of an experience you may have had. See Chapter One of *How They Carried the Mail,* by Joseph Walker.

An Assignment for the Roving Reporter

Write an article for a popular magazine on conditions in the Fertile Crescent today. Consult recent magazines, or see *Camel-bells of Baghdad,* by Janet Miller.

A Subject for Debaters

"Resolved: That the peoples of Mesopotamia made greater contributions to civilization than did the Egyptians."

Candidates for Your Album of Famous People

Ashurbanipal, Cyrus, Darius, Hammurabi, Nebuchadrezzar, Zoroaster. Write a biographical portrait of one of these famous people for your *Album of Famous People.*

INTERESTING READING ABOUT MESOPOTAMIA

CHIERA, EDWARD. *They Wrote on Clay.* "The clay tablets discovered by archeologists speak clearly to us today."

Compton's Pictured Encyclopedia. "Babylon: Empires that Flourished when the World was Young," and Index.

DAVIS, W. S. *Belshazzar.* "A tale of the fall of Babylon."

ENGBERG, ROBERT MARTIN. *The Dawn of Civilization.* "History Begins with Writing."

MILLER, JANET. *Camel-bells of Baghdad.* An unusually colorful account of a journey to lands of the past, written with beauty and humor.

MILLS, D. *The Book of the Ancient World.* "Assyria was the great robber nation of the ancient world."

THORNDIKE, LYNN. *A Short History of Civilization.* "The Sumerians fought with one another as well as against the Semites."

VAN LOON, H. W. *Ancient Man.* "Flowers were made to grow upon the many walls of the city. . . ."

VAUGHN, D. M. *Great Peoples of the Ancient World.* "If the document is a letter, it is . . . addressed before being baked."

WALKER, JOSEPH. *How They Carried the Mail.* Chap. I. "There shall be no word save that of Sargon the Great."

WALLBANK, T. W. and TAYLOR, A. M. *Civilization — Past and Present.* "The Egyptians used the wheel but probably borrowed it from their Fertile Crescent neighbors."

PART FOUR

THE HEBREWS AND THE PHOENICIANS MADE NEW CONTRIBUTIONS TO WORLD PROGRESS

HEBREWS AND PHOENICIANS

Nicosia

CYPRUS

MEDITERRANEAN

SEA

NILE DELTA

Sidon

Tyre

PHOENICIA

LEBANON MOUNTAINS

LAND OF CANAAN

Damascus

SYRIA

Nazareth

SEA OF GALILEE

Samaria

Tel Aviv

ISRAEL

Jerusalem

Bethlehem

Jordan River

JUDAH

DEAD SEA

EDGE OF THE FERTILE CRESCENT

THE ANCIENT BRIDGE BETWEEN EGYPT, SYRIA AND MESOPOTAMIA

Gaza

LAND OF GOSHEN

Heliopolis (Cairo)

ROUTE OF THE EXODUS OF THE HEBREWS

EGYPT

MOUNT SINAI

Nile River

Arabian Desert

RED SEA

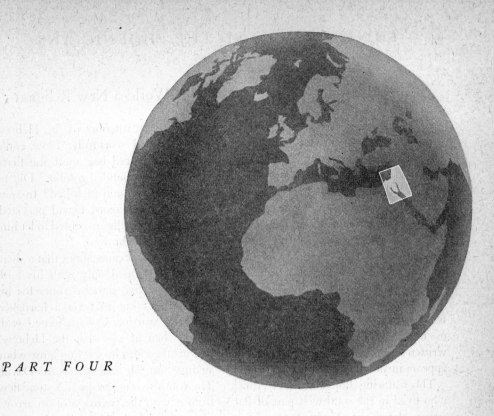

A Religious People and Their Merchant Neighbors

GREAT size does not make a great man; neither does great size make a great nation. Some of the biggest contributions to civilization have been made by small nations. One such nation was Phoenicia, on the eastern shore of the Mediterranean Sea. And to the south of Phoenicia lay the two little countries of the Hebrews, Israel and Judah, which in later times have, together, come to be known as Palestine. Though neither the Phoenicians nor the Hebrews held vast lands, one gave the Western world an alphabet and the other, a religion.

The story of the Hebrews and Phoenicians will be more interesting to you if you know the location of the places which are mentioned. What two historic seas are to be found in Israel and Judah? Where is the Jordan River? What mountains lie between Phoenicia and Syria? Locate Jerusalem, Bethlehem, Nazareth. What are the two seaports of Phoenicia?

Trace the route of the Hebrews as they wandered through the desert to reach their "Promised Land." Do you find the mountain where Moses gave his followers the Ten Commandments? Read the story of these peoples and you will appreciate why we call the Hebrews a religious people and the Phoenicians the merchants of the Mediterranean.

Chapter 1 ~ The Hebrews Gave the World a New Religion

A shepherd boy met a giant in single-handed combat. For centuries the idea of devotion to one God has been identified with the Hebrews. Their land of Palestine was smaller than other important ancient kingdoms, such as Assyria and Persia, and they never attained the great power of those nations. But the ideas of religion and of right and wrong taught by their prophets were a lasting contribution to the world.

One example of great faith in God, as well as great courage, is told in the story of the shepherd boy, David. It was written down by Hebrew historians and appears in the Old Testament.

The seafaring Philistines [fi lis'tinz], who lived in the southwest part of Palestine along the Mediterranean Sea, were at war with the Hebrews. From the camp of the Philistines there came a giant dressed in a coat of mail and bearing a shining metal shield and a heavy pointed spear. Boldly he strode into the open crying out that the Hebrews should choose a man from their army to come forward and meet him in single combat. If the Hebrew should kill him, he cried, then the Philistines would bow before the Hebrews; but if he, the giant, should kill the Hebrews' champion, the Hebrews must serve the Philistines.

When they heard this thundering challenge of the giant Goliath [goh lai' uth], terror and dismay gripped the hearts of the Hebrews. While the camp was still in the turmoil of fear, there came to it a boy who had been herding sheep in the wilderness. Sure that his God would help him, the shepherd boy, David, went to King Saul and said, " I will go and fight with this Philistine."

The sturdy warriors of the Hebrew army laughed scornfully. How could this inexperienced boy meet the fierce giant in single-handed combat? Did he not know he would be killed? In spite of laughter and scorn David persisted, and the king finally consented to let him fight for the Hebrews.

This is how it came about that a shepherd boy — armed only with his faith in God and five smooth stones for his sling — went out to meet a hardened Philistine warrior. Goliath roared with anger when he saw that the Hebrews had insulted him by sending a mere boy against him. He rushed toward David. The youth swung his sling. A stone flew from it with the swiftness of an arrow, and struck the middle of the giant's forehead. Goliath crumpled to the ground. The Philistines, seeing that their champion had fallen, fled in wild disorder. David's moment of victory is illustrated in the picture on page 95.

Palestine was at the crossroads of ancient civilizations. David and his fellow Hebrews lived at the far western end of the Fertile Crescent, in Palestine. This land of the Hebrews was not large. In fact, one could stand on a mountain peak in the center of Palestine on a clear day and see the entire length and breadth of it. It reached from the great, parched Arabian Desert to the south and east, where earlier Hebrew tribes had lived, to the Lebanon Mountains on the north. To the west rolled the blue Mediterranean.

Today it does not take long to travel the 150 miles from the green hills and valleys of the north to the almost desert land of the south. Parts of Palestine are

Drawing by John C. Wonsetler

DEATH OF A GIANT

The shepherd boy David, armed with his faith in God, and with five smooth stones for his sling, overthrew the giant Goliath, and saved the Hebrews from Philistine rule.

still very beautiful with olive groves, forests of mighty cedars, and green pastures. It is easy to see why the Hebrews, when they wandered in from the hot sands of the desert, called this the "land flowing with milk and honey."

Although Palestine was a much better homeland than the desert, its small size and a lack of natural resources kept it from becoming a nation of power and wealth. Nevertheless Palestine had an important part in world affairs. This country was the bridge between the great empires of Egypt to the southwest and Mesopotamia to the east. Across this bridge the mighty armies and glittering chariots of the Egyptian pharaohs and the Assyrian general-kings thundered many times. Usually they left behind a torn and bleeding Palestine. Like Poland in World War II, Palestine was a battleground for larger nations.

Turn to the map on page 92 to see how Palestine stood at the crossroads of the Egyptian and Mesopotamian civilizations. Find the famous city of Jerusalem. Notice that the northern part of Palestine was called Israel and the southern part Judah [joo'duh]. (It was only for a brief period that they were closely united in one kingdom.) See how the historic river Jordan makes its way straight down from the northern highlands, pauses at the Sea of Galilee, and flows on through the lower plains and deserts. Finally it sinks into the salty waters of the Dead Sea, whose level lies almost 1300 feet below the level of the ocean. The Nile gave us Egypt; the Tigris and Euphrates watered Mesopotamia; and the Jordan helped to make Palestine the " Promised Land."

The early Hebrews were desert wanderers. We know little about the earliest Hebrews who, long before the time of David, wandered with their flocks of sheep and goats through the Arabian Desert. There they sought whatever pasture land and water they could find. Probably their lives were much like those of desert tribes today. Wild tribes still rove across deserts, with no homes except goatskin tents, no possessions that cannot be moved on a few hours' notice, no law except the word of the patriarch [pay'tri ahrk], or the wise old man, of the tribe.

The Hebrews were made slaves in Egypt. Gradually some of the Hebrew shepherds drifted out of the Arabian Desert. The Bible tells us about some of them who wandered into Egypt and set-

tled on the eastern part of the Nile Delta in a region called the Land of Goshen. For a time, the Hebrews were well treated by the pharaohs of Egypt. Some of them held high places in the government. Probably you remember the story of Joseph and his many-colored coat, and how he was sold by his brothers into slavery to an Egyptian. After a number of years he came into the service of the pharaoh, who was so impressed by Joseph's wisdom that he made him governor over all Egypt.

However, a pharaoh came to the throne who made slaves of the Hebrews in Egypt. After this there was no happiness for them; there was only work and suffering. They toiled under the lash in " hard bondage in mortar and in brick and in all manner of service in the field."

Moses led the Hebrews out of Egypt. At last a leader arose among the Hebrews who was strong enough to help them to escape. This man was Moses. You will recall the Bible story telling how he was found in the rushes along the bank of the Nile by an Egyptian princess, who brought him into the royal palace and had him educated there.

Although Moses was brought up as an Egyptian prince, he became interested in the plight of his fellow Hebrews. One day he was aroused beyond endurance when he saw an Egyptian overseer beating a Hebrew. Impetuously Moses rushed over to them and in his fury killed the Egyptian.

Moses was now a criminal forced to flee from the palace and the country. He went far into the desert. There he thought about the condition of his people and became convinced that God had called him to be their leader. He resolved to go back to Egypt to see if by any means he could lead his people out of

Brown Brothers

THE MIRACLE OF THE RED SEA

An artist's idea of the escape of Moses and the Hebrews through the Red Sea. The sea is rolling back to engulf the pursuing pharaoh and his followers.

bondage. He was able to return in safety because his former enemies had died.

The Bible tells how Moses tried to reason with the pharaoh, but the " pharaoh's heart was hardened." A number of terrible plagues then visited the Egyptians, and at last the pharaoh became convinced that the God of the Hebrews had sent the plagues. In desperation he told Moses to lead the Hebrews away. Even so, when he learned that they had gone he regretted that he had given his slaves their liberty. Gathering his nobles and armies together, the pharaoh hurried after the Hebrews, who had crossed over a part of the Red Sea. He ordered his armies to follow them. The Bible relates how the onrushing waters of the Red Sea drowned the pursuers. The escaping Hebrews are shown above.

Even when they had escaped from Egypt, and reached the Sinai peninsula on the southeastern edge of the Arabian Desert, many of Moses' followers were afraid and wanted to turn back. Some of them had adopted the religion of the Egyptians. They believed that their Egyptian gods had been left behind, and that they now had no gods to protect them.

Moses gave his people the Ten Commandments. Moses led his followers to a mountain called Sinai. Here he left them for forty days and forty nights while he went to the top of the mountain to pray and receive help from God. When he returned Moses brought with him the Ten Commandments.

The people promised to obey the Ten Commandments and worship no other God but Jehovah [ji hoh′vuh]. Their belief in Jehovah gave them a new strength, and the Ten Commandments were a code by which to live. In the midst of a vast, barren desert the Hebrews found a real faith in God, which helped to bind them together as one people.

Desert life prepared the Hebrews to conquer the "Promised Land." For about forty years these former slaves wandered in the desert, sometimes hungry and thirsty, often doubting the wisdom that had led them out of Egypt. Food was scanty, and water was scarce. Because of their ceaseless search for new pastures and water for their flocks, the Hebrews could never camp long in one place. Also, there was always danger of attack from fierce desert tribes. But in this life the Hebrews grew strong, hardy, and fearless. They were becoming ready to conquer Palestine, the "Promised Land."

The Hebrews waged war to gain possession of the "Promised Land." Among the tribes already living in Palestine were the Canaanites [kay'nun-aitz]. At that time Palestine was called the land of Canaan. Probably some time before 1200 B.C. the Hebrews began to force their way into Canaan east of the Jordan River. The desert invaders had to fight the Canaanites, Hittites [hit'aitz], and Philistines in order to wrest the fertile land from them. The Old Testament gives vivid accounts of the plunder and pillage which resulted.

For more than a century the struggle continued. Gradually the Hebrews subdued their enemies and took the control of most of Palestine from them. Now the lives of the Hebrews changed. They had been shepherds wandering from place to place, but now they settled down to till the land as well as to herd their sheep. In the desert only tents had protected them from heat and storms; now they lived in comfortable homes.

Not all of the Canaanites were driven out of Palestine. From those who remained the Hebrews learned many things. They took off their sheepskins and put on the fine woolen clothing of the Canaanites. They learned the trade and business methods of the conquered people. Gradually they drifted into towns, and the old simplicity of the des-

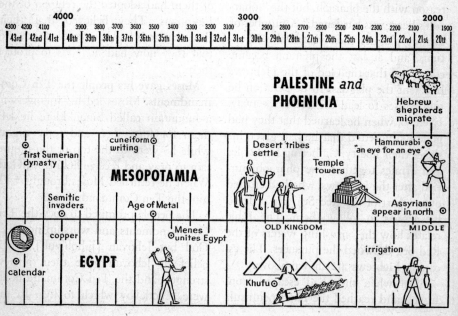

4000														3000												2000
4300	4200	4100	3900	3800	3700	3600	3500	3400	3300	3200	3100		2900	2800	2700	2600	2500	2400	2300	2200	2100		1900
43rd	42nd	41st	40th	39th	38th	37th	36th	35th	34th	33rd	32nd	31st	30th	29th	28th	27th	26th	25th	24th	23rd	22nd	21st	20th

PALESTINE and PHOENICIA

Hebrew shepherds migrate

first Sumerian dynasty

cuneiform writing

MESOPOTAMIA

Semitic invaders

Age of Metal

Desert tribes settle

Temple towers

Hammurabi "an eye for an eye"

Assyrians appear in north

calendar

copper

EGYPT

Menes unites Egypt

OLD KINGDOM

Khufu

irrigation

MIDDLE

ert disappeared. Some of the Hebrews even adopted the Canaanite idols.

With this changed way of living the Hebrews needed a new kind of government. Enemy tribes on every side caused them to form a strong union among themselves. They decided to organize their nation into a kingdom with one ruler at the head.

Saul and David were early kings of the Hebrews. The first king of Israel, in the northern part of Palestine, was King Saul who ruled about 1000 B.C. at the time David went out to meet Goliath. Up to that time and even during Saul's reign, there was never a strong central government in either Israel or Judah; both were made up of tribes that warred among themselves. When the shepherd boy, David, grew older he became a great military leader. He put down civil wars and also led the Hebrews in campaigns against their outside enemies — the Philistines, the Ammonites [am''n aitz], and the Syrians.

David became king of Judah and then united the peoples of both Judah and Is-

rael in one strong kingdom. He made Jerusalem the capital city of the Hebrews and the center of their religion. He brought the Ark of the Covenant to Jerusalem. The Ark was the sacred chest containing the stone tablets of the law which Moses had received on Mt. Sinai. David had many of the faults of a bold warrior, but he was beloved by the people. In later generations he was remembered not only for his battle prowess and kingly qualities but as a gifted harp-player and poet.

The splendor and extravagance of Solomon divided the Hebrew kingdom. David's famous son, Solomon, came to the throne at the age of twenty. He resolved to give great pomp and splendor to his court in order to glorify God and firmly establish the greatness of the Hebrew religion. To pay for this magnificence, it was necessary for the Hebrews to build up a large trade with other countries. Solomon's ships brought horses and chariots from Egypt, and " gold, silver, ivory, apes, and peacocks " from Mediterranean ports. From his

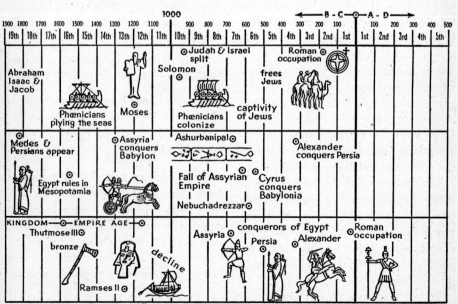

ally, the king of Tyre [tair], Solomon obtained trained navigators to sail his ships. You will learn more about these seagoing men of Tyre, and of other towns in Phoenicia, when you read the next chapter.

Solomon was a great builder. He erected a splendid temple at Jerusalem in honor of Jehovah. Near the temple, which is shown on page 101, Solomon built his own magnificent palace. Its great hall had forty-five large pillars carved from cedars brought from the forests of Lebanon. Visitors traveled from distant countries to see the splendor Solomon had created, and they also proclaimed the wisdom and learning of Solomon. He is remembered as one of the wisest kings of ancient times.

Solomon's reign was long and peaceful, but he required much money and labor for his many undertakings. The money was wrung from the people by heavy taxes, and the labor was obtained by forcing the men to work without pay. When the people complained of bad treatment, Solomon turned a deaf ear. Some of the people were also dissatisfied with the king because they believed that he was less devoted to Jehovah than his father, David, had been. When Solomon died, Israel withdrew from the kingdom. Solomon's extravagance and love of luxurious living had helped to divide the Hebrew people. From about 930 B.C., there were two separate kingdoms in Palestine, Israel in the north and Judah in the south.

Assyria destroyed the northern kingdom. The division of the kingdom made two weak states out of one small but prosperous nation, and so brought great danger to the Hebrews. Assyria on the north and Egypt on the south constantly menaced their freedom.

At last Assyria gathered her armies together and marched toward Israel to lay siege to Samaria [suh may'ri uh], the capital of the northern kingdom. For three dreadful, bloody years the Hebrews withstood the Assyrian hosts. At last the city walls were broken down, and in 722 B.C. Samaria was conquered. The inhabitants were herded together and marched across the hot plains to be held captive in Assyria. The Assyrians then repopulated the town with natives of Mesopotamia. (Later these people became known as the Samaritans.) But the fall of Samaria had brought the northern kingdom to an end.

Babylonia destroyed the southern kingdom. Judah lasted long enough to see the fall of Nineveh, the capital of Assyria (in 612 B.C.), but long before that time its own days of glory had departed. The splendor of Solomon's time was a mere memory. One mighty nation after another exacted tribute from the little land, until Nebuchadrezzar, king of Babylonia, wrecked Jerusalem in 586 B.C. As in the northern kingdom, the citizens were marched away into slavery. They were taken to Babylon. The sorrow of the people still echoes in the verses of the Bible:

By the rivers of Babylon, there we sat down, yea, we wept, when we remembered Zion (Jerusalem).

We hanged our harps upon the willows in the midst thereof.

How shall we sing the Lord's song in a strange land? [1]

The Hebrews gained a new idea of God. Among these downtrodden captives, who believed that they had been deserted by their God, there arose a great poet and teacher, whose name is not known to us. He cried to the homesick exiles, " Be comforted, ye people, be com-

[1] Psalms 137:1–4.

New York Public Library

KING SOLOMON'S TEMPLE

King Solomon was not only a philosopher but also one of the first great engineers. This temple was built according to his plans, at Jerusalem, in honor of Jehovah. Does the design of the temple look ancient, or could you imagine it in a modern city?

forted," and gave them hope once more. He reminded the people of Jehovah, whom he called their only God and the Creator of the world. He explained that the suffering of the Hebrews was their preparation for service in the world. Later this prophet's sayings were made part of the Book of Isaiah [ai say′uh], in the Bible.

The Hebrews came to see Jehovah not as a fierce, jealous, tribal God, but as a kindly father of all people. This belief was monotheism [mahn′oh thee iz′m], or the belief in one God. You will re-

FARMING IN THE HOLY LAND

The primitive farming methods in modern Palestine are somewhat made up for by the use of the versatile camel, such as you see in the foreground above.

call that the Egyptians, too, had developed a primitive idea of one God of the universe.

While the Hebrews waited for the day of their deliverance, which they felt sure God would bring them, some of their wise men gathered together their sacred writings to form a history of their people. Into it they wove the stories of their past triumphs and sufferings and their hopes for a greater future. Many of these stories are in the Old Testament.

Cyrus the Great granted the Hebrews their freedom. At last a brighter day dawned for the Hebrews. Cyrus, the mighty Persian, took Babylon in 538 B.C., as you learned in the story of Mesopotamia. At the same time he set the exiled Hebrews free, and permitted them to return to Jerusalem. He allowed them to rebuild their holy city and restore the temple. Now they could also publish the religious laws that they re-

vered so much. The joy of returning to their homeland and rebuilding their temple inspired Hebrew poets to write and arrange a remarkable book of religious songs, the Book of Psalms, to be found in the Bible.

The Hebrews have long endured persecution. When Cyrus the Great restored Jerusalem to the Hebrews and assured their right of freedom to worship their one God, Jehovah, that did not mean the end of the persecution of the Hebrews. Rome and other military nations were to seize their country. Again they were to be driven from the " Promised Land." Throughout the ages, they were to migrate to many lands, becoming citizens of other nations. Without having developed in later times a nation of their own, the Jews are to be distinguished primarily by their religious inheritance.

If we were to unroll the script of this *Story of Nations* to the present day, we would find, as you know, that the Jew n certain lands is still persecuted. In Germany, to give the most flagrant example of recent times, the Jews were stripped of their social, political, and individual privileges to an unbelievable extent. By the fanaticism of the Nazis [nah'tsiz], the Jews were singled out and blamed for many of the weaknesses of the Nazi state. Thus the Nazi leaders were able to whip up the German people into a fury of intolerance and misdirected national fervor.

The Nazis could point to times in the past when the Jews had been viciously persecuted. In the Middle Ages Christians were forbidden by the Church to engage in the business of lending money at interest. At that time, many Jews, whose religion did not forbid their taking interest on loans, became moneylenders. When the Jews prospered, singly or as a group, people often resented them. Many times their wealth was confiscated and sometimes the resentment was so bitter that brutal treatment resulted. This background of persecution made it easier for the Nazis to inflame their people to intolerance and brutality in modern times. Though it is difficult for us who live in free countries to believe, literally hundreds of thousands of Jewish civilians (in addition to other peoples) have been put to death wherever the hand of the Nazi conqueror has been laid. The health and the happiness of millions of other Jews in foreign lands have been injured almost beyond our understanding.

The Jews have continued to migrate. Before World War II, a good many Jews in Germany had managed to migrate to countries with more liberal governments. Since our country is traditionally known for its religious and political freedom, many such refugees have been attracted to the United States. In this migration, they followed the example of the Pilgrims, the Irish, the Germans, and countless other immigrants who came to the American "Melting Pot" for "life, liberty, and the pursuit of happiness." Some countries of Central and South America have also served as a haven of security for many persecuted Jews of modern Europe.

Modern Jews return to Palestine. Among many persons of Jewish origin there has been a longing to return to Palestine, the home of their forefathers. At the end of the 19th Century, a nationalistic movement known as Zionism urged groups of Jews to settle in Palestine. At present there are approximately 375,000 members of their race living in their old homeland. The government is administered under a mandate (for supervision and protection) to Great Britain, set up by the League of Nations at the end of World War I. While it is probable that no great numbers of Jews will continue migrating to the settlement in that small country, the government there, and the many co-operative ventures, such as farming, are interesting examples of economic and social co-operation.

Chapter 2 ― The Phoenicians Sailed the Seas and Helped Spread Civilization Westward

The Phoenicians were daring sailors. Most of us are thrilled when we hear the story of daring adventurers who go places none have gone before. A whole nation of daring sailor-adventurers once lived on the narrow coast of Phoenicia, just north of Palestine.

The Phoenicians were probably an early offshoot of Semitic-speaking peoples. They had thick black hair and broad hooked noses. They were first known about 1600 B.C., when the Egyptians were extending their empire into Asia.

In their small strip of homeland the Phoenicians did not have much fertile land for raising food; so they took to the sea. In time they became skilled workmen in many crafts, but their prosperity was based on their shipping trade. They established many trade routes in the Mediterranean. In time they even ventured past the Pillars of Hercules [her′ kyoo leez], as the Strait of Gibraltar was then called, and then further out into the Atlantic Ocean. In those days it took courage to sail toward the meeting place of the earth and sky, for there, according to legend, dwelt the monsters of the sea. Some of the Phoenicians, blown off their course by trade winds, may even have reached America, though we cannot be sure of this likelihood. No one knows, since the Phoenicians kept their routes a secret from the other ancient peoples. For example, the story was told of a Phoenician captain who was on his way to Sicily for tin. He saw a ship following him. Rather than disclose his course, he ran his ship aground.

PHOENICIAN SHIPS

The Phoenicians were daring sailors who ventured into enchanted waters and carried their wares and civilization to many parts of the Mediterranean world.

Mountains and the sea served to protect Phoenicia. Turn again to the map on page 92 to find Phoenicia. Notice what a narrow strip of country it was. This land was less than two hundred miles long, and only thirty-five miles broad at its widest part. Its situation was somewhat similar to that of the country of Chile [chil'i] which stretches along the western coast of South America. Chile, of course, is much longer.

Unlike Palestine, Phoenicia was somewhat protected against the armies that so often invaded and despoiled her neighbor. On the north and east were high mountains. On the west was the sea. But just beyond the mountains were powerful neighbors strong enough to conquer the small land of the merchant people. Instead they demanded tribute from the Phoenicians as the price for leaving them alone. These trading people were not fighters, and found it easier to raise the tribute money by their commerce than to go to war. Among the foreign powers who, in turn, became their overlords, were Assyria, Babylonia, Persia, Egypt, Greece, and Rome. Under Roman rule in the First Century B.C., Phoenicia finally became a part of Syria, and was no longer known as a separate nation.

Usually the Phoenicians lived at peace with their neighbors. The Hebrews borrowed their skilled builders as well as navigators, and bought supplies from them to build the temple of Solomon. At the time of Egypt's supremacy, the Egyptians allowed the Phoenicians to build a temple to their own gods in the Egyptian capital. Later when the Persians conquered the Phoenicians, they allowed them to keep their own king and taxed them very lightly.

The Phoenicians worshiped Baal. The religion of the Phoenicians was very much like that of the Canaanites, who were distant relatives of theirs. Like the Canaanites the Phoenicians had as their chief god Baal [bay''l]. The anger of Baal, it was believed, must be appeased by sacrifices of the things that were dearest to them. This belief led the people to offer up even their children to insure his protection. Possibly you remember the story of Jezebel [jez'uh b'l], daughter of the Phoenician king, who married Ahab [ay'hab], king of Israel. She carried many of the barbarous religious practices of the Phoenicians into Palestine.

The religion of the Phoenicians lacked spiritual ideals. They had no belief in a hereafter, but called the period after death the "time of nonexistence." Those who died "went down into silence and became mute."

Tyre and Sidon became the great trading cities. From the ports of Tyre and Sidon [sai'd'n], their two chief cities, the Phoenicians sailed west on their trading adventures. Today we find practically no traces of these once powerful cities.

Though few ruins are left to remind us of the greatness of Tyre and Sidon, these cities are often mentioned in ancient literature. They were two of the world's greatest trading centers. It was said that Tyre, the capital of Phoenicia, had such a well-fortified natural harbor that its merchant fleet could lie there at anchor "as if within a house whose doors were bolted."

The Phoenicians became expert shipbuilders and navigators. On page 104 you will see a picture of two Phoenician ships. Notice that one is small with a square sail in the center and is rowed by men sitting on one level. This was the earliest type of ship developed by the Phoenicians. The one in the foreground, which had two banks of oars, was called a bireme [bai'reem].

Although to us these ships appear small and poorly equipped, they seemed almost like miracles to the people with whom the Phoenicians traded. Herodotus, the Greek historian of whom we have already spoken, tells about going down to the water's edge and talking with the " lookout man " on board a Phoenician ship. This is what he says:

. . . I saw this man in his leisure moments, examining and testing everything that a vessel needs when at sea. . . . I asked him what he was about, whereupon he replied, " Stranger, I am looking to see, in case anything should happen, how everything is arranged in the ship and whether anything is wanting or is inconveniently situated; for when a storm arises at sea, it is not possible to look for what is wanting, or to put to rights what is arranged awkwardly."

Phoenician ships and caravans brought treasures from Europe, Africa, and Asia. When the ships of the Phoenicians set out on their voyages they usually carried four things: purple dye, glass, woven fabrics, and fine metalwork. The purple dye, which was made in Tyre, came from a shellfish found in the Mediterranean Sea. Tyrian purple was considered a great luxury, and kings eagerly bought it to color their robes.

The craftsmen of Tyre and Sidon were also famous for fine metalwork. Homer, the blind Greek poet, wrote in one of his poems:

A silver bowl well wrought,
By Sidon's artists cunningly adorned,
Borne by Phoenicians o'er the dark blue sea.

Although the craftsmen of Phoenicia learned the art of glass-blowing in

TREASURES FOR KING SOLOMON

The Hebrews used Phoenician navigators to transport goods overseas. Phoenicians brought supplies to be used in the building of Solomon's Temple. Do you know where the peacock in this picture might have come from?

Egypt, they soon became better workmen than their teachers. Beautifully decorated bowls, cups, and vases were sent from Phoenicia in almost every merchant ship that sailed.

In exchange for their wares the Phoenicians brought back gold, incense, and myrrh from Ethiopia; and bronzes and other works of art from Greece. In Egypt they loaded their ships with grain, fine linen, and embroidery. Pearls, spices, ivory, ebony, and ostrich plumes came from India. Silver, iron, tin, and lead were brought from southern Spain.

Not content with trade by sea, the Phoenicians sent caravans by land up toward the Black Sea to bring back slaves and horses, and to obtain the copper vases made by mountaineers. Some caravans went as far as China to purchase shimmering silks for the Phoenicians and their wealthy customers on the shores of the whole Mediterranean. Phoenicia had become the first really great commercial power. Her control of the Mediterranean was so effective that her peoples became the leading merchants of the Mediterranean.

The Phoenician merchants established strategic centers of trade in the Mediterranean. About two thousand years have passed since the Phoenicians sailed throughout the Mediterranean world. The great Phoenician cities of Tyre and Sidon are no more. Yet even today we find trace of the merchant empire of Phoenicia. Such cities as Marseille [mahr seh′y] in southern France and Cadiz [kay′diz] in Spain still boast of their origin as early Phoenician centers of trade.

The Phoenicians founded a great trading center which later surpassed both Tyre and Sidon in size, wealth, and beauty. This was Carthage [kahr′thij] in North Africa, almost directly across the Mediterranean from the toe of Italy. The map on page 182 will show you its strategic location for trade or conquest in northern Africa. Carthage was in the

Canaanite-Phoenician-Aramaic	Greek	Latin
Ӄ Ӿ	Λ	A
⅁ 𝟓	B	B
⅂	ΓC	CG
◿ ◿	ΔD	D
⅂ ⅂	F E	E
Y	F Y	FVUWY
エ ☲	I	Z
Ⴂ H	H	H
Ꙁ	I	IJ
Ⴞ Ⴟ	K	K
Ꮐ Ⴑ	ΛL	L
ᙏ ᙏ	M	M
Ɣ Ꙅ	N	N
ⱻⱻⱻ	✝ ☲	X
○○	O	O
ᎢᏋᏋ	ΠΓ	P
ⴋⱨⴋ		
ϤϤϥ	Ọ	Q
Ϥ	PR	R
ᴡ	Σ ς	S
✕	T	T

ANCIENT PEOPLES GAVE US OUR ALPHABET

The alphabet was the means by which the contributions of ancient peoples have been preserved and handed down to modern civilization. In reading across the three columns, you will see how our alphabet gradually developed.

section of North Africa held by American soldiers in World War II. You will learn more about this city of Carthage when you read the story of the Romans.

The Phoenicians carried the alphabet to the Western world. Not much is known about the origin of the Phoenician language. Some of its words and forms of grammar were similar to those of the Hebrews, but it appears that the two languages developed independently. The Phoenicians were not a literary people, but they had a practical use for writing in their business orders and bills of sale. In time they developed a simple alphabet, which is shown on page 107.

Since the Phoenicians were the only people whose trading took them all over the western Mediterranean, their alphabet was the first to be widely introduced into Europe. At first the Greeks, it is said, looked with mistrust at the strange black marks on bits of yellow paper, believing that they might be some charm that would bring bad luck. But gradually the mistrust disappeared. Finally the Phoenician alphabet became the foundation of Greek writing. The Greeks improved the Phoenician alphabet, adapted it to their own use, and handed it on to the Romans and the peoples of western Europe who in turn passed it on to us. Thus the course of civilization moved westward as Phoenician ships carried their cargoes to ports farther and farther away from their home on the shore of the eastern Mediterranean.

The Hebrews Gave the World a New Understanding of God

Palestine, the land of the Hebrews, is located at the western end of the Fertile Crescent. The northern part of Palestine was called Israel; the southern, Judah.

The early Hebrews were a wandering desert people. Some of them settled in Egypt, where, after a time, one of the pharaohs made them slaves. Moses, a strong leader, finally led the Hebrews out of Egypt. Moses brought the people the Ten Commandments. The Hebrews promised to obey these rules, and to worship only one God. They wandered for forty years in the desert of the Sinai peninsula, becoming strong and hardy. Probably some time before 1200 B.C. they began to force their way into Palestine, their " Promised Land," which was then inhabited by peoples called the Canaanites, Hittites, and Philistines.

The struggle for control of Palestine lasted nearly a century. The Hebrews learned new skills and ways of living from the people they conquered. David, ruler of Judah, united Israel with his kingdom. He made Jerusalem the capital city of the joint kingdom. David's son, Solomon, built a magnificent temple and palace. He was famous as one of the wisest kings of ancient times, but his lavish expenditures and heavy taxes caused discontent. When he died, Israel withdrew from the kingdom. This made Palestine into two weak states instead of one strong kingdom.

Assyria finally conquered Israel in 722 B.C. About a century and a half later, the Babylonians destroyed Judah, the southern kingdom. When Cyrus, the Persian, took Babylon, he released the captive Hebrews to return to Palestine and rebuild Jerusalem. Later, Rome and other nations seized Palestine, and the Hebrews were driven from their country to migrate to many lands and become citizens of other nations. Today the Jews are still persecuted, and are driven to migrating to any land that offers them a refuge. Within the last century the Zionist Movement has attempted to settle many Jews in Palestine once again. Today the government of Palestine is under a mandate to Great Britain.

Jewish men and women are proud of the part their people have played in history. They have made many lasting contributions to the world's progress in science, medicine, music, drama, and poetry. Probably one of the greatest gifts of the Hebrews to the world has been their steadfast example of a belief in one God. Among all the ancient peoples their religion was the most idealistic. They were the first to consider God as a loving father who ruled the world with kindness. It was a Hebrew who said of Jehovah —

> He hath shewed thee, oh man, what is good;
> And what doth the Lord require of thee,
> But to do justly,
> And to love mercy,
> And to walk humbly with thy God?

The Merchant Adventurers of Phoenicia Helped Spread Civilization

Phoenicia, a small narrow country on the Mediterranean Sea to the north of Palestine, was the homeland of daring sailors and skillful craftsmen. Many foreign powers in turn were overlords of the Phoenicians, until finally the country became a part of Syria in the First Century B.C., and ceased to exist as a separate nation.

Tyre and Sidon were the great trading ports of Phoenicia. Phoenician sailors were expert shipbuilders and navigators. They traded all over the western Mediterranean, and established strategic centers of commerce in other lands, such as Marseille in France, Cadiz in Spain, and Carthage in North Africa. Their ships usually carried purple dye, glass, woven fabrics, and fine metalwork, for these were the products of the celebrated Phoenician craftsmen. The Phoenicians also sent out caravans overland to trade. As these people carried their cargoes far and wide, they also spread their alphabet. The Phoenician alphabet was the foundation of Greek writing, and thus indirectly of our own. The greatest contribution of the Phoenicians was the effect their trading had of carrying new learning and skills to all parts of the Mediterranean world.

SELF-TEST

I. Select the word or phrase which best completes the following statements:

1. The earliest Hebrews lived on (*a*) the Sahara Desert, (*b*) the Arabian Desert, (*c*) the grasslands of northern Europe, (*d*) the Nile Delta.

2. The Hebrews were led out of bondage in Egypt by (*a*) Moses, (*b*) David, (*c*) Joseph.

3. The river which helped make Palestine the "Promised Land" was (*a*) the Tigris, (*b*) the Nile, (*c*) the Jordan.

4. The most grave result of Solomon's rule was (*a*) the building of Solomon's temple (*b*) dividing the Hebrews into two weak kingdoms, (*c*) Solomon's alliance with the King of Tyre.

II. Complete the following statements:

1. The best-known writings in which we find much of the history and literature of the Hebrews are commonly called ——.

2. One of the greatest contributions of the Hebrews was their belief in ——.

III. Tell whether each of the following statements is correct, and discuss each briefly.

1. The geographical position of Palestine in the ancient world was of no great importance in her history.

2. Because of the power of Joseph, the Hebrews gradually conquered the Egyptians.

3. The ancient Hebrews were monotheists.

Look back upon the story of the Phoenicians by testing yourself on these exercises.

IV. Select the three adjectives which most nearly describe the Phoenicians: (1) adventuresome, (2) idealistic, (3) shrewd, (4) warlike, (5) ignorant.

V. Tell whether each of the following statements is accurate and discuss each briefly.

1. Phoenicia was on the Mediterranean coast north of the land of the Hebrews.

2. In appearance the Phoenicians were somewhat like modern Englishmen or Swedes.

3. The Phoenicians were the first to reach the coast of North America.

4. Rather than go to war the Phoenicians willingly paid tribute to strong foreign nations, in order to carry on their trade.

5. The worship of Baal in Phoenicia was accompanied by cruel practices.

6. The belief of the Phoenicians about life after death was more like that of the Babylonians than that of the Hebrews.

7. Phoenicians carried on their trade both by land and by sea.

8. The Phoenicians introduced the alphabet into western Europe.

VI. Complete the following statements:

1. Monarchs especially desired the dye known as Tyrian —— for their royal robes.

2. The city of —— in Spain and the city of —— in France owe their origin to Phoenician traders.

3. The most famous and wealthy colony established by the Phoenicians was ——.

INTERESTING THINGS TO DO

Topics for Talks

1. "The arts and crafts of the Phoenicians." See "Phoenicia" in *The World Book Encyclopedia.*

2. "The world's greatest work of literature." This statement is often made with reference to the Bible. Prepare a talk explaining the many types of writing contained in the Bible, such as poetry, stories, etc., and then read to the class a portion which you think has special qualities as literature.

3. "The civilizations of the Hebrews, Egyptians, and Phoenicians." Prepare a talk comparing these three peoples, and describing the main contributions made by each of them to civilization.

Assignment for the Roving Reporter

Pretend you are a reporter writing on the Zionist Movement. Write an article for your paper about the collective farms set up by the Jews in Palestine, and about other developments in Palestine in recent times. Consult books or magazines, such as *Life,* October 11, 1943.

Adventures for the Amateur Author

1. Write an account of an imaginary trip of a Phoenician trading vessel which departs from Tyre or Sidon, sails westward as far as Spain or the British Isles, and returns to Phoenicia. Your account should indicate a reason why the Phoenicians became a seafaring people; give any information you are able to secure concerning ports visited and the products important in the trade of that time. See the Bible, *Ezekiel,* Chap. 27, verses 1-25, and "Phoenicia" in *The World Book Encyclopedia.*

2. Write an historical sketch entitled, "The ABC's Go Westward." Read on the subject of the alphabet in encyclopedias and reference books.

3. Write a description of the splendid temple of King Solomon. See the

Bible, *I Chronicles,* Chap. 28, verses 11–21, for David's plans for the temple; *II Chronicles,* Chaps. 3, 4, and *I Kings,* Chap. 6, for a description of the temple Solomon built according to David's plans.

Ideas for Your Little Theater

1. Dramatize for presentation before the class an incident in the life of Joseph, Abraham, Ruth, Solomon, or some other famous Biblical character.

2. Using films, slides, or pictures from magazines, present to the class a travelogue program on the Holy Land.

3. Arrange a program of Hebrew music for the class. In choosing phonograph records, try particularly to include such ancient melodies as "Kol Nidrei" and "Eili, Eili."

INTERESTING READING ABOUT THE HEBREWS
AND PHOENICIANS

The Holy Bible

HAGEDORN, H. *The Book of Courage.* See the spirited biographical sketches of Moses and Saul, who dared to follow their convictions.

HUNTING, H. B. *Hebrew Life and Times.* A source of information on life in Biblical times.

MILLS, D. *The Book of the Ancient World.* ". . . they went . . . out into the Atlantic, which was supposed to be the abode of monsters . . ."

——, *The People of Ancient Israel.* ". . . he saw in the distance a bush that was aflame with fire . . ."

National Geographic Magazine, February, 1944. "On the Trail of King Solomon's Mines," by Nelson Glueck. ". . . almost 3000 years ago, Solomon's men employed what is essentially the principle of the Bessemer blast furnace. . . ."

——, December, 1927. "The Pageant of Jerusalem," E. Keith-Roach. "Where one's word is one's bond."

PARKER, GILBERT. *The Promised Land.* "A story of David in Israel."

VAN LOON, H. W. *The Story of Mankind.* "The Jews had come upon evil times. . . ."

WELLS, H. G. *The Outline of History.* "But the nature and the position of their land was against the Hebrews. . . ."

The World Book Encyclopedia. "Jews," "Phoenicians," and Index.

PART FIVE

LEARNING, ART, AND CITIZENSHIP
BROUGHT GLORY TO GREECE

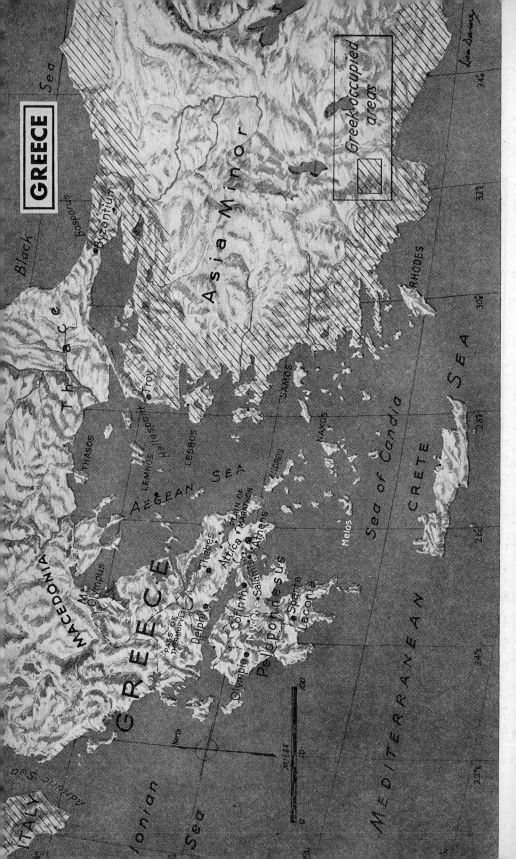

This Is Immortal Greece!

THE land of the ancient Greeks was made up of the Greek peninsula and of islands in the Aegean, Mediterranean, and Ionian seas. On the map opposite, notice the islands scattered between Asia Minor and the Greek peninsula, which juts out into the Mediterranean. These islands served as stepping-stones on the path of civilization. From the eastern end of the Mediterranean came the customs and learning of Egypt, Mesopotamia, Palestine, and Phoenicia. Then on these islands and on the Greek mainland there sprang up a new civilization — in some ways the most remarkable of all time.

Notice the mountain ranges, harbors, and deep inlets of the sea. Why do you think the Greeks became a trading people? The shaded areas on the opposite map show the overseas colonies founded by the Greeks. The Greeks founded so many cities that we show you the names of only the most important ones. But dots indicate the location of many others. How do you account for their location? The ancient Greeks never became a single nation; their land was divided into many city-states. The names of only the two most important ones are shown here, but the boundaries of others are shown to give you an idea of how the land of Greece was broken up.

Chapter 1 ~ Greece Was the First Home of Western Civilization

The role of ancient Greece was an important one. There are many good reasons why an intelligent person should be familiar with the story of ancient Greece. The ancient Greeks have given us many things which we find in the world today. There is not a high school in the land that has not emphasized the kind of physical fitness which the Greek youths brought to such a high degree of perfection. Even some of our athletic equipment, such as the discus, shown in the picture below, and the javelin, are directly derived from ancient Greece. And still that is not all.

The University Prints, Newton, Massachusetts
DISCUS THROWER
This reproduction of a statue of a young Greek athlete shows the physical perfection and grace which the Greek ideal demanded, as a supplement to harmonious development of mind.

The Greeks taught the worth of the individual man; they had caught the vision of democracy (itself from a Greek word), even though they restricted it to a privileged group. Their leaders were thinkers. They learned the value of discussion, of speaking one's mind in public, of satisfying one's curiosity by a scientific kind of thinking. And the alphabet, the language, and the literature they developed are closely interwoven with the very fabric of modern civilization. But perhaps the height of their self-expression is to be seen in the exquisite works of art they created: beautiful statues, perfect buildings which are a symphony of line and form, and articles such as vases, cups, and jewelry — all made with superlative skill and an unusual sense of refinement.

Greece is a land of seas and mountains. Many times in this *Story of Nations* we have seen that the geography of a region played a significant part in its development. The same was true of ancient Greece. Look first at the map on page 114. Then turn to the large reference map of Western Europe reproduced at the back of this book. Let the four fingers of your right hand rest on France and England. You will find that your thumb extends downward over the Balkans to the peninsula of Greece. You should note that the Grecian peninsula is a part of the European mainland. It juts out into the Mediterranean with the Ionian [ai oh'ni'n] Sea on the west and the Aegean Sea on the east. But in ancient days, as in modern ones, Greece included a sprinkling of many islands in these waters, particularly on the east, which extend as far south into the Medi-

OROC

THE SHORE LINE OF THE ISLAND OF CORFU

This picture gives a glimpse of the beauty of Greece. The Island of Corfu is in the Ionian Sea off the shore of Albania. It is shaped somewhat like a sickle, to which it was compared by the ancients.

terranean as the island of Crete [kreet]. These islands were steppingstones of civilization from the ancient oriental nations of the Near East to the Greek mainland, which became the first home of Western civilization.

Greece was separated by mountains and united by seas. If you will turn again to the map on page 114, you will notice that the various parts of the country are separated by rugged mountains. Also you will see that the coastline is indented or cut up with numerous arms of the seas. Many of these reach far inland. The Gulf of Corinth [kor'inth] practically cuts the Grecian peninsula into two parts, a northern and a southern part. Because of this fact no place in the interior of Greece is very distant from the sea.

Water all about, even extending inland, resulted in the Greeks' becoming skillful sailors. The difficulty of travel by land led them to turn to the use of boats as the easiest means of getting from one part of the country to the other. Thus the seas became their highways. An old Greek proverb says, " Mountains divide; the seas alone unite."

Mild climate and varied resources make Greece an attractive land. The climate of the Grecian peninsula and the near-by islands is warm and mild. It is well suited for the development of an out-door type of people, which the Greeks became. The peninsula and the islands are midway between the hot winds of Africa on the south and the cold blasts of the mountains to the north of Greece. As you know, the warm waters of the Mediterranean wash the beaches of Greece. In the winter, or the rainy season, sometimes chill winds blow over the lands.

Though the highest mountains are too rocky to support vegetation, laurel, oleander, and myrtle are found at lower altitudes. When the plentiful rain clothed the uplands with rich green grass, the shepherds allowed their sheep and goats to roam over the hillsides. On the more fertile lowlands, wheat, olives, barley, and grapes could be raised without cultivation. These products were changed into the three articles which were essential to the ancient Greeks — bread, wine, and oil. The oil was used as butter for their bread and for lighting and cleansing purposes. Bread and wine were served at nearly every meal. In spite of the variety of her products, however, Greece did not produce enough food to feed her people. The land is not very fertile and even in ancient days much of the food supply for Greece had to be im-

ported from other countries. Of course, this is still the case today.

Greece was more fortunate in having an abundant supply of stone for building, clay for pottery making, and fine marble for sculpture. From early days pottery was exported from Greece in exchange for grain. Grecian marble furnished the material for the most beautiful sculpture and buildings that the world has ever seen.

The civilization of Greece can be traced back to earlier Aegean peoples. About 800 years before the time of Christ, the civilization of the ancient Greeks began. But hundreds of years before that time — perhaps 2000 B.C. — an earlier civilization had flourished in this region of the Mediterranean. It began with people who lived on the Aegean islands, those steppingstones of civiliza-

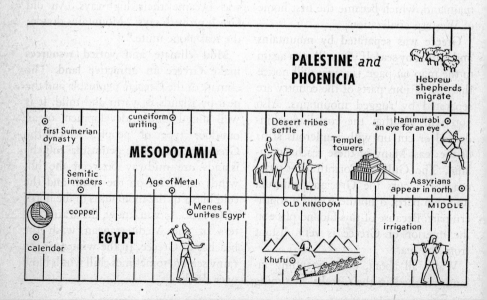

4000													3000										2000
4300	4200	4100	3900	3800	3700	3600	3500	3400	3300	3200	3100		2900	2800	2700	2600	2500	2400	2300	2200	2100		1900
43rd	42nd	41st	40th	39th	38th	37th	36th	35th	34th	33rd	32nd	31st	30th	29th	28th	27th	26th	25th	24th	23rd	22nd	21st	20th

tion between the Near East and Europe. As their power and trade increased, they founded colonies on the shores of the Greek peninsula. For a clear picture, see again the map on page 114. At the same time, other less civilized peoples were coming down from the northern mountains and grasslands to mix and mingle with, or destroy, the civilization they found on the peninsula of Greece and the near-by islands. In a few words the story is that the roots of ancient Greece were deep in the past. There is not space to tell here all that might be said of the beginnings of Greece. But there are some early peoples of whom we should know. Among these are the peoples of the Aegean islands, and especially those of Crete, called the Cretans.

The civilization of Crete was remarkable. Centuries before the Greeks, we find Aegean peoples, particularly those on the islands of Crete and Melos [mee′los], had developed a remarkably civilized way of life. You can see these islands on the map on page 114. The Cretan writing of these Aegean peoples has not yet been deciphered; so there are many things which are not known about them. Their civilization may have begun as early as that of the Egyptians with whom they traded. By 2000 B.C., at any rate, they were making fine pottery and had begun to use weapons of copper.

Later the Cretans established thriving settlements on the Greek mainland. By 1600 B.C. they had passed out of the age of copper and were making articles of bronze. Their civilization was at its height about 1500 B.C., when they dominated the shores of the Greek peninsula as well as the islands of the Aegean.

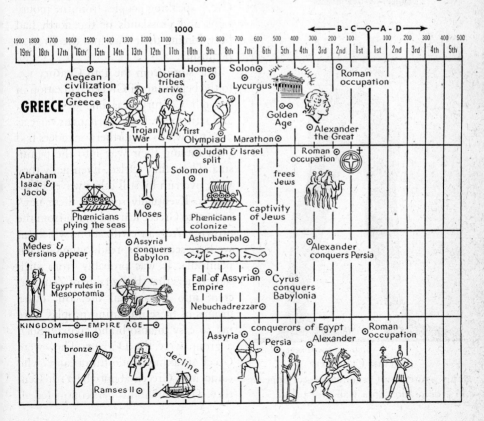

Though the Cretan ships had sailed to Egypt, to Phoenicia, and to Sicily and Spain, whatever the Cretans learned they made their own; Cretan civilization, itself, was distinctively their own.

Metropolitan Museum of Art
CRETAN CUPBEARER
This figure of a Cretan cupbearer appears in a decoration on a wall of a palace.

In 1400 B.C., the palaces of the kings of Crete were burned by enemies, possibly from the Grecian peninsula where Cretan colonies had been established. From then on, the centers of Aegean civilization and power shifted from the islands to the Grecian peninsula. After this the Aegean culture is called Mycenaean [mai'see nee''n] from the town of Mycene [mai see'nee], which you can find on the map on page 114. But it was not very different from the Cretan civilization. Only a few new customs, such as the worship of Zeus [zyoos], appeared, and they suggest to us that a newer people had mingled their ideas with those of the Cretan colonizers. Yet the civilization was still Aegean in its nature.

Waves of invaders settled in Greece. Through the centuries when Aegean civilization had been developing, various Greek-speaking peoples from the mountains and grasslands of the north had been forcing their way into the Grecian peninsula.

The story from the 12th Century B.C. to the beginning of Greek civilization in the 9th Century was one of invasion and settlement. From perhaps as early as 2000 B.C. waves of northern invaders had been forcing their way into the peninsula. There they settled. Eventually they were overrun by still other waves of invaders. Eventually some of these newcomers to Greece learned much from the growing Aegean civilization, which, as we have seen, had spread to the Grecian peninsula. It was probably from such newcomers that the worship of Zeus had crept into Mycenaean life. But other groups of these migrating peoples were not so easy to absorb and civilize. Such a group were the Dorians. They were Greek-speaking Indo-Europeans who came into Greece about the 11th Century. The Dorian invaders conquered all

THE TROJAN HORSE

The great wooden horse loomed at the Trojan gates after the Greek besiegers had apparently withdrawn. The Trojans, curious, brought it into their city. At night, the Greeks emerged from the wooden horse and captured the city. Homer tells this story in the *Iliad*.

of Greece and the islands of the Aegean as well. But instead of absorbing the ways of Aegean civilization, they remained unaffected by it and almost wiped out Aegean culture. The Aegean peoples were killed, absorbed, or enslaved, and their language was lost.

Glorious Greece was built by the descendants of many peoples. The Greeks who built the famed cities of Sparta and Athens, who searched for wisdom and created beauty, were the descendants of many early peoples. First, as you know, were the original inhabitants of the Grecian peninsula about whom little is known. Then also there were the Aegean

peoples with their remarkable civilization, from approximately 2000 B.C. to 1000 B.C. At the same time there were Greek-speaking Indo-European invaders from the north, who first settled in the Grecian peninsula, then gradually came into contact with the Aegean civilization. Finally one of these groups, the Dorians, swept down upon Greece, as you have learned, about 1000 B.C., to conquer the peninsula and the islands. The 11th and 10th Centuries B.C. were dark years of conquest and disorder. The descendants of all these different peoples spoke the Greek language, but the art of writing was lost and the people had all but forgotten the story of their origin.

The only remaining echo of the Aegean days was heard in legends which told of the siege of Troy, in Asia Minor, in the 12th Century B.C. Years later these legends were woven into the epic poems called the *Iliad,* supposedly by the blind poet Homer. This great poem came to be regarded as a national epic and helped to give these early Greeks of different tribes a feeling of unity. The heroes of these ancient legends came to be regarded as great national heroes by all the Greeks. The picture on page 121 illustrates the episode of the Trojan Horse from Homer's *Iliad.*

Civilization was revived in Greece. Apparently the Dorians in the 11th Century B.C. had not done a complete job of destruction. Traces of the knowledge, the art, and the skills somehow survived. With another factor, it was enough to furnish a foundation for a new civilization in Greece. This other factor was trade. The Greeks shared the trade of the eastern Mediterranean with the Phoenicians, about whom we read in Part Four. Even in the dark years following the Dorian conquest, Greeks sailed to Syria, Cypress, and Phoenicia. You can see these countries on the map on page 92. And the Phoenicians also came to Greece to trade. With trade comes the exchange of ideas, knowledge, and skills. From the Phoenician traders the Greeks learned of the advanced civilizations of Egypt and of the Fertile Crescent. Early in the Ninth Century the Greeks took the Phoenician alphabet and adapted it to their own language. (From the Greek alphabet, in turn, our own English alphabet has grown.)

Thus from the meager remnants of the civilization of the peoples of the Aegean islands, and from the knowledge of the ancient civilizations of the Near East passed on by the Phoenician traders, the Greeks, in the Ninth Century B.C., began to develop a new civilization of their own. As we shall learn in the next few chapters, it soon became the most brilliant and glorious civilization of the ancient world.

Chapter 2 ~ The Greeks Founded Colonies and Developed City-States

Kings gave way to the aristocrats. During the Ninth Century B.C., when Homer wrote or sang his poems of earlier days, the Greeks were divided into many little kingdoms. By the Eighth Century B.C., power in most of the Greek states had been taken into the hands of small aristocratic groups. Under these groups there developed a new type of political organization — the city-state. A city-state is a city which is ruled by its free citizens, who also govern the outlying lands around the city. The city-state gave Greece an opportunity for developing a unique and very high form of civilization. It also had certain limitations, and caused a great deal of trouble, as we shall see.

The age of colonization. At first the aristocracy oppressed the mass of free citizens in the cities so badly that many of them left the peninsula in the Eighth and Seventh Centuries B.C. and founded Greek colonies all around the shores of the Mediterranean — even in Sicily and southern Italy. The map on page 114 will give you an idea of the extent of Greek colonies at this time. Another reason for the founding of the colonies was the desire for land. Land in Greece at that time was owned by families and acquired only by inheritance. Thus if a man did not happen to be in the direct line of inheritance he had better go elsewhere and make a new home. Fortunately the Greeks, like the English in later days, were interested in trade and were adventurous. They were natural colonizers and they took their civilization with them to new lands.

It was the nature of the Greeks to be independent. We have seen that the many mountain ranges of Greece tended to separate the Greek peoples into various groups between which communication was difficult. But this alone does not account for the fiercely independent character of the different Greek city-states. Intense independence seems to have been part of Greek nature, from the days when the invading tribes fought against one another as well as against the original inhabitants and the Aegeans. By the Ninth Century B.C. the Greeks liked to feel that they were one in language and culture and past history. But their great loyalty remained to the city-state. It was their home as well as their nation, partly because it was so small. With only a few thousand people living in a city-state, a man counted for something. As a youth he took part in its athletic contests. As a man he bore arms for the city-state and might take a direct part in its government. If he were gifted, he could become an important figure in the city-state's artistic or literary life. Whatever he did well his neighbors and fellow citizens could take pride in and boast about to Greeks of other cities.

During the second half of the Seventh Century B.C., when industry had become more important in the Greek city-states, the mass of the free citizens struggled to obtain greater rights from the aristocracy. They largely succeeded, and their success laid the foundations for constitutional and representative government in the Western world. You may have noticed that we have spoken particularly of the "free citizens" of the city-state. Only about one-fifth of the inhabitants of a Greek city-state were citizens. The great majority were either alien residents or slaves. As was said, Greek citizenship was given only by inheritance. An alien could not become a citizen of a Greek city-state.

Ancient Greece had a civilization built on slavery. The Cretans had had serfs, and the Greeks of earlier days had taken captives in war for use as domestic slaves. But in the Seventh Century B.C., when Greek trade and industry began to require more laborers, slavery in Greece became serious and widespread. Slaves were captured and imported on a large scale from Asia Minor, Thrace, and the shores of the Black Sea. The map on page 114 will show you where these places were.

The lot of the slaves was somewhat more harsh than that of the earlier Cretan serfs. The slave system of the Greeks left a well-to-do Greek citizen free to devote himself to the welfare of the city-state and to the greatest development of his own individual abilities. But slavery made it harder for free Greek laborers and craftsmen to make a living, and the whole history of some Greek city-states was affected by slave rebellions and threats of rebellions.

The Greek republics are sometimes spoken of as democratic. The word *democracy* comes from two Greek words meaning "people" and "power," and can be translated as "government by the people." But when you hear of the democracy of the Greeks remember that it was democracy for the few. The Greek idea of representative government was remarkable because it emphasized self-government (by certain classes) in small city-states. In contrast was the autocratic power of a ruler of a large empire, as in Egypt and in Mesopotamia. The Greeks laid the foundation for democratic government as it has been developing in modern times and is still continuing to develop.

Chapter 3 ~ Sparta Trained Her People to Be Warriors

Sparta and Athens became the leading city-states of ancient Greece. The Greek city-states differed greatly from one another in government, laws, and customs. The most famous of these city-states are Sparta and Athens. Sparta was the stern, totalitarian, military city. Athens, on the other hand, was the center of art and learning and the champion of the rights of citizens. So completely different were the civilizations of Athens and Sparta that we must look at each separately. In most ways Athens was the leading city-state of Greece and the other states tended to follow her in thinking and in culture. But let us look first at Sparta. There men and women had few privileges; the state was supreme, and war was the chief occupation. Sparta, we shall find, played a vital part in the history of the Greek peoples.

Sparta became the chief city-state in southern Greece. Sparta (sometimes called Lacedaemon [las'i dee'm'n]) was the chief city of southern Greece. It stood at the tip of the peninsula, called the Peloponnesus [pel'oh puh nee'suhs], which you can see on the map on page 114. The land Sparta ruled was called Laconia [luh kohn'yuh]. Most Greek cities were built on high ground and were surrounded by high walls. Sparta, however, was "low-lying among the caverned hills," and had no wall to protect her. But the Spartans were ready to give their lives if necessary to protect their city from invasion. As Lycurgus [lai ker'guhs], the wise man of Sparta, once said, "The city is well fortified which hath a wall of men instead of brick." The site of the Spartan Acropolis is pictured on page 125.

Sparta was transformed into a military power. At one time Sparta was no stronger than the city-states about her and had much the same literary and artistic interests. But in the Seventh to Sixth Centuries B.C., Sparta was transformed into a military state, whose citizens lived under iron discipline. The state was all-important, and individual citizens and families were of value only as they served the state and fulfilled its ends. In some ways the Spartan state was very much like ancient Crete in its organization, community life, and emphasis on militarism. The Spartans believed that their rise to power was largely

Acme

THE ACROPOLIS AT SPARTA

This hill was the site of the Spartan Acropolis. When you compare this site with that of the Acropolis of Athens, page 129, you see that the Spartan capital city lacked the inspiring grandeur of the setting of Athens.

owing to the law-giver Lycurgus. Although many legends cluster about the name of Lycurgus, history does not tell us a great deal about his life. It is probable that many rules and institutions credited to Lycurgus had grown up naturally among the Spartans or had been taken over from an earlier civizilation.

Sparta had both private estates and common land. Because Spartan citizens devoted all their energies to the state, some provision had to be made for the support of their families. The Spartan nobles owned great estates, which were farmed for them by slaves. Sparta, as a state, owned certain common land also. This land was divided among the citizens. A parcel of land could pass from father to son by inheritance but could not be sold or divided. These parcels of land, like those of the nobles, were farmed by slaves. The slaves owed only a certain amount of produce each year

to the landowner, which was sufficient to support him and his family. The rest the slave might keep. The landowner was thus free to devote all his energies to war and government. It was possible for a man to gain land, by gift or inheritance, in addition to his own government-assigned parcel of land; so the other Greeks of the peninsula did not take too seriously the claims of the Spartans that they shared and shared alike.

Sparta was a great military camp. The Spartans had conquered all the original inhabitants of Laconia, and then conquered neighboring Messenia [meh seenee'ah], which you can see on the map on page 114. Thus a small number of Spartan citizens were ruling over thousands of subjects and slaves. The rule of the Spartans was constantly threatened by rebellion. This is probably one reason why the Spartans became so strongly militaristic. Sparta in historic times was practically one great armed camp. The Spartans had a system of secret police which might have been the envy of a modern totalitarian nation.

Luxury was discouraged in Sparta. The Spartans were a traditional people and clung to the old, simple ways. They wished to discourage trade and luxury lest it weaken the state. Instead of adopting gold and silver coins as the other states did, they clung for centuries to the use of iron bars as coins. These bars were so heavy and worth so little that it was almost impossible to use them for money.

There was no more means of purchasing foreign goods; merchants sent no shiploads into Laconian ports; no gold or silversmith, engraver, or jeweler set foot in a country which had no money so that luxury wasted to nothing and died away of itself.

Of course, by practically banning the use of money, the Spartans had made commerce, as well as luxury, impossible. They were not much interested in the better living which commerce could have brought about. Their concern was solely with the military future of Sparta and the ruling and enslaving of other peoples.

The training of good soldiers was the chief purpose of Spartan education. The Spartans believed that the training of good soldiers must begin early in life. Therefore strict laws were made for the training of children. Upon the birth of any child it was taken to —

. . . the elders of the tribe to which it belonged; their business it was carefully to view the infant, and if they found it stout and well made they gave order for its rearing, but if they found it puny and ill-shaped, ordered it to be taken to a cavern on Mount Taygetus, where it was left to perish, for they thought it neither for the

good of the child itself, nor for the public interest that it should be brought up, if it did not, from the very outset, appear made to be healthy and vigorous.

Sparta regarded boys as assets of the state. The boys did not live as members of their families but were under the control of the city-state. The Spartan boys were cared for in their own homes only until they reached the age of seven; then the state made them live in public barracks. In later years when Hitler and Mussolini were making totalitarian military states of Germany and Italy, they allowed the children to live at home, but the state took strict control of their education from the age of six or seven onward. Italian and German boys were also organized for military drill at an early age.

The training of Spartan boys was stern and severe. Everything possible was done to increase endurance and make the boys better soldiers. Even in winter they wore only one garment. No covering for their feet was allowed, though the hills and countryside were rough and rocky. As soon as the boys were twelve they made their beds with the rushes grown by the banks of the river. It was difficult to get enough rushes for a bed because the stiff, tough stems had to be broken off without the use of knives.

Since the boys were being trained only as soldiers and not as all-round citizens, the ethical standards of their training were not very high. Food was coarse and so scanty that the boys had to steal from the neighboring farmyards and gardens to keep from starving. If the lads were caught they were severely whipped — not for stealing, you will be surprised to hear, but for being so clumsy as to be found out. This training in stealing was intended to teach the boys to forage for

SPARTAN BOYS AT SCHOOL

Physical vigor, skill, and endurance were the goals set before these Spartan boys — not philosophic minds or adventurous spirits.

themselves in time of war and to be stealthy and silent fighters.

So seriously did the Lacedemonian [las' i di moh'ni'n] children go about their stealing that a youth, having stolen a young fox and hid it under his coat, suffered it so to tear him with its teeth and claws that he died rather than let it be seen.

When the boys grew older, each year they were beaten in public to teach them to endure pain in silence. It is reported that some boys died as a result of this whipping but made no outcry.

Tradition says that Lycurgus, the Spartan ruler, wanted the boys to become very modest and so made special rules for them.

In the very streets they were to keep their two hands within the folds of the cloak; they were to walk in silence and without turning their heads to gaze . . . but rather to keep their eyes fixed upon the ground before them. And you might sooner expect a stone image to find a voice than one of those Spartan youths.

The speech of the Spartans became very short and abrupt. Today we call this way of talking " laconic " [luh kahn'ik] after Laconia, the country of the Spartans.

The Spartan soldier enjoyed special privileges in time of war. So that they might enjoy warfare, the treatment of the young men during a war was less severe than during their training at home. Their food was better and more plentiful. The men marched away to war carrying their large heavy shields and chanting their battle song:

Now we fight for our children, for this
    land;
Our lives unheeding, let us bravely die.
Courage, ye youths! together firmly stand;
Think not of fear, nor ever turn to fly.

Spartan women were disciplined patriots. Spartan girls, like the boys, were trained in gymnastic exercises and taught to be fanatically loyal to the state. When the Spartan mother gave her son the battle shield, which was so large that he could never flee without leaving it behind, she said, " Return either with your shield or upon it." The story is told of a mother, with five sons in the war, who hastened out to meet the returning soldiers. Upon being informed that all five of her sons had been killed she exclaimed, " This is not what I wish to know. Did Sparta win? " "Yes." " Then let us give thanks."

Probably you will think that the Spartans carried their patriotism too far or expressed it in the wrong way. Certain it is that they gave no great gifts to the civilization of the world like those of their less warlike neighbors, the Athenians. But we need to know about the Spartans because they played a vital part in the history of Greece and also because some of their ideas influenced ambitious nations in modern times.

Spartan life was simple and severe. All the Spartans were required by law to marry. Here again we have a parallel with the interest of certain modern dictator nations in increasing their population. Even after marriage the men had to take their meals at the barracks. At the large tables, which seated about fif-teen, the men were served very simple food. Their most common dish was a black broth, which one cook admitted was worth " nothing without the seasoning of fatigue and hunger." Besides the black broth, cheese, figs, wine, and barley meal were the daily fare of the Spartans. Fish and meat were luxuries that were enjoyed only on special occasions. After dinner was over " every man went to his home without lights, for the use of them was on all occasions forbidden, to the end that they might accustom themselves to march boldly in the dark."

For many years the code of laws in Sparta was unchanged and strictly followed. As long as the Spartans lived simply, built up their health and endurance, and allowed no luxury to creep into their city, Sparta continued to be one of the strongest of the Greek city-states. As we shall see in Chapter 5, Sparta was jealous of her neighbors and did not use her strength wisely. But the Spartans did prove to the world that by simple living and by lack of luxury they could develop a strong state.

Chapter 4 ~ Athens Gave Training in Citizenship

Athens became the leading city of Greece. As Sparta was the greatest city of the Peloponnesus, so was Athens the greatest city of Attica [at'i kuh]. Furthermore, Athens was the most beautiful city in all Greece. Look again at the map on page 114 to see the small peninsula of Attica which juts out from central Greece into the Aegean Sea. Although Attica is smaller than Rhode Island, our smallest state, it supported the city which became so well known in the ancient world.

The soil of Attica was so stony and barren that the Greeks who settled there had a hard struggle to make a living. But they believed that the great beauty of the country made up for the lack of fertility of the soil. Around the little peninsula the azure blue waters of the Aegean Sea surged and sparkled; overhead the sky was dazzlingly bright with

Brown Brothers

ATHENS

The Acropolis rises in the distance in this modern view of the ancient city of Athens. In the foreground is part of the Stadium. Note how the modern architecture blends with the ancient.

sunshine; near by the rugged mountains stood in bold relief against the heavens.

Athens was first built upon a massive rock formation a few miles from the sea. This rock plateau, which is one of the most famous in history, was known as the Acropolis [uh krop'uh lis]. It is pictured above. In later years this rocky height was kept for the temples of Greek gods. The city spread out at the foot of the plateau. For protection, a high wall was built around Athens. Within this wall the finest and best of Greek civilization flourished and then declined. Except for Sparta, most of the other Greek states patterned themselves after Athens in learning and culture.

Athens developed a representative government. We Americans are proud of our government because we have a part in it. We call our government a representative democracy or republic. It

was the city-state of Athens that developed this democratic form of government, but she did not always have it; it took time to develop. Like other Greek city-states Athens was ruled in her earliest days by a king, and then later by a number of powerful men called archons [ahr'kahnz]. The rule of these officials was not always wise. Too often they disregarded the rights of others, particularly the rights of the common people. For instance, when crops failed they allowed the farmer to be sold into slavery to pay for his debts. The Athenians were taxed too heavily. Injustice was common.

Solon was the lawgiver of Athens. Finally there came into power in Athens a man who gave the city a better government. He took the power out of the hands of a few and gave it equally to all citizens. More than any other man

THE MARKET PLACE OF ATHENS

The color and liveliness of the people must have contrasted with the lofty marble buildings of the market place in Athens.

he was responsible for making Athens a more democratic republic. This man's name was Solon.

Although Solon was a noble by birth, he understood the troubles of the common people because he himself was poor. Toward the end of the Sixth Century B.C. when he was elected archon (the chief ruler), he immediately set all those free who had been sold into slavery because they could not pay their debts. He repealed the laws of Draco [dray′koh], an earlier lawgiver of Athens—

because they were too severe, and the punishment too great; for death was appointed for almost all offenses, so that in after times it was said that Draco's laws were written not with ink, but blood.

Although Solon did not make a division of the land as the Spartans had done in Laconia, he set a limit to the amount that any noble could hold. All mort-

gages on land were declared canceled. Men were forbidden to pledge the freedom of their wives and children as a security for a debt. A new constitution for Athens was written in which every citizen, including the lowest class, who had hitherto been excluded from citizenship, was given important political rights. A citizen who lost a lawsuit could appeal his case to a panel of his fellow citizens. Moreover the written constitution gave all citizens a right to vote in the general assembly of the people.

Athenian citizenship was limited to the few. Not everyone living in Athens had the right to vote. Like the members of other Greek city-states, the Athenians had slaves, and the great mass of slaves had no voice in the government. Moreover, Athens was very slow in giving citizenship to strangers who moved into the city. Children born in Athens were not citizens unless both of their parents were free citizens. So, in reality, Athens was ruled by only a limited number of the people. Yet despite this fact, here we have a beginning of representative government.

"Not life, but a good life" was expected of every Athenian citizen. From the time of Solon every Athenian citizen felt that he had a duty toward his city and took a great interest in its government. The affairs of the state concerned him as much as his own private business. He believed that his wealth was held only in trust for the state. The more money and land a man had, the more he was expected to contribute to the state to build its ships, erect its beautiful buildings, and pay for its public festivals. This idea reminds one strongly of the modern systems of graduated income taxes. Because the Athenian had a definite share in making his city, he was loyal to it. He felt that he owed to his state the highest patriotism and a life of real service. As the Greek philosopher Aristotle [ar'is taht″l] said, "Not life, but a good life" was expected of every citizen. Except that the rights of citizenship were withheld from many, no people have ever had finer ideals of citizenship than these ancient Greeks.

Athenians discussed important state affairs in their assembly. Greek laws originated in a small governing body called the Council, but after the time of Solon, Athens had an assembly of male citizens which decided important state questions. Owing to the small size of the city-state, the Athenian came into closer touch with his government than do we with our government today. One of the first duties and privileges of the Athenian citizens was to attend the meetings of the assembly, which were held at least forty or fifty times each year.

The meeting place was a natural amphitheater [am'fi thee'uh ter] west of the Acropolis. This huge semicircle, hollowed out of the land by nature, made a splendid open-air auditorium. On meeting days hundreds of voters could be seen seated there waiting for the assembly to be called to order.

The assembly was opened with prayer. In this prayer the Athenians asked that the favor of the gods be bestowed upon them and their friends, and that a curse be placed upon any scoundrel who would deceive the people with bad counsel. Next the loud voice of the herald would open the business for the day by crying, "Who wishes to speak?" Those desiring to debate an important question or to bring a matter before the attention of the assembly mounted the platform. After a question had been discussed the vote on it was taken by a show of hands.

Justice in Athens was secured by courts of law. Like the United States today, Athens had courts where one's rights might be protected, or punishment might be imposed for wrongdoing. Since anyone who was a citizen might accuse another of a crime, the Athenian courts of law were very busy. In fact, unless a citizen was unusually peaceful or very insignificant he would be sure to find himself in the courts at least once in every few years. As Aristophanes [ar'is tahf'uh neez] said, "The cicada [si kay'duh] (locust) sings for only a month, but the people of Athens are buzzing with lawsuits and trials their whole life long."

At a trial both the accuser and the accused were allowed a certain time to speak. The length of time was marked by a water clock. Free men testified under oath as they do today, but the oath of a slave was counted as worthless. Here again democracy was for the few.

ZEUS

Zeus, the ruler of the Olympian gods and goddesses, was deeply respected by the Greeks. They pictured him as the impressive figure shown in this statue.

Slaves were believed to tell the truth only under torture; so an accuser might insist, " I demand that my enemy submit his slaves to torture," or a man sure of his case might scornfully announce, " I challenge my enemy to put my slaves under torture."

The idea of a trial by jury developed. To judge a trial, a jury was chosen from the members of the assembly who had reached thirty years of age. The Athenian juries were very large, often consisting of 201, 401, 501, 1,001, or more men, depending on the importance of the case being tried. The juryman swore by the gods to listen carefully to both sides of the question and to give his honest opinion on the case. His oath ended with this statement: " Thus do I invoke (the gods) Zeus, Poseidon [poh sai'd'n], and Demeter [di mee'ter] to smite with

destruction me and my house if I violate any of these obligations, but if I keep them I pray for many blessings." Each juryman gave his decision by depositing a white or black stone in a box. This method of voting was the origin of our expression, "blackballing." To keep citizens from being too careless in accusing one another, there was a rule which provided that the accuser was condemned in place of the accused if he did not receive a certain number of votes.

The jury not only decided whether a man was guilty but also gave him his sentence. Sometimes there was a penalty of death, exile, or fine, but almost never of imprisonment. Jails were not used as commonly as were the stocks and the whipping post. You may remember reading from your American history how commonly these forms of punishment were used in some of the American Colonies. When the death sentence was imposed upon a citizen he was given a cup of poisonous hemlock juice to drink. After death his friends were allowed to give him a suitable burial.

Tyrants were banished from Athens. Because Athens several times in her history had been seized and governed by powerful men, the Athenians were fearful of any man who became too powerful. The Athenians called these men, who seized power and ruled illegally, *tyrants*. Today we call such men *dictators*.

Not all modern peoples have found a successful way of preventing dictators or would-be dictators from arising. But the Athenians, knowing that too much power is bad for any one man as well as for all the people, found a way to prevent the development of so much centralization of power. Once each year all Athenian citizens were called together in a public assembly. They were asked to write on a piece of broken pottery, called an *ostrakon* [ahs'truh kahn], the name of any man whom they believed dangerous to the liberty of the state. From this comes our verb to "ostracize." If a prescribed number of votes were cast against a citizen, he was banished, or ostracized, for ten years. In this way the Athenians hoped to prevent any man from becoming powerful enough completely to rule the state. Sometimes Athens' finest citizens suffered this fate. For example, Themistocles [thi mis'toh kleez], who you will find saved Athens from the Persians, was ostracized in spite of all he had done for the Athenian people.

Chapter 5 ~ The Greeks Drove Out Foreign Invaders

Athens encouraged a revolt in the Persian Empire and Darius promised revenge. Although the city-states of Greece frequently quarreled and fought among themselves, no great foreign power threatened their existence until about 500 B.C. Then Athens and Sparta found themselves clenched in a life-and-death struggle with Persia, the greatest military power of that time. This is the way it happened.

Darius, the great Persian organizer and general, extended the boundaries of his empire until it stretched east to the Indus River in India, west to the Nile River, and north to the Black Sea. Some of the people in this great Persian empire, however, were not satisfied with the Persian rule. The Greeks of Asia Minor revolted and the Athenians sent a few men to help them regain their freedom. Because so few troops were sent, Darius easily suppressed the revolt. He then punished the people by burning their homes and sending their women and children into slavery. Darius, having noticed that outsiders helped in the rebellion —

. . . inquired who the Athenians were; and when he had been informed, he asked for his bow, and having received it and placed an arrow upon the string, he discharged it upwards toward the heaven, and as he shot into the air he said, "Zeus, that it may be granted me to take vengeance upon the Athenians!" Having so said, he charged one of his attendants that when dinner was set before the king he should say always three times: "Master, remember the Athenians!"

Darius advanced upon Athens. Although Darius was determined to punish Athens, he first decided to give her the opportunity to save herself from destruction by submitting to his rule. Before he started his expedition into Greece, he sent messengers to the cities of Greece asking that they send earth and water as a sign that they acknowledged him ruler of both land and sea. Most of the Greek cities meekly agreed to the demands of Darius, but both Athens and Sparta were enraged. In their anger the Athenians forgot their sense of honor and threw the messengers into a deep pit. The Spartans dropped the messengers into a well with the remark that they would find all the earth and water there that they would want. After this insult Darius immediately began to gather his army and ships together to advance upon Athens and Sparta to avenge their insults.

Athens was divided by political quarrels. Athens was not in a good political condition to withstand an attack. Her political life was split by two bitterly opposing groups. One of these was a conservative party, the other a radical party, as we would use those terms today. The radical party was actually in alliance with Persia and believed that the invasion was in its own interest. The Persians expected that this party would take the Persian invasion as a signal to rise in revolt against the Athenian government, and that Persia could thus conquer all the Athenians very easily and take over Attica. In short, Persia thought she had a quisling party planted in Athens. But when the radical party was put to the test, it did not rise in revolt.

Athens turned to Sparta for help. The Athenians sought help from various parts of Greece, but were refused. Then they turned to Sparta, which for years had been in sympathy with the Athenian conservative party. Surely, they thought, Sparta with her well-trained soldiers would help drive out the invaders. Accordingly, Pheidippides [fai dip' i deez], the swiftest Athenian messenger, was sent to Sparta to ask for aid. Although the distance between Athens and Sparta was 150 miles, it is told that Pheidippides reached Sparta the day after he started. He burst into the Spartan assembly crying, "Men of Lacedaemon, the Athenians implore you to come to their aid!" The Spartans were in no hurry to send their men because they had a superstition that it was ill luck to go to war before the full moon. They said certainly they would come, but not for five days, at which time there would be a full moon. With a heavy heart, because of the bad news he carried, Pheidippides started on his long journey home.

The Greeks met the Persians at Marathon. When Pheidippides reached Athens he learned that the Persian army had landed twenty-four miles from Athens on the plain of Marathon [mar' uh thahn]. In spite of his long journey, Pheidippides joined the army to fight the invaders. The Athenian army marched over the hot, rough road to meet the Persian foe. The only help which had come to Athens was about a thousand men from a neighboring Greek city-state.

Herodotus tells us that the Persians outnumbered the Greeks ten to one, but it is thought that this is an exaggeration. The Greeks, fired with the desire to protect their women, children, and city, flung themselves upon the Persians "like madmen." Soon the invaders were fleeing in terror to their ships. Their defeat is shown in the picture on page 135.

After the victory, Pheidippides was once more called upon — this time to carry the good news back to Athens. In his last great race he flung himself along the rough road shouting, "Athens is saved." But his heart could not stand the terrible strain. After he had delivered his message, he fell lifeless to the ground.

The Battle of Marathon in 490 B.C. was a most important event. The victory of the Greeks at Marathon made it possible for representative government to continue in the Western world.

Xerxes decided to avenge Marathon. Although Darius returned to Persia beaten, he did not give up the hope of humbling the Greeks. Slowly and carefully he began to make plans for another expedition. He died before this second expedition could be launched. Xerxes

Brown Brothers

AT MARATHON

The Athenian soldiers, outnumbered ten to one, hurled themselves upon the Persians on the plain of Marathon. They routed the enemy in one of the decisive battles of the world.

[zerk′seez], the son and successor of Darius, tried to carry on the war that his father had begun. His determination to avenge the defeat of Marathon was as great as his father's had been. In the meantime the Athenians were preparing to defend themselves against the Persians.

Themistocles urged Athens to build a navy. At this time there appeared in Athens a statesman and general who was to guide her through the trying days ahead. This man was Themistocles. He had risen from a very humble boyhood to a position of great influence as a political leader.

Themistocles was alarmed at the growing power of the Persian Empire. He felt that the Athenians must look to the defense of Attica, and that they should immediately build a great fleet. It was no easy task for Themistocles to persuade the Athenians that their only hope for safety lay in becoming a strong sea power. Yet, owing to his power and ability, within a few years Athens had two hundred triremes (vessels with three tiers of rowers), which were second to none in that day.

The Persians crossed the Hellespont. For ten years after the battle of Marathon, Persia found so many important matters to occupy her time in the East that she was not able to consider the settlement of the old score with Athens. But in the spring of 480 B.C. the startling news came to Greece that Xerxes had reached the Hellespont [hel'uhs pahnt] with the greatest army and navy that had ever been brought under the command of one man. There he waited until his ships were tied together to make a floating bridge on which his warriors could pass across the narrow strait.

Ahead of the king marched a special force of picked men armed with gold and silver spears. Next came the sacred chariot of Zeus. Next, the king's chariot rumbled along, surrounded by special bodyguards with crowns on their heads. After the king there followed another band of carefully chosen troops. Behind them straggled the motley hordes that had been drafted from the four corners of the mighty Persian Empire: Assyrians, Bactrians, Egyptians, Lydians, and many others, including troops from distant Ethiopia. Each man wore the costume of his own people, and bore the weapons of the place from which he came. It was a colorful procession, bent on the destruction of Greek civilization.

It is said that before the army had crossed the Hellespont there was an eclipse of the sun, which badly frightened the superstitious Xerxes. In terror he summoned the wise men to tell him the meaning of this sign. They answered him, " Fear not, O great King. The sun gives warning to the Greeks, but the moon to the Persians. The sun has vanished from the heavens, and so will the cities of the Greeks vanish from the earth." The army of Xerxes marched on to meet the Greeks.

The Greeks disagreed about their plans for defense. When the news reached Athens that the army of Xerxes had crossed the Hellespont and was rapidly making its way down the eastern coast accompanied by the Persian fleet, great was the consternation among the Athenians. Messengers were sent to all parts of Greece and to all the leading colonies, asking help to save Greece from its enemies.

Messengers were also sent to Delphi [del'fai] to ask the advice of the oracle, of which you will learn more later. The oracles often replied in obscure symbolic language which could well have more than one meaning. This time the answer given was even more confusing than usual, for it said, "Safe shall the wooden walls continue for thee and thy children." There was much discussion in Athens about this strange reply. Some of the Greeks remembered that the Acropolis had once had a wooden wall around it; so they said that the people must take refuge on the Acropolis. Themistocles was sure that the " wooden walls " meant the walls of the Grecian ships.

The Greek states called a council of war to plan their defense against the Persians, but they could not agree. The Athenians, in the north, wanted to fortify the northern mountain passes and keep the Persians out of the Greek peninsula entirely. The Spartans, far to the south, argued that the Athenians should abandon Attica to destruction, retreat southward, and set up their defense below the Gulf of Corinth. You can imagine that this plan did not appeal to the Athenians. Finally the Spartans, because they did not dare lose the support of the splendid Athenian fleet, agreed to defend northern Greece also. But the Spartan government actually proved to be half-hearted in its attempts to do so.

Spartan soldiers held the Pass of Thermopylae. The Persian host marched down through Thessaly, keeping as close to the sea as possible. To enter the central part of Greece, Xerxes' army had to be led through the Pass of Thermopylae [ther mahp'uh lee]. Here, commanded by the Spartan king, Leonidas [lee ahn'i-duhs], the Greeks made their first stand. They are shown in the illustration below. But the struggle was sure to be unequal, for the Persians far outnumbered the Greeks. Only a tiny fraction of the Greek force was in the field. Leonidas regarded his small army merely as an advance force and expected large reinforcements from southern Greece. Reinforcements were never sent, however, though Leonidas sent back desperate appeals to Sparta for help. Thus, division of council among the Greeks was nearly their ruin, and the fate of Western civilization hung for awhile on the devotion and fanatic courage of a few fighting men.

Time after time during the following hot summer days the Persians rushed the pass. At each attempt they were pushed back by the fierce fighting of the Greeks. Even though the Greeks were exhausted, they held the mighty army of the Persians at bay for three whole days. Xerxes was almost completely baffled until a Greek traitor appeared in camp and offered to lead the army through a secret pass across the mountains if he were rewarded with enough gold. Soon a picked force of Persians was pouring through the other mountain pass.

At dawn those keeping watch at Thermopylae found the enemy approaching from the rear. After a heroic defense, the Greeks were finally overcome. Some four thousand of them had fallen in battle with the Persians. Among them were Leonidas and his three hundred Spartans, whose laws forbade them to flee. They had fought to hold the pass as long as they lived, though they knew it meant certain death. At the end of the battle not one Spartan was left to tell the story.

To the Greeks the word "Thermopylae" became immortal. It was to be re-

Drawing by John C. Wonsetler

THERMOPYLAE

At the Pass of Thermopylae Leonidas and his three hundred Spartan soldiers fought off the Persian Army for three days — as long as any Spartan in the band remained alive.

THE BATTLE OF SALAMIS

Here Xerxes sees his eight hundred ships rammed and destroyed by the Greek fleet of only half that number. Apparently he watched the contest much as we do a football game.

membered forever. Leonidas and his men were buried where they made their last stand. In memory of their bravery a marble lion was placed at the entrance of the pass. On one of the pillars which was erected were written these words:

Go, stranger, and to Lacedaemon tell,
That here, obeying her behests, we fell.

Centuries later, in the early days of World War II, British troops awaited Nazi forces in this famous pass.

The Athenians left their city and Athens was burned. When the brave Spartans failed to hold the Persians at Thermopylae, the people of Athens knew that nothing could save their beautiful city. They decided to take the advice of Themistocles and seek safety within the " wooden walls " of the ships. The Athenians rushed wildly about, gathered together their choicest treasures, and put their women and children into boats that they might be taken to a safer place. This was accomplished none

too quickly. The invaders swept down upon Athens when the boats were barely out of sight of the city. Soon the city was in flames. Nothing remained but piles of smoking ruins. The Persians had destroyed the proud city of Athens.

The Persian king saw his navy destroyed at Salamis. In this time of trouble Themistocles was the acknowledged leader of the Greeks. He hoped to meet the Persians in a naval battle before the Persians were fully prepared. So he sent a secret messenger urging the Persian general Xerxes to attack at once. Xerxes believed that the message came from a Greek traitor and decided to act upon the advice. At dawn the great sea fight began, at the narrow strait of Salamis [sal'uh mis], which you can see on the map on page 114. The Athenian fleet was joined by ships from other Greek city-states but the Greeks still had fewer than four hundred ships in all.

Before the battle Xerxes took his place on the golden throne which " full in view of all the host . . . stood on a high knoll hard beside the sea." Close beside the throne stood the scribes who were to record the brave deeds of the Persians. But the outcome of the battle was to be very different from that which Xerxes so confidently expected.

With horror the waiting king saw his eight hundred ships rammed and shattered by the determined Greeks. Everywhere were the smashed hulls of Persian ships. This terrible fight continued until

> . . . no more could one discern the sea,
> Clogged all with wrecks and limbs of
>   slaughtered men:
> The shores, the rock-reefs, were with
>   corpses strewn.
> Yes, every keel of our barbarian host,
> They with oar-fragments and with shards
>   of wrecks
> Smote, hacked, as men smite tunnies or a
>   draught
> Of fishes; and a morning, all confused
> With shrieking, hovered wide o'er that
>   sea-brine
> Till night's dark presence blotted out the
>   horror.

After the battle, in great disgust and disappointment, the Persian monarch decided to leave Greece forever. Realizing that the Greeks might break down his bridge of boats across the Hellespont before his army could march across, he and most of his troops hastened toward Persia.

Even in their homeward flight, bad luck pursued the Persians. They could find little to eat besides grass, leaves, and the bark of trees. Great numbers of soldiers died of starvation and plague. In the end Xerxes arrived in Persia with a broken army and a sad heart.

The Persians withdrew from the land of the Greeks. Xerxes left behind a general who promised to conquer " the rest of Greece " if he were given three thousand men. The general sent a messenger to Athens, saying:

> I will give you back your own land and any other in addition, and you shall remain independent; and I will rebuild all your temples, provided you will make a treaty with me.

But the proud Athenians answered:

> So long as the sun goes on the same course by which he goes now, we will never make an agreement with Xerxes, but trusting to the gods and heroes as allies, we will go forth to defend ourselves against him.

The Athenians met what was left of the Persian army the following year and defeated them thoroughly. The Persians were so completely humiliated that they withdrew forever from the land of the Greeks. At last Greece was free! Throughout all their internal quarrels the Greeks had fervently believed that the subjects of a despot, such as Xerxes, were no match for free citizens defending their homeland. Events had proved them to be right. The democracy of ancient Greece was saved from Asiatic despotism.

Chapter 6 ~ A Period of Peace Brought Progress in Art, Literature, and Philosophy

Athens became an empire. After the Persians had been driven from the Greek peninsula, the Greeks who had settled in Asia Minor revolted against Persia and appealed to Athens for help. Athens organized them into a Naval League, with herself at the head, and helped them drive out the Persians. Athens then extended the League to include most coastal cities of the Aegean Sea. Some members of the League wished to withdraw when the Persian danger was passed; but Athens refused to release her allies. If they rebelled, she conquered them and made them into subject states paying tribute to her. Thus, although a democracy at home, Athens had become an empire in relation to many other Greek city-states. Her sea power was so great that she became the shipping center of the whole Aegean. Athenian industry and commerce boomed.

Athens entered her Golden Age. Such prosperity was a great factor in the Golden Age of Athens, or the Age of Pericles [per'uh kleez], as it has also been called. This was really a short period of about fifty years during the middle part of the Fifth Century B.C. During the Golden Age Athens erected magnificent buildings to replace those destroyed by the Persians. Her artists and sculptors set standards of skill and beauty that have never been surpassed. Her writers gave to the world plays and dramas. Her

The University Prints, Newton, Mass.

THE ACROPOLIS IN THE GOLDEN AGE OF ATHENS

This restoration shows the Acropolis as it was at the height of Athenian greatness. The Propylaea [proh'pi lee'ah], whose name means " before the gate " in Greek, is the main structure in the center of the foreground. Do you recognize the Parthenon?

philosophers presented new interpretations of the meaning of life. Athens was at her greatest height. A restoration of the Acropolis as it was in this period is shown on page 140.

Homer played a distinguished role. Several times in the story of Greece we have mentioned the name of the Greek poet Homer. His work had a remarkable effect on the Golden Age of Greece. He furnished ideas which for centuries inspired poets, painters, sculptors, and dramatists of Greece and other lands. Even today we find the beauty of his words undimmed. It is thought that Homer was blind and that he lived in the early days of Greece sometime in the Ninth Century B.C., long before the Golden Age of Athens.

There was a time in the story of Greece during which epic poems were created that have never been surpassed. Verses from the *Iliad* and the *Odyssey,* the poems thought to have been written by Homer, were told and retold for generations. These poems describe some of the extraordinary adventures of Greek heroes and tell of early Greek myths.

Pericles became the "First Citizen" **of Athens.** The Athenians continued to improve their city government during the Golden Age. The leader in these improvements was a statesman by the name of Pericles. Although he belonged to a noble family, Pericles often championed the cause of the people. Because of his strong character, and his eloquence as an orator, he gained control of public affairs in Athens. The writers of the time realized the great influence of Pericles. One said, "The democracy existed in name; in reality it was the government of the first citizen." Another said, "He got all of Athens into his own hands." Though the personality of Pericles was so strong that he held

The University Prints, Newton, Mass.

PERICLES

The calm, intelligent face of Pericles makes it easy for people living twenty-three centuries later to believe in his wisdom.

the reins of the government in his own hands, he never abused this privilege or tried to become a tyrant.

The fine character of this distinguished statesman is shown by his last words. As he lay stricken by the plague that had already carried away his favorite son, his friends gathered around his bed to pay their last tribute. Not realizing that he would understand what they were saying, they began to speak of the outstanding things he had accomplished during his life. Opening his eyes, Pericles interrupted them to say —

What you praise in me is partly the result of good fortune, and, at all events, common to me with many other commanders. What I am most proud of, you have not noticed. No Athenian ever put on mourning for an act of mine!

Courtesy Nashville Chamber of Commerce

A RECONSTRUCTION OF THE PARTHENON

This reproduction of the Parthenon is in Nashville, Tennessee. It shows, better than the ruins on the Acropolis or a small model, the beauty of the original structure. Can you imagine the brilliant beauty of this building in the sunlight?

Pericles was a patron of the arts. Like most of the ancient Greeks, Pericles was a lover of beauty. Today we remember him chiefly for the magnificent buildings and statues which were created at his command. Do you recall that the buildings on the Acropolis were burned just before the battle of Salamis when the Persians invaded Athens and the Greeks took refuge in the "wooden walls" of the ships? Pericles determined to cover this barren hill with masterpieces of Greek architecture and sculpture.

The Greeks built the Parthenon. The noblest of all the temples built to crown the Acropolis was the white marble Parthenon [pahr′thuh nahn]. This beautiful building was created by Ictinus [ik-tai′nuhs], the architect, and Phidias [fid′i uhs], the sculptor. See the picture of the ruins of the Parthenon on page 143. In the photograph of a reconstructed

model of the Parthenon which is shown above, notice the frieze [freez] or band of sculpture running around the building just above the columns. This frieze, which showed a scene from Greek mythology was beautifully tinted in gold, blue, and red. Many magnificent temples and buildings have been erected since the Parthenon was built about 2400

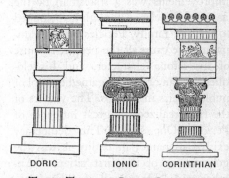

DORIC   IONIC   CORINTHIAN

THREE TYPES OF GREEK COLUMNS

In designing these columns the Greeks created patterns for the architecture of all time.

years ago, but none has ever surpassed it for sheer beauty and grace.

Another example of the perfection of Greek architecture is the manner in which the columns were constructed. Have you ever noticed that two parallel lines seem to bend inward toward each other? Scientists have long known of this optical illusion. The Greek architects also realized this peculiarity. They offset it by chiseling their columns with a greater diameter in the middle than at either end. The curved line which this construction produced made the columns appear straight to the human eye. Such careful adjustment to offset optical illusion shows what skillful workmen the Greeks had come to be.

The Greeks created three beautiful columns. Look carefully at the picture on page 142. The columns supporting the Parthenon are built in the simple, stately Doric style. In deciding which kind of graceful column should be used to support the roof of the Parthenon, the Greeks had three styles from which to choose. The three orders of Greek architecture were the Doric, the Ionic [ai ahn′ ik], and the Corinthian [koh rinth′i′n]. On page 142 are sketches of each.

The simple Doric column tapers slightly up to the thick slab of stone

Meerkamper from Monkmeyer

A FRAGMENT OF THE PARTHENON

The central part of the Parthenon was destroyed in the war between Turks and Venetians in the 17th Century. The Turks had been using the Parthenon as a powder magazine, and a Venetian bomb fell through the roof. Sculptures from the Parthenon were removed to London by Lord Elgin in the 19th Century.

The University Prints, Newton, Mass.

STATUE OF ATHENA

This statue of Athena stood in the main hall of the Parthenon. It was 39 feet high and was made of ivory with golden drapery and precious jewels.

forming the capital. The capital, itself, instead of being a plain block of stone, is artistically curved to blend with the upright lines of the column. Unlike the other two orders, the Doric column has no base, but stands directly upon the temple floor like the Egyptian columns in the temple of Karnak, shown on page

62. The Ionic style is a more slender column, and its capital is carved in spiral form. The delicate Corinthian column is capped with a cluster of exquisitely carved acanthus leaves. No architect has ever designed more beautiful columns than these three carved by the ancient Greeks. When modern architects wish to use graceful, stately columns they usually choose the Doric, the Ionic, or the Corinthian type.

The Parthenon glorified the Goddess Athena. Since the Parthenon was dedicated to the goddess Athena [uh thee′ nuh], two magnificent statues of her were erected for the temple. One was placed inside and the other in the open area between the Parthenon and the colonnaded entrance to the Acropolis. The figure within the building stood thirty-nine feet high and was made of ivory with golden drapery and precious jewels. This use together of ivory and gold had been a favorite combination of the Cretans, centuries before. Outside the building the colossal bronze statue of Athena towered seventy feet into the air. As protectress of Athens she stood there armed with shield and spear. The gilded point of this spear could be seen from a great distance. It is said that sailors returning from foreign lands would see it glittering in the sunlight as they rounded the southern tip of Attica. Then they would know that they had reached home at last.

Phidias became the leading sculptor of the Golden Age. Phidias was the artist who created the beautiful statues and friezes on the Parthenon. Such artists as Myron [mai′rahn], who created the statue of the discus thrower, which is shown on page 116, had lived before the Age of Pericles. But the work of Phidias surpassed all that which had been done up to his time. The figures of Phidias were strong and majestic, lofty and formal. It is said Phidias used to stand out of sight of the people who came to visit his work and listen to their comments. If their criticism revealed a flaw, he was never happy until it had been corrected, even though that flaw might be very slight. Verses written by the American poet, Edwin Markham, describe Phidias at work.

Once Phidias stood with hammer in his hand,
Carving Athena from the breathing stone,
Tracing with love the winding of a hair,
A single hair upon her head, whereon
A youth of Athens cried, " O, Phidias,
Why do you dally on a hidden hair?
When she is lifted to the lofty front
Of the Parthenon, no human eye will see."
And Phidias thundered on him, " Silence, fool!
Men will not see, but the Immortals will! "

The greatest work of Phidias was the statue of Zeus in the temple of Olympia in the Peloponnesus. This statue was so masterfully carved that —

. . . those who entered the temple there no longer think that they are beholding the ivory of India and the gold from Thrace, but the very deity translated to earth by Phidias.

The pilgrims who came every four years to the Olympic games went reverently to the temple to gaze at the great statue. It was counted a misfortune to die without having seen the Olympian Zeus. Some said that Zeus must have come down from heaven and shown himself to Phidias so that he might make a lifelike statue. Others believed that —

. . . when the image was completed Phidias prayed that the god would give a sign if the work were to his liking, and immediately, they say, Zeus hurled a thunderbolt into the ground.

HERMES OF PRAXITELES

The statue of the Greek god Hermes reveals why the sculptor, Praxiteles, is considered one of the greatest sculptors of all ages.

The face of Zeus as sculptured by Phidias showed such kindness and understanding that —

. . . if anyone who is heavy-laden in mind, who has drained the cup of misfortune and sorrow in life, and whom sweet sleep visits no more were to stand before this image, he would forget all the griefs and troubles of this mortal life.

Praxiteles created lifelike figures. Another artist, who lived about a century after Phidias, and whom some believe to be even greater than Phidias, was Praxiteles [praks it'uh leez]. Instead of making his statues of gods lofty and forbidding as did Phidias, Praxiteles made his figures seem very human and graceful. Many of his individual figures were life size. The statues of Phidias stood very straight and exalted, but those of Praxiteles could be found in attitudes of repose. Although many of the Greek statues have been preserved for us only through copies, we still have the original of Praxiteles' Hermes [her'meez] with the infant Dionysus [dai'oh nai'sus]. See the photograph of this statue above.

The right arm of Hermes has been broken away, but it is believed that he once held a bunch of grapes in his right hand.

Drama was important in Athenian life. The Greeks not only expressed their genius in remarkable buildings and beautiful statues, they also wrote and enacted many plays. Twice each year all the citizens of Athens went to the Theater of Dionysus on the Acropolis to see plays. A reconstruction of this theater is pictured on the facing page. It consisted merely of row after row of stone seats built upon a hillside, forming an arc around the level space where the plays were given. The great open-air amphitheaters of today resemble the Theater of Dionysus.

Pericles, believing that drama was so important that none should miss it, ordered that all male citizens who could not afford to attend the theater should be admitted free. The plays were about the legends and history of Greece and did much to educate the people.

The men who attended the plays had to go to the theater early in the morning in order to get good seats. Usually they took their lunches with them so that they would not have to leave their places until the end of the program. All day long one play followed another in quick succession. The actors wore huge, grotesque masks to portray the different characters.

No woman was ever allowed to take part. The men interpreted the lines of women characters if the play called for such parts. The well-trained voices of the actors and the beauty of their lines held the attention of the audience.

The Greeks enjoyed both comedy and tragedy. The Greeks liked light, merry comedies in which the actions of their most prominent citizens were ridiculed, but they enjoyed dignified tragedies even more.

The Greek tragedies, in many of which the ending was wretchedly unhappy, told the story of real or legendary heroes of the Greeks and the part played in their destiny by fate and the gods. The favorite type of Greek tragic hero was a strong and gifted leader whose fate it was to be undone by circumstances and by some flaw in his own character. The Greek tragedians also liked to portray noble men or women who, with a stern sense of duty, went bravely to their deaths — not through any fault of their own but because of the fate in which their family or city was enmeshed.

Today almost every tragedy on the stage or screen has a few comic characters to relieve the tension when the situation becomes too trying for the audience. But in those days comedy was felt to have no place in the tragic drama. Instead a dramatic scene was usually followed by a beautiful chant from a chorus of male voices. This chorus helped to set the atmosphere for the play and to interpret its action to the audience.

Three great poets wrote tragedies for the Greek theater. When all the plays had been presented, a state prize was given to the man whose play was voted the best. Thirteen times this prize was given to the first Greek tragedian, Aeschylus [es'kuh luhs]. Today he is often called the "Father of Greek Tragedy." This man, who was a soldier as well as a writer, fought for Athens both at Salamis and at Marathon. If you will look on page 139 you can read again a few lines from his famous play, *The Persians,* which described the defeat of the Persian navy at Salamis.

The second well-known Greek dramatist was Sophocles [sahf'uh kleez].

Schoenfeld Collection from Three Lions

THE THEATER OF DIONYSUS

The Theater of Dionysus at Athens was partly hollowed out of the cliffs of the Acropolis. Here some of the plays of Sophocles were performed.

When only twenty-eight years of age, he won the first prize for the best play at the festival. You can imagine how happy he must have been over his success. It is said that Aeschylus, who was nearing sixty, was so disappointed when his play was not given first prize that he left Athens to live in Sicily. One of Sophocles' heroines, *Antigone* [an tig'uh ni], is considered among the finest in literature. According to an old legend (retold in the play *Antigone*) this brave young woman of royal family incurred the death penalty by dutifully sprinkling dust on the bodies of her slain brothers who had been denied burial by their conquerors.

The third great Greek dramatist was Euripides [yoo rip'i deez]. He wrote the most emotional plays of all the poets. Tradition says that he was born on the island of Salamis on the very day of the important battle of Salamis. In his great play, the *Trojan Women,* he tells of the misery and suffering brought about by war. On page 158 there are a few lines from this play.

Historians wrote of the glory of Athens. The Greek writer, Herodotus, who lived in the middle of the Fifth Century B.C., has been called the "Father of History." This noted traveler, whom we have quoted several times, wrote the first extensive history that has come down to us. Herodotus was a charming writer and storyteller because he always noticed the interesting little incidents that make history more than a listing of facts. Unfortunately, however, he was not always as sure of his facts as he should have been. Unlike a true historian, he was likely to substitute his

SOCRATES

In his search to find the truth and in his efforts to teach young Athenians to reason, Socrates disregarded his personal safety.

personal opinion for what really happened. Nevertheless, we have no better account of the Persian wars than that written by Herodotus. He himself said that he wrote his history that "the great and wonderful deeds done by the Greeks and Persians should not lack renown."

Thucydides [thyoo sid'i deez], who was thirteen years younger than Herodotus, was more accurate and impartial in his writing than his predecessor. Of his own work he said:

Men do not discriminate and are too ready to receive ancient traditions about their own as well as about other countries; and so little trouble do they take in the search after truth. . . . I have described nothing but what I either saw myself, or learned from others of whom I made the most careful and particular inquiry. The task was a laborious one. . . . If he (who

seeks the truth) . . . shall pronounce what I have written to be useful, then I shall be satisfied. My history is an everlasting possession, not a prize composition which is heard and forgotten.

The claim of Thucydides that his history of the civil wars of Greece is an "everlasting possession" has been well proved.

Socrates dedicated his life to the search for truth. If you had lived in Athens about 400 B.C. you might have seen walking through the streets of the city a short, ugly old man with a flat nose and massive forehead, much as he appears in the picture at the left. Although he was poorly dressed and had only one coat to his name, this man was proudly received and greatly respected by people of wealth. His name was Socrates [sahk' ruh teez], and he was a famous philosopher. The word *philosopher* means one who seeks wisdom, truth, and the meaning of life. So Socrates was the wise man who tried to find the right way of living.

Even though his father had been a poor stonecutter, Socrates seems to have had a fine education. He tells of having studied "the treasures which the wise men of old have left us in their books." Besides knowing what others had thought about important questions, Socrates learned to think for himself.

Socrates was frequently to be found teaching on the streets of Athens. Even though he was very poor he would take no pay from his pupils. He taught others by asking them questions. Plato, one of his most admiring pupils, tells us that he asked such questions as, "What is friendship? When one man loves another which is the friend — he who loves or he who is loved? Or are both friends?" By means of these questions Socrates set people to thinking. One of his pupils said, "Socrates makes me acknowledge my own worthlessness. I had best be silent, for it seems that I know nothing at all."

The maxim of Socrates was "Know Thyself." By helping his pupils to understand themselves this philosopher encouraged them to lead upright lives. Plato once wrote:

Socrates has often brought me to such a pass that I have felt as if I could hardly endure the life I am leading. For he makes me confess that I ought not to live as I do, neglecting the wants of my soul. And he is the only person who ever made me ashamed, and there is no one else who does the same.

Socrates was falsely accused and condemned to death. Like other educated men of his time, Socrates did not believe in the poets' tales of many gods. He believed instead in the existence of one supreme being, and he felt that he had a divine mission to lead those around him to examine their thinking and beliefs and strive for a good life. Unfortunately, among Socrates' younger friends and students were one or two self-willed young aristocrats who later became very unpopular with the people. Socrates was accused, unjustly, of teaching them false beliefs. His enemies finally charged him with corrupting the thoughts of the young men of Athens. Since this charge was scarcely probable, they also charged him with not believing in the Greek religion. He was tried and condemned to die. It is said that no one ever received his sentence more calmly or " ever bowed his head to death more nobly." With great courage he said, " Now the time has come and we must go hence; I to die, and you to live. Whether life or death is better is known to God and to God only."

Surrounded by his faithful followers and friends, Socrates drank the fatal cup of hemlock. Plato, who was with him at the time of his death, says:

Such was the end of a man who, I think, was the wisest and justest and the best man I have ever known. . . . I could not help thinking that the gods would watch over him still on his journey to the other world, and that when he arrived there it would be well with him, if it was ever well with man.

Plato and Aristotle carried on the work of Socrates. The work of Socrates was carried on by Plato and Aristotle. Plato lived half a century longer than his beloved teacher, and wrote down many of his teachings with such grace and conviction that people began to think he was descended from Apollo [uh pahl' oh], the god of eloquence. In his most famous work, the *Republic,* he tells about the ideal state and the kind of education that should be given to young men to make them good citizens.

Many think Aristotle, a pupil of Plato, was the greatest of the three philosophers. You would be astonished to learn on how many subjects he was an authority. For two thousand years after his death his books on astronomy, mathematics, poetry, physics, logic, and rhetoric were studied by students, as the highest authority in all matters of science and philosophy.

Mathematics, astronomy, and geography became true sciences. Aristotle was not the only Greek who was interested in such sciences as astronomy, mathematics, and physics. Like the Egyptians and the Babylonians before them, Greek scientists studied the stars, used numbers to solve their problems, and looked for the principles which would explain the natural world about them. Furthermore, unlike their predecessors, they were not content merely to observe and record the facts; their keen minds asked not merely

ARCHIMEDES

In this painting, the scientist and inventor Archimedes is shown in the garden of his home, working on a problem in geometry.

"what," but also "how" and "why." So carefully was the information organized and analyzed that many natural laws of the universe were discovered. It was the Greeks who developed mathematics, astronomy, and geography into true sciences.

Let us consider what these talented Greeks were able to do. They could measure the heights of their many mountains and the distances to brilliant stars by using trigonometry. Trigonometry is the science of measuring triangles. The principles of plane and solid geometry were well known to the Greeks. In fact, a Greek by the name of Euclid [yoo' klid] wrote a book called *Elements of Geometry* which is still considered a basic text in geometry. It is said that no modern mathematician has ever been able to surpass his methods.

The Greeks knew that the earth is a sphere [sfeer] which revolves upon its axis. Greek astronomers had already determined that the sun's year was 365¼ days; so they based their calendar upon this knowledge. Long before the Age of Pericles a Greek astronomer was able to predict an eclipse of the sun. About 200 B.C. a geographer calculated the circumference of the earth to be 28,000 miles, which was an error of only three thousand miles. Remember that this was in the time when Spain was the western boundary of the known world! This same geographer predicted that by traveling westward from Spain one would eventually arrive in India. About two thousand years later Ferdinand Magellan [muh jel'n] was to prove the truth of the Greek geographer's prediction.

Hippocrates wrote an oath for all good doctors. It is not strange that the Greeks began the practice of medicine in the modern sense of the word. About the middle of the Fifth Century B.C. a Greek priest-physician, Hippocrates [hi pahk' ruh teez], began to insist that every disease resulted from some special cause. Like Socrates, Hippocrates was a teacher, and a splendid one. Before he would permit his students to practice medicine he made them take an oath that they would be true doctors and help anyone in need. You will often see a copy of this same oath which Hippocrates taught his medical students, framed and hung in a doctor's office. Today the medical profession considers Hippocrates to be the father of its science and honors him for setting the high standards which are followed by all worthy members of the profession.

Archimedes: A great Greek scientist. Of all the Greek scientific geniuses, Archimedes, a native of the Greek colony of Syracuse in Sicily, was perhaps the greatest. He lived after Alexander the Great, about whom you will read in the next chapter, had welded the Near East and Greece into an empire.

By drawing upon the accumulated knowledge of the Greeks, the Babylonians, and the Egyptians, this mathematics genius, Archimedes, was able to build a rich background of information. The previous inventions of other ancient people suggested new principles and devices to him. From the spiral staircases of the Babylonians, Archimedes got his idea of the spiral screw, which lifts things higher and higher. By studying the lever which the Egyptians used, he formulated the principles of the lever. Archimedes also found the principle of specific gravity, or the relative weight of objects. Today we find the discoveries and inventions of Archimedes used widely in such modern mechanical contrivances as the automobile, the motorboat, and the airplane.

Chapter 7 ~ The Greeks Combined Simple Living With Idealism

The Greeks liked moderation in all things. Greek life was simple in the early days because food and other supplies were scarce and people had to live frugally. The Greeks developed an ideal of simplicity, self-control, and moderation in all things. They sought beauty, wisdom, and accomplishment rather than luxury and rich possessions.

Slavery was part of Greek life. Even households which had slaves might be very simple. Domestic slaves helped in the daily work of the household, sometimes working side by side with the housewife herself. We should not think of all the Greek slaves as being ignorant. Many of them were well-trained and capable persons whom the fortunes of war had thrown into slavery. A number of them did the work of business or professional men. A Greek slave might keep his master's accounts or be a tutor to his master's children. Skilled slave craftsmen were sometimes hired out by their masters to work in the same shop with free Greek laborers. Unless a Greek farmer was exceptionally well-to-do he might work in the fields with his slaves.

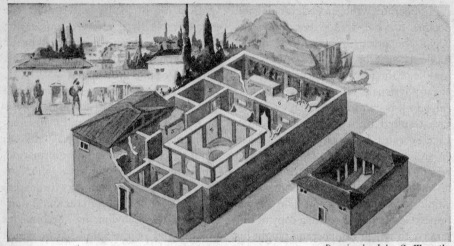

Drawing by John C. Wonsetler

PLAN OF A GREEK HOUSE

In this Greek house the sections are numbered as follows: 1. entrance; 2. shop or space for keeping animals; 3. porter's cell; 4. court; 5. small room; 6. large room. The court was open, as shown in the smaller-scale drawing.

Although the Greek slaves had but few privileges, they do not seem to have shown any great discontent or tendency to rebel. This, however, was not true in Sparta, which was constantly threatened by slave rebellions.

The Greek house was unattractive and inconvenient. An Athenian gentleman once said, " I do not spend my days indoors; my wife is quite capable of managing our domestic affairs without my aid." If you could see an ancient Athenian house you would be able to understand one reason why the men preferred to stay out of doors. Large amounts of money were spent each year to build stately temples, but very little money was used to beautify the homes of the Greeks. A plan of a Greek house appears above.

No green, well-kept lawn or garden of bright flowers separated the house from the street. The big, solid door of the home opened directly upon the street itself. When the massive door swung outward it revealed an open central court. This open court was by far the most pleasant part of the house. There under the sunny skies the family spent much of its time. The small, dark rooms grouped around the court were much like cells. In the daytime no light entered them except through the doors. In the evening olive-oil lamps gave dim, flickering light. The beds had no springs or sheets. The kitchen had no running water, no drainage, no modern conveniences of any kind. How different were the dark, uncomfortable homes of the Greeks from the spacious, airy houses of the Egyptian upper classes!

The Greek woman lived within the home. The woman, who usually managed the household and directed the domestic slaves, was treated very much like a grown-up child. Indeed, as a Greek writer said, she was " most carefully trained to see and hear as little as possible, and to ask the fewest questions."

The childhood of a girl was probably happy enough, although she was not sent to school or given an education as her brothers were. Until she was fifteen most of her time was occupied with domestic training. Every girl was reared with the distinct idea that she must marry.

When the girl was fourteen or fifteen her parents arranged a marriage for her without consulting her wishes in any way. Sometimes the marriage was planned by the parents of the bride and groom, with the man having little more to say about the matter than the girl. Frequently, however, the man was about twice as old as the girl; then the bargain was made by the groom with the parents of the bride. This is what one of Sophocles' characters says about these conditions in one of his plays:

We women are nothing; — happy indeed is our childhood, for then we are thoughtless; but when we attain maidenhood, lo! we are driven from our homes, sold as merchandise, and compelled to marry and say, " All's well."

Since the average girl was brought up in such a way that she expected nothing more from her marriage, she was probably not so unhappy as the poet represented her to be.

Before the wedding ceremony the young bride tearfully dedicated her ball and jackstones and all her childish toys and treasures to the goddess Artemis [ahr′ti mis] who had watched over her childhood. Then when the moon was full, the girl was draped in her most beautiful robe, crowned with a wreath, and closely veiled before she was led into the courtyard where the bridegroom and guests awaited. This might have been the first time she had ever seen the man who was to be her husband. After the father had offered a sacrifice to the gods and the ceremony was finished, the bridal chariot was drawn up before the door. Surrounded by the guests and accompanied by her mother, who carried the marriage torch with which the fire on the hearth of the new home was to be lighted, the bride went to the home of her husband.

It was the Greek ideal of citizenship that the man should give his best to the state, and the woman her best to the

Drawing by John C. Wonsetler

COURT OF A GREEK HOME

This picture shows a scene in the court of a Greek home around 300 B.C. The open court made up in some degree for the small windowless rooms grouped around it.

Brown Brothers

ATHENA

The goddess Athena was the protector of Athens. She represented wisdom and peace, and was loved and honored by the Athenians.

home. The well-born lady rarely left the house after her marriage. A Greek orator said, "The woman who goes out of her own home ought to be of such an age that when men meet her the question is not, 'Who is her husband?' but, 'Whose mother is she?'" There in her home, carefully guarded from the outside world, managing her household, nursing the sick slaves, singing lullabies to her children, the Athenian woman gave herself unselfishly to her work.

The school day lasted from sunrise to sunset. When he was seven years old the Athenian boy started to school. He toiled in the schoolroom from sunrise until sunset. Indeed, the schoolday was so long that Solon once made a law, saying that the school must not open before sunrise and must be closed before sunset so that the boys would not have to walk through the dark, empty streets.

Athenian education stressed good character. The Athenians believed that "if you plant good education in a young body, it bears leaves and fruit the whole life long, and no rain or drought can destroy it." Unlike the Spartan education, the education of the Athenians was intended to build strong characters and to make boys good all-round citizens. The young man must be physically fit and well developed in order to defend his city in time of trouble; he must appreciate beauty and art; his standard of conduct must be the highest; he must learn to be industrious and thrifty; he must be taught to think of his city before thinking of his personal welfare.

Only three main subjects — letters, music, and gymnastics — were taught in the Athenian schools. Since there were practically no books, the boys often stood in front of their masters and repeated the lesson word for word until they had learned it by heart. Every boy was expected to memorize parts of the poems of the great Greek writers. Not one of the three main subjects was neglected. "He can neither swim nor say his letters," and "He doesn't know how to play the lyre" were phrases for describing the man who had no education. Evidently the Greeks considered their system of education quite effective, for Plato said it turned the boy from "the most unmanageable of animals" into the "most amiable and divine of living beings."

The Athenian youth took the oath of citizenship. Usually the young man finished school before he was twenty. At that age he was considered old enough to be given the privilege of citizenship and to understand the duties which go with service to the state. He was summoned before the highest officers of the city to receive the shield and sword which symbolized his citizenship. There he swore in the name of the Athenian gods —

. . . Never to disgrace his holy arms, never to forsake his comrade in the ranks, but to fight for the holy temples, alone or with others; to leave his country, not in a worse, but in a better state than he found it; to obey the magistrates and the laws, and defend them against attack; finally to hold in honor the religion of his country.

Athenian children were taught to worship many gods. When the Athenian children were very young they were taught to worship the Greek gods. They were told that these gods dwelt on Mt. Olympus, the loftiest mountain in Greece.

The three greatest Olympians were Zeus, Apollo, and Athena. Zeus, with the lightning in his hand, ruled all the other gods. Though the Greeks believed him to be the protector of all those who were in distress and the guardian of the home, his anger was terrible to behold. They believed that he hurled the thunderbolt, sent the storm cloud, and threw the forked lightning. One movement of his overhanging eyebrows could shake Mt. Olympus like a leaf on a tree.

Athena was the most beloved goddess of the Greeks. The city of Athens was named after this goddess, and to her the Athenians looked for protection. It was believed that Athena could give aid in turning away the foe and in bringing home a victorious army. It was also believed that Athena helped the women to weave and do beautiful handiwork and gave knowledge of how to care for the olive tree. Athena was so wise that she was often consulted by the other gods and goddesses. For the Greeks Athena was the symbol of the ideals of courage, self-control, and dignity —

APOLLO

Apollo was the sun-god and the god of music. He was a skilled archer, as well, and had the power of seeing into the future.

traits which are evident in the statue of Athena on page 154.

The fair-haired sun-god Apollo, who was such a deadly archer that "the Gods tremble, yea, rise up all from their thrones as he draws near with the shining bended bow," was the inspiration for all poetry and music. He played beautiful music upon his lyre as he went about protecting the flocks in the fields. But greatest of all, he could look into the future and tell what would happen years hence. These powers made him even more loved by the Greeks than Zeus himself.

Besides these three great divinities there were other gods and goddesses. The stately wife of Zeus was Hera [hee′ruh]; she was the protectress of marriage. The laughter-loving Aphrodite [af′roh dai′ti] was the goddess of love and beauty. You probably know of this goddess as Venus, the name by which the Romans called her. It was she who "gives sweet gifts to mortals and ever on her lovely face is a winsome smile." Aphrodite had a plump, rosy little son who was called Eros. In later days the Romans called him Cupid. This mischievous child played about the earth, piercing the hearts of men and women with his love darts.

Hermes, with his winged sandals, was the messenger of the gods and the god of trade and commerce. When he started out to carry a message —

. . . he bound on his fair sandals, golden, divine, that bear him over the waters of the sea and over the boundless land with the breathings of the wind.

From his shining palace deep under the sea, Poseidon ruled the ocean. Although he usually preferred to remain at home, he could sometimes be seen traveling to Olympus over the foaming waves in a chariot drawn by tossing white horses. To him all sailors looked for protection.

To the Greeks every shaded nook, stream, and rocky crag had a spirit to protect it. The best known of these spirits was Pan —

. . . the goat-footed, the two-horned, the lover of din and of revel, who haunts the wooded hills. . . . Lord is he of every snowy crest and mountain peak and rocky path. . . . Ever he ranges over the high white hills and at evening returns piping from the chase breathing sweet strains on the reeds.

The Greeks believed in prayer and in an uncertain after-life. The Greeks had no particular day of each week on which to worship, but various days during the year were set aside for the worship of certain gods and goddesses. Most homes had an altar where prayers were offered. Also there were altars outside of the beautiful temples dedicated to the gods. When the Greeks prayed they did not kneel, but stood upright, bareheaded, with their hands upstretched to heaven. They prayed before undertaking difficult tasks, before athletic contests, and before the opening performance in the theater. The great Greek statesman, Pericles, always prayed before he spoke in public that he might "utter no unfitting word."

The Greeks thought that after death one went to the shadowy underworld called Hades [hay'deez]. This was ruled over by King Pluto. A few of the heroes and those greatly loved by the gods were allowed to go to the Elysian [i lizh''n] Fields, or the Isles of the Blessed, which lay far to the west on the edge of the unexplored ocean. There all was endless bliss and happiness.

The Greeks visited the oracles to learn the will of the gods. The Greeks believed that one way of learning the will of the gods was to visit an oracle. These oracles were usually situated in wild, gloomy spots. The most famous of all was the Oracle of Apollo at Delphi, to the south of Mt. Olympus. You will remember that Apollo was thought to have the power to look into the future.

At Delphi from a deep cleft in the rocks a mysterious vapor arose. The Greek who wished advice from Apollo brought the richest gifts he could afford, placed them in the hands of the priest, and waited for the answer to his question. A priestess in the innermost sanctuary drew close to the vapor rising from the rock, and the vapor soon made her half-unconscious. The priests wrote down the words she uttered, often turning them into verse, and took them out to the one who wished advice.

The priests, who really determined the nature of the answer, must have been very wise men, for they often gave clever replies. These men kept in touch with

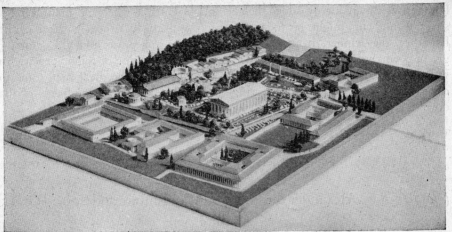

Metropolitan Museum of Art

OLYMPIA

This reconstruction shows a part of Olympia, the site of the Olympic games held in honor of Zeus. These were the most famous of all Greek games.

the affairs of the world, and their wide experience well fitted them to give advice in difficult matters. For instance, one oracle said of the poet Homer: " He shall be deathless and ageless for aye."

The Greeks held athletic festivals to honor their gods. One of the most interesting events of the Greeks, who believed that their gods liked to watch athletic contests, was the Olympic Festival. Homer told of these games in the Ninth Century. No one knows how much earlier they were held. In 776 B.C. the Greeks began to record the names of the victors. Beginning in that year the Olympic festivals were held every four years. The four years between the contests were known as Olympiads [oh lim′pee adz]. The Greeks began to date events by saying that an occurrence took place in one of the years of a certain Olympiad.

Although there were games in many of the Greek cities, the greatest festival was at Olympia in honor of Zeus. This festival was held in late summer and lasted for several days. Only young men of Greek blood, who had sound, well-

trained bodies and good morals, were allowed to compete.

A week or so before the games all roads were officially declared safe for the thousands of travelers who came from many parts of Greece. Highway robbers were to suffer especially severe punishment if they molested the wayfarers. During an entire month all warfare had to stop. Pleasure and the worship of Zeus took the place of ordinary business. On the morning which marked the beginning of the festival, the men could be found long before dawn in their seats in the stadium. Since they believed Zeus to be present at the games given in his honor, they sat in the burning sun all day long with their heads uncovered. The main features in the contest were foot races; javelin, discus, and spear throwing; jumping; and wrestling matches. In later times there were four-horse chariot races.

On the fifth day prizes were given to the winners. These were merely olive-wreaths which had been cut from a sacred olive tree with a golden knife, but they were more highly valued than a silver loving cup might be today. In honor of the winner, banquets were given, poems were written, and statues were sculptured. A triumphal procession carried the victor home, often tearing down a portion of the city wall that he might enter it where no man ever before walked. In Athens a victor of the Olympic games was invited to dine for the rest of his life at public expense in the hall where the great men came to eat and talk over the problems of the city.

Chapter 8 ~ Alexander the Great Built an Empire and Spread Greek Culture

Athens and Sparta fought a great civil war. For a number of years, the Greek city-states built great navies, constructed magnificent buildings to beautify their cities, and in many other ways surpassed the other countries of the ancient world. But they never were able to unite under one government for the good of all. When a city-state became more powerful than the others, it tried to impress its authority upon the weaker cities. Because of their jealousy and their selfish desires to dominate, Athens and Sparta eventually lost their independence and began to decline.

About the middle of the Fifth Century B.C. a group of city-states joined Sparta in an attempt to overthrow the Athenian Empire. A long series of civil wars began. These conflicts are called the Peloponnesian [pel oh puh nee'zh'n] Wars. This series of wars makes up the saddest and most pitiful chapter in Greek history. While peace reigned over the sunny country of Greece, the talented Athenians were able to produce masterpieces of art and architecture, which are still imitated throughout the civilized world. When the Greeks turned against their brothers, civil war took the place of peace, happiness, and creative effort.

A few Greeks realized that war could bring only horror and downfall to Athens and Sparta. Euripides wrote of war in this way:

And there, at home, the same long dearth!
Women that lonely died, and aged men
Waiting for sons that ne'er should turn again,
Nor know their graves, nor pour drink-offerings,
To still the unslaked dust. These be the things
The conquering Greek hath won!

After Athens began her death struggle with Sparta, bad luck seemed to wait for the Athenians at every turn. A terrible plague struck the city, taking many of the strongest and greatest men. Pericles died of the pestilence, and none was left who could fill his place. Whole cities were destroyed; hundreds of the most promising young men were killed. Year after year armies overran Greece, leaving a path of destruction behind them. Athens and Sparta never recovered from the ruinous war which they had inflicted upon each other. They soon sank into the background, and another country began to lead the way.

Philip united the Macedonians. To the north of Greece lay a wild, rugged country called Macedonia [mas i doh′ nyuh]. The men who lived in Macedonia were no less wild and rugged than the country itself. Although they spoke Greek, they had no art, no science, no literature, and no written laws like those of the other Greeks. Some of them tended flocks and herds, but for most of them fighting and hunting were the chief occupations. In fact, a man was not allowed to sit at the table with other men if he had not killed a wild boar in the hunt. Those who had not slain their man in battle were required to wear cords around their waists.

After the Greek city-states had been weakened by civil wars a strong man arose among the Macedonians. This was in the middle of the Fourth Century B.C. He is known in history as Philip of Macedon. Within a few years Philip's boundless ambition had changed Macedonia from a weak state, whose barbarian mountain tribes were continually at war with one another, into the strongest nation on the Greek peninsula.

Philip set out to do three things. First, he created a standing army and invited his troublesome countrymen to join it. Thus he changed some of his enemies into allies. Next, and this was more difficult, he united all of Macedonia into a real kingdom. No king had ever before been able to subdue the barbarian hill tribes. Finally, Philip planned to bring all other Greek states under his power and to extend his rule beyond the seas.

This was an ambitious program for the able king, but he never faltered in carrying it out. Many city-states fell before his new but well-trained forces. Other cities were won because Philip did not hesitate to bribe a traitor. At least, there is a story that when one of his generals reported that a certain fort could not be taken, Philip said, "No fortress is inaccessible if one can only introduce within it a mule laden with gold."

Demosthenes warned Athens against Philip. One man in Athens viewed the conquests of Philip of Macedon with alarm. This was the orator Demosthenes [dee mahs′thuh neez]. In fiery speeches he urged the Athenians to organize an army against Philip. He told them that their future and the safety of Athens depended on the stand they made against the Macedonians. His bitter speeches against Philip of Macedon have been called "Philippics" [fil ip′iks]. Today we still call a speech which attacks a cause or man relentlessly a philippic.

In spite of all his persuasion and pleadings, Demosthenes could not get the Athenian people to realize the danger that threatened them from the north. The Athenians were blind to their peril, just as, more than two thousand years later, the English and the Americans underestimated the danger of the Nazis and the Japanese warlords. Even though he was inspired by love for his city, Demosthenes could not save it. Like the other Greek city-states, Athens fell before the power of Philip.

Alexander showed unusual ability. Though Philip of Macedon made a great name for himself, his career was not so brilliant as that of his son, Alexander. When Alexander was only ten or twelve years old his father and the courtiers saw that he was an exceptionally clever lad. This story is told of how he tamed the horse Bucephalus [byoo sef′ uh luhs]. The prancing steed had been offered to Philip for a large sum of money, but when the attendants tried to mount him he kicked and snorted until they believed him unmanageable. They were about to lead Bucephalus away when Alexander said to his father, "What an excellent horse do we lose for

Metropolitan Museum of Art

THE CONQUEROR AND THE PHILOSOPHER

Alexander meets Diogenes, the old philosopher, who has no interest in worldly power or in conquerors. All that Alexander can do for him is to move so that he will not block off the sunlight.

want of boldness to manage him!" "Boy," cried his father, "do you find fault with those older than yourself as if you were better able to manage him than they?" "I could certainly manage this horse better than the others." "If you fail what will you forfeit for your rashness?" "The whole price of the horse," answered Alexander.

The young prince had noticed that Bucephalus was afraid of his own shadow. Turning him directly toward the sun and stroking him gently, he sprang upon his back. At first the king was alarmed, but he was overjoyed when he saw that the boy kept his seat. "O my son," he cried, "seek another empire, for Macedonia is too small for thee!" And, in time, this seemed to be the case.

Aristotle tutored Alexander. This incident convinced Philip that his son

should have the best teacher that could be found; so he sent this letter to the famous philosopher, Aristotle:

Be informed that I have a son, and that I am thankful to the gods not so much for his birth, as that he was born in the same age with you; for if you will undertake the charge of his education, I assure myself that he will become worthy of his father, and of the kingdom which he will inherit.

So Aristotle journeyed to Macedonia to become the tutor of Alexander.

Young Alexander became king of Macedon. Alexander inherited his father's kingdom in 336 B.C., retained it by force. Like many other overly ambitious rulers, Philip of Macedon died at the hand of an assassin. Alexander was then only twenty years old. No ordinary young man had succeeded Philip.

Gathering his army together, Alexander marched through Greece, demanding that the city-states give him the same promise of allegiance they had made his father. When the rebellious Greek city of Thebes refused, Alexander completely destroyed it. The other cities then more readily pledged allegiance to Alexander. All the Greek cities remained under Macedonian rule.

Alexander built a vast empire. With peace once more restored on the Grecian peninsula, Alexander turned his eyes to the Persian Empire, which his father had always dreamed of conquering. The story of Alexander's crossing the Hellespont, his march through Palestine, his freeing of Egypt from Persian rule, and his capture of the king of Persia, is too long to tell here. But the campaigns he planned and directed in conquering his great empire mark Alexander as one of the great generals in history. In the twelve years that Alexander ruled Macedonia he conquered and established an empire that stretched from India in the east to include Greece and Macedonia in the west, and from Egypt in the south to the Black and Caspian seas in the north. The map on page 162 will show you the extent of his empire.

The adventures of Alexander revealed the man. Many heroic legends cluster about the name of Alexander the Great. A few of them may help you to understand better his character and personality. It is said that Diogenes [dai ahj'i-neez], the philosopher, was living in Corinth when the Macedonian and his army passed through the city. Crowds gathered to praise and flatter the young conqueror, but Diogenes paid no attention to him whatever. Noticing the philosopher lying in the sun, Alexander asked, " Is there any way in which I can serve you? " " Yes," growled Diogenes without looking up, " stand out of my sunshine." His followers laughed, but Alexander thoughtfully remarked that if he were not Alexander, he would like to be Diogenes.

One day while passing through Asia Minor, Alexander came to the city of Gordium where he saw the famous Gordian knot. This knot was so twisted and tangled that no one had ever been able to untie it. An old prophecy said that the man who could untie the knot would rule the world. Alexander tried for a time to loosen the cord but finally, losing his patience, he drew his sword and cut the knot. Today when anyone finds a short way out of a difficulty we say he has " cut the Gordian knot."

Alexander was worshiped almost as a god by the men of his army. In one of his campaigns he led them on a " long, painful march of eleven days during which his soldiers suffered so much from want of water that they were ready to give up." They came across some Macedonians who were carrying skins filled with water. The Macedonians, seeing Alexander almost choking with thirst, poured water into a helmet and offered it to him.

. . . when he took the helmet into his hands, and looking round about, when he saw all those who were with him stretching their heads out and looking earnestly after the drink, he returned it again with thanks without taking a drop of it. " For," said he, " if I alone should drink, the rest will be out of heart." When the soldiers heard him speak in this way, they one and all cried out to him to lead them forward boldly, and began whipping on their horses. For whilst they had such a king, they said, they defied both weariness and thirst, and looked upon themselves to be little less than immortal.

Alexander introduced Oriental luxury into his court. The time finally came when many of Alexander's friends

ALEXANDER'S EMPIRE

turned away from him. Dreaming of a world empire, he offended his Macedonian countrymen by showing favor to the Persians whom he had conquered. He dressed as a Persian. He adopted many Oriental customs, even insisting that all who came to him on business bow down to the earth and kiss his feet. He began to allow his temper and passions to get out of control.

The climax of trouble with his friends came one night when he was feasting at a banquet. A countryman who had once saved Alexander's life criticized him for allowing a song to be sung which ridiculed the Macedonian officers. After a heated argument in which he lost his self-control, Alexander sprang up, snatched a spear from a guard, and thrust it through the body of his friend. For three days Alexander sat speechless in his tent. But no mourning could bring back to life the man whom he had killed.

Shortly after this incident Alexander fell ill with the fever. Many of his old friends, willing to forgive the sick man, came to his chamber. The next day the startling announcement was made that

Alexander was dead. Lacking his personality and leadership, the army and the empire of Alexander soon fell apart.

Alexander the Great carried Greek civilization through the Western world. Alexander's career was like that of the rocket that arches brilliantly but briefly through the sky. Short though it was, his career had a lasting effect upon the world. The undefeated army of Alexander the Great did more than conquer an empire for its leader; it carried the civilization of the Greeks to all parts of the known world. Everywhere Alexander went he founded cities and planted Greek colonies. These cities became new centers for literature, art, religion, and Greek ideals.

Under Alexander, Greece and western Asia were united into one empire. The long struggle for supremacy was at an end. Greek thought and civilization now flowed into the Orient. The chief seaports of the eastern Mediterranean were placed in the hands of the Greeks, who for a time controlled the commerce of the ancient world. Thus it was in large part Alexander the Great who spread the civilization of Greece throughout the Near East. But as Greek culture spread, it was thinned out and mixed with the learning and customs of the conquered peoples of the Near East. Thus the Greek civilization that spread was somewhat different from the civilization of Greece itself. This later Greek civilization of Alexander's empire centered in the new city of Alexandria in Egypt, shown on the map on page 162, and in cities on the coast of Asia Minor. Later, much of this civilization was acquired by the Romans, as you will learn when you read Part Six of this *Story of Nations*.

The Greeks Developed a Wisdom and a Love of Beauty that Have Lighted the Pathway of Civilization

Surrounded by mountains and sea the Greeks developed a civilization that has endured through the ages. This culture was based partly on the remains of old Aegean civilization and partly on knowledge of Egypt, Babylonia, and Phoenicia which the Greeks acquired through trade.

Separated by mountain ranges and inlets, the Greeks organized a number of city-states, instead of one central government. The city-states often quarreled and fought with one another. These city-states did not extend citizenship to conquered peoples or to aliens, and their citizens also held slaves; so only a small fraction of the inhabitants of a Greek city-state were citizens. The governments of Greek city-states, however, were the beginning of representative government and were much unlike the governments of the despotic rulers of the Near East.

Sparta, in the Seventh Century B.C., ruled over an unusual number of slaves and subject peoples and conquered neighboring territories. It had become a militaristic state and its citizens had little time for art or literature. The state was supreme in Sparta, and the individual and the family were important only insofar as they served the state.

Athens was in many ways the greatest city-state of Greece. In their search for truth and happiness the Athenians emphasized "not life, but the good life." Instead of a military camp, they developed a form of government in which every citizen had a part. Co-operation and justice were made their ideals. In Athens democracy was born. Unfortunately the Athenians could not live in peace at all times. There were conflicts among the different Greek states, and attacks by their foreign foe, the Persians. The Greek city-states displayed barely enough co-operation to defeat the Persians. Athens was burned, but the Persian army and navy were defeated and the Athenians lived to build the finest civilization the world had yet known.

After the defeat of the Persians the Athenians became a great commercial power and built up an empire. The Greeks' greatest contributions were made by Athens in the Age of Pericles, or the Golden Age. Under the leadership of Pericles, Athens flourished and her people were contented and happy. During this period of prosperity the Parthenon, dedicated to the goddess Athena, was built. It has remained unsurpassed as an example of beauty and grace in architecture for over twenty-four hundred years. It was during this Golden Age that Greek artists, dramatists, historians, and sculptors did their greatest work. The three men who most influenced the thinking of other people, even to the present day, were the Greek philosophers, Socrates, Plato, and Aristotle.

In contrast with the Spartan youth who was reared in a military camp, the Athenian boy lived at home. He received gymnastic training for the body, and a musical and literary training for the mind. Life in the home and in the school stressed good character. When an Athenian boy reached manhood he took the oath of citizenship and participated in the religious festivals as well as the affairs of the state.

The downfall of Athens was brought about by the Macedonians, under the leadership of Philip and, later, his son Alexander, who has become known in history as Alexander the Great. Alexander first conquered the other Greek states, then invaded Asia Minor, Egypt, the Fertile Crescent, Persia, and a part of India. In the wake of his conquests Greek civilization spread throughout the Mediterranean world and was merged with the civilizations of the peoples that were conquered.

SELF–TEST

Look back upon the story of Greece by testing yourself on these questions.

I. The first great civilization of the —— world developed in Greece. This land is one vast fertile plain (T or F?). Its coast line is indented by numerous narrow arms of water (T or F?). The effect of the geography of the land upon the life of the people is seen in the old Greek proverb, " —— divide; seas alone ——."

Much of the beginnings of Greek civilization came from the —— of the Ionian sea and the —— sea. A highly developed culture flourished there, particularly in —— and ——, before the civilization of the mainland. About —— B.C. barbarous peoples from the (north, south) began overrunning the Greek peninsula. A few centuries later, the —— also had established settlements on the coast of the mainland.

II. During the —— Century B.C., the time of Homer, the Greeks were divided into little city-states. Since the city-states were small, a man had a good chance to become important, and his accomplishments to be noticed (T or F?). The Greeks formed many new colonies all around the shores of the Mediterranean. This colonization was brought about by the desire for —— and for an escape from the —— of the aristocracy. Greek " free citizens " were few, for Greek citizenship could be given only by ——. No —— could become a citizen. Slavery in Greece was widespread (T or F?). Our word democracy comes from Greek words meaning —— and ——.

III. Of the Greek city-states, the most powerful came to be —— and ——. —— was the chief city of the Peloponnesus. Her rise to power was credited to the ability and character of an early leader, a man by the name of ——. He probably lived about (300 B.C., 500 B.C., 800 B.C., 1000 B.C.). Under the code of laws which this man gave to the ——, they were led to live (poorly, richly, luxuriously, simply), and developed a state in which the first concern of every man was to become an efficient ——. Training for this purpose, however, had little effect on the lives of the boys or the women (T or F?). The educational methods of these people set a pattern for ambitious nations in later times (T or F?).

IV. Athens was less warlike than her sister city, Sparta (T or F?). The Athenians, however, were expected to take part in the affairs of government (T or F?). They were just as patriotic as the Spartans (T of F?). In Athens a new type of government was developed which came to be known as a ——. The leader who was responsible for making government in Athens more democratic was ——. This was about the year (400 B.C., 500 B.C., 600 B.C., 700 B.C.). He (*a*) built a strong army; (*b*) secured a new constitution; (*c*) repealed unjust laws; (*d*) made the nobles responsible for the government; (*e*) abolished slavery for the nonpayment of debts. One of the best known landmarks of Athens is a high plateau called —— ——.

V. Until about —— B.C., the Greek city-states were never seriously menaced by a foreign power. Then the Athenians became involved in a war with Darius, emperor of ——. Although Darius was defeated by the Athenians at the battle of —— in —— B.C., this defeat did not prevent his successor, ——, from invading Greece ten years later. Leonidas, with his —— hundred picked countrymen of ——, met the Persian host at the Pass of ——. In spite of the bravery of the ——, the —— army swept down upon (Sparta, Athens) and that beautiful city was soon in flames. But the Greeks, with —— for their leader, avenged the burning of their city in a sea victory at ——. Following this battle, —— and his army withdrew from the land of Greece never to return.

VI. In the years which followed the defeat of the Persians, Athens built a wonderful civilization under the leadership of the great ——. This brief period during which Athens reached her greatest height occurred in the middle of the —— Century B.C. It is known as the —— —— —— ——, or —— —— ——. During this age, magnificent temples were erected upon the —— to replace those which were burned by the Persian invaders. Of these temples, the most famous is the ——, created by the architect —— and the sculptor ——. This stately building, with its (*a*) Ionic, (*b*) Doric, (*c*) Corinthian columns, was dedicated to ——, the patron goddess of Athens. The genius of the Greeks was expressed in other fields besides architecture and sculpture. Three dramatists, ——, ——, and ——, produced some of the finest plays which have ever been written. Three renowned philosophers, ——, ——, and —— , vitally affected the thought of the Greeks and of the Western world. The glory of Athens was recorded by two famous historians (*a*) Herodotus, (*b*) Praxiteles, (*c*) Thucydides, (*d*) Demosthenes.

VII. The Greek ideal included —— and —— in all things. A Greek slave had many privileges but was often likely to rebel (T or F?). The Athenian husband shared with his wife the responsibilities of directing the household (T or F?). Girls were trained to take part in civic affairs and to choose their husbands wisely (T or F?). If an Athenian boy were to attend your school, he would find the hours easier (T or F?). The three main subjects of the Athenian school were ——, ——, and ——. The Athenian oath mentions: (*a*) service to country, (*b*) religion, (*c*) individual rights, (*d*) loyalty to fellow men, (*e*) freedom, (*f*) respect for law. The home of the Greek gods was thought to be —— ——. It was thought that the will of the gods could be heard at an ——. Zeus was the ruler of all the gods; —— the god of music; —— the goddess of love and beauty. The Greeks believed in an after-life (T or F?).

VIII. The jealousy and quarreling between the Greek city-states of —— and —— is an example of the saying that "united we stand; divided we fall." The wars fought by these cities are called the —— Wars, and took place about the (Third, Fourth, Fifth, Sixth) Century B.C. A country to the north, called ——, then became important. The king of this land brought all of Greece under one rule. His son —— built a vast empire which stretched on the east to ——, on the west to —— and ——, on the south to ——, and on the north to the —— and —— seas. When —— died his great empire soon fell apart. Many Greek scientists helped to lay the foundation of science in the modern sense. Among them were ——, ——, and ——.

INTERESTING THINGS TO DO

Projects for the Chart Maker and Artist

1. Sketch columns representing the three orders of Greek architecture. Make a collection of snapshots of buildings in your community that show the influence of Greek architecture; or, for this same purpose, collect pictures from newspapers and magazines. See also *Art through the Ages,* by Helen Gardner.

2. Make a copy of both the large and the small letters of the Greek alphabet and compare them with the corresponding letters of the English alphabet.

Topics for Talks

1. "The Olympic games, yesterday, today, and tomorrow." How do our modern Olympic games differ from those of the Greeks? See "Olympian Games" in *The World Book Encyclopedia.*

2. "If we could exchange places—" If a Spartan or an Athenian school-boy were suddenly to appear in your school today, what things about your school life do you think would appeal to him most? If you were to be carried suddenly back in time to ancient Greece, what features of your school life would you miss most? Are there any characteristics of a Spartan or Athenian school that you would like to see adopted by your own school today? See *Boy through the Ages* or *Girl through the Ages,* by Dorothy M. Parker.

3. "The Greeks established colonies." Why did some of the Greeks leave their homes to establish colonies? How do their motives compare with those of the early American colonists?

Adventures for the Amateur Author

1. Write a short essay comparing and contrasting the governments of Athens, Switzerland, and the United States. In what ways are they similar? How do they differ? Which do you think comes nearest to attaining pure democracy? Which representative democracy?

2. Write an essay explaining why the Athenians trained their young men to speak well in public. Was this ability more important to the Greek than to the young American citizen?

3. Write a poem describing some person famous in the story of Greece, or some stirring event, like the Battle of Marathon, or the death of Socrates.

4. Write a dispatch for an imaginary Athenian newspaper of the time, de-scribing the heroic defense at Thermopylae. The account should be a thrilling one, foreshadowing the immediate flight of the people of Athens from the path of the victorious invaders.

Ideas for Your Little Theater

Dramatize one of the following: a visit to a famous Greek oracle; a scene in an Athenian home; one of the old Greek myths; an incident from the *Iliad, Odyssey, The Persians, The Trojan Women,* or the like.

Candidates for Your Album of Famous People

Aeschylus, Alexander, Archimedes, Aristotle, Demosthenes, Euripides, Herodotus, Hippocrates, Homer, Leonidas, Pericles, Phidias, Plato, Praxiteles, Socrates, Sophocles. Write biographical portraits of at least four of the people listed above for your "Album of Famous People."

INTERESTING READING ABOUT GREECE

BERRY, E. *The Winged Girl of Knossus.* A tale of life in early Crete.

BULFINCH, THOMAS. *Book of Myths.* Stories of the ancient gods and goddesses of Greece and Rome.

Compton's Pictured Encyclopedia, "Greece: The Land Where European Civilization was Born"; and Index.

DAVIS, W. S. *A Day in Old Athens*. ". . . clumsy wagons are bringing down marble from the mountains. . . ."

GARDNER, HELEN. *Art through the Ages*. A clear, accurate, and beautifully illustrated book that will continue to be a valuable source of information as you progress from ancient to modern peoples.

HALL, J. *Buried Cities*. " The artist had great skill who could chisel out of such marble such a . . . rider and such a . . . horse."

HALLIBURTON, RICHARD. *Glorious Adventure*. The adventurous author followed the trail of Ulysses, and climbed Olympus, visited the Delphic oracle, swam the Hellespont, and ran from Marathon to Athens.

HAMILTON, EDITH. *Great Age of Greek Literature*. A beautifully written study of Greek thought and the Greek way of life, enlivened with amusing stories of the great Greek writers.

MILLS, D. *The Book of the Ancient Greeks*. ". . . for it was believed that to run gracefully was as important as to run swiftly. . . ."

National Geographic Magazine, Dec., 1922. " The Glory That Was Greece," by A. W. Wendell. " Athens honored victors in contests of the arts."

——, March, 1944. " The Greek Way," by Edith Hamilton. " The Greeks were the first people in the world to play, and they played on a grand scale." " Greece — The Birthplace of Science and Free Speech," by Richard Stillwell. " Conquered, Greece still ruled the world of letters." " The Glory That Was Greece," by H. M. Herget. A series of thirty-two paintings showing Greek people, scenes, customs, occupations, and recreations, with a page of anecdote or explanation to add to the enjoyment of each picture.

QUENNELL, MARJORIE, and QUENNELL, C. H. B. *Everyday Life in Homeric Greece*. The stories of Homer and the discoveries of the archeologists give us an unusually good picture of Greek life and culture in this valuable and interesting book.

TAPPAN, E. M. *The Story of the Greek People*. " To have ugly things around them made them uncomfortable."

TUCKER, T. G. *Life in Ancient Athens*. A reliable and entertaining book dealing with the social and public life of a classical Athenian family from day to day.

VAN LOON, H. *The Story of Mankind*. " That night the people of Athens watched the sky grow red with the flames of burning ships."

WEBSTER, H. *Historical Selections*. Part II, Greece and Rome. ". . . he will have his hair cut frequently and will keep his teeth white. . . ."

WHEELER, BENJAMIN I. *Alexander the Great*. A good biography of a most extraordinary character.

The World Book Encyclopedia. " Greece: The Story of Greece "; and Index.

THE ROMANS ORGANIZED A VAST EMPIRE

ROMAN EMPIRE
NORTHMEN
GOTHS
NORTH SEA
SCOTLAND
HADRIAN'S WALL
ANGLES
Baltic Sea
GOTHS
SLAVS
IRELAND
BRITAIN
SAXONS
LOMBARDS
VANDALS
HUNS
FRANKS
Rhine R.
ATLANTIC OCEAN
BELGIANS
Plains of Chalons
OSTROGOTHS
VISIGOTHS
Caspian Sea
GAUL
Danube R.
Black Sea
Byzantium (Constantinople)
Po R.
Rubicon River
APENNINE MTS.
Massilia (Marseille)
PYRENEES MTS.
Adrianople
CORSICA
Rome
ITALY
ASIA MINOR
IBERIA
GREECE
SARDINIA
MESOPOTAMIA
MEDITERRANEAN SEA
SICILY
Pillars of Hercules (Gibraltar)
Carthage
NUMIDIA
CRETE
CYPRUS
PHOENICIA
MAURETANIA
PALESTINE
Dead Sea
BOUNDARY BETWEEN EASTERN & WESTERN EMPIRES, A.D. 395
MILES
0
300
600
Alexandria
EGYPT
ARABIA
Liam Dunne

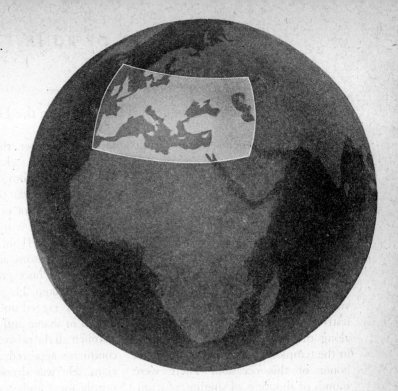

Rome Expanded from a City to an Empire

FIND the heart of the Roman Empire, the city of Rome. In the story of Rome, which follows, you will learn how this city came to rule a great nation, and finally a great empire. Whether a Roman citizen stood beside Hadrian's Wall in Britain or on the warm sands of northern Africa; whether he stood on the shores of the Dead Sea or sailed through the Pillars of Hercules, he still was within the Roman Empire. Roman soldiers and wonderful works of Roman engineering helped to bind the empire together. (The globe above shows the part of the world covered by the map on the facing page.)

Notice the location of the land we now call Italy — a peninsula extending into the Mediterranean Sea. And study the location of the mountains in this map. What would you expect to be the natural boundary of the lands ruled by the ancient Italian peoples? In the story that follows you will see how the Romans extended their empire to include the homelands of the Egyptians, the Mesopotamians, the Hebrews, the Phoenicians, and the Greeks. From this map can you name some of the leading modern nations whose lands were once a part of the Roman Empire? Do you see why the languages of some of these modern nations were derived from Latin and called Romance languages?

Chapter 1 — The Land of Italy Helped Shape the Destiny of Rome

A victorious general marched into Rome.[1] From earliest dawn there was confusion and hurrying in the valleys around the seven hills of Rome. The victorious army returning from the East spent the night just outside the city walls. At sunrise the Porta Triumphalis [pohr′tah tree um fahl′is], the gate which is opened only for a conqueror, was thrown wide to let the victors in. The citizens, dressed in their festival garments, crowded the hills along the route. Priests stood waiting in the temples which were decorated in honor of this occasion. There were sounds of shouting, of singing, of trumpets and of lutes. At last the procession came winding its way along the river and through the streets of Rome, as you may see in the picture on page 173.

First came the senators; then the trumpeters; and after them the abundant spoils of war. Armor, banners, silken stuff, jewels, marble and bronze statues, and rich furniture were drawn in carts heaped high with booty, or borne aloft by slaves. The East had been stripped of priceless treasures to make this triumph the most magnificent ever staged by a returning general. The carts of loot passed one by one, so that all might see what had been brought to Rome.

Beautiful white oxen lumbered awkwardly along. Each had been brushed until he shone, and his horns were gilded and tied with ribbons. Later in the day these oxen would be sacrificed

to Jupiter. After them came strange animals — lions, elephants, camels — brought home from distant lands.

Before the great conqueror's chariot marched gangs of prisoners. They will become slaves or will meet their death in the Colosseum [kahl′uh see′′m]. There, with his two sons and little daughter, marched the once proud monarch of a great kingdom. He walked barefooted, in chains, ragged and forlorn, his head bowed in shame and humiliation.

When all the prisoners had passed, the conqueror appeared, preceded by musicians. He was dressed in a gold and purple toga, and stood proudly in his high chariot drawn by four horses abreast. He held a laurel branch in his right hand and an ivory scepter in his left. With him in the chariot were his children, and two slaves. One held above the conqueror's head the golden wreath that belonged to the god Jupiter. The other, lest the victor become arrogant, constantly whispered the caution, "Remember thou art a man." Under the chariot tinkled a small bell, similar to the one which tolled when a criminal paid for his misdeeds with his life. It reminded the conqueror that he, too, must obey the laws of Rome.

Behind the conqueror marched the legions of soldiers who fought for him. By the thousands they came, shouting, singing, rejoicing. For the glory of this day they have endured hardships. And for this day some of their comrades had died.

Rome left her mark on the world. Such a triumph as we have described was held not once but often in the history

---

[1] This description of the triumph is adapted from "The Splendor of Rome," *National Geographic Magazine*, June, 1922.

Drawing by John C. Wonsetler

A ROMAN TRIUMPH

Following the procession of captives, the conqueror rode in his chariot. One of his slaves is holding the golden wreath of Jupiter over the conqueror's head.

of Rome. Many generals were sent to distant countries to enforce the rule of Rome. Sometimes they failed in their missions, but usually they returned victorious. For hundreds of years Roman soldiers conquered the Western world and Roman governors ruled it. Such a record has never been made by any other nation. A nation which ruled the known world for centuries must have left its mark on civilization. As a matter of fact, as we shall learn, many of our practices in government and law, as well as in other fields, had their beginning with the Romans.

To understand Rome's contributions to civilization we must learn many things about her. We must see why and how she conquered the ancient world; how she organized her vast dominions; and how her people lived. We must see what made Rome great and why she fell. By knowing the mistakes Rome made in her career, we should be able to shape our own course among the na-

tions in a more intelligent fashion.

The story of Rome presents a fascinating account of great leaders, great achievements, and great mistakes. Though the story is not entirely military in nature, it is the record of one of the most efficient aggressor nations of all time. Like many other great empires, however, Rome, too, finally declined and fell. We shall first look at the land of the Romans to see what influence it had on the lives of the people who lived there three thousand years ago.

Sunny Italy is a pleasant land. Italy has a California-Mediterranean climate. Regions having such a climate are to be found in South Africa; on the southwestern coasts of Australia, South America, and North America; and, of course, in the Mediterranean itself. Having this kind of climate, Italy is warm and sunny, with mild weather. The soft winds of the Mediterranean blow over this boot-like peninsula which projects southeast from the mainland of Europe.

ROME ON THE TIBER RIVER

The seven hills and the River Tiber are the two main geographical features of the site of Rome. In this modern picture, the dome of St. Peter's Church shows. The present structure was built in the 16th Century.

As you can see from the map on page 170, Italy, like Greece, has the seas on both sides. A long rib of mountains runs the length of the peninsula; these are the Apennine Mountains, the "backbone" of Italy. The Italian Alps to the north shut off some of the cold winds; they also make travel into the country from the north a matter of some difficulty. The waves of the Adriatic [ay'dri-at'ik] and Mediterranean lap softly upon the sandy beaches. And the sparkling seas reflect the Italian sky in brilliant blue.

Because of her many rivers, Italy is well-watered. From the top of the Italian boot to its heel, Italy has a long coastline. True, there are but a few good harbors, and these are mostly on the western coast and in the south. Rain and cold there are, of course, and snow drifted deep in the mountains. But for the most part Italy is a land of beautiful lakes, swiftly running rivers, magnificent scenery, and a soft, mild climate.

Many peoples have been attracted to Italy. Men were living on the Italian peninsula as early as the New Stone Age. But the people who are known as the Italic tribes were various groups of Indo-European people who came into Italy in the Age of Bronze and overcame the inhabitants. Again it is the old story of conquest, such as we saw when the barbarian Greeks came south into the Greek peninsula and took possession, and when the desert and mountain tribes filtered into Mesopotamia. In the broad valleys watered by the Tiber [tai'ber] and Po rivers, farmers could raise their crops and tend their flocks of sheep, pigs, and cattle. Here were grown luscious grapes for wine, grains for bread, and olives for rich oil.

The Italic tribes were not the only peoples to find their way into this land. About 800 B.C. a people called Etruscans [ee truhs'k'nz], who probably came from Asia Minor, settled on the western coast of Italy. Within the same century, the Greeks made settlements in southern Italy and on the near-by island of Sicily. And about 500 B.C. a group of northern barbarians called Celts [seltz], or Gauls [gawlz], found their way through the passes of the Alps and settled in the Po Valley between the Alps and the Apennine Mountains.

Italy faced the uncivilized western lands. The long narrow peninsula of Italy divides the Mediterranean world into two parts, the eastern and the western. In ancient times the countries to the east of Italy were inhabited by people who had become civilized early in the history of the world. You have read the stories of some of these peoples. They were the Egyptians, the various peoples of the Fertile Crescent, the Phoenicians, and the Greeks. To the west lay the lands where uncivilized or barbarian peoples lived.

Italy is said to face the west because the land generally slopes westward. The good harbors, as was said, are on the western and southern coasts. By looking at the map on page 170 you will see that the Apennine Mountains lie close to the eastern shores. Much of the good farming land of Italy, therefore, lies west of the Apennines.

Italy was threatened not only by the barbarians along the western seacoast but also by the uncivilized people from the lands to the north. Since Italy was a warm and fertile country, the barbarians looked with envious eyes on this fruitful land. The snow-capped Alps, which tower skyward in northern Italy, offered some protection to the inhabitants. But the northern hordes could find their way into Italy through the high mountain passes.

The geography of Italy favored the development of small independent states. In the beginning, the Italic peoples formed a number of separate little communities or nations much as the Greeks had done. They remind us, too, of the early Egyptian communities along the banks of the Nile. The rugged geography of the Italian peninsula tended to further the establishment of these separate communities, or independent peoples. However, in certain coastal areas and in long interior valleys communication between these peoples was not too difficult.

Some of the Italic states at first went their own way, often fighting for their rights with their neighbors. They were also menaced by warlike people from outside Italy.

Rome was built on the Tiber. Near the western seacoast (south of the Etruscan settlements) lay the city of Rome. Rome was built a short distance inland on the Tiber River. This position gave protection from the pirate ships which sailed through the Mediterranean, attacking the coastal cities as well as capturing merchant vessels. The site of Rome had other advantages. It was on a north-south road and so was a convenient trading center. The fertile plain surrounding the city furnished food for its inhabitants. The seven hills upon which Rome was built made a stronghold which was easy to protect.

It was natural that Rome should become a strong city. To understand how it became the power which united Italy and finally ruled the Western world, we need to know something about the mind and character of the Roman people themselves.

Chapter 2 ~ The Romans Learned to Govern and Ruled Italy

A legend told of the founding of Rome. No one knows a great deal about the early period of Roman history. Written records were rare. However, a wealth of legend has grown up around those days. Some of the stories are based on fact; others are likely to be pure fiction. Most Romans themselves believed these tales about the origin and early development of their city. They told their children that Rome was founded in what we call the year 753 B.C. by the twin brothers Romulus [rahm'yoo luhs] and Remus [ree'muhs].

They described how these boys, when babies, had been thrown into the Tiber by their wicked uncle, who had seized the throne that should have been theirs. The babies' cradle drifted ashore, and they were kept from starving by a she-wolf. When they grew up, the boys learned of their origin, killed their wicked uncle, and built the city that was to rule the Western world.

The Romans had another story to explain why Rome was named for Romulus instead of Remus. When the brothers began to lay the city wall they could not decide which one should give the city his name. A heated argument arose and developed into a quarrel. Superstitious friends of the twins suggested that Romulus and Remus wait for a sign from the gods. So the brothers climbed a hill and watched all day and all night. Just as the sun was creeping over the crest of the hills, Remus shouted aloud in joy. He had seen six vultures flying across the sky. Before Remus could be hailed as king, the cry arose that Romulus had seen twelve vultures. Each

brother was sure he had been favored by the gods. Again angry words passed between the twins, and finally Remus —

contemptuously jumping over the newly raised wall, was forthwith killed by the enraged Romulus who exclaimed: "So shall it be henceforth with every one who leaps over my walls." Romulus thus became sole ruler and the city was called after him.

Rome was founded in the Eighth Century B.C. As a matter of fact, Rome probably was founded in the Eighth Century B.C. Some farming villages on the Tiber in the little country of Latium [lay'shee'm] united and formed the city-state of Rome.

These little villages, like many others in Italy, were used to some self-government, so they set up that kind of government for their new city-state. There was a "town meeting," or assembly, which all male property holders could attend. This fact reminds one of the New England town meetings in Colonial America. Two consuls [kahn's'lz] were elected each year to call meetings, hold elections and direct the army. And there was a senate, which was made up of the heads of the leading families. This senate was very powerful. The consuls had to ask the advice of the senators and get their approval on any important matter before it was taken to the assembly. Of course, none of these developments took place rapidly; they grew over a number of years.

Along with this government, the Romans kept the patriarchal system in which women, children, and slaves were under the power of the "patriarch," or male head of the family.

Rome sought security in electing rulers for life. Some time after Rome became a city-state it began having trouble defending itself against the Etruscans. These people lived in near-by Tuscany, which you can see on the map on page 170. The Romans did not like to keep changing officials during times of danger; so they discontinued electing the consuls every year and elected princes who held office for life. These princes were not very different from kings, and therefore this period in the story of Rome is sometimes called the kingdom. But the assembly of property holders still met.

Early Rome was a farming community. During these early years of Rome, the people lived a simple life. They tilled their farms outside the earthen city walls and built up their city. When Rome was in danger, the farmers left their work to protect their homes. As soon as their army was victorious, the Roman citizens returned to their fields.

At the beginning of her career no one could have foreseen the great future of Rome. The simple, hard-working Roman citizens probably did not realize that they were laying the foundation for a mighty empire.

Rome expanded beyond her city walls. Many changes came to Rome in the Sixth Century B.C., when the Etruscans, who long had been the enemies of early Rome, finally gained control of the city. It was the Etruscans who first made Rome a power in the Italian peninsula. First they enlarged the city and surrounded it by a great stone wall, which was built largely by forced labor. They built up a strong army and went out from Rome to conquer the surrounding country, until they had brought much of Latium under their control and all of it under their dominance. In time, they even abolished the assembly of property holders. Yet the Etruscans did encourage building and trade, and a great new working class grew up in the city. Mediterranean countries to the east became interested in trading with Rome, and the seaport at the mouth of the Tiber was opened to commerce. For a hundred years the Etruscans ruled Rome, along with their own land of Tuscany.

Rome became a republic. About 500 B.C. the Romans were able to drive out their Etruscan rulers and set up a republic. At first, this Roman Republic tried to control all the communities that the Etruscans had been ruling when they were in power in Rome. But the other Latin towns objected strenuously. Like Rome, they wanted their independence. They were, moreover, in a position to demand it, for the Romans still were occupied with the Etruscans who wanted to reconquer Rome. The Etruscans kept coming back, time and again, to attack the city.

Under those circumstances, it was possible for the small Latin communities to withdraw entirely from the dominance of Rome. These smaller cities joined together and formed a league to resist Rome's claims over them. But the Romans, even this early in their history, showed genius for government. Instead of combating the unruly Latin communities who were resisting them, Rome wisely proposed a Latin league which would join the small Latin cities into one group. Thus the foundation was laid for a Roman republic. You should remember that this league was established early in the Fifth Century B.C., a number of years before the great Empire was developed.

The Patricians gained control of Rome. The Roman government had done well to co-operate in the Latin league. But the Romans themselves had trouble at home. For one thing the government was not nearly so democratic as it had been when Rome was first founded. It was the senators who had led in driving out the Etruscans, and it was they who had set up the new government. These senators continued to keep much of the power of government for themselves. Also they set themselves up as a class apart from the other people. This ruling class, and their descendants, were now called *patricians*. Only a patrician could be a magistrate, or a priest, or could interpret the laws. The

assembly could not pass a law of which the patricians did not approve. The common people, or *plebeians* [pli bee′y′nz], as they were called, were not allowed to hold office or to marry into patrician families. Great class differences had grown up. During the hundred years that Rome was ruled by the Etruscans, many people had become little more than serfs, or slave-like laborers bound to their work. Others had made money through trade or by exploiting the other Latin cities.

After the Romans had driven out the Etruscans, conditions in Rome were bad

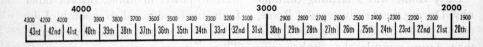

4000											3000										2000
4300	4200	4100	3900	3800	3700	3600	3500	3400	3300	3200	3100	2900	2800	2700	2600	2500	2400	2300	2200	2100	1900
43rd	42nd	41st	40th	39th	38th	37th	36th	35th	34th	33rd	32nd	31st	30th	29th	28th	27th	26th	25th	24th	23rd	22nd	21st	20th

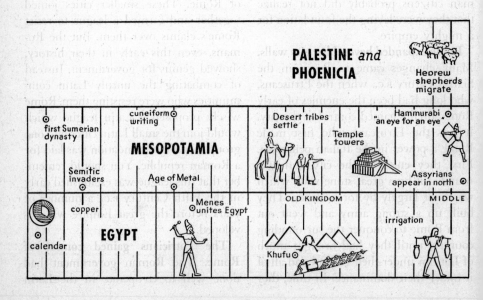

for a time. Building ceased. Commerce by sea fell off. And of course open trade with the Etruscans was out of the question.

Wealth no longer came in from the other cities in the rest of Latium which Rome tried to dominate. The Romans, and the plebeians in particular, suffered from the constant wars against the Etruscans. And since the select group of patricians had the use of most of the public land, many of the plebeians did not have a means of livelihood and could not pay their debts. Rome was ripe for change.

The people struggled to gain their freedom. The common people who could not pay their debts had an especially hard time, because the Roman laws about debt were harsh. A man might be thrown into jail or even sold into slavery for debt. Often the plebeians did not even know what the laws were, for Roman laws at that time were not written down. The laws could be interpreted only by the haughty patricians. In order to protect themselves, therefore, the plebeians demanded the right to elect officers called *tribunes,* who would hear their appeals and shield them

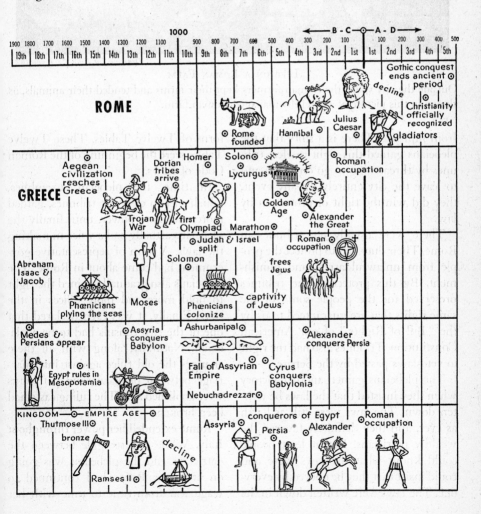

Drawing by John C. Wonsetler

LIFE ON A ROMAN FARM

Outside the city walls, the Roman farmers kept their farms and tended their animals, as shown in this picture of a carefully managed Roman farm.

from injustice. There is a story that the plebeians gained this right to elect tribunes by threatening to go on strike and to leave the city entirely. In any event, they did win the right of protection by law.

There were usually ten tribunes in Rome. Their duty was to protect the people from unlawful arrest and punishment. By this protection the tribunes preserved for the people some of the same rights that are guaranteed to us by the " Bill of Rights " of our American Constitution. Tribunes also had the right to veto laws passed by the Senate.

The plebeians gained another victory when they insisted that the laws be written down. The laws were still as harsh as ever, and they definitely favored the wealthy patricians. But at least people could know what the laws were and could insist that they be obeyed by everyone. The laws were written down in the form of Twelve Tables. These Twelve Tables were the beginning of the Roman Code of Laws.

In time, the plebeian assemblies, which met to elect the tribunes, gained more and more power, until finally the plebeians actually had a voice in making the laws. A form of representative government had come about in Rome. The plebeians also gradually gained the right to hold more and more offices in the state. Finally, it was even declared that one of the two consuls had to be a plebeian. Naturally, along with all these changes the old rules against intermarriage between plebeians and patricians were abolished also. The ruling caste had been broken.

Rome extended her power throughout Italy. While this struggle between the patricians and the plebeians was going on at home, Rome had continued to wage war from time to time with her

THE ROMAN FORUM

The Roman Forum was the center of political and commercial activities of the city. A forest of marble columns and arches grew up in the Forum. The central building in this picture is the Temple of Vespasian.

neighbors. Sometimes these wars helped the patricians hold their authority. At other times the wars gave the plebeians an advantage at home because the patricians needed their support against the enemy.

About 400 B.C. Rome itself had been invaded by the Gauls from the Po Valley. The towns of the Latin league had been serving as buffer states between Rome and her enemies, and were becoming irked at this situation. Too, they did not like Rome's growing dominance over them in the Latin league. So instead of helping Rome to drive off the Gauls, the towns of the Latin league made the invasion an opportunity for revolt. But as soon as Rome recovered from the Gallic invasion, which she did very quickly, she forced the Latin cities back into line — and in an inferior position. Then Rome went on to conquer and annex the southern part of Etruria.

The various tribes of the Italian peninsula were perhaps responsible, at first, for the fact that Rome continued to make conquests and grow in territory and power. These tribes were constantly warring among themselves. So Rome, to protect her neighbors (as well as to gain new power) was constantly at war in Italy over a period of years. Thus Rome would go to war and conquer more territory. Usually she gave the conquered people the rights of Roman citizens after they had proved their loyalty to their conquerors.

Rome first conquered the peoples of central Italy. Then she conquered the Greek settlements in southern Italy. By 265 B.C. Rome was the mistress of all Italy. The map on page 182 shows how, from 500 B.C. to 265 B.C., Rome extended her territory and brought the Roman system of law to practically all of the land of Italy.

Chapter 3 ~ Rome Conquered the Western World

Rome became the rival of Carthage. Just across the Mediterranean Sea, on the northern shore of Africa, lay Carthage, then the greatest sea power in the ancient world. You will recall that the site of ancient Carthage in North Africa, about two thousand years later in World War II, was taken by the United Nations. They used it as a springboard from which to make an attack on Fascist [fash´ist] Italy. Thus you can see how its position could be a threat to Italy in both ancient and modern times. Locate it on the map below.

Carthage, as you will recall from the story of the Phoenicians, had been founded as a trading post in the Eighth Century, B.C. In time, Carthage had become a great commercial center. The fast triremes [trai´reemz] of Carthage, with their three banks of oars, plowed through the Mediterranean. Silks, spices, ivory, ostrich feathers, and other luxuries were carried to countries that bordered the sea.

Year by year Carthage became more arrogant. Her prosperous trade brought her great commercial and political influence. She even controlled parts of Spain and a part of Gaul, the land we now call France. At one time she had no powerful rivals in the western Mediterranean world. She declared that the Mediterranean was a Carthaginian [kahrth´uh jin´ i´n] lake and that no one dared even to wash his hands in it without her permission.

It was difficult for Rome to avoid conflicting with Carthage. After all of Italy had been brought under Roman control, Rome herself began to take a greater in-

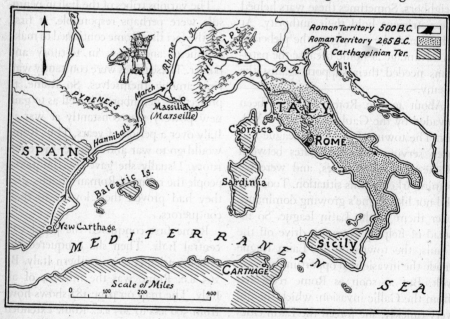

ANCIENT ITALY

This map shows the early growth of Rome and the route of Hannibal's march over the Alps into Italy.

terest in Mediterranean commerce. Naturally Rome resented the attempts of Carthage to control all trade in the western Mediterranean, and Carthage feared that Rome might shortly become a real rival. The two cities grew more hostile and more jealous of each other every day. Each began to rally her forces for battle.

If the strong points of Rome and Carthage had been weighed against each other, they would have been almost equal. The population of each city was probably about a million. Rome had the greater army but Carthage boasted a larger and better navy. The commerce of Carthage had brought her more ready money to buy supplies for a long war. But the Carthaginians did not follow the practice of giving citizenship or other privileges to people in other lands when they extended their rule as the Romans had done. So the Carthaginian troops were made up largely of mercenaries [mer'seh ner'eez], or soldiers who fought only for hire, whereas the Roman army contained many patriotic Roman citizens and allies. A man living in 264 B.C. would have found it hard to foresee which of the two great powers would be triumphant in the bitter struggle that was to last more than a hundred years. But he would have seen that this conflict, like many in later days, had its roots in rivalry for trade.

Rome and Carthage clashed in Sicily. The trouble first broke out in Sicily. The Carthaginians had already taken most of Sicily from the Greeks who had been in possession of it. Sicily was the last remaining island Carthage needed to give her a complete encircling control of the western Mediterranean. A few people from Italy had settled in Sicily, too, and a quarrel between them resulted.

As the protector of the entire Italian

A ROMAN WARSHIP

The high decks of the Roman warships gave the Roman fighting men protection from attack and enabled them to drop down upon their enemies.

peninsula, Rome did not care to have such a great power as Carthage within sight of Italian shores. She did not want Carthage in Sicily at all. Since all Italy was now under Roman control, Rome was ready to turn to the task of driving the Carthaginians out of Sicily and reducing the power of her great rival.

Rome built a great navy. In the war which followed, the Romans were handicapped. They could not expect to defeat a city that was mistress of the sea, without adequate ships. With great energy and determination, they cut down trees and transformed them into ships. Since the Romans were not so skillful in rowing and maneuvering ships as the Carthaginians were, they fitted their ships with grappling bridges. When a Roman ship could get close enough to the enemy ship, the Roman sailors would let down the grappling bridge, with its giant hook, and hold the other ship fast. The

Drawing by John C. Wonsetler

HANNIBAL CROSSING THE ALPS

Hannibal accomplished the tremendous labor of leading an army and elephant-borne supplies over the Alps. Difficulties of temperature as well as of terrain challenged Hannibal's progress.

Romans would mount by this bridge to the Carthaginian ship. In a hand-to-hand combat, they had confidence they could win. In this manner they defeated the fleet of their enemy. They won the first war with Carthage and gained the island of Sicily. And from that time the Romans were powerful upon the sea.

Hannibal promised to avenge the defeat of Carthage. The peace which followed the first war between Carthage and Rome was an armed peace. The first clash proved to be only the beginning. As her own trade increased, Rome continued to resent the arrogance of Carthage. The Carthaginians wanted revenge. Few men in Carthage had a greater longing for revenge than the dashing young general Hannibal. His father, Hamilcar, bitterly hated the Ro-

mans whom he had fought in the first war, and Hannibal had grown up with this hatred.

When Hannibal was only nine years old his father was starting off to a battlefront in Spain. As the religious sacrifices were being offered to insure a safe journey, Hamilcar turned to his young son to ask, " Would you like to go to war with me? " " Yes," cried the boy, " take me with you now." " I will take you," answered the father, " if you will make a promise to me." Placing the boy's hand upon the altar, which was prepared for the sacrifice, he said, " Promise me that you will never, as long as you live, be a friend to the Romans." Until his dying day Hannibal kept his promise. For many years he was a most powerful and dreaded enemy of Rome.

Hannibal may be ranked among the cleverest and most fearless generals of ancient times. Even the Roman writer Livy [liv´i] acknowledged his dauntless courage:

He was fearless in exposing himself to danger, and perfectly self-possessed in the presence of it. No amount of exertion could cause him either bodily or mental fatigue; he was equally indifferent to heat and cold; his eating and drinking were measured by the needs of nature, not by appetite; his hours of sleep were not determined by day or night; whatever time was not taken up with active duties was given to sleep and rest, but that rest was not wooed on a soft couch or in silence; men often saw him lying on the ground amongst the sentinels and outposts, wrapped in his military cloak. His dress was in no way superior to that of his comrades; what did make him conspicuous were his arms and his horses. He was by far the foremost both of the cavalry and the infantry, the first to enter the fight and the last to leave the field.

Hannibal crossed the Alps to conquer Rome. The second war between Rome and Carthage broke out in Spain, early in 218 B.C. The Carthaginian soldiers under Hannibal defeated the Romans, and then this bold Carthaginian determined to invade Rome. In the spring he gathered together thousands of foot soldiers and cavalrymen, and many elephants (which served much the same purpose as modern tanks) and set out for Italy. Hoping to surprise the enemy, he decided to go by land rather than by sea. Over the Pyrenees [pir´i neez] Mountains and across Gaul marched Hannibal and his strong army of invasion. The hardest part of the journey was before them — the Alps. A scene from this journey is shown on page 184.

It was late autumn before Hannibal reached the towering Alps that shut him out of Italy. Little wonder his men were discouraged when they saw the steep, dangerous, snow-covered mountains. Day by day the army crept along a narrow pass. The men were hungry, cold, and weary. Unfriendly natives rolled huge stones down upon them. Snowslides hurled some of them to destruction over the dizzy precipices. A trail had to be opened so that the elephants could pass. Half of Hannibal's men were lost in crossing the Alps, but those who survived made their way into Italy.

The war in Italy. The Romans were astonished and alarmed to find Hannibal approaching from the north. With great speed they organized an army to defend their country. Many battles were fought. The Romans lost thousands of men.

At first Hannibal was successful, but he was disappointed in one important respect. He had really hoped to stir up trouble among the Roman allies on the Italian peninsula and turn them against Rome. He claimed to be delivering the other Italic peoples from Rome. Hannibal did not understand that Rome's policy of extending either citizenship or other privileges to her conquered neighbors had been highly successful. With only two exceptions the neighboring Italian cities remained loyal to Rome. Hannibal and his soldiers found they were enemies in Italy.

Rome brought the war home to Carthage. The tide turned when a brilliant Roman general carried the war across the Mediterranean into Carthage. Soon Carthage sent a message to Hannibal begging him to leave Italy and return to protect his home city. Historians report that Hannibal nearly wept when he received this summons. But like a true patriot, he obeyed the order, leaving his campaign in Italy unfinished.

Not even Hannibal's courage and generalship could save Carthage. The

Drawing by John C. Wonsetler

ROMANS ATTACKING A WALLED TOWN

The Roman attackers lowered themselves on platforms and raised themselves on scaling ladders to deal savagely and effectively with their walled enemies.

Romans were victorious and Hannibal was put to flight. Rome took possession of the parts of Spain which Carthage had been ruling, but was not content until Carthage itself was completely crushed. Cato [kay′toh], the Roman statesman, who was known for his upright life, ended every speech he made in the Roman senate by saying, "Carthage must be destroyed."

In 146 B.C. the order was given that Carthage should be completely wiped out. The Roman army was glad to carry out the command. Those Carthaginians who were not killed during the siege of the city were liquidated or sold into slavery. Carthage was plundered and then burned. After that the ground on which Carthage had stood was turned under with a plow, and it was claimed

that a terrible curse was laid on anyone who should ever try to rebuild the city. Thus the great Phoenician trading center of the Mediterranean passed out of existence. Rome became the undisputed ruler of the Western world.

The Roman Empire grew even greater. Even before the destruction of Carthage, the Roman armies had made conquests in many other places. In order to keep, or enforce, peace in the eastern Mediterranean, the Romans conquered Macedonia, Greece, and Asia Minor. Between 200 and 168 B.C. Rome took most of the lands that had made up the empire of Alexander the Great, of whom you read in the story of Greece. The Roman citizens were proud of the famous generals who added more land to the vast territories of Rome, and honored them with power and magnificent triumphs such as we have described.

A new kind of government was designed for the Roman provinces. Rome had to work out some practical way of governing her vast empire. To the various peoples on the Italian peninsula itself, Rome allowed a large measure of self-government. But this method did not prove satisfactory in ruling a huge empire made up of many different peoples, many of whom were not used to self-government. So Rome sent out officials to govern the different provinces.

Since these officials were allowed to hold their posts for only a year or two, they did not get experience enough to become really efficient. Many of them were chiefly interested in lining their own purses by collecting more than was legally right. Although this practice was known to the government in Rome, the dishonest officials of the provinces were seldom corrected. The poor farming people of the provinces suffered the most, for the rich were likely to evade their taxes.

Many changes were made in the government in Rome. As a result of her great wars, the Romans made a number of changes in their own government. It is true that Rome remained a republic for some time after she won her vast empire. But this republic was quite different from the republic of the earlier days.

We have seen in Chapter 2 how the plebeians, after a struggle, had gained a voice in the government of Rome. One might expect that the early plebeian office-holders would try to make the government more democratic. But things did not work out that way.

The senators, who really ruled Rome, were all nobles. And the families of plebeians who had been consuls and gone into the Senate, began to be considered as nobles too. In a short time these plebeian families that had arisen to some power began to join with one another and with the patricians to form a powerful kind of little clique, which became a new ruling caste. This "new nobility" used its money and its influence to keep all the high offices in Rome among the members of its own families, as well as to keep any further newcomers from breaking into their group. There were actually no laws of Rome which said that only the nobles could hold high office. But in practice the new nobility made it very difficult for anyone but themselves to be elected. We sometimes refer to this group as the "senatorial class."

It is true that for many years the new nobility ruled Rome efficiently. They did have a great deal of knowledge and experience in governing. It was this group that brought Rome through the wars with Carthage in triumph. But it seems that no self-chosen body of rulers is likely to remain efficient and uncorrupted forever. By the time Rome had acquired a vast empire, the government within Rome had become corrupt.

The Roman conquests brought economic changes. The wars which enlarged the empire had some bad results for the people throughout Italy. For one thing, wars had made the rich richer and had reduced many people of the middle class to poverty. You have probably heard the middle class referred to as the backbone of America. The middle class was the backbone of Rome, too, particularly the free laborers and the small independent landholders.

Farming in Italy suffered from the wars in several ways. Many of the young farmers had been killed. Then, too, some of the veterans who returned from the

Brown Brothers

THE ROMAN SENATE

The togaed Roman Senators listen to the orator Cicero in their stately chamber. The scene is a fresco wall painting in the Palazzo Madama, in Rome. It pictures the trial of Catiline, a conspirator against the republic.

wars found that their small farms had been sold for unpaid taxes. With no money to buy more land, such farmers drifted into the city to take any work they could find. Here they fared little better. They discovered that the wealthy had found it cheaper to buy slaves to work for them than to hire free men.

The veterans who did return to their neglected farms found it harder and harder to make a living farming. And again slavery was one reason. Men who had grown rich in business, or in government, or from Rome's foreign conquests were buying land to form vast estates, and they were buying slaves to farm their lands. The small independent farmers found that they could not sell their farm produce at such a low price as could the rich man who used slave labor. When the free farmers could no longer compete, they found work themselves on one of the large estates as serfs, or they drifted into the cities. Many free laborers, as well as the farmers, faced the

same discouraging prospects. Rome had reached the place where only big business really paid. And war and government were the biggest businesses of all.

Slavery became common in Rome. When Rome conquered a country outside of Italy, she often took large numbers of captives to be used as slaves. In so doing, Rome was following the old customs of eastern empires, not the newer method of co-operative government which she had worked out for herself in dealing with the other people in Italy.

Every year thousands of captives of war were brought to Rome to be sold into slavery. Slaves were so easy to obtain that every Roman of rank had at least a few of them. Many wealthy citizens owned hundreds of slaves, so many that they did not even know their names. We have already read of some of the effects of this slavery on the middle class.

Conditions in Rome resulted in civil war. Class hatred increased in Rome as a result of all these unhappy conditions

—the lack of work or land faced by re-
urning veterans, concentration of the
and into the hands of a few, slave la-
)or, and an exclusive new noble ruling
:lass. There were some leaders who hon-
·stly tried to reform affairs, but their at-
:empts were met by violence and blood-
hed from those who wanted things as
they were. Two patriotic brothers by the
name of Gracchus [grak'uhs] tried to
have state land allotted to independent
farmers and to bring about other important reforms. The popular assembly
gave them enthusiastic support, but the
senators, who represented the great
landowners, opposed them bitterly. In
the end the senators had one of the
Gracchus brothers murdered. The other
killed himself.

As often happens in time of disorder
and discontent, the frustrated mob next
turned to a military leader for help.
They found him in the general, Marius,
who had repeatedly been a consul. Unfortunately, the landowners also had a
military leader, Sulla. Sulla likewise
was a general, and furthermore, he was
the consul at that time.

While Sulla was fighting enemies
abroad, Marius, the people's leader,
marched on Rome, took it by force, and
killed many of his enemies. But Marius
happened to die just then. Sulla was very
angry when he heard how his rival had
seized Rome. As soon as he had defeated
Rome's foreign enemies he marched
back to the city at the head of his army
and in his turn slaughtered the followers of Marius.

Julius Caesar gained office. After Sulla
died, the government was taken over
by three prominent leaders known as
the *triumvirate* [trai um'vi ruht]. They
hoped to save the country from any more
civil war. One of these three men was
Julius Caesar [see'zuhr], who is thought

Brown Brothers

JULIUS CAESAR

This calm-looking man was the conqueror
of Gaul and Britain and the ruler of
Rome. Julius Caesar was also a writer of
excellent Latin prose.

by many to have been the greatest of all
Romans. It was not to be very long before the entire power of the Roman state
was centered in Caesar's hands alone.

Caesar was born about 100 B.C. into
an old-fashioned patrician family. To his
mother he owed the splendid training
and discipline which helped to mold his
character. In his early years he had been
a leader among the younger nobles who
enjoyed the gay life and amusements
of Rome. He was interested in politics,
however, and became a leader of the people's party. As a follower of Marius, he
had narrowly escaped death at the hands
of Sulla's soldiers.

**Caesar proved his ability in Spain and
Gaul.** Before he was forty years old, Caesar had become so prominent in Roman
affairs that he was sent by the Senate to
govern the province of Spain, then called

Iberia [ai bee'ri uh], which Rome had taken from Carthage. Fighting was necessary to subdue this unruly province and Caesar proved himself both a remarkable general and a good governor. But Caesar felt that he was capable of holding a higher position. It is said that one day he sat a long time in thought after reading the story of Alexander the Great. At last he burst into tears. His friends were surprised and asked him the reason for it. "Do you think," said he, "I have not just cause to weep, when I consider that Alexander at my age had conquered so many nations, and I have all this time done nothing that is memorable?" From the beginning of his career Caesar knew that he would never be satisfied with anything less than supreme power.

After Caesar returned to Rome political conditions favored his ambition. He became one of the three members of the triumvirate which was to rule the Roman Republic. He served as consul for a year and then was sent to Gaul as military governor. This gave him his chance to build up his military reputation. For nine years he fought the Gallic chiefs. Messengers from Gaul brought back stirring stories of Caesar's campaigns. They told how strong bridges and good roads were built so that his conquering armies might pass. They told how the enemy was conquered in surprise attacks, how Gallic chiefs bent their proud heads in submission to Rome, how towns were destroyed by the Roman war machine.

Rumors reached Rome about the British Isles, which could be seen from the coast of Gaul on clear days. It was reported Caesar had crossed the channel in small ships and defeated the warlike Britons. You will read of them later.

Caesar wrote an account of the Gallic wars in his *Commentaries*. His writings are in such simple, excellent Latin prose that they are still read by young people in our high schools.

Caesar "crosses the Rubicon." In the meantime things were not going smoothly for Caesar in Rome. Pompey [pahm' pi], one of Caesar's fellow-members of the triumvirate, who was also a famous general, became jealous of Caesar's good fortune and popularity. Now he began to stir up enemies against Caesar. Under these conditions Caesar realized that he must return to Rome to protect his interests. When he neared the Rubicon [roo'bi kahn] River in northern Italy a messenger approached bearing a decree from the Senate. The Senate, urged on by Pompey, had declared that Caesar must disband his army before entering Italy. If he failed to do so, he would be pronounced a public enemy. What should he do? Did he dare obey the Senate's order? Without his army would he not find himself at the mercy of his enemies?

At the river Rubicon . . . he paused for a while, and realizing what a step he was taking, he turned to those about him and said: "Even yet we may turn back; but once cross yon little bridge, and the whole issue is the sword."

For a moment he stood in doubt, but not for long. Then, leading his army, he crossed the Rubicon. Since that time the expression, "He has crossed the Rubicon," has been used to describe a decision which cannot be changed. The famous crossing is pictured on page 191.

Although Pompey had boasted that he could fill Italy with armed men by merely stamping his foot, he made no attempt to meet Caesar there. With many of the senators he fled from Italy into Greece and raised an army that

Caesar defeated. Soon after Pompey was killed in Egypt. Caesar became dictator for life and turned his attention to improving the conditions of the common people.

Caesar demonstrated his statesmanship. In the few brief years (49–44 B.C.) that Caesar was the ruler of Rome he did much for the people. He ruled justly and with great wisdom. He sent the poor out of the cities to live on the farms. Caesar increased the number of senators, allowing some of the common people, as well as the nobility, to become members of the Senate. He limited the amount of land one man could hold. He reformed the system for taxing the colonies so that the governors could no longer collect money that did not belong to them. He made new laws for the settlement of debts. He extended the privilege of citizenship to those conquered provinces in which he was sure it would be appreciated. He revised and improved the calendar so that it was almost the same as it is today.

Caesar proposed to do many other things for the people. He planned to make a great collection of Greek and Roman books; to gather the Roman laws together into a single code; to drain the unhealthful marshes; to rebuild Carthage (as a Roman city, of course); to build a canal through the Isthmus of Corinth, a road along the Apennines, and an aqueduct for Rome; and to erect magnificent public buildings. Caesar planned to spend the enormous wealth

Brown Brothers

CAESAR CROSSING THE RUBICON

Once Caesar had led his army across the river Rubicon, he would have disobeyed the Senate, which had forbidden him to bring his soldiers into Italy. Resolutely, Caesar took the step and marched on to the destinies awaiting him at Rome.

From the painting by Gérôme

THE ASSASSINATION OF CAESAR

Crying out, " Et tu, Brute," Caesar pulled his cloak over his face and fell wounded at the foot of Pompey's statue. The conspirators are here pictured as leaving him alone on the floor to die.

which had resulted from his conquests to glorify Rome at the expense, of course, of the conquered lands.

Caesar was assassinated by conspirators. Most men of action in public life have enemies, and Caesar was no exception to the rule. Some men believed that Caesar was too ambitious, and that he intended to make himself king. The Roman Senate, in particular, mistrusted his ambitions as they saw them conflict with theirs. Brutus [broo'tuhs], whom Caesar loved and trusted, formed with others a plot against Caesar's life. March 15, 44 B.C., was the time set for his assassination. Shakespeare, in his play, *Julius Caesar,* writes that Caesar had been warned of this time — the " Ides [aidz]

of March " — by a soothsayer. But Caesar merely declared, " It is better to die once than to be always in fear of death. That kind of death is best which is least expected."

When Caesar took his place in the Senate on the fifteenth of March the conspirators drew close to him. Upon a signal they rushed at him with drawn daggers. It is said that Caesar first tried to break through the ring, but when he received a blow from his friend Brutus he struggled no longer. After crying out, " Et tu, Brute! " (" You too, Brutus "), he fell to the floor, wounded and bleeding. Silence fell over the city. Caesar was dead. Afterward the people came to think of him as a god.

Chapter 4 ~ The Glorious Roman Empire Flourished and Faded

Rome became an empire under the rule of Augustus. Caesar had no son, so he had bequeathed his fortune to his nephew, Octavius [ahk tay'vi uhs], who was then eighteen years old. Octavius, who was with the army at the time of Caesar's death, hastened to Rome to establish himself. Though young in years, he soon proved that he was able and far-sighted.

At first a new triumvirate was formed, but in a fairly short time the power was divided between Octavius, who ruled the western part of the empire, and Caesar's friend, Mark Antony, who ruled the eastern part. There was trouble between the two. Antony cherished dreams of founding an independent eastern empire which he and the Egyptian queen, Cleopatra, would rule from Egypt. Antony and Cleopatra may even have hoped to bring the western part of the Roman Empire under their power as well. After about twelve years the Senate revoked Antony's command in the East and open war broke out between Octavius, on the one side, and Antony and Cleopatra on the other. Antony and Cleopatra were defeated in a great naval battle, and Octavius was left as sole ruler of the entire Roman Empire, in both the East and the West.

Unlike his famous uncle, Octavius had no desire to enlarge the empire. He felt that Rome had conquered enough territory, and that now she should try to rule it more wisely. Octavius proved to be an able, determined ruler. He continued many of the reforms which Caesar had started. He defended the frontiers, and he made the governors of the provinces responsible to him or to the Senate so that they could not become corrupt or too powerful. The provinces of Rome once again became prosperous under his rule.

Octavius realized that the Romans did not want the outward form of their government changed. Therefore he did not attempt to make himself king. Finally, the Senate gave him the title of Augustus, which meant " majesty " or " honored." Since that time Octavius has been known by the name Augustus Caesar. The eighth month of the year was renamed in honor of Augustus Caesar,

AUGUSTUS CAESAR

Octavius, or Augustus Caesar, as he came to be known, became emperor of the Roman Empire, which was established shortly after the death of Julius Caesar.

and the seventh month was renamed for Julius Caesar.

Even though Augustus did not try to make himself king, the supreme power of the empire was really in the hands of one man, and that man was Augustus Caesar.

When Augustus died, early in the First Century, there was great sorrow in Rome. Sacrifices were offered for him; temples were built in his honor. Even though his rule marked the end of the Roman republic, he had brought justice and order to his people. He had given them forty years of peace. He left an empire which reached from the Sahara Desert in Africa to the lands of the Rhine and Danube [dan'yoob] rivers on the north, from the Atlantic Ocean on the west to the far-off Euphrates River in the east. Rome ruled most of the known world.

Augustus founded a dynasty. After the time of Augustus the rulers of Rome no longer pretended that Rome was a republic, but openly took the title of emperor. Augustus had been concerned about what would become of the empire after his death. He had therefore adopted his stepson as his heir, and had let him rule with him for the last ten years of his reign.

Augustus' forethought proved to be wise, for when he himself died the rule passed peacefully to his heir. For more than fifty years Rome was ruled by emperors who claimed descent by adoption from Augustus or from Julius Caesar. Some of these emperors were more able or more likable than others. Under them southern Britain was conquered, and the West was largely Romanized. The last of this dynasty, the demented Nero, whom tradition credits with fiddling during a great fire in Rome, left no heir to rule the empire.

Rome profited under the " Good Emperors." After a short period of civil war and military despotism, the empire settled down to a long period of good government under emperors of another line. During most of the Second Century Rome was spared further wars for the throne. By chance several emperors in succession had no children, but they chose heirs and the people approved their choices; so there was no trouble. Under one of these " Good Emperors," northern Britain was conquered. New provinces were also added near the Rhine and in the East. These were the last additions made to the Roman Empire, but the defenses of the empire were improved. Government both at home and in the provinces was well conducted. The emperors chose able officials and made them personally responsible to themselves. The Senate was no longer very powerful.

A hundred years of civil strife weakened the empire. But the reign of " Good Emperors " ended when one of them, unwisely, appointed his son to succeed him. The new emperor happened to make neither a good nor a capable ruler. His reign was followed by nearly a hundred years of recurring civil wars, during which the military group made and unmade various emperors so fast that the position of emperor became of lesser consequence. The result was the imperial government was disastrously weakened and the people were impoverished.

Rome was no longer enlarging her territories, but was now on the defensive. This internal strife made it all the harder to defend the empire from barbarian invaders. She suffered both from the warfare of her own political groups and from the foreign invaders. The power of the empire was breaking down.

THE ARCH OF CONSTANTINE

This arch was erected in Rome in A.D. 315, in honor of the victory of Constantine the Great over another emperor, Maxentius. It is one of the many triumphal arches erected in honor of Roman heroes and rulers. Triumphal marches passed from the Appian Way through the Arch of Constantine into the city of Rome.

Diocletian helped to restore the power of the empire. At last in A.D. 285 there came into power a strong emperor, Diocletian [dai'oh klee'sh'n]. Diocletian strengthened and reorganized the imperial government so that it was as autocratic as that of an oriental monarch. He surrounded himself with pomp and splendor. For a time he lived in Asia Minor rather than in Rome, and divided the rule among four co-emperors, with himself the final authority. Diocletian did keep the empire strong, but the expense of his many officials was almost more than the heavily taxed people could bear.

Constantine presided over a crumbling empire. Diocletian left the position of emperor, that is, abdicated, in 305. His rule was followed by twenty years of civil war. As many as six men,

including Diocletian's recent co-emperors, claimed the throne. The victor was Constantine [kahn'stan tain]. As ruler of the whole empire, Constantine found himself in a difficult situation. Diocletian had followed the custom of hiring German mercenaries to keep out their fellow Germans. Such a policy had proved somewhat unsuccessful. More and more German barbarian peoples seemed to be infiltrating into Italy. These German immigrants complained about the high taxes and other abuses even more forcibly than the native Romans.

Constantine moved his capital to a city in Turkey which he renamed Constantinople [kahn'stan ti noh'p'l], and left to a co-emperor in Rome the difficult task of ruling over the western part of the Roman Empire. Upon Constantine's death the empire was divided among his three sons. They plunged into civil war against each other. From then on the empire tended to break into pieces.

The last emperor to rule over both the eastern and the western part of the empire died in A.D. 395. After that, for a time, the Romans kept up the fiction of one undivided Roman Empire. But for purposes of government the empire was divided into two parts with the western capital at Rome and the eastern capital at Constantinople.

It should be clearly understood that Rome had been declining for years. There were many reasons, as we have seen. Not only had the seat of the government of the whole empire been split into the western and eastern centers, but there were also many other factors. Slave and free labor conflicted and that mean the end of economic freedom for th lower classes, farmers, merchants, an the like. A crushing burden of taxes t support the vast empire fell on the mas of people, and on the wealthy when th latter could not evade it. A number o weak rulers, who tolerated a corrupt o ficialdom, weakened the structure o government. The infiltration of migrat ing barbarians, gradually but steadily changed the nature of the population And, as we shall see, vigorous fighting men of the barbarian hordes on the fron tiers of the empire were attacking and pushing in at any sign of weakness Rome therefore fell partly by its own weight and partly because of new peo ples who were ready to take it over.

Chapter 5 ~ A Weakened Rome Yielded to Barbarians

The northern barbarians pushed into Italy. The storm which was to destroy Rome finally swept down from the north and northeast. There lived the fierce German barbarian tribes. A Roman historian tells us something of these people. They were giants in size, with blue eyes and blond or red hair. They loved warfare, and laughed at wounds and even at death itself.

When the fighting begins, it is shameful for a chief to be outdone in bravery, and equally shameful for the followers not to match the bravery of the chief: to survive one's chief and to return from battle is a foul disgrace which lasts as long as life.

When they are not fighting, they spend little time in hunting, much more in doing nothing. They devote themselves to sleeping and eating. Even the bravest and most warlike are quite idle, for they give over the care of the house and fields to the women and the old men . . . they love idlenes yet hate peace.

Besides being gluttonous eaters, these early Germans drank heavily. They sometimes gambled away everything they possessed, even staking their liberty on a single game.

But the German barbarians had other and better characteristics; they were brave, their love of liberty was strong and they were an honest people. To quote our historian again:

Almost alone among the barbarians they are content with one wife. No one in Germany laughs at vice, nor is it the fashion to corrupt and be corrupted. Good habits are here more effectual than good laws elsewhere.

Although the Romans built high walls to keep them out of the empire, the Germans gradually drifted across the frontiers. Attracted by the warm, sunny country and the luxurious life of the Romans, they pushed their way into Italy. Some settled down to till the soil; others became servants; still others joined the Roman army.

The barbarians defeated the Roman army. In the Fourth Century a tribe of Germans called the Visigoths [viz'i-gahths] were settled on the north bank of the Danube River. They begged the Romans to let them cross the river to seek safety from their enemies. They told stories of a fierce people called Huns who came from Asia and who had swept over eastern Europe like a destructive tornado. These Huns were little men with "big heads and small pig eyes." Their nostrils were so short and broad that the people of Europe said they had two holes in their faces. The terrified Visigoths thought that the Huns were either beasts or children of witches and demons.

In answer to the imploring message of the Visigoths, the Roman emperor, during the latter part of the Fourth Century, sent permission for them to come into Roman territory. Great numbers of Goths are thought to have crossed the Danube to the south and west. All might have gone well, but the Roman officers who were sent to protect the Germans, instead robbed and mistreated them. Angered by this injustice, the barbarians came to blows with the soldiers. In a battle fought at Adrianople [ay'dri uh-noh'p'l] in A.D. 378 the Roman army was routed and the emperor slain. The barbarians had proved their strength. The new emperor of the Eastern Roman Empire was able to persuade the Visigoths to turn toward Italy and Rome instead of pressing on to Constantinople. Now it was only a matter of years until they would conquer the western half of the empire.

Alaric plundered the city of Rome. A few years later a powerful leader, Alaric [al'uh rik], arose among the Goths. He gathered his men together and swept

Brown Brothers

ALARIC PLUNDERING THE CITY OF ROME

Rome, for so long the center of civilization and ruler of the world, fell to the invading Visigoths led by Alaric. He is pictured here as the central figure, on horseback.

Drawing by John C. Wonsetler

ATTILA THE HUN

The savage, Mongolian-featured Attila had no respect for Western civilization. The Hun
and his horse made a powerful mobile unit of destruction.

down through Greece. After Corinth and Sparta had been ravaged, Alaric advanced on Rome. For days the barbarians besieged the city. At last the starving people sent out a messenger to ask Alaric his terms. "Give me all your gold, all your silver, and all your movable property," said Alaric. "What will be left to us?" "Your lives," was the haughty answer.

When Alaric allowed his followers to enter and plunder the city of Rome, the world was horrified and dismayed. Though Rome was no longer at the height of her power, many had believed her to be unconquerable. For the first ime people saw that the Roman world could fall. There were to be similar times in later history, when people could scarcely believe that a great power could be reduced. The spell of Rome was broken.

Alaric marched southward, carrying his rich booty with him. But this barbarian — who had mastered Italy, conquered southwestern Gaul (now part of France), and established his kingdom there — was not to have many more years to live.

The Huns overran Europe. About 450 the terrible Huns from Asia, who had settled in what is now Hungary, began to plunder far and wide. Their bold leader was Attila [at'i luh]. So complete was the destruction that he left behind him, Attila is said to have boasted that grass never grew where the hoof of his horse had trod.

At first the Roman emperors tried to bribe the Huns not to invade Roman territory, but Attila was not to be satisfied with so small a reward. The invaders mounted their horses, drew their swords, and advanced into Gaul. The Romans and the Goths feared Attila so greatly that they decided to join forces to withstand him. Those combined forces defeated Attila in Gaul. Thousands were slaughtered in this fierce battle. Only the coming of night saved Attila from being taken by his enemies. Next morning the Huns retreated eastward and a few years later they returned to Asia from whence they had come into Europe.

Other barbarians destroyed and ravaged Italy. Encouraged by the success of Alaric and his Goths in their conflicts with the Romans, many other barbarian tribes had penetrated into the Roman Empire. Thousands of crude, uncivilized German barbarians roamed through Italy, sometimes burning, stealing, and ravaging. One group, the Vandals, sailed from North Africa across to Italy, plundered Rome, and returned.

For years Germanic, or Gothic, officers in the Roman army had been setting up their own puppet emperors in Rome. At last one of the Germanic high officers decided to make himself the ruler. He deposed the last of the Roman emperors in the West. This man who had been an officer in the Roman army was Odoacer [oh'doh ay'ser]. He became ruler of all Italy. This final blow to the Roman Empire was in 476. The Western Empire had fallen. The eastern portion, known as the Eastern Roman Empire, continued to exist many centuries with its capital at Constantinople, but never again was Rome, the " Eternal City," to hold the central position in a great empire.

The Dark Ages closed in upon Italy. For three centuries after the fall of Rome, the civilization of Europe gave way to barbarism. Time and time again cities and villages were burned and plundered by new hordes of barbarians from the north and east. The fields of Italy which had once raised food for the people were now overgrown with weeds. Most of the livestock was killed. Roads crumbled and bridges fell. Highwaymen lurked in shadowy places to rob the traveler. Pirates made the Mediterranean Sea unsafe for commerce. Law and order seemed to disappear entirely from the European world. The centuries following the fall of Rome were dark indeed as far as the progress of civilization was concerned. In the story of the feudal world we shall see how the Church alone remained the guardian of learning and later, in the story of the Renaissance, how Europe once again awoke to make new progress.

Chapter 6 ~ Roman Life Reflected the Fortunes of the Roman State

The Roman father was the head of the family. The Romans did not spend all their time as soldiers conquering the world. Neither did they give all of their attention to organizing and ruling the provinces they conquered. There was plenty of time left to spend at the public games, at home, or in the country. Like other people, the Romans had many interests besides war.

From the earliest time the family was the most important and sacred of all the Roman institutions. The Roman family was larger than the families of today because it included not only the parents and unmarried children, but the married sons and their wives and children. The father was the undisputed ruler of the family.

The Roman wife was highly honored. She shared her husband's interests and had more privileges than the women of Greece. Greek women were seldom allowed outside the women's quarters and were almost never seen on the streets. A Roman matron entertained her guests, sat beside her husband at the table, did the buying in the market place, and rode about town in her chariot. In time Roman women were granted the right to hold property. Roman women did not themselves have the right to vote, but Cato complained that they were openly campaigning and influencing elections.

Drawing by John C. Wonsetler

A ROMAN BRIDE

This Roman girl is admiring her jewels and her wedding gown in a mirror made of highly polished bronze. Notice the Roman lamp on the table, and the jars which contain cosmetic preparations. From the furnishings, this appears to be a well-to-do home.

The Romans made the Greek gods their own. The father had charge of all the religious ceremonies for the family. Each day all the members of the household gathered around the hearth to worship their gods. The early Romans had a simple religion suited to their agricultural life. They worshiped various spirits of nature, but they did not at first picture these spirits as existing in the form of men or women.

Later the Romans borrowed many of their ideas about the gods from the Greeks. (Turn again to page 155 to find what the Greeks believed about some of their gods and goddesses.) The Romans had almost the same beliefs, though they changed the names which the Greeks had given to the gods. They worshiped Jupiter as king of the gods, who hurled the thunderbolt and held the forked lightning in his hand. Mars was the god of war; Juno, the wife of Jupiter and the protectress of women; Neptune, the ruler of the waters; Mercury, the messenger of the gods; and Venus, the queen of love and beauty. During the days of the empire, Rome tolerated in the city the public worship of the gods of all lands. But everyone was also compelled to revere the statue of the emperor.

Vesta protected the hearth and household life. One of the most honored of the goddesses was Vesta, protectress of the hearth, who watched over the household. Her symbol was the fire which glowed upon the hearthstone. Temples were built in her honor. Six maidens chosen to be her priestesses saw to it that the sacred fires in these temples never died out. These girls promised to remain unmarried for the thirty years in which their lives were dedicated to Vesta. All honor and respect were given to the Vestal Virgins, because the safety and pros-

The University Prints, Newton, Massachusetts

MARS

Mars, the Roman god of war, is shown in this reproduction of a Roman statue. "Mars" was the name under which the Romans revered the Greek god Ares.

perity of the city was believed to depend upon the faithfulness with which they performed their duties and kept their vows.

The Romans believed in signs and omens. The Romans looked upon worship as a sort of contract or bargain with their gods. They believed that their prayers would be answered if they prayed at the right time, in the right place, and with the proper form. When a man wanted to receive favors from a god, he would promise to do certain things, such as make gifts to the god if his prayers were answered. The Romans believed that they would be punished if they failed to make proper sacrifices, but that many favors would come to them if they gave due respect to the gods.

You will remember the oracle of Delphi from the story of Greece. The Ro-

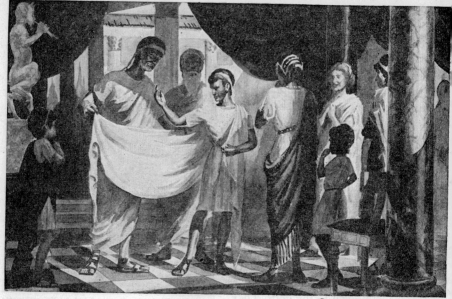

Drawing by John C. Wonsetler

THE TOGA OF MANHOOD

At sixteen, the Roman boy put on the pure white toga of manhood. All members of the household celebrated the occasion. Until then he had worn a toga with a purple border. The word toga comes from a Latin word "tego" meaning "I cover."

mans also had great faith in oracles. Too, they thought the future was revealed in such things as the flight of birds, the appearance of a comet in the sky, or the croaking of a raven. The entrails of a sheep which had been killed for sacrifice were carefully examined in the belief that something about them would foretell coming events.

A Roman spent a full day. Roman trade flourished after the defeat of Carthage, and in the first two hundred years of the Empire, Rome was a thriving center of business and government. A day began early in Rome. It was not unusual for a Roman to rise at five in the morning and have most of his day's letter writing done before breakfast. Then about nine he would descend to the Forum, which was an open market place or square in the lower part of the city. The Forum was surrounded by temples, colonnades,

and large, elaborately designed buildings for the use of judges and merchants. In or near the Forum a man could count on finding anyone of consequence with whom he would have business or political dealings. Much business was transacted in the Forum.

In the middle of the day the Roman would return to his home for a light lunch, followed by a nap. Then, if he were well-to-do, he would probably spend the afternoon in the gymnasium or in the public exercise field, have his bath, either at home or in the magnificent public baths, and be ready for dinner.

The Roman matron spent part of her time supervising work in her household, looking after her own and the children's clothes, training and caring for the younger children, shopping, marketing, no doubt gossiping a bit with her

Drawing by John C. Wonsetler

A ROMAN SLAVE MARKET

The slaves waiting in the market to be bought would be purchased for many purposes. Some would act as personal servants; others would spin and weave and make shoes. Some, if they were gifted, might teach the children of their owners, or entertain the household with music.

friends, and furthering her husband's and her own social life.

Dinnertime in a Roman home was made as pleasant as possible, and the time after dinner was given over to relaxation and sociability. People might enjoy music or poetry or might discuss with their guests the latest plays or translations from the Greek or the latest political developments in the empire.

Rome was an out-of-door city. Because of the mild climate of Rome, much of the life was carried on out-of-doors, particularly in the summer. The Forum, like some of our city parks, was a place for discussion and argument. Public orations were sometimes delivered out-of-doors. Rome contained numerous open-air amphitheaters for plays or public games. And in the mild evenings the young people enjoyed strolling, as is always true, along the banks of the Tiber River.

Roman education was thorough. In the early days of the Republic, parents taught their own children in the home. The children learned reading, writing, arithmetic, and courteous behavior. Mothers taught their girls to be good housekeepers. The boys were taught Roman history by their fathers and given an understanding of Roman law and government.

Later, in the larger cities, the government provided schools. Both boys and girls were sent to school at the age of six or seven to learn to read and write. This first school covered about six years and was something like our elementary school.

At the age of twelve the boys went on to another school where they learned rhetoric and oratory. Every Roman citizen was expected to be able to present his own case in court and perhaps speak his mind in public assemblies. The boys

A ROMAN BANQUET

The Romans who spent hours reclining at luxurious banquets, eating elaborate foods, and being entertained by musicians, were not the sterner men who had built the empire.

also studied Greek and Latin literature; Latin, of course, was their native language; it was the speech they heard daily.

A more advanced school, which the boys entered at fifteen, was attended largely by those who were being trained to become public leaders. There the boys continued their study of oratory and learned Roman law and history as well. Some studied medicine, mechanics, or music. A few boys of wealthier families were sent on to finish their education at the universities of Alexandria in Egypt and of Athens in Greece.

Roman life lost its early simplicity. During the earlier days of Rome's history her people lived a simple, hardy life. One cannot read about the early citizens of Rome without respecting their vigor, simplicity, and determination. In time, however, the Romans lost many of their virtues. As we have seen, the wars in the East brought great wealth

and many slaves into Rome, so that many people did not have to work hard for a living. There was plenty of time for play and amusement. Well-to-do young people spent most of their days at the public bath, the circus, and the banquet. With life a continual round of pleasure, and little work to balance the play, the Romans became soft and dissipated.

It should be understood that these conditions were true not only in the city of Rome, itself, but in many parts of the Roman Empire. Wherever large groups of people lived in communities, the middle and wealthy class lived somewhat as described. The Romans might once have been Gauls, Germans, Greeks, or peoples of the Near East. But Roman citizenship was gradually extended throughout the empire and all these people came to be citizens of Rome, with the privileges and duties of such citizens.

Their accomplishments in trade, politics, and the fine arts thus became Roman achievements. Likewise their failures and their vices were also those of Romans. Hence Roman civilization was a grand mixture of the contributions of all ancient peoples.

Captive slaves became a curse to Rome. The bringing of thousands of captive slaves into Rome naturally affected daily life in many ways. The slaves did almost everything for the master. They prepared his food in the kitchen. They waited on his table. They played music on the lyre while he reclined on a couch to eat his dinner. With everything done for the well-to-do Romans, it is little wonder they grew increasingly soft and easygoing.

Conditions among the slaves were almost unbelievable. In the eyes of the law they had no rights. The master might punish them in any manner he chose, even flog them to death. So that they could be easily recognized, slaves were not allowed to wear the same kind of clothing as free citizens. They could not marry without the consent of their owners. To keep them from running away, they were often chained together as they toiled in the fields. The attitude of most Romans toward their slaves was well expressed by the prominent Roman statesman, Cato, when he said, " Worn-out cattle, sick sheep, broken tools, old and sick slaves, and all other useless things should be sold." This attitude toward less-privileged people has re-

Drawing by John C. Wonsetler

PLAN OF A ROMAN HOUSE

Like the Greek house, the Roman house contained small windowless rooms opening on a court. The Roman house, however, was likely to have two courts — the atrium [ay'tri'm] and the peristyle. These were open, as shown in the small-scale model at the right. The parts of a Roman house are designated as follows in this drawing: *a.* shop; 1. entrance; 2. stairway to upper floor; 3. porter's room; 4. atrium; 5. master's room; 6. sleeping room; 7. wing or ala; 8. sleeping room; 9. passage; 10. peristyle; 11. shrine for household gods; 12. sleeping room; 13. back door; 14. kitchen; 15. dining room.

Brown Brothers

A GLADIATORIAL COMBAT

The spectators decree, by pointing "thumbs down," that the victor shall put his vanquished opponent to death. Note that the Vestal Virgins join in this demand while the emperor calmly looks on.

curred again and again throughout history. As we know, the Nazis in World War II showed this same kind of attitude in their treatment of conquered peoples.

There were vast differences in the position and treatment of slaves. Well-educated household slaves often served as tutors or as advisers and agents to the master and were given many privileges. Slaves from the commercial countries of the Near East sometimes managed their master's business and were permitted to do a little business on their own. Skilled artisans were also sometimes permitted to keep part of their wages. But for the most part the lot of a captive sold into slavery was bitter, indeed. The slave in the city could sometimes earn enough money to buy his freedom. But there was

in the country little hope for the slave. If he ran away there was small chance for him to escape undetected. If he were caught and returned to his master he would have the letter *F* for *Fugitivus,* meaning "fugitive," branded on his forehead with a red-hot iron. He might even be nailed to a cross and crucified as an example to the rest of the slaves. We must remember that some of the slaves, educated Greeks for example, were far more learned and cultured than their masters. They were slaves simply because their lands had been conquered and they had been made captives.

Most of the independent small farmers, who had fought the battles of Rome and had made her the ruler of the Western world, lost their fine spirit of independence as it became harder and harder for them to make a living against slave competition. Thus the poor freemen became idle and troublesome. They even depended upon the state for their food since it had become the custom in Rome regularly to distribute free food to the masses. The common people grew lazy.

The homes of the wealthy were beautiful. While the great mass of the population under the later empire existed in squalor, poverty, and misery, the wealthy class lived in luxury. This was true of cities all through the empire. Pompeii [pahm pay'ee] is an example of a smaller city whose ruins showed evidence of luxury such as Europe would not see again until the 18th Century. Instead of the old-fashioned Roman houses that had had but one room with a square hole in the middle of the roof for the smoke to pass out, the wealthy throughout the empire began to build more elaborate structures with many rooms. Fine mosaic work, bronze statues, Greek paintings, inlaid furniture, rich hangings, and carpets from the East now made the homes of the wealthy the most luxurious that had ever been built. In the kitchen could be found running water, pipes carrying warm air to other rooms, shining bronze pans and kettles. A plan of a Roman house is shown on page 205.

Tenement districts developed. In sharp contrast were the living conditions of the poor, who were crowded into miserable houses of several stories which commonly faced on narrow, dirty streets. The tenement house, with its lack of sanitation, space, and privacy, had appeared. Thus we see that the Romans had housing problems much like those of our own large cities today.

Graft undermined Roman statesmanship. There were periods in the history of Rome when civic honesty was the

The University Prints, Newton, Mass.

THE SEATED BOXER

This bronze statue of a boxer was made in the First Century B.C. The boxing gloves of this period reached almost to the elbow. This boxer has had his nose broken in one of his bouts.

rule. During less fortunate periods, such as the last days of the Republic or the later days of the Empire, corruption was felt even in the distant provinces. Roman officials and governors practiced graft, and took money that was not rightfully theirs. Also, in order to win elections, Romans would frequently spend huge sums on elaborate public entertainments and in bribing the voters.

The Roman found amusement at the Colosseum. Today when a player is hurt in a football game the sympathy of the crowd generally goes out to the injured man. This was not true of the Roman people. Romans went to the Colosseum to watch others suffer and even die violently.

Hand-to-hand combats between two captives were often held for the amusement of the populace. For a time only slaves or condemned criminals were matched against each other. Sometimes these unfortunate men were promised their freedom if they proved their bravery in many combats. Soon the people grew tired of seeing unskilled fighters. Schools were established where men were taught how to fight more expertly. These combatants came to be known as gladiators, from the Latin word *gladius* meaning " sword."

Gladiatorial combats were usually held in the huge Colosseum which seated thousands. Though practically in ruins, it is still used occasionally for very large gatherings.

Not satisfied with combats between gladiators, the Romans arranged fights between wild animals or between men and ferocious beasts. In later times the persecuted Christians were often sent unprotected into the arena to fight hunger-maddened beasts. In this manner the Romans celebrated a holiday — a " Roman holiday," as we use the term.

Chapter 7 ~ Rome Passed on the Torch of Civilization

The Roman Empire established order in a world of confusion. Rome did more than conquer the ancient world; she organized it. She brought peace as well as war to western Europe and the lands surrounding the Mediterranean Sea.

But what is of greatest significance is that Rome spread civilization. True, we may call it Roman civilization, but it was more than Roman. It included the learning of the Greeks, the skills of the Phoenicians, the ideas of the Hebrews, and elements of civilization from both Mesopotamia and Egypt. Moreover, the barbarians from the north and east also contributed to what we call Roman civilization. Yet it was the Roman Empire that spread the culture of the ancient world.

For the first time in the story of civilization we find a period during which all people of the Western world were living in peace. From the time of Augustus until the fall of Rome in the Fifth Century, Rome ruled the world. Except

for the brief struggles for the throne which followed the death of Nero, the people of the Western world lived in peace for nearly two hundred years. The smaller nations, instead of bringing about their own destruction by warring among themselves, had been forced to accept the rule of the Roman Empire. Those who lived within the Empire merged their nationality with that of Romans and became Roman citizens.

After the last of the " Good Emperors," barbarian invasions and repeated wars for the throne weakened the power of the Empire. By the time Rome was extending citizenship to all freemen in the Empire, her power had already weakened to such a degree that Roman citizenship no longer gave a man the legal protection which it would have insured in an earlier day.

Although the Roman rule of conquered peoples has often been pictured as cruel, it was more just than that of any conqueror before her day, and more just than that of some conquerors since ancient times. The peoples conquered by the Romans were usually allowed to keep their native culture, religion, and customs, and much of their local government. Thus the Romans proved their ability not only to make laws but to rule wisely.

Rome gave the Western world a code of laws. The Greeks, who loved beauty and wisdom, made their greatest contributions in art, sculpture, architecture, drama, and philosophy. In contrast to the Greeks, the Romans were less imaginative and more worldly. They are remembered particularly for their achievements in engineering and architecture, and in government and law.

The Romans loved order in the home, where the father's authority was supreme but where everyone had a part and had a keen sense of duty in performing that part. These same traits — a respect for authority and a sense of duty — are found in their community life and government. Law among the Germanic tribes had consisted largely of a set of rules providing vengeance or repayment for injury. Roman statesmen developed laws which would help to bring about a fair settlement of disputes. The Roman courts were interested in justice; they tried to learn the truth and consider the merit of each case. Roman law had changed and expanded greatly since the plebeians had won their struggle to have the original Twelve Tables written down. As the years passed, Roman laws were not to be found in any one place or in any one set of books, but were scattered through the records of the courts and the decisions of judges over a period of many years. It was not until 530, during the reign of Justinian [juhs-tin'i'n], one of the last great rulers of the Eastern Empire, that the Roman laws were collected and organized into a code. This Justinian Code became the basis of the laws of many of the civilized countries of the Western world.

Roman engineering. The Appian [ap' i'n] Way is one of the most famous roads built by the Romans. This great highway led south and east from one of the gates of Rome. It was paved with huge blocks of lava laid on a foundation made of a kind of concrete. The Romans had discovered how to make a mortar, by mixing lime and volcanic soil, which would hold stones in one hard mass. Portions of the Appian Way, built in this way more than two thousand years ago, are still in use. In World War II many Americans walked along the Appian Way.

The Appian Way is only one of many fine roads constructed by the Romans. By means of these highways various parts of the empire were connected with the city of Rome. The saying, "All roads lead to Rome" really has some meaning. These roads, intended for military purposes, were also used for commerce, so that Rome became a center of travel and trade. Roads made it possible to extend Roman rule and trade. Wherever Roman legions were established in conquered territory, Roman engineering as well as Roman law was brought to the native people.

Besides building great networks of highways, the Roman engineers drained marshes and built bridges and docks. The ruins of the Claudian [klaw'di'n] Aqueduct also bear witness to engineering genius. Ten such great aqueducts supplied the city of Rome with water carried through tunnels, in stone-protected beds, and across ravines and narrow valleys. Some sources of water were more than sixty miles from the city. These aqueducts were so well built that two of them are still in use. The remains of many of the old Roman roads and aqueducts may still be seen not only in Italy but in France and Spain and other countries once under Roman rule.

Roman artistry found expression in architecture. The Romans never equalled the Greeks in painting and sculpture. The realistic Roman sculpture and the Roman bas-reliefs depicting the deeds of soldier-emperors are rightly famous, but Rome made a far greater contribution to architecture.

In architecture, the Romans adopted the columns of the Greek and combined with them the Etruscan idea of the arch. The arch, with its keystone, was perfected by Roman builders. They used the arch extensively in vaultings and huge domes, and for the support of the channels of the great Roman aqueducts. The use of the arch and the vaulted dome might be seen in the many temples of Rome dedicated to different gods of many lands. The most famous of these was the Pantheon [pan thee"n], a temple dedicated to all the gods.

The temples and other public buildings in Greece were extremely beautiful but are quite small when compared with the large structures erected by Roman genius. Credit is due to the Romans for renewing interest in large-scale building, first done by the Egyptians, and for passing on much knowledge to the architects of a later date. The use of concrete as a building material, as well as the use of the arch, made the large buildings of the Romans possible. Instead of building with solid blocks of marble the Romans used only slabs of this fine building material as a facing for their buildings.

The abundant supply of water made possible magnificent public baths. These buildings included lounges, reading rooms, gymnasiums, and sometimes museums and libraries. Public baths and other large buildings were erected in many of the cities and villages of the empire from North Africa to the British Isles and from Spain to the Near East.

The gigantic Circus Maximus, built for chariot races and public games, was over 2000 feet long and seated about 250,000 spectators. The Colosseum, one of the largest of the Roman open-air theaters, seated about 50,000 persons.

Rome preserved Greek culture and learning. It has been said that "into Rome all the life of the ancient world was gathered; out of Rome all the life of the modern world arose." To the credit of Rome, she seldom destroyed the civilizations of the peoples whom she conquered. Indeed, she often copied the best that she found in them.

The Romans collected and arranged the medical works of the Greeks. They themselves organized a public-health system, and a hospital system which first grew up in connection with the army.

Greek slaves were brought to Rome to educate the children. Greek comedies were translated into Latin so they might be enjoyed in the theaters. The Romans also wrote comedies in imitation of the Greek ones. Greek statues and other works of art were carried away by the Roman conquerers as part of the valued plunder in their triumphs. To a large extent Rome preserved for the modern world the culture which the Greeks had originated.

The practical bent of the Romans may be seen in their literature. At first Roman writers did little more than translate or imitate the works of Greek authors. After they had broken away somewhat from the influence of the Greeks, Roman writers turned their attention toward problems of the day. They wrote books on grammar, rheto-

THE APPIAN WAY

This ancient highway leading to Rome is still in use. The ruins of tombs stand beside the road.

ric, oratory, geography, natural history, medicine, agriculture, military tactics, and many other subjects.

Rome also had historians, poets, and other writers of literature. Cicero, one of Rome's greatest orators, delivered a number of orations which are still famous. They are models of the best form of Latin composition and are read in high-school and college Latin classes today. He also wrote letters which give us a glimpse of the daily life of the upper-class Romans of his day.

Julius Caesar wrote a description of his military campaigns. These writings are called *Commentaries on the Gallic Wars*. Two other historians won recognition among Roman writers. One of these was Livy, who wrote a complete history of Rome, most of which has been lost. The other was Tacitus [tas'i tuhs], who gives us a picture of conditions in Rome during the days of the emperors and our only full description of the life and customs of the early German barbarians.

Vergil [ver'jil], Horace, and Ovid [ahv'id] are three of Rome's greatest poets. In his *Aeneid* [i nee'id], Vergil relates the Roman myths. His poetry is read by many students of Latin today. Horace wrote odes and satires (literary compositions making fun of abuses or vices). His odes have been imitated in many languages for centuries and have had considerable influence on English poetry. The satire was about the only form of Roman literature that was not copied from the Greeks. The poetry of Ovid was influenced by the imagination of the Greeks. In turn Ovid's writings have influenced the literature written centuries later. His works were probably more extensively read by such English writers as Spenser, Shakespeare, and Milton than those of any other ancient author. The Roman authors not only helped to preserve and arouse interest in Greek literature, but added their contribution to the literary heritage of civilization.

Latin became the language of the Western world. During the five hundred years Rome ruled the world, her language was spread over all parts of the empire. A popular form of Latin gradually displaced the languages previously used in most of the conquered provinces. To protect their rights in the courts or to trade with the Roman merchants, the Roman colonists found it desirable to know Latin. Thus the Latin language, as well as the Roman army, helped to bind Rome and her provinces into one great state. In a later story we shall learn that Latin became the language of the scholar, of the courts, and of the Church in the Middle Ages.

After the fall of Rome, many Roman provinces again became separate nations. Although each developed its own language, Latin influenced them all. Some of these languages, including modern Italian, French, Spanish, and Portuguese, are directly based upon Latin and are therefore known as the Romance languages. That is, they are derived from the language of the Romans. Others, such as English, although they are not so closely related to Latin as are the Romance languages, have borrowed many words traceable to the Latin.

Rome Influenced the World

In this story of Rome we saw a small group of simple people living on the Tiber River near the western coast of the Italian peninsula develop a mighty Empire. At first a more civilized people, the Etruscans, conquered them and ruled them tyrannically. But the Etruscans taught them much about building, craftsmanship, industry, and commerce.

In time the Romans drove out the Etruscans. They then set up a government which was a republic, but it was not what we would call democratic. After a long struggle the people gained a voice in the government.

In the meantime the Romans often had to defend themselves against their quarreling neighbors. They fought many battles and conquered neighboring peoples. Unlike earlier victors, the Romans made the peoples they conquered either citizens or allies of Rome. By 265 B.C. Rome ruled in this way the whole Italian peninsula.

As the power of Rome grew, she came into conflict with the commercial center of Carthage, in Africa. The rivalry and wars with Carthage lasted for more than one hundred years, but in the end Carthage was completely destroyed.

Rome had been extending her power in the Mediterranean even before the final destruction of Carthage. Greece was taken, then gradually portions of Asia Minor fell to Rome. Syria and Palestine followed, and the rich land of Egypt. By the time of Augustus, Rome ruled Spain and France, southeastern Europe up to the Danube River, the Near East, Egypt, and North Africa.

In the meantime, the representative government of Rome had, in practice, given way to the control of the senatorial class. For years this class gave Rome efficient rule. But in time it became corrupt and began to use its great power selfishly and unwisely. Other great changes had taken place in Rome and throughout Italy during the years of warfare and empire building. Captives of war were brought into Italy. Free farmers and laborers suffered from slave competition; land was bought up by a few rich men; and serfdom increased.

The nobility met any attempt at reform with violence. No reform could be made in Rome unless the reformer had an army behind him. Civil war broke out between military champions of the people and those of the nobles. Then in 48 B.C. Julius Caesar, the general who had been subduing Gaul, marched on Rome with his legions and made himself dictator. Although Caesar ruled only a short time before he was assassinated, he started a number of popular reforms. Neither Caesar nor Augustus, who followed him, changed the outward form of government, but in reality Rome was no longer a republic but an empire. There was a real change in the method of carrying out the laws, and actually a great improvement in the government of the provinces.

For about two centuries the Roman Empire flourished. An orderly government kept the world at peace; cities grew, trade flourished, and schools were maintained. It was during this period of peace that the Romans showed their genius in government both at home and in the provinces.

During the last three centuries of the Empire, Roman civilization declined. The army made and unmade emperors and there were numerous wars for the throne. The people became poorer and the government became more corrupt and expensive. German barbarians were admitted to Roman territory and began to hold important positions in the army and even in the government. Also, the Empire was tending to break into two parts, the Eastern and the Western. Two strong emperors, Diocletian and Constantine, restored order and strengthened the government for a time. Diocletian lived in Asia Minor part of the time, and Constantine made his capital in the East at Constantinople, now Istanbul [is tan bool'], leaving a co-emperor in Rome to rule the West.

The German barbarians within and without Italy grew stronger and more threatening. Finally they defeated the Roman army, and crowned a German in Rome king of Italy. The Western Empire had fallen. Only the Eastern Empire remained, with its capital at Constantinople.

Life in Rome during the earlier years of the Republic showed a marked contrast with her wealthier days of the Empire. In the earlier days home life was simple and wholesome. The Romans adopted the Greek gods, but gave them Roman names. The goddess Vesta, who protected the home, was one of the most honored.

As Rome grew to be an empire, the Romans lost many of their virtues. The upper class lived in lavish extravagance and luxury. Slave labor further weakened the people. The poor through enforced idleness grew corrupt and lazy.

The Roman Empire broke up, but in time modern nations sprang up from its ruins. The Latin language became the basis for the Romance languages—French, Spanish, Portuguese, Italian, Romanian—and other languages adopted many Latin words. Rome preserved the culture and learning of Greece for later civilizations through the writings of her great authors. She also contributed much knowledge of her own in engineering and in architecture, particularly in developing the arch. But perhaps the greatest contribution of the ancient Romans to civilization is Roman law.

SELF-TEST

Look back on the story of Rome by testing yourself on these questions.

In the following brief sketch of the story of Rome you will find different kinds of statements. Some of these you are to recognize as true or false, others you are to complete, some are to be arranged in proper time order, and in still others you are to choose the correct response from a number of words. Do whatever the test calls for. *Do not mark your book.*

I.

1. There are legends, but few known facts, about the origin of Rome (T or F?).
2. The city of Rome was built on the banks of the —— River, a short distance inland on the (eastern, western) coast of the peninsula.
3. The plebeians had no trouble in gaining a voice in the Roman government (T or F?).
4. By about (700 B.C., 500 B.C., 300 B.C., 100 B.C.) Rome had conquered all of Italy.
5. From that time her commerce grew (T or F?).
6. Rome came into sharp rivalry with the city of —— whose great fighting force was her ——.

7. This city was located on the northern coast of —— and her leader whom the Romans most feared was ——.

8. Rome conquered most of the territories which had belonged in the empire of ——.

9. During the wars with —— the nobility gained control of the —— and for many years really ruled Rome.

10. The —— brothers attempted to make peaceful reforms in Rome but failed.

11. Slave labor in Rome gave the rich greater leisure and threw the poor out of employment (T or F?).

12. Some of the important milestones in the life of Julius Caesar are: (Rearrange in correct order.) (*a*) Gaul, (*b*) "crossing the Rubicon," (*c*) Spain, (*d*) "You, too, Brutus," (*e*) 100 B.C., (*f*) ruler of Rome.

II.

1. A Roman husband would probably have said to his wife, "May I go down to the Forum today?" (T or F?).

2. The Roman style of architecture was very similar to that of the Greeks (T. or F?).

3. Because of their high degree of education the Romans were not superstitious (T or F?).

4. Of the several reasons for the decay of Rome, four significant ones are ——, ——, ——, and ——.

III.

1. The barbarians who first invaded Rome came from (*a*) northern Africa, (*b*) Mesopotamia, (*c*) Phoenicia, (*d*) central Europe.

2. Because the barbarians understood the art and learning of the Romans, they wished to conquer the Romans and thus take over their civilization (T or F?).

3. Alaric at Rome is an example of the foregoing statement (T or F?).

4. The Huns who had come out of ——, and were led by ——, were defeated at the battle of —— about A.D. ——.

5. About A.D. 500 the Roman Empire in western Europe ceased to exist, but a portion of the empire in the Near East continued with its capital at ——.

IV.

1. It can be said truly that for long periods Rome brought peace, not war, to the Western world (T or F?).

2. The —— Code, assembled and brought together Roman laws, which had been changing and developing throughout the Empire (T or F?).

3. Roman engineers and architects built many remarkable things, among

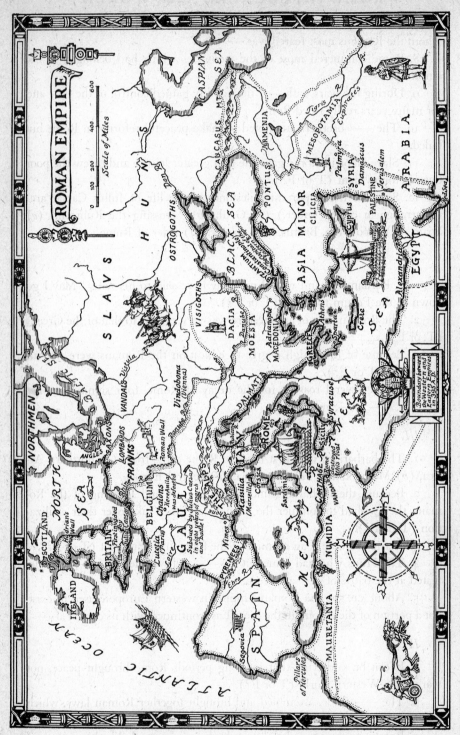

ROMAN EMPIRE

Scale of Miles
0   100   200   400   600

Boundary between
the Western and
Eastern Empire
in 395 A.D.

ATLANTIC OCEAN

NORTHMEN

IRELAND

SCOTLAND
Hadrian's Wall
BRITAIN
First invaded
by Julius Caesar

NORTH SEA

ANGLES
SAXONS
LOMBARDS
FRANKS
BELGIUM
Lutetia (Paris)
Chalons
Nemetacum
was defeated

GAUL
Subdued by Julius Caesar
in eight years of much
fighting and battle

Loire
Nimes
Rhône
PYRENEES
Ebro R.
Segovia
SPAIN
Pillars
of Hercules

Roman Wall
Vindobona
(Vienna)
Danube
VANDALS Vistula

SLAVS

HUNS

OSTROGOTHS
Don R.

CASPIAN SEA

CAUCASUS MTS.
ARMENIA
Tigris
Euphrates

BALTIC SEA

VISIGOTHS

DACIA
MOESIA
Danube
Adrianople
MACEDONIA
GREECE
Athens
Sparta
Crete

BLACK SEA

PONTUS
BYZANTIUM
Constantinople

ASIA MINOR
CILICIA
Cyprus

MESOPOTAMIA
Palmyra
Damascus
SYRIA
PALESTINE
Jerusalem

ARABIA

MEDITERRANEAN SEA

Alexandria
EGYPT

Massilia
(Marseilles)
Corsica
Sardinia
Rome
ITALY
ROME
DALMATIA
Syracuse
Sicily
CARTHAGE
VANDALS
sacked
Rome

NUMIDIA
MAURETANIA

216

which are a road called the —— Way; ——s to supply water; the great —— in Rome where the gladiatorial combats were held; and the —— or temple of the gods with its domed roof.

4. Among the famous writings of the Romans are the orations of —— and the *Commentaries,* by ——. Three famous Roman poets are ——, ——, and ——.

5. Examples of countries speaking Romance languages are (*a*) Norway, (*b*) England, (*c*) France, (*d*) Russia, (*e*) Spain, (*f*) Italy.

V. Study the map of the Roman Empire on the opposite page. Then answer the following questions on a separate sheet of paper.

(1) What nations that you have already studied became a part of the Roman Empire?

(2) What modern nations have grown up in lands that were once part of the Roman Empire?

(3) What works of engineering illustrated in sketches on the map show the widespread influence of the Romans?

(4) What symbol of Roman authority is illustrated in the sketches of the map border?

(5) Name at least ten towns located on the map that are still important cities today.

(6) What type of transportation is shown in the sketches?

(7) What do the sketches of warriors tell you about the armor of that time?

INTERESTING THINGS TO DO

Topics for Talks

1. "The Roman military machine." Why did the Romans find it necessary to develop a strong army? Do modern nations develop powerful military machines for the same reasons or for other reasons?

2. "If I had been a Roman boy (or girl) — " What sort of home, recreation, and education would you have had? Compare and contrast Roman and American family life. Were the pioneer families in America more like the Roman or the Greek families?

3. "The conquest of the Dacians." Trajan was one of Rome's greatest emperors. Tell in your own words the story of how he was able, with the help of his brave courier, Laurentius, to conquer the Dacians. See Chapter 5 in *How They Carried the Mail,* by Joseph Walker.

4. "Blow-by-blow account of a great gladiatorial combat" or "A radio announcer's description of a Roman triumph." Choose one of these topics and imagine it would have been possible for you to broadcast one of the events by radio.

Adventures for the Amateur Author

1. Write an account for an imaginary Roman newspaper of the unexpected approach of Hannibal's army after their crossing of the Alps.

2. Imagine you are a Roman household slave, perhaps a tutor to your master's children, and write a few pages from a diary you might have kept.

3. Suppose you were a soldier who had returned from the war against Carthage and found your farm sold for taxes. Write a letter to your cousin in Rome, explaining your problem and your feelings.

Candidates for Your Album of Famous People

Augustus Caesar, Cicero, Constantine, Diocletian, the Gracchi, Hannibal, Horace, Julius Caesar, Marius, Mark Antony, Ovid, Sulla, Vergil. Choose at least two of the above for biographical portraits for your Album.

INTERESTING READING ABOUT ROME

BENTLEY, PHYLLIS. *Freedom, Farewell!* A story with the downfall of the Roman Empire as background.

BOTSFORD, G. W., and BOTSFORD, L. S. *The Story of Rome as Greeks and Romans Tell It.* Readings from the works of Plutarch, Caesar, Horace, etc.

COLES, MANNING. *Great Caesar's Ghost.* An unusual mystery story that involves two boys in adventures against a background of ancient Roman life and customs.

Compton's Pictured Encyclopedia. "Rome: How Rome Won and Lost the World"; and Index.

DAVIS, W. S. *A Day in Old Rome.* "Augustus wrote out his intended conversation with his wife . . . lest he should say. . . ."

——. *Friend of Caesar.* A story of the adventures of a young Roman.

HAGEDORN, H. *The Book of Courage.* The story of Hannibal.

JOHNSTON, H. W. *The Private Life of the Romans.* An attractive book of information concerning the domestic life of the Romans.

KING, GORDON. *The Rise of Rome.* Great men and important events in the rise of Rome.

SHOWERMAN, G. *Rome and the Romans.* "The diners reclined upon their left elbows, three on a couch, facing the table. . . ."

TAPPAN, E. M. *The Story of the Roman People.* "He provided wild beasts by the hundred and gladiators by the thousand."

VAN LOON, H. *The Story of Mankind.* "They were going to hang him. . . . 'The boy is too young.'"

WALLACE, L. *Ben Hur.* "The people rose and leaped upon the benches, and shouted and screamed. . . ."

The World Book Encyclopedia. "The Story of Rome"; and Index.

PART SEVEN

THE FAITH OF MANKIND IS EXPRESSED
IN MANY DIFFERENT RELIGIONS

A World of Many Faiths

Wᴇ live in a believing world. We do not all worship in the same way, but some form of religious faith is followed by millions of different people all over the world. Naturally, peoples' beliefs and faiths affect their attitudes and their actions. The history of the world's different religions has often affected the history of the nations themselves. So we shall want to learn something about the different great religions in our *Story of Nations*.

The map on the facing page shows a large part of the Eastern hemisphere — just how much you can tell by looking at the globe above. The great religions of mankind originated in Arabia, China, India, and Palestine. Some of them of course have now spread over much of the earth's surface. Compare the globe above with the globe on page 3. Roughly speaking the area in which the great religions originated is much the same as the area in which the oldest remains of early men were found.

Consult the map opposite as you read the story of religions. It will help you follow the story of the religious beliefs which have influenced the story of nations and helped shape the world we live in today.

Chapter 1 ~ We Live in a Believing World

Religion is hard to define. A mother throws her baby into the River Ganges [gan'jeez] in the name of religion; another mother, with a different religion, founds a baby-welfare clinic. The writers of the early parts of the Old Testament thought that Jehovah was a God of Battles; to Jesus he was a loving Father, a God of Peace. Jesus taught one thing, Mohammed [moh hahm'ed] another, and before either of them, Confucius [k'n fyoo'shuhs] and the Buddha [bood'uh] taught their followers still other beliefs.

You may find it hard to think of the beliefs or practices of primitive men as religions. Their rites, bloody sacrifices, and exhausting ceremonial dances were all a part of their worship. To you they may seem crude, foolish, and useless. But suppose you knew nothing of the forces of nature that make wind and rain and lightning and the changes of the seasons. Suppose you saw one of your friends carried away in a raging torrent, blown over a precipice, or struck down by lightning. Suppose you did not know why the volcano roared and belched forth molten lava. Suppose you saw your field of corn, planted to provide food for the winter, drying up for lack of water. Might you not get the idea, as did early men, that there were spirits in everything? Might you not believe that there were good and helpful spirits, with whom it paid to be on friendly terms? Might you not believe also that there were evil and harmful spirits who needed to be favored in order that they would do what you wanted done? These beliefs, which are very natural, still sur-

vive in the form of superstition in many countries. For that matter, we all share them a little. It is hard not to feel at times that there is a living spirit in nature which is personally friendly or spiteful toward us. How often have you heard people say that it would not rain because they wore their rubbers and carried an umbrella? Or that it would probably rain because they were planning a picnic?

When you look at all the world's religions, from the most primitive belief in many spirits to the highest belief in one God, you have a hard time writing a definition that will cover them all. Probably this statement is as good as any other: "Whenever men have felt the experience we call religion, they have believed that there is a power beyond themselves (a God, or gods, or a shaper of destiny) that is of greatest importance in the direction of human affairs. Religion is the attitude of men toward what they regard as divine or all-powerful."

As you will see later in this section, some religions have been founded by a person or else built around a personal founder like Jesus, the Buddha, or Mohammed. Others are what we might call national or racial religions, since they have grown up through thousands of years of history along with the spiritual life of the people and without any special founder. These latter ones are religions like Hinduism [hin'doo iz'm] and Shintoism [shin'toh iz'm].

Religious beliefs were found in the earliest civilizations. Since early man left no written record, we do not know what his beliefs were. Yet, from the round

Wide World Photos

A COUNTRY CHURCH

Everywhere we go we see evidences of man's religious beliefs. Little white churches such as this can be found in all parts of the world. And many thousands of buildings, quite unlike this one, have been built as places of worship.

graves, the many strange stone monuments, and other relics, it is safe to conclude that primitive man had some sort of belief in powers greater than his own. But in early historic times, when man was first able to write down his beliefs, religion played an important part in his life. In their *Book of the Dead* the Egyptians told about their faith in a life after death. The great tombs and massive pyramids, built to house the bodies of ancient pharaohs and nobles, still stand as an expression of this belief. From the myths and hero stories of the ancient Greeks and Romans we learned that they had many gods and goddesses who they thought directed the lives of men and the fate of the world. Again, we

found that the Hebrews who lived in ancient Palestine made a great contribution to religious thought. They were the first to believe that one mighty force, one spiritual God, controlled the world.

Religion is important to modern men. Religion continues to sway the hearts and change the lives of men. We find about us, every day, evidences of religion: in our magnificent churches, in the announcements of services, in the sermons broadcast over the radio. Great hospitals and universities are built in the name of religion. Men travel to distant countries, leaving their friends and families, even enduring persecution, to help spread religious teachings throughout the world. It may be a priest in a leper colony, a missionary in a strange land; everywhere, it seems, the faithful are at work. The spirit of true religion is a power that could bind together all peoples, and make all men brothers.

Millions of people follow great religious leaders. We who live in the United States are likely to think that most of the people in the world are using forms of worship similar to those we find about us. Do you realize that only two-fifths of the earth's inhabitants are Christians and that the other three-fifths have some other religious belief? As a citizen of a nation which stands for freedom of religious belief, you should know more about the beliefs of the millions of people in other parts of the world.

As you will learn, different parts of the world are inhabited by the peoples of these various religions. For example, the Mohammedans cover Asia Minor and northern Africa; Christianity is the principal religion of Europe and the two Americas; and most of the people of China believe in Buddhism [bood'iz'm] or Confucianism [k'n fyoo'sh'n iz'm].

You might start in the interior of India and travel northeast through China for several thousand miles without meeting a human being who has heard of Christmas, Easter, or the story of Jesus. All along the journey you would see reverent men and women worshiping at the jeweled shrines of Buddha or in the temples of Confucius.

If you started just west of India and traveled on westward, over miles of glaring hot sand, past green oases fringed with palm trees, across the peninsula of Arabia, through northern Africa to the place where Europe and Africa almost meet at the Strait of Gibraltar, your whole journey would be through the lands of the Moslems [mahz'luhmz]. They are the followers of Mohammed. Many of these tanned men with turbaned heads are willing to unsheath their weapons and fight to the death in the name of their prophet Mohammed. It is of him they tell their sons as they gather in the evening about the smoldering desert fire.

What would you like to know about the great religions? Perhaps you have seen an oriental prayer rug. Why is it given this name? You may have seen a Chinese tapestry on which there was woven a saying from Confucius. Who was he and why is he honored by the Chinese? Perhaps you have seen the image of Buddha and never suspected that he rendered great service to his people. What did he do to cause the people to make images of him after his death?

Such questions can be answered by learning something about the great religions of the world and the life stories of some of their founders. To find the beginnings of these religions, we turn to the mysterious Orient, their birthplace. Let us go first to India, homeland of Hinduism and Buddhism.

Chapter 2 ~ Hinduism and Buddhism Originated in India

Long ago a new civilization was begun in India. South of the snow-capped Himalaya [hi mah'luh yuh] Mountains of Asia lies the warm, fertile country of India. This land, shaped like a triangle, extends like a wedge south into the tropical waters of the Indian Ocean. Many centuries before the birth of Christ, a certain race of white men — Indo-European tribes, like the forefathers of the Persians, Greeks, and Romans — broke through the passes of the Himalaya Mountains on the north of India. They entered the region along the Indus River. Here they found a climate so warm that little clothing and shelter were needed, and soil so fertile that juicy fruits and leafy vegetables grew without much cultivation. They had no desire to wander farther, and they settled down near the tribes of dark-skinned natives.

For some time the Indo-Europeans and the natives continued to share the region along the Indus River. These peoples together came to be known as Hindus [hin'dooz], from *Hindus,* another spelling of *Indus.* The cultures and customs of the two groups began to merge as the new civilization of the Hindus developed. The Indo-Europeans took the lead in government.

Newcomers to India introduced a caste system. Gradually the Indo-Europeans imposed their codes and customs on the natives' way of life. But they began to fear that their people would mix with the dark natives and lose the pure Indo-European blood strain. They therefore set up rigid social barriers that forbade intermarriage and all business,

social, and religious association. These barriers and taboos gradually developed into a caste system. The Indo-Europeans of course put themselves at the top, and the natives were classified into three lower castes based on occupation.

But the caste system failed to prevent the intermingling of blood of the Indo-Europeans and the natives, as may be seen by looking at the present-day natives of India. Whether of high or low caste, the East Indians commonly have dark eyes, dark skin, and black hair.

Hinduism is the oldest religion of the Far East. Hinduism is one of the most difficult religions to describe in a relatively few words. In trying to tell of its story briefly, a story thirty-five centuries long, we must skip over details and give you only a few of the outstanding characteristics and beliefs.

The origin of Hinduism is not clear. It must have sprung from ignorance, fear, or primitive beliefs as other early religions did. Men felt their weakness against the mysterious powers of nature, and the need of appeasing them. Scholars today divide Hinduism under six or more heads. But we shall present but three, Vedism [vay'diz'm], Brahmanism [brah'm'n iz'm], and Hinduism. Indeed, it would be better to think only of one religion, the major one, Hinduism, which has absorbed many other religions. But Hindus do not call their religion by any of these names. They call their faith simply Arya-Dharma, the Religion of the Aryans.

The Vedas were the religious books of the Brahmans. The pure, ancient "Vedic" religion of the Indo-Europeans

Metropolitan Museum of Art

THE HINDU TRIMURTI

The Trimurti, or three-bodied god, was formed by the merging of Brahma, Vishnu, and Siva. Brahma was the creator; Vishnu, the preserver; and Siva, the destroyer.

who came down into India was founded on writings called the Vedas. These were written fifteen hundred or a thousand years before Christ. They include more than a hundred books of hymns and mystic rituals. Some of these remind us of the most beautiful parts of our Bible. Read, as an example, this poem telling the believer that the light of Brahma, the supreme being, is brighter than any other light. And as you read it, think of an East Indian looking from his open door, past the shining stars, to the light of Brahma:

The sun shines not there, nor the stars;
These lightnings shine not, much less this
    earthly fire!
After him as he shines does everything
    shine.
The whole world is illumined with his
    light.

Others seem contradictory and hard for us Westerners to understand. Read, as an example, this description of Brahma:

The being and the beyond;
Expressible and inexpressible;
Founded and foundationless;
Conscious and unconscious;
Reality and unreality.

There was no idol worship in the Vedas. But the poets who wrote the Vedas would be astonished at the many thousands of gods that are worshiped in India today. The story of how that happened is the story of what happens to any highly spiritual religion which tries to take over spirits and gods and beliefs of other religions.

Hinduism developed from a composite of beliefs. Wherever the home of the Indo-Europeans who came down into India was, whether it was on the Baltic Sea, by the Caspian, or somewhere north of present-day India, these people brought with them their Vedistic religion. It was a religion based on their sacred Scriptures, the Vedas. We can properly call these writings the Hindu Bible. Because Brahma, the One Spirit, the World Soul, was their one god, their religion came to be called Brahmanism.

It happened that these Indo-Europeans who came into India were not content to dominate merely the governmental affairs of the Hindus; they also wanted to direct their religion. The natives worshiped many gods and goddesses, and refused to give them up to embrace the Brahman religion of the Indo-Europeans.

Two of the most popular gods of the natives were Vishnu [vish'noo] and Siva [see'vuh]. In their efforts to convert the natives to Brahmanism, the Indo-Europeans absorbed these two gods into their god Brahma. The Trimurti [tree moor' tee] thus formed was a kind of three-bodied god. It was composed of Brahma, the creator; Vishnu, the preserver; and Siva, the destroyer. With this triple-god the Brahmans were more successful in making converts to their beliefs. The merged or combined religion thus developed came to be known as Hinduism. The Trimurti is pictured on page 226.

Yet the Brahmans themselves continued to worship only Brahma. They became priests directing the Hindu religion. The natives worshiped one, two, or three parts of the combined god, and sometimes other gods as well. Generally today, the Hindus (except the Brahmans) worship Brahma only through the lesser gods, of which there are many.

Hinduism not only has a composite or combined god; it also has complex directions for everyday living. Many of the old native beliefs and customs mixed with the beliefs of the Brahmans. Brahmanism, like Hinduism, is both a religion and a social code of laws; Hinduism has become the religion of the majority of the people of India. About two-thirds of the Indians — over 250,-000,000 — are believers in Hinduism.

The idea of transmigration is part of Hinduism. The Hindus believe in transmigration, or reincarnation — the passing of the soul, when the body dies, into another body. Thus Hindus believe in life in various forms. According to their belief, the soul of the dead escapes to the moon, but soon sinks back again to the earth. The soul then enters another body, that of a person, an animal, or even a plant. If a man had lived a very bad life, he might return as something lesser like a dog, a pig, or a snake. If he had lived a moderately good life, he would, perhaps, return as a person of higher caste. If he had lived a very good life, he might return as a Brahman. And

Metropolitan Museum of Art

KUAN YIN

In China, Kuan Yin is the Buddhist Goddess of mercy. This statue shows her as a gentle, human-looking person, with an intelligent face.

this was the only way a man could become a Brahman — to be reborn after a successful life in some lesser form. Thus Hinduism offers to the members of low caste only a weary perpetual struggle in this life today.

Nirvana and the goddess of mercy are part of the Hindu belief. According to the Brahmans there is only one way to escape this horrible cycle of unending life, and that is by losing one's individual self through absorption into the Great Being. If man could entirely destroy his own desires he would be free, and could escape to Nirvana [ner vah'nuh] or freedom. Nirvana is a state of mind, in the Hindu belief, not a place, like the afterworld of the Greeks.

There is a legend about a girl called Kuan Yin [gwahn yin] who once turned back from the desirable state of Nirvana. After striving for many bitter years to lose herself in the Great Being, Kuan Yin reached the threshold of Nirvana. But there she paused, appalled and dismayed by the cries of anguish from the earth. Horror-stricken, she found she could not go on into Nirvana. So she turned back to the world to accept life once more and to do her part in lessening the sufferings of mankind.

Both Nirvana and Kuan Yin have been absorbed into the religion of Buddhism. Buddhism itself was a heresy, or an offshoot, of Hinduism. You will soon learn more about this religion called Buddhism. These two beliefs — Nirvana and Kuan Yin — are now more important in Buddhism than in Brahmanism. Kuan Yin became the Buddhist goddess of mercy. The next time you see a little statue of her in the home of a friend or in a Chinese store, remember that although she is thought of as the Buddhist goddess of mercy in China, she had her origin in the Brahman religion of India. An image of Kuan Yin appears on page 227.

The caste system determines the life of the untouchables. As the years passed, Hinduism has changed from century to century, taking on new gods and forgetting old ones. But one thing has remained nearly the same. It is the caste system of India.

The caste system did not prevent the intermingling of dark and white peoples, as it was designed to do. Still it did not die out. This unfortunate system, with the high-caste Brahmans at the top and the " untouchables " at the very bottom of the social scale, is still in existence today. The untouchable is an outcast. He is not permitted to be a member of any caste. He is so low on the social scale that a Brahman will not even allow the shadow of one to fall on him as he passes in the street. He believes this would

make him "unclean." A group of untouchables are shown on page 229.

There are more than fifty million untouchables in India today whose living conditions are more like those of animals than of men. These underprivileged people have almost no education, few opportunities, and little hope of any kind. They believe they were fated to live as untouchables because of inadequate behavior in a previous life in a different form, or incarnation. The only way they can improve their lot is by being born again a little higher up in the social and economic scale. Therefore the untouchables are fatalistic about their present living conditions and make no effort to change them. And the caste system promotes this attitude.

In spite of every attempt to change or eliminate the caste system, the people of India have never been able to pull themselves out of the quicksands of religious fear and social taboo which are so much a part of the caste system. The Brahman priests have never wavered from their belief in rigid castes. As in the days of early Brahmanism, the modern Hindu is born into a caste in which he remains throughout his life.

Hinduism is to be condemned for fostering this rigid system. It is responsible for the social backwardness of the Hindus. Because of this fact, India presents a serious problem to the modern world. Such enlightened Hindus as Gandhi [gahn'dee], a modern political leader, have tried to improve conditions among the untouchables. But many devout Hindus have bitterly resisted their proposed reforms. Progress, if any, has been slow. It may take centuries for the Hindus to throw off the binding chains of their caste system. Furthermore, outsiders of other lands have been able to do almost nothing about the caste sys-

Ewing Galloway

UNTOUCHABLES

These ragged people are some of India's fifty million untouchables — so called because to touch them would disgrace the members of the castes. The untouchables are outcasts, condemned by the caste system to live wretchedly in settlements like the one pictured.

tem of India. Perhaps a better standard of living through economic assistance may someday help to break down a caste system which gives no consideration to equality of opportunity as a basic freedom.

In India a great religious leader was born. In the interior of India, south of the Himalayas and near the sacred river Ganges was born the founder of another of the world's great religions. His name was Gautama [gou′tuh muh], but later he came to be known as the Buddha. His father was a wealthy rajah [rah′juh], the rajahs being the rulers of certain of the Indian states. Little is known of Buddha's early life, but he probably lived in the princely luxury common among nobles. When he was nineteen years old he married a beautiful princess.

Buddha saw "the way of life." As he neared the age of thirty, a great change came over Buddha. The legend runs that one day while he was driving with his trusted servant Channa, he saw an old man, bent and feeble. "Such is the way of life," said Channa. "To that we must all come." Soon afterward they came upon a man suffering with a loathsome disease. Again Channa said, "Such is the way of life." While still pondering over these things, they saw an unburied body. Once more Channa repeated, "Such is the way of life."

Buddha felt as though his eyes had suddenly been opened to all the miseries of life. He was no longer content to live for mere pleasure and he no longer felt at ease in his luxurious palace with so much poverty and unhappiness outside the palace walls.

Culver Service

BUDDHA ANSWERING QUESTIONS

Buddha, seated, is shown answering the questions of a divine being. One of these questions was " What is it fire cannot burn or moisture corrode? " Buddha is said to have answered, " Blessing. Neither fire, moisture, nor wind can destroy the blessing of a good deed, and it will reform the whole world."

Buddha searched for wisdom. That night, accompanied only by Channa, Buddha fled into the darkness in search of someone or something that would show him the deeper meaning of life. He paused in his flight to cut off his flowing hair and beard. He exchanged his silks and linens for the ragged clothing of a beggar whom he met on the road. He tore off his jewels and ornaments and gave them to Channa to be returned to his wife.

But Buddha himself did not turn back. He joined a group of hermits who lived in caves of the mountains. These men sat under the trees talking of the mysteries of life. Their most earnest desire was to forget the unhappiness of this world by sleeping forever. For a while Buddha stayed to talk with them. But when he had learned all they had to teach him he was still not satisfied.

Many people in ancient times, and many since then, believed that fasting and torturing the body gave man a greater power and deeper knowledge than could be gained in any other way. So Buddha tried fasting and self-torture. But they brought him no new knowledge.

One day Buddha was seated beneath a great banyan tree thinking how unsuccessful his search had been. Suddenly the truth seemed to come over him, and he felt free. He rushed off to tell other men of the new meanings and beliefs he had just learned under the banyan tree. Thus a new religion was born.

Many of the beliefs and practices, the gods and the ways of worshiping, were carried over from Brahmanism to Buddhism. Transmigration, Nirvana, and Kuan Yin are three of these you have already read about.

Buddha taught his beliefs as " Four Truths." The gospel Buddha preached has been called the " Four Truths." These can be described in this way: (1) Life brings grief, misery, and discontent: " The waters of the four great oceans are naught compared with the tears of men as they tread the path of life." (2) But this misery and discontent is caused by the selfishness and greed of man. (3) If one wants contentment, he should forget himself and serve his fellows. (4) The road to salvation is not fasting, self-torture, and punishment, but right conduct and intelligent living. Everlasting peace comes only to

Ewing Galloway

BUDDHA

This tranquil statue of Buddha is in the grounds of a monastery in Kamakura, Japan. The statue is over forty-nine feet high. The jewel in the forehead, representing the radiance which Buddha is supposed to cast through the universe, is composed of thirty pounds of silver. The eyes of the statue are said to be made of pure gold.

him who overcomes the sin in his life. These beliefs were the basis of Buddhism.

Buddhism became an organized religion. Years passed and men came to hail Gautama as the Buddha, the "chosen one through whom wisdom returned to the earth." After his death, people looked upon him as a god. As is so common, even with Christians, they forgot the real personality of their leader and neglected to follow his teachings. Buddhism became an organized religion with sacred cities and sacred rivers, with monasteries and temples, with an elaborate order of saints and priests, and with great sacred images like the statue of Buddha on page 231.

In time, Buddhism became less powerful in India, the birthplace of Gautama, but grew in strength and influence in other countries. A few centuries after the birth of Jesus, Buddhism penetrated Burma, Siam [sai'am] now Thailand [tai'land], China, and Japan. Gradually it spread into Tibet [ti bet'], Turkestan [toor'kuh stahn], and the Malay Archipelago [may'lay ahr'ki pel'uh-goh]. Look once more at the map on page 220 to find these strongholds of Buddhism. When we remember that the followers of this religion number 150,-000,000, we can see why Buddhism must be recognized as one of the great religions of the world.

Chapter 3 ~ Confucianism, Taoism, and Shintoism Arose in the Far East

Confucius was born in China. Journeying still farther east, where ancient China spreads across almost one-third of Asia, we find the birthplace of another great religion. Here about the middle of the Sixth Century before Christ (550 B.C.) and not long after the birth of Buddha in India, the founder of Confucianism was born. His Chinese name was Kung-fu-tze, which means Kung the philosopher, or Reverend Master Kung. The Latin form of his name, Confucius, was used long after his death, by Jesuit missionaries. A likeness of Confucius is reproduced on the facing page.

Little is known of the early life of Confucius except that he was born into a family which was poor even though it belonged to the nobility. When Confucius was complimented on his knowledge of many arts, he said that the poverty of his youth had forced him to learn all he could about the common activities of life.

Confucius stressed standards of conduct. When he was in his early twenties, Confucius was already an extremely popular teacher. His pupils were not children, but young men who wished to learn about their great ancestors, their standards of conduct, and government. Confucius spent much time collecting the ancient writings of his people and teaching others to revere the wisdom of their forefathers.

Confucius believed that good rulers make for good people. He taught that public officials (in the service of their fellowmen) should be wise, righteous, and loving. The opportunity came for Confucius to put his beliefs about good government into practice when he was appointed chief magistrate of a city in the Chinese province of Lu. He was so successful that he was later appointed minister of crime for the entire province. According to the story, within a year Confucius had practically put an end to crime in that province. He did this by supplying the people with an elaborate system of rules to regulate their every-days acts. It was not necessary for them to think whether a thing was right or wrong; all they had to do was to obey the many strict laws.

For a time all went well in Lu, but finally a neighboring ruler began to fear the increasing power of the province of Lu. He sent to Lu a large group of beautiful women musicians and dancers, and a troop of fine horses. Their performances, probably like those of our circuses, led the people away from their strict way of life under Confucius and to a life of pleasure. Gradually Confucius lost his power and influence, and the people ceased to follow his code of laws. Sorrowing, Confucius withdrew from the province and began his search for people who would accept his moral teachings.

Confucius suffered for his cause. The rest of Confucius' life was full of disappointment. Although he traveled from court to court for thirteen years, offering his services to the different princes, no one had a place for him. But even though he was without a home and probably often without food, Confucius never lost faith in his cause. When he was advised to leave the country, his answer was "It is impossible to withdraw from the world — with whom should I associate but suffering man?" When he had no food and no money with which to buy it, he merely said, "The superior man may have to endure want, but he is still the superior man; a small man

Schoenfeld Collection from Three Lions
CONFUCIUS

Like Kuan Yin, Confucius devoted himself to the cause of suffering human beings. He attempted to serve humanity by perfecting government, and by substituting rules for reasoning. Do you remember reading about a Greek philosopher who tried to serve humanity through far different means?

in the same circumstances loses his self-command."

Confucius gave a golden rule to the Chinese. After Confucius died, his teachings and works lived on. Devoted disciples wrote down his sayings, which later found a place among the sacred books of the Chinese. Although Confucius contributed nothing new to the religion which he had inherited from his ancestors, he did try to teach the Chinese how to live justly and happily together. The golden rule which he set for his followers was "What you do not like when done unto yourself, do not do to others." We must understand that Confucianism is more a code of conduct than a religion in the usual sense.

Today Confucius, who lived in pov-

LAO-TZE

This Chinese painting shows Lao-tze at work on his book, the Tao-Teh-King. This book contains the principles of Lao-tze.

erty, lies in a magnificent tomb with a marble statue, approached by a beautiful avenue lined with cypress trees. On the statue are the words, "The most sagely ancient teacher; the all-accomplished; the all-informed king." More than fifteen thousand temples have been erected in his honor throughout China. Thousands of followers worship at his shrine. Truly Confucius, like so many religious leaders, is greater in death than he was in life.

China produced another great religious leader. Lao-tze [lou dzu] was born in China, somewhat before the birth of Confucius, which was about the Sixth Century B.C. Lao-tze, whose name may be translated "Old Scholar," is said to have been court librarian in the province of Chou [joh]. Tradition says the young reformer, Confucius, met Lao-tze when he went to deposit some books in the royal library. Great was Confucius' surprise when in conversation with Lao-tze he learned that this scholar refused to support his suggested reforms of certain laws. In fact, Lao-tze rebuked Confucius for his efforts to reform society, thus "introducing disorder into the nature of man." Lao-tze has been

sharply criticized for shunning reforms and withdrawing into "convenient irresponsibility." Such actions appear strange for a man who is considered by many to be one of the world's great philosophers, but let us examine some of the convictions of this remarkable Chinese, Lao-tze.

The three great principles of Lao-tze were Inactivity, Humility, and Frugality. The ideal of life, said Lao-tze, is inactivity or passivity. These, he said, can be learned by contemplation of nature. Water is strong by being weak; the soft overcomes the hard, the weak the strong. For a man even to defend himself from injury was against the religious principles of Lao-tze. "To them that are good, I am good, to them that are not good, I am also good; thus all get to be good," he declared. Thus over five hundred years before Christ, a Chinese philosopher told the world that it was best to return good for evil.

Humility was the virtue next emphasized by Lao-tze. "He who overcomes others is strong; he who overcomes himself is mighty." Only as one learns to claim no credit and to exert no authority can one accomplish great things:

"Keep behind and thou shalt inevitably be kept in front." With humility Lao-tze taught unfailing kindness and gentleness.

Lao-tze also believed in frugality, or being thrifty. As strength comes from weakness, he believed, and prominence out of humility, so liberality comes out of frugality. To quote Lao-tze, "The wise man does not accumulate. The more he expends for others, the more doth he possess of his own; the more he giveth to others, the more hath he for himself."

Lao-tze wrote the Tao-Teh-King. After Lao-tze retired from his position as librarian, he decided to leave China. As he approached the gate leading out of the kingdom, the gatekeeper recognized him as the "True Man" and begged him to leave behind him a record of his teachings. The gatekeeper set before him a cup of tea, and thus, it is said, originated the custom of serving tea to a guest. Lao-tze interrupted his journey long enough to write his book, called the Tao-Teh-King [tou'teh king]. He is shown at work in the picture on page 234.

Taoism became an established religion. Lao-tze made no attempt to found a religion. Indeed, he did not believe in temples, ritual, and priests, yet he seemed to have believed in worshiping "the Unknown." In his book he mentioned a God, "the Heavenly Emperor," but only once, saying that before even He existed there was Tao. To Lao-tze, Tao was the supreme power and governing principle of the universe, not a personal being or God.

Strictly speaking, Lao-tze was not a religious leader, but a philosopher like Confucius; not a prophet, but a sage. Yet his teachings had much in common with the loftiest ideals of the greatest religions.

After the death of this great teacher, the religion of Taoism [tou'iz'm] developed. Temples were built to Lao-tze, who did not believe in ritual. Priests hailed him as the discoverer of magic potions to make life everlasting, though Lao-tze believed life to be the sorriest of vanities. And, the greatest irony of all, the little old wise man who laughed at gods was himself worshiped as a god. For more than two thousand years he has been worshiped throughout China. Taoism has become a religion of superstition and magic rites. It must be clear that the Taoism of Lao-tze, himself, was much nobler than the organized religion of his followers.

Shintoism became a national religion in Japan. East of China, home of Confucianism and Taoism, is Japan, where another religion, Shintoism, developed. At the dawn of Japan's history, most Japanese were Shintoists. Shintoism was similar, in many respects, to the religion of other primitive, superstitious people.

Around them the Japanese found many things which excited their wonder and reverence: volcanos and rivers, the moon and the stars, birth and death. Greatest of all these wonders was the huge red ball of fire which rose every morning in the east and set each night in the west. The Japanese explained these mysteries, as the early Greeks had done, by means of gods and goddesses. The Shintoists worshiped many gods, but chief of all was the sun goddess, from whom they believed the emperor of Japan was directly descended.

About the Sixth Century, Buddhism began to flow into Japan from India and China. Other religions, too, were followed by the Japanese. Shintoism never died out, but it came to have a different form. It became a national religion — one based on love of country and worship of ancestors and royalty. Most Japanese were Shintoists and also members of another religion, such as Buddhism, which did not conflict with the national faith.

Shintoism is today a religion of patriotism. From a spiritual faith based mainly on reverence of nature, Shintoism has become, for the Japanese people, an intense expression of national patriotism. Japanese who believe in Shintoism have learned to worship their ancestors and the national heroes of Japan, to make pilgrimages to Shinto shrines, and to love the beauty and grandeurs of their

country, such as the sacred snow-capped Fujiyama [foo'jee yah'mah], and to offer sacrifices to Japanese military heroes. They believe, as did their forefathers, that the emperor is divine, that he descended from the sun goddess whose emblem appears on their flags as a red sun in a field of white. The Japanese people have been taught that nothing can be more honorable than death on the battlefield in the service of the emperor. Shintoism has become an intense worship of everything having to do with the Japanese nation, the land, its history, and its people.

Chapter 4 ~ Mohammedanism Was Founded in Arabia

Arabia is the birthplace of Mohammedanism. Southeast of Palestine, as you have learned, lies the arid expanse of the Arabian Desert. Many scattered tribes lived here. They wandered from place to place, depending upon their flocks for food and clothing. From the Arabian civilization we learned our simple system of Arabic numbers (although it originated in India), as well as algebra.

The Arabian was first to use oval windows and domes in temples and public buildings. He was first to discover that the coffee berry could be used in preparing a delicious drink. He learned to make the famous Damascus [da mas'kus] steel which was so strong and flexible that it could be bent almost double without breaking. And, as we shall learn, these Arabians developed one of the world's most widespread religions.

Mohammed was born in Mecca. When Christianity was not quite six

hundred years old, there was born in the city of Mecca [mek'uh] a child who was later to be called Mohammed, the founder of the religion known as Mohammedanism. His parents died when he was very young. After that Mohammed made his own living. He became a shepherd and a camel driver. With such a difficult start in life it is probable that Mohammed never learned to read or write. When he married a wealthy widow, he was relieved of the necessity of working for his living. He then had time to consider the great problems of life.

Mohammed founded a religion and was forced to flee. Mohammed, who was subject at times to spells of melancholy, had a strong desire to get away from other people. He often hid in a cave so that he might think in peace. On one of these occasions, Mohammed had a marvelous dream. He believed he had been visited by a heavenly angel and had been appointed as the prophet to lead all Arabia away from the worship of idols to the acceptance of the one god, Allah.

When Mohammed told the story of his dream to his wife, she believed he had been inspired. His friends and relatives were also impressed. Mohammed began to draw about him a large number of believers in his new religion. By his teachings, however, Mohammed made many enemies too. Some of the people of Mecca became angry when he tried to force them to give up the worship of idols. On a July night in A.D. 622, Mohammed had to flee for his life. He went to near-by Medina [meh dee'nah], where he had been offered the position of ruler of the city, which had fallen into great disorder. This escape of Mohammed from Mecca to Medina has been called the Hegira [hi jai'ruh], which

means "flight." Mohammedans reckon time from the date of the Hegira, just as Christians reckon the years from the birth of Jesus. Thus the year one in the Mohammedan calendar is 622 in the Christian calendar.

Mohammed became both a civic ruler and religious leader of Medina. In the next ten years he tried to win all Arabia to both his government and his religion. He soon became complete ruler of Arabia. A painting of Mohammed is reproduced below.

Mohammedanism improved the lives of its followers. When Mohammed began his teaching, the Arabians were quite uncivilized. Mohammed tried to make his religion attractive enough to them so that they would give up their barbaric ways of living and accept both religion and civilization. His teachings of a simple way of life, guided by a sim-

Culver Service

MOHAMMED

The mounted Arab with brandished scimitar is Mohammed, leading his fervent, militant followers in the spreading of Mohammedanism.

ple and practical moral code helped his followers toward more civilized ways.

The religion of Mohammedanism is primarily a system of religious observances which show devotion to Allah. "Allah" is the Mohammedan's word for God. In the Mohammedan religion the muezzin [myoo ez'in] calls out the hours of prayer from the minaret [min-uh ret'] of the mosque.

Christianity and Judaism may be considered as the forerunners of some of the teachings of Mohammedanism. In common with Hinduism, Mohammedanism includes the belief that a man's behavior and his fate are determined long before he is born. Therefore, somewhat like the Hindu caste system, it caused its followers to accept life with a fatalistic attitude.

Mohammedanism does not permit altars, pictures, or images. Mohammedans, or Moslems as they are sometimes called, are not permitted to gamble or to drink intoxicating liquor. They are taught to be kind and obedient to their parents, to protect the weak and helpless, and to be gentle with animals.

The Mohammedan bible is the Koran. Mohammedanism is based on the Koran [koh'ran]. That book is the Mohammedan bible. It is a collection of the prayers, speeches, and other sayings of Mohammed. Mohammedans believe that the Koran is an inspired book, just as Christians think of the Bible. Mohammedans believe the Koran contains the revelation from Allah which the angel sent to Mohammed when he was in his religious trances.

The Koran teaches five things that every Moslem should do: (1) He should recite with understanding and belief the short creed, "There is no god but Allah; and Mohammed is his prophet." (2) He must pray five times a day: at dawn, just

after noon, before sunset, just after sunset, and at the end of the day. Before prayer, he must wash his face, hands, and feet; during prayer he must turn toward the city of Mecca and bow his head to the ground. If you have ever seen a genuine Mohammedan prayer rug, you may have noticed worn spots where the knees of the Moslem owner have rested and where his forehead has touched the rug as he bowed toward Mecca. (3) A strict Mohammedan must fast from sunrise to sunset during one month of each year. (4) He must give alms to the poor. (5) And, if he is able, he should make at least one pilgrimage to the sacred city of Mecca.

Mohammedanism was spread at the point of the sword. Mohammed died about ten years after the Hegira to Medina, but the Moslems continued his work of converting people to Mohammedanism. Mohammed sent out armies for military purposes; he spread Mohammedanism by the sword in conquered territories. After his death the Arabs, united for the first time by their religion, began to conquer the surrounding countries. The Arabs were poor and warlike; their neighbors were richer and more peaceful. It was again the old story of those who have and those who have not. The rulers became known as Caliphs [kay'lifs]. They were the successors of the prophet Mohammed and so were heads of both religion and government. The Arab aggressors conquered eastward to the borders of India, northward to the border of Asia Minor, and westward along the whole North African coast and up through Spain.

For centuries the Mohammedan Caliphs ruled this vast empire, and under their rule most of the conquered people were converted to the Mohammedan religion. Later Mohammedanism spread even beyond the limits of the empire into India. In this empire a great civilization arose. It was much more highly developed in many ways than any civilization of the Western world in the year 1000.

All Moslems had to be able to read the sacred Koran, and the Arabic language became the common language from Persia to Spain. The Caliphs ruled first from Damascus on the eastern shore of the Mediterranean, and then from Bagdad in Persia. You can see these cities on the map on page 220. The Caliphs were immensely powerful and lived in more than oriental splendor. The most famous ruler was, perhaps, Haroun-al-Rashid [hah roon'ahr ruh sheed'], whom you may remember if you have read the *Thousand and One Nights.*

By A.D. 732, exactly one hundred years after the death of Mohammed, some of the Moslems, Moors from North Africa, had invaded Europe as far as Tours

[toor], France. Near that city they were defeated, and the tide of Mohammedanism was turned. Driven back into Spain, the Moors built a great civilization which lasted for nearly eight hundred years. Some buildings remain in Spain as remnants of Moorish civilization there, as you will learn in the story of Spain.

Although the spread of Mohammedanism was halted at Tours in France, it still must be recognized as one of the great religions of the world. It is the principal religion of North Africa, the Arabian peninsula, and Asia Minor, and it has many followers in India, Persia, and Turkestan. And as it spread throughout much of the Mediterranean world and parts of the Orient, it brought with it the craftsmanship and knowledge of Arabian civilization. Europe, as well as the Orient, has learned much from the Mohammedans.

Chapter 5 ~ Jesus Became a Messenger of Peace and Good Will

Christian teachings developed in a world of religious belief. The Hebrew peoples were deeply religious by nature. They believed in their one God, Jehovah. Their religion controlled their daily lives, gave them hope for the future, and kept them unshaken in their faith through slavery, war, persecution, and death. Of the religious beliefs of Judaism [joo'deh iz'm] we learned in Part Four.

The teachings of Christianity are familiar to most of us. The children of the so-called Christian nations of Europe and the Americas have studied them or

heard them told. We should understand that the teachings of Christ and his Twelve Apostles [uh pahs'l'z] began in the land of the Hebrews in Palestine. We should not overlook the fact that most of these men were Jews themselves and had grown to manhood among people who accepted the teachings of the Old Testament of the Christian Bible. Those books of the Bible tell of the Hebrew laws, of religious history, and of the sayings of the ancient Hebrew prophets. It was in such an environment of religious faith that Christianity developed.

Jesus grew up in a humble home. Here it will only be necessary to sketch the life of that great religious teacher, Jesus of Galilee. He grew up in the humble home of Joseph the carpenter. Little is known of his early life except that he worked at carpentry. At the age of twelve he was found —

. . . sitting in the midst of the doctors, both hearing them, and asking them questions. And all that heard him were astonished at his understanding and answers.

Jesus became a great teacher. When Jesus grew to manhood he was recognized as an authority on Jewish law and the writings of the Hebrew poets and prophets. In his new explanations of the old Hebrew teachings, he pointed the way to a better life. Wherever he went men and women gathered to hear his message. In simple language, often by means of a story or parable, he led people to see their shortcomings.

Jesus taught that the way to eternal life was not only through sacrifice and obedience to the letter of the law, but also through the worship of God and service to one's fellowmen. His own manner of living bore out his statement of the Golden Rule: " Therefore, all things whatsoever ye would that men should do to you, do ye even so to them." His ideal of brotherhood is expressed in his saying, " Love thy neighbor as thyself." He helped the sick and brought new hope to the downtrodden.

Jesus also taught his followers that he was of divine origin, the Son of God, and that his mission was to bring the Will of God on earth. He pictured to his followers an immortal life after death in the Kingdom of Heaven. As we shall see, it was some of these teachings that led him to be feared by the priesthood of the established temples and the civil rulers of what was then the Roman province of Palestine. The priests and governors wanted no conflicting power to grow up, even though Jesus was speaking in terms of the spirit, not of worldly matters. Thus they feared him.

Jesus visited Jerusalem and was betrayed. After spending three years teaching the people of Galilee, Jesus carried his teachings to Jerusalem. The time chosen for this visit was just before the Jewish feast of the Passover, about which you may read in the Bible in Exodus XIII. Jews from all parts of the country had gathered in Jerusalem to celebrate that feast. When Jesus, with his twelve disciples [di sai'p'lz], reached Jerusalem, they found that his fame had preceded him. Great crowds rushed out to greet him. The Jews hailed him as the long-promised Messiah, or Savior. They believed that he had come to deliver them from the iron hand of Rome. But great was their disappointment when they learned that Jesus had not come to lead them to battle against the Romans, but to preach a gospel of peace and good will.

Almost overnight the people turned away from Jesus. In his hour of greatest need, Jesus found himself deserted by most of his followers. Judas [joo' duhs], one of his disciples, for thirty pieces of silver, betrayed him to the soldiers who came to take him prisoner.

Jesus was taken into custody, accused of being King of the Jews. He was tried for treason against the Roman Empire, for being false to Caesar, the title which was used by the head of the Roman Empire, of which Palestine was a part. His few brief statements at the trial were misunderstood, and he was sentenced to death. He was crucified with two thieves whose crosses stood on either side. Even

From the painting by J. James Tissot. John H. Eggers, N. Y.

JESUS AND HIS DISCIPLES

Jesus is seen here blessing his disciples as he sends them out, two by two, to carry his message to many lands.

in the anguish of death, this messenger of peace cried, "Father, forgive them; for they know not what they do."

The teachings of Jesus were spread by his followers. Although Jesus had suffered and died on the cross, his life and ideals became a mighty force among the people of the Western world. His vision of the brotherhood of man appealed especially to the poor and unfortunate. His teachings offered hope to the humble and distressed, if not in this world then in the future world of immortality. The slave and the workman could understand the sympathetic beliefs of Jesus, which offered peace and good will.

After his crucifixion, his followers, ashamed that they had forsaken him, remained in Jerusalem to tell the story of his life and teachings. In spite of persecution, each year more people were attracted to the ideals of Jesus. There was one man in particular whose conversion to the new faith was important. This was Saul, or as he was later called, Paul.

Paul organized Christian churches in many lands. Paul, who lived in Asia Minor, was a Jew and a Roman citizen. He was noted for his violent temper and his strong likes and dislikes. For some time he had persecuted those who believed in Jesus. One day, as he was on his way to Damascus to continue his persecutions, a strange thing happened to him.

According to one account, a vision of the risen Jesus suddenly appeared to Paul. From the "light from Heaven" which surrounded Jesus a voice cried out, "Saul, Saul, why persecutest thou me?" When Paul had ceased his trembling and become calm once more, a great change had come over him. He no longer wanted to persecute the followers of Jesus, but to aid them in spreading their gospel of peace and good will. Paul threw himself wholeheartedly into this new work. He traveled from Asia Minor to Greece and then to Italy, establishing churches in the name of Jesus.

The apostles had called Jesus "The Christ," which comes from a Greek word meaning "Anointed One." The religion spread by the Apostle Paul has come to be known as Christianity, and, as you know, its followers are called Christians. Through the work of Paul and other disciples, Christianity was carried throughout the Roman world. You can see the great extent of the Roman Empire from the map on page 170.

Early Christians were cruelly persecuted. The first followers of Christianity were often cruelly persecuted. In Rome the early Christians were executed because they refused to make sacrifices to the Roman emperors and because they openly prophesied the fall of Rome. The emperor Nero had murdered thousands of Christians whom he falsely accused of setting fire to the city. Many devout believers were thrown to hungry wild beasts in the arena. Such actions were considered by many early Romans as entertainment for themselves, as you read in the story of Rome.

In spite of severe persecution, the number of Christians rapidly increased. Martyrs went to their death without dismay; slaves rose to unexpected heights of heroism. Had not their Savior died for the truth, they asked? Surely he would not desert his followers who gave their lives for the same cause. Death held no fear for these suffering Christians, for they believed in a beautiful immortality in the Kingdom of Heaven.

The early Christians who lived in Rome found one way to protect themselves. They made use of underground galleries, called catacombs, where they might bury their dead and hide in time of danger. Secret entrances admitted believers to this network of passages which lay under the city of Rome. Sometimes the Christians lived for long periods in these dark hiding places, afraid to venture into the open. The catacombs still remain as a grim reminder of the persecution and misery endured by the followers of Jesus.

Constantine ended the persecution of the Christians. In the early part of the Fourth Century, Constantine the Great became Emperor of Rome. According to the story, Constantine, while marching to battle against a rival emperor, saw in the sky a fiery cross upon which was written *In Hoc Signo Vinces*. These Latin words mean "By this sign thou shalt conquer." At the end of the battle Constantine, in the presence of his victorious troops, pledged that he would support the religion whose sign was the cross. Having been recognized as Emperor of the western part of the Empire as a result of his victory, he and the Eastern Emperor together issued a decree granting complete freedom of worship to the Christians. Later, after Constantine became sole ruler of the Eastern and Western Roman Empires, Christianity came to be recognized as the official religion of the Romans.

Christianity is the principal religion of the Western world. From that time Christianity gained more rapidly in numbers and in power than ever before. Later, in Part Eight, you will see how the Church became the great force in the Middle Ages. When Rome fell before the invasion of the German barbarians, men turned to the Church as the only institution that stood firm in the midst of the wreckage.

Most of the peoples of Western Europe became interested in the teachings of Jesus and adopted the Christian faith. And later, when these same peoples began to explore and settle the New World, they brought their religion with them. Thus Christianity was spread throughout Europe and the Western Hemisphere.

Our calendar, as we have learned, reckons time from the beginning of the Christian era; B.C. means " Before Christ," and A.D. (*Anno Domini*) means " In the year of our Lord." December twenty-fifth, as you know, is celebrated throughout the Christian world as the anniversary of the birth of Christ. Pal-estine, in which Jesus was born, came to be known as the Holy Land, and Jerusalem as the Holy City.

Almost two thousand years have passed since Christ was born. Today it is estimated that about two-fifths of all the people in the world, or about 600,-000,000, are Christians. There is hardly a country where Christian missionaries have not worked. Christianity has held out a way of salvation through worship and the gospel of brotherly love. It has been a great force in the struggle to civilize the world. Many of the principles of Christianity are also principles of democracy.

Religions Play an Important Part in the Life of Mankind

The word " religion " covers far differing beliefs and customs. It includes primitive sacrifices, the worship of innumerable spirits, and the belief in one supreme being. But in all its meanings, the word implies an " attitude of men toward what they regard as all powerful." And the history of all peoples contains a record of their religious beliefs.

We have finished the story of the great religious leaders who tried to teach people to live better lives. Each of them had a message to bring to believing multitudes. The peoples of the Western world have been most influenced by the Christian religion, but those who live in other parts of the world have been influenced by other religions.

In the present world two-fifths of the earth's inhabitants are Christians. Mohammed, Buddha, and Confucius have their millions of followers in the other parts of the world. And millions more are faithful to one or another of the great racial or national religions such as Hinduism. Yet no matter how the faiths of men may differ, we have come to see that the spirit of religion is a common heritage of mankind.

Hinduism is a composite religion that has absorbed the earlier religions of the peoples of India. Out of Hinduism the Buddhistic faith developed through the teachings of Gautama, the Buddha. From India, Buddhism spread to Burma, Siam, and China.

In China the teachings of two great philosophers formed the bases for two religions. Confucius taught high standards of conduct and the reverence for one's ancestors. Lao-tze taught the value of modesty, humility, and frugality. His teachings grew into the organized religion of Taoism. In Japan Shintoism, another national religion, combined nature worship and patriotism.

The great monotheistic religions of the world are Judaism, Christianity, and Mohammedanism. Judaism was the first of these. It has many followers today. Moreover, it prepared the way for Christianity. After a dark period in which the Christians were persecuted, Christianity was spread by conversion. It became the most powerful religion of the Western world, and a supreme civilizing force. Mohammed, the prophet of Allah, originated the faith that bears his name and that spread by conquest from Arabia far into Africa, India, and for a time into parts of southern Europe.

Peoples in other parts of the world have, in general, the same hopes, the same needs that we have. Almost every religion teaches honesty, consideration, kindness, and hope. Because the modern world of invention brings all peoples nearer to one another, it is important that we understand people all over the world. An understanding of people requires an understanding of their religions. This understanding carries with it a willingness to respect the right of others to believe according to their own consciences. Intelligent understanding of other peoples' ideas and customs will help us to respect them and their efforts to live a good life according to their best beliefs.

SELF–TEST

1. Match the items in the following columns by writing on a piece of paper the numbers at the left, and beside each the letter of the word or phrase at the right that is most closely connected with the word or phrase of each number at the left.

(1) Lao-tze	(a) The way of life
(2) Nirvana	(b) Patriotism
(3) Confucius	(c) Apostle
(4) Judaism	(d) Brahmanism
(5) Mohammed	(e) Kuan Yin
(6) Jesus	(f) Hegira
(7) Shintoism	(g) Old Testament
(8) Paul	(h) Standards of conduct
(9) India	(i) Peace and good will
(10) Gautama the Buddha	(j) Inactivity, humility, frugality

2. In the following story of the great religions, complete the statements as indicated. More than one word may be needed in some cases.

Throughout the story of man we find that most people (have, have not) some form of religion. Learning about religions other than our own (*select the best phrase for completion of this sentence*) (a) helps us to understand our own; (b) helps us to understand other people; (c) tends to make us set apart from us people of different faiths. Hinduism came about because the followers of —— modified their religion to convert the natives of India. This composite religion is based partially on religious books called ———. The Hindu Trimurti is composed of ———, the creator; ———, the preserver; and ———, the destroyer. The worst feature of Hinduism is ———. Buddhism was founded by Gautama ———, who saw a new " way of life." He taught his beliefs as " Four ———." Confucius set up certain standards of ——— for the people to follow. His golden rule was: ———. Taoism was founded by ———, which means ———. His three great principles were ———, ———, and ———. Taoism today is (*a*) very much as he taught it; (*b*) very different from his teachings. The national religion of Japan is ———, which is based on worship of the ——— goddess, nature, ———, and heroes. Most Japanese follow (only one, more than one) religion.

Mohammed was born in ———, where he founded the religion known as ———; this city has become the ——— city for his followers. His escape to ——— is called the ———. This flight was in the year ———, which is important because ———. Mohammed spread his religion by ———. His book of religion is called ———. Christianity is founded on ———, as can be seen from the first half of ———, which consists of ———. The founder of Christianity, ——— ———, was a great ———; he made use of the story or ——— to spread his message. He taught a ———, similar to that of Confucius, and advised people to return ———, as did Lao-tze. One of his greatest apostles was ———, who was great because he ———. Christianity spread rapidly because of the work of the Emperor ———, who was converted to it when he ———. The Christian Holy City is ———, and the Holy Land is ———. Our calendar reckons time from the beginning of the ——— era; B.C. to us means ———, and A.D. (from ———) means ———. Christianity offers salvation through worship of God and the Gospel of ———.

INTERESTING THINGS TO DO

Projects for the Chart Maker and Artist

1. Make a chart that shows some of the similarities of the great religions. Use such headings as "Leaders," " Time of Beginning," " Books," and " Principal Points of Belief."

2. On an outline map of the world show by different colored crayons in what parts of the world the different great religions are largely followed. Include a key in your map so that others can understand it.

Topics for Talks

1. " The parables of Jesus." Tell one of the parables of Jesus to the class. Explain its meaning, and give your own interpretation of how its moral operates in a particular case.

2. " The birthplace of a religion." Give an illustrated travel-talk about India, China, Arabia, or Palestine, locating and describing places that are significant in the story of one of the great religions.

3. "Thoughts and ideas that have influenced millions of people." From the writings of the founders of great religions, collect as many quotations on similar subjects as you can. Read a few of these quotations to the class, and make comparisons of the underlying ideas in each. See *Tree of Life*, by Ruth Smith, or the last chapter in *Founders of Great Religions*, by Millar Burrows.

Adventures for the Amateur Author

1. Write a letter or story, or compose a poem or song, which deals with an incident in the life of one of the leaders of great religions. See *Master Kung*, by Carl Crow, or *Founders of Great Religions*, by Millar Burrows.

2. Write an article on religious intolerance that describes an incident of intolerance not mentioned in your book. Is intolerance ever justifiable?

Candidates for Your Album of Famous People

Buddha, Jesus, Lao-tze, Mohammed. Write condensed biographies of at least two of the great religious leaders for your Album.

INTERESTING READING ABOUT RELIGIONS

The Holy Bible

Asch, Sholem. *The Nazarene*. The life of Jesus forms the core of this beautifully written novel.

Atkins, G. G. *Procession of the Gods*. " There is pathos, humor, and splendor in it all. . . ."

Browne, L. *This Believing World*. " He spoke without the slightest flourish, using plain words and homely parables."

Burrows, Millar. *Founders of Great Religions*. " He tried to penetrate the hearts of the men whose lives he describes."

Compton's Pictured Encyclopedia. " Brahma "; " Buddha "; " Confucius "; " Lao-tze "; " Mohammed "; " Shinto "; " Jerusalem "; " Jesus."

Gaer, J. *How the Great Religions Began*. " All the religions in the world in the days of the Buddha were national religions."

National Geographic Magazine, December, 1929. " Bethlehem and the Christmas Story," J. D. Whiting. ". . . recognizing by the costumes that the Three Wise Men were Persians, the vandal hordes spared the church. . . ."

Smith, Ruth. *Tree of Life*. " Treasures of beauty and wisdom " in sample selections from the world's sacred literature.

Wells, H. G. *Outline of History*. " He amazed and horrified his five companions by demanding ordinary food."

The World Book Encyclopedia. " Brahma "; " Buddha "; " Confucius "; " Lao-tze "; " Mohammed "; " Shintoism "; " Jesus Christ."

PART EIGHT

CHIVALRY, SERFDOM, AND THE CHURCH CHARACTERIZED THE FEUDAL WORLD

NORWAY
SWEDEN
SCOTLAND
DENMARK
LITHUANIA
IRELAND
WALES
ENGLAND
London
NETHERLANDS
Hamburg
Berlin
POMERANIA
SLAVS
POLAND
RUSSIA
HOLY
ROMAN
EMPIRE
Frankfort
Rhine
Reims
Seine R.
NORMANDY
Paris
Tours
Oberammergau
HUNGARY
Danube R.
Black Sea
Caspian Sea
Clermont
FRANCE
BURGUNDY
CROATIA
Bologna
ITALY
Assisi
Rome
Pyrenees Mts.
Marseille
CORSICA
PAPAL STATES
SARDINIA
Salerno
SERBIA
BULGARIA
EASTERN
(BYZANTINE) EMPIRE
Constantinople
ASIA MINOR
DOMINIONS OF THE
TURKS
MOHAMMEDANS
SPAIN
Madrid
Toledo
Lisbon
Cordova
GREECE
Mediterranean Sea
SICILY
CRETE
CYPRUS
Antioch
PALESTINE
Jerusalem
KINGDOM ESTABLISHED BY CRUSADERS
MOORISH DOMINIONS
EGYPT
ARABIA
MILES
0
300
600
North
Liam Dunne

A Map of Unorganized Europe

AFTER the fall of the Roman Empire and before the forming of modern European nations, Europe was in a state of disorder and confusion. There were no strong central governments. Many petty kingdoms sprang up — more than can be shown on this map. Each ruler felt free to attack his neighbor.

On the map opposite, some modern nations are shown, to help you orient yourself as you read the story of the feudal world. There you will also find features typical of feudal times. The Eastern Roman Empire, with its capital at Constantinople, for centuries kept alive something of the old Roman power and influence in the Middle East. In the West, a new kind of empire grew up, combining the old idea of the Roman Empire with the new idea of a single Christian Church. This new empire came to be called the Holy Roman Empire.

Notice on this map the neighbors of the medieval states. To the north were the Vikings or Northmen. To the South, in Africa and Spain, were the Mohammedans. In the story of the feudal world much is said about the Crusades, the attempts of the Christians in Europe to get possession of Palestine. Find the Holy Land to which the Crusaders went and the kingdom they established in the East.

Chapter 1 ~ Feudalism Became the Pattern of Life in Western Europe

When law and order went, insecurity and disorder remained. A fight without rules becomes a free-for-all with no holds barred. A family without control begins to quarrel. And a state without law and order falls into anarchy and disorder. Security of business, trade, or even one's own person is gone.

In Part Six we learned how the Romans governed the Western world and spread their civilizing influence throughout Europe. But we also saw the power of Rome weaken by decay from within and by pressure of the barbarians. Finally, in the Fifth Century, the power and grandeur that was Rome was no more. What was left in Europe is about what you would expect: disorder and confusion; lawlessness and aggression; the weak trampled on by the strong; and the progress of mankind brought to a halt.

Western Europe sank into ignorance and disorder. After the break-up of the mighty empire of the Romans, Europe sank into ignorance and disorder. The German barbarian tribes continued to migrate from the northern to the southern and western parts of the European peninsula. As there were no strong governments, these tribes plundered at will and waged more or less continual war among themselves. Many of the Roman homes, manners and customs, and institutions that had been spread over western Europe were either destroyed or lost because of the hordes of ignorant barbarians who overran the land. What had been carefully tilled fields reverted to a tangle of weeds and underbrush. Cities which had bustled with trade became empty shells. The Roman roads fell into disrepair and disuse. Bridges and aqueducts were destroyed. And with uncontrolled highwaymen at every turn, travel from one part of Europe to another almost ceased. This meant, too, that trade and commerce came almost to a standstill, and Europe lost the invigorating effect of commerce in the life of a region.

Learning almost disappeared. If men had wanted to read, they would have found few manuscripts. Many libraries containing copies of the works of famous Greek and Roman writers had been wrecked or burned by the fierce invaders. Few people appreciated art, beautiful buildings, fine plays, and poems. For a time the culture of the Greeks and Romans seemed in danger of being completely lost.

Charlemagne built an empire. It was during these days of disorder and little learning (from the Fifth through the Seventh Centuries) that the Franks gained control of much of northwestern Europe. The Franks had been one of the invading barbarian tribes. They conquered and settled in what is now part of France, Belgium, and the Netherlands. For three centuries they ruled this territory with varying success. One of their more famous leaders, Charles Martel [shahrl mahr tel'] was the ruler who stopped the invading Saracens at the Battle of Tours (A.D. 732) and thus prevented the Mohammedan civilization from spreading in Western Europe. We learned of that significant event in Part Seven, when studying the story of the Mohammedan religion, and shall hear of the Franks again in the story of the French.

It was the grandson of Charles Martel who rescued Europe, for a time, from the darkness into which she had plunged. This strong and enlightened man became king of the Franks. He is known in history as Charlemagne, or Charles the Great. This man was truly an unusual person to appear in Europe at this particular time. He was a bold warrior, an ardent Christian, and a natural leader. He became the ruler of a number of loosely organized states located in what is now France, Belgium, and parts of Germany and the Netherlands. His subjects were descendants of the German tribes who had swept across the Rhine more than three centuries before his time.

Charlemagne devoted himself for more than forty years to the tasks of building up a strong government, defending his kingdom from invasion, and extending the power of the Church. The map below shows the territory he added to his kingdom.

After years of fierce fighting, the heathen Saxons acknowledged his rule and accepted the Christian faith. He conquered barbarian tribes along the Danube. He not only prevented the Saracens from settling in the southern part of France, but won some territory from them south of the Pyrenees. One of his most important campaigns was against the Lombards in Italy. He defeated their king, and placed the rule of a number of Italian cities in the hands of the Pope. On Christmas day of the

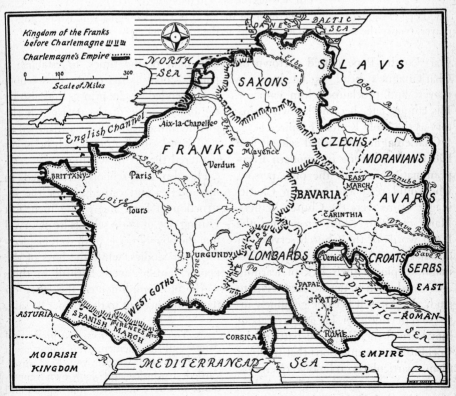

THE GROWTH AND EXTENT OF CHARLEMAGNE'S EMPIRE

Culver Service

THE CROWNING OF CHARLEMAGNE

The Pope is shown placing the crown on the head of Charlemagne, who is kneeling in prayer. Notice the soldiers and lesser clergy in the foreground.

year 800 the Pope placed a crown on Charlemagne's head as he knelt in prayer, and proclaimed him emperor. His empire later became known in history as the Holy Roman Empire.

Charlemagne established schools and laid the cornerstone for modern European nations. About the only persons who could read and write in Charlemagne's time were the Church Fathers. Many of them could pronounce the Latin words of the Church service but did not know their meaning. Charlemagne deplored their lack of learning and urged them to devote themselves to study. He himself became genuinely interested in education. He gathered about him learned men from all parts of the world to discuss questions that troubled them, particularly religious questions. He sent a messenger to England and invited Alcuin [al'kwin], the most schol-

arly man of the times, to establish a palace school at his court. This school was attended by the princes and also by the older people of the palace. Charlemagne himself attended, and learned to read Greek and Latin, though he never mastered the art of writing.

He also had schools established in monasteries and cathedrals for the instruction of boys and young men. On visiting one of these schools he observed that the boys of noble birth were neglecting their studies, while the boys of the poorer families were faithful in their work. He complimented the latter on their diligence but to the former he said,

". . . You sons of princes, you pretty and dainty little gentlemen, who count upon your birth and wealth, you have disregarded my order and your own reputations; you have neglected your studies and spent your time in games and idleness, or in foolish occupations! I care little for your noble birth, and your pretty looks, though others think them so fine! And let me promise you this: if you do not make haste to recover what you have lost by your neglect, you need never think to get any favors from Charles!"

Charlemagne will always hold a conspicuous place in the history of Western Europe for bringing order out of confusion within his kingdom, for building a great empire, and for his support of Christianity and education. One important result of his work, however, should not be overlooked. When the Holy Roman Empire was established, Italy and that part of Western Europe which had been under the control of the Romans became a part of it. You will remember it was stated in the story of Rome that there was no strong central government in Italy after the fall of Rome in the year 476. The only leadership came from the emperor at Constantinople, where the Eastern Roman Empire continued to exist. But Constantinople was so far away and the emperor was usually so lacking in power that there was little influence upon conditions in Italy. Civilization on the Italian peninsula gave way to barbarism. People lost the culture of the ancient Romans. But with the formation of the Holy Roman Empire under Charlemagne, conditions changed. Interest in the old Roman culture revived. People began to look to the past, rather than to Constantinople, for cultural and intellectual leadership. This brief revival of learning laid the foundation of a civilization which was to develop centuries later in the modern countries of Western Europe.

Europe again sank into disorder and strife. While the Holy Roman Empire lasted nearly a thousand years and had

Schoenfeld Collection from Three Lions
CHARLEMAGNE

This picture of the Emperor Charlemagne was made from a portrait painted by the German painter Dürer.

a great influence on the history of Western Europe, it ceased to be a great power soon after Charlemagne's death. Neither his sons nor their successors were able to rule so vast a territory. The bitter struggles between groups or states within the Empire and attacks from without caused Western Europe to sink again into disorder and confusion. The Slavs, attacking from the east, left a trail of bloodshed and destruction. The Northmen, daring adventurers from Scandinavia, seized many towns and took possession of lands in France and England. The Saracens renewed their attacks on the southern part of France and Italy. While Charlemagne may be said to have laid the cornerstone of modern nations of Western Europe, nearly three centuries elapsed before further progress was made in building them.

The weak sought the protection of the strong in exchange for services. Most kings of the time following the collapse of Charlemagne's empire did not have enough power to establish order. The lack of good roads made it hard for an army to put down a distant rebellion. Trade, which brought gold and silver, had died out, and the kings had nothing with which to pay the nobles and knights who fought for them, except land. As the nobles gained more land they also gained more power.

The people were always in danger of invaders from foreign lands, sometimes from Scandinavia and sometimes from eastern Europe. They also had to fear warring neighbors. They managed as well as they could to defend themselves. At first they tried building stockades, such as the American pioneers built to protect themselves from the Indians. But these were not strong enough to withstand a siege. Then the larger land-owners built round stone towers, which were secure against onslaught by simple weapons such as existed at that time. Later, when Europe became more prosperous, great castles such as the one shown on page 257 were built.

Of course only a wealthy landowner could afford to build a castle. A freeman with but a few acres of land was at the mercy of any invader. Such a man lived in fear of having his property destroyed and his family carried away into slavery. His ruler might be some distant king, but in times of peril he had to look for protection to the nearest powerful noble or landowner, to someone with a castle

in which to take refuge and a following of fighting men to give protection. As a result, most freemen made bargains with the rich nobles. They gave these lords their lands and received back only the use of them.

Vassals gave up their land for protection. When a freeman exchanged his land for the protection of someone more powerful, he became the *vassal* of the stronger lord. The lord promised to protect him, and the vassal in turn promised to do military service for his lord, thus adding to the lord's power. The land which the vassal held under these circumstances was called a *fief* [feef]. The bargain between the vassal and his lord was a hereditary bargain. It was also an honorable relation, since both were nobles, that is, fighting men. This relation extended from top to bottom of the noble land-holding class. When the lords in their turn found it necessary to seek the protection of those stronger than themselves, they would become vassals of some still greater lord above them. The system worked both ways. The king and also the great nobles needed soldiers; so they gave land as fiefs to men who became their vassals. Also, the kings who were not strong enough to govern gave the powers of government to the lords who were their vassals, but who had ceased to be subjects of the king as had been true in the past. The whole of noble society was thus held together by a complex series of personal vassal-lord relations.

Below the noble class were the great mass of the peasants. Some of these had been freemen with small farms who were forced to give up their land and seek protection. But unlike the more fortunate freemen, who had enough land to become fighting vassals, they were forced to work for the lord. Manual labor

Drawing by John C. Wonsetler

VASSAL DOING HOMAGE TO HIS NOBLE

This picture shows the freeman placing his hands between those of the lord. Notice that he has removed his head covering, and his sword and spurs. These acts formed the first part of the ceremony which made him a vassal.

was not regarded as an honorable service and they lost their freedom, becoming the property of the lord. Others of the peasants were descended from workers who never had been free. Others again were given land to work when the lord needed laborers. In any case, they were semislaves, bound to the land and ruled by the lord. They were known as serfs.

One of the chief obligations of the vassal of a noble lord was to take up arms for his lord for at least forty days each year. He might be called upon to provide arrows, spears, horses, grain, and other supplies when his lord went to war. The vassal was also expected to attend the court of the lord to help settle disputes among other vassals.

When the lord's son became a knight or his daughter was married, his vassals were expected to help pay the expenses. If a lord were captured in war and held for ransom, his vassals must help to buy his freedom. If a lord decided to visit one of his vassals, the vassal had to entertain him and any company he might bring with him.

A regular ceremony sealed the bargain which made a freeman a vassal. After uncovering his head and laying aside his sword and spurs, the freeman knelt before his lord, placed his hands between those of the lord, and promised to be " his man." The lord raised him up and gave him the kiss of peace. When the vassal had sworn solemnly to be faithful to his lord at all times, the lord gave him a piece of earth, a stone, or a branch as a symbol of the land, or fief, which was given into the vassal's charge. This ceremony was repeated when either lord or vassal died and was succeeded by his heir.

The Holy Roman Empire revived. In 962 a German king, Otto I, revived the idea of a Christian Roman Empire which had first taken form under Charlemagne, and he was crowned emperor. His empire included some of the same land that Charlemagne had ruled: Germany and a part of Italy. For nearly a thousand years, until the early 19th Century, this institution continued to exist and to exert a claim over greatly varying territories, which at times included eastern France. Its emperors, usually Germans or Austrians, were elected by the German nobility and crowned by the Pope. The Holy Roman Empire was partly religious and partly political in nature. In time it lost most of its power through a long struggle between the popes and the emperors. It became in the later Middle Ages a kind of shadowy over-government of a number of principalities, but did not exert much actual control.

Chapter 2 ~ The Life of the Castle Was Supported by the Toil of the Serf

The castle was built for security. The word *castle* sounds imposing. If you were to visit one of the medieval castles today, such as those still found in Normandy, France, you would agree that the medieval castles were impressive. The stone walls were often twelve to fifteen feet thick. The rooms were damp and dark because of the few, narrow windows, infrequently spaced in the cold, damp walls. Castles were usually huge places, and you can imagine the difficulty of heating them even with a fireplace in almost every room. There was, of course, no plumbing as we know it. In fact from the angle of domestic comfort the castles were gloomy, drafty, and often unclean — in short, they were rather uninviting piles of stone masonry.

But castles were built for a purpose. They were places of refuge from attack. The lord of the castle and his serfs, who worked the surrounding land, looked upon the castle as an island of safety in unsafe times. The castle was the home of the lord and his family, a temporary place of safety for his dependents in time of attack, and all in all the center of life in feudal times.

Feudal times lasted for many hundreds of years — from about the time of the breakup of Charlemagne's empire to the 14th Century, and even later in some countries. A castle such as we have described could not have been built in early feudal times for lack of wealth and even skilled masons to build it. It was, therefore, not until after the 11th Century that feudal castles as we have described them could come into being. Before that time cruder methods of protection and simpler strongholds were used.

Gunpowder and cannon had not yet come into use in Europe, and they were not generally used until nearly 1500. So the lord located his castle to withstand the cruder weapons of that time. These weapons included catapults for hurling stones weighing as much as three hundred pounds, battering rams for breaking down heavy gates, and movable towers from which the attackers could throw a bridge across the moat to the castle wall. Since the chief reason for building

A MEDIEVAL CASTLE

Steep cliffs, thick walls, and deep moats provided safety for the noble, his household, and his dependents. Why would such devices be ineffective today?

the castles was security, the lord tried to build his castle in a place where it was difficult to move these machines close enough to do any harm. A hill-top or an island made a good site. Otherwise a broad ditch, or moat, could be dug, and a high protective wall placed around the castle.

The moat around a castle might be' thirty feet wide and forty feet deep, and was filled with water. Inside a high outer fence, or stockade, sentries kept watch. A stone roadway led to the top of the pier on which the drawbridge rested when lowered across the moat, as shown in the illustration above.

Between the towers guarding the castle entrance were swung heavy wooden doors which could be securely barred. A heavy iron grating, called a portcullis, was suspended above the entrance. It could be lowered quickly if an enemy managed to cross the drawbridge. At strategic points the walls were protected by strong circular towers in which were

stairways leading to the battlements above. Some towers jutted out over the edge of the walls, and had narrow openings in the floors through which arrows could be shot and hot water or molten lead poured down upon the foe. In early times the walls and towers were built with square corners, but these gave way to round towers which had no corners where an enemy could find shelter.

A feudal castle was like a small community. The outer wall of the castle sheltered stable and shops. The main entrance led to an outer court where the lord kept his horses. Here the near-by villagers stored their food and sought shelter in time of war. The outer court often resembled a small village. There were the carpenter shops, the great oven where bread was baked, and the shops of the tailor, saddler, swordsmith, and other craftsmen.

Sometimes the outer court was separated from an inner court by another heavy wall quite like the outer one.

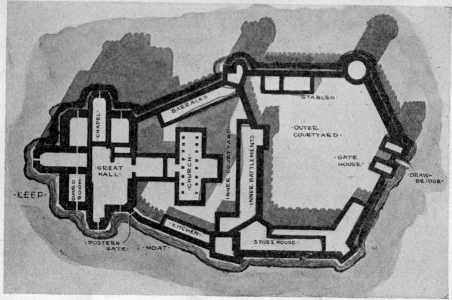

Drawing by John C. Wonsetler

PLAN OF A TYPE OF ENGLISH CASTLE

This plan shows why many of the feudal castles were practically impregnable. Notice the thick walls, the protective moat, and the numerous massive towers. The keep, which served as a final inaccessible refuge for the lord and his family, is shown at the left.

Should the enemy gain entrance to the outer court he had not yet taken the castle. In fact, he might find himself trapped in the outer court, with defenders on both sides.

Provisions were generally stored in buildings in the inner court. There also was the kitchen, a building shaped like a great jug with a chimney, something like a modern charcoal or lime kiln [kil]. The food was cooked over an open fire. In order to roast the fowl or other meat evenly, it was slowly turned on a spit, or stick. When just right it was said to be "done to a turn."

In most castles there was a small church or chapel in which the lord and his followers worshiped. Sometimes, in attacking a castle, an enemy would hurl a spear or throw stones against the chapel. Then the lord could send a messenger to a neighboring lord saying that the

church had been attacked. He knew the neighbor might then come to the rescue when he would not have come for any other reason.

The keep was the stronghold of the castle. The most important building in a castle was located in the spot that was hardest to reach. It was known as the keep, and was the home of the lord. The keep was the real stronghold of the castle where the lord and his followers made their last stand against the enemy.

The floors of the main hall were usually of stone covered with rushes. Here and there a suit of shining armor, a cluster of lances and swords, or embroidered banners and tapestries decorated the walls.

The earlier castles that were built had no separate bedrooms. At night coarse mattresses were laid on the hall floor for the lord's family. Later, when castles were built higher and larger, separate rooms with crude beds were added. If a lord accumulated wealth, the bedroom furnishings became more elaborate. Then there would be ornate beds, perhaps with gilt bedposts inlaid with ivory, as well as silk bed covers.

Dinner was served in the main hall. The main room or great hall of the keep where the lord and his family lived had a huge fireplace, or perhaps two fireplaces, one at each end of the room. At mealtime a long table was set up; it was made by placing boards on trestles so that it could be put away after each meal. These board tables were the origin of our words *board* and *boardinghouse*.

In those days there were no forks, plates, saucers, or napkins. Sharp steel hunting knives were used for carving meat into portions. The people ate from trenchers, which were crude plates made of thick slices of stale bread; often two people used the same trencher. Later the trenchers were made of wood. Everyone ate with his fingers and licked them or wiped them on his clothes. Though forks were in use in Italy at an earlier date, they were not common in Western Europe until well into the 17th Century. Bones were thrown to dogs that were allowed to stay in the room to eat the scraps from the unswept floor. When the meal was over a large bowl and towels were brought in for those who wanted to wash the grease and food from their fingers. A meal is shown in progress in the drawing below.

The ladies of the castle wore gorgeous costumes. In later feudal times, when the nobles had amassed wealth, the lord and his family lived in some degree of luxury. The ladies of the castle spent much time on their elaborate costumes. Some of these costumes are shown on the following page. During one period they wore tight-fitting dresses with long, full skirts and tight-fitting sleeves which extended to their knuckles. Sleeves were often decorated with fifty or sixty buttons. The more colors that were combined in one costume, the more fash-

DINNER IN A CASTLE

Pages and squires, and sometimes a vassal, served the nobles and ladies. The dogs were always eager attendants at the dining table at mealtime.

COSTUMES WORN IN THE 14TH, 15TH, AND 16TH CENTURIES

Both men and women of wealth wore elaborate costumes during the Middle Ages. Head coverings were particularly fanciful, as shown here by the high peaked cap on the small lady at the left. Notice that heavy, brocaded materials were in great favor.

ionable the garment seemed to be. Their clothes were not often washed or cleaned, in spite of their elegance. People usually slept between sheepskins in the same clothes in which they worked all day. Perfumes and powders took the place of cleaning and washing. The lack of personal cleanliness was a characteristic of feudal peoples of all classes.

The style of headdress for ladies often changed, but it was nearly always elaborate, as you can see from the illustration above. At one time the hair was covered with a net of gold threads. At another time the hair was puffed out to give the appearance of horns, butterfly wings, a crescent, or a harp. At one time the women wore a headdress shaped like a tall cone with yards of lightweight cloth fastened to the tip. Men also wore vivid colors and rich costumes which were the forerunners of the elaborate court costumes of a later time.

Young men and girls lived at the castle. In a lord's household were a number of boys and girls of noble birth. These were sons and daughters of vassals or other lords, who had been sent to the castle to receive their education. The girls were taught to manage a house-

hold, to card wool, to spin and weave, to sew, and to embroider. They were carefully taught how to dress the wounds of an injured knight. They also learned to sing, dance, ride, and hunt so that they could join the knights in these pleasures.

Pages were trained to be squires. Until a boy of the noble class was seven years of age, when his education for knighthood began, he was left to the care of his mother and the other women of the castle. From the age of seven to fourteen he was called a page. Probably not much of his education was book learning. He studied a little reading and less writing. It was no disgrace for a knight not to know how to read or even write his own name.

A page learned to sing and to play backgammon and chess. Such accomplishments were looked upon as marks of a gentleman. A page was taught to say his prayers and show respect for religion. The main ideal of his training was service. He must wait upon the ladies and lords of the castle and do their bidding. He must always be gentle and polite, for a knight was a gentleman who should never fail in courtesy.

A page had to learn to care for and
de his horse; to sit securely when jump-
ng a ditch or wall; to spring to the sad-
le without the aid of a stirrup. He
ad to help the squires keep the lord's
eapons and armor in good condition.
He was trained in swimming, fencing,
nd boxing. He had to meet other boys
n sham contests to show that he could
ecome a valiant knight. He learned
o assist lords and ladies in the sports
f hunting, and to train the hawks that
ere used in falconry and the dogs for
he chase.

A boy who was a page looked forward
o the time when he would enter the
econd stage of training for knighthood,
nd become a squire. The training he
nad begun as a page became more in-
ensive. The squire was trained to use
all the weapons, such as the lance, ax,
sword, and mace.

**The squire took the vows of knight-
hood.** When a squire was made a knight
he had to go through a number of ceremonies. First came the bath of purifica-
tion, after which he put on garments of
red, white, and black. The red stood for
the blood he was willing to shed for
the oppressed and for the Church. The
white signified that he was pure and
clean in mind. The black was to remind
him of death which comes to all.

After a night of " watching the arms "
and fasting and praying in the church,
the squires assembled in the courtyard.
A great number of knights and ladies
gathered for the ceremony of knight-
ing. After friends had helped each
squire to gird on his armor and sword,

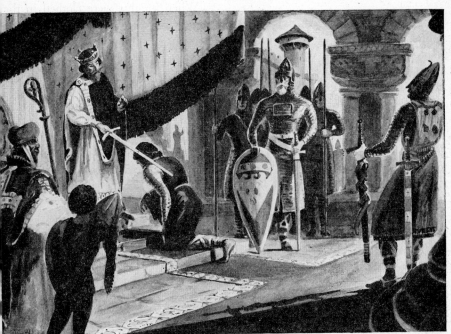

Drawing by John C. Wonsetler

THE ACCOLADE

The young squire in this picture has reached the final step in the ceremony of becoming
a knight. As he kneels, the lord touches him on the shoulder with the flat of his sword.
The new knight is then ready to start his career.

Metropolitan Museum of Art

A KNIGHT IN ARMOR

A knight had to be well protected and well armed, since he had to depend upon himself for the safety that government gives us.

he was ready for the climax of the ceremony. The squire's father or lord advanced and gave him what was called the accolade [ak'oh layd'], a stroke on the shoulder with the flat of his sword. At the same time the lord said, "In the name of God and St. Michael and St. George I dub you knight. Be brave and loyal." In different localities the names of different saints were used.

A suit of armor protected the knight. A knight had to be prepared to defend himself on a journey, when waging war, or when defending his own castle. He wore a coat of mail or armor to protect himself against lances, swords, and battle-axes. Such armor is worn by the knight in the illustration above.

The complete suit of armor was not devised at one time. In the early days of knighthood a knight wore a leather tunic, or shirt, and breeches of the same material. For greater protection rows of small metal rings were fastened onto the leather. Gradually other parts of the armor were added until some coats of mail were so heavy that a knight could not mount his horse without help.

Each part of the armor was carefully shaped to fit the body, as you can see from the picture at the left. The part that protected the hand was called a gauntlet, a word which we use to describe a certain kind of glove. A metal helmet protected the head. Some helmets were very much like those worn by our soldiers today; others were broad-brimmed like a large hat, or shaped like a cone with a visor that protected the entire face. These visors hid the face so well that the knight raised his visor when approaching friends. From this we get our custom of tipping the hat. A knight often added to his helmet a metal crest in the form of an eagle, lion, or dragon.

When knights were clothed in their complete armor with their visors down, it was impossible to tell friend from foe. So they began to use certain signs drawn on the shield or breastplates. These insignia developed into coats of arms, and were embroidered on a knight's coat and upon the trappings of his horse. The coat of arms, and the crest on the helmet, were handed down from generation to generation in many families.

Wealthy nobles gave tournaments. Just as the Greeks had their Olympic games, the Romans had their chariot races and gladiatorial combats, and American universities have football games, so the knights of the Middle Ages engaged in a sport which was a kind of sham battle with other knights. When such a contest was limited to two men it was called a joust [juhst]. When two teams of several men each took part it was known as a tournament.

Tournaments were given by wealthy nobles, and attracted the knights and

Culver Service

A JOUST

The joust and the tournament filled a larger place in the life of the Middle Ages than collegiate football occupies in modern times. Notice the royal box on the left, the plumes on the knights' helmets, and the trappings of the horses.

their ladies from far and near. Possibly you remember that the ancient Greeks were always guaranteed a safe journey to the Olympic games. The same right was given in the Middle Ages to those who traveled to a tournament. Even in time of war, rulers of hostile countries would usually allow those who wanted to attend a tournament to pass through their territory without harm.

On the day of a tournament great crowds gathered. The galleries, which had been built for the occasion, were decorated with rich tapestries and floating banners and were filled with gaily dressed men and women. When the heralds cried, " Come forth, knights, come forth," the knights dashed upon the field dressed in glittering armor, with the bright colors of their favorite ladies fluttering from helmets and lances. Victory went to the knight who unhorsed his opponent or broke the greatest number of lances. A defeated knight sometimes forfeited his horse and armor to the victor or paid for his defeat in some other way. Sometimes he lost his life, especially when real weapons were used instead of blunted lances or swords without points.

The nobles fought almost continually. The nobles gave much of their time to fighting. They regarded the waging of war on one another as a privilege that should not be interfered with by either the king or the Church. The stronger grew more ambitious and conquered the property of the weaker. There was continual fighting and disorder.

The Church tried to stop the constant fighting of the knights. It encouraged them toward higher ideals and customs of knighthood. There developed a code of knightly behavior called *chivalry,* from a French word meaning "horseman." The good knight who respected his word and rendered service to others was said to be chivalrous. Many romantic stories have been written about ideal knights, but evidently such knights appeared more often in stories than in history. However, many knights did strive to live up to their code. Some of our modern customs, characteristics of dress, and ideals of conduct can be traced to the days of chivalry.

The peasant provided luxury for the noble. How could the nobles give so much time to warfare and to their own pleasures? Who provided their food and clothing, who built their castles and paid their expenses for waging war on one another? The nobles of the Middle Ages thought that they were a privileged class and had the right to live by the hard work of others. They were not the only ones who believed this. One writer has quoted a bishop of the Middle Ages as saying:

God has divided the human race, from the beginning, into three classes. These are the priests, whose duty it is to pray and serve God; the knights, whose duty it is to defend society; and peasants, whose duty it is to till the soil and support by their labor the other classes.

During the Middle Ages there were not many people in the upper classes who thought much about what happened to the peasant, though his hard work provided all their needs and luxuries alike. In feudal times there was no consideration given to equality or freedom from want. Many peasants were *serfs,* who had to remain on the lord's lands and do his bidding, as you learned in Chapter 1.

The peasants lived in villages for protection. The peasants did not live on scattered farms as most American farmers do, but in small communities or villages. In the mornings they led their sheep, cattle, or geese to the fields to feed, and then worked on the land. But in the evening they returned to the village for security. This practice has come down to the present in certain parts of Europe, especially France and the Balkan states. Some household or stable servants, of course, lived in their lord's castle.

Most serfs worked on the land. Each village had a blacksmith, a leather worker, and a carpenter, but most of the men worked in the fields. Usually there was a small plot of ground close to the huts in the village, where each family was expected to plant fruit trees and raise onions, cabbages, and carrots. Potatoes were not grown in these gardens; the Americas, where potatoes were first found, had not yet been discovered. Each man was held responsible for the cultivation of several plots outside the village in addition to the village gardens. Instead of giving a serf one piece of land to work, the lord gave him several long strips scattered in different fields among those worked by other serfs. It was thought that this plan would give each man some good and some poor land. The amount of land worked by one man would vary from a few to a hundred or more acres.

The medieval farmer would have been amazed by the large crop an American farmer can raise on one acre of ground. Where a modern farmer gets twenty-five or thirty bushels of grain to an acre, a serf seldom got more than six or eight. Since he did not know about prepared fertilizers or other modern ways of caring for land, he allowed his fields to rest one year out of three to keep them from becoming unproductive. He used crude farming implements, such as wooden plows which seldom even had iron points.

The peasants lived in rude huts. The houses in the village of serfs were something like the huts of the early American pioneers, only they were more crudely built and had thatched roofs. Sometimes the walls were of stone and the roof of clapboards. The small rooms were dark and unsanitary. Usually there were no glazed windows, since glass was very rare. When a window was cut through the side of a hut, it was covered with oiled linen or paper that let in very little light.

While most castles had fireplaces and chimneys, though these were often defective, the fires of the peasants were usually built on a hearth in the center of the room. The smoke escaped through cracks and through the door. The door was sometimes built so that the upper half could be left open to let out the smoke while the lower half remained closed. The cattle were usually housed under the same roof with the peasant's family, a custom which has not entirely disappeared in some parts of Europe. The bed of the whole family often consisted of a pile of straw, in the corner or in the loft, covered with the skins of animals. If the serf were a little more prosperous he might have beds or bunks made of stakes and poles. The packed-down earth which served as the floor was covered with rushes. Carpets were a luxury which the villagers seldom saw. Instead of chairs they had stools. In place of cups and glasses the serf drank out of horns and gourds. All the furniture was rough and crude.

Peasants wore coarse clothes and ate coarse food. The clothing of the peasants was of animal skins or homespun wool. Generally they wore only one garment, a loose, sacklike dress which hung from

A VILLAGE SCENE IN THE MIDDLE AGES

Village life in the Middle Ages was as lacking in comfort and conveniences as life in American pioneer days. The villagers had to toil for the noble who lived in a castle, but the pioneers were free to work for themselves and their families.

Ewing Galloway

A MEDIEVAL CASTLE

In the Middle Ages this medieval castle dominated and protected the serfs who lived under its shadow. The castle has survived the feudal period. The peasants in the roadway enjoy more privileges and comforts than did the serfs of the Middle Ages.

the shoulders to the knees. This was gathered in at the waist with a leather belt or rope; the arms and legs were left bare.

The food of the peasants was coarse and had little variety. The two chief articles of diet were cabbage and a dark bread made of barley, oats, and beans. The bread was coarse and heavy. White bread was eaten only by the well-to-do and nobles. Although the rich had a great deal of meat on their tables, a servant was fined or beaten if he had meat at his table without permission. Sometimes he had fish, caught in near-by rivers.

On special occasions the serfs were invited to take part in merrymaking at the castle, and there were times, especially when the lord was generous, when the peasants had good meat and ale on their tables. But generally their fare was poor and monotonous.

Many articles of food that we find on the average American table today were great luxuries during the Middle Ages. Salt was scarce because it had to be brought long distances over muddy roads where robbers lurked. Often the salt supply was so low that the meat which was preserved in brine for winter use spoiled; this often caused disease. Many people kept swarms of bees for honey. It was used as we use sugar. Coffee and tea had not yet been introduced into Europe.

In times of war, or when one bad season followed another, there was great suffering from lack of food. The serfs usually had no provisions saved; sometimes they were forced to live on roots and the bark of trees. Many died of starvation. As in all times of conquest or famine, the poor suffered the most.

There were severe laws for the peasant. Laws and punishment for the peasant were much more strict than for any other class of people. The Church claimed the right to hold a special court for members of the clergy and they were often let off for wrong-doing with only light penalty. Many nobles were so powerful that no court was strong enough to punish them. But there was no one to uphold the rights of the serf. He could not even marry without his lord's consent. Inhuman penalties were often inflicted for even slight offenses. Men were sometimes hanged for no greater crime than killing a pig belonging to a noble. Peasants might be branded, and carry the scars for the rest of their lives. For the serf there was no real justice, unless the lord was kindly.

The lack of hope for justice had the effect of making the people more lawless. One writer has said:

A violent ruffian knew if he robbed a man he would be hanged, and that the punishment could be no worse if he murdered him. He had nothing to gain by letting him live, and nothing to lose if he cut his throat. Rather than be captured he might as well make a good fight and kill as many as stood in his way of escape.

The peasant paid heavy taxes. The hardships of a peasant were increased by his duties to his lord. He paid the rent on his plots of ground by giving the lord a certain share of what he raised. Part of each week he had to help cultivate the lord's land in payment for the land and the protection which the lord furnished him. He had to present the lord with a lamb, a pig, or a calf for the use of his pasture. He had to grind his grain at the lord's mill; bake his bread in the lord's oven; and press his grapes at his wine press. And he had to pay well for these privileges. He had to pay extra taxes when the lord's daughter was married, or if the lord were captured and held for ransom.

Sometimes while fighting or hunting, the nobles rode carelessly over the peasants' crops, destroying them. The peasants had no real protection against such injuries. Some effort was made to end these oppressions, especially through the Truce of God, about which you will read in the next chapter. But conditions were still so bad in the 11th Century that a bishop tried to get the feudal barons to take this oath:

I will not take away a cow nor any other beast of burden. I will not seize the peasant nor the peasant's wife nor the merchant's. . . . From the first of March to All Saints' Day I will seize neither horse nor mare nor colt from the pasture. I will not destroy and burn houses; I will not uproot and devastate vineyards under pretext of war. . . .

Although this attempt to better the conditions of the serf had little effect, the oath shows how very difficult were the conditions under which the serfs existed.

Chapter 3 ~ A Strong Church Held Sway in the Feudal World

The Church discouraged fighting. During the Middle Ages some men of the Church tried to improve the conduct of the knights and their treatment of the serfs. To be sure, sometimes the clergy themselves acted very much like the feudal lords when they themselves fought, as sometimes seemed necessary, to protect Church lands. But in spite of its darker pages, the Church had much influence for good. As it grew in influence the Church managed to issue a decree (about A.D. 1000) known as the Truce of God. This order forbade the nobles to fight from Wednesday evening to Monday morning in each week, and also on certain sacred days such as Christmas and Easter, and during Lent. Although the nobles did not always obey the Truce, it did curb their fighting to some extent.

The Church also established sanctuaries, or holy places where no blood was to be shed. If a man was accused of any crime and was in fear of being killed he came to the church. There he could be safe until the priest could settle the dispute.

The Church could disgrace the disobedient. If a noble disobeyed the orders of the Church, he was excommunicated, which means he was cut off entirely from the Church. This was both a punishment and a disgrace. If a noble was cut off from the Church in this way he lost all his property. No one could speak to him or give him food or shelter. When he died he could not be buried in sacred ground or hope for heavenly reward. Sometimes, to punish a whole community or country, the priests closed the doors of the churches and refused to carry on services. This practice w[as] feared by the people. It meant that:

> The music of the bells was silenced a[nd] the bodies of the dead lay unburied, stri[k]ing the beholders with fear and horr[or.] The solemn joys of the church servic[e] were no longer known.

Gradually the Church grew strong[er] and stronger. From the middle of t[he] 11th Century to the end of the 13th, t[he] Bishop of Rome, called the Pope, w[as] usually more powerful than any Eur[o]pean king or noble.

St. Benedict founded a monastery. I[n] the midst of the fighting and turmoil [of] the Middle Ages there were some me[n] of the Church who sought peace an[d] quiet. Having no desire for the riche[s] over which people quarreled and foug[ht,] they believed that they could get close[r] to God by a life of prayer, fasting, an[d] self-discipline. These men banded to[get]her in monasteries and were know[n] as *monks,* a word which means " alone." At the beginning of the Sixth Centur[y] Saint Benedict founded a monaster[y at] Monte Cassino [mahn'teh kahs se[o] noh], in Italy. He made rules for th[e] conduct of the monks which came t[o] serve as models for the other monas[]teries of the Middle Ages. Unfortunatel[y] this ancient monastery was destroye[d] during World War II. German troop[s] held the monastery and it was necessar[y] to bomb and shell it to dislodge them.

A monk took a threefold vow. O[n] entering a monastery a monk took [a] threefold vow committing him to pov[]erty, chastity, and obedience. This mean[t] that he must give up all his propert[y] and turn everything he had over to th[e] monastery. He did not even own th[e] ough shirt he wore, the sheepskins he hrew down on the cold stone floor to leep on, or the quill pen with which he copied old manuscripts. When a monk ook the vow of chastity he promised hat he would never marry. Since he had no responsibility for a wife and children, his greatest interest could be his religion.

The monk's oath of obedience made him responsible to the abbot who was at the head of the monastery. At the command of the abbot he worked for long hours, cooking, washing the home-spun clothing, or raising vegetables in the garden. Saint Benedict believed that hard work was the salvation of every monk. "To work is to pray," he said. Another man wrote, "A laboring monk is troubled by one devil; an idle monk by a host of devils." When a monk worked in the field or appeared in pub-lic, he wore a long, black, hooded cloak. The dark, simple clothing of the monks made a sharp contrast with the elaborate and richly colored costumes of the no-bles.

The monks preserved ancient learn-ing. To the monasteries we owe some of the best things that the Church did dur-ing the Middle Ages. Had it not been for the monks, much of the ancient learning would have been lost. Roman writings had been made on papyrus or parchment of goat, calf, or sheepskin. When these began to crumble, or if the work were rare, the monks copied them with painstaking care. They also illu-minated their manuscripts; that is, they decorated them with beautifully colored letters and pictures. You can see part of a page of this old manuscript at the top of the next page. It took hours to draw and decorate one of the elaborate capital letters. It took so many years to copy one manuscript that several monks

Metropolitan Museum of Art

A MONK AT WORK IN A SCRIPTORIUM
The monks of the Middle Ages spent many years preserving Greek and Roman learn-ing for later civilizations.

might make this their life work. When one died, another took up the task.

The monks taught nobles and peas-ants. Not only did the monks keep alive the learning of the past, but they were the teachers of their period. Many of the monasteries kept two kinds of schools. One was for those who wanted to join the order, and the other for sons of no-bles and freemen. In these schools the students were taught something about reading, writing, and arithmetic, as well as the ideals of a gentleman.

The men of the neighborhood learned many things about raising crops as they saw the monks plant and care for their own vegetables and grains. The monks helped them to build dikes to keep out the flood waters and to drain swamps so there would be more land to culti-vate. They taught the peasants all they knew about breeding domestic animals.

Metropolitan Museum of Art

PART OF A PAGE OF ILLUMINATED MANUSCRIPT

Many of the illuminated books were works of art in which the artist-monk illustrated the ideas on the page in pictures. Beautiful colors were frequently used.

The monks were respected. Some of the monks mingled with the people, and did much to make their burdens easier. When peasants were ill, the monks gave them simple medicines made in the monastery. A traveler could be sure of food and a bed at the monastery. The monks were usually greatly respected by men, women, and children alike.

Of course, life in a monastery appealed to some men who were not very religious. It was an escape from war and trouble, and it offered quiet for study. In the course of time many monasteries became very wealthy through gifts of land. In periods when the religious spirit of a monastery declined, some monks might live a rather luxurious life.

The Order of St. Francis served the poor. Other kinds of religious orders were founded during the Middle Ages. One of the most remarkable men of those times was St. Francis of Assisi [ahs see'zee] in Italy, founder of the Franciscan Order. His followers were called friars. They preached to the people in the towns rather than staying to themselves in monasteries as the monks did. They lived humbly, devoting their lives to the poor. They were not allowed to have any possessions and had to work for their bread or even beg for it if necessary.

Great Christian cathedrals were built. The Church was responsible for the building of magnificent cathedrals, such as the one shown in the illustration on page 271. Nothing portrays more clearly the important place religion had in the daily lives of the people than the churches, which it sometimes required hundreds of years to build. The cathedrals were gifts of labor and love from the people, both rich and poor.

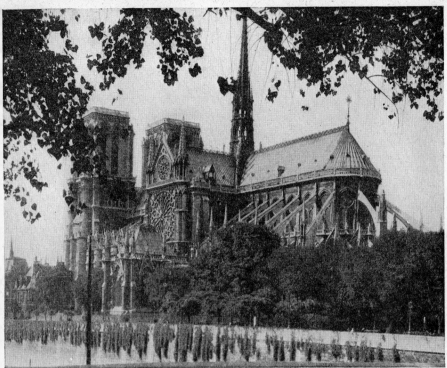

NOTRE DAME CATHEDRAL

Notre Dame Cathedral is built on an island in the Seine River, which flows through Paris. This photograph shows a rear view of the Cathedral. Notice the flying buttresses. On the larger tower are gargoyles, the grotesque figures that personify evil spirits. The Cathedral is famous for the beauty of its early Gothic architecture and for the history associated with it. Napoleon was crowned ruler of France in Notre Dame, and the marriage of Mary Queen of Scots took place there.

Not everyone could write earnest prayers or beautiful hymns, or go on a pilgrimage to some spot sacred in Church history. But almost everyone could take some part in the building of a cathedral. Sometimes an artisan might work for years carving one beautiful figure in stone. Care, patience, skill, and devotion helped to make these churches among the finest ever erected.

The first Christian churches were Romanesque. Until the 12th Century Christian churches were usually built in what is known as the Romanesque [roh'm'n-esk'] style of architecture. They had heavy, thick walls to support the vaulted stone ceiling. The windows had to be small and narrow so that the walls would not be weakened. The windows were rounded at the top like the arches the Romans had used in their bridges. Because of the thick walls and small windows, the interiors of the churches were cold and dark.

A new type of architecture developed. A new style of architecture called *Gothic* developed in Western Europe in about the 12th Century. In contrast to the Romanesque style, it had thin walls and many tall, beautifully designed win-

GARGOYLE ON NOTRE DAME CATHEDRAL
Gothic buildings were often adorned with
weird, half-animal or birdlike stone figures
like the one pictured here. Some of these
figures served as waterspouts, and so came
to be called gargoyles, from a French word
meaning "throat." Later, similar decora-
tions were also called gargoyles.

dows. This change was made possible
by the discovery that a flying buttress, a
column-like support outside the walls,
would hold up a heavy ceiling as well as
the walls. It is one of the main characteristics of Gothic architecture. You can
see flying buttresses in the illustration on
page 271. The large windows were made
of small pieces of colored glass skillfully
leaded together. There were many beautiful designs. One of the most famous
was the rose window of the cathedral at
Reims [raNs], pictured on page 422.
The designs were sometimes pictures,
often illustrating stories from the Bible.
The people who could not read could
learn something of the life of Christ
from these pictures. Probably you have

often seen similar colored windows in
our American churches. Churchmen in
Europe attempted to preserve these
structures from damage during the
World Wars. Many glass windows were
removed for safekeeping. Sandbags were
stacked about the stone carvings. However, considerable damage was done to
some of these structures.

**The Gothic church symbolized Chris-
tianity.** A Gothic church is always built
with its floor plan in the form of a cross
to remind people of the crucifixion of
Christ. Its towers pierce the sky and its
windows have pointed arches as if to
draw the worshiper's thoughts upward.
Groups of stone figures represent many
of the Bible stories and lives of the
saints. And, strangely enough, grotesque gargoyles, such as the one pictured at the left, sometimes glare down
from the upper ledges.

Gothic architecture took its name
from the barbarian Goths who entered
Rome early in the Fifth Century. The
Romans always thought of the Goths as
uncivilized people who had no respect
for the fine arts and architecture. When
the new architecture first appeared in
Italy, the Italians did not like it, and
called it Gothic to imply that it was the
work of barbarians.

**Christians made pilgrimages to gain
spiritual blessings.** A stanch Christian
often showed his reverence for the
Church by going on a journey to some
sacred shrine or even to the Holy Land.
These journeys were called pilgrimages.
Some pilgrims who were ill walked for
miles in the hope that they would be
cured if they prayed before a certain
shrine or touched a sacred relic. Others
were sent on pilgrimages by their priests
as penance for sin. Sometimes they wore
heavy chains or walked with peas in
their shoes, for they believed that these

iscomforts would somehow help to ake them more holy.

A pilgrim was easy to recognize on ie road. He wore a rough gray cloak nd a round felt hat. Over his shoulder vas slung a bag in which he carried any ood that was given him. A water bottle ung from his long walking staff. With iis meager equipment, a pilgrim some- mes walked hundreds of miles.

Priests and nobles sometimes made ong pilgrimages, and many of them vent as far as Palestine. Those who were prominent carried letters from their kings asking for protection from rulers in the countries through which they passed.

Some of the pilgrims, who were mer- chants, came back from the Holy Land with heavier purses than they had when they started. They had bought silks, spices, fine linens, and laces from the Eastern caravans, and then sold them at huge profits on the homeward journey. In this way the Church unconsciously helped commerce and trade.

Chapter 4 ~ The Crusades Helped to Break the Barriers of Feudalism

The Turks captured Jerusalem. Since ie Seventh Century, Jerusalem had een ruled by the Mohammedan Arabs, ho had permitted the pilgrims to pass ack and forth through the land with- ut molesting them. They were even villing to allow the Christians to live in erusalem provided they paid a tax of vo gold pieces each year, dressed dif- erently from the Mohammedans, did ot place the cross on any of their build- ugs, and stood up when a Mohamme- an came among them. Although the Christians may not have liked these ules, still they saw in them no great ause for complaint.

Then in the 11th Century Jerusalem vas captured by the warlike Turks. "hese new conquerors, who were also f the Mohammedan faith, were not so onsiderate as the Arabs had been. Of- en pilgrims who walked peacefully long the roads in their journey to the holy places in Jerusalem were killed without pity. Devout priests were dragged from the churches and thrown into dungeons. Everywhere Christians were mobbed and murdered.

Peter the Hermit urged the rescue of Jerusalem. One of the pilgrims, who was very angry at this cruelty, was a monk called Peter the Hermit. As Peter knelt in prayer before the Holy Sepulcher [sep"l ker] in Jerusalem, thought by many to be the burial place of Christ, he believed that he heard the voice of Christ saying, " Peter, arise; hasten to proclaim the suffering of my people; it is time my servants should receive help." So Peter hastened back to Italy to tell his story to Pope Urban II. The Pope listened gravely while Peter told of the suffering of the pilgrims and advised Peter to do as the voice had directed him.

Dressed in the coarse, gray mantle of a pilgrim, bareheaded and barefooted,

Brown Brothers

CRUSADERS ON THE MARCH

Priests and soldiers march at the head of the Crusade; women and noncombatants follow in the procession. The zeal of the crusaders kept them from realizing the enormousness of their undertaking — to march from Germany to Jerusalem. In the 11th Century, when the Crusades began, travel was dangerous for civilians.

and carrying a heavy cross, Peter journeyed through France to urge people to support his cause. He told them that he had seen Christians loaded with irons, carried into slavery, and harnessed to the yoke like animals. He had seen priests dragged from their churches, beaten with rods, and condemned to death. " Repent! Repent! " he cried. " You now have a chance to win pardon for all your sins. He who strikes a blow to rescue the Holy Sepulcher from the pollution of the unbelievers has thrown open the door of heaven for himself."

It was not long before Pope Urban took up the cause of the pilgrims. He called a great assembly at Clermont [kler mon'] in France, and urged the nobles to declare a holy war. " If you are slain," he said, " you will indeed have lost your bodies but you will have saved your souls. Do not refuse for love of your families; for you must love God more than these."

The nobles shouted, " God wills it! God wills it! " and this became their war cry. The nobles received crosses of red cloth which they were to wear upon the breast on their way to the Holy Land and upon the back during the homeward journey. To those who in this way "took the cross" was given the name of crusaders.

Excitement swept the feudal world. August (1096) was set as the time of departure of the First Crusade. Many people were carried away with eagerness. Priests left their churches; whole towns were deserted. Many persons sold everything they owned to buy arms and other equipment. If a servant wanted to join the expedition, his master did not dare deny him. "God wills it!" cried the criminal in prison, and the doors of his dungeon were thrown open so that he might become a crusader.

The enthusiasm became so great that some of the people did not wait for the day of departure. Two large companies set out early, one under the leadership of Peter the Hermit. Thousands in these companies traveled on foot, carrying swords, iron clubs, and rude weapons. Many women and children joined the band.

Poor misguided people! They did not stop to think how much food would be needed for such an enormous army. Some of them expected God to send manna to his followers as he had in the stories in the Bible. They did not stop to consider that high mountains and hot deserts must be crossed before they reached the Holy Land. Many had no idea how far it was to Jerusalem. Whenever they came in sight of a new city the children cried, "Is this Jerusalem?"

While the men and women in this first group were on French and German soil, they were fed and kindly treated. But when they crossed the boundary into what is now Bulgaria, they found the people unfriendly. The Bulgarians refused to give food to the crusaders; so they stole flocks, burned houses, and even murdered some of the people. The

Culver Service

THE STORMING OF CONSTANTINOPLE

The leaders of the Fourth Crusade turned their forces to conquests rather than to the liberation of Jerusalem. Constantinople was twice captured. The second time, it was sacked.

Bulgarians took up arms and rushed into battle. The crusaders were hopelessly defeated, and their women and children were carried off as slaves.

The First Crusade gets under way. The nobles of France, Germany, and Italy continued their preparations for the real First Crusade that had been planned at the time of the Pope's appeal. On the day set, the crusaders started for Jerusalem in five large companies, each made up of well-trained and well-armed knights. Knowing of the failure of the advance forces, the leaders of the First Crusade insisted upon good order and military discipline. They found the journey long and difficult, but they did not suffer as did the unfortunate people who preceded them.

The crusaders finally reached the city

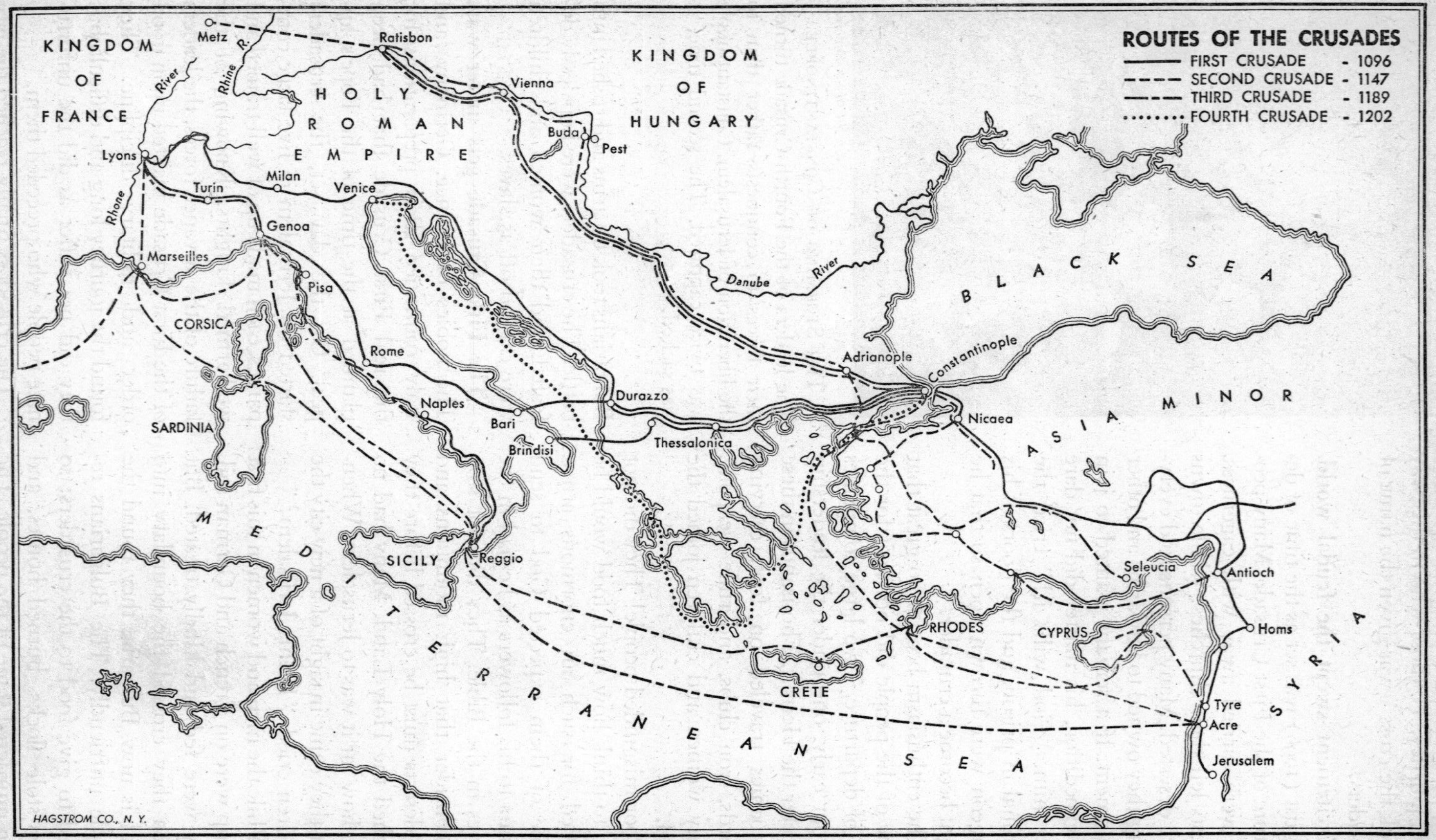

ROUTES OF THE CRUSADES

FIRST CRUSADE - 1096
SECOND CRUSADE - 1147
THIRD CRUSADE - 1189
FOURTH CRUSADE - 1202

HAGSTROM CO., N. Y.

of Antioch [an'ti ahk], where they defeated twelve thousand picked Turkish horsemen who came to the aid of the city. The city of Antioch can be found on the map on page 276. See how the route of the First Crusade passes through the ancient city of Constantinople and then through Antioch.

The crusaders took Jerusalem. From Antioch the crusaders marched to Jerusalem. It was a march in which both men and horses suffered agonies from lack of water. Priests had visions in which they were promised victory if they marched barefoot around the city for nine days. So the crusaders did this, and priests and bishops chanted hymns and prayed as they led the procession.

At the end of nine days the Christians made a fierce attack upon Jerusalem. The Turks threw huge stones and boiling pitch and oil from the city walls, but the crusaders could not be checked. After much bitter fighting and slaughter the Christians took the city. A description written by one crusader tells of great cruelties which the crusaders inflicted on their defeated victims. Having completed the conquest of the Holy Land the crusaders organized it as a feudal kingdom, called the Kingdom of Jerusalem, and many settled there permanently.

About fifty years later, the Turks recaptured the northern portion of the Kingdom of Jerusalem, and the Second Crusade was organized. Two armies, under the French king and the German emperor, started out. The expedition, however, was a complete failure.

Saladin captured the Holy Land. About a century after the First Crusade Mohammedans from Egypt set out to conquer the Holy Land. Their leader at that time was Saladin [sal'uh d'n], one of the greatest rulers the Mohammedans

ever had. He was simple in his habits, kind and upright, and a brave general in battle. As you will remember from the story of Mohammed, all wars fought by his followers were "holy wars"; so for Saladin the war with the Christians was a holy war.

After conquering the outlying country, Saladin laid siege to Jerusalem itself. Within two weeks the Christians surrendered. The Mohammedan leader allowed great numbers of the Christians to go free and unharmed. The churches were changed into mosques where Mohammedans could worship. Once again the Holy Land was lost to the Christians.

The Third Crusade also failed. The victory of Saladin caused great excitement in Europe. The rulers of England, France, and Germany took up the cross and set forth on what is known as the Third Crusade. This was toward the end of the 12th Century, about a hundred years after the First Crusade. The old Emperor Frederick, of Germany, who was called "Barbarossa" [bahr'buh-rohs'uh] because of his long red beard, was the first to lead his great army toward the East. All went well until they reached Asia Minor, where the emperor fell into a river and was drowned. His army went to pieces and was lost in the desert or destroyed by the Turks.

King Philip Augustus of France and Richard the Lion-Hearted of England were more successful. They reached Palestine, and fought many battles. It was not long, however, before the two kings quarreled. Finally Philip angrily gathered together his knights and followers and led them back to France. Not long after, Richard heard that his brother was trying to seize the English throne and so he hastily started for England. This left the Mohammedans in possession of the Holy Land. Thousands of

Monkmeyer

A CRUSADER'S SHIP

Many crusaders found travel by ship more comfortable than the long march across the land. Do you recognize any of the royal shields mounted on the ship?

lives had been lost; many men had suffered, but Jerusalem was still held by the Turks.

The Children's Crusade. People began to believe that only those free from sin could recapture Jerusalem. Because of this idea a French shepherd boy gathered together a band of children to win back the Holy Land. Thousands of boys and girls joined them.

Can you imagine little children starting out on foot, without food or weapons, for a city thousands of miles away? It is not hard to imagine what happened. Many of the children died of cold and hunger; others were captured and sold as slaves. Very few ever again saw their homes or their parents.

The Crusades were successful failures. There were several other lesser Cru-

sades but none of them was successful. Yet the Crusades may be called successful failures. Although the crusaders did not hold Jerusalem, in other ways they accomplished more than they knew. For one thing they helped to educate the people of Europe. Many people learned that great nations existed in parts of the world about which they had known nothing before, that the men and women of the East had different customs from those in Europe.

Commerce and trade had begun to spring up again between Italy and the Near East by the 11th Century. The Crusades hastened the development of trade. The crusader had seen many luxuries in foreign lands that he wanted. There were the spices from the East — cloves, cinnamon, nutmeg, and pepper to season his coarse food. There were dates and oils from the desert, sugar from the East, calico from Calicut [kal'i kuht] in India, and muslin from Mosul in Mesopotamia. The crusader brought back many new fruits that were until then unknown to the people of Europe. Lemons, apricots, and watermelons were introduced.

The crusaders adopted some of the customs of the Arabs. They learned to shave and to bathe regularly. Up to this time the knight had allowed his beard to grow long and tangled, and he had been even more indifferent in the matter of personal cleanliness. The European was never again to be quite so unkempt as he had been before the Crusades.

Larger ships were built as a result of the Crusades and the growing commerce with the Near East. The first knights to go to the Holy Land found that the journey by land was so long and tiresome that they urged their friends to go by water. So later crusaders sailed to Palestine on the Mediterranean, in sailing vessels.

In earlier times a sailor had to rely entirely upon the sun, moon, and stars in guiding his ship, but now seamen began to learn more about navigation. From the Arabs they learned about the compass and its magnetic needle which pointed northward in stormy as well as fair weather. It is believed that the compass had come first from China.

Another remarkable invention that crusaders brought back into Europe at this time was the windmill. This they used to grind their corn and furnish power. In the Netherlands today there are windmills which have been in use for hundreds of years.

One important result of the Crusades was a more general use of money. During the early Middle Ages many men actually lived and died without ever having seen a piece of money. Up to the time of the Crusades both the lord and

the serf commonly paid their bills in grains, vegetables, and meats from the farm. Of course this practice was out of the question when a knight started on a journey of many hundreds of miles to the Holy Land. He could not carry dozens of eggs or loads of meat to pay his expenses. But now merchants had begun to bring money into circulation, and by exchanging his produce for money in the town, a knight had something much easier to handle on a long journey. Sometimes for money, the lord gave to the townspeople certain privileges such as the right to fish or hunt on his property. The granting of these privileges helped to break down the power of the nobles and to give more freedom to the people.

After the Crusades, life in Europe was never quite so narrow as before. The Crusades upset the old ways of thinking and doing, and helped to prepare the way for great changes in Europe.

Chapter 5 ~ Towns Fostered Trade, Learning, and Freedom

"**City air is free air.**" From the time towns began to develop, the townspeople had more rights than those living on farms. Although the serf was bound to the land, the townsman was free to move about when he chose, to buy and sell goods. He was not a slave, but a free man. And if a serf could escape from a farm and hide in the city for a year and a day he was given his freedom. This led to the saying, "city air is free air."

During the early Middle Ages commerce and skilled trades had almost disappeared and city life disappeared with them. About the beginning of the 11th

Century, Italian merchants reopened trade with the East and gradually commerce spread northward through Europe. As the number of merchants and skilled artisans increased, cities came to life again everywhere. Merchants could not carry on business in isolated country villages and so they naturally gathered together in cities. They therefore banded together to acquire personal freedom and some rights of self-government.

Usually the lord of a region would grant a town new privileges for a price. Thus the towns would buy the right to govern themselves, and would be given

By Burton Holmes from Ewing Galloway
A STREET IN STRASBURG

In Strasburg, capital of Alsace, medieval-looking buildings with out-jutting upper stories still stand.

charters listing the new rights they might enjoy. Taxes collected in the towns were welcome sources of income to the lords. With this money they could pay the expenses of going on crusades and of their battles at home.

To us who live in a free country the privileges given to the medieval townspeople in their charters do not seem many, but to them those rights meant much. The agreements were different in different cases. Sometimes the ruling lord agreed to take only a fixed amount of rent or taxes, or to limit military service to a distance of one day's journey. Or he might promise the free use of the town's oven. In most instances, however, the charter also gave the citizens the right to elect officers and establish a city government. Very often the cities had their own laws and courts as well.

The townsmen built better homes. Towns grew wealthier in time through trade and industry. The houses could be larger and much better furnished than the huts of the peasants. But these houses were built very close together. Even though more people moved into the town each year, the space inside the city walls remained the same.

The crowded conditions in the towns brought about a characteristic style of architecture. The houses usually had a lower story of stone and heavy hewn beams, and an upper story of wood and plaster. The householder had his shop and workrooms downstairs and the family's living quarters above. In order to have more room, the second stories often jutted out over the narrow streets. The picture at the left shows a street in a medieval town where the houses still appear as described. The large attics sometimes served as storerooms or as sleeping quarters for apprentices and servants.

The medieval towns were not clean. The narrow streets that wound through the town were dirty, unpaved, and often cluttered with rubbish. There were no sewers. People threw refuse into the streets, where it was eaten by the dogs and pigs that roamed at will. It was necessary to wear high boots as a protection from the filth. If anyone ventured forth at night he had to carry his own lamp, for there were no street lights. Night watchmen guarded the city and insisted that everyone give a strict account of himself. As the watchman passed through the streets, he announced the hour and cried "All is well!"

Painted signs advertised the shops. The shops of each trade were grouped together. On one street were the goldsmiths; on another the cloth merchants. In one part of the town were the tanners, and in another the money changers,

OROC

GUILD HOUSES

These guild houses on the Grande Place, Brussels, have been restored to look as they did centuries ago. They represent the following guilds, reading from left to right: bakers (with patron saint, Nicholas), seamen, tapestry weavers, goldsmiths, and painters.

or bankers. Over the streets hung many signs, on each of which was painted some design to suggest the business of the house. These pictured signs were needed then because many people could not read, but the custom has lasted into the present time. The head of a wild boar was often used as the sign for an inn. A mortar and pestle [pes'l] was the sign of the druggist. Since barbers were also surgeons or bleeders, they used a striped pole to indicate flowing blood and the bandages used when bleeding patients.

The tradesmen organized guilds. Just as today we have trade unions in which plumbers, electricians, or carpenters organize to protect their business, so in the Middle Ages men in the same trades organized guilds. The guild set up standards of quality and fixed the prices for the goods made and sold. It prevented outsiders from coming in to sell their goods unless a tax or toll was paid. Members paid dues but if a member was sick or in want, or had been thrown into jail, the guild came to his rescue. Each member of the guild called a fellow member "brother," as do the members of a lodge today.

Some of the guilds, especially the merchants' guilds, became very powerful and wealthy. They loaned money, promoted commerce, supported the Church, and established schools.

An apprentice learned a trade. You will remember that the son of a noble who was trained for knighthood first served as a page, then as a squire, and finally was dubbed a knight. In a similar way a boy who wished to become a full-fledged member of a craft guild had to pass through three stages of training. First he was an apprentice, then a journeyman, and last a master-workman. As an apprentice he learned a trade under the guidance of a master-workman.

If a boy planned to become a goldsmith, for instance, his parents arranged with a master goldsmith to take their son as an apprentice for a fixed length of time, ranging from three to eleven years. He was to obey his master, work faithfully at the trade, and keep his master's secrets. The master in turn agreed to give the boy a home, including food and clothing, and to teach him all that he himself knew about the trade.

The apprentice advanced to journeyman. When a boy had served his apprenticeship he became a journeyman working for wages under a master-workman. While most journeymen looked forward to the day when they would become master-workmen, only a small number

Culver Service
BANNER OF A BOOT AND SHOE MAKERS
GUILD
The banner above represented the craft guild of shoe makers.

ever reached this goal. Then if they had been industrious and saved their money, they might be able to open shops in their own houses, hire journeymen, and accept apprentices. No one was allowed to become a master, however, until he had presented a masterpiece of his craft to the guild to prove that he could do fine work. The guild required every master to prove his ability, just as the state now requires every lawyer, doctor, and pharmacist to pass an examination before he can practice his profession.

The fair was a place of trade. Because the merchants needed a place to exchange their goods, fairs became common both on the Continent and in England. The word *fair* comes from a Latin word meaning " holy day " or " holiday." Fairs were often opened on days set apart in honor of some patron saint, and they usually lasted for several weeks. They were something like our county fairs. The purpose of the fair was to give merchants of other cities and countries, as well as the local merchants, a place to sell their goods.

People sometimes came even from distant lands to attend the fairs. Knights and ladies came to see the fine displays and to purchase. Stewards of the abbeys and castles came to lay in a year's supply of spices, wines, furs, linens, and silks. The peasants came to buy a few necessary articles and an occasional luxury. Jugglers, gypsies, and minstrels came to entertain the crowds and earn money. Iron goods, copper, gold, horses, hay, grain, cattle, hides, cloth, velvet, ribbons, silk, satin, laces, flax, fish, wax, honey, oil, resin, spices from the Far East, and armor were a few of the things that were for sale. Fair day was a gala time when people might look, buy or sell, talk to travelers from other lands, and laugh at the antics of the entertainers.

The fairs helped to break the monotony of daily life in the Middle Ages.

The guilds gave miracle plays. Mystery and miracle plays which represented Bible stories and the lives of the saints developed during the Middle Ages. It was one of the religious duties of the guild to present a religious play each year. Sometimes these plays had as many as thirty different scenes and lasted for several days. A group of plays would tell the whole Bible story, from the creation to the destruction of the world.

At first these plays were given in the church, and later in an open theater or courtyard. Often the large stage was divided into three parts, one on top of the other. The lower part was curtained off for dressing rooms; the second floor was the stage for most of the acting; and the third floor represented heaven. Although no elaborate stage settings were used, the manager tried to make the plays realistic. For instance, animals were used in the scene showing the creation of the world and a boat was drawn across the stage in the scene of the flood.

In recent years dramatic performances something like the old miracle plays have been given in some parts of Europe. The most famous is the play telling the story of the life of Jesus which is presented at Oberammergau [oh'ber am' er gou'], Germany. The story is that the people pledged that if they were spared from a famine and plague which seemed to threaten them, they would present the story of the life and death of Jesus every ten years. Some performances have been missed. The 1940 performance, for example, was postponed because of World War II.

Teachers and students met in the towns. With the return of the crusaders and the development of towns, people

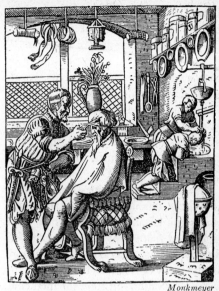

Monkmeyer

A MEDIEVAL BARBER SHOP

This engraving shows in amusing detail how greatly the barber shops of the Middle Ages differed from those you see today. Notice particularly the barber chair, and the shampoo equipment at the right.

began to take a new interest in education. Universities were established in some of the larger cities. The early university, however, had no beautiful buildings, no expensive equipment, no lecture halls, no gymnasium. At first, any man who thought he had something worth while to say about religion, science, or philosophy found a place in which to lecture. If he became noted, his followers grew in number and would go with him wherever he went. If the students did not like what he had to say, they could leave him and turn to someone else. One of the greatest of these university teachers of the Middle Ages was Peter Abelard. He felt that scholars should start on a basis of doubt, and proceed by questioning and reasoning. His lectures became so famous that they drew students from many countries to

France. Consequently he had considerable influence on the minds and thoughts of the scholars of his time.

As time went on, some cities, in order to attract teachers and students, would give them special privileges such as freedom from taxes and exemption from the laws of the city. Thus these wandering students and teachers had their own laws, their own courts, and their own jails.

In time the universities became more definitely established in certain places and some became noted for their work in special fields. For example, the University of Paris was noted for theology, or the study of religious beliefs; the University of Salerno in Italy for medicine; the University of Bologna [boh loh' nyah] in northern Italy for law.

Students often wandered from one university to another. As learning was connected with religion, and the great majority of students expected to become priests or monks, the people thought it a duty to give students food, shelter, and clothing on the way. The medieval student wore a hood similar to those worn by holders of degrees of our colleges today. Sometimes he would allow the hood to hang down his back so he could carry in it a loaf of bread or other food given him by some kindhearted person.

The medieval university represented a distinct forward step in educational progress. Great thinkers came from some of these institutions and thus knowledge was to spread throughout the countries of Europe.

The Black Death took a heavy toll. Throughout the centuries there had occasionally been plagues or pestilences in Asia and Europe. The worst ever known in Europe was a cycle of plagues in the 14th Century called the Black Death.

These epidemics of disease (most of which we now know as the bubonic [byoo bahn'ik] plague) spread most swiftly and cruelly in the cities, where the people were crowded closely together. The scourge, which seemed to come from Asia, reached France and England in the middle of the 14th Century. Millions of lives were lost. The pestilence was no respecter of persons; neither the baron in his castle nor the peasant in his hut was safe. One Frenchman wrote:

It is impossible to believe the number who have died throughout the whole country. . . . Travelers, merchants, pilgrims declare that they have found cattle wandering without herdsmen in the fields, towns, and waste lands. They have seen barns and wine cellars standing wide open, houses empty, and few people to be found anywhere. In many towns where there were before twenty thousand people, scarcely two thousand are left.

In some parts of Europe as many as three-fourths of the people died. In all Europe probably a fourth of the people, about twenty-five million, lost their lives. Fields lay uncultivated. It was difficult to find laborers for the farms and workers in the towns.

The peasant revolt in England. In England near the end of the 14th Century there was an uprising of the peasants which for a short time threatened the power of both the king and the nobles. The peasants did not have weapons, a trained army, or any means of meeting in large numbers to protest their wrongs. Yet terror reigned while mobs of peasants and town workmen demanded equality for the common people.

The people had become emboldened partly because of the extra hardships which followed in the wake of the plagues, and also because of their anger at some new, harsh taxes. The many deaths in the plagues caused a shortage of labor; thus the workers were much more important. One of their leaders spoke of their grievances in these words, according to a writer of that time:

Are we not all descended from the same parents, Adam and Eve? And what can they [the lords] show, or what reason can they give, why they should be more masters than ourselves? They are clothed in velvet and rich stuffs, ornamented with ermine and other furs, while we are forced to wear poor clothing. They have wines, spices, and fine bread, while we have only rye and the refuse of the straw; and when we drink, it must be water. They have handsome seats and manors, while we must brave the wind and rain in our labours in the field; and it is by our labour they have wherewith to support their pomp.[1]

The peasants alarmed the city of London. A mob of peasants marched on London. They raided certain palaces in the city, set prisoners free, and committed a number of murders. The king met a large body of the rebels outside the city gates and heard their complaints. They demanded the end of serfdom and of certain rules restricting their work and trade. They insisted that all classes of the people should have equal rights. The king promised to grant all these demands, as long as the authority of the crown was respected, and he persuaded the throng to disperse and return to their homes. Later all the promises were withdrawn, and the leaders of the peasants were hunted down and slain.

To the king and others of the noble class, such uprisings were the works of "wicked men," and they felt no guilt about breaking the promises they had been forced to make. They saw all order and government threatened by such acts.

[1] From Froissart's Chronicles (Dutton), p. 208.

The peasant revolt was a complete failure. Yet it was a sign of a ferment for freedom that was at work among the common people, and that was to become more active in the following centuries. The revolt reminded those in power that the common people could be dangerously strong against the rulers, and that they would continue to demand their rights.

Nevertheless, the serfs in many parts of Europe were granted freedom during the 14th and 15th Centuries. The demand for their farm produce in the growing towns was making them more prosperous. Thus they could pay their lords in money instead of in labor. Therefore there was less reason for keeping them in serfdom. The growth of trade and commerce had a direct effect on the growth in the freedom of the common people.

The peoples of Europe adopted Arabic numerals. If you have ever tried to multiply Roman numerals, you know what an impossible task it soon becomes. Yet the peoples of western Europe had little knowledge of the Arabic system until sometime during the Middle Ages. About the Ninth Century, the Arabic system of numbers — 1, 2, 3, etc. — was brought by the Mohammedan Moors across the desert of Arabia, into North Africa, and up into Spain. There the Moors established schools and universities. Gradually the peoples of Europe realized that the Eastern culture taught by the Moors had much to offer in the way of superior learning. The Arabic system of numbers spread rapidly and became the basis of our modern arithmetic. Commerce, too, helped to spread a knowledge of Arabic numbers. Traders on land and sea, such as Marco Polo, no doubt helped to spread the Arabic system.

Wars and Disorder Held Back Civilization in the Middle Ages

The centuries following the breakup of the Roman Empire are known as the Middle Ages. During the first part of this time the civilization of the Greeks and Romans was forgotten. In the latter part of the Eighth Century and the early years of the Ninth Century, Charlemagne ruled in Europe. His reign was like a bright light in the darkness. He conquered many peoples and built a great empire. He was an ardent Christian who promoted the influence of the Church. He also did much to spread an interest in learning. After Charlemagne's death, however, his empire broke up. Europe slipped back into disorder. There developed feudalism, a system in which powerful lords owned the land and gave protection to the serfs and freemen who did their farming and the other work of the manor, as well as fought in the armies. Feudalism and the Church were the two important institutions of the period and they brought some order out of chaos.

In feudal days a lord's castle was the center of community life. It was the fortress and home of the noble, and a place of refuge for all his dependents in time of war. Since a feudal lord required his dependents to provide food and do all the work, he devoted most of his time to fighting, eating, drinking, and gaming. Few people could read or write and education was neglected almost entirely, except for the training given boys of noble birth who were preparing to be knights.

The serfs were bound to the land. They spent long hours in hard work and lived in crude huts. They could be tried in a lord's court and were often punished severely for small crimes. The Church gradually grew in strength during feudal days. What ancient learning had been saved was owing to the efforts of the Church. A new type of architecture, the Gothic, was developed.

Devout pilgrims and zealous knights joined in Crusades to the Holy Land to take Jerusalem from the Turks. The Crusades seemed to be failures but they taught the people of Europe how other people lived. Trade developed and more progressive ways of thinking began to spread.

The increase in the demand for goods kept the craftsmen and shopmen busy. Towns and cities grew. Cities became free when feudal lords needed money and granted rights to cities for cash. Workmen organized guilds to protect their industry and trade.

The plague known as the Black Death brought new hardships to the common people and caused terrible loss of life. Since the loss of life caused a shortage of labor, the people were in a position to demand more democratic rights. In England the peasants revolted and for a short time the king's power seemed threatened. Although this revolt was put down, the oppressed peasants were beginning to insist upon a better life. The darkness of the Middle Ages was breaking; civilization in Western Europe was about to be reborn.

SELF-TEST

See how well you have pictured for yourself life in feudal times by trying this self-test.

1. Rearrange the following in the time order in which you think they most nearly belong: (*a*) the invasion of the barbarians, (*b*) lords and vassals of the feudal system, (*c*) the breakup of the Western Roman Empire, (*d*) Charlemagne.

2. Here is an imaginary story of a feudal serf who was still a young boy in the year 1200. In it you will find different kinds of statements, some true or false, others possible or impossible, some incomplete. Be able to read the story aloud correctly.

Adam was born a serf. The time in history was that which we now call the ——. Like most of the serfs who lived in the village, his father was a ——. Sometimes his father would take him out to work on the land which the —— had assigned to him. One day Adam's brother rushed in saying excitedly, "Father, Father, the lord wants Adam to work in the kitchen of the castle, and he is to bring two of the suckling pigs from the last litter!" (Possible?) "What," exclaimed the father, "must we send to the lord both our boy and our food, and get nothing in return!" (T or F?) "Hush," said the mother, "the —— gives you —— from those who would attack and rob us, and he furnishes you —— upon which to raise food. (T or F?) Do not complain, for if you do not like the treatment, you can leave this land and live elsewhere." (T or F?)

Adam did not mind going to the castle. Grasping a pig under each arm, he almost ran across the drawbridge over the waters of the ——. Servants rushed him to the kitchen. (Possible?) There he saw the pigs dressed and put to roast on ——. Afterward he was allowed to make his way to the great hall. Reaching the main hall, he was given a large bowl of water and a towel and told to take it to the table where the nobles were finishing their meal. (Probable?) Just as he approached the table, he stepped on a bone on the greasy floor and down went the bowl. (Possible?) To his chagrin there was a roar of laughter. Refilling his bowl, he determined to keep his wits about him so that he might learn the latest news from near and far. He overheard some of the young men say that there was to be an expedition, called a ——, to the Holy Land to drive out the —— and restore the birthplace of —— to Christians. He heard another claim that the saying "—— —— ——" showed that the Church was encouraging these ventures to Jerusalem. (T or F?) Adam admired the eager young ——, who were practicing feverishly so that they could take their vows of knighthood in time to join the expedition to Jerusalem.

Years passed and Adam grew to manhood. He became the head of a family but, unlike his father, served his lord by his skill as a blacksmith. But he was not contented. Many people, both good and bad, had left to go to the Holy Land. (T or F?) The lord would be gone for long periods and when he returned seemed to be willing to give any privilege in exchange for that new form of wealth, called ——, which was coming into use. (T or F?) Adam had been able to save from the sale of some of his iron work. (Possible?) He purchased his freedom from the lord and moved into a town not far distant. (Possible?)

In the town he lived on a wide, clean street in a little bungalow. (T or F?) His neighbors were also blacksmiths. Soon, from his trade, he came to be known as Adam Smith. With other iron workers, he became a member of a —— of his craft. (T or F?) Soon he became skillful enough to be called a master craftsman. One of his sons had finished his apprenticeship to a goldsmith. His other son wore a cloak with a hood which showed that he was a —— at one of the new ——. Adam was called upon to work upon a wonderful cathedral, called —— in style, and later, because of his particular skill, was sent to another town to do the same kind of work on still another church. The people of both these churches were of exactly the same religious belief. (Probable?) On the way back to his own town, he met with a monk who explained to him the vows of ——, ——, and ——. The monk explained to Adam how the —— —— of the new cathedrals made possible the high walls and many large windows. He told also how his brother monks in the —— would spend years copying the ancient writings of the —— of whom Adam had never heard.

INTERESTING THINGS TO DO

Projects for the Chart Maker and Artist

1. Make a drawing entitled "The Stream of Civilization" that will show what branches of culture flow into this stream and at what points. See *The Middle Ages,* by Dorothy Mills.

2. Make a sketch of a medieval castle, or a large-scale drawing, for use by the class, of a floor-and-ground plan of a castle, its inner and outer courts, its defenses, the village, and the surrounding areas. See *Famous Buildings,* by C. L. Barstow, or *When Knights Were Bold,* by E. M. Tappan, pp. 52–74.

Ideas for Your Little Theater

1. Prepare a program of medieval music. Your school music teacher may be able to help you locate illustrations, phonograph records, or other materials. For general information about the musical instruments of that time look up dulcimer, bagpipe, harp, and recorder, in any encyclopedia.

2. Prepare to tell the class some of the best-known stories from medieval times, such as those of Siegfried, Roland, Robin Hood, and the tournament from Scott's *Ivanhoe.* See *Legends of the Middle Ages,* by H. A. Guerber.

Adventures for the Amateur Author

1. Suppose you had gone on one of the Crusades. Write a few pages of a diary you might have kept, or write an account of a thrilling experience you might have had. See *National Geographic Magazine,* Dec., 1933. See also *Durandal,* and *The Crusades: Iron Men and Saints,* by Harold Lamb.

2. Write a brief history pamphlet about a medieval city-state such as Venice. Illustrate your history with an outline map of Europe during the Middle Ages on which you show the chief trade routes radiating from the city you write about. Explain the origin of the phrase "When my ship comes in."

3. Write an essay comparing and contrasting the guilds of the Middle Ages with the trade unions of today. Touch on their purposes, work, and contributions.

Topics for Talks

1. "Tanks on two feet." Prepare a talk on the kinds of armor worn in the Middle Ages, giving the names, uses, and advantages of the different kinds. Consult *The Encyclopaedia Britannica,* "Arms and Armour."

2. "Through medieval glasses." Pretend you are a boy or girl of the Middle Ages and try to look upon life today as it would seem to one of them. From their viewpoint, prepare a talk on such a subject as training of skilled workmen then and now, or on farming in the Middle Ages and in modern times.

3. "The Crusades were successful failures." Discuss the changes in thought and action brought about as a result of the Crusades.

4. "The monks of the Middle Ages served mankind in many ways." Describe the life and work of the monks in the Middle Ages, and explain some of the problems of the different peoples they served.

Questions for Round-Table Discussion

1. Was feudalism a necessary and natural outgrowth of the breakdown of the strong central government of the Roman Empire?

2. Was the lot of the serf during the Middle Ages better or worse than that of the unemployed in modern times?

3. Did medieval cities promote the growth of democracy?

4. Did the growth of power of the Church promote or hinder progress?

Candidates for Your Album of Famous People

Choose one of the following for your Album: St. Benedict, Peter Abelard, Peter the Hermit, Charlemagne, St. Francis of Assisi.

INTERESTING READING ABOUT THE FEUDAL WORLD

BALDWIN, J. *The Story of Roland.* " But no one of all the great company who met to view the tournament there in the Seine meadows could excel Roland in grace and strength and skill."

BARSTOW, C. L. *Famous Buildings.* " The castle is the building of fairy story and romance, for here dwell the princes and princesses of our early dreams. . . ."

Compton's Pictured Encyclopedia. " Crusades: When Christians Fought Infidels for Palestine ": " Feudal Age: Lords and Vassals "; " Middle Ages: One Thousand Years of Europe's History "; and Index.

DAVIS, W. S. *God Wills It.* A story built around the Crusades and the medieval Church, with glimpses of several famous people of medieval times.

——. *Life on a Medieval Barony.* A clear idea of what life was like in the 13th Century in the typical feudal community.

HARDING, S. B. *The Story of the Middle Ages.* " When we read of all the things that Charlemagne did, we wonder that he was able to do so much."

HILL, F. E. *Canterbury Tales.* In this book, many of Chaucer's unusual stories have been translated into modern English, without losing their special charm.

LAMB, HAROLD. *Durandal.* A vivid story of a young French Crusader.

MILLS, DOROTHY. *The Middle Ages.* The story of the Middle Ages told intimately and informally, and illustrated with contemporary pictures and a useful time chart.

National Geographic Magazine, Dec., 1933. " The Road of the Crusaders " by Harold Lamb. " I started from central Europe to follow the ' Road of God,' the trails that lead to Jerusalem."

SCOTT, W. *Ivanhoe.* " He is fitter to do the juggling tricks of the Norman chivalry than to maintain the fame and honour of his English ancestry. . . ."

TAPPAN, E. M. *When Knights Were Bold.* " When the pilgrims had reached their journey's end, some went straight to their prayers, others wandered about the church curiously."

VAN LOON, H. *The Story of Mankind.* " Indeed, the Crusades . . . became a course of instruction in civilization for millions of young Europeans."

WILMOT-BUXTON, E. *The Story of the Crusades.* " The great army of the Crusades began to move toward the East."

PART NINE

THE MEDIEVAL WORLD AWAKENED: THE RENAISSANCE AND THE REFORMATION

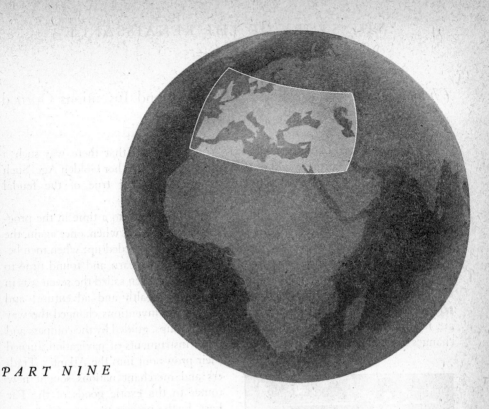

PART NINE

A Medieval World Becomes Modern

THE awakening of the medieval world was a time of exploration, discovery, and great change. Notice that the Byzantine Empire no longer appears on the map opposite. It fell to the Turks in 1453. Later, in Part Eighteen, you will read how a new country, Russia, carried on part of its civilization. Notice also that the Moors no longer held part of Spain. They were driven out in the 15th Century. But the knowledge which they had brought into Spain helped awaken the medieval world. The Holy Roman Empire is not shown on this map either. It continued to exist until the 19th Century, but it was no longer of much importance.

Study the towns and cities on this map. Can you find Lisbon and Seville? Notice that they are on the Atlantic side, not the Mediterranean. Europe had begun to send her ships westward to seek out new sea routes and new lands. In northern Europe you will find a section that is marked off from the rest. A conflict of ideas caused these lands to break away from the medieval Church. As you read the following story of adventure, strife, and change, refer often to the map which shows the Western world when it was fast becoming the modern world we know today.

Chapter 1 ~ New Wealth, Explorations, and Inventions Opened the Way for Progress

The medieval world became modern. There is no doubt that the world of the Middle Ages changed its ways and finally became modern. You and everything about you are proof of that fact. But it did not happen all at once; nothing in history does. Yet there seem to be times in mankind's story when events move more rapidly; when there is a remarkable surge of activity; when there is a noticeable outburst of creative energy in art, learning, discovery, invention, or in changes in the ways of doing things.

The University Prints, Newton, Mass.

THE BANKER AND HIS WIFE

The first great banks in the modern sense of the term were founded in the 17th Century. Not much is known of the history of banking, but it is certain that the circulation of money was increased during the latter part of the Renaissance by the large imports of gold and silver from the New World. The banker pictured here is carefully weighing different-sized coins to find their true value.

You will recall that there was such a time in Greece in her Golden Age. Such progress was not true of the feudal world.

Now we come to a time in the progress of civilization when, once again, the tempo of life speeded up; when men became eager to learn and found time to learn; when men sailed the seven seas in search of wealth and adventure; and when new inventions changed the way of life. Ships, guided by the compass and other instruments of navigation, turned their prows out into the Atlantic. Traders and merchant nations sought new routes to the exotic goods of the Far East. In the process the astounding discovery of the Americas occurred; routes by sea around Africa and into the Indian Ocean were charted; and a world which most people believed to be flat was proved to be round.

Inventions and discoveries were made which greatly changed the life, and the thinking, of the peoples of Western Europe. Their world in government, religion, learning, and trade had been centered in the Mediterranean area. Their daily life in the Middle Ages had been that strip of land tilled by the lowly serf, the battles fought for the feudal lord, and the life of castles and chivalry. Their religious world had been the medieval Church, centered in Rome. And the geography of their daily lives in the feudal ages had been as limited as the horizon which they could see about them.

In Part Eight, which you have just read, you learned that the feudal world had begun to change. Money, a new

Swedish State Railways

A MEDIEVAL TOWN

This Swedish seaport was one of the scenes of growing medieval commerce.

thing, began to circulate, and people began to circulate too. Teachers and students gathered together to establish universities. Small villages grew into towns, and some towns grew into cities. Guilds of craftsmen were organized. Centers of trade prospered; and some men became wealthy. These well-to-do city dwellers, as relatively few as they may have been, had leisure to learn. Furthermore, they became ambitious to learn; and it was good for their business and trade. Learning gradually became the style, and a sign of the times.

Crafty or keen-minded monarchs, urged on by the merchants and traders who were their subjects, wanted to find new markets and new ways to old markets. These men, outside of Italy, were discontented with the Italian monopoly of the Mediterranean trade routes. They were not satisfied that the Mediterranean should be the only seaway to

wealth. So explorers and adventurers were backed and the new routes, to the west and to the south, were found.

Necessity became the mother of strange, new inventions. Needs of all sorts demanded improvements: for shipbuilding, for trade, for record-keeping, for combat, for life in towns and cities. And the inventions came along with the discovery and exploration. Sometimes, however, inventions and discoveries seemed to lead the way to change.

With the kettle of Western civilization boiling so merrily, it is a simple matter to understand why no one can truthfully say, " This and this alone was the cause." So, as we shall see, from a combination of circumstances, the medieval world began to awaken from its Rip van Winkle-like sleep of some four or five hundred years. It was as though the feudal world shook itself, reached out, and found a whole world to develop. It was a world to exploit, to improve, to fight over, to populate. It was a world to fill with ideas.

Of course, we must not be so naïve as to think that all men and women, say in the year 1500, were aware of an awakening world. Thousands of people went about the daily routine of their lives in the field and in the shop untouched by the significance of the changes going on in the world. A day's labor had to be done and there was not time or inclination for vast numbers of the common people to understand. As is usually true, progress was made and known by the few. It was much the same as. is true today in some of our own backward or provincial communities where " the news " is seldom felt and life goes on as it has for years.

The awakening of the medieval world meant a rebirth of interest in life. The period of awakening is known by the long French name, the Renaissance [ren' uh sahnce]. You will find upon looking up the word *Renaissance* in a dictionary that it means " rebirth " or " revival." Before you have finished this part of our story you will agree that the name was well chosen. You should keep in mind that there are no sharp breaks in the history of man's progress. One thing leads to another. Even the Roman Empire was tottering long before it fell. The Renaissance is not a sharp break in the story. When we tell you that this period during which the medieval world was awakening is included in the two hundred years between 1350 and 1550, remember that these are only approximate dates. Much happened before and much happened after this time, which might be included in the change from the Middle Ages to modern times.

The medieval world awakened in many ways. In many ways the Renaissance was the Golden Age of Europe.

Men in various lands were eager to do well what the ancient Greeks and Romans had done, and to accomplish other things which never before had been undertaken. Already we have told you of the inventions and explorations. But the world was also progressing in many other ways. There was a renaissance: (1) in discovery and inventions; (2) in the learning of the ancient world; (3) in religion; (4) in science and education; and (5) in the fine arts.

The awakening of the medieval world began in Italy. From there it spread like a wave across Europe until it reached England. Two centuries saw its progress from the Mediterranean to the North Sea. Since the Renaissance began in Italy, let us begin with the unusual story of an unusual man, Marco Polo, with whose name you may already be familiar.

Marco Polo studied geography at firsthand. Fate decreed that an Italian youth named Marco Polo was the first of the famous adventurers to leave Europe and explore the world. The Far Eastern lands had many luxuries to sell to the peoples of Western Europe. Among these goods of the Far East were silks, jewels, and the spices which were so prized by the Europeans to make their foods more palatable.

Marco's father and uncle were engaged in trade with the East. When only fifteen years old, Marco went with them to the court of the Great Khan [kahn], or ruler, of the Mongols in far-off Pekin. The Great Khan, who was then an old man, took a strong liking to the young Polo. Though Marco was very young for such a mission, he was made a special envoy, or minister, and sent throughout the vast realms of the empire to observe and to report on what he saw. The Khan preferred Marco Polo's

Drawing by John C. Wonsetler

VENETIAN TRADERS IN THE ORIENT

Traders from Venice came to the Orient to barter for rare and precious stones. In an Oriental palace a group of these men are offering cloth brought from their native land in exchange for jewels that would be worth millions of dollars today.

reports to those of all his other officials because they were so interesting.

With not too much modesty, Marco Polo himself tells us:

Marco . . . sped wondrously in learning the customs of the Tartars, as well as their language, their manner of writing, and their practice of war; in fact, he came in brief space to know several languages. . . . And he was discreet and prudent in every way, inasmuch that the Emperor held him in great esteem.[1]

For twenty-four years, during the latter part of the 13th Century, Marco Polo traveled the length and breadth of Asia. In his writings he speaks of having seen Persia, the Mongolian deserts and highlands, China, India, and many other regions.

[1] For an interesting account of the travels of Marco Polo, which is illustrated with pictures of present-day Asia, see the *National Geographic Magazine,* November, 1928.

Marco Polo saw strange sights in Asia. During his travels Marco Polo saw many wonderful sights. In the southern part of the Mongolian realm he found " serpents " thirty feet long, " with jaws wide enough to swallow a man." They were probably crocodiles. In another place he saw the natives using " a sort of black stone [that was coal] which they dug out of the mountains. When lighted, it burns like charcoal and retains the fire better than wood." He also observed that crude oil was in use in Asia. " There is a fountain from which oil springs in great abundance. . . . The oil is not good to use with food, but 'tis good to burn and is also used to anoint camels that have the mange."

The Polos returned to Venice and told of wonders they had seen. Finally after a quarter-century of wandering about Asia, Marco Polo, with his father and

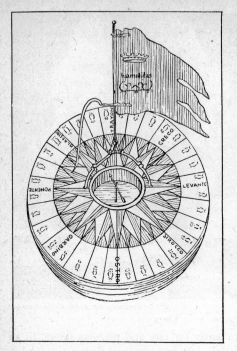

AN EARLY COMPASS

Before the use of the compass, European sailors had to guide their ships by landmarks, sun, and stars. After they learned about the compass from the Arabs, they ventured to sail uncharted seas.

uncle, returned to Venice. At first they were not recognized, and little wonder:

There stepped ashore in Venice one late afternoon in the nineties — the nineties of the thirteenth century — a bedraggled, weather-beaten trio, in queer, coarse garments. Their faces were leathery and bronzed, scorched perhaps by the tropic sun, yet scarred as if they had been frostbitten, too.

The Polos gave a dinner for some of their friends. At the end of the dinner the travelers brought out the ragged clothes that they had worn upon reaching Venice, and ripped open the seams. Out poured rubies, sapphires, large diamonds, and many other precious stones.

These had been stitched carefully into the clothing so as not to arouse the suspicion of robbers. This display of precious stones caused the people to believe that these were really the Polos who had left Venice so many years ago, and that they had been in the Far East. But many of the stories that the Polos had to tell were so unbelievable that they were considered as fanciful tales of good storytellers.

The stories had little influence on the knowledge of those times. The world was still thought to be very small indeed. But the romantic adventure of Marco Polo did arouse the imagination of a few adventurous minds of those times and heightened the desire to explore which was to be so characteristic of the next two centuries.

Four remarkable inventions change ways of living and ways of thought: (*1*) *The ship's compass*. Out of the Far East, perhaps from China, came a knowledge of four remarkable inventions. One of these was a steel magnetic needle, which, when balanced in the middle, would swing freely about and point northward. This was the forerunner of the mariner's compass. It could tell the captain, when out of sight of land, which way to head his ship. It could direct the caravan on the desert, or the traveler in the deep woods, to his desired destination. The success of Columbus, in piloting his tiny ships across the Atlantic, was partly due to this instrument. An early compass is pictured above.

(2) *Gunpowder* vs. *castle walls*. Gunpowder is another invention which came out of the Orient. It meant the death blow to feudalism. There was a time when the baron was safe behind the heavy stone walls of his castle. But with gunpowder the feudal lord could be blasted out of his retreat. The soldier on

foot became more powerful than the armored knight. Though the introduction of gunpowder into Europe was the beginning of the terrible tools of modern warfare, at least it did hasten the breakdown of the feudal system.

(3) *Cheap paper gave a new means of spreading ideas.* A third invention which hastened the change from medieval to modern times was paper. It may truly be said that modern civilization is set down on paper. It may seem that paper has been used for a long time, but its first use in Europe is of comparatively recent date. You remember that the men of the Stone Age drew crude pictures on the cave walls and on pieces of bone. The Egyptians made a writing sheet from the papyrus plant. The people of Mesopotamia placed their cuneiform marks on soft clay tablets. The writers of the Middle Ages used parchment made from the skins of lambs and goats, on which were transcribed the pen-and-ink copies of early manuscripts. But

parchment was expensive. Today we use it only for diplomas and other important documents.

The knowledge of papermaking had been introduced into Europe by the Arabs centuries before. They had learned the process from the Chinese who probably had made use of paper even before the time of Caesar. Paper came into common use in Europe about 1300, or a hundred and fifty years before the printing press became common. Thus paper was at hand to carry the printed word.

(4) *Gutenberg invented a press with movable type.* The fourth great invention of the Middle Ages, which was to play a large part in the awakening of the medieval world, was the printing press. Since the invention of an alphabet by the Phoenicians, the printing press is by far the most important development in the story of man's civilization. Although the art of printing from engraved wooden blocks was known to the Chinese several hundred years be-

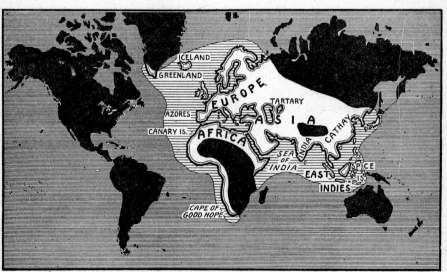

THE KNOWN WORLD BEFORE 1492

The black portions of the map are those parts of the world that had not yet been discovered by early Europeans. Can you name the countries that were totally unknown before 1492?

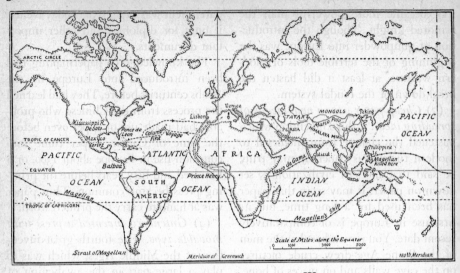

MAGELLAN'S ROUTE AROUND THE WORLD

Magellan's trip around the world verified the belief held by some scientists that the earth was round. Notice that the routes of other early explorers are included.

fore printing was done in Europe, it was not until about 1450 that a German by the name of Johannes Gutenberg [yoh-hahn'uhs goo't'n buhrg] was printing full pages from movable type.

If you can imagine a world without the telegraph, telephone, radio, books, magazines, and newspapers, you will have some idea of how slowly news spread in the medieval world. Cheap paper and the printing press made it possible to spread news and learning both quickly and well.

Columbus, seeking a new route to the Far East, found America. There were many great discoveries in the late 15th and early 16th Centuries which also had a tremendous effect in bringing about new ways of living and thinking. The Arabian astronomers knew that the world is round, and the Moors had brought this knowledge into Spain. From the works of the ancient Greeks, also, the scholars of Europe had learned that the earth is round. But the great masses of people did not believe so. And

no one had actually tried to go around the world until the Italian navigator, Columbus, made the attempt in 1492 in the hope of finding a new route to India

We all know the story of Columbus, who had the courage to test his idea. With financial aid from Queen Isabella of Spain, he started across an unknown ocean with three little boats, any one of which could be carried on the deck of a modern ocean liner. And, in that well-known year of 1492, the great discovery was made — Columbus found a new world. It is regrettable that Columbus did not live long enough to learn that it was a new world which he had discovered, not a new route to the Orient

Two other courageous explorers About the time of the discovery of America the Portuguese Diaz [dee'ath] discovered the Cape of Good Hope. Soon afterward, sailing under the flag of Portugal, Vasco da Gama [vahs'koh dah gah'mah] rounded the Cape, and reached India.

The first round-the-world voyage wa

organized and commanded by Ferdinand Magellan, a Portuguese who sailed under the colors of Spain. The attempt, as you know, was successful, but it was costly. In 1519, five ships and about three hundred sailors left the port of Seville [sev il']. Enduring many hardships, they battled the treacherous currents in the straits now called the Straits of Magellan. Mutiny broke out among the crews. The food became putrid, the water foul;

scurvy, that dread disease of the sea, took its toll. Magellan himself perished in the Philippines. But in 1522 one ship and less than twenty men sailed proudly back into the harbor of Seville. They were the first living proof to the peoples of Europe that the world was round.

There were many other daring explorers sailing uncharted seas during the 15th and 16th Centuries. Some of them you will meet later in *Story of Nations*.

Chapter 2 ~ The Revival of Learning Began in Italy

Petrarch made collecting his hobby. One of the early leaders in the Renaissance was Petrarch [pee'trahrk], who lived in Italy during the 14th Century. He knew Latin well, but Greek was his despair. He wanted to know Greek so that he could read the ancient Greek writings in the language in which they were written. There were no books on Greek grammar and only poor teachers. Petrarch consoled himself by saying that in all Italy there were not eight men who knew the ancient language of the Greeks.

Though Petrarch failed to learn Greek, he made a hobby of collecting ancient writings. Wherever he traveled in Italy, France, Germany, and Flanders he searched for the forgotten writings of the Greek and Roman scholars. Sometimes an old castle, a merchant's shop, or a monastery would yield manuscripts which had been neglected for over a thousand years. The enthusiasm of Petrarch caused others to become interested in finding the ancient masterpieces and in learning Greek. By his

practice of collecting ancient writings he helped to bring about one of the early steps of the Renaissance — the revival of the learning of Greece and Rome. Following his example the great majority of Italian scholars for the next two hundred years studied the classics with enthusiasm and used the classical form of Latin for their own writings.

An Italian prince also was a collector of ancient learning. Petrarch was, of course, not the only person who had a part in the revival of learning. There were many other scholars and men of wealth and influence who became interested in bringing a knowledge of the civilizations of Greece and Rome back into the world. Another, a century later, was Lorenzo de' Medici [loh ren'zoh day med'i chee], a prince of the powerful and famous Medici family of Florence, Italy. He lived in the latter part of the 15th Century. Lorenzo, as a wealthy merchant prince, was able to rule the city of Florence.

From his grandfather, Lorenzo had inherited a fine collection of ancient writ-

THE FIRST SHEET FROM CAXTON'S PRESS

The illustration above shows an excited group crowding about Caxton, all eager to examine the first sheet from his miraculous new printing press. Caxton, an English man, learned the art of printing on the Continent, and upon his return home established the first printing shop in England.

ings. It is said that the elder Medici had given instructions to his agents in all parts of the Mediterranean world to keep on the lookout for manuscripts on any subject in any language, and to buy them without regard to price. The result was that Indian spices and Greek manuscripts often reached Italy in the same vessel. Lorenzo continued to build up the library he had inherited.

In the northern part of Italy there were a number of small, but powerful, city-states. They were quite as independent and quarrelsome as the city-states of Greece had been. But the very wealth and independence of the Italian city-states made it possible, despite wars and politics, for rulers to advance the arts.

By his position, wealth, and interest, Lorenzo helped the medieval awakening in many ways. For example, he filled the Medici gardens with ancient statuary. This was probably the first collection of sculpture made since the time of the Romans, a thousand years before Lorenzo's day. Distinguished visitors admired the furniture, oriental rugs, and gems which his agents had purchased for him in the Near East. To worthy young artists he gave financial aid, so that they might carry on their studies. Nor did he, himself, neglect learning. He studied Greek and Latin, and as a pastime wrote many verses in the language of the common people of Italy — an early form of Italian. To a yearly banquet he invited the learned men of Italy. After dinner the works of Plato were read and discussed by the host and his guests.

The revival of interest in learning was not common. From what has been said of Petrarch and Lorenzo de' Medici, it would be a mistake to believe that everyone in the 15th Century was like these men. They were exceptions, but they show that the interests of many people were slowly broadening. The great mass of people were probably as ignorant of the world and its wonders as the people of feudal times had been. News traveled slowly. What few books there were, were written in Latin, a language which the common people could not understand. And, as you remember, these books were written with quill and ink on expensive parchment. Even if the common people could have read Latin, they could not have afforded to buy the rare manuscripts.

The printing press spread both the old and the new ideas. The invention of cheap paper and of the printing press, as we have explained, was to make it easier for the people to have news of current events and knowledge of past civilizations. Printers were busy at their presses. In Venice, for example, there was a printer by the name of Aldus Manutius [ahl'duhs muh noo'shuhs] who undertook the ambitious task of printing all the Greek classics. In his own shop the type was cast, ink made, and a book-bindery set up. In the year after America was discovered he finished the first book of the series. Wars among the city-states of Italy greatly interfered with his work. But during the twenty-two years before his death he had printed twenty-eight Greek and Latin classics and a number of books in Italian.

The type which Aldus used was called Aldine [ahl'dain]. It is said that the printer had it engraved after a model of Petrarch's handwriting. We call this type form "italic" and we often use it now to call attention to important words and statements. (*This sentence is in italic type, or italics.* This is roman type.)

Oddly enough, not everyone was in favor of printing the classics of ancient literature. Some people, who did not take to new ideas easily, thought that to print the classics and put them into the hands of the common people would be disrespectful to the great writers of the past. Even after printing had begun, one man kept thirty or forty copyists busy with ink and quill copying the classics. The statement was made, " all the books are . . . written with pen, not one printed that it might be disgraced thereby." Of course, it was not many years before printing won out against almost all objectors.

The Renaissance swept across Western Europe. From its beginning in Italy, the Renaissance swept across Western Europe as far north as Scandinavia and the British Isles. The progress, it is true, was gradual in the years from 1350 to 1550, but the spirit of rebirth of learning, religion, and the arts nonetheless spread and grew.

It is not possible here more than to mention a few Renaissance names. There was Erasmus, the brilliant scholar whom you will read more about in the story of the Netherlands. There were the great Dutch painters and men of science whom you will also read about in Part Twelve. And in England there were many brilliant men. Among these was Sir Thomas More, who wrote *Utopia* [yoo toh'pi uh]; a host of scientists; and that great man of literature, William Shakespeare, who has never been surpassed. You will learn more about them in the story of England.

Chapter 3 — The Spirit of the Renaissance Influenced Religion

People began to question traditional ways. By 1500 the stage had been set in Europe for another of the steps by which the medieval world was to change into the modern world. The explorations, the inventions, and the revival of interest in the older civilizations of Greece and Rome had aroused the people of Europe to new interests. After more than a thousand years of unquestioning acceptance of ideas and customs, people began to wonder whether there might not be better ways of living.

This spirit of questioning began to invade the realm of religious thought during the later years of the 14th Century. John Wycliffe [wik'lif], an Englishman, translated the Bible from Latin into English so that it could be read by the common people as well as by the scholars who understood Latin. But Wycliffe's religious teachings were so contrary to the usual religious opinion of his day that he was severely criticized. The Pope summoned him to Rome to answer the charge of heresy, or opposing the teachings of the Church. He refused to answer this summons. Not many years after this incident, John Huss of Bohemia, hearing of Wycliffe's teachings, began to preach to the people of his own country against the authority of the Church and the Pope. He was tried by a Church council, was declared a heretic, and was burned at the stake.

For the next two hundred years the Church kept its authority in religious matters over most of Europe. But the movement away from the Church was joined by an increasing number of people who, for various reasons, began to question that authority. In the early years of the 16th Century this movement broke out in a widespread revolt which was to lead many men and women to break entirely with the Church. This movement became known as the Protestant Reformation.

Luther was the leader of the Protestant Reformation. Martin Luther was the man who led the revolt. He was the son of a German miner who lived in a small village in Saxony. His father was ambitious that his son should become a lawyer, so the young man entered the University of Erfurt [er'foort] in central Germany. There he made a good record, particularly in public speaking and composition. Luther was religious by nature and finally became convinced that God had called him to the service of the Church. Instead of completing a legal training, Luther took the vows of a monk. Two years later he was ordained a priest. It is said that he spent much of his spare time studying original Hebrew and Greek texts of the Bible.

Luther became a professor and stirred the religious world. Luther's ability as a scholar won him an appointment as a professor of religion in the University of Wittenberg [vit'uhn buhrg]. His reputation as a speaker and his original outlook on religious ideas attracted wide attention and a number of followers. Soon he began to make direct attacks on some of the practices of the Church, particularly those relating to the forgiveness of sins and ways of collecting money.

In those days, before newspapers existed, it was not unusual for one who wished to put his ideas before the public to write a bulletin and post it in a public place where people might read it. Luther prepared a bulletin of ninety-five statements against what he considered wrongs in the Church. In accordance with the custom he nailed his bulletin on the door of the church at Wittenberg.

Luther was called to account. We must not forget that Luther was a priest in the medieval Church. Moreover, it should be recalled that the Church played an important part in the lives of the people of Europe and was the only religious institution of widespread influence. Luther was called to Rome to explain his statements, but he refused to go. A council of the Church in Germany then gave him an opportunity to recall his statements, but he again refused. Finally he was excommunicated, or completely cut off from the Church and denied its privileges. The Pope then called on the emperor Charles V to punish Luther also. Luther was brought to trial but refused to take back anything he had said. Luther's friends hid him for awhile for fear he might be put to death. But so many of the North German princes favored Luther that the Emperor did not dare do anything more severe than declare him an outlaw. Since many people agreed with Luther this punishment was not in reality very severe. Thus what started with criticism within the Church itself, ended in a complete break with the Church by Luther and his followers.

The Reformation led to strife and disagreement. The Lutheran revolt against the Church was now well under way and could not be stopped. Many churches and other church properties, especially in North Germany, were taken over by the Lutherans. Lutheran services were conducted in German, and the Lutheran clergy were allowed to marry. When the Catholic princes tried to stop this swing toward Lutheranism, the Lutheran princes drew up a protest. From this protest, all non-Catholic Christians came to be called Protestants.

Some of the Catholic princes in Europe felt that the Lutheran princes were supporting the Protestant Reformation because they wanted to weaken the power of the Holy Roman Emperor and the Pope, and make their little realms as independent as possible. Feeling between the two factions grew high and finally their sharp differences led even to war, which became known as the Thirty Years War. In Germany conditions were bad. For thirty years these religious wars plunged the many little German states into bloodshed and destruction. These bitter religious disagreements did much to delay the final union of the German people into a strong nation.

The Church of England became independent of Rome. In England, several years after Luther posted his bulletin, King Henry VIII quarreled with the Pope at Rome. You will read more of this quarrel in the story of England. To settle the quarrel he had Parliament declare that he himself was " the only supreme head of the Church of England." Thus England cast off the control of the Church at Rome and set up an independent national church.

Other leaders established religious sects. Not only England, but the Scandinavian countries and parts of Germany and Switzerland were in large measure lost to the medieval Church. In several countries other religious leaders came to the front and new religious sects were formed. Though these leaders were Protestants, they did not follow all of Luther's teachings. In fact each of the more important leaders had positive views of his own that differed from all the others. That is why there are so many forms of Protestant worship. We cannot here describe many of the leaders for lack of space, but we can mention, as examples, two men. John Calvin, of France, was a strict reformer who laid the foundation for the religious beliefs of the Puritans — those serious-minded people who played so many leading parts in the story of our own nation. Later Calvin carried his religious ideas to Switzerland. John Knox, who was a follower of Calvin, established the Presbyterian Church in Scotland. Many of these Protestant sects were in time brought to America by English and European settlers.

The Church responded to the spirit of the times. We have seen how many of those who disagreed with the Church at Rome turned from her religious guidance to seek new forms of worship. But these disagreements did not always go so far as to cause them to leave the Church. Many who felt that certain reforms ought to be made within the Church did not consider breaking the religious ties which they held in great respect. They argued that where there was a wrong in the Church, the individuals responsible should be dealt with; the Church should not be condemned as an organization. However, it was generally recognized that something must be done to restore the prestige of the Church and prevent the further spread of heresy. Thus began a movement known as the Counter Reformation.

The Pope began a reorganization of the government of the Church and insisted upon higher standards on the part of the clergy and the correction of undesirable practices. In these ways the Church recognized the spirit of the times and strengthened its defenses against the danger of further losses.

Loyola spread the teachings of the Church of Rome. One day in the early part of the 16th Century a young Spanish captain broke his leg in battle. During his slow recovery he passed the time in reading. It happened that the books at hand told about the life of Christ and the lives of the saints. He decided to give up his knightly adventures and became a soldier of Christ, spreading the teachings of the Church. In this way the Catholic Church gained one of her most able servants, Ignatius Loyola [ig nay' shuhs loh yoh'lah]. Loyola spent eleven years preparing himself for the cause he wished to serve. Finally, with a group of companions, he founded the Society of Jesus.

Four vows were taken by the members. The first three, poverty, chastity, and obedience, were the same as those vows taken by the medieval monks. In the fourth, the members promised to obey the Pope and to undertake any missionary service, at home or abroad, which he might require of them.

Unlike the monks who sought the quiet of the monastery, the members of the Society of Jesus mingled with the people as preachers, teachers, and missionaries. The Jesuits [jez'yoo itz], as they came to be known, were the soldier-crusaders of the Church, exerting one of the strongest forces in the Counter Reformation. Their schools, which had a high standard of teaching, were especially influential. Through the Jesuits some of the peoples who had turned Protestant were brought back to the Catholic Church. Later, in the 17th Century, the Jesuits spread the doctrines of the Church of Rome throughout the New World. One famous Jesuit was Marquette, who taught the religion of his Church to the Indians of our Great Lakes region. Many schools and colleges all over the world were established by the Jesuits and are still run by this Society.

Chapter 4 ~ The Spirit of the Renaissance Gave Rise to New Ideas in Science, Philosophy, and Education

Science grew out of " the Black Art." During the Middle Ages science had been largely an array of odd-shaped bottles, peculiar mixtures, and black magic. It was frequently called " the Black Art." But with the spirt of the Renaissance at work, men became more ready to drop their superstitions and to seek the facts. As with all progress, the changes in scientific thinking centered around a few leaders.

One of the forerunners of modern science was Roger Bacon, an English monk who lived during the 13th Century. Though he believed in some of the superstitions and magic of medieval science, Bacon was impatient with the stupidity and ignorance of many of his fellow-scientists. He believed that scientific facts could be reached by making experiments. In this belief he showed a truly modern attitude. He predicted quite rightly that experimental science would result in discoveries and inventions more wonderful than the works of magic. Here is a passage from one of his letters. As you read it, remember that it was written over five hundred years before his interesting predictions came true.

Courtesy Fisher Scientific Company

THE YOUNG ALCHEMIST

Even though the alchemists wasted their time trying to make gold out of crude metals, they learned some things that paved the way for the science of chemistry. The early laboratory pictured here is certainly vastly different from a modern laboratory.

Instruments for navigation can be made which will do away with the necessity of rowers, so that great vessels . . . shall be borne about with only a single man to guide them and with greater speed than if they were full of men. And carriages can be constructed to move without animals to draw them, and with incredible velocity. Machines for flying can be made in which a man sits and turns an ingenious device by which skilfully contrived wings are made to strike the air in the manner of a flying bird.

In Italy Leonardo da Vinci [lay'oh-nahr'doh dah veen'chi] was a leader in science and art. He experimented and kept a careful record of what he observed. By using mathematics he tried to figure out some of the laws of nature. The story is told that da Vinci purchased the bodies of criminals from the hangman in order that he might study anatomy instead of simply guessing how the organs of the human body work. He built birdlike machines, for da Vinci, like Roger Bacon, was convinced that man would fly as soon as more laws of nature were known. One of his drawings for an airplane is shown below. Da Vinci also kept a book on the mechanics of bird flight. He designed a helicopter and a parachute, though these things remained only ideas with him.

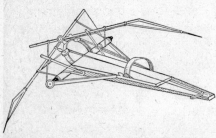

LEONARDO DA VINCI'S FLYING MACHINE
Leonardo da Vinci was so far ahead of his time in scientific thought that he recognized the possibilities in many inventions that have only recently been perfected.

Other men in these times were making marvelous discoveries and giving unbelievable explanations of the world and life about them. For a time after the learning of ancient Greece was rediscovered, European scholars had accepted the beliefs of most of the Greek writers. They thought that the earth was the center of the universe and that the sun and planets revolved around it. This idea was upset by Copernicus [koh per' ni kuhs]. He dared to tell the people that the sun was the center of the solar system and that the earth and planets revolved about it. He wrote a book in which he explained his new ideas about the earth and the heavens. His work caused him to be known as the founder of modern astronomy.

At first the European scholars had been limited by superstition and ignorance. Then they had come to rely absolutely on the writings of the ancient Greeks and Romans, particularly Aristotle. Finally they came to insist upon careful observation, experimentation, and the use of mathematics. With these changes taking place in science, the medieval world took another step toward becoming modern.

Philosophy ceased to be arguments about trivial things. The discussions of the medieval philosophers often centered about trivial matters in a way that can hardly be understood in the light of present-day knowledge. They argued seriously such questions as " How many angels can stand on a point of a needle? " and " Can God make two hills without an intervening valley? " Even in less extreme cases, philosophy was generally used to support current teachings rather than to seek new truths.

Such conditions in the field of philosophy disgusted the Dutchman Erasmus, one of the keenest thinkers who lived during the Renaissance. In a book called *The Praise of Folly* he wrote:

. . . But alas! Those notional diviners, however condemned by the sober judgment of others, are yet mightily pleased with themselves, and are so laboriously intent upon prosecuting their crabbed studies that they cannot afford so much time as to read a single chapter in any one book of the Bible. . . . They thus trifle away their misspent hours in trash and babble.

The substitution of ideas based on facts for the hairsplitting arguments of some of the medieval thinkers is another evidence that the world was becoming modern.

Francis Bacon, an Englishman, also attacked the shallow thinking of the medieval philosophers. Like his countryman, Roger Bacon, who lived many years earlier, he was a courageous thinker who insisted upon seeing things as they were. Like other Renaissance thinkers, Francis Bacon thought that instead of starting with an opinion borrowed from some ancient Greek philosopher, men should discover truths for themselves. He believed they should gain knowledge by firsthand observation and then base their conclusions on what they observed.

The spirit of the Renaissance invaded the schools. Why do you suppose Latin is taught in so many high schools today? It is largely owing to the revival of learning which took place in the early years of the medieval awakening. Before the revival of learning, you will recall, the sons of nobles received their training in the castle. You will also remember how the lost manuscripts of Greek and Roman writers were finally discovered and collected. Many of these writings, sometimes in Greek but usually in Latin, were studied in the schools of the Renaissance. To read them the students had to be able to read the languages in which they were written. Thus Latin and Greek became the chief subjects taught in the schools of the Renaissance. For hundreds of years the pupils in the higher schools of Europe spent from one-half to three-fourths of their time studying the classics. In fact, many of the schoolmasters became so interested in the study of the Greek and Latin languages that they had no time for anything else. Even today we find that Latin has a place in the program of studies.

Luther advocated reforms in education. Some time after the revival of interest in the classics, there was a tendency away from the study of Greek and Latin. Early in the 16th Century Martin Luther asked the mayors and councilmen of the German cities to have schools built at public expense and require children to attend. He urged that the children study their own language instead of Greek and Latin.

Luther also insisted that every boy and girl, rich or poor, be taught to read, write, and figure. He even asked that children who had to work should attend school a few hours each day. These demands sound quite modern. They show us how people were getting away from the medieval notion that education was only for the noble classes and the clergy.

Rabelais described the complete education. Rabelais [ra′buh′lay′], of France, was one of the leaders during the Renaissance who criticized the schoolmasters for spending so much time in the study of the languages. He accused them of trying to make young Romans out of their students. He argued that it was more useful to learn about the manners, the customs, and wisdom of the Romans than about their language, in order that the pupils might be better educated to meet the needs of their own time.

Half-humorously Rabelais wrote a story about the education of a boy. The student of his story took long walks in which he studied trees and plants and brought specimens home with him. The boy was taught horsemanship and the use of arms — the training of a knightly gentleman. He was also taught the skills of the workshop. Books were not neglected; six hours a day were spent in serious study. Rabelais' ideas were not popular with the schoolmen of his day. His plans were years ahead of his time; but from his writings we can see that medieval education was gradually giving way to modern schooling.

Montaigne insisted that education should help people live wisely. Montaigne [mahn tayn'], another Frenchman, who lived a few years later than Rabelais, also had new ideas about education. He, too, helped to change medieval schools into modern schools. Montaigne said that the learner was of first importance, not the facts of textbooks. He did not think it important to possess knowledge unless it was helpful in daily life. Here is a quotation from his writings:

Except our mind be better and our judgment the sounder . . . I had rather my scholar had employed his time playing tennis. . . . We are ever ready to ask — hath such a one any skill in the Greek or Latin tongue? Can he write well in prose, in verse? But whether he be grown better or wiser — which should be the chief drift — that is never spoken of.

Because much in modern education is practical, it may be difficult for us to realize why Montaigne felt so strongly about bookishness. But we should remember that he was objecting to the schools of the 16th Century.

Comenius modernized the Greek idea, "Know Thyself." "Look at the facts about you" was the spirit of the Renaissance science. This idea was also voiced by a schoolman named Comenius [koh-may'nee oos], who lived in Bohemia (now part of Czechoslovakia) during the 17th Century. He believed that if science should present a study of real things, certainly the schools should train boys and girls in this field of learning in order to meet real conditions in everyday life.

Thus Comenius was one of the first great realists in education. To him the business of the schools was to improve the abilities which nature had given a person, so that he might have a full knowledge of himself and the world about him. This was a revival of the Greek idea of "know thyself" as an important purpose of education. Too, Comenius is the father of illustrated textbooks.

Chapter 5 ~ The Spirit of the Renaissance Led to an Amazing Development in Creative Art

The medieval awakening brought about a rebirth in the fine arts. Before the Renaissance the fine arts were largely influenced by the religious ideas of the times, and religious subjects were often selected. Medieval painting was remarkable for its beautiful design and color. To us it may seem rather formal nd unlifelike for two reasons: the medieval artists had not worked out the law of perspective, and they did not know much about human anatomy. Literature of medieval times was limited almost entirely to the writings of the Churchmen. They, of course, wrote in Latin, the language of the Church, instead of the language used by the common people. Architecture was also influenced by the ideas of the Middle Ages and found expression in the wonderful Gothic cathedrals of Western Europe. Then came the Renaissance. A rebirth took place in the fine arts just as it did in the fields of science, education, and philosophy.

Italian artists first learned, during the 15th Century, to get a three-dimensional effect in their paintings so that they could paint human figures which appeared to have some weight and substance like real people. With the new interest in science, Renaissance artists also had a greater knowledge of human anatomy to aid them in their work. They also worked out the laws of perspective perfectly and could paint landscapes which suggested distance amazingly well.

The artists of Italy saw the beauty of life. The rediscovery of the culture of Greece and Rome was not limited to old manuscripts. Men of the Renaissance collected statuary also. In places covered by debris and rubbish, from the ruins of ancient cities, and from peasant farmers who had come upon buried statues, they collected the ancient masterpieces of Greece and Rome. You may remember that Lorenzo de' Medici placed many rare and beautiful pieces of statuary in his garden in the city of Florence. The young artists of that day would come to the garden to study and to copy. There were other collectors of classic art, especially in Italy. And so the artists of the Renaissance gradually became interested

Underwood and Underwood

MONA LISA

Leonardo da Vinci painted this picture of an unknown Italian woman. Her slight smile has puzzled art lovers for centuries. Is it sympathetic or amused?

in the beauty of line and color to be found in the human face and form, and in every flower, tree, cloud, and horizon. Once the beauty of life was again realized, the renaissance in art spread across Europe.

Leonardo da Vinci: scientist and artist. One of the remarkable artists of the Renaissance was Leonardo da Vinci, also of Florence, who began his work toward the end of the 15th Century. Already we have spoken of him as a scientist. As a painter, he produced pictures which have made his name unique. " The Last Supper," one of his most famous, pictures Christ at the Last Supper with the Twelve Disciples; He has just said, "Verily I say unto you, that one of you shall betray me." Judas, who had betrayed his Master, is the second figure to the right of Christ. He sits clutching his bag of money. His face and posture

The University Prints, Newton, Mass.

"DAVID"

Michelangelo's "David" is a tremendous statue eighteen feet high. The statue is so heavy that forty men were needed to roll it from the workshop.

plainly show the fear and consternation which he feels. Though da Vinci used a religious topic for his picture, it is a typical Italian Renaissance painting. The figures and the feelings which he shows us are most real. Should you some day visit the city of Milan [mi lan'], step into the old dining room of the convent church of Santa Maria [sahn'tah mah-ree'ah]. There you will see extending along one wall da Vinci's "Last Supper." It has faded and cracked, but it still is firsthand evidence of the genius of a master artist of the Renaissance.

Another painting by which we remember da Vinci is his "Mona Lisa" [moh'nah lee'zah] which is shown on the preceding page. It is the portrait of a young Italian woman. In painting the picture da Vinci used oil paints on canvas. The use of such materials was still fairly new, having been developed early in the 15th Century in both Italy and the Netherlands. Da Vinci was a pioneer. The picture is not large, the dimensions

being about twenty by thirty inches. One of the interesting things about the young woman, who sits calmly gazing at us, is her mysterious smile. It is difficult to tell whether she is smiling at us or laughing to herself as she watches her admirers. The Mona Lisa is one of da Vinci's best known pictures.

Michelangelo: sculptor, painter, and architect. When Leonardo da Vinci was about twenty-three, a boy was born to a poor but proud family in the city of Florence. The boy was Michelangelo [mee'kel ahn'jay loh]. The young Italian had a tempestuous and determined disposition. He gave his father no end of worry by insisting that he wanted to become an artist. And an artist he became. In his student days he quarreled with one of his fellow pupils and received a blow on the nose which disfigured him for life. Yet with all his stormy temper and unsociable traits, he is one of the wonderful men of the world. A sculptor, a painter, an architect, Michelangelo is another great figure by whom we shall remember the renaissance in art.

As a youth of thirteen Michelangelo became an apprentice to one of the foremost painters of Florence. Soon, however, he took up his studies in the gardens of Lorenzo de' Medici. There, among the rich collection of ancient statuary, he studied the skill of the Greek and Roman artists.

His rare abilities, his training, and his fierce application to work made it possible for Michelangelo to surprise even his fellow townsmen with a burst of skill. Returning to Florence one day from a stay in Rome, he was urged to see what he could make out of a huge block of marble that had been spoiled by an artist some forty years before, and had been standing neglected ever since. Working only from some sketches and wax models which he prepared, Michelangelo applied his chisel and mallet. For two years he drove himself to his task and hewed out of the solid block the statue of a magnificent young athlete. The popularity of the statue and its sculptor was immediate. The massive sculpture was of David, the Hebrew youth who slew the giant Goliath. A picture of this " David " can be seen on page 312.

One day the Pope asked Michelangelo to decorate the ceiling of the Sistine [sis′teen] Chapel in Rome. At first Michelangelo objected, protesting that his field of art was sculpture. However, the Pope was so insistent that Michelangelo promised to attempt the new type of work.

When he began he found himself intensely interested in the art of painting. On a high scaffold he lay, face up, in a cramped position. He sketched and applied his colors. Finally, after three years, the paintings were finished. They told the Bible story of Genesis [jen′uh sis] from the Creation to the Flood. There were hundreds of human figures. These figures show the knowledge of anatomy he gained from his work as a sculptor. Many American soldiers saw these paintings on the ceiling of the Sistine Chapel during the occupation of Rome in World War II. The pictures are faded, for over three hundred years have passed; but they still are proof of the remarkable skill of Michelangelo. They show us an artist who broke away from the more formal traditions of the Middle Ages and established new standards of art.

Michelangelo was not only a sculptor and a painter, he was also an architect of great ability. The Pope called upon him to complete the design of the Church of St. Peter's in Rome, and to design the massive dome. This he did when he was past seventy years of age.

The University Prints, Newton, Mass.
" THE SISTINE MADONNA "

" The Sistine Madonna " by Raphael is considered by many to be the greatest Madonna painting in the world.

In his ninetieth year, Michelangelo died, but his name will never be forgotten. He left many masterpieces of painting, sculpture, and architecture of which we have mentioned only a few. We have seen that he helped to revive the art of the ancient world and to raise art to new heights. His work is part of the heritage of the modern world.

Raphael became " the Perfect Painter " of the Renaissance. Leonardo da Vinci and Michelangelo, who were masters of technique and form, were inspirations to many other artists of that day. And so they proved to be to the aspiring artist, Raphael [raf′ay el].

Raphael was born at Urbino, Italy, where he spent his years of apprenticeship in painting. Later he worked in Rome and Florence, as did the other two artists we just mentioned. Raphael was about ten years younger than Michelangelo and about thirty years younger than da Vinci. Although he lived only about half as long as the other two masters, he became known as the perfect painter of Italy.

Some three hundred years after Raphael's time, Goethe [gœ'tuh], the German poet, wrote of him:

Raphael's nature and achievement were so perfectly balanced that . . . no modern artist ever attained to such purity and completeness of thought, or to such clearness of expression. His art is as it were a draught of fresh water from the purest spring. He feels, thinks, and works exactly as if he were a Greek.

Even though Raphael lived but thirty-seven years, he is responsible for several hundred paintings. The most famous of these is the " Sistine Madonna " which Raphael painted for a chapel in Rome. This priceless picture now hangs in the art gallery in Dresden, Germany. The painting shows the old Pope Sixtus and Saint Barbara as they kneel in worship of the Virgin Mother and Child. Though the picture is not in perfect condition, because of its age, one can still see the rich colors, the flowing garments, and the beautiful expressions of the Mother and Child. The Sistine Madonna is one of the best known pictures in the world. There is a reproduction of it on page 313. A printed illustration can give you only a meager idea of a canvas, about ten feet in height and seven feet in width, done in rich oil colors.

The spirit of the Renaissance in art swept across Europe. Just as the interest in the revival of learning of the Greeks and Romans had spread from Italy to England, so the spirit of the renaissance in art traveled. In Germany, France, Spain, the Netherlands, and England, artists were becoming skillful in painting the beauty of life in the world about

them. Later, as we take up the story of each nation, we shall become acquainted with some of the pictures of these artists.

Greek columns and Roman domes marked the architecture of the Renaissance. The feudal strongholds of the Middle Ages had been designed to serve as fortresses for the lords. The beautiful Gothic cathedrals, which the people of northern Europe built during the Middle Ages, were dedicated to the worship of God. You may well wonder how a rebirth in architecture could result in more beautiful buildings. It is true that the changes which took place in buildings of the 14th and 15th Centuries were not so remarkable as the changes which took place in painting and sculpture. But the revival of ancient learning interested men in the buildings of Greece and Rome. During the Renaissance the architects copied the Greek columns, Roman domes, and other features of the ancient buildings. Yet somehow the perfect harmony and the artistic simplicity of the ancient buildings were lost.

One of the foremost examples of Renaissance architecture is the cathedral of St. Peter's. As you know, it was designed by Michelangelo. The massive dome rises over four hundred feet above the floor. The many Greek columns, the steps and portico, and the decorative statues remind us of the Greek temples. St. Peter's is the largest church in the world. With its connected buildings it covers thirteen acres. In its style of architecture we can easily see the influence of Greece and Rome. There are many modern buildings in Europe and America which are fashioned in the Renaissance style. It is interesting to know that our capitol building at Washington, with its high dome and many columns, can trace its ancestry to the buildings of the 16th Century.

Dante set a new style in literature. In spirit Dante [dahn'tay] belongs to the Renaissance, though he actually lived in the Middle Ages. He did much to change the world of literature from medieval into modern ways. Like so many of the other leaders he was an Italian and a native of that remarkable city of Florence. Because of political trouble he was exiled by his fellow townsmen. In middle life he found himself wandering up and down Italy, disappointed and discouraged.

He wrote a poem by which he made his name everlasting. It came to be called the *Divine Comedy*. In it he describes an imaginary trip through heaven and hell. In hell, of course, he finds his enemies and many others. As you remember, the people of the Middle Ages were very much interested in salvation. Dante's poem shows the religious interests of his time. It was different from the usual medieval literature, since Dante wrote about himself and other people. He used many illustrations which he drew from the actual life about him in Italy.

Dante also wrote in his native language, Italian. For a man of learning to write in anything but Latin was considered by many to be vulgar and bad form. But by doing so Dante called the attention of educated people to the beauty in the language of the common people. So we may say that he helped to found modern Italian language and literature.

The *Divine Comedy* opens with lines which show how Dante felt at being forced to leave his home town. As you will realize, the quotations which follow are translations from the Italian.

> Midway of life's journey I again
> Found myself in a dim forest;
> For the right road was lost.

Other writers of the Renaissance followed Dante's example. They wrote about themselves and the interesting things which their fellow men did. They described in words the beauties of nature which the painters and sculptors were brushing on canvas and cutting in marble. Each country began to develop a literature of its own, in the language of the common people. Dante, we should remember, was the earliest of many authors who began to write in their native languages.

Modern musical forms and instruments developed as a result of the Renaissance and the Reformation. With the great interest in learning and art, music also began to be affected. The invention of printing soon led to improvements in musical notation that did away with confusing and useless signs, and made music easier to read.

Martin Luther started a change in the world of music. He wanted church congregations to be able to take part in the church music, and therefore he himself gathered material for new and simple songs for the people to sing during the service. In all, Luther wrote thirty-seven hymns. Perhaps the most beautiful is " A Mighty Fortress Is Our God," with which many of you may be familiar. It has been called the " Battle Hymn of the Reformation." Hymns for congregational singing were being written in countries throughout Europe at the time. Although some of the early hymn melodies were original, many were adapted from folk melodies and from the Catholic masses and chants.

While Lutheranism was sweeping through Europe, the Church itself, as you have read, was undertaking many reforms. Church leaders recognized that music was one of the matters that required change; the indiscriminate use of the same tunes for religious masses and for popular songs seemed objectionable. Models of what church music should be were furnished at this time by the masses composed by a gifted young musician called Palestrina [pal' uh stree'nuh], who devoted his whole life to music. He produced hundreds of compositions. When he died, the words "Princeps Musicae" (Prince of Music) were engraved on his tombstone. Many of his sacred compositions are still admired today.

Instrumental as well as vocal music underwent changes as a result of the current of the Renaissance. Musical instruments such as the lute, viol, and oboe up to this time had been used to accompany singers, carrying the melody and merely adding to the volume of sound. But composers now began to write music for instruments alone. Solo singing began to be popular also, and the oratorio, a sacred drama with music, became a favorite type of religious music. From these beginnings at the end of the 16th Century, the first of the popular modern operas developed.

The Renaissance and the Reformation helped music to become a full-fledged art. Within a few years so many changes had occurred that, in artistic importance, music had come to equal painting, architecture, and sculpture.

The Medieval World Awakened

The Renaissance, or rebirth, of Europe, was a current that set in motion the sluggish thinking and living of the medieval world. Most men and women of the Feudal Age were landlocked in the spot in which they had been born; they had scant means of getting new ideas or information. Somehow, in Italy as early as the 14th Century the mysterious current of the Renaissance began to stir men's thinking and acting and to swing them away from tradition toward a free appraisal of their world, past, present, and future.

In the 15th Century the feudal world was showing change. The introduction of money, the increase of trade, the growth of cities and towns, and the accumulation of wealth were making people's lives freer and the people themselves more receptive to the new ideas of the Renaissance. The new wealthy class in the cities had the leisure and the desire to learn. Moreover, merchant traders and merchant-minded nations were eager to break the hold of the Italians on the sea lanes to far-eastern markets. Explorers and adventurers were beginning to chart routes to the Americas, around Africa, and even around the globe. Necessity brought many important inventions and discoveries. The compass was improved; gunpowder came into use; the invention of the printing press and the availability of paper made it possible to spread ideas and information.

In Italy this awakened excitement and interest in living, both past and present, had led such men as Petrarch and Lorenzo de' Medici to collect ancient manuscripts and works of art. The old manuscripts were translated, and

a revival of learning swept across Europe. Through translations from literature and history, the beauty of Greece and the glory of Rome gradually became familiar to the people of the Western world, and influenced their lives.

In religion the force of the Renaissance tended to make men critical.
Protestantism grew strong in Europe and spread to the New World. The
Roman Catholic Church, critical of itself, carried on reforms from within.
Loyola and his Jesuit followers carried the Catholic faith to many parts of
the world. Almost all the fields of man's activities were touched by the spirit of
change. Under the genius of men like Roger Bacon and Leonardo da Vinci,
science ceased to be the " Black Art " and became more nearly an ordered
process of thinking and experimenting. Leaders in thought, such as Erasmus
and Francis Bacon, criticized certain philosophers of the Middle Ages and insisted that men who talk about the meaning of life should see life as it
really is.

The schools, too, felt the influence of the Renaissance. The revival of
learning had made the study of Greek important. Dante, in his famous poem,
The Divine Comedy, had used the native Italian instead of Latin, thus
strengthening the standing of modern language, and opening the possibility
of literary expression to men who were not classical scholars. Rabelais and
Montaigne, writers, and Comenius, an educator, spurred interest in new
methods of schooling. Education, they claimed, should be suited to life and
should develop an all-round person.

The Renaissance would be an epoch famous for its artists alone, if for no
other reason. Leonardo da Vinci, Michelangelo, Raphael — these three perhaps above all the other painters and sculptors — made the Renaissance the
" Golden Age " of European art.

Through all these changes we have seen the awakening of the European world. This world was not altered entirely, for traces of medieval ways
can be found even today. But the current of the Renaissance brought unmis-
takable evidence of the beginning of a modern age.

SELF–TEST

Take this self-test to see if you have understood how the medieval world
awakened.

I. In the following, select the clause or clauses that correctly complete
each statement.

(*a*) The story about Marco Polo shows (1) that the people of the Middle Ages traveled widely; (2) that the people of the 13th Century in Europe
knew little about the world; (3) that Marco could tell exaggerated tales.

(*b*) The four remarkable inventions changed the ways of living and ways of thinking because (1) travel became more common and ideas spread more rapidly; (2) castles could now be built more strongly; (3) men could now make a record of what they had done; (4) luxuries from the Far East added to the comfort of life in Europe.

(c) In the awakening of the medieval world the revolt of Luther was a result of (1) the Counter Reformation; (2) the spirit of the Renaissance; (3) the division of Christian peoples into a number of different religious faiths; (4) the spread of Jesuit teaching throughout the New World.

II. Name five ways in which the Renaissance led to the awakening of the medieval world.

III. Match the following by writing on a piece of paper the numbers and letters of the items which belong together or are most directly connected with each other. Do not mark the book.

(1) Michelangelo	(a) Renaissance in religion
(2) Gutenberg	(b) Mona Lisa
(3) Turks	(c) Sistine Madonna
(4) Marco Polo	(d) printing press
(5) Rabelais	(e) founder of modern astronomy
(6) Leonardo da Vinci	(f) dome of St. Peter's
(7) Dante	(g) 1453
(8) Raphael	(h) first to sail around the world
(9) Petrarch	(i) Renaissance in education
(10) Copernicus	(j) helped found Italian language
(11) Magellan	(k) collector of ancient writings and sculpture
(12) Lorenzo de' Medici	(l) illustrated textbooks
(13) Calvin	(m) revival of ancient writings
(14) Comenius	(n) Pekin
(15) Wycliffe	(o) Puritans

IV. Tell why each of the following statements is true or false:

(a) The variety of religious faiths which resulted from the Reformation has made a real need for tolerance in Christian nations.

(b) Loyola's actions showed he believed that religious reform could be brought about without breaking away from the medieval Church.

(c) Though Leonardo da Vinci was a great artist, he was not a man of wide accomplishments.

(d) Roger Bacon showed some traces of "Black Art" in his thinking, but even so was one of the first to suggest that science should be based on experiment.

INTERESTING THINGS TO DO

Projects for the Chart Maker and Artist

1. Make an illustrated book of the artists of the Renaissance. Select a suggestive title such as "The Golden Age of Art." If possible, include prints of some of the great masterpieces. You may want to enlist the aid of an " ama-

teur author" in expanding your book to include brief biographies of some of the artists, or stories concerning some of the pictures.

2. Make an illustrated map of the journeys of Marco Polo. Use cut-outs and sketches. If possible, read Marco Polo's diary. See also *Vast Horizons,* by Mary S. Lucas.

3. Draw a cartoon entitled "The Bridge of the Renaissance," which will show how the Renaissance led from the medieval world of feudalism to the world of modern nations. Use as many original ideas as you can.

4. Make a tree cartoon showing how the Christian peoples have branched out into many churches because of happenings of the 16th Century.

5. Draw "tree-trunk" charts of the Romance and German language families with their subdivisions.

Topics for Talks

1. "The needle points the way, or the story of the compass." See "Compass" in *Encyclopaedia Britannica.*

2. "The making of a book, or the story of printing." See any encyclopedia or *Wings for Words,* by D. C. McMurtrie and D. Farran. See also *Historic Inventions,* by R. S. Holland.

3. "Gunpowder, or the story of the changes brought about in warfare by explosives." See encyclopedias.

4. "Papyrus, parchment, and paper, or the story of paper." See encyclopedias or *Black on White,* by I. I. Marshak, pp. 115–129.

Adventures for the Amateur Author

1. Write a poem about the Mona Lisa, Lorenzo the Magnificent, Magellan, or some other colorful personality or some moving event that highlights the Renaissance.

2. Write an article for a popular magazine on the magic of the alchemists, or the beginnings of chemistry. Include descriptions of the early laboratories, elixirs, the philosopher's stone, and the theory of transmutation of the elements with reference to radium in recent times. See *Story of Chemistry,* by F. L. Darrow; *Makers of Chemistry,* by Eric Holmyard, and also "Alchemy" in *The World Book Encyclopedia.*

3. Write an essay about the work of some great figure of the Renaissance not mentioned in your text, such as Paracelsus, Vesalius, or Titian. See encyclopedias, or ask your librarian about books of collected biography from which you may secure more information.

Ideas for Your Little Theater

1. Congregational hymn singing began in the Reformation. Arrange a musical program with phonograph recordings of some of these early hymns,

and also of madrigals and chorals. If possible, obtain records also of some of Palestrina's compositions.

2. Dramatize for the class an incident from the life of Marco Polo. See *Travels of Marco Polo*, by Manuel Komroff, *Messer Marco Polo*, by Donn Byrne, or *Vast Horizons*, by Mary S. Lucas.

Candidates for Your Album of Famous People

Roger Bacon, Columbus, Comenius, Erasmus, Vasco da Gama, Gutenberg, Loyola, Luther, Magellan, Lorenzo de' Medici, Michelangelo, Montaigne, Petrarch, Marco Polo, da Vinci.

Choose at least three of the above people for biographical portraits in your Album. If you wish to, you may substitute other famous people mentioned in your text for some of those listed above.

INTERESTING READING ABOUT THE RENAISSANCE

BARSTOW, C. L. *Famous Buildings*. ". . . all the chairs were piled up in the choir and set on fire. . . ."

COTTLER, J. *Man with Wings*. A biography of Leonardo da Vinci that pictures his personal charm and his brilliant achievements as an artist, sculptor, engineer, and inventor.

ELLSWORTH, LINCOLN. *Exploring Today*. " What is there left to explore? "

HEWES, AGNES D. *Spice and the Devil's Cave*. A story of Portugal's attempt to find the " Way of the Spices." An adventurous tale that involves a mysterious girl, Vasco da Gama, and Magellan.

HODGES, C. WALTER. *Columbus Sails*. A book that cleverly weaves old legends and stories into eye-witness accounts of Columbus' first voyage to America.

JOHNSTON, MARY. *1492*. A novel about Ferdinand and Isabella of Spain and the explorations and discoveries in the New World.

LUCAS, MARY S. *Vast Horizons*. Songs, maps, charts, and the adventurous stories of men " who set out to conquer the unknown " combine to make this an absorbing history of discovery.

MILLS, DOROTHY. *Renaissance and Reformation Times*. Numerous quotations, well-chosen illustrations, and a time chart help this book to present a clear, unprejudiced picture of the political, economic and religious changes of the Renaissance.

National Geographic Magazine, Nov., 1928. " The World's Greatest Overland Explorer," by J. R. Hildebrand. " The Winter Palace at Peking, set in a maze of walls, Marco explained, was a literal Chinese puzzle."

VAN LOON, H. W. *The Story of Mankind*. " If he was an interesting speaker, the crowd came and stayed."

WELLS, H. G. *The Outline of History*. " Europe begins to think for itself."

PART TEN

THE BRITISH PEOPLES BUILT AN EMPIRE
AND SPREAD IDEAS OF SELF-GOVERNMENT

BRITISH ISLES

PART TEN

The Setting for the Story of the British People

Just as a stage setting reveals something of the play to be presented, so the geography of a country gives us some idea of the life of the people who inhabit it. Before the curtain rises on the story of the British people, look at the map of the world at the back of the book. See also the globe above. We see that the British Isles provide a very small stage for a people who have carried their civilization to all parts of the world. Why do you think the British became a great seafaring and industrial people?

Now look at the map on the opposite page. Can you tell why the British Isles have a temperate climate? You have already read about Stonehenge and, later, about Hadrian's Wall. Can you find them on the map? What part of England was of great interest to the peoples of ancient times?

North of Hadrian's Wall you will find Edinburgh, the old Scotch university town. On the western coast of Scotland is Glasgow, famous for its shipbuilding. In Ireland, notice the two divisions, Eire and Northern Ireland. In the story of the British people, which follows, you will also learn about the other countries which make up the British Commonwealth of Nations.

Chapter 1 ~ The British Were an Island People

"The English." What do you think of when you hear "the English"? Perhaps you recall pictures of the "Redcoats" of Revolutionary days or the old song about London Bridge. It may be that you think of Shakespeare's *Merchant of Venice,* Dickens' *Christmas Carol,* or the bombing of London during World War II. Whatever it is we may think about, the words, "the English" mean many things to us in the United States.

It is not strange that we should be interested in the people living in the British Isles. Many of the founders of our country came here from England. One of the strongest ties that bind us to what the American colonists used to call "the mother country" is language. It is true that there are differences. In England an automobile truck is a lorry; a radio tube, a valve; a policeman, a bobbie. There are also some differences in pronunciation and the inflection of the voice, but the language of the people in both England and America is English.

Who are the British? We use the terms England and English, Great Britain and British, quite loosely; it would be wise to define them now. England, "that tight little isle," is actually only a part of an island. England, Scotland, and Wales are a single island, called Britain or Great Britain; and Eire [ehr'uh] (or Ireland as it is frequently called) is another. These are the major islands of the British Isles. The English, Scotch (or Scots), Welsh, and Irish are all Britishers — as are the inhabitants of many other parts of the British Empire.

There is a saying that "the sun never sets on the British Empire." Look at the map on page 363. The shaded parts are lands occupied by the British in 1939. It seems odd that those little islands off the west coast of Europe exercise such great influence or control over about one-fourth of the earth's surface and about one-fifth of the people in the world. You will learn more about some of these lands and peoples in Chapter 6 of this Part.

Strong are the ties that bind. The story of Great Britain is especially interesting to Americans. It gives us an understanding of the conditions that led to the forming of our own nation. It also touches other nations so that we shall learn something about the French, the Spanish, and many other peoples as we study the story of the British Empire. Had the world map at the top of page 363 been made during the 17th Century or the first half of the 18th Century, it would have shown a shaded area on the eastern coast of what is now the United States. The ports of Charleston, New York, and Boston, for example, were then British harbors.

Many distinguished leaders in the early history of the United States were either British or sons of men who were born in the British Isles. Some of the strongest traits of these early Americans were British. George Washington showed the dignity, the ability to command, and the manners of an English country gentleman. These characteristics were typical of his ancestors. Benjamin Franklin gave us his wise sayings in *Poor Richard's Almanac* first as a loyal British subject and later as an American. English blood ran in the veins of Abraham Lincoln. His unforgettable phrase, ". . . that government of the people, by the people, and for the people shall not perish from the earth" recalls the long struggle for freedom and justice which was waged and won by the English of an earlier day. When we enter a court of law, use parliamentary procedure, or speak our native language, we are following American ways that had their beginning in the British Isles.

The seas separate the home of the English from the Continent. We have often seen in this *Story of Nations* how the life of a people has been affected by their natural surroundings. You will recall how the Egyptian civilization grew up along the fertile banks of the Nile. We have seen how the Greeks developed a number of independent states, partly because of the mountains that separated one group of people from another. As might be expected, the life of the early English was greatly influenced by the isolation of their homeland.

Although the British Isles are separated from the mainland they are in many ways a part of it. The English Channel is only a narrow strip of water. On clear days a Frenchman can stand on his home shore and see, about twenty miles distant, the white cliffs of Dover. Yet this narrow channel with its rough waters made it possible for the English to develop a separate nation, with characteristics decidedly different from those of the people on the Continent. The seas surrounding the British Isles have been like the moat of a feudal castle. They have been a protection without being a barrier to the customs and ideas of the other nations of Europe. Shakespeare, the English writer, has said —

This little world
This precious stone set in the silver sea,
Which serves it in the office of a wall,
Or as a moat defensive to a house
Against the envy of less happier lands. . . .

The English Channel and surrounding seas, however, did not give complete protection to the islands. Invaders, sometimes as pirates, came on these same seas to lay waste the coast and often to occupy the conquered land. But each time invaders settled in England they found themselves so separated from their native lands on the continent that they became more and more like the people they had come to conquer. Thus the isolation of the British Isles helped the English to build a nation distinctly their own.

The British Isles have resources and beauty. You may wonder why the peoples of Western Europe found these islands of the North Atlantic so attractive. People like to live in a country where nature has supplied many resources, a good climate, and a pleasant countryside. England has these attractions.

The British Isles are in the same latitude as Labrador, but the warm ocean current from the Gulf of Mexico sweeps across the Atlantic and up along the western coast of the British Isles. Thus the climate of England is neither very cold in winter nor very hot in summer. There are many rolling hills, numerous fine rivers and safe harbors, and beneath the surface of the land is a good supply of tin and coal, and some iron. Also, the sea provides an abundant supply of fish, which has proved a most important resource.

There is an old English fishing song that runs —

The husbandman has rent to pay
(Blow, winds, blow,)

And seeds to purchase everyday
(Row, boys, row,)
But he who farms the rolling deeps
Though never sowing always reaps;
The ocean's fields are fair and free
There are no rent days on the sea.

The British Isles are very small compared to our country. The state of New Mexico has about the same number of square miles as the British Isles, and Texas is twice their size. Because of the limited size of the islands, and the need for trade and for defense, the British became great shipbuilders. They took advantage of the sea to become sailors and merchantmen, and to carry goods to all parts of the world.

The climate of the British Isles is warm and moist, and the rainfall is ample. Frequent rains on the fertile soil have produced green fields and verdant forests. One of the islands, Ireland, has come to be known as the "Emerald Isle." There are regions of the British Isles, of course, that are rugged and mountainous, and other parts that are low and desolate. But in some of these less favored regions rugged peoples, such as the Scots and the Welsh, have developed.

Chapter 2 ~ The Blood of Courageous Adventurers Flows in the Veins of an Englishman

England was inhabited during early times. In the story of early men we learned about the discovery of the bones of the Piltdown man on the British Isles. He must have lived over a million years ago. There are also evidences that people lived on these islands during the Stone Age. Many years before Christ, and long before Julius Caesar ruled the Roman world, there were people living on the British Isles about whom we have some reliable information. They lived in the Age of Bronze. Men of the Bronze Age needed tin to melt with their copper. This need brought the people of early England to the attention of the ancient world because they had tin. The Phoenicians in sailing the seas had discovered that fact. They became rich by supplying tin from the mines of Cornwall, England, to the countries of the Mediterranean.

During the Bronze Age Britain was conquered by the Celts. The people who lived in Britain during the Bronze Age were not able to hold the country for themselves. The islands were too attractive to outsiders. About a thousand years before the birth of Christ, the Celts from Western Europe came to England and conquered the native inhabitants. The Celts were strong, tall fighters who used bronze weapons as well as horses and war chariots in battle. They learned to mine the tin of Cornwall and to carry on trade with their neighbors. They absorbed the early inhabitants of Britain and became the ancestors of the Scotch, Irish, and Welsh peoples. The Celts who remained in what is now called England came into contact with several other invading peoples before they became the Englishmen we know today. Let us see who some of these invading peoples were.

CAESAR LANDING IN BRITAIN

The British archers and spearmen could not prevent Caesar and his legions from landing in England in 55 B.C.; but the conquest of Britain took the Romans over 200 years.

The Roman legions reached the British Isles. For hundreds of years the Celtic British enjoyed the British Isles unmolested. As we might expect, they saw something of the other peoples of Europe. They traded with the people who lived just across the English Channel. Phoenician and Greek traders visited their shores.

When Caesar was waging war against the Gauls in what is now France, he discovered that his enemies were receiving aid from the island which could be seen in the distance. So, about half a century before Christ, Caesar led an expedition against the Britons. The landing of Caesar is pictured above.

The legions of Rome were surprised at the resistance they met. There, near the white cliffs of Dover, stood the Briton warriors with glistening bronze spears. The soldiers of the mighty Caesar rushed amid flying arrows, spears, and rocks, and scattered their foe. But not until the following year could Caesar and his legions force their way up the river now called the Thames to a muddy village of thatched huts. Little could

Caesar have imagined that some day London, for long the world's largest city, was to stand near that marshy spot. Caesar found that although he had defeated the Britons he had not subdued their spirit and, when the Roman soldiers left, the island ceased to be a part of the Roman Empire.

Caesar described and named the Britons for us. As many high-school pupils know, Caesar left some accounts of the people he found in Britain. He speaks of them as being tall, blue-eyed giants with long yellow hair. To make themselves appear terrible to their enemies, the Britons stained their bodies with a deep blue dye. This practice caused the Romans to call them *Brythons* [brith"nz], meaning "painted folks." From this name has developed the term *Britons*. They wore short cloaks made of heavy skins and carried massive skin shields and sharp bronze weapons. These Celtic Britons made wagons with wheels, built thatched huts, wove wicker boats, and designed many ornaments.

Caesar was particularly interested in the strange religion of the Britons. Their priests carried on mystic rites in the depths of the oak forests. The oak tree was held in great reverence, and the mistletoe which grew on the oaks was sacred. The people wove baskets of the mistletoe in which the priests offered up sacrifices of animals and sometimes human beings. This form of worship is called the Druid [droo'id] religion, or Druidism.

A century later the Romans came again. For nearly one hundred years the Britons had their island to themselves. But about a century after the birth of Christ the Romans came again, conquering most of that part of the main island which we know today as England. Many of the natives fled before the Romans into the mountainous parts which we now call Scotland and Wales, where they kept their independence.

The Romans found the savages of the north so strong that a wall was built by the emperor, Hadrian [hay'dri'n], to protect the new Roman colonies. Hadrian's wall stretched across England from the Irish Sea to the North Sea. It was eighty miles long, eighteen feet high, and nine feet thick. About every twenty miles a fort was built and manned by Roman soldiers. The ruins of Hadrian's wall may be seen today.

We may think of the wall, of course, as a monument to the military genius of the Romans. But it is also a monument to the spirit of independence and courage of the ancestors of the hardy Scotchmen of today. Later, many centuries after the Romans had left, the Englishmen themselves had a most difficult time in bringing Scotland under their rule.

The Romans contributed to English civilization. As we learned in the story of Rome, wherever the Roman legions went they carried Roman civilization. South of Hadrian's wall a network of fine roads was built, some of which still remain. About the Roman camps, villages and cities grew. The Latin word for camp is *castra* [kahs'trah]. When we hear of such English cities as Lancaster, Manchester, or Chester we know that they probably had their beginnings in a Roman camp or fort.

Over fifty walled cities were built by the Romans. In these cities and about the countryside, beautiful homes were constructed which included spacious rooms and luxurious baths. Occasionally, when an excavation is made in England, ruins of these homes are found, giving evidence of the Roman occupation.

For three and a half centuries, Britain was a Roman colony. The Romans treated the Britons harshly. But the Britons learned many things from the higher civilization of the Romans in language, customs, and methods of constructing roads and buildings. During the time of the Roman occupation, Christianity was brought to Britain.

Britain became England with the Anglo-Saxons in control. The Britons had come to depend upon the soldiers of Rome. When the Roman legions were recalled to defend their capital city in the early part of the Fifth Century, the Britons became the prey of the barbarian tribes north of Hadrian's wall and the barbarians from across the sea. Hurriedly the Britons sent a plea for protection to a Roman general, saying, "The barbarians drive us to the sea; the sea throws us back on the barbarians." But the Romans themselves were in too great danger to send help.

The savage tribes of the north broke over Hadrian's wall. German barbarians from the shores of northern Europe sailed down the coast of Britain. Towns were burned, crops destroyed, and people slain or made captive. These plundering invaders from the continent were the Angles, the Saxons, and the Jutes. These tribes are generally referred to as Anglo-Saxons. Within two and a half centuries these invaders had conquered and occupied much of Britain. Then the country ceased to be called Britain and became "Angleland" or "England." The Anglo-Saxons drove back the northern tribes and killed or made slaves those Britons who had not fled to the mountains of Wales. From this period of history have come down those wonderful legends of one of the British warrior kings, King Arthur, and his Knights of the Round Table. The Britons fought the invaders valiantly, but were overcome. The Latin language and other signs of Roman civilization almost completely disappeared. England became Anglo-Saxon. The Christian Britons gave way to their pagan conquerors.

The Anglo-Saxons made England their home. When the early Anglo-Saxons came to England they planned to make it their home. Like their descendants who settled much of our own country, they brought with them their wives and children. The English may well be proud of their Anglo-Saxon ancestors. They had a deep respect for women. To friends they were hospitable and against their enemies they were fearless. They believed in what we would call the simple life. Town life held little attraction for them. They lived on their homesteads and cultivated the soil. Their religion was that of other Northmen; you will learn more about it in the story of the Scandinavians. They stood in awe of the powers of nature and of fate or destiny, which they called *wyrd* [weerd]. It is from this Anglo-Saxon word that our own word *weird* is derived. The Anglo-Saxons expected little help from their gods. They felt that they had to

work out their own problems, within the limits of fate, which no man could foresee or change. They were sternly self-reliant people, with a strong sense of duty.

The Anglo-Saxons told thrilling tales about their brave ancestors. One of these was Beowulf [bay'oh wuhlf], a young warrior prince, who had come from the southern part of the land now called Sweden. Beowulf killed a terrible monster and thus saved the lives of the Danish king and his followers. For hundreds of years the story of Beowulf was handed down by word of mouth and through the songs of harpists. It was finally written down in Anglo-Saxon, a language so different from modern English that you would not be able to read it. But the story has been translated into modern English from an old Anglo-Saxon copy which is kept in the British Museum.

Christianity returned to England. The Anglo-Saxon hordes in England, with their gods of nature, had almost stamped out the Christian belief. An energetic missionary, now called Saint Patrick, had established Christian churches in Ireland, but Anglo-Saxon England was heathen. In the last few years of the Sixth Century a Christian missionary by the name of Augustine [au'guhs teen] reached England and again brought the Christian faith to its inhabitants. Convents were established and churches were built. Anglo-Saxon England gradually became a Christian country once more.

The Anglo-Saxon kingdoms. For a time Anglo-Saxon England was divided into a number of separate little kingdoms, each with its own warrior-king. This division resulted in constant quarreling among the many rulers. Finally Egbert, the king of Wessex, which was one of the small kingdoms, showed himself to be the most powerful of these kings and became the overlord of the others. This move, however, did not bring the Anglo-Saxon kingdoms into close union.

The northeast wind was an ill wind for England. The Northmen whom the early Britons had feared were the Angles, Saxons, and Jutes. The Anglo-Saxons also had Northmen to fear — the Danes, whose very name terrified them. The Danes began to visit the eastern shores of the British Isles near the beginning of the Ninth Century, some 350 years after the Anglo-Saxons had come to England. These Danish invaders came from the same parts of northern Europe where hundreds of years before the Anglo-Saxons had lived. But the Danes did not care to settle down and till the land. Neither did they care to give up their gods Thor [thawr] and Woden [woh'd'n] for the one Christian God. They liked a life of adventure, pillage, and war.

Where there were riches, there was booty for the Danes; and England was tempting. Grain was in the fields; wealth was in the households; and gold, silver, and jewels were kept in the monasteries. In their Viking boats, equipped with colored sails and long oars, the Danes would swoop down the coast upon the unsuspecting Anglo-Saxons. Sometimes they would quietly steal up some river and attack a village under the cover of night. We can picture their horned helmets glistening in the light of their torches. They broke into churches, monasteries, and dwellings; they stole the valuables, captured slaves, and set fire to the buildings. When the Danes returned home, their plunder and slaves excited others to ravage England. In those days, certainly, "the tight little isle" was neither safe nor merry. By the third quarter of the Ninth Century the Danes had turned from raiding to organized conquest. They had conquered all the Anglo-Saxon kingdoms north of the Thames. Only Wessex remained independent and it was seriously threatened.

King Alfred outwitted the Danes. The English are noted for their resourcefulness and perseverance. These traits were shown by Alfred, a grandson of King Egbert. Alfred became king of Wessex about the middle of the Ninth Century, when he was twenty-eight. He well understood that his biggest task was to rid the country of the Danish robbers. Alfred gathered together an army and defeated the invaders. He forced them to stay in the northeastern part of England. During the remainder of Alfred's reign, the English no longer feared the Northmen.

Alfred the Great was a man of learning. The Danes driven back, there was now time to develop the arts of peace. Alfred used his opportunities. In his own words, his aim was "to live worthily while I was alive, and after my death to leave to those that should come after me my memory in good works." He accomplished this aim so well that he will be remembered as Alfred the Great so long as the story of nations is told.

First, he protected his hard-won peace by organizing a strong army and navy. But Alfred was more than a warrior. As a man of learning he translated Latin writings into English so that they could be read by his people. Schools were established much like the palace schools that Charlemagne had introduced at his court. Furthermore, Alfred made attractive offers to learned men on the Continent to come to England to teach his people. With the help of some of the monks, he wrote what was called "the Anglo-Saxon Chronicle," a history of

Culver Service

KING CANUTE WAS REALISTIC

King Canute chose a dramatic way of showing that he understood the flattery of his courtiers. Could you imagine Canute writing a book such as Hitler's *Mein Kampf?*

England from early times, as far as the writers knew the facts. Everything important that happened in England down to two hundred and fifty years after Alfred's death was written in this record by the monks who had charge of the work thus started.

Canute, a Dane, became a good English king. Alfred the Great died at the beginning of the 10th Century. During the next fifty years his descendants reconquered all of England from the Danes and united it for the first time into one kingdom. Within about a hundred years after Alfred's death, however, England had fallen completely under the control of the Danes. The Danish warrior Canute [kuh nyoot'] became King of England. The responsibilities of his new position seemed to change him. He was no longer the ruthless Dane, but became the wise ruler of England. He married an Anglo-Saxon queen and accepted Christianity. By protecting the churches and the monasteries he showed that, even though he was a Dane, he was willing to follow in the footsteps of the Anglo-Saxon kings.

There is an interesting story told about King Canute. It may be partly legend, but it gives us an idea of the kind of man he must have been. The people of his court tried to flatter him by saying that so great was his power that even if he told the waves to recede they would obey. Ordering his chair to be placed on the beach at the edge of the incoming tide Canute forbade the waves to come farther. Of course the tide continued to rise. Then, turning to the men of his court, he said, " Let all men know how empty and worthless is the power of kings; for there is none worthy of the name but Him whom heaven, earth, and sea obey." An engraving of King Canute appears on page 331.

King Canute's peaceful rule lasted about twenty years. After his death, dark days came upon England. With the passing of his weak, cruel sons who followed him on the throne, one after the other, the last of the Danes had ruled England.

The English had Northmen neighbors just across the Channel. Other descendants of the adventurous Northmen, however, were to get control of England. But to understand the story we shall have to go back to the time of Alfred the Great. While Alfred was fighting the Danish invaders, other sea rovers, the Vikings from the eastern shores of the North Sea, were visiting many parts of the world. Then, during the early part of the 10th Century, some of these Vikings raided the northern shores of France. Finding the country attractive, they settled near the mouth of the Seine [sayn] River. This part of France, just across the Channel from England, became known as Normandy, and the Northmen who had settled it were called Normans. As you can see, both these names come from the word Northmen.

The Danes who had settled in England had gradually become English. The Anglo-Saxon customs had really conquered them more completely than

they had conquered the English. Much the same thing happened to the Normans in France. They intermarried with the French. They adopted the French language and many of the French customs. In time, they gave up the Viking gods for the one God of the Christians.

The Vikings in Normandy became civilized. The Normans in France, about the year 1000, were learning new, easy ways of living. Knights and their ladies, the manners of chivalry, and the duties of lords and vassals changed the rough Northmen. They probably found that their own respect for women fitted in well with the ideas of chivalry. The feudal system was not yet highly developed in England, and the Anglo-Saxons and the invading Danes had not come in touch with the more polished customs of the Continent. The Englishman was content with the independent life on his farm or hunting in the forests.

When Northmen were again invading and settling England, the Normans, their cousins in France, would sometimes send their fighting men to aid the Danish invaders. To end this aid and to bring about more friendly relations with the Normans, an Anglo-Saxon king of England married a Norman girl. This union did not accomplish its purpose, for it was not long before the queen's Norman relatives used the excuse of relationship to lay claim to the English throne.

In 1066 William of Normandy became an Englishman. In the autumn of 1066 the last and greatest conqueror of England reached her shores. He was William, Duke of Normandy. It is not necessary for us to go into all the promises and quarrels which led William to claim the English throne. He wanted it; so he crossed the Channel to take it.

Drawing by John C. Wonsetler

HARVEST TIME IN A FEUDAL VILLAGE

The feudal castle which overlooks the peasants' harvesting must have been a central landmark for them. Probably they would have had difficulty in imagining a life not centered
in the feudal castle.

The king of England had just died. The king's council, composed of his great vassals, had elected Harold, a great Anglo-Saxon noble, as the new king. But Harold knew that he would have to defend his title.

When in 1066 William of Normandy arrived with his well-trained band of followers, Harold met him with his army near Hastings, a small town in southern England. The fierce Battle of Hastings is one of the most important in the history of the world. In it Harold was killed and his army defeated. As a result of this success the Normans quickly gained control of England.

Oddly enough, much of our information about the Battle of Hastings comes from a tapestry named for the town of Bayeux [ba'yoo'] in northern France through which United Nations troops passed in their invasion of Normandy in World War II. It is about two feet wide and two hundred feet long. On it are pictured scenes of the struggle between Harold and William.

A new race of Englishmen begins. You will remember that the Anglo-Saxons came to England as invaders and settled down to become Englishmen. The Danes did likewise. And now we find the Normans becoming Englishmen. Within a century and a half they had adopted many of the English ways and had intermarried with the Anglo-Saxons and the Danes. But, as we shall see, the Normans also brought many changes to England.

The Normans were great organizers, and William the Conqueror was not content with conditions as he found them in England. He wanted a strong central government. After many bitter contests he took the lands away from the

Anglo-Saxons and parceled them out to his followers. William strengthened the feudal system in England, with himself as the chief feudal lord. All lands were received directly from him, and thus all allegiance was due directly to him, the king. This plan made the power of the English throne much greater than it had ever been. The feudal system, which had brought protection for the weak and power for the lords of the Continent, also brought law and order to England. By establishing direct royal control of all parts of England, and by taking real power for the throne, William the Conqueror laid the foundation for the English nation.

The Normans brought about other changes in England. Norman art and architecture became common. Along with their organizing ability, the Normans brought new interests and skills to the Anglo-Saxons. The manners and ideas of continental chivalry were added to the earlier feudalism of the Anglo-Saxons. The Anglo-Saxon language was enriched by new words from the Norman French. In the main, these were words which had been used by the upper classes in France. For example, Anglo-Saxon *lamb* was called *mutton* by the Norman lord; *pig* became *pork;* and *cow* became *beef,* and *calf* became *veal.* These terms, however, did not come into common use in England for several generations after the Norman conquest.

Norman ideas and customs merged with those of the Anglo-Saxons. Intermarriage also took place. The result was a new sort of Englishmen. Surely we may consider the year 1066 an important milestone in the long story of the English peoples.

The later Norman kings made England a strong nation. For almost a century after the Battle of Hastings, Norman kings ruled England. Because of the lands which they held on the Continent, the English people were inclined to look upon the Norman kings, and their successors of French ancestry, as foreign intruders. The common people resented the establishment of forest preserves where only the king might hunt. They disliked, too, being forced to list all their property in a record called the Domesday Book. This listing made it too easy for the king to know what they could pay toward the support of the kingdom. But these measures and many others were forced upon them. Under the driving force of the Norman kings, the people were compelled to consider the commands of their king before their own wishes, and the good of the kingdom before the local interests of their town, village, or countryside. England was becoming a nation.

Chapter 3 ~ The English Struggled for Justice and the Right of Self-Government

William the Conqueror began a new age for the British. You will recall that at the Battle of Hastings, in 1066, William of Normandy met and defeated the English king, Harold. We have already told you of the many fine things accomplished under the new English king, William of Normandy. Under his rule and during the reign of his second son, England had the strongest government of any country in Europe.

Then came a brief period of civil war and anarchy. For a time it seemed that all of the good work of the early Norman kings would be undone.

Henry II brought law and order to England. About a hundred years after the Battle of Hastings, Henry II became king of England. He found conditions bad. Powerful barons had been building strongly fortified castles. They were ignoring the sovereignty of the king and were little better than armed robbers. Henry II was no weakling. He sent his men through England to tear down many of the castles. He also released prisoners whom the barons had thrown into their dungeons, and he protected the common people against the unfair demands made upon them by the barons. You probably have heard of jury trials, circuit judges, and grand juries. All these ways of securing justice can be traced back to the time of Henry II. They are among the most important contributions of the English to the progress of civilization.

Courts and juries were created to insure justice. Before the days of Henry II the Anglo-Saxons depended on the old medieval custom of using ordeals to determine the innocence or guilt of an accused person. An ordeal was the required performance, by the accused, of a dangerous, painful feat such as walking barefooted over red-hot plowshares. If the accused performed such a feat without suffering injury or death, his innocence would be established. The decision had nothing to do with legal inquiry, but was based on the theory that a superior power would, if the accused were innocent, intervene to protect him. The Normans settled their personal

differences by fighting duels. In the baron's court, the one who could pay the highest fee usually won his case. To correct these evils, King Henry created a jury system and sent justices to hold court in all parts of England.

Under the jury plan the king's officer called in twelve men from each neighborhood to tell under oath of any crimes committed in the neighborhood. This was something like our grand jury. The justices, or judges, would then decide the case. A century or more later, special juries began to be used to decide whether the accused was guilty or innocent. By means of these "petty juries" as they were called, the accused gained the right of trial before his peers, or equals, a right held dear in all civilized countries. In this way our modern grand and petit (or petty) juries were started.

The principles of justice are expressed in the English common law. During the time of Henry II another step toward law and order was taken. It was the development of the English "common law." As the judges of Henry II went about on their circuits holding court, they kept a careful record of the decisions that were made. Finally these decisions grew into a group of principles, or accepted ideas, to which judges could refer when a new case had to be decided. In this way the English common law had its beginning. Many of the rules of justice which are used today by lawyers and judges in American courts are based on the principles or ideas of English common law.

Henry II made the kingship important in the eyes of the people. The fact that this new system of courts and justice had been established by Henry II made the English people think more favorably of their king. Englishmen were gradually becoming nation-minded. The money fees from the courts, which poured into the royal treasury, also helped to strengthen the position of the king. But Henry II did not stop here. He issued orders that all men should equip themselves with weapons. These they must not sell or pawn, for they must hold themselves in readiness to fight for their king when called upon. The king further strengthened his position by encouraging the payment to him of money instead of the performance of the many feudal services. When the king no longer had to depend upon the armies of the barons, but had funds with which he could raise his own army, the English throne became more powerful than ever. Henry had laid the foundation of monarchy for England but English kings did not have armies of their own until the 14th Century.

Henry II had difficulties with the Church. It was during Henry II's reign that a struggle between the power of the medieval Church and the English kings reached a climax. Thomas à Becket had been appointed Archbishop of Canterbury by Henry for the purpose of uniting the Church and the rulers for the benefit of the monarchy. Becket proved to be stubborn, and did not obey Henry II's orders. Becket warned Henry that if he persisted in trying to run the affairs of the Church, "this friendship would soon turn to bitter hate." Henry, becoming angry, remarked that he wished Becket were dead. Some of Henry's own soldiers took the king at his word, followed Becket to Canterbury, and murdered him. This act placed the king in the wrong, and he was forced to set aside his plans to limit the power of the Church.

The kingship gradually lost power to the barons. William of Normandy had conquered England only by the help of his own barons. Henry II had to bring about order by crushing the barons and feudal lords, and asking for the help of the so-called middle class and of ministers raised from the ranks. The rulers that followed used their own methods to stay on the throne.

Toward the close of the 12th Century, Richard I, for example, tried to make the people forget his many abuses of power by leading a Crusade to the Holy Land. He was a born soldier and loved adventure, and with it all inherited some of the bold statesmanship of his father, Henry II. Part of Richard's plan was to hold Normandy at all costs. He built a powerful fort on the border of Normandy; it is considered the greatest warlike monument of the Middle Ages. But Richard was more interested in conquest and power than he was interested in carrying out governmental reforms for the benefit of the English people.

How Englishmen got their first charter of liberties. Have you noticed that thus far in our story of England the laws were made to control the people and not the kings? The kings were supposed to rule wisely and justly. Many of them, however, were interested more in their

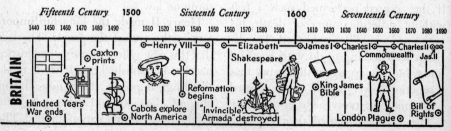

Fifteenth Century 1500   Sixteenth Century   1600   Seventeenth Century

1440 1450 1460 1470 1480 1490   1510 1520 1530 1540 1550 1560 1570 1580 1590   1610 1620 1630 1640 1650 1660 1670 1680 1690

BRITAIN

Caxton prints — Henry VIII — Elizabeth — James I · Charles I — Charles II · Commonwealth Jas. II

Shakespeare

Reformation begins

King James Bible

Hundred Years' War ends   Cabots explore North America   "Invincible Armada" destroyed   London Plague   Bill of Rights

own pleasures than in watching out for the good of their people. This was particularly true of King John, another son of Henry II, who followed Richard on the throne. He ruled England during the early part of the 13th Century. He was cruel, unjust, and generally unpopular. He did not respect the rights his father had sold to the English towns and the English people. He persecuted the Jews for their wealth. His subjects were thrown into prison without trial. Violators of the law found that they could win their freedom by gifts to the king. The barons particularly, who knew their rights, were angered by the unjust acts of King John.

As you might expect, the barons revolted and joined forces against the king. Early in the summer of 1215, King John met the barons, and bishops and abbots, who, being the king's vassals, rated as barons. The meeting was at Runnymede on the banks of the Thames River, a few miles from London. An artist's picture of this scene is on page 338. The king saw that it would be useless either to fight or to argue with the rebellious nobles; so he promised to respect their rights. The barons forced him to sign a document listing these rights. Copies were then sent throughout England to let the other barons know about their new freedoms. No king after John was able to ignore entirely this early charter of the rights of the nobles. The document is so famous that it is called the Great Charter; sometimes it is given the Latin form, *Magna Charta* [mag'nuh kahr'tuh]. Here are some quotations from it.

No freeman shall be taken . . . imprisoned . . . or exiled or in any way destroyed — except by lawful judgment of his peers or by the law of the land.

To no one will we (that is, the king) sell, to no one will we refuse or delay, right or justice.

No constable — of ours (the king's) shall take any one's grain or chattels (property) without immediately paying for them in money.

Did you find in these quotations beginnings of constitutional government?

The Great Charter contained many other guarantees of the barons' special feudal liberties and rights. The king was no longer to ask unfair money payments from the barons who gave him military service. The Church also received certain rights. Its property was not to be touched by the king. And before the king could collect any special taxes, he was required to call a meeting of the barons and the churchmen to get their permission.

One of the most important things about the Great Charter was that it insisted that the king act according to law instead of his own personal wishes. This partly explains why there developed in England what is known as a "constitutional monarchy," or a kingship based upon law. English law was made to apply to the king as well as to the people. The Magna Charta gave the barons more power than ever before over any king

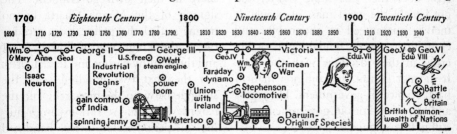

1700	Eighteenth Century	1800	Nineteenth Century	1900	Twentieth Century

1690 1710 1720 1730 1740 1750 1760 1770 1780 1790   1810 1820 1830 1840 1850 1860 1870 1880 1890   1910 1920 1930 1940

KING JOHN SIGNING THE MAGNA CHARTA

The Magna Charta, which a reluctant king is being forced to sign in this picture, was brought to the United States for safety during World War II. Together with the Constitution of the United States, the Magna Charta was hidden in a secret place until the fall of 1944, when all danger of bombing was considered over in the Western Hemisphere. Why has the Magna Charta been so carefully protected?

who might rule England. It is well to remember that this same charter did not benefit the great mass of people. It merely guaranteed to the nobles and churchmen certain feudal rights or liberties in their dealings with the king. It did not permit the common man to have a voice in government. His rights and responsibilities in government were still to be recognized.

The English people began to take a share in their own government. The signing of the Magna Charta by no means settled the political disputes between the kings who followed John, and the wealthy barons and feudal lords. For the next two hundred years the struggle between the monarchy and the barons went on. At various times during this period certain events happened which helped in the gradual building up of a more representative form of government for the great mass of the English people. But the "commoners," or middle class, were not always to be silent. Here is how the first steps were taken toward creating a representative government such as now exists in England and such as we have in the United States of America today.

During the time of King John and the ruler who followed him, the king's council had met frequently. Gradually the king's council came to be known as the Parliament [pahr'li m'nt]. The word "parliament" comes from the French *parler* [pahr lay'], which means "to speak." Sometimes the discussions of this group were heated and the feelings bitter. The trouble was usually over the levying of taxes. The great nobles and the high clergy were wealthy and so were much concerned about matters of this kind. But there were also large landholders in the country, and rich merchants in the rapidly growing towns, who had to pay taxes but who had no voice in the Parliament. These last mentioned belonged to the so-called middle classes.

Just as we found the barons revolting against King John in 1215, so we find the leading barons fifty years later revolting against Henry III, a ruler who was ignoring the provisions of the Great Charter. The barons threw the king into prison and called a meeting of the Parliament. The barons sought the support of the suppressed English themselves and invited the towns to send representatives for the first time. This was about two hundred years after the Battle of Hastings. Thus some of the middle classes were given a vŏice in the government. Such a procedure did not become customary at once, but was taken up

Culver Service

QUEEN ELIZABETH AT A SESSION OF PARLIAMENT

Queen Elizabeth attended the session of Parliament which is shown here. The meeting was held in a palace chamber. The Commons are shown crowded outside a barrier.

again some sixty years later and then did become customary. The common man was winning his rights.

In the earlier sessions the representatives of the middle classes met in the same room with the barons and clergy. Later they met in a separate room, and became known as the House of Commons. The barons and clergy came to be known as the House of Lords. Ever since that time Parliament has been divided into two branches — the House of Lords and the House of Commons. As the story of England grows, notice the ever increasing strength of the House of Commons and the weakening of power in the House of Lords.

Parliament controlled the nation's purse. At first Parliament was not a law-making body. It simply met to consider the king's requests, which were usually for money. When an English king needed money badly, however, the members of Parliament sometimes would grant taxes only in exchange for rights granted by the king. In such cases Parliament would send a petition to the king. If he signed it, Parliament would grant the taxes he wanted. Because the petition bore the king's signature, it would become binding on the whole nation. In this way Parliament won the right to make laws.

The next step, of course, was for Parliament to insist upon knowing how the money from taxes was to be spent before it was granted. Soon Parliament claimed the right to say who should inherit the throne upon the death of a king. All these rights were won by the end of the 14th Century. The kings' need of money for the Hundred Years' War with France gave Parliament more and more opportunity to ask for privileges in return for taxation. Because Parliament controlled the purse of the nation, its power gradually grew until now it is very much greater than the power of the English king.

Chapter 4 ~ The British Developed a Limited Monarchy and Established the Church of England

Rivalry for the throne of England led to civil war. The long political history of England is really the story behind the kings of England. There were intrigues, plots and counterplots, and local wars among many groups. The barons disregarded democratic processes in government to build up their own power against the kings. The House of Lords was in constant struggle with the king; the House of Commons gradually took over the work of getting through constitutional reforms. This movement began in the 13th Century.

In the 15th Century the struggle for the rule over the English people came to a head in civil war. The rival families of Lancaster and York then fought for control of the English throne. This struggle has come to be known as the Wars of the Roses because a red rose was the badge of the House of Lancaster and a white rose was the badge of the House of York. At the close of these wars, the House of York was victorious, and the throne of England went to one of its members.

Taxation continued to cause trouble in England. During these years of rivalry for the English throne, there was no advancement toward sound constitutional government. After the Wars of the Roses there followed more years of turmoil and conflict. You may wonder why the people stood for all this strife. There seem to be several reasons for its duration: (1) the people had great reverence for the king; (2) the king controlled the army by appointing its officers and paying their wages; (3) the loyalty of the army was to the king, not to the people. A maxim of the day was " he who controls the army controls the government." But it was the common people who really paid the bills for the long wars — by heavy taxation.

From the 13th Century on, there was conflict between the powerful barons and the rich merchants for control of taxation. Every king had to declare his belief in the principles of the Magna Charta before Parliament would approve his decisions and give him the necessary funds to continue his power. By 1500, however, with the establishment of the Tudor line of kings, a new system of taxation had come into use. This included direct taxes on personal property, as well as upon income from land rents, and fees. There were also taxes on Church property and income. Taxes from whatever source, however, were difficult to collect. Consequently, kings were constantly seeking new means of raising funds to maintain their armies. Naturally, these efforts led to trouble between the king and Parliament.

Henry VIII broke with the medieval Church. In the midst of all this political turmoil, the Reformation was beginning on the Continent. Back in the 14th Century John Wycliffe, the forerunner of the Reformation in England, attacked many of the beliefs and practices of the Church. He also translated the Bible into the language of his countrymen, so they could read it for themselves.

These were courageous things to do in a time when so many people respected and feared the power of the Pope. In many ways Wycliffe was like Luther, about both of whom you have read.

Luther began his attacks against the Church in the early part of the 16th Century. Henry VIII, one of the kings of the Tudor line, was on the throne of England during that time. King Henry was then a devout Catholic, and was shocked at Luther's bold criticism of the beliefs

Metropolitan Museum of Art

HENRY VIII

To the German portrait painter Holbein, King Henry VIII must have been an arresting subject — although he might have been an extremely restless poser. Holbein's portrait shows the king at the age of 49.

and practices of the Church of Rome. Henry even wrote a pamphlet against the teachings of the German monk. The Pope was so greatly pleased with the support that Henry VIII had given the Church that he bestowed on him the title "Defender of the Faith." A portrait of Henry VIII is reproduced above.

All English rulers have since been called "Defender of the Faith." The faith, however, which the English king today promises to defend is that of the Church of England, a Protestant, not a Catholic, church. It may seem surprising that the same Henry VIII who, with his pen, came to the defense of the Catholic Church was the king who broke off relations with the Pope. The break marked the beginning of England's turn to Protestantism.

The story of King Henry's break with

the Pope is too complicated to give in detail here. The English king disliked the influence that some Churchmen had in English political matters. Then, too, there were rich Church lands that Henry wanted for himself or for his favorites. Moreover he wanted a son who would be heir to his throne. Because his wife had not given birth to a son, he asked the Pope to declare his marriage illegal. When the Pope refused his request, King Henry decided to take matters into his own hands. He brought the Church in England under his control, made himself its head, and proclaimed that the power of the king, and not the Pope, was supreme in religion as well as in politics.

Of course the Pope declared King Henry a religious outcast and excommunicated him. Once before, when an English ruler, King John, had been threatened with excommunication, he had followed the dictates of the Church. But that was in the 13th Century. Henry VIII was living in the 16th Century and times had changed. He ignored the Pope and set about to make his position secure. He appointed his own bishops and other church officers. These officials declared his marriage illegal so that he was free to marry again. He seized church lands. He distributed a part of this land among his friends but kept a goodly portion of it for himself. He took over, plundered, and destroyed monasteries and other church property, including many schools. He used some of the money to build new schools, but most of it went into his private coffers. Since the people had had some part in these activities and no longer had to pay money to the Church, they were loyal to Henry VIII. This was especially true of the nobles who had been given church lands. This seizure of church property

greatly lessened the burden of taxation on the common people. The wealthy classes benefited also, because their taxes were not greatly increased. Consequently there was little clash between king and Parliament. The House of Lords and the House of Commons continued to meet, but only occasionally and only to approve the king's actions. Thus you can understand that as the Tudor kings continued in power, the English government became more absolute. The king settled all political disputes without the consent of Parliament. The people had no say in their own government.

Queen Elizabeth re-established the Church of England. Great religious turmoil followed the death of Henry VIII. He had broken off relations with the Church of Rome, but the English people were still divided in their religious and political beliefs. The faithful Catholics tried to restore the power of the Pope. The Protestants were persecuted and many were put to death. About ten years after the death of Henry VIII, his daughter Elizabeth came to the throne of England. (She had been preceded in turn by a brother and a sister.) There has been no greater period in English history than the years of Elizabeth's reign. Many reforms were made under her rule. England gained great power and respect among the nations of Europe. For these and other reasons this time has come to be known as the Elizabethan period. So we often hear of the Elizabethan period in art, in drama, and in other fields. A painting of Queen Elizabeth is shown on page 343.

Everyone was wondering which side the new queen would take. Would she, like her brother during his short reign, aid the Protestants, or, like her sister who preceded her on the throne, give strong support to the Catholics? Eliza-

eth was well educated, resolute, im-
perious, shrewd, and, above all, devoted
o her country. She was determined to
ule for all the English people and not
be controlled by any foreign power.

Elizabeth did not turn either to the
Catholics or to the most extreme Protestants, who differed from the beliefs of
he English Church. She chose a middle
ourse and re-established the Church
of England, carrying on the work her
ather had begun. This church was
Protestant in belief, but retained the
ystem of organization and many of the
orms of worship of the former church.
Under her leadership all matters of religion were placed under the control of
he government. She appointed her own
hurch officials who prescribed the form
f worship that should be followed. The
emaining Catholic churches were gradually brought into the national Church
of England, and the clergy were required to swear allegiance to the queen
nd to the national church or give up
heir positions.

**A strong government added strength
o the Church of England.** Religion was
only one of the many problems that
Queen Elizabeth had to face when she
ame to the throne. It can easily be un-
erstood that support given to the new
ational church would depend upon the
ower of her government. She was
hrewd and bold in attacking problems.
The nobles were depriving the peas-
nts of their lands and thereby increas-
ng the number of the poor and home-
ess. Queen Elizabeth had laws passed
gainst this practice and levied a tax to
eed the hungry. The guilds about which
ou learned in the story of the feudal
world could no longer control their ap-
rentices and other workmen or the
oods they made. The laborers were suf-
ering from lack of work and the people

Metropolitan Museum of Art
QUEEN ELIZABETH
Queen Elizabeth outwitted kings and made
England one of the leading nations of
Europe. In this portrait the titian-haired
queen is costumed with the elaborateness
that she strove for, although it did not suit
her mentality and temperament.

were in need of the craftsmen's goods.
The government drew up regulations
that ended many of the difficulties.
Trade was growing less year by year because the different kinds of moneys used
had no fixed values. Elizabeth's government took over the coinage of money
and established relative values of different coins which are still recognized.
Commerce, both at home and with other
countries, began to increase.

In meeting these and other problems
so effectively, Queen Elizabeth gained
the good will and support of the people and undermined the power of the
nobles. No one, not even Parliament,
was able to oppose her successfully.
Naturally this power of Queen Elizabeth's government added strength to the
Church of England.

Queen Elizabeth protected England and the national church from foreign foes. When Elizabeth became queen, two questions, which were sometimes regarded as one, were of great interest to her people. Whom would Queen Elizabeth marry, and with what country would she form an alliance? Elizabeth, however, was determined to avoid being drawn into foreign wars and to keep her shores free from invasion. This policy of peace was difficult. The Pope had opposed Queen Elizabeth's efforts to make England a Protestant nation. King Philip II of Spain was a Catholic and felt that he should aid the Catholics in England. He offered to marry Queen Elizabeth and continue the alliance between the two countries. The Queen had many other suitors, among them the King of France, who also hoped for an alliance with England. She held her royal suitors in suspense for years, but finally declined both a marriage and an alliance which might plunge England into war.

When it seemed that Elizabeth would not marry and leave an heir to the throne, her cousin, Mary Queen of Scots, a devout Catholic, sought to be named as her successor. The Catholics in England even plotted to put Mary on the throne. The plotters were discovered and put to death. In the end, Mary suffered a like fate.

The Spanish ruler felt that he should avenge Mary's death as well as punish the English for breaking with the Church of Rome. Furthermore, he resented interference by the English with Spanish trade and colonization of America. In the war that followed, Spain was defeated. England was saved from invasion and the Church of England was protected from the vengeance of the Spanish Catholics. You will learn a lit-tle later the details of this English vic-tory and why the defeat of the Spanish was one of the great events in the history of Western Europe.

The Reformation in England laid foundation for religious freedom in England and America. The Church of England was opposed by the Catholics, and also by some Protestants who objected to it because it retained so much of the beliefs and forms of worship of the Catholic Church. They came to be known as "Puritans" since they were continually insisting upon what the considered a purer form of worship than that of the established church. Many of the Puritans, as well as some Catholics came to America to gain religious freedom. Queen Elizabeth was able to make the Church of England secure during her reign, but she could not settle the many questions of religion for all of the English people.

While these religious struggles were going on in England, the spirit of the Reformation was bringing about changes in other parts of the British Isles. Under the influence of the great reformer, John Knox, the people of Scotland became Protestant. The Irish also struggled for greater freedom, but for the most part they remained loyal to the Catholic Church. After Queen Elizabeth's death the religious conflict continued for years. There was not only quarreling between those who wished to follow the established Church of England and those who wished to follow the Pope, but the various Protestant sects often carried on heated discussions and even conflicts among themselves.

As a result of these many religious differences, the English people gradually came to see that there should be freedom of religious worship for all. We may consider this principle of religious freedom another contribution of the English peoples to the progress of civilization. Today throughout the British Empire we can find many different faiths, each of which is allowed to worship as it sees fit. It is interesting to note that the men who drew up our Constitution had in mind the experience of the English in regard to freedom of worship. We find in the first amendment these words:

Congress shall make no law respecting the establishment of religion, or prohibiting the free exercise thereof. . . .

English kings continued to battle Parliament for the right to govern. The English monarchs of the 16th and part of the 17th Centuries had again become very powerful. Some of them were industrious, clever, and capable. At the same time the barons, who were constantly opposing the kings, had become less powerful. Long wars had thinned their numbers. Feudalism was gradually dying out and with it the feudal powers of the great lords decreased. Englishmen began to look more and more to the king as the head of the nation. Gunpowder came into use at about this time, and as the king controlled all cannon, he found it comparatively easy to keep down any ambitious baron. Furthermore, England was beginning to carry on trade with other nations, which meant not only a richer and more contented country but also a new source of funds when the king needed money. All of these advantages to the king made it begin to look as though Parliament would need to take steps to protect the rights which it had won.

Under such conditions it is not surprising that a few of the English rulers should come to the conclusion that they were all-powerful. In the early part of the 17th Century we find a king who boldly proclaimed that he ruled by " divine right."

James I tried to rule by " divine right." Queen Elizabeth was the last of the Tudors. When she died, early in the 17th Century, there was no successor to the throne. Before her death, however, Elizabeth had said she favored James VI of Scotland. He was a Stuart, a distant relative of the Tudor family, and the nearest heir to the throne. The House of Parliament thought that because he was an outsider (from Scotland) they could easily control him and gain more power at his expense. They permitted him to become king. He took the name of James I of England.

But James I had other ideas. He declared he ruled by " divine right " and not by the will of the people or any group. He went so far as to say —

The state of the monarchy is the supremest thing upon earth, for kings are not only God's lieutenants upon earth and sit upon God's throne, but even by God himself they are called gods. . . . I will not be content . . . to make the reason appear of all my doings. . . . I would wish you to be careful . . . that you do not meddle with the main points of government; that is my craft. . . .

If James I had respected the rights of Englishmen as set down in the Great Charter, there might have been no trouble. At it was, there was trouble in abundance between the king and Parliament. Each struggled for the power to control and rule the nation. James I passed laws without asking Parliament for their approval. He demanded large sums of money to finance his extravagant plans. Both the House of Lords and the House of Commons resented his deeds, and Parliament refused to grant him money. The king then persuaded friends to loan him money with the understanding he would pay them back. But he never paid his loans. Instead he sold titles to these people as a substitute for payment.

Friction between the king and parliament increased. Constitutional, financial, and religious disagreements all worked together to increase the friction between England's kings and the Parliament. The Tudor rulers had done as they pleased but had been careful to keep up the appearance of respecting the rights of Parliament. James I frequently gave in to the demands of Parliament but at the same time irritated the members by lectures on the divine right of kings. In short, James talked too much.

Meanwhile, England's growing prosperity and security was giving the members of the House of Commons a stronger feeling of independence than they had had in the previous century. The majority of the members of the House of Commons were Puritans and were strict in their moral views as well as being thrifty and prosperous. They disliked the king's extravagance on both economical and moral grounds.

Finally, their desire to change the form of church worship was firmly opposed by the king. The Puritan members of Parliament realized that they could not make these changes in the Church until they had the right to pass laws against the king's wishes.

For all of these reasons the feeling between James I and Parliament became more tense. There was no open break, however, while James I lived.

His son, Charles I, inherited this tense situation, but made it worse by an even more stubborn pursuit of his father's policies. War with France and Spain, very badly managed, forced Charles to ask for more money. When Parliament refused his request, Charles tried in vain to finance the war by illegal means. Parliament therefore drew up the Petition of Right, the second great charter of English freedom. Charles was forced to accept the Petition of Right because he was in desperate need of money. Some of the many rights granted were:

1. No one could be taxed without consent of Parliament.
2. No one could be tried in a military court during peace time.
3. No one could be put in prison without trial by his peers (equals).
4. No one could be compelled to take in soldiers in his home.

Charles I tried ruling by divine right and lost his head. Once peace was declared and Charles needed less money, he ignored the Petition of Right. He ruled for eleven years without calling Parliament into session. Like his father, Charles I sincerely believed that he was answerable only to God for his actions, certainly not to the members of the House of Commons. Then a rebellion broke out in Scotland. Charles needed money again. He summoned Parliament, but this time the House of Lords and the House of Commons made a concerted effort to whittle down the king's power.

The result was that the long struggle between king and Parliament reached a climax. The country was stirred. A party of royal officers and many of the country gentlemen stood by the king, but the middle classes, the Puritan gentry, and most of the House of Commons were against Charles I. Civil war broke out. Under the leadership of a man by the name of Oliver Cromwell the people's party defeated the king and his party.

Then an unusual thing happened. The king was brought to trial. Charles I, a "divine right" monarch, was taken be

CROMWELL REFUSED A CROWN

Someone who knew Cromwell said of him, "A larger soul, I think, hath seldom dwelt in a house of clay." Other views might have been less flattering. His refusal of the crown, for instance, might have been considered a dramatic gesture, for Cromwell was in actuality a dictator.

fore a high court of justice. The clerk of the court read aloud, "Charles Stuart, king of England, you have been accused on behalf of the people of England of treason and other crimes; the court has determined that you ought to answer for the same."

Charles I was beheaded. By order of Parliament a king had been executed! To give the credit due to Charles I, we must say that he honestly considered himself to be in the right. Furthermore, he showed himself to be a man of courage when, without losing his self-control, he mounted the scaffold and died, as he thought, for the sake of his country.

Oliver Cromwell became dictator of England. Charles I was executed in the middle of the 17th Century. The next few years were troublesome ones for England. There was no king, but there was a controlling power in Oliver Cromwell and his army. The House of Commons met and voted to abolish the office of king and the "useless and dangerous" House of Lords. It also declared the people of England to be a "Commonwealth and Free State."

But the English people became dissatisfied with Parliament, for it refused to hold new elections. Apparently the members wanted to keep their seats in Parliament and thus retain their power. Finally Cromwell and his soldiers drove the members of the House of Commons out of the halls of the Parliament building. Cromwell had the doors locked and pocketed the key. The government of England was then the army with Cromwell at the head. He was given the title of "Lord Protector," but we would simply call him a dictator.

There is no doubt that Oliver Cromwell was a strong ruler. He was deeply religious and believed that what he did was a religious duty. He came from the middle class, not from nobility. In all but name he was king. He moved into the palace. Like a king, he signed state papers with his first name only, " Oliver." His rule in the beginning was efficient and strict. He had the interests of the people at heart. Whether the people liked his measures or not, they were forced to do what Cromwell thought best for them.

Englishmen of the Seventeenth Century wanted their rights and their king. During Cromwell's dictatorship Parliament never really functioned. In fact, under the Protectorate, Cromwell's first government, Parliament consisted of only one house. For the first time Ireland was represented. But this kind of government was certainly not democratic — it was absolute autocracy, a military dictatorship.

Democracy took a step backward under Cromwell. Of course, in all these political struggles between the kings and various groups opposed to the kings, the people were benefiting in the long run. They could not realize this at the time of the ceaseless struggles and conflicts; nevertheless, the government was slowly moving toward a more liberal rule. Oliver Cromwell had gone too far for the English people. Englishmen then, like the Americans a hundred years later, believed in " certain unalienable rights." They were more interested in those rights than in having a dictator tell them what was best. Also, the English people were used to a king. They were unhappy without one. Their rights they must have, and a king as well. Fur-

thermore, the calmness and courage which Charles I had shown at the moment of his execution had made a strong impression on the people.

When Oliver Cromwell died, his son tried to carry on the strenuous work of his father, but in the end he was forced to resign. The two houses of Parliament met and decided to communicate with Holland, where the late king's son was living in exile. With great pomp and ceremony, King Charles II was placed on the throne of England. From that day to this, the British have had a king.

Parliament assumed the right of electing the king. The return of the king did not mean the victory of the royal power over representative government. The king had been asked to the throne by Parliament and had promised to respect its rights and obey its laws. It is true that for the next quarter of a century the kings tried to control Parliament. But when James II, who was a Catholic, threatened to destroy the Church of England, general rebellion followed. This gave Parliament the opportunity to depose the king. Then Parliament elected a new king and queen from members of the royal family whom it felt could be trusted. By this action Parliament made itself the chief power in the government. Thus was settled, for all time, the bitter quarrel between the English kings and Parliament for the power to rule. The system of representative government had won. The Englishmen had kept their king and had been successful in their struggle for the right to govern themselves.

Now, in the latter part of the 17th Century, Parliament had assumed so much authority that it could name who should be king. The ruler of Holland, William of Orange, and his wife Mary, grand-daughter of Charles I, were sked by Parliament to become king and ueen of England. But before they could ecome England's rulers they were told f the conditions which they must accept. These conditions were in the form f a written document called the Bill f Rights. In 1689, William and Mary igned the Bill of Rights, and came to he throne of England. This was an outtanding achievement in a more democratic form of government. It is so imortant a document that it became a part f our own Constitution a hundred ears later.

The Bill of Rights repeated and made more emphatic the other two great charers, Magna Charta and the Petition of Right, which you read about in earlier ages. Among the conditions stated in he English Bill of Rights were:

1. The king should execute only such laws as are authorized by Parliament.
2. Neither excessive bail nor fines should be imposed nor cruel and unusual punishments inflicted.
3. No taxes should be levied without the consent of Parliament.
4. The election of members to Parliament should be free.
5. There should be freedom of speech and debate in Parliament without fear of impeachment or questioning in court.

From this list you can see that the representatives of the people in Parliament made sure that the king would have to respect the rights of Englishmen.

The Bill of Rights was a turning point in England's political history. It was brought about by the pressure of Parliament, particularly of the House of Commons. The rise of the middle class in England was in the background of this whole story from about 1500 onward. By 1700 democratic government had really begun for England. Democracy did not come to the English people within a few short years. Democracy as we know it today took over a thousand years to develop.

England became more democratic and developed political parties. There were many political conflicts among many groups in England during her development into a great nation. The king fought against the barons, the rich merchants against both, the businessman for his own rights, the Church for its privileges. They all wished to so control the government that whatever the government did would be for the benefit of that particular group. The first job of all these groups was to weaken the power of the king to such an extent that he could no longer dictate and enforce his will upon the English people. This very thing had been accomplished in England by the end of the 17th Century. But once the power of the king was subject to the will of Parliament, the various factions in Parliament began to wrangle among themselves as to who should dictate the policies of the government. Barons, merchants, churchmen, and country gentry could not agree on any one plan. They therefore split into various groups or parties. Thus we have the rise of the first political parties in England.

The people who felt that the government should have great power classed themselves as a group called *Tories*. Those who wished for a more liberal and representative government of the people grouped themselves into a party called *Whigs*. The *Tories* were made up of country squires, clergymen, and men who had become wealthy because of gifts from the kings. The *Whigs* were composed of merchants, businessmen, and some barons of great wealth who feared the power of the kings. The

Tories believed in a strong rigid central government. The *Whigs* were much more democratic in their beliefs; they claimed that the great mass of people should have representation, and they feared a strong autocratic government headed by a king.

These two parties, which began in the 18th Century, have kept those general beliefs even to the present day. The only noticeable change is the change of name: the Tories are now called the Conservatives, and the Whigs are called the Liberals.

The House of Hanover came to the English throne. After the death in 1714 of Queen Anne who had reigned after William and Mary, there was no immediate heir to the throne. Parliament named George I, a German elector and a descendant of James I, as the next king of England. He came from a German state called Hanover. He was the first of a long line of kings, still on the throne of England, although today the House of Hanover is called the House of Windsor.

For over 200 years the descendants of George I have ruled England without further civil wars. These kings have been satisfied to take a place of less importance and to let Parliament do the actual governing. And since 1714 England has progressed steadily toward a more democratic government.

When George I came from Germany to assume the role of King of England, he spoke only German. Not being able to understand what his own Parliament was talking about, he selected a group of advisers to instruct him on government affairs. This group of advisers was the king's cabinet. This idea of a cabinet of special advisers was not new. As early as the 1500's the king of England had a small select group of men around him

called a Privy Council. But this Privy Council in time became too large and unwieldy and gave way to a smaller and still more select group of personal advisers called a "Cabinet." At first, the king tried to include in his Cabinet persons from both political parties. But this was not successful, for the members could seldom forget party affiliations enough to co-operate. Thus the Cabinet came to be composed of members from the *majority* party. Government in England has run much more smoothly since this idea has been in operation. It also means that the majority party in Parliament really runs the English government and they rise or fall on election by the people.

The Prime Minister speaks for the government. Members of the Cabinet are the various heads of departments of the government. There are approximately nineteen positions, such as Secretary of State for Foreign Affairs, Chancellor of the Exchequer, First Lord of the Treasury, Secretary for War, and First Lord of the Admiralty. George I, not able to understand English, did not attend even the meetings of his own Cabinet. As a result, one member of the Cabinet assumed the role of spokesman for the Cabinet and thus for the government. He became known as the Prime Minister. Since he and his fellow Cabinet members were all members of Parliament, they had to attend meetings of either the House of Lords or the House of Commons. This practice goes on to this day. Every so often you will read or hear of the Prime Minister appearing before a session of Parliament, giving the opinions of the government and defending them if necessary. Thus in a sense the Prime Minister, and not the king as you might expect, is the real head of the English government.

The first Prime Minister — and one of the greatest — was Sir Robert Walpole. A leader of the Whig Party in the House of Commons, he proved to be a great financier, politician, and statesman. He came from a rural section of England, and seemed more interested in farming and hunting than in fierce political conflicts. Even his wealthy and powerful opponents in the House of Commons and House of Lords admired him for his frankness and simple truthfulness in debate. There was no sham about Sir Robert Walpole.

A new kind of revolution brought reform to the government. But with all the advancement of the English form of government, the great mass of people still had no way of expressing their own will. During Walpole's time it could be truthfully said that government was by the rich, the well-born, and the able. The House of Lords was composed of nobles or peers who had inherited their titles, and of bishops of the Church of England. Elections to the House of Commons were carried on openly, and anyone could check the records to see how his neighbor voted. The common people were afraid to go against the wishes of local men of wealth and influence, and generally voted the way they were told. William Pitt once exclaimed in the House of Commons, " This House is not a representative of the people of Great Britain. . . ." To become a member of Parliament required some form of wealth, land, or high position in the church.

The Industrial Revolution had been going on in England since 1750, as you will read in the next chapter. By the middle 1800's another group of people was growing in power. These people were the " middle class," owners of banks and manufacturing plants, shipowners and merchants of world trade. They began to feel their power, and tried unsuccessfully at first to get Parliament to pass laws for their benefit. The Industrial Revolution also greatly increased the class of industrial workers who gradually learned to organize and to use their numerical strength for political purposes.

During the 19th Century, the struggle for the rights of the common man continued. At intervals, various reform bills were passed. Finally, in 1867, the industrial workers received more representation and the right to vote. These workers had a real leader in John Bright. Living at the same time was William Gladstone, member of Parliament and leader of the Whig Party. The Whigs were opposed to the Tories, led by Disraeli [diz ray'li]. Between these two parties, fighting for power and influence, the workers benefited. In 1872 the Australian Ballot Act was passed, making all voting secret. This was an important step forward in democracy, for it did away with the evils of bribes and open voting. It has been in operation ever since. We in the United States use the Australian method of voting. These democratic steps forward in the interest of the common people, it is interesting to note, came through the efforts of the members of the House of Commons.

The House of Lords lost its hold on the government. The House of Lords, from the early 17th Century, took little or no part in passing laws for the benefit of the average Englishman. They were satisfied to keep things as much as possible as they were. They fought many of the changes which the House of Commons tried to force through, and many times they succeeded. But in the early years of this century, the House of Commons was in power and still is. In 1918, the right to vote was given to all men and women over 21, regardless of property qualifications. Democracy in England was at last a reality!

Under a limited monarchy, England experienced a " Golden Age." From the middle of the 19th Century to World War I, England had economic prosperity under her new-found democracy. This has been called Britain's " Golden Age." Great political reforms had been accomplished down through the centuries since the Battle of Hastings in 1066. The people had won a hard fight for their rightful representation under a limited monarchy. The next big job was to consolidate the huge British Empire and to work for the benefit of all.

From the ordeal of World War I, England emerged on the victors' side, with her empire intact but with an increasing number of economic and political problems abroad. At home, the one social and political upheaval was the renouncing of his throne by Edward VIII (now Duke of Windsor) to marry Wallis Simpson, an American born in Baltimore, Maryland. This incident caused great concern and much publicity throughout the British Empire, for England was experiencing difficult times. The abdication of King Edward brought to the throne his brother, the Duke of York, who probably never wished to be king, but who accepted the inevitable and became George VI, the present king of England.

Chapter 5 ~ A Century of Invention Changed Life in England — The Industrial Revolution

Political struggles made little change in the life of the common people. Now we back up in our story of England to tell of another force at work during the last two centuries — The Industrial Revolution. Kings and Parliament might struggle over the right to govern; but the common people of England carried on from day to day in the first half of the 18th Century, much as their grandparents had before them. There had been little change for centuries in the daily lives of the common people or the ways in which they made their living.

A new kind of revolution transformed life in England. Beginning about 1750 an immense change took place in England.

Some writers say that it was the most important development in the long story of mankind. The ways of living, working, playing, and thinking were changed almost beyond belief. No longer were the people dependent upon oxen and horses as a means of travel; instead, they could go by train or steamship. No longer did the farmer plant his little strips of grain, peas, and beans; instead, he planted crops in larger fields, and grew in addition such products as clover, turnips, beets, and sweet potatoes. No longer were goods slowly made by hand in the cottages of the workmen; instead, they were produced by machines in great factories. The words " to manufacture," which originally meant " to make by hand," came to mean " to make by machine."

As a result of these new methods of production, people lived more and more in the cities instead of on the estates of the nobles or in small country villages. Their lives were very different from what they had been before factories were established. These and many other such changes have come to be known as the Industrial Revolution. The period of most rapid change was from about 1750 to 1850, but we must remember that the Industrial Revolution is still going on.

Many new inventions brought on the Industrial Revolution. During the latter half of the 18th Century in England, the greatest changes were in the methods of making cloth, in the use of iron, and in the use of steam for power.

Look at the pictures on page 354 and see how the methods of spinning and weaving were improved by inventions. In the early days thread was spun by holding in one hand a distaff on which was a bunch of wool, flax or cotton from which a thread was drawn by the whirling spindle in the other hand. About the middle of the 16th Century the spinning wheel was invented; then it was used instead of the hand spindle. A spinning wheel is shown in the first picture. It increased the amount of thread or yarn that the spinner could produce.

The second picture shows a hand-and-foot loom on which the thread was woven into cloth. These methods of spinning and weaving (except the use of the spinning wheel) had been in use from the time that cloth was first made.

The third picture shows a " spinning jenny " invented by James Hargreaves a few years before the American Revolution. A mishap gave him the idea for this machine. His wife happened to upset her spinning wheel. He saw that the spindle continued turning in the upright position as well as it did in its horizontal position. This gave him the idea of constructing a row of vertical spindles to be turned by the one wheel so that each machine would produce as much thread as eight people could produce in the same time with the old spinning wheel. Wishing to compliment his wife, whose name was Jenny, he called his new machine the " spinning jenny."

About five years later a barber by the name of Arkwright improved the spinning jenny by adding rollers through which the threads of wool or cotton were drawn and twisted. He first used horse power but later used water power to run this machine; so it came to be called a " water frame." Arkwright built many factories, became quite wealthy, and was knighted by the king.

The thread produced by the spinning jenny was not of uniform size or strength, and the thread produced by the water frame was coarse. It remained for a young man by the name of Samuel Crompton to take the good points of these machines, add some improvements of his own, and construct a spinning machine that, with some other improvements, is still in use today. This machine was called a " mule " because it was a cross or hybrid, like the animal so named.

With more thread ready to be made into cloth, the next need was for a machine which would make cloth faster. This called for improvements on the hand loom. A flying shuttle was first designed which could be tossed from one side of the loom to the other. A little later, an English preacher, Edmund Cartwright, invented the power loom shown in the fourth picture. With this new machine one man could produce as much cloth as a dozen weavers working

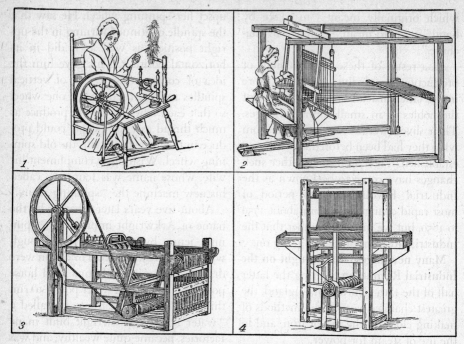

SIMPLE INVENTIONS LEAD TO GREAT CHANGES

Primitive machines used through the ages gave way to new inventions. Such changes brought the Industrial Revolution into being. The inventions shown here are as follows: 1) spinning wheel; 2) hand loom; 3) Hargreaves' spinning jenny; 4) Cartwright's first power loom.

at hand looms. When we compare the spinning wheel and hand loom with the machines in a modern factory, as shown on page 358, it is easy to understand what great improvements were made in the manufacture of cloth. The effect of the use of these machines on the life of the people, as we shall see a little later, was far reaching.

A number of other inventions added to the production of cloth and the expansion of the textile industry. One was a machine which stamped colors on white cloth much as a newspaper used to be printed on a hand press, making this white cloth into calico.

An American inventor increased the production of cotton cloth. Another remarkable invention which speeded up

the textile industry was made by Eli Whitney in the newly established United States of America. This was the cotton gin, a machine which would take the seed out of cotton. As you will see by the picture on page 355, this consisted of cylinders on which were teeth or brushes. Seeding cotton by hand had been slow and laborious. With Whitney's new machine one man could " gin " as much as a thousand pounds of cotton a day. This made it possible for the growers to meet the increased demands for cotton. In twenty years the amount produced in our Southern states grew from two to eighty million pounds per year. What became of all this cotton? Much of it went to England, where it was manufactured into cloth by the newly developed spinning jennys and power looms.

James Watt provided new factories with new power. Machines must have a steady driving power. It was well enough for the early spinning and weaving machines to be run by the long-used water wheel or windmill. Factories with many machines, however, had need for greater and more reliable power. This need was supplied by James Watt, a Scotchman, who was an instrument-maker by trade. A customer brought to him to be repaired a model of a steam engine designed by Newcomen, an English mechanic. Watt was a student and experimenter. He became interested in improving the steam engine and increasing its efficiency. He improved the steam engine so greatly that it could be successfully used for many purposes, including the turning of the wheels of the spinning and weaving machines.

The steam engine was first used in 1785 to run a spinning machine in an English factory. Five years later Arkwright began to use it in place of water power in his factory. As early as the first part of the 19th Century the use of steam power was as common in England as was the use of water or wind power. Since the use of steam power did not spread rapidly to the other countries of Europe, England, with her newly invented machinery and factories, gained an advantage in manufacturing which long made her the leading industrial nation.

Transportation was speeded up. We all know the story of how the American, Robert Fulton, with a British-built engine in his ship, the *Clermont,* steamed up the Hudson River in 1807. A little later the first ocean liner, the *Savannah,* with paddle wheels and sails crossed the Atlantic Ocean in 1819.

WHITNEY'S COTTON GIN

An American, Eli Whitney, invented this machine, which caused cotton to become the staple crop of the United States. The cotton gin that is used today differs only slightly in principle from the original invention.

With factories rapidly turning out machine-made goods, there was need for improved transportation. No one city was likely to consume all the output of its own factories. For a long time the bolts of cloth and other products were brought to London by pack horses or in broad-wheeled wagons and shipped from there to the markets throughout England and in other countries. But roads were bad and such transportation was expensive. Here is a description of the roads in the middle of the 18th Century, written by an unhappy traveler who was making a trip through England:

Of all the cursed roads that ever disgraced this kingdom, in the very age of barbarism, none ever equalled that from Billerica [bil'rik uh] to the King's Head at Tilbury. It is for near twelve miles so narrow that a mouse cannot pass by any carriage; I saw a fellow creep under his waggon to assist men to lift, if possible, my chaise over a hedge. The ruts are of an incredible depth. . . .

Some improvement in the means of transportation had been made by the beginning of the 19th Century. A Scot by the name of McAdam invented a new way of building roads. You probably have heard of roads made of crushed rock and gravel called "macadam" roads after the name of this man. Also, several large canals had been built. But still there existed a great need for means of transporting goods and passengers quickly and cheaply.

An Englishman by the name of Stephenson was the first to try to meet this need for better transportation in a large way. He built a steam engine into a locomotive in 1825, and sent it puffing slowly on metal tracks. His work was the beginning of the English railroads, which grew rapidly. In twenty years — by the middle of the 19th Century — the British Isles and the continent of Europe were covered with networks of steel rails. In America, too, railroads spread from the eastern cities, binding the nation together.

Old industries took on new life. Inventions and new ways of doing things were not confined to the textile industry and transportation. Old industries took on new life. Coal was needed to run the steam engines. A little later it was discovered that coal could be substituted for charcoal in the smelting of iron. Fortunately Great Britain was well supplied with coal, so that mining became, and has continued to be, one of the chief industries of the British Isles.

For making the new machines much iron was needed. New inventions and new processes brought about as great a change in the iron industry as had taken place in the textile industry. It was discovered that by the use of large bellows for blowing currents of air into the blast furnaces, a much higher quality of iron could be made. The hotter fire thus produced consumed more of the charcoal or coal used in smelting the iron ore. It was discovered that by stirring or "puddling" the hot iron, most of the impurities could be removed. A little later it was discovered that hot iron could be rolled into sheets. Thus, by improving the quality of the iron, as well as by increasing the quantity, better machines could be made.

The weaving of wool by hand had been an important industry in England ever since the 16th Century. With the invention of textile machines, the woolen industry became even greater than the manufacture of cotton textiles. English woolen cloth came to be recognized as superior in quality to that manufactured elsewhere.

Growth of the woolen industry even before the Industrial Revolution in England caused great poverty among the peasants. Landowners wanted to raise sheep for the wool. Consequently the little farms rented by the peasants were taken over by sheep growers. The poor farmer and his family were often left jobless. Many drifted to the cities in vain search of work.

Many inventions mark the trail of industrial progress. We have not here the space to tell about all the inventions and new machines that were made during the century between 1750 and 1850. Only a few of the more important inventions are listed on page 357 to mark the trail of the industrial development upon which our 20th Century civilization rests. The dates are given merely to show the onward march of the Industrial Revolution. There is no need to memorize them.

Industry moved from the home to the factory. The introduction of machinery was revolutionary, but even greater

The Trail of Industrial Progress

Date	Inventor	Invention	Nationality
1767	Hargreaves	Spinning jenny	English
1768	Arkwright	Spinning machine	English
1769	Watt	Steam engine	Scotch
1779	Crompton	Spinning mule	English
1785	Cartwright	Power loom	English
1792	Murdock	Gas lighting	English
1793	Whitney	Cotton gin	American
1800	McAdam	Macadam roads	Scotch
1807	Fulton	Steamboat	American
1829	Stephenson	Railroad locomotive	English
1831	McCormick	Reaper	American
1832	Faraday	Electric dynamo	English
1839	Daguerre	Photography	French
1844	Morse	Telegraph	American
1846	Howe	Sewing machine	American

changes took place in the home and community life of the workers. Before the factories were built, the workers lived in the country or small villages. They were neighborly; they worked together; they cared for each other when ill; they attended the same church. Each family had a garden plot, a few animals, and perhaps some crops to provide the household with food. When not busy in the garden or field or with the duties about the simple home, many people spent their time spinning and weaving. Of course each family made its own clothes.

The new inventions, however, brought about a great change in home life. Machine-made goods were produced so much more cheaply than handmade that the workers no longer could afford to spin and weave at home. Since the average person had neither the money to buy machinery nor the power necessary to run it, the textile industry moved from the home to the factory. For these reasons those who remained in the country often found themselves deprived of their only source of income, so that in the end they lost their cottages and became paupers, or migrated to America or some other land. Many workers were forced to move to the cities that sprang up about the factories. Here they found living conditions quite different from those they had known in the country or villages. They lived in miserable little houses or dark cellars with no conveniences. Sometimes a number of families occupied a single room. Contagious diseases were hard to control and often spread rapidly under such conditions. Since workers had no gardens they could not raise their own food. Wages were so low that the women and children, as well as the men, had to work long hours to earn money for their meager supply of food and poor clothes. Often tired children were kept awake at their work in the factories by the foreman's cane or strap.

The skilled hand could not compete with the machine. We know from our own experience that almost everyone likes to plan and to make things for himself and for others. We saw that under the guild system the master

Courtesy U.S.D.A. Photograph by Forsythe

How Many Spinning Wheels?

Think of the thousands of spinning wheels and spinners that would be required to spin the yarn produced by one modern factory. Do such inventions cause unemployment or increase the possibilities of leisure? The cotton yarn pictured here is being spun for use in a textile mill where sheets are manufactured.

workman designed whatever he made and was so proud of his work that he put his own stamp on it. The invention of machines changed these conditions. Under the factory system the workman neither planned nor completed the article on which he worked. He merely tended a machine which did the work. He had little interest in what he was doing and did not care what became of the product. All that was left for him was the meager pay he received for his hard labor.

Another undesirable result of the factory system was that the routine of doing the same kind of work day after day and week after week made a man unfit for any other kind of work. If the machine on which he worked were improved so that he was no longer needed, he was out of a job and had to learn to do something else. If he were a young man he might be able to make this change, but if he were an older man he was like an old horse turned out to shift for himself. The possibility of unemployment constantly faced the workman. Of course for the engineer, the artist, and the like, there remained the personal interest in creating something fine and the ability to adjust himself to new conditions. The problems of the laborer's lack of interest and security and his lack of ability to adapt himself to changing conditions remain unsolved, although many gains have been made.

The nobility gained luxuries but lost power. When we think of the misery the inventions brought to the poor, we cannot but wonder how they affected the lives of the aristocracy and the so-called middle class. Before the Industrial Revolution the land held by the nobles was the chief source of wealth. The demands for more wool caused these country gentlemen to extend their holdings by taking land from the small farmers as had been done in earlier years. For the nobility the industrial development brought greater comfort and more luxuries. Many large houses were built of brick or stone, with magnificent stairways and beautifully decorated rooms. New styles of furniture such as Chippendale, Sheraton, and Queen Anne added to the beauty of their homes. Some large households kept many servants dressed in gorgeous liveries and white wigs.

Manufacturers and businessmen unwittingly promoted democracy. England has been fortunate in having a larger so-called middle class than most European countries. During the industrial development, hundreds of commoners gradually accumulated wealth and gained power and influence through organizing and developing industrial enterprises. These men owned the factories, bought the raw material, hired the workers, and sold the manufactured goods. Because they had the capital, or money to finance these industries, they came to be called capitalists. Successful merchants were also included in this group.

Under the guild system, you may remember, there were regulations and laws governing both the master and his apprentice. Under the new factory system, however, the capitalists were free to do much as they pleased. They paid the laborers whatever they wished. Since their object was only to make money, they gave no thought to the health of their employees or the conditions under which they worked in the factory or lived at home. If a worker became ill, another was hired to take his place. Naturally the capitalists joined together to see that no laws were passed that would affect their profits.

The statesmen of the 17th and 18th Centuries believed that industry and trade should be regulated. The capitalists would have none of such regulation. Owing to their influence with the government, they were permitted to make whatever they wished and as much of it as they pleased.

It might seem from the conditions of the poor and the growing influence of the capitalists that civilization was going backward; but it was not. In spite of the misery and turmoil some progress was being made. Although the capitalists did not recognize the needs or the rights of the laborers or their responsibility for them, they were breaking the hold of the old aristocracy, or the nobility.

Workers were no better off than serfs. When the Industrial Revolution began, the owners of the factories encouraged the poor to seek employment in industry. Most of the manufacturers, however, paid as low wages as possible. The factory workers were made to toil long hours under deplorable working conditions. The discipline was very severe. The whip was often used. Brutal bosses would strike down workmen with their fists on the slightest pretext. The laws were such that the laborers found it difficult to move from one place to another in order to find work.

Labor conditions improved gradually. Early in the 19th Century, in order to get higher wages, less harsh treatment, and better living conditions, the laborers began to organize. A group of cotton weavers asked Parliament to regulate wages. When no action was taken, the labor union resorted to strikes and compelled others to join them. But the manufacturers easily secured legislation prohibiting unions.

There were, however, a number of factory owners who were interested in the welfare of the workers. They finally secured legislation regulating conditions under which laborers had to work, and a limitation on the number of hours of employment for children.

Labor became more powerful. Living and working conditions in England gradually improved. In 1825 a law was passed that permitted laborers to organize. Twenty-five years later labor unions were permitted to persuade others to join in their efforts to bring about better wages and working conditions. A trade-union act was passed in 1906 that gave workers the same freedom as employers to enter into contracts. The labor group increased its membership in Parliament. Although some of the members were inclined to promote impractical schemes, others worked to promote the purposes of trade unionism and to provide for the needs of the workers. After World War I the Labor Party liberalized its program and became a great force in the political affairs of Great Britain. There are now many labor representatives in Parliament, and the party has gained a strong position.

The Industrial Revolution created a demand for raw materials and markets. With the migrations of workers from the country to the industries in the cities, and the increased demand for wool,

many landowners turned their small farms into large pastures for sheep. This worked in reverse also. As more landowners began to raise sheep — a profitable business — fewer farmers were needed. With no farms to till, people went to the city for work. Soon England could not raise enough food for her people and had to import grain and other foodstuffs from the United States, Canada, and other countries. Since England needed more iron than she could produce for her industries, iron ore was imported from Spain and Sweden. So much of the cotton used in the cotton mills of England was shipped from our Southern states, that when the boll weevil destroyed a large part of the crop in America, factory workers in England were thrown out of work. Food supplies, iron, and cotton were only three of the many kinds of raw materials England had to import. As her industries multiplied, her need for new materials increased and her commerce grew.

Her commerce grew in another way. If more goods are manufactured than can be sold at home, markets in foreign lands become desirable. From the beginning of the Industrial Revolution to the present day, the English have been particularly interested in markets as well as in raw materials. Turn again to the map of the British Empire at the top of page 363. The vastness of the British possessions is explained in part by the need of raw materials and markets where the products of the English factories could be sold. India, for example, furnished cotton fiber for the textile mills of the British Isles, and in turn bought the cotton goods that these mills produced.

About one hundred years before the Industrial Revolution, England passed navigation laws to aid her merchants in

Courtesy Caterpillar Tractor Co.

A COMBINE

This versatile machine is combining the processes of reaping and threshing. It can cover 3½ to 4 acres an hour on 2 gallons of fuel. The combine is one of the machines that have revolutionized agriculture, and made modern large-scale farming possible.

their foreign trade. These laws required that all goods from Asia, Africa, and America be brought into England in vessels owned and manned by Englishmen. You will recall that the American Colonists objected to these laws. The English capitalists of the period of the Industrial Revolution also opposed them. They were repealed just two centuries after they had been put into force, and Great Britain adopted a policy of free trade, or trade without tariff barriers. In the meantime, however, England, under the protection of her navy, had so extended her commerce that she gained rather than lost by this change of policy. As a result of these gains, Great Britain became and still holds her place as one of the leading nations of the world in ocean commerce.

The Industrial Revolution has never ended. While the years 1750 to 1850 have been given as the time of the Industrial Revolution, or the century of rapid industrial development, it must not be thought that the latter date marks the close of the period of remarkable change. There have been other periods of rapid and even greater development since that date, especially the second and third decades of the 20th Century. And this has been true not only in Great Britain but in other modern nations. We have told of the Industrial Revolution here in the story of England because the changes there were earlier and more pronounced than in other nations.

Results of the Industrial Revolution. The Industrial Revolution built machines that do much of the heavy work and drudgery that was once done by hand. It has reduced the number of hours of labor and increased the number of hours of leisure.

Working conditions have been greatly improved; factories and shops are becoming clean, sanitary, comfortable places to work. Modern sanitation, transportation, libraries, educational institutions, research laboratories, hospitals, and so on are largely products of the Industrial Revolution.

It has also given us the telegraph, the telephone, and the radio that place us in communication with all parts of the world. Many other improvements in living conditions have resulted.

But now, as in the past, when a new machine is invented or a labor-saving device is introduced, many new economic and social problems have to be met. Labor-saving devices often throw workers out of jobs, and many unskilled laborers are almost daily replaced by machines. Earlier machines are replaced by improved machines which require only unskilled attendants — and skilled labor is no longer required. Also, assembly-line construction means that many workers must spend their days at jobs which are routine, uninteresting, and not at all stimulating.

The solution to these and many similar problems does not lie in decreasing the use of machines. The Industrial Revolution has put power and machinery into the hands of man. Whether he will become the master or the slave of his discoveries and inventions remains yet to be seen.

Chapter 6 ～ England Is the Heart of the British Empire

How England expanded and became the United Kingdom of Great Britain. Many interesting events mark the growth of a nation. We have learned that the earlier part of England's story was a period of turmoil and conflict. The rulers of petty kingdoms fought among themselves, and attacks on them by foreign foes were numerous. Gradually, however, that part of the British Isles now known as England came to be the home of one people under one ruler. England had become a sturdy nation.

England grew by conquering other nations of the British Isles, the Irish and the Welsh. This was no easy task. These peoples were independent, fierce fighters; and devoted to their own countries. Scotland and England were officially united when the Act of Union was passed early in the 18th Century. These four peoples came to be called the United Kingdom of Great Britain.

What is the British Empire? The British Empire is the largest political unit in the modern world. It embraces one-fourth of the world's land surface, and more than one-fourth of the population — slightly more than that of China. The empire includes people of many branches of the human family, and of widely differing religions and cultures.

Two fundamental ideas apply to the whole empire: (1) All people owe allegiance to a common Crown, which participates in every government, normally through its representative, the governor; (2) the Parliament of Great Britain is

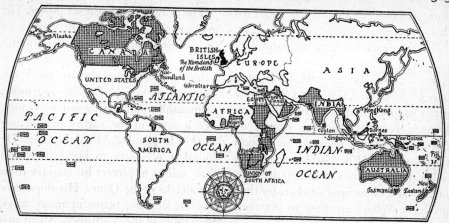

THE BRITISH EMPIRE AT THE BEGINNING OF WORLD WAR II
This map shows why it has been said that the sun never sets on the British Empire.
Which hemisphere contains more British territory?

over the entire empire, though it no longer legislates for the self-governing peoples of the empire without their consent.

In general, the British Empire consists of: (a) the British Commonwealth of Nations—Great Britain, Eire (Ireland), Canada, Australia, New Zealand, and the Union of South Africa; (b) Crown colonies, such as Bermuda, the Bahamas [buh hahm′uhz], Barbados [bahr bay′dohz]; and (c) "in-betweens," such as India and Rhodesia [roh dee′zyuh]. There are also mandates, or supervised territories, which are not actually a part of the empire.

The members of the British Commonwealth of Nations, listed above, have the status of Dominions of the British Empire. Prior to World War I these dominions gradually gained control over their internal affairs, but through their governors, Great Britain handled all external, or foreign, affairs for them. During that war the leaders of the Dominions gradually became recognized on an equal footing with the leaders of Great Britain. In 1931 the British Parliament relinquished all control over the govern-ments of these Dominions. Now the Dominions are independent nations, except that each owes allegiance to the King of England. They select their own Governor-General, have their own diplomatic representatives in foreign nations, and direct their own international affairs. They are now bound to Great Britain only by the King (who has no governmental authority), common interests and purposes, and social and cultural ties.

Why do nations build empires? We have learned that "the sun never sets on the British Empire"; we know that in a few hundred years a small island off the coast of Europe gained control over much of the land and many of the people of the world. Why and how did this come about? Why do nations wish to expand, and how do they do it? Especially, why do nations wish to expand by gaining control of foreign territory — territory that cannot be incorporated within their own natural boundaries and government? Why do they want to rule people who have manners, customs, and beliefs quite foreign to their own?

As you study the geography and resources of modern nations you will learn that no nation is entirely self-sufficient, that is, in possession of all the natural resources necessary for economic and social well-being and progress. Such countries as the United States and Russia are better supplied than most other nations. Densely populated nations usually do not have sufficient resources to support the population. Where and how are they to get the necessary raw materials? Too, industrial nations need markets for their products. Where are they to get these markets?

The chief reasons for the desire to expand, then, are to secure natural resources and to develop trade. Of course there are other reasons, such as needing more room for a nation's people, wanting better self-protection, or even merely showing power.

Throughout history, nations, like individuals, have acted on the principle, "The finder is the keeper," and have taken not only discovered resources, but also the territory where the resources were found. This practice explains, for example, why so many expeditions were sent by different nations to the Americas, after their discovery by Columbus.

Sometimes the claims of one nation, based on discovery or possession, have not always been recognized; and possessions have been seized by another nation. One indication of the advance of civilization is that in more recent times this practice has been frowned on by civilized nations, especially the democracies, even when they were not immediately concerned. This disapproval did not prevent Mussolini from taking Ethiopia, or Japan from seizing Manchuria. But the approved method today is to arrange by mutual agreement for a fair exchange of natural products and manufactured goods.

The growth of British sea power. The greatest single factor in the growth of the British Empire was Great Britain's control of the seas. This control was gained only through many bitter encounters in which English ingenuity, seamanship, and daring led to victory. We learned in the earlier part of our story of England of Alfred the Great. He found it necessary to build ships and train sailors to protect his country from the attacks of the Danes. His ships were swifter, steadier, better in many ways, than those of the Northmen. About two centuries later, when sailing vessels took the place of oar-driven boats, Great Britain continued to build more and better ships.

For many years the kings of England were content to rule and defend their homeland. However, the startling discovery by Columbus, and the explorations of Cabot and of English seamen during the last decade of the 15th Century, showed the English rulers the possibilities of conquest and of a greater overseas trade. They encouraged foreign commerce by granting aid to English merchantmen. New and larger warships were built and equipped with cannon, especially during the reign of Henry VIII.

But it is to their great Queen Elizabeth that the British are indebted for the first achievements that really led to the mastery of the seas. The queen was determined to defend her country against all foreign foes, especially Spain and France. She had a new type of war vessel built to protect exploring and commercial expeditions, as well as to prepare for the defense of England.

The struggle with Spain. In the meantime, Spain's growing hostility toward England broke out into war. Spain thought Columbus's discovery gave her

QUEEN ELIZABETH CONFERS KNIGHTHOOD UPON DRAKE

In 1580 Drake returned from a voyage round the world. He was the first Englishman to circumnavigate the globe. In honor of his achievement, Queen Elizabeth boarded his ship, the *Golden Hind,* and conferred knighthood upon Drake. This picture is a reproduction of a painting by the artist John Gilbert.

the first claim to the whole of North America as well as to South America and the islands of the Caribbean Sea. She resented the fact that English privateers were interfering with Spanish commerce, particularly in the West Indies. She also objected to the rapid growth of British occupation of the New World. As a climax to the situation, the daring Englishman, Drake (who later made a voyage around the world), " singed the King of Spain's beard " by boldly sailing into the harbor at Cadiz with only four of England's new ships and destroying a Spanish fleet. The picture above shows Drake being knighted by his queen.

Defeat of the Spanish Armada. The year 1588 will never be forgotten by the

English, for in it the Spanish Armada [ahr mah'duh], or fleet, set sail from Spain to attack the English. Storms crippled many of the ships, and when the Armada reached British waters her numbers were greatly reduced. The large Spanish galleons sailed up the English Channel in a majestic half-moon formation. But the English had received warning and were prepared. Their war vessels did not wait but went out to meet them. Rough seas and high winds made the heavy Spanish galleons hard to handle, while the newer and faster English ships were more easily managed. After many desperate encounters, which lasted for nearly two weeks, what remained of the Armada was driven into the North Sea from which they tried to return home by way of the west coast of Ireland. Even then many more of the Spanish ships were destroyed by a fierce gale before they reached their ports in Spain. Spain never again challenged the English on the high seas, and Britain was well on the way toward becoming "mistress of the seas."

British settlements were enlarging the Empire. While England was fighting Spain for naval supremacy, British expeditions were being carried on all over the world. During this period the British were settling such territories as Newfoundland and Nova Scotia; Barbados, Bermuda, and Honduras [hahn doo' ruhs] in the West Indies; and Gambia in West Africa.

The struggle with the Netherlands. About fifty years after the defeat of the Armada, England became engaged in a number of wars with the Netherlands for the control of the North Sea and trade in the East Indies. Many of the conflicts on the waters ended without glory for the English and with disaster to British trade. In the end, however, the Netherlands were exhausted and England was left stronger on the sea than any other maritime country. It was during this conflict that New Amsterdam became New York.

During this period, too, England gained possession of territories including the African Gold Coast, the Bahamas and Jamaica, and parts of Canada.

The struggle with France. Scarcely had peace been made with the Netherlands when England began a hundred-year contest with France for control of lands in America and India. During this time the French came to the assistance of the American Colonists in their struggle for liberty. Many fierce battles between the English and the French were fought on sea and on land, in many parts

of the world. This contest ended in a complete victory for the English off the coast of Spain near Trafalgar [truh fal' ger] in 1805.

Admiral Nelson, who led the English fleet to victory at Trafalgar, became one of the outstanding national heroes. Just before joining in battle with a larger fleet of French and Spanish vessels, he had hoisted that famous signal, "England expects that every man will do his duty." Through his daring and skillful seamanship the English won one of the greatest victories in naval history. Toward the end of the battle Nelson was fatally wounded. Resting in the arms of an old comrade, he murmured, just as the guns ceased firing, "Now I am satisfied. Thank God, I have done my duty." In recognition of Nelson's victory a square in London has been named Trafalgar and a tall monument erected there in Nelson's honor.

Great Britain gained control of both gates to the Mediterranean. Gibraltar [ji brawl' ter] stands at the western entrance to the Mediterranean Sea. This rocky cape near the southernmost point of Spain was known to the mariners of ancient times. It was the scene of numerous conflicts between the Moors and the Spaniards, but finally was held by Spain. In 1704 Gibraltar was captured by the British and the Dutch, at war with Spain; and in 1713 it was granted to Britain by a treaty. Gibraltar then was so strongly fortified by the English that all efforts on the part of Spain to recapture it failed. This control of the western gate to the Mediterranean made possible the movements of British ships which brought about the victories of Trafalgar and the Nile. "As strong as the rock of Gibraltar" has come to be a common expression to describe great strength and endurance.

The eastern gateway to the Mediterranean was the Suez Canal, built by a French engineer, de Lesseps [duh luh′ seps′], between 1859 and 1869. The funds for the canal had been provided by a French company and by the Mohammedan governor of Egypt. England gained control of the canal by diplomacy rather than by military prowess. The crafty English statesman, Disraeli, very early saw the importance of this canal to England and watched his chance to get possession of it. At a time when the governor of Egypt was in great need of money, Disraeli was able to purchase Egypt's share of ownership in the eastern gate to the Mediterranean, and thus to control the canal.

This was only the beginning of English influence in northeastern Africa, an influence which grew until it had brought about control of Egypt. After the close of World War I, Egypt regained much of her independence, but England continued to hold the Suez Canal. This control of the gateways to the Mediterranean enabled England not only to carry on her commerce and hold her power in eastern Africa, but to play an important part in Asia as well.

Many territories were added to the British Empire. Throughout the 18th and 19th Centuries, the British Empire was growing rapidly. Much of Canada, Australia, and South Africa was settled, and much of India was brought under British control. We shall tell the stories of these territories a little more fully in the following pages.

The Far East was also invaded by British merchants and controlled by British power. The Chinese island of Hong Kong was seized and made into a British naval base. It became one of the greatest commercial centers of the Far East. Shanghai, Canton, and other Chinese

British Press Combine

AIR VIEW OF GIBRALTAR

Britain's west gate to the Mediterranean is the strategic Rock of Gibraltar, placed at the point where Europe comes closest to Africa. On the left in this picture is the naval harbor. The white areas on the right are reservoirs, or catchments, which collect rain water for Gibraltar's water supply.

cities were opened up to foreign trade and partial foreign control, principally owing to British pressure. Singapore [sing'guh pohr'] and the rest of the Straits Settlements were also taken over as a colony, and another great commercial center was developed there.

During this period the British flag was hoisted over many more islands and territories, all important to British sea power and commerce. Britain had gained an empire which stretched around the world. Let us see how she obtained some of her more important territories.

British Influence in the Western Hemisphere

Our American forefathers aided British expansion. In your study of the early history of our country you learned of the courage and endurance of our forefathers in their struggles for greater religious and political freedom. They made determined efforts to establish homes on American soil. Behind them was Great Britain's desire to gain control of as much territory as possible in North America.

While colonists from Britain were making their settlements in New England, Spain was taking possession of Florida and much of what is now Latin America. The French were establishing trading posts and settlements in the region of the St. Lawrence River. You may recall that the Jesuit missionary Marquette, the trader Joliet, and the explorer La Salle traveled down the Mississippi River and gave France a basis for laying claim to the Mississippi Valley.

The rivalry between France and Great Britain for colonial possessions in India and America led to a number of wars. In one of these, known to us as the Seven Years' War, or sometimes as the French and Indian War, George Washington and Colonial militiamen, as loyal British subjects, joined the British regulars who were sent over to keep the French from encroaching on British territory. In this conflict, England was victorious

and France yielded to Great Britain her claims to Canada and the territory east of the Mississippi River. Thus English civilization was definitely established in the Western Hemisphere. Great Britain became the leading naval, colonial, and commercial power in the world. Her possessions came to include not only the territory on the North American continent, but also British Honduras, British Guiana, and the Bahama Islands off the coast of Florida.

An imaginary line separates two great nations. To our north, across a completely unarmed boundary, lies Canada. This boundary line is about 3000 miles in length, stretching from the Atlantic to the Pacific. No forts or other forms of military defense are to be found along it; no armed vessels appear on the Great Lakes to guard the water boundary between the two nations. The boundary has stood unchanged for more than a hundred years, bearing witness to the fact that neighboring nations can live in peace and without fear of each other. In 1932, at the dedication of the International Peace Garden in the mountains on the boundary between Manitoba [man'uh toh'buh] and North Dakota, fifty thousand people from Canada and the United States raised their hands and solemnly swore, " To God in His Glory, we two nations dedicate this garden, and pledge ourselves that as long as men

AN OUTLINE MAP OF PRESENT-DAY CANADA

shall live we will not take up arms against one another, so help us God."

Canada is geographically similar to the United States. Canada stretches across the northern half of North America, including all of it except Alaska, Newfoundland, and Labrador. (Newfoundland is a separate portion of the British Empire; Labrador is a dependency of Newfoundland.) The total area of Canada is slightly less than that of the United States including Alaska. The land is a huge basin, with mountains along both sides — much as is the United States. Along the Canadian coastline are many fine harbors, a large number of which are open all year. Hudson Bay, however, although important for trade since the early days of New World settlement, is ice-free for only about four months of the year. The Great Lakes, which form part of the Canadian boundary, are important to Canadian shipping, as is the mighty St. Lawrence River. Canada has many other lakes and rivers as well. The climate is as varied as is our own. The range of temperature is actually about the same as in our country. But the temperature is lower, owing to the increased latitude. The climate of southern Canada is much like that of the northern part of the United States. Northern Canada is of course colder than any part of the United States, and has not been as well developed.

Canada is a rich land. Canada's plant and animal life is similar to our own, and so are her natural resources. From early times to the present, her mines have yielded gold, copper, silver, lead, zinc, nickel, and asbestos. Her dairy industries and fur trade are of major im-

Courtesy Canadian Pacific Railway

QUEBEC

This old walled city on the St. Lawrence River has played an important part in the history of Canada, ever since Champlain chose its site over three hundred years ago. It was the scene of the battle that decided England's struggle for Canada. It has been the capital of the province by the same name — the province that is still strongly French. And it was the scene of international conferences in World War II.

portance. Canadian waters yield large quantities of fish and her forests are abundant. Over an excellent transportation system, Canada exports wheat, lumber, pulp, paper, and minerals. Cheap water transportation makes profitable the movement of these bulky products. It is understandable that Great Britain wanted this vast, rich land.

Our neighbor on the north is both French and British. We generally think of Canadians who come into the United States very much as we do of people from a different section of our own country. Their language, manners, customs, and thinking are very much like our own. If we should visit such places as British Columbia or Ontario, however, we would see and hear many things that are markedly British. And if we should visit the province of Quebec [kwee bek'] it would be almost as if we were in a different country. The provincial lan-

guage is French. The business establishments, the streets, the architecture, the manners and customs, have much in common with those of France of a somewhat earlier period. Naturally we wonder why the French, the British, and other immigrants from Europe have not been fused into one Canadian people. The answer is to be found in the history of Canada.

French beginnings in Canada. France based her claim to the territory along the St. Lawrence River on the explorations made by Jacques Cartier [zhahk' kahr' tyay'] about fifty years after the discovery of America. About half a century later, Samuel de Champlain [duh sham' playn'], who explored the lake that now bears his name, established at Quebec a settlement which was the capital of New France for almost two hundred years. A view of this city is shown above.

The French were not interested in establishing homes in America as were the English colonists south of them. The Jesuit church fathers came to Canada to establish missions among the Indians; these missions became centers of French civilization. The fur trade with the Indians lured adventurous Frenchmen to the uncharted forests of Canada. They became explorers as well as hunters and traders. The first French colonies in Canada were autocratically controlled by both the government of France and the Catholic church.

English beginnings in Canada. When England took over the government of Canada in 1763, the French Canadians were assured freedom in religion, that is, the Catholic faith, and the continuance of French laws and customs. In the United States at the close of the Revolutionary War, the Loyalists were in a difficult situation. Since they had favored the cause of the British, and the Colonists had won their independence, the Loyalists wanted to find some other place to live. Many of them migrated to Canada. Families from the British Isles, especially from Scotland and Ireland, also moved to Canada.

The differences between the French and the English developed into bitter antagonisms. In order to meet this situation, the British government first divided Canada into two provinces, each with its own local government under a central British administration. Upper Canada was British and Protestant. Lower Canada was French and Catholic. Out of a total population of about eleven million in a recent year, approximately three million were French Canadian.

Canada became an independent nation. Today Canada is an independent, democratic nation. Numerous problems had to be solved and a few conflicts had to be won by Canada in gaining her present freedom and standing. There have always been differences that had to be adjusted between the conservative French Canadians and the more liberal English-speaking Canadians. The conditions that caused the French Canadians and British Canadians to unite were similar to the conditions that led the American Colonists to unite. Local misunderstanding and conflicting trade laws interfered with their commerce. There was also a growing fear of the power of a foreign nation, in this instance the United States. The confederation finally developed in Canada was composed of the provinces of Quebec, Ontario, New Brunswick, and Nova Scotia. As the new provinces of Prince Edward Island, Manitoba, Saskatchewan, Alberta, and British Columbia were organized, they were added to the Union. The governments of the provinces of Canada are much like the governments of the states in our country, but the central government of Canada is more like that of Great Britain.

The addition of western provinces brought to the fore the problems of communication and transportation. These were solved by the building of a government railroad and by the invention and development of the automobile, the airplane, and the radio. Canada attained full independence by becoming a member of the British Commonwealth of Nations, which extends to each of its members full responsibility to make its own laws and its treaties. The ties between Canada and Great Britain today are those of common backgrounds, manners, customs, and institutions. The common purposes and interests of the United States and Canada also have, during the last few decades, drawn the two countries closer together.

British Influence in Africa

Great Britain controls a large part of Africa. The British control large areas in the west, in the south, and in the east-central parts of Africa. These territories have been gained through conquest, exploration and settlement, annexation, and mandates.

The types of control exercised by Great Britain range from a colonial government that is entirely in the hands of the British, as in the Gold Coast and Nigeria, to an independent dominion like the Union of South Africa. Between these are protectorates, such as Egypt and Rhodesia; joint protectorates, such as that with Egypt in the Sudan; governments administered under a council of the League of Nations, or mandates, such as Tanganyika.

The Union of South Africa is made up of four provinces. The Union of South Africa is a dominion of the British Commonwealth. It is the largest and most important British territory in Africa. More than four times the size of the combined British Isles, it consists of four provinces: (1) Cape Colony, (2) Natal [nuh tal'], (3) Transvaal [transvahl'] and (4) Orange Free State. The government of the Union of South Africa is similar to that of the other dominions. About one-fourth of the population is white, of British and Dutch ancestry; the remainder of the people are Negroid natives.

The land is a mixture of steep hills and plateaus, of vast plains and veld, or grasslands. There are few natural harbors, although good ports have been developed.

More gold and diamonds come from the Union of South Africa than from any other place in the world. Much of the territory has too little rainfall to support much agriculture, but irrigation is gradually making more of the land productive. Maize, sorghum, and cotton are grown in these areas, and in the more humid sections tropical fruits, sugar, tea, and tobacco are grown. The Union of South Africa exports quantities of minerals and some agricultural products. It imports textiles and clothing, food products, and machinery.

The history of the Union of South Africa. The colonial history of the Union of South Africa may remind us of the early history of our own country. In South Africa the Dutch built forts and trading stations. Then, since the soil was fertile, they established colonies. But they did not manage their colonies well. Through mismanagement and wars with England, the Netherlands lost their Dutch territory in South Africa to the British. The British freed all slaves in South Africa, as they did throughout the empire, but they did not adequately compensate slaveholders in South Africa. The British were unwise in their government of the liberty-loving Boers [boors], as they are called, from a Dutch word meaning " farmers." As a result, many of the Dutch migrated from the province of the Cape of Good Hope and established colonies farther north, which became the provinces of the Transvaal and the Free State.

The discovery of gold in the Transvaal and diamonds in the Orange River attracted great numbers of foreigners, many of whom were British. The conflicts that followed resulted in a war, but the Boers did not gain their independence as the American colonists had done more than a century earlier. The Boers

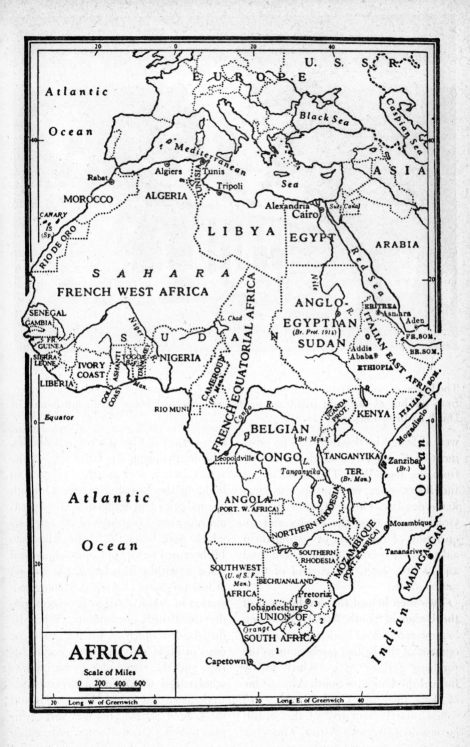

AFRICA

Scale of Miles
0   200   400   600

Courtesy South African Railways and Harbors

A HOME IN SOUTH AFRICA

The Union of South Africa is a land of great variety. The homes of the inhabitants range from the hut of the Zulu tribesman to the well-designed house of the inhabitant of Dutch or British descent.

were defeated by the British. The provinces of South Africa suffered greatly from the Boer War. The homeland of the Boers, once very prosperous, was made desolate. However, after the war Great Britain won the loyalty and cooperation of the Boers by giving them aid in the restoration of their homeland and, a little later, the control of their government.

Two men helped the development of the Union of South Africa. Two men became recognized leaders in the development of the British possessions in the southern part of Africa which finally formed the Union of South Africa. One of these men was Cecil Rhodes [ses'l rohdz], a representative of the British government in South Africa. The other was Jan Christiaan Smuts, a native of

the province of Capetown. Cecil Rhodes, who lived during the latter half of the 19th Century, was greatly interested in building the British Empire. Through his activities and leadership Great Britain came into possession of the territory which now bears the name Rhodesia. He became Premier of Cape Colony, and ruled it with a firm hand. He was an ardent promoter of a self-governing federation of South African provinces, under the British government. When he died he left much of his fortune to be used to build universities in South Africa, and the remainder to be used as scholarships to Oxford University for students in the British Dominions and the United States. This was part of his plan to bring about a better understanding among all English-speaking peoples. To be selected as a Rhodes scholar is a great honor.

Jan Christiaan Smuts, son of a Dutch farmer, devoted much of his life to the freedom and union of South Africa. He fought in the Boer War and became a general. After a hard fight, he accepted defeat calmly and put forth every effort to bring peace and harmony between the defeated Boers and Great Britain, and in doing so gained the confidence of the British government as well as the people of South Africa. It was largely through his efforts that the provinces in the southern part of Africa became the Union of South Africa. He was a member of the first cabinet of the new government, and later served as premier for a period of four years. When Great Britain declared war against the Axis in 1939, General Smuts became Premier of the Union of South Africa a second time; he was responsible for the decision of his government to join Britain in World War II.

British Influence in the South Pacific

World War II made the southwest Pacific one of the strategic parts of the world. If you will turn again to the map of the British Empire on page 363 you will notice that the British possessions extend southeastward from India to beyond New Zealand. First, find Singapore on the peninsula of Malaya. Observing the position of Japan, you can understand why, at the tip end of this narrow neck of land, Great Britain built what she thought was an impregnable fortress to safeguard India and the islands of the South Pacific. Further on, you will find the islands of Borneo and New Guinea. The largest British possession in this region is Australia, south of which is Tasmania. Twelve hundred miles to the southeast is New Zealand. Australia provided the base from which Australian and American forces under General MacArthur halted the Japanese in their conquest of the South Pacific in World War II.

Australia is an unusual land. The native Australian animal and plant life is markedly different from that of other countries. Australia is the home of marsupials, or animals that carry their young in a pouch like the American opossum. They range in size from the small bandicoots to the kangaroo, the largest animal in Australia. Plants of early geological times, which have disappeared from other parts of the globe, are still found in Australia. Although Australia is nearly as large as the United States, it has nothing comparable to our great Mississippi Valley. The central portion of Australia is an arid tableland. Only the coastal regions are naturally suitable for agriculture.

A daring explorer added a continent to the British Empire. There is only one instance in history where a nation has come into possession of a continent — the British acquisition of Australia. Its peaceful conquest by Great Britain was possible because Australia was quite far removed from modern nations and the principal lines of ocean transportation. Also, the exploration and colonization, and the discovery of great natural resources, were made when Great Britain was in a position to maintain her claim.

About the middle of the 16th Century the Portuguese reported finding land beyond the East Indies. A number of

Courtesy Australian News & Information Bureau

ON THE AUSTRALIAN COAT-OF-ARMS

The kangaroo, which is native to Australia, appears, with the emu, on the coat-of-arms of Australia. There are many live kangaroos off the coat-of-arms, too. They live in the less settled areas of the country, and are protected by game laws.

Dutch explorers also had learned something about this unknown land. About a century after the Portuguese reported the discovery of Australia, Abel Jansen Tasman discovered, south of Australia, the island named Tasmania.

The natives of Australia were rather backward in their mental, physical, and social development. They had no fixed homes and lived on whatever they killed, often eating their food without cooking it. They had not discovered, nor made use of, any of the natural resources; so the early explorers were not encouraged to establish settlements or trading posts in Australia. Therefore Australia, which was called New Holland until the middle of the 19th Century, lay undeveloped for more than a hundred years.

In 1770 Captain James Cook, a famous English navigator who devoted his life to exploration, was in command of a scientific expedition to the Pacific Ocean. He visited New Zealand, and discovered and explored that part of Australia now known as New South Wales. The first settlement was made by British convicts, many of whom had been thrown into prison for very minor offenses. For many years this settlement was little more than an open-air prison. Later, other settlers came into the country and a number of model colonies were established. Sheep raising was introduced, gold was discovered, and Australia began to develop more rapidly. Today over five million persons occupy the more desirable parts of the three million square miles of this last-discovered continent.

In earlier years, the present provinces or states in Australia were separate colonies. Owing to differences and conflicts they, like the American colonies, found it necessary to arrange a common central government. A constitution, somewhat similar to that of the United States, was adopted, and approved by the British Parliament, at the beginning of the present century. The new federal government, not handicapped by traditions, enacted many new governmental laws and practices that were startling to older nations. Some of these will be discussed a little later. One of the less startling, and one that was later adopted by the United States and Great Britain, was the Australian Ballot System, which insures secrecy in voting.

New Zealand, the most " British " of British possessions. New Zealand is noted for its beautiful scenery and delight-

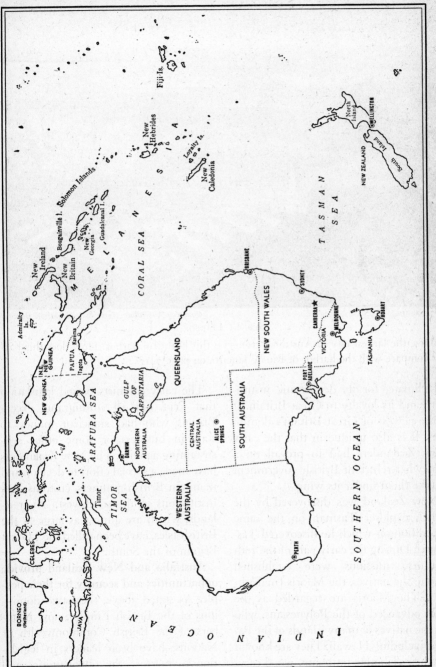

AUSTRALIA, NEW ZEALAND, AND PART OF THE SOUTH PACIFIC

Courtesy Australian News & Information Bureau
SYDNEY HARBOR

Sydney, the largest city in Australia, fronts on this beautiful harbor. How does this harbor compare with the harbor of Rio de Janeiro, on page 741?

ful climate, for its democratic institutions and its loyalty to Great Britain. It is the newest of Great Britain's dominions. It is also unique in that the early New Zealanders had to prevail on a somewhat reluctant British government to take them under its wing.

New Zealand was discovered by the Dutch explorer Tasman on the same expedition on which he discovered Tasmania. During the early part of the 19th Century, missions were established among the natives, the Maoris [mah'ohriz]. The Maoris are regarded as the most advanced of the Polynesians, who are the natives of many islands of the Pacific, including Hawaii. They are known for their elaborate tattooing, wood carving, and their poetic nature myths. They learned rapidly to adapt themselves to new conditions, and are now citizens.

The early colonists passed legislation that kept out all immigrants except Britons who had sufficient money to start in business or some other self-sustaining activity. The New Zealanders have made a special effort to develop and maintain British manners, customs, and institutions in the southwest. Their islands, which are almost as large as the British Isles, have been called the " Great Britain of the South."

Australia and New Zealand provide opportunities and security for their people. As stated above, these two dominions of the British Empire, now members of the British Commonwealth of Nations, have been leaders in legislation to increase the opportunities and welfare of their citizens. Owing to their fine systems of public schools, illiteracy is much lower in these countries than it is even in the United States and Great Britain; in fact, it has almost reached the vanishing point. Immigration is restricted so that only persons who are self-supporting and can be easily assimilated may become citizens.

New Zealand, which is only slightly more advanced in industrial and social legislation than Australia, has government ownership of railways, telephone and telegraph systems, other public utilities, and all natural resources. Before 1900, an income tax was adopted; the right to vote was given women; the arbitration of disputes between capital and labor was made compulsory; and a system of old-age pensions and a minimum wage were established. The two democracies of Australia and New Zealand, unhampered by tradition and long-established group distinctions, have been able to pass and enforce legislation that has been considered Utopian or quite visionary by the older nations.

British Influence in India

India is a land of contrasts. You probably have read or heard fabulous stories about the strange, romantic land of India — tales of wealthy Indian princes and reports of impoverished natives. Most of these are undoubtedly true; India is a land of great contrasts. You may have heard of the " Black Hole of Calcutta," the name given to a small, poorly ventilated prison into which an Indian prince crowded 146 helpless English, all but twenty-three of whom died before morning. Kipling's *Jungle Book* and *Kim* have given many people their first glimpse of life in India. Probably you have read about and seen pictures of Gandhi or Nehru [nay'roo], leaders of the people of India in their struggle for self-government.

India is large in area and population. The triangular peninsula of India juts down in the Indian Ocean. To the east is the Bay of Bengal, to the west the Arabian Sea. India is about the same size as Europe west of Russia, and has about the same population. Its people comprise almost one-fifth the total population of the world — and three-quarters of the population of the entire British Empire. Its population of about three hundred million is second only to that of China.

The land of India is divided into three large areas: the Himalayas on the north form the mountainous region; the central plains region is the gift of the Indus, Ganges, and Brahmaputra [brah' muh poo'truh] rivers — just as Egypt is the gift of the Nile; and to the south the hill country reaches toward the equator.

The peninsula has a coastline about 3000 miles long, and much of it is regular except where rivers have built up large deltas. The climate of India varies greatly from the Himalayas to the southern tip, for the peninsula extends from the temperate zone (at about the latitude of New York City) almost to the equator.

India has only two seasons — wet and dry; and the monsoons and floods sometimes do incredible damage to the land. There are forests and jungles throughout the country, and insect and animal life abound. The great number of animals living in India may be owing in part to the Indian religious belief that

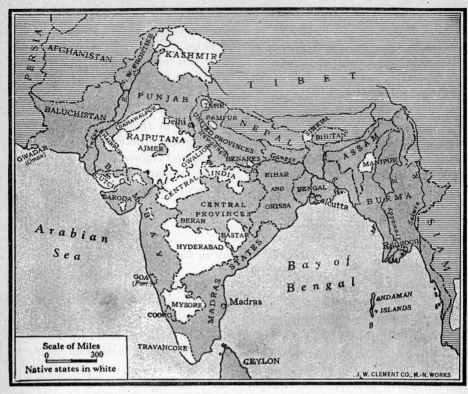

INDIA, SHOWING BRITISH INDIA AND THE NATIVE STATES

no animal should be killed. Even poisonous snakes, of which there are many, are permitted to live unmolested, and every year many Indians die of snake bites.

India had an impressive early civilization. Little is known of the earliest inhabitants of India, but it is likely that they were Negroid, Mongoloid, and Malay. Many European and Asiatic peoples swarmed into India in very early times, so that the Hindus of today are a complex mixture. As early as 3000 B.C. there was a high form of civilization in India; it may have been as great as that of Egypt and Mesopotamia. The civilization was quite individual, for water and Himalayas cut India off from the rest of the world. Little is known about this early civilization, for many of the relics are buried in the mud deposits of the rivers. But it is known that art, industry, and city life were highly developed. The early Brahman literature, as you learned in the story of religions, includes some of the finest of early writings.

India's trade brought her many rulers. As early as the Seventh Century B.C., India's trade had brought her to the attention of many other peoples. Darius the Great invaded India about 500 B.C., in an effort to take over her profitable trade. Alexander the Great made a similar invasion about two hundred years later. India also became part of the Mohammedan Empire, and still later part of the Mongolian Empire. For centuries the power shifted from overlords to first one local prince and then another.

In the 16th Century Portugal seized several Indian ports, and soon the Dutch,

English, and French also had territory there. Again, trade was the principal reason for such holdings. These nations struggled for trade supremacy for many years, but by the middle of the 18th Century, Great Britain — represented by the East India Company — was supreme.

How did Great Britain gain control of this far-off land of India? During the reign of Queen Elizabeth the desire for natural resources and trade led English merchants and manufacturers to organize trading companies. These were given special privileges by the British government. One of these companies was the British East India Company, which gained a monopoly on trade with India. Another was the London Company, which promoted the settlement at Jamestown. The French likewise were setting up trading posts both in India and in America. The French and the English soon took over the Indian trade established by the Portuguese and the Dutch.

Since India was thickly populated and at times under the rule of strong native princes, the English and French made no attempts at colonization. But they did set up trading posts. As trade in spices and other Eastern products increased, these trading posts grew in number and in size. The rivalry between the traders was keen, and there were frequent clashes between them in India. An American phase of this conflict was the French and Indian War. As a result of the Seven Years War, France was ousted from India by the British. You have already read how France lost Canada in that struggle. Thus it was that after 1763 Great Britain took over a large part of India that had been controlled by the French. She gradually extended her rule to include the whole of India, either by defeating local princes, or maharajas, or by making agreements with them.

Problems of British rule in India. When thinking about the British government and its problems in India, we must keep in mind a number of unusual situations in that country. In the first place, the population of India is not composed of one fused people into which invaders or immigrants have been assimilated. Although there naturally has been some assimilation, the population of India is made up of many different races. This fact explains why there are eighteen languages and more than two hundred dialects in use today.

The people are divided into hundreds of castes and subclasses, with restrictions and traditions governing each. One of the greatest problems is what to do about the lowest class, the " untouchables," for whom life is almost intolerable. You learned something about this problem in the story of religions. The British government has tried to help this situation by not recognizing caste distinctions in its provisions for schools, the use of railways, and opportunities for government service. Some of the leading citizens of India have also worked to win recognition and opportunities for the untouchables. But little progress has been made in this work.

The customs in India that seem strange to us have grown out of many and varied religious beliefs. Many different gods are worshiped in different parts of India, but the Hindus and the Mohammedans dominate the life in this Asiatic country. Religious differences, particularly between the Hindus and Mohammedans, cause bitter conflicts in India. A proposed change in government favored by one group may be opposed by the other.

As you learned in the story of religions, Hinduism is a philosophy and a guide to living as well as a religion. It is

Three Lions

A MAHARAJAH'S WELL-DRESSED ELEPHANT

The maharajah, or native prince, who owns this elephant, probably thinks him well ornamented, with his capped tusks, his braceleted leg, and the painted design on his face. The maharajah's other possessions are as splendid as the elephant.

estimated that two-thirds of the total population of India follow the Hindu religion.

Mohammedanism was introduced into India by a series of Arabian invasions beginning about A.D. 1000. Today about one-fifth of the Indians are Mohammedans. Most of these live in the province of Bengal, along the Ganges in the eastern part of India. As you will remember, the followers of Mohammed were not averse to spreading their religion by the sword. The Hindus, on the other hand, are inclined toward nonresistance and pacificism. This difference in reli-gious beliefs also keeps the Indians from becoming united.

India has two governments. An unusual situation exists in India: the amount of British control differs in two parts of the land. In what is known as British India, control is great; in what are known as the Indian States, British control is light. The way Great Britain inherited this situation is interesting. The East India Company, not the British government, was originally in control of British affairs in India. The British Parliament ruled a company which in turn was dominating and exploiting an empire greater and more populous than that of the king of England. The Indian mutiny — a revolt of the Bengal native army in the middle of the 19th Century — brought an end to all this, however, and the British government took over the control of Indian affairs.

The Indian States, ruled in an autocratic manner by princes, were somewhat like the feudal states of Europe ruled by nobles during the Middle Ages. The states were even more extensive, and the princes attained much greater wealth and maintained their courts in greater splendor. Gradually these princes learned that they were able to gain a certain amount of security from attack by neighboring states by coming under the general supervision of the British government.

At first these princes feared social reforms in British India, because of the power they might lose over their subjects. In recent years, however, some of the princes have improved the living conditions of their subjects and granted them greater freedom in government. At the present time these states have agreements with the British government which permit them to handle local affairs but give the British government full control of foreign affairs. The representative of the British Crown for the Indian States is known as the "Viceroy." He is also the governor-general of British India.

The struggle for self-government. The British govern India under a constitution, and Indian representation in legislative bodies has been increased from time to time. The franchise [fran'chaiz], or right to vote, has also been extended to an increasing number of the natives. But the people of India have hoped and struggled for still greater freedom. Nevertheless, at the outbreak of World War I practically all agitation for reforms ceased and the whole of India remained loyal to Great Britain. The Indian princes raised large sums of money for the purchase of greatly needed equipment. Soon after World War I, a new constitution was drawn up by a commission sent to India for this purpose. Yet the revised constitution failed to provide for full self-government, and the conflict between Great Britain and the Indian Nationalists was resumed.

About this time Mohandas K. Gandhi became a leader in the Indian efforts toward self-government. Under his leadership, many of the Indians have carried on a more or less continuous campaign of non-co-operation and civil disobedience. At a series of conferences held in London in 1930, at which Gandhi was the outstanding figure, the Indian princes agreed to the establishment of a federal union in India. Owing to differences between the representatives of British India and the Indian princes on the kind of federation to be established, no actual agreement was reached. These discussions, however, did lead to a new, more liberal constitution.

The attitude of the people of India toward Great Britain at the outbreak of World War II was different from their attitude in 1914. The Indian National Congress demanded full independence as the price of co-operation. In 1942 the British Government agreed to full dominion status, or local self-government, for India after the War. But Gandhi and his followers demanded immediate and full independence; so nothing was accomplished. Although Gandhi lost prestige through his failure to accomplish his purpose, the struggle for independence in India continued. The problem, however, was not so much what should be done but rather the discovery of a "how" that would command the co-operation of the different factions in India. In addition to the violent religious differences, the states of India are separated by their rulers' desires to preserve as great a degree of independence as possible. It is somewhat the same struggle that we had in the early days of the United States, when a battle went on between those who favored states' rights and those who favored a strong central government. Until this problem is solved in India, little progress can be made toward the democratic self-government that the Indians want. In a sense, we have in India the largest single experiment ever attempted in the growth of a democracy.

Under British control, India's social conditions are gradually improving.

Certain developments within India as a result of British control seem to be of unquestionable value. Illiteracy is slowly decreasing. When Great Britain took over the direct rule of India, it was customary for women to remain in seclusion; for girls from ten to twelve years of age to be given in marriage; and for a widow to become a servant in her husband's family, not being permitted to marry again. The British have made numerous reforms. Laws were passed prohibiting child marriages and giving widows the right to remarry. The practice of seclusion of women is gradually being abandoned. Hospitals are being built and sanitary conditions are being improved. However, there are still many improvements to be made in social conditions in India.

Chapter 7 — British Writers, Artists, and Scientists Have Enriched Civilization

The British have developed the fine arts as well as the art of government. If the British Empire were to pass away as did the civilizations of Greece and Rome, there would still be left the great contributions to civilization made by British writers, artists, musicians, and scientists.

First let us consider England's poets, dramatists, and novelists whose works have helped to make the English language so important in the world. It would be possible to list thirty or forty great writers, many of whose names you would probably recognize; but here we can mention only a few.

Above all other writers stands William Shakespeare. Not only his countrymen but also the peoples of other nations recognize William Shakespeare as one of the greatest writers of all times. He was the leader among those who made the 16th Century the Golden Age of English literature. Oddly enough there is little known of Shakespeare's life. In his youth he was a handy-boy about a theater, occasionally taking minor acting parts. He soon learned, however, that his talent lay in writing plays. By the time he was twenty-eight, his ability as a playwright was recognized. He died when he was only fifty-two.

Though he did not have much school-ing, Shakespeare was keenly apprecia-ive of human nature. He was a close observer of his fellow men and seemed to know and understand all human feel-ings. What his fine training and experi-ence in the theater did not furnish him, his wonderful imagination did.

His play *Julius Caesar* makes the days of Rome live again for us. Listen to Antony bemoaning the murder of the great Caesar:

Friends, Romans, countrymen, lend me
  your ears;
I come to bury Caesar, not to praise him;
The evil that men do lives after them;
The good is oft interred with their
  bones. . . .

Not all of Shakespeare's plays are seri-ous or tragic. Read, for example, these lines from *As You Like It*.

All the world's a stage,
And all the men and women merely
  players.
They have their exits and their entrances,
And one man in his time plays many parts,
His acts being seven ages. At first the in-
  fant,
Mewling and puking in the nurse's arms.
And then the whining school boy — with
  his satchel
And shining morning face, creeping like a
  snail
Unwillingly to school. And then the lover,
Sighing like a furnace, with woeful ballad
Made to his mistress' eyebrow. . . .

Here are a number of quotations from his various writings. Notice how they show Shakespeare's understanding of the strength and weakness of mankind.

Cowards die many times before their
  deaths;
The valiant never taste of death but once.
                          — *Julius Caesar*

Neither a borrower nor a lender be;
For loan oft loses both itself and friend. . . .

This above all: to thine own self be true,
And it must follow, as the night the day,
Thou canst not then be false to any man.

There is nothing either good or bad, but
  thinking makes it so.

Rich gifts wax poor when givers prove unkind.
                                  — *Hamlet*

We cannot all be masters, nor all masters
Cannot be truly follow'd.

O, beware, my lord, of jealousy!
It is the green-eyed monster which doth
  mock
The meat it feeds on.
                                 — *Othello*

To business that we love we rise betime,
And go to 't with delight.
                   — *Antony and Cleopatra*

Many other writers have brought glory to the name of the British. Of the other writers who have brightened the pages of English history, we can say little here. Perhaps you have read, or your interests will lead you to read, some of the follow-ing: Chaucer's [chaw'serz] *Canterbury Tales;* Robert Burns' *The Cotter's Sat-urday Night;* Walter Scott's *Ivanhoe;* Charles Dickens' *David Copperfield;* Robert Louis Stevenson's *Treasure Is-land;* Rudyard Kipling's *The Jungle Book*. These are but a few works of the many British authors who have contrib-uted to Britain's fame.

Reynolds was a master portrait paint-er. Sir Joshua Reynolds is one of the famous English painters. He lived dur-ing the 18th Century. At the age of twenty-three Reynolds had become a portrait painter of such ability that or-ders for pictures poured in on him. One of Reynolds' pictures, "The Age of In-nocence," shows clearly how this painter was able to catch and place on canvas the spirit of childhood. Reynolds was likable and generous, and had many close friends among the writers of the day.

Brown-Robertson Co.

"THE AGE OF INNOCENCE"

Sir Joshua Reynolds painted this child's portrait. How does it compare in lifelikeness with Velazquez's portrait of the Infanta, on page 484?

The story is told of a drawing of a wall and window which Joshua, at the age of eight, had made in his Latin book. His father, not realizing what fame his son would attain, wrote under the sketch, "This is drawn by Joshua in school, out of pure idleness."

Gainsborough created "The Blue Boy." Another name of which the English may be proud is that of Thomas Gainsborough. He was a contemporary of Reynolds; that is, he lived at the same time. Gainsborough grew to great fame as a landscape and portrait painter. One of his most famous works is "The Blue Boy." Reynolds had said, "The masses of light in a picture ought to be always of warm, mellow color — yellow, red, or yellowish white; and the blue, the grey, or green colors should be kept al-

most entirely out of the masses." Gainsborough sharply disagreed. It is said he painted "The Blue Boy" to disprove Reynolds' statement. In it he skillfully blended the blue of the boy's suit, the blue sky, and the green background of the foliage and grass. A reproduction of "The Blue Boy" appears below.

Turner captured the spirit of an old man-of-war. Joseph Turner is usually considered the greatest artist of the English school of painters. He did his work in the first half of the 19th Century. His paintings were brilliantly designed and brilliantly colored. Turner loved to paint the rich, luminous colors of the setting sun as its rays reflected against the clouds. Brilliant reds, blues, and yellows are characteristic of his works. His most famous picture is "The Fighting Té-

Brown-Robertson Co.

"THE BLUE BOY"

In Gainsborough's famous painting, "The Blue Boy," the brilliant blue of the boy's suit is the most impressive detail. The sensitive face is sometimes overlooked.

méraire " [tay'may rayr']. The story is told that one day Turner was boating on the Thames River near London. A steam tug approached, towing an old fighting vessel of the English navy. The glorious days of that ship were past, and it was now being escorted to its last berth by the golden rays of the setting sun. Turner thought he saw a fitting end to the old man-of-war, so with oil colors he developed his idea on canvas.

British songs are well known in America. From the many songs which the British people sing, and by the enthusiasm of their concert audiences, we know that they love music although they themselves have had almost no great symphonic composers. In the late 16th and early 17th Centuries England had been the leading musical nation of Europe. The national anthem of the English is " God Save the King." The tune is an old, old air. The words have been in use for almost two hundred years. Other nations — Germany, Switzerland, and the United States — have put their own words to the same music. It may surprise you to learn that the national hymn, " America," is set to the same air as the British anthem, " God Save the King." As a national song the Scotch have their "Scots Wha Hae wi' Wallace Bled." The Welsh have their stirring " Men of Harlech," and the Irish lustily sing the " Wearing o' the Green."

In addition to their national hymns and songs, the British peoples have many favorite songs. These are not only the heritage of British boys and girls, but they are well known, too, by us in America. In the partial list which follows, you will probably find some old friends:

Drink to Me Only with Thine Eyes (English)
Sweet and Low (English)
Onward Christian Soldiers (English)
Comin' Thro' the Rye (Scotch)
Annie Laurie (Scotch)
Auld Lang Syne (Scotch)
All Through the Night (Welsh)
Deck the Hall (Welsh)
Believe Me, if All Those Endearing Young Charms (Irish)
Kathleen Mavourneen (Irish)
Mother Machree (Irish)

British scientists have helped to solve the mysteries of nature. You will recall that in the story of the awakening of the medieval world we spoke of the disappearance of the black magic of the medieval scientists. Francis Bacon, an Englishman of the 17th Century, was the leading scientific thinker of the late Renaissance. He was the forerunner of an astounding period of scientific progress during the 18th and 19th Centuries. The English, the Scotch, and the Irish all contributed names which stand high in the record of scientific discoveries and theories. Of the many men who could be mentioned, the following will give you a good idea of the contributions of the British to the advancement of science.

Newton saw an apple drop and began to wonder. The neighbors of Isaac Newton thought him a bit odd. He did so many things and had so many ideas which were different from those of most people. As a boy, Newton was interested in tinkering. He would build doll furniture for his sisters, make windmills, waterclocks, sundials, and the like. As he grew older his interest in mechanical contrivances increased. He began to suspect that nature had certain definite ways of acting.

The story is told that one day Newton was sitting in his garden. Some apples fell from a near-by tree. That set him pondering. Do apples drop at the same speed throughout the distance which they are falling? Does the earth attract them or do they attract the earth?

To his problem Newton applied a new kind of mathematics, called calculus, which he had invented. Finally he came to some remarkable conclusions. Scientists say that these conclusions are the greatest contribution to science ever made by any one man. Newton had discovered the laws of gravity. They tell us such things as these: a falling object gains thirty-two feet a second in speed; objects weigh slightly less at the equator than in higher latitudes because they are farther from the center of the earth at the equator.

Newton's theories made him famous even in his own day. He was a modest and retiring man who disliked publicity. He was made a knight by the king, and thus gained the title of "Sir." Though much of Newton's life falls in the 17th Century, his work added glory to the first quarter of the 18th Century. It was a good beginning to a golden age of science in the British Isles.

Faraday learned how to generate electricity. Did you ever wonder how man learned to generate electricity? Michael Faraday discovered the means. Like many another great man, Faraday came from a family in modest circumstances. His father was a blacksmith who lived near London. As a boy, Michael became an apprentice to a bookbinder. He must have been more interested in reading books than in making them. At any rate he used his spare time to read many of the scientific books which found their way into the shop of his master. A customer noticed the boy's interest in science and encouraged him to attend the lectures of one of the great scientists of the day. This scientist, Sir Humphry Davy, made Faraday his assistant. When Davy was asked later on what he considered his greatest discovery, he replied simply, "Faraday."

Once when experimenting, Faraday rotated a coil of wire between the ends of a horseshoe magnet. He noticed that a current of electricity had been set up. He had discovered how to generate electricity. The same principle that Faraday discovered makes it possible for immense power stations to produce the current used to light streets and homes, to move trains, and to turn the wheels of industry. Wherever a dynamo generates electricity or a motor revolves, the contribution of Michael Faraday is being used. Since the 19th Century when Faraday did his work, the world has almost left the age of steam power and entered an age of electricity. This remarkable change has been made possible by the discoveries of the British blacksmith's son who became a world famous scientist.

Charles Darwin wondered how living things grew. Another name which adds luster to British science is that of Charles Darwin. His life covers about the first three-quarters of the 19th Century. According to his own statement, Darwin gave no special indications of greatness as a boy. "I was considered by my masters and my father as a very ordinary boy, rather below the common standard in intellect." Charles, however, was interested in collecting shells, coins, and the many other odd things that alert boys like to get together.

When Darwin was but twenty-two he had the good fortune to go as a naturalist on a scientific expedition. He spent many years in the study of the life of the South Seas. He made interesting discoveries on the Galápagos [gah lah'pah gohs] Islands, which lie off the west coast of South America. Darwin received no pay, but he made many collections of plants and animals, and filled his notebook with descriptions of the things he saw. From his observations of nature he thought out a new theory. It concerned the way by which plants and animals have come to be what they now are. In his day this theory caused great excitement and bitter debate. Today, too, we still find Darwin's theories the sub- ject of much argument. His two best known works are: the *Origin of Species* in which he explains how new kinds of living organisms can be developed by cross-breeding and by changing their surroundings, or environment; and *The Descent of Man*.

Progress Marks the Story of the British People

The little islands off the west coast of Europe, whose inhabitants speak our language and share ancestors with a good many of us, are the seat of a government that exercises control over almost a fourth of the earth's surface. The English Channel and the seas surrounding the British Isles have made it possible for the British to develop separately from the peoples of Europe, but have not protected them in the past from invasion and occupation — by Celts from Western Europe, Romans, Anglo-Saxons, Danes, and finally, in the 11th Century, by Normans led by William the Conqueror. Out of the mingling of custom and blood, the British people as we know them have developed; and the English language, founded on the Anglo-Saxon, enriched by the Norman, with traces of the earlier Celtic and rich borrowings from other tongues, has grown into its present form.

The nation which today we know as Britain has reached its present strength and established its democratic institutions through centuries of struggle between conflicting classes and ideas. The seeking of power by different classes and groups, and the adjustment of power among these groups, is a dramatic chronicle in itself. In following this story, you have read how King Henry II heightened the king's prestige by strengthening the legal system of the nation, and laying the foundations of common law. You have read of the conflict between barons and churchmen in his reign; and of the conflict between barons and the king, which was settled when King John signed the Magna Charta, the first of the great documents that defined the rights of certain groups of people. The rights of the barons were protected by the Magna Charta. The middle classes were to win the recognition of their rights more slowly, through representation in Parliament.

Wars and violence accompanied the conflict of interests and beliefs. The Wars of the Roses were civil warfare between two families who claimed the throne. At the end of this strife, the first of the Tudor rulers came to the throne. The reign of Henry VIII, the second of the Tudors, had its share of conflict — between the crown and the Roman Catholic Church. Henry broke away from the Roman Catholic Church, and declared that the king, not the Pope, was the real head of the Church of England. Queen Elizabeth strengthened the Church of England. Her reign was marked by the defeat of Spain's

Armada; a great literary awakening climaxed by the writings of Shakespeare; and a growth of foreign commerce. The reign of the Stuart monarchs who followed the Tudors was the period of struggle between Parliament and the kings who believed in their divine right to rule alone — the period in which Charles I was deposed and beheaded, and the Puritan Cromwell made ruler. Two other great charters of human liberty came out of these stormy years — the Petition of Right and the Bill of Rights. Parliament — particularly the House of Commons — emerged as the dominant force in the government of Britain. But the struggle for power and adjustment of power was not over. Although the middle classes were represented in Parliament, the masses, largely because they were not landowners, were not represented. When membership in the House of Commons was finally broadened to represent the masses, democratic government in Britain was firmly established. It was one of the sources of strength which enabled the nation to endure, and be victorious in, the period of world wars which was to come in the 20th Century.

Another great force which had been at work in England was the Industrial Revolution, which, beginning in 1750, transformed life through the invention of machines, and the use of power. Transportation was speeded up; industry moved from the house to the factory. Manufacturers and merchants gained in power. Factory workers — including young children — labored under conditions that would seem criminal today. Organized protest by the workers, and the occasional sympathy of an exceptionally humane employer finally resulted in change. Parliament passed laws to protect the workers. Labor unions grew in strength, and the Labor Party took its place beside the other political parties in England.

While the nation was developing internally, it was developing externally into an empire. First the British had brought the Welsh and Scotch and Irish under one rule. Through later centuries, other peoples all over the world were joined to the Empire. The expansion of Great Britain was largely a result of her need to secure resources and to develop trade and was made possible by the growth of British sea power, from the days of Queen Elizabeth and the defeat of the Spanish Armada through the brilliant victories of Nelson in the Napoleonic Wars. Today the British Empire consists of the Commonwealth of Nations — Great Britain, Ireland, Canada, Australia, New Zealand, and the Union of South Africa; crown colonies such as Bermuda; other dependencies, such as India; Newfoundland, now governed by a commissioner; and mandated territory.

The nation which has spread so far geographically has reached equally far in the region of the intellect and culture. The genius of Shakespeare and Chaucer, of Sir Joshua Reynolds and Joseph Turner has enriched the literature and the painting of the world. British scientists — Francis Bacon, Newton, Faraday, and Darwin, for examples — have added brilliant scientific achievements to the long, famous chronicles of the nation to which they belonged.

SELF–TEST

Look back upon the story of the British peoples by trying this self-test.

The following is a sketch of the story of the British peoples in test form. In it you will find various kinds of statements. Some you will need to be able to recognize as either true or false; some you will need to complete; other statements you will have to arrange in proper time order; and in some you will have to decide which of several things given is correct. Do whatever the test calls for. Keep the record of your answers on a piece of paper. Do not mark the book.

1. There are a number of good reasons why we should be interested in the English, among which are their influence upon our (*a*) ——, (*b*) ——, (*c*) ——. All Englishmen could be British, but all British are not English. (T or F?) The famous saying that " the sun —— —- —— the British —— " is well illustrated by sailing westward across the Atlantic from England to ——, which is a member of the British Empire; then southwest on the Pacific to another member, the small continent of ——; then northwest up to British controlled —— with its millions of people; then up through the Red Sea and through the —— Canal, controlled by the British; into the Mediterranean Sea and out into the Atlantic again through the Strait of ——, also controlled by the British. Once the British Isles were part of the continent of Europe. (T or F?)

2. The courageous adventurers whose blood flows in the veins of an Englishman arrived in the British Isles in the following order (arrange correctly): Saxons, Celts, Romans, Normans, and Danes. The traces of Roman civilization still left in England show that the Romans with their efficient army found it a simple matter to subdue the Celtic Britons. (T or F?) The Saxons were good settlers. (T or F?) Christianity was first taught in England by ——. This was during the time of the Saxons. (T or F?) Three of the several reasons why Alfred the Great may be called great are: (*a*) ——, (*b*) ——, (*c*) ——. William the Conqueror laid the foundation of the English nation by: (*a*) adding many new words to the English language; (*b*) introducing the customs of chivalry; (*c*) bringing the small kingdoms together into a strong central government.

3. Some of the early steps in the protection of human rights, which were taken during the time of Henry II, were (*a*) ——, (*b*) ——, (*c*) ——. Another important step in the struggle for justice was the Great Charter which was forced by the barons from King —— in the year ——. It deserves to be called " great " because, among other reasons, it called upon the king to act according to ——, not his own wishes. The main reason why the power of

Parliament became great was because Parliament managed to gain control of the ——. During the four-hundred-year struggle between the English monarchs and the Parliament over the right to rule, the age-old idea of the —— —— to rule was insisted upon by such kings as —— and ——, who lost his head in the civil revolt led by —— ——, who became military dictator of England. But the English people preferred a king. (T or F?) By the end of the (14th, 16th, 17th Century) the power of Parliament had become supreme, and the English had drawn up a statement of their rights in a document known as the —— of ——. Ideas found in the Constitution of the United States can be traced back to it. (T or F?) Two of its provisions were —— and ——.

4. From the time of the coming of St. Augustine in the (Fourth, Sixth, Eighth, Tenth Century), until the time of King —— ——, England, like the rest of medieval Europe, was —— —— in its religious belief. For a time the monarch named —— defended the faith against the teaching of the German monk, ——, who had begun the religious movement known as the ——. But the king wanted to take over the church lands and taxes for himself, and he wanted to remarry; so he broke away from the —— —— ——. His daughter, Queen ——, strengthened the Church of England, which was —— in belief. The principle of religious freedom in our own Constitution can be traced back to these times in the story of England. (T or F?)

5. During the hundred years between the middle of the —— Century and the middle of the —— Century, many changes took place in the life of the peoples of the British Isles and the Continent. This series of changes is still going on. (T or F?) It is given the name of the —— ——. Names which are closely connected with the invention of the following things are: (a) steam engine, ——; (b) power loom, ——; (c) cotton gin, ——; (d) locomotive, ——; (e) dynamo, ——; (f) telegraph, ——. Inventions in this list show that these changes were going on in America also. (T or F?) Because of the changes brought about, people began to live more in —— near large —— where they worked at tending ——. The need for new markets and for raw materials has been an important reason for the growth of the British Empire. (T or F?) That Empire includes such important lands as (a) ——, (b) ——, (c) ——, (d) ——, and others. From the time of Alfred the Great, sometimes called the father of ——, down to the defeat of the Spanish ——, in the time of Queen ——, and to the present, Great Britain's —— has been an important factor in the growth of the Empire. The British Empire now includes about one-fourth of the earth's surface and one-fifth of the people of the earth. (T or F?)

6. Many able British men and women have made outstanding contributions to civilization. The names most closely connected with the following are: (1) " The Blue Boy," ——; (2) " Rich gifts wax poor when givers prove unkind . . .", ——; (3) laws of gravity, ——; (4) generating electricity, ——;

(5) *Treasure Island,*——; (6) " The Age of Innocence,"——; (7) *Origin of Species,*——; (8) *Ivanhoe,*——; (9) *The Jungle Book,*——; (10) an English song,——.

7. Study the illustrated map on the following page, and on a separate sheet of paper answer the following questions.

(*a*) What evidences do you find that early man once lived in the southern part of England? (*b*) What point in the British Isles was of great interest to ancient peoples? (*c*) On what river is London? (*d*) What natural conditions caused this part of the British Isles to become the heart of the British Empire? (*e*) Do you see any reason why the English Channel is a " choppy sea "? (*f*) Note where the Spanish Armada was defeated. Why should the English have decided to give battle to the galleons of Spain at this point? (*g*) Locate Hadrian's Wall. What people built this wall and why was it built? (*h*) What different types of vessels do you see in the waters about the British Isles? (*i*) What does each type of vessel tell you about British history or trade?

INTERESTING THINGS TO DO

Projects for the Chart Maker and Artist

1. Make a comparison chart similar to the one on pages 599–600 for the British colonial empire. Use headings such as " Location," " Size," " Peoples," " Government," " Products," etc. See encyclopedias, or *British Empire,* by Stephen Leacock.

2. Make a trade chart of the British Commonwealth of Nations that shows what the British possessions supply to the mother country and what they receive from her. See *British Empire,* by Stephen Leacock, or look up the individual dominions and colonies in an encyclopedia.

Topics for Talks

1. " Strong are the ties that bind." Imagine that you are the newly arrived American ambassador, and that you are about to make your first speech in London at a dinner given in your honor. Prepare a short after-dinner talk that will show your understanding of the British people by describing some of the many ideas and customs we have in common with them, and by expressing our appreciation for the debt our civilization owes to theirs.

2. " The rise of the factory system." Prepare a short talk in the nature of a lecture by a professor which explains the growth of the factory system in England, and describes its effects on the life of the people. See *The Industrial Revolution,* by Charles Beard, and *Story of English Life,* by A. Williams-Ellis and F. J. Fisher. Read *Hard Times,* by Charles Dickens, or *The Story of Weaving,* by Louise Lamprey.

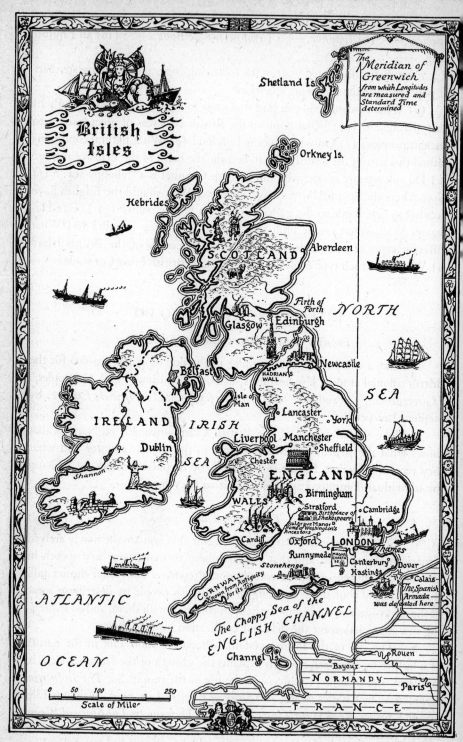

British Isles

The Meridian of Greenwich from which Longitudes are measured and Standard Time determined

Shetland Is.

Orkney Is.

Hebrides

SCOTLAND

Aberdeen

NORTH

Firth of Forth

Glasgow · Edinburgh

Belfast

Newcastle

HADRIAN'S WALL

SEA

Isle of Man

IRELAND

IRISH

Lancaster

York

Liverpool Manchester

Sheffield

Dublin

SEA

Chester

Shannon

ENGLAND

WALES

Birmingham

Stratford
Birthplace of Shakespeare
Sulgrave Manor
Home of Washington's
Ancestors

Cambridge

Cardiff

Oxford

LONDON

MAGNA CHARTA

Thames

Runnymede

Canterbury

Dover

CORNWALL
Known from Antiquity
for its Tin

Stonehenge

Hastings

Calais
The Spanish
Armada
was defeated here

ATLANTIC

The Choppy Sea of the
ENGLISH CHANNEL

Channel Is.

Rouen

OCEAN

Bayeux

NORMANDY

Paris

0 50 100   250
Scale of Miles

FRANCE

394

3. "Blood, sweat, and tears, and money besides." All these things have gone into the making of the British Empire. Choose one of the British dominions or colonies, and discuss its history, telling how the British gained possession of it, and what they had to do to develop the land or civilize its people. See *Building an Empire,* by Louise Lamprey, *British Empire,* by Stephen Leacock, or *Here Is Africa,* by E. M. Gatti and A. Gatti. See also "The British Commonwealth of Nations," by Eric Underwood, *National Geographic Magazine,* April, 1943.

4. "Cromwell and Hitler." Prepare a talk contrasting and comparing England's famous dictator of the past and the fateful German dictator of recent times. Show how these men differed in ideas and ideals, although they were somewhat alike in some of their methods of governing. See *Men of Power,* by Albert Carr.

Adventures for the Amateur Author

1. Write a letter or a few pages of a diary that reveal an experience in the life of Drake, Newton, Darwin, Shakespeare, Cecil Rhodes, or Queen Elizabeth. See books of collected biography such as *Van Loon's Lives,* by W. H. Van Loon, or *Masters of Science and Invention,* by F. L. Darrow.

2. Write a vivid description of the coronation of King George VI in 1937. Picture the pomp and ceremony of this colorful and thrilling occasion. See "A Long London Coronation Route," by M. O. Williams, *National Geographic Magazine,* May, 1937.

Ideas for Your Little Theater

1. Form a group of amateur actors to present scenes from Shakespeare's plays. Before the scenes are presented, have a master of ceremonies give a brief biography of Shakespeare, and, before each scene, the story of the play from which it is taken. Perhaps your English teacher will help you select scenes suitable for such a program.

2. Arrange a music program from records of English, Scotch, Welsh, and Irish folk songs. Also, play for the class Elgar's "Pomp and Circumstance," and explain how it carries the spirit of the public ceremonies of royalty.

Candidates for Your Album of Famous People

Cromwell, Disraeli, Queen Elizabeth, Henry II, Henry VIII, Kipling, Nelson, Pitt, Sir Joshua Reynolds, Rhodes, Sir Walter Scott, Smuts.

The candidates listed above are only a few of the famous people who have been important in the political and cultural development of the British Empire. Choose five famous people in all, either from this list, or from those mentioned elsewhere in your text, to represent the British in your Album.

INTERESTING READING ABOUT ENGLAND

Compton's Pictured Encyclopedia. " England: Motherland of the World's Greatest Empire "; and Index.

DAVIS, W. S. *Life in Elizabethan Days.* Through sport, education, superstition, costumes, and the theater, the author paints a picture of the customs and social life of Elizabethan England.

DICKENS, C. *Oliver Twist.* " ' I bought them from the man and woman I told you of, who stole them from the nurse, who stole them from the corpse.' . . ."

GUERBER, H. A. *The Story of the English.* " Elizabeth was extravagantly fond of dress and display."

KINGSLEY, CHARLES. *Westward Ho!* A story of adventure during the period of the rivalry between England and Spain.

KIPLING, RUDYARD. *Puck of Pook's Hill.* Puck, the spirit of English history, who can " think for centuries at a time," entertains two young people with his stories of how England was born.

LLEWELLYN, RICHARD. *How Green Was My Valley.* A beautifully written story of a Welsh family in a flourishing mining village of the last century.

MAJOR, CHARLES. *When Knighthood Was in Flower.* A romantic tale of the time of Henry VIII.

PYLE, HOWARD. *Men of Iron.* " A wonderful picture of the days of chivalry."

QUENNELL, M., and QUENNELL, C. H. B. *A History of Everyday Things in England.* " Wigs, long and much curled, were seen on every man."

RUGG, H. *Changing Civilizations in a Modern World.* How England Became Modern Industrial Great Britain. " She is the center of world trade and one of the most powerful empires of the earth."

——. *Changing Governments and Changing Cultures.* England's March toward Democracy. " ' Tory ' . . . had been the nickname applied to certain Irish outlaws."

SALZMAN, L. F. *England in Tudor Times.* " At the other end of the social scale were hordes of beggars, hungry and half-naked."

TAPPAN, E. M. *In the Days of Alfred the Great.* ". . . you shall be hanged like a Dane to the nearest tree."

——. *In the Days of Queen Elizabeth.* ". . . declared she to her council, ' a queen does not lend aid to rebels.' "

TICKNER, F. W. *Social and Industrial History of England.* " Wherever enclosure for sheep-farming went on, the yeoman and tenant-farmers suffered."

WILLIAMS-ELLIS, A., and FISHER, F. J. *Story of English Life.* A valuable source of information on the position of the common people in England as the nation progressed in art, science, and invention.

The World Book Encyclopedia. " England."

PART ELEVEN

THE FRENCH PEOPLE ESTABLISHED A NATION AND SPREAD THE IDEAS OF LIBERTY, EQUALITY, AND FRATERNITY

FRANCE

GERMANY

NETHERLANDS

BELGIUM

LUXEMBOURG

RUHR REGION

Brussels

Waterloo

Lille

Calais

Dover

London

Hastings

ENGLAND

North Sea

English Channel

Cherbourg

Le Havre

NORMANDY

BRITTANY

Paris

Versailles

Seine

Reims

Verdun

Meuse

Ardennes Mts.

Moselle R.

Meuse R.

Marne R.

Oise R.

SAAR

LORRAINE

ALSACE

Strasbourg

Vosges Mts.

Jura Mts.

SWITZERLAND

THE ALPS

ITALY

Rhine R.

Main R.

Orleans

Tours

Loire R.

Limoges

Bordeaux

Garonne R.

Pyrenees Mts.

SPAIN

Bay of Biscay

ATLANTIC OCEAN

Lyon

Rhône R.

Avignon

Nîmes

Marseille

Riviera

CORSICA

5°N.

10°E.

5°E.

North

100   200

200 MILES

0

So This Is France!

Fʀᴀɴᴄᴇ is known as the land of liberty, equality, and fraternity. From its location, do you see why we say that France stands at the crossroads of civilization? What neighboring countries do you think must have played an important part in the story of France? What parts of France are fairly well protected from neighboring countries by mountains and seas? Where has nature given her the least protection? What did the lack of natural barriers along this one frontier have to do with strategy in World War I and World War II?

Trace the great rivers that form the beautiful valleys of France. These valleys are fertile as well as beautiful. From the map, what way of getting food, besides farming, do you think the French people have? In southern France, on the Mediterranean, is the important port of Marseille, which was founded in ancient times by the Phoenicians. Perhaps you know of some products which the French export. In the story which follows, you will learn that other countries have imported vital ideas as well as manufactured goods and art objects from the French. You will also learn of the French people's dramatic struggle for freedom and the effect that it had on many other lands.

Chapter 1 ~ The Geography of Their Land Has Influenced the
Story of the French

The stories of America and France touch at many points. Benjamin Franklin is quoted as having said, "Every man has two mother countries: his own, and then France." Though some of us may give other lands second place in our affections, there are many reasons why Americans are interested in the story of the French people. During our Revolutionary War the gallant Frenchman, Lafayette [lah feh'et'], helped us win our independence from the British by taking part in our battles and by winning sympathy and aid from France for the American cause.

There are names of many places, from Marquette on Lake Superior to New Orleans at the mouth of the Mississippi, which remind us that a great section of what is now our country once belonged to France. Many of our Middle-Western states were carved out of the Louisiana Territory which we purchased from France at the beginning of the 19th Century. The Statue of Liberty in New York harbor was designed by a French artist, Bartholdi [bahr'tohl'dee] and given to the United States as a symbol of the ideals of freedom common to both the American and French republics.

But the tie which binds us to the French, perhaps more strongly than any other, is the part which we played in World War I and World War II. In both these wars American soldiers went to France, lived among the French people, and fought on the historic battlegrounds of that nation. Hundreds of the sons of America now lie buried in French soil.

The geography of France places her at the crossroads of Western Europe. France is larger in area than any state in our United States except Texas, and is almost as large as that state. Yet France is a remarkably small country when one considers her importance as a nation. The distance from the southernmost to the northernmost border is only about six hundred miles and from the eastern border to the shores of the Atlantic is a little over five hundred miles. But what France may lack in size has been made up in the importance of her location. She is at the crossroads of Western Europe. The traveler is likely to cross France several times as he visits Spain, Italy, Switzerland, Germany, and Belgium.

The armor of geography leaves France with but one weak spot. France is shaped roughly like a hexagon, as you can see from the map opposite page 399. Five of the six sides are formed by natural boundaries — seas, rivers, and mountains. These boundaries we might consider a geographic protection behind which the people of France have been able to develop a language, customs, and a national spirit entirely their own.

On the northwest, the narrow but rough English Channel has helped to separate the French and the British. To the west are the choppy waters of the Bay of Biscay. On the south, between France and Spain, the mighty Pyrenees form a natural fortress over nine thousand feet high and 250 miles long. Farther east the warm waters of the Mediterranean wash the coast until the border between France and Italy is reached.

There the famous Alps begin almost at the water's edge and extend northward; the mountain ridges and peaks, for the most part, form the eastern border of France. For about the last hundred miles of the eastern border the historic Rhine River forms a natural boundary.

The northeastern part of France, as you will see by the map on page 398 is naturally protected by the rough, hilly country in the region of the modern city of Verdun [ver′duɴ′]. There the earth layers slope gradually toward the interior of France, but are sharply upturned against any foreign foe who might come from the northeast. But from this point to the English Channel, France has no geographic armor. The low coastal plains which extend along the Belgian border form a smooth path into the heart of France. Invading enemies have often taken advantage of this fact. However, since natural boundaries long protected France from neighboring peoples, to so large an extent, it is possible to say that geography has helped the French to develop a distinctly separate nation.

France is a country of many rivers and canals. In France there are over four thousand miles of rivers and over three thousand miles of canals. Together these give France a network of water transportation. The long, heavily-laden canal boats being slowly drawn from lock to lock are a common sight in France.

The map at the beginning of the chapter will give you an idea of the location and length of the four most important rivers. The greatest is the Rhone, up which French and American troops drove into German-held territory in World War II. The Rhone rushes southward down its beautiful valley, passing through busy manufacturing cities and finally emptying into the Mediterranean Sea.

The other three chief rivers have their mouths on the western coast of France. The Loire [lwahr], over 625 miles in length, is the longest of all. It rises in the highlands of south-central France, and empties into the Bay of Biscay. The Garonne [gah′ron′] rises in the high Pyrenees, drains southwestern France, and empties into the large bay of the Gironde off the Bay of Biscay. Bordeaux [bohr′doh′], an important French city, is situated near the mouth of the Garonne.

But of all the great rivers, the Seine, with its tributaries, is bound up most closely with the story of France. In a graceful curve, it flows through the heart of Paris. There, in midstream, is a small island called the Cité [see′tay′], which hundreds of years ago was the original city of Paris. Though Paris is over a hundred miles from the coast and deep-draft ships cannot reach it, the Seine has made the city a river port.

Paris lies at the center of a basin — the Valley of the Seine. This valley of some fifty thousand square miles is the most fertile and best farmed region in France. From the air it gives the impression of a vast park with patches of green woodlands and neatly cultivated fields.

The Marne [mahrn] is the most important tributary of the Seine. Time and again it has served as a feudal moat for France, holding back the first rush of the invaders.

The wide coastal plain and the mild climate favor agriculture. A wide and fertile plain extends along the coast of France from the Pyrenees in the south to the boundary of the Low Countries in the north. This coastal area is a region of many small farms which are carefully worked by hardy French peasants. In recent times French farms have been able to supply the bulk of the nation's food requirements. Fruit, root crops, and cereals are raised. Conditions are particularly good for the raising of wheat, and France is the leading wheat-producing country of Western Europe. But in order to supply enough of the long loaves of coarse white bread which are a common article of food in the daily diet of a French family, some grain must still be imported. In many parts of France the fertile soil and the temperate climate nourish hundreds of vineyards, and France is one of the greatest wine-producing nations in the world.

The raising of livestock is also an important part of French farming. In fact, the average French farmer depends on the sale of animals and animal products for a large part of his cash income. Dairy cattle are raised chiefly along the coastal plain and in the northwest. The sheep-raising industry is centered in the Paris basin and in the hilly area of southeast France. Ewes' milk is used in some sections in the manufacture of cheese, such as the famous Roquefort. Great Britain is the largest market for French agricultural products, receiving from France considerable quantities of fruit, flowers, seeds, vegetables, butter, and cheese.

The seas yield resources to the French fishermen. About a hundred thousand of the French people make their living as fishermen. Small fishing boats travel to the coasts of Iceland and Newfoundland in search of the valuable cod. Also, millions of pounds of sardines, herring, and mackerel are caught. Lobsters, oysters, shrimp, and other sea delicacies are supplied to markets, not only in the towns of the coast but far into the interior of the country.

"Made in France" is considered a guarantee of quality. French industry developed in small units that concentrated on producing quality products. The rest of the world has come to expect that things made in France will be articles of both quality and beauty, for the French standards of workmanship are high. France's reputation is well established for pottery and porcelain, perfumes, textiles, ladies' fashions and cosmetics. French wines find a ready market in many foreign lands.

The textile industry in France has had a long history. In recent times the manufacturers have had to import the greater part of their raw materials, wool from Argentina and Australia, cotton from the United States, silk from China and Japan, and flax from Belgium. But French textiles are of such high quality that exports of lace, silk, carpets, flannels, and cotton materials command a high price in foreign markets.

Delicate and valuable porcelains have been made for more than two hundred years at Sèvres [sehv'r] near Paris. The well-known Haviland china industry, located at Limoges [lee'mohzh'], was founded a century ago by an American family named Haviland.

Large-scale manufacturing has developed in recent times. France has deposits of coal, of iron and other metals. Iron and steel, and various metal products have long been manufactured by the French, but these industries were greatly expanded after World War I. The war itself, with its heavy demands for large quantities of materials, was one cause of expansion in industry. The enemy occupation of the greatest manufacturing area, in northern France, made it necessary for the French to establish factories in other regions. World War I was also responsible for the increased development of electric power in France. When coal mines were ruined during the war, the French turned to "white coal," or the electric power which could be developed from the rushing waters of their mountain streams. Much of this electric power is used in industry, but still France has to import some of the coal she requires.

Another factor in increasing the total output of industry was the territory France regained from Germany at the end of World War I. Alsace-Lorraine [al′zas′ loh′rayn′], previously held by Germany, contains large iron and potash deposits, as well as textile and chemical industries.

France is an important commercial nation. The great French ports of Cher-bourg [sher′boor′], Le Havre [luh-ahv′r], Dunkirk, Bordeaux [bohr′doh′], and Marseille handle a tremendous volume of foreign trade in normal times. Foodstuffs and raw materials are imported, but France is much more nearly self-sufficient than Great Britain. In normal times exports of machinery, metal goods, and chemical products have increased. Agricultural and textile products, however, are still the most valuable items of export. Many of the goods which France exports are high quality, or luxury, goods.

Chapter 2 ~ The French Formed a Nation and Their Monarchs Became Supreme

The story of France reaches back into the dim past. Who were the first people to live in that part of Europe we now call France? The question is hard to answer. From our story of early men we know that the primitive Neanderthal Man once lived in this region, but that these people disappeared from Europe. The first permanent inhabitants of this land which is now France were Cro-Magnon men who came into Western Europe about 25,000 years ago. They were the " first settlers " and seemed to have been replaced by other peoples in France by the time written records began.

The written story of France began with Gaul. Hundreds of years before the birth of Christ a tribe of people called the Celts lived in this region. They belonged to the same group of people as the Celtic invaders of the British Isles. We have seen that about a half century before the birth of Christ, the Romans became interested in this land of the Celts, conquered the people, and began to rule their country, which they called Gaul. For over four hundred years — until the Roman Empire began to crumble in the Fifth Century — the Romans ruled the Gauls with an iron hand.

The Roman occupation of Gaul made a permanent impression on the country. The Romans built immense buildings, roads, bridges, and aqueducts, many of which were so well constructed that they are still standing. There is an aqueduct near Nîmes [neem] which once carried water to that city of Southern France. Traces of Roman laws are to be found in the French civil code of modern times.

Perhaps the greatest contribution of

the Romans to the Gauls was language. When Caesar conquered Gaul, he found the natives speaking a crude Celtic tongue. The conquering Romans, of course, spoke Latin. And during the centuries of Roman rule, Latin became the common language of Gaul, so that the Celtic language almost disappeared. Later Gaul was conquered by German invaders who brought their own language which was gradually mixed with the spoken Latin of the conquered peoples. From this combination modern French developed. This mixing of the Celtic tongue with the Latin language of the Romans explains why French is known as a Romance language, as you learned in the story of Rome. Even the beginning student of French who has studied some Latin will recognize many similar words in the two languages, such as *father: pater, père; mother: mater, mère; sister: soror, sœur; brother: frater, frère.*

When Rome weakened, barbarian tribes came into Gaul. From our stories of the Romans and the English, you will remember that in the Third Century the Roman Empire began to weaken. Gradually the German barbarian hordes from the north and east began coming into southern and western Europe to find new lands and homes. These invaders from northern Europe were glad to come into Gaul because they, themselves, were being hard pressed in their homelands by a yellow-skinned race of people from Asia called Huns.

Screen Traveler from Gendreau

IN THE HARBOR AT MARSEILLE

A small section of the harbor at Marseille, the chief commercial port of France. Not long before World War II Marseille was connected with the extensive network of waterways in France by means of a large canal through a tunnel excavated in the mountains back of the city.

Drawing by John C. Wonsetler

MIGRATING BARBARIANS

Barbarian Germanic tribes like the hardy group pictured above migrated into Gaul. They used covered wagons to transport their women and children, and all their household possessions. The long procession was protected by scouts who rode ahead, and armed guards who rode beside and behind the formation.

Three different barbarian peoples settled in Gaul. A group known as West Goths, or Visigoths, took up their homes in the south near the Pyrenees; the Burgundians settled in the beautiful valley of the Rhône River; and the most able of all the invaders, the Franks, began to spread westward from the Rhine Valley. The Gauls, whom the Romans had helped to civilize, gradually mixed with the conquering German tribes and occupied the central part of the country. The descendants of these four peoples — the Romanized Gauls, and the Germanic West Goths, Burgundians, and Franks — are the French of modern times. A picture of a band of Goths is reproduced above.

The Franks won control of Gaul and Gaul became France. It was not long before the Franks had won control of most of Gaul. By keeping in constant

touch with their people in the Rhine Valley, the Franks, unlike the other invading barbarians, were continually reinforced. They avoided being cut off and absorbed by the Gallic tribes. Largely for this reason they were able to conquer the other peoples in Gaul. From the name of the Franks, the most successful of the barbarian invaders, Gaul gradually came to be known as France.

An outstanding king of the Franks was Clovis [kloh'vis]. This name, which later was changed in form to Louis, is one which many of the kings of France have borne. Clovis made his headquarters in Paris and from there directed the conquests which made him master of an area that included almost all of what has become modern France. Clothilde [kloh'teeld'], his wife, was a Christian, and through her influence Clovis was baptized. Because their ruler had accepted the new faith, the Franks became Christians.

France became a part of the empire of Charlemagne. When Clovis died early in the Sixth Century, his kingdom was divided among his sons. The first successors of Clovis continued to conquer new lands until the territory of the Franks extended far into what is now central Germany. But the later descendants of Clovis quarreled and fought with one another. Sometimes the kingdom of the Franks was united under one ruler, and sometimes it was redivided among several heirs to the throne.

Civil wars weakened the Frankish kingdom. The authority of the king also lessened because of the transfer of power to strong nobles. The chief officers of the government were counts who represented the king in the parts into which the country was divided. These great nobles began to ignore the authority of the Frankish king. At the same time the palace officials began to take the real power out of the king's hands, leaving him little more than an empty title. As the king's prestige grew weaker, a number of the counties broke away from Frankish rule and set up their own rulers.

Finally in the middle of the Eighth Century the king's minister, Pippin, grew so powerful that he was able to sweep away the old line of kings begun by Clovis. But first he asked the permission of the Pope. This point is more important than it seems at first, for the new king thus became in theory a representative of the Church. Thereafter it became a religious duty to obey the king —an early instance of the "divine right" idea of which we heard so much in the story of the quarrel between the English kings and Parliament.

Pippin, as the new king of the Franks,

strengthened his kingdom and passed it on to his famous son Charlemagne. You will remember from the story of feudalism how well Charlemagne ruled his domains. The people who lived in France benefited by the good order Charlemagne brought to the country. France was a part, but only the western part, of his vast empire. The name of Charlemagne brings our story of France down to the early years of the Ninth Century.

Charlemagne's successors set a bad example for the jealous dukes and counts of their realms, and they began to quarrel with one another for land and power. The task of bringing all the people together into one strong nation seemed hopeless.

The Northmen invaded France. While the strong feudal nobles were fighting one another, and thus weakening and disorganizing the kingdom of the Franks, a new danger appeared. You have already read in the story of Great Britain how the Northmen raided and settled areas on the coast of England. In the latter part of the Ninth Century about twenty thousand Northmen with seven hundred ships landed on the northern shores of France and attempted to take possession of the country.

By the beginning of the 10th Century, these Northmen, or Normans, had become so strong in northern France that the French king decided it would be wise to come to terms with them. So he gave them a rich section of farming land in northwestern France which even today is called Normandy.

To the Norman chief the king gave his daughter in marriage. The chief, in turn, became a Christian and a vassal of the king of France. It was a later Norman duke who in 1066 crossed the Channel from Normandy to become William the Conqueror of England, about whom you read in the story of the British people.

During the invasions of the Northmen one of the French nobles showed himself to be a man of great courage and action. This man was Hugh Capet, duke of Paris, a feudal noble who controlled the land in the region about Paris. Because Capet had won the confidence of the people and his fellow nobles, the nobles deposed the king descended from Charlemagne, and chose Capet to be king. This new line of kings which began in the 10th Century ruled France for hundreds of years.

The king of France was king in name only. When William the Conqueror became king of England, he strengthened the feudal system and saw to it that he himself was the foremost feudal lord. Such was not the case on the Continent. The duke of Paris, who was also recognized as the king of France, was a strong feudal lord and held much of the fertile lands in the Paris basin. But there were other feudal lords holding various parts of France who considered themselves just as important as the king. Like the king, these lords had strong armies, they had vassals who were dependent upon them, and they owned vast areas of land. So for two centuries the king of France was king in little more than name.

The king of France became the real head of the nation. Gradually, however, the power of the king of France became greater than that of the other lords. There were several reasons for this change. In the first place, the practice of dividing the kingdom among the king's sons was no longer followed. Also, in the line of kings which Hugh Capet began, it happened that there was always a son to take the place of the king when he

Courtesy French Government Tourist Information Bureau

PORTE D'ORANGE, AT CARPENTRAS
IN SOUTHEASTERN FRANCE

This towered gateway is all that remains of the medieval fortifications in the old town of Carpentras. Notice the openings in the parapet at the top of the tower. Through these openings missiles were dropped upon the attackers below.

died. The first kings of the Capet line took the precaution of having the heir to the throne crowned while the old king was still alive. Thus, on the death of the old king, there could be no dispute over who should succeed to the throne. The people became accustomed to look upon the duke of Paris as the real king of France. Then, too, the Church seemed to favor the French kings against the feudal lords. The Church knew that a strong Christian king meant protection and power for its beliefs and practices.

The Crusades, which took place from the end of the 11th to the 13th Centuries, drew many of the French nobility from their feudal estates to the Holy Land. With powerful rivals out of the country, the king found his own army

MONT ST. MICHEL

On the border of Normandy stands rocky Mont St. Michel. The houses of the little town nestle between the lofty 15th Century church at the top, and the ring of ancient ramparts and towers at the base. At high tide Mont St. Michel is completely surrounded by water. At low tide it is far out in the bay in a sea of sand.

more effective. He gradually added the lands which had been ruled by other feudal lords to the royal holdings.

With trade springing up, money coming into circulation, and cities and towns gaining greater freedom, the new middle class, made up of tradesmen, businessmen, and the like, came into being. These people were not much interested in the petty quarrels for power between great feudal lords. They wanted peace and security, and they gradually came to see that these could best be given by a strong national government directed by the king of France.

For a hundred years France struggled against England for her national boundaries. The feudal lords were not the only enemies of a United France.

When William of Normandy became king of England he thereby gave the English kings who followed him a reason for claiming as their inheritance the sections of France which he had controlled. Also, by the marriage of English royalty into the families of French feudal lords, the kings of England found themselves in control of other French lands which had belonged to their French wives. At the beginning of the 12th Century, the possessions of the English crown in France included practically all the western seacoast plain from the Pyrenees north to the English Channel. The English kings held these lands as vassals of the king of France while ruling England as kings in their own right. In theory the fiefs they held were part of the French kingdom, but in practice they seemed to belong to England. The English kings, too, found it profitable to unite with the nobles of France against the one who was king of France. Thus the kings of France were faced with the double problem of conquering some of the French nobles and driving the English out of France. Fighting between the French and English kings continued at intervals throughout the 12th and 13th Centuries, until in the 14th Century what had been a series of feudal quarrels blazed up into a national war.

Many disagreements set the stage for the Hundred Years' War. The quarrel with England was many-sided. The French and the English each wanted to gain control of the fishing rights in the English Channel and the North Sea. The two nations were trade rivals as well. Flanders was at that time the greatest manufacturing center of woolen cloth, and the weaving industry depended on the importation of English wool. When the French interfered in the wool trade, the laborers and manufacturers of Flanders united with the English against the French.

Finally, by the 14th Century, the feudal system was breaking up and the kings of England and France were beginning to think of themselves as national monarchs rather than as feudal lords. Thus the old fiction that the English held their French lands as vassals no longer meant anything.

While these disagreements over the fisheries and the wool trade were developing, the last of the Capet kings died without leaving a male heir to the throne. A new king of France was chosen from another branch of the Capet family. The king of England (whose mother had been a French princess) attempted to weaken the power of the French king by putting forward his own slight claim to the throne of France. He hoped in this way to win for himself the support of some of the French nobles.

Rivalry between the French and English for territories and for trade then drove the two nations headlong into war. In history this conflict between the French and the English became known as the Hundred Years' War, because it lasted from about the middle of the 14th Century to the middle of the 15th Century. Of course there was not continuous fighting during all this time. Sometimes, between periods of actual warfare, there were long periods when the kings of the two countries were occupied in trying to raise money and to recruit armies to continue the struggle.

The Black Death invaded Europe. A twin brother of War seems to be Pestilence. Early in the Hundred Years' War a terrible epidemic of bubonic plague swept across Western Europe. By the middle of the 14th Century the epidemic, commonly called the Black Death, had reached France and England. As you read in the story of feudalism, it took its toll of life from the humble homes of the peasants and from the castle halls of the feudal nobles. So many of the laboring class died that it was difficult to get men for necessary work in the fields and shops.

Dark days for the French. The Hundred Years' War had been going very badly for the French. The King of France had recently died and the Dauphin [daw'f'n], the name the French gave to the uncrowned successor to the throne, just as the English speak of the Prince of Wales — had not yet been crowned. Furthermore the city of Reims, where the French kings had been crowned since the time of Clovis, was held by the English. In fact, the English

THE CORONATION OF THE DAUPHIN

This photograph shows a well-known painting of the coronation of the Dauphin, with Joan of Arc standing beside him. The painting is in the Pantheon, a famous public building of Paris, which has been used as a national burial place for many French notables.

had conquered all the northern part of the country and had even occupied Paris. The weak Dauphin fled south for safety. His military leaders were poor and he was not sure whether money and men could be obtained to expel the English.

A peasant girl led the French armies to victory. It was not a brilliant general nor a courageous king who changed the course of events. It was Joan of Arc, a simple peasant girl. Though still in her teens, Joan felt sure that she could aid the cause of France. She believed that she had the power to help the French Dauphin become recognized as king. Her self-confidence did not come alone from her courage and patriotism; it sprang mainly from her religious faith. Joan of Arc, or Jeanne d'Arc [zhahn dark] as the French call her, told of having visions in which she was commanded to help the Dauphin and to deliver France from her enemies. These visions promised her the help of the saints in her great task.

Joan's faith in the visions and "voices" that advised her was very strong. After much difficulty she received permission to speak with the Dauphin. She implored the uncrowned king to allow her to lead a force against the English who at the time were trying to capture the city of Orleans [or'leh' ahn'] just south of Paris. The timid Dauphin finally gave his consent.

Mounted on a horse and wearing the dress of a feudal page, Joan led the French soldiers against the English. The sight of this young French girl courageously leading an army against the invaders kindled the spirit of the French. They fought as soldiers had seldom fought before, and Orleans was saved.

The English were struck with awe. They looked upon Joan as a witch. Cities which had sided with the English threw

THE CATHEDRAL AT REIMS

The famous cathedral, where French kings were crowned, is an outstanding example of the splendor of medieval architecture.

open their gates to the Maid of Orleans. Finally, on the march northward, the city of Reims was taken, and there, with Joan standing by him, the Dauphin was crowned as the King of France. This coronation ceremony is the subject of the painting reproduced on page 410.

With the crowning of the king, Joan felt that her services should be at an end. But since the weak, ease-loving king did little to follow up the victories, Joan continued to resist the English. Within a few months she was taken prisoner.

The English were anxious to try her for heresy. The trial was held in the city of Rouen [rwahɴ] on the river Seine. Joan was condemned to death. In the Old Market Square of Rouen she was chained to a stake. Fuel was piled high about her and the torch applied. According to legend, one of the English soldiers present who had come to rejoice at the death of this enemy was heard to cry out, " We are lost — we have burned a saint! "

Indeed, the English cause in France was lost. During the next few years the French made slow but steady progress in defeating the English invaders, until finally only Calais [ka'lay'] was left in English hands. The faith of Joan of Arc had aroused the patriotism of her countrymen, and had stimulated the growth of a national feeling. Today in France the spirit of Joan of Arc still lives. In the present century, she has been officially declared a saint by the Church of her faith.

The power of the French monarch became supreme. At the close of the Hundred Years' War, the king was the leading feudal lord and also the master of all France. In the two centuries that followed the Hundred Years' War the king's power increased until he became a supreme and absolute monarch.

A number of changing conditions favored this growth of the royal power. In the first place, the kings gradually broke up the remaining powerful dukedoms or absorbed them. Also, the kings had acquired the right to tax people throughout the kingdom and so could maintain a national army, without depending on the vassal service of the nobles. As long as the nobles continued to enjoy their social privileges, however, they made no strong opposition to the increased strength of the king. Occasional rebellions were put down by force or turned aside by bribery. The Estates-General, or legislative parliament, was practically suspended.

During these centuries following the Hundred Years' War, new and unpopular taxes were levied against the people. But these common people, called the Third Estate, were not united or organized and so their resentment had little effect. If the nobility and the Third Estate had joined forces, their combined opposition would have been a serious threat to the growth of the king's power. No such alliance came about, however, for so long as the nobles retained their feudal powers, the middle class felt it necessary to support the king who was the only power that could keep peace and order. Later, when the nobles became mere courtiers, they in turn supported the king and depended on him to preserve their social privileges against the demands of the rising middle class. Like some of the monarchs of England, the French kings claimed to rule by " divine right." They considered that they themselves were the state. They believed that there was no national will except as expressed in their own wishes.

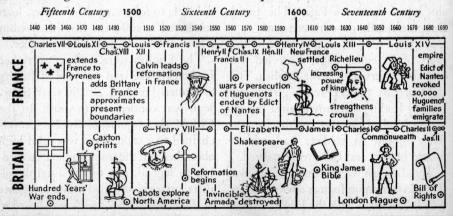

Louis XIV became the grand monarch of France. About the middle of the 17th Century, a five-year-old lad inherited the French throne. He was destined to become one of the most interesting kings that ever ruled any nation. His reign of seventy-two years is the longest of any monarch in European history. His rule and personality had a marked effect on his times in France and other nations.

Louis XIV was an absolute, or all-powerful, ruler who, like the English king, James I, believed in his divine right to rule. The nobles, who had been largely occupied with defeating the will of the king, were now content to live at the palace in his favor. If Hugh Capet, the feudal king of France who lived some seven hundred years before this time, could have seen the pomp of Louis XIV he would have been amazed. He would have seen the nobles handing the king his clothes when he arose in the morning and standing respectfully by when the monarch was at his meals. He would have seen these nobles forming an appreciative audience for the many great artists and writers whom Louis XIV brought to this court.

True, the French king had become powerful, and had brought about the unity of the nation. But the extravagance and selfishness of divine-right

FASHIONS AT THE COURT OF LOUIS XIV
The humorous drawing above exaggerates the elaborate hair styles of that period.

monarchs were bound finally to lead to dissatisfaction and rebellion in France as they had in England.

Louis XIV made French language and French fashions popular in European courts. Louis XIV and his court became the wonder of Europe. French manners and dress were imitated in the courts of other nations. The French language became the fashionable tongue of polite society and the official language of many royal courts of Europe. Following the example of Louis XIV, the rulers of other nations began to patronize and en-

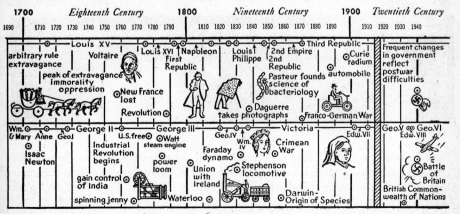

| 1700 | *Eighteenth Century* | 1800 | *Nineteenth Century* | 1900 | *Twentieth Century* |

courage writers and artists. A few rulers even tried to duplicate the splendor of the French court.

The dress and the customs of the upper classes were dictated by this king. His wars upset the peace of Europe. The interest which he showed in art, architecture, and the other fine arts has caused the French to refer to his time as the Grand Century. Louis XIV himself came to be known as the Grand Monarch, the Sun-King.

The palace of Versailles reflected the grandeur of the court of Louis XIV. Louis XIV did not like the narrow streets and unruly mobs of Paris. He decided to have a magnificent royal residence built about twelve miles southwest of Paris on a sandy and marshy plateau where his father had often hunted. The

Palace of Versailles [ver'sah'ee] and the park surrounding it show us to what length this French king went to surround his court with elegance and splendor. The photograph below shows only a small part of the beautifully landscaped gardens.

The foremost architects and artists were commanded to build and decorate the palace and the grounds of Versailles. In the hundreds of rooms ten thousand people could live comfortably. The stables could house twenty-five hundred horses. A beautiful green lawn swept down from the palace to a grand canal. Shrubs, trees, and flower beds were laid out in extensive geometric patterns, and hundreds of fountains and beautiful pieces of marble statuary decorated the gardens.

Culver Service

THE PALACE OF VERSAILLES

The fabulous cost of the Palace of Versailles, with its charming gardens, innumerable fountains, and smooth green lawn, increased the already heavy burden of taxes laid upon the poor French peasants. The lawn pictured here is called the *Tapis Vert,* or " green carpet."

Though Versailles was a dreamland for Louis XIV and the men and women of his court, it meant a nightmare of suffering and taxation for the common people. Thousands of peasants and soldiers were forced to work without pay. Quite a few were killed in the process of constructing the buildings. The extravagant monarch is said to have destroyed the records showing how much had been spent, but it is probable that the royal residence cost the people of France about a hundred million dollars.

There are few spots in Europe more steeped in historic interest than Versailles. In the Hall of Mirrors, oddly enough, more than two centuries later the modern German Empire began. In that same immense hall with its polished floor and rows of mirrors, the peace treaty of World War I was signed.

Though the extravagance of the royalty at home was a serious menace, the brilliancy and the military power of the French in the 17th Century were well known. France was respected as a world power. She was a feared rival of the English. Her aid, in the form of money and arms to the new American republic was a decisive factor in the Revolutionary War. Her traders and missionaries had made their influence felt in the New World.

The costly grandeur of Versailles was, however, only a veneer of elegance covering the hardship and poverty endured by the majority of the people. The oppression they suffered and the rebellious feelings it aroused led to a bloody revolution that changed the entire course of the story of France and affected other countries as well.

Chapter 3 ~ The Spirit of France Broke Forth in Revolution and the People Struggled for Liberty

The lot of the French people was hard. Abraham Lincoln, who was famous for his common-sense wisdom, is reported to have said, "You may fool all of the people some of the time, and some of the people all of the time, but you cannot fool all of the people all of the time." An idea such as this never seemed to have occurred to Louis XIV or to the two spendthrift monarchs who came after him. In France, in the middle of the 18th Century, neither the king and nobles, nor the higher churchmen bothered much about the rights of the common

people. They thoughtlessly enjoyed their pleasures and privileges while the common people bore the burden.

French peasants lived in much the same way as the poor peasants in the story of the feudal world. They still paid many of the dues of feudal times to the nobles who owned their lands. Furthermore, many payments had to be made to the Church and to the tax collectors of the king. The peasants could not even kill the rabbits or birds which might be eating their crops, for these only the lords could hunt. If a party of nobles should destroy a peasant's crops while fox-hunting in his fields, all the humble peasant could do would be to doff his cap and hold his tongue.

The common people of the towns, businessmen, tradesmen, and craftsmen, also had cause to complain bitterly. If they wished to sell their goods at a fair or market, they often found that a tax for the privilege had to be paid to some noble. If they wished to send their goods to other parts of France, they had to face toll charges at many bridges. The king's tax collector watched every growth in business with a sharp eye and asked for more money on every pretext. The Church, too, expected and received its share. Despite all this, however, the upper middle class was becoming wealthy and well educated, and as a result was becoming more aware of its grievances.

Louis XIV gave France glory — at a price. Louis XIV had been extravagant in his life at Versailles, yet he had some claim to consideration. He had provided France with a strong and effective central government.

In his wars with foreign nations Louis XIV had been successful also. Such successes, of course, pleased the French people and strengthened the position of France as a nation.

In the 17th Century such hardy French explorers as Champlain, Marquette, Joliet, and La Salle had given France claim to much of the New World. The French were early explorers of our great Mississippi Valley. They had claimed the whole of that region for France and had named it Louisiana in honor of their king, Louis XIV.

Conditions grew worse under later kings. The two monarchs who followed Louis XIV were chiefly interested in their own selfish pleasures and glory.

The court at Versailles became increasingly corrupt. Wicked men and women bought favors of the kings. The political enemies of the king were condemned without a chance for a fair trial and thrown into the dungeons of that famous prison-fort in Paris, the Bastille [bas'teel']. There they were often forgotten and left to die. The bitterness of the common people continued to increase.

The next king, Louis XV, paid little attention to the French colonies which had been established in America. When war came with England, it was therefore not long before that country was able to win the French holdings in what is now Canada. But Canada was not the only loss in the time of Louis XV. Like several other European nations, France had made some successful settlements in India, which was a source of raw materials and a promising market for European merchants. Here again the English and the French clashed. Since Louis XV was not interested, the French soon lost their foothold in India as they had in Canada.

When the American Colonies revolted against England in 1776, Louis XVI, who had recently become king, had an opportunity to strike back against the English. He listened willingly to the arguments of Benjamin Franklin that France should aid the colonies. The American Revolution cost France two and a half million dollars.

The extravagance of the king and the court at Versailles continued to increase. The burden was more than the French people could bear. The nation was on the verge of bankruptcy. Louis XVI ordered his officials to raise more and more money. When they could not raise enough money to please him, he dismissed them and appointed others.

Able French thinkers championed the cause of justice. The nobles in France were quite satisfied with their special privileges such as exemption from taxation, and did not want to see conditions changed. But during the 18th Century there were a number of keen, critical Frenchmen who did voice the cause of the common man. The writings of these French reformers, aimed at the injustices of the times, did much to stir the people to action.

Voltaire ridiculed the established order of things. One of these men was Voltaire [vohl'tayr']. With keen mind and quick wit he heaped ridicule upon the narrow-mindedness of the nobility and the clergy. Voltaire was twice made a political prisoner in the Bastille, yet he was so clever that even royalty entertained him. Voltaire took part with other reformers of the 18th Century in writing a series of books called the *Encyclopedia*. In this work the reformers attacked the old beliefs concerning Church and State and explained the scientific ideas of the Renaissance. Naturally the upper classes looked upon Voltaire as a radical.

Here are a few lines from one of Voltaire's letters. They will give you an idea of how he used words to scorn the conditions of his times.

. . . I agree with you that it is somewhat a reflection on human nature that money accomplishes everything and merit nothing: that the real workers behind the scenes have hardly a modest subsistence, while certain selected personages flaunt on the stage: that fools are exalted to the skies, and genius is in the gutter. . . .

It is sad to see . . . those who toil, in poverty, and those who produce nothing, in luxury: great proprietors who claim the very birds that fly and the fish that swim: trembling vassals who do not dare to free their houses from the wild boar that devours them: fanatics who want to burn everyone who does not pray to God after their own fashion: violence in high places which engenders violence in the people: might making right not only amongst nations but amongst individuals.

Rousseau claimed that government is based upon the consent of the governed. Another reformer whose writings stirred the French people was Jean Jacques Rousseau [roo'soh']. In *The Social Contract*, Rousseau attacked the right of kings to rule without the consent of the people they governed. " Man," he said, " is born free and yet is now everywhere in chains. One man believes himself the master of others and yet is after all more of a slave than they." He then went on to say that men were born to be good and happy and that by the selfishness of kings and politicians they were made wicked and miserable. The people, he claimed, had a right to decide for themselves how they were to be governed.

The stage was set for revolution. The king, Louis XVI, needed still more money. His officials were no longer able to wring it from his overburdened subjects since they could not tax the nobles or the clergy. So the king was forced to call a meeting of the Estates-General, the legislative parliament, which had not met for years. This assembly was made up of members of the upper classes — the nobility and the clergy — and members from the Third Estate, or middle class.

When the Estates-General met at Versailles, the Third Estate, who had as many numbers as the other two put together, wanted to have the three Estates meet as one body and vote as individuals. When the king ordered them to meet in separate Estates, each Estate casting a single vote, the members of the Third Estate refused, knowing that the first two Estates would outvote them.

The Estates-General declared that the king must not levy any more taxes without its consent. This made Louis XVI so angry that he ordered his soldiers to prevent a further meeting in the palace. The members of the Third Estate were determined and held their next session where they would not be disturbed. They met in an indoor tennis court in Versailles. There they took the name National Assembly and agreed by oath not to adjourn until they had given France a constitution. Louis finally agreed and ordered the three Estates to meet together as a National Assembly. The days of divine-right monarchy in France were almost over; the power of Louis XVI was crumbling.

July 14 became the French Independence Day. The people of France were wrought up. They were disgusted with the king and knew that their only hope for equal rights lay in overthrowing the old order of things. Throughout the country, feudal castles were attacked and burned. In the towns, angry mobs took matters into their own hands. In Paris, the half-starved workmen and shopkeepers armed themselves. On July 14, 1789, the mobs stormed and took the Bastille, that grim fortress which to them seemed a symbol of the oppression they had suffered for so many years. Ever since that day, July 14 has been the French national holiday. The motto " Liberty, Equality, Fraternity " became the watchword of the Revolution, and in the years following it became the custom in France to inscribe these words on public buildings. (*A Tale of Two Cities,* by Charles Dickens, the English novelist, gives us a vivid, though fictional, description of these days.)

The monarchy was overthrown. After two years of work the National Assembly finally gave France a consti-

tution calling for an elected Legislative Assembly, and with the king acting as chief executive. Had Louis XVI and his queen, Marie Antoinette, been wise they might have continued to rule under this constitution. Instead, Louis intrigued with the nobles who had left the country and was proved to be in secret alliance with the other kings who wanted to suppress the Revolution for fear it would spread to their lands. The Legislative Assembly, as the new legislature was called, then proclaimed that the king was no longer to rule. They ordered a National Convention to be elected for the purpose of setting up a new government and a new constitution.

When the National Convention met, their first act was to agree in the abolishing of the monarchy. Although the members of the Convention had many differences of opinion, they were all republicans, that is, against the monarchy. Louis XVI was summoned for trial, and condemned to death on the guillotine. Marie Antoinette was executed a few months later.

The execution of the king greatly increased the indignation of the other kings of Europe, who were fearful lest the revolutionary movement spread and endanger their thrones as well. Foreign armies from many lands began to march against France. This stirred the French to a new patriotism, and republican armies were quickly raised for the defense of the nation. At this time a young French army captain Rouget de l'Isle [roo'jhay' duh leel'], composed a stirring marching song which was caught up and made popular by the lusty voices of the young republican volunteers as they made their way to Paris. This song, the " Marseillaise " [mahr'say'yaiz'], has become the national song of France.

Under the stress of a defensive war the

Brown Brothers

STORMING OF THE BASTILLE

The storming of the old prison-fortress, the Bastille, on July 14, 1789, marked the beginning of mob rule in revolutionary Paris. Since that year, July 14 has been Independence Day in France.

leaders of the Convention voted themselves dictatorial powers to organize resistance. At the same time, to prevent counter-revolution they opened a Reign of Terror against all suspected of sympathizing with the old system. The new government was ruthless but efficient, and it managed to hold off the invading armies.

The people grew sick of bloodshed. Revolts throughout France were at last ruthlessly crushed. The horrible Reign of Terror that had taken so many lives had almost burned itself out. France was to be a republic, and the National Convention had nearly completed drawing up the new constitution that provided for a new legislature, and also an executive body of five men called the Directory. But those in favor of restoring the monarchy organized a rebellion and marched against the Convention.

Napoleon helped establish the authority of the government. The task of holding off the mob and protecting the Convention was entrusted to a young officer named Napoleon Bonaparte. When the rioting mob appeared, Napoleon dispersed them with a volley of grapeshot from his cannon. Many were killed, and the others fled. This harsh treatment of the Paris mobs taught them a lesson: violence and rioting were no longer to be tolerated. The authority of the government had made itself felt.

Napoleon rose to power under the Directory. The new government under the Directory turned its attention to the foreign armies attempting to invade France. The republican armies had won a number of victories against the invaders while the Revolution within France was still in progress but there was still trouble. Great Britain and Austria were the chief remaining enemies of the Republic at this time. The Directory planned a widespread campaign against the Austrians. As a reward for his action in defending the Convention, Napoleon was made a general and given command of a small army to carry out a minor part of the Austrian campaign by attacking the Austrians in Italy.

General Bonaparte directed his small force with such military skill that he was completely victorious. His brilliant campaign in Italy forced the Austrians to make peace with France, and also established French influence in much of northern Italy. Napoleon's first success was followed by a defeat in a campaign against the English in Egypt. But in spite of this setback, when he returned to Paris, Napoleon was greeted with enthusiasm by the people as a national hero.

The new government of France, under the Directory, had proved corrupt and inefficient, and had not been faring well. So in the last year of the 18th Century, Napoleon overthrew the Directory and made himself First Consul of the French Republic. Already popular with the French people, he suppressed with a strong hand small rebellions within France. Then he turned to the French frontiers and cleared them of foreign enemies.

Napoleon made himself emperor. In less than five years after he had become First Consul of the Republic, at the age of thirty-five, Napoleon Bonaparte stood in the famous cathedral of Notre Dame in Paris. There he had come to be crowned emperor. Seizing the crown from the hands of the Pope, he placed it upon his own head and became "Napoleon I, Emperor of the French." "Liberty" went into an eclipse. France was to feel again the hand of an organizer such as she had not known since the days when France was Gaul and the organizing hand was that of Julius Caesar, the conqueror.

Napoleon, the master of men. Napoleon Bonaparte was not a native Frenchman. He was born on the island of Corsica [kohr'si kuh] which lies just off the southern coast of France in the Mediterranean. In a crowd there would have been reasons for overlooking Napoleon. He was short, only five feet and one inch in height, and of sallow complexion. But Napoleon had matchless ability to inspire others with faith in himself. He believed so thoroughly in his own superiority that he made others believe in it also, as other dictators have done in more recent times. Once he said of himself, "I am the child of destiny. . . ." And again, ". . . I began to make mistakes only when I listened to advisers."

Once Napoleon had decided upon a course of action he let nothing stand in his way. Those who had helped him he rewarded with high positions and other honors. To his enemies and those who were of no use to him he was heartless. In order to strengthen his own position, he placed members of his family and favorite military leaders at the heads of the states which he had conquered.

Napoleon, the soldier. Napoleon is most famous as a great military commander. His name was feared by all the monarchs of Europe. The rulers of other nations were eager to punish the French for revolting and for beheading their king, Louis XVI. At various times Napoleon's Grand Army had to face the combined forces of many enemy nations. But Napoleon was usually the victor. He freed France from invaders, and then he set out to conquer all those who had opposed him: Spain, the Italian States, Switzerland, Austria and the Germanic States, Russia, Great Britain, and the Netherlands. His ideal was to bring all of Europe under one emperor — himself — with his friends set up as kings in the various states of the empire. Napoleon's success was with land forces. England, his greatest enemy, he could not attack successfully because of her control of the seas. In the end, his widespread conquests were Napoleon's undoing, for he had conquered more than he could hold.

Napoleon, the statesman. Napoleon was interested in improving the land he ruled. Like the Roman emperors, he constructed roads and other public works. Buildings and triumphal arches were erected to commemorate the victories of his armies. The most famous of the arches is the Arc de Triomphe [ahrk' duh tree'ohnf'] which towers 165 feet above one of the prominent squares of Paris. Today it shelters the grave of the Unknown Soldier of France of World War I.

Napoleon also set legal minds at work collecting and rearranging the laws as well as improving outworn statutes. A group of laws known as the Code of Napoleon resulted. This code became the model for legal systems in other countries of Europe and is the basis of modern French law. In the constitutions of some of our states it is possible to find traces of the Code Napoleon, for the Louisiana Territory sold to the United States by Napoleon was formerly part of the French Empire.

Napoleon was responsible for many other things that show he was a statesman as well as a soldier. During the Revolution the Church had been frequently scoffed at. Napoleon reached an agreement with the Pope which helped the Church again to carry on its work. He also reorganized the school system of France. It is interesting to note that Napoleon required that loyalty to the emperor be taught to children in the schools.

Napoleon seemed to realize that the spirit of the French would thrive on glory and honor. He founded the famous Legion of Honor to which are still elected men and women who have done something outstanding in war or in peace. Many Frenchmen wear the little red ribbon of a member of the Legion of Honor, showing that they have achieved something unusual of which France is proud.

Napoleon met his Waterloo. The tide in Napoleon's affairs turned against him at last. As another ambitious dictator was to do almost a century and a half later, Napoleon invaded Russia. Although his armies managed to reach Moscow, the Russian winter, the length of the supply line, and the resistance of the Russians forced Napoleon to retreat from Moscow in one of history's most disastrous routs.

The next year, combined armies of the nations allied against Napoleon defeated him in Europe. He was sent to the island of Elba, off the coast of Italy, as a prisoner, and a king was again placed on the throne of France. But Napoleon escaped to Marseille, in southern France. He made a triumphal march to Paris. When the soldiers who had been sent by the king to stop Napoleon again saw their " Little Corporal," as Napoleon's men affectionately called him, tears came to their eyes. They begged to be forgiven, and shouted, " Vive L'Empereur! " (" Long live the Emper-

NAPOLEON ON THE "BELLEROPHON"

In 1815 Napoleon, on his way to permanent exile at St. Helena, gazed sadly at the disappearing coast of France from the deck of the English ship "Bellerophon."

or! ") Under the spell of Napoleon's personality they were ready to fight again under the tricolor — the banner of the Revolution and Napoleon.

Napoleon quickly raised an army and met the allied forces of England, Holland, and the German states at Waterloo. There after a hard-fought and bloody battle he was at length defeated. His power was forever crushed and the old line of kings was again placed on the throne of France. Napoleon threw himself on the mercy of his most bitter enemies, the English, and was exiled to the faraway island of St. Helena [heh-lee'nuh] in the South Atlantic, where he died six years later.

Napoleon I became a glowing legend. To many of the French, the name of Napoleon has become more glorious with the passing years. His deeds, like those of Joan of Arc, have become a patriotic legend. Forgotten are the thou-

sands of men whose lives he unhesitatingly sacrificed in his wars for more power; forgotten are his selfish ambitions. To many the name of Napoleon has come to stand for the ideals of the Revolution, for law and order at home, and for power and respect among foreign nations.

There is, however, another side to the story. In his *Outline of History* the modern English writer, H. G. Wells, gives us his opinion of Napoleon:

The figure he makes in history is one of almost incredible self-conceit, of vanity, greed, and cunning, of callous contempt and disregard of all who trusted him, and of a grandiose aping of Caesar, Alexander, and Charlemagne which would be purely comic if it were not caked over with human blood.

The Congress of Vienna sowed the seeds for future trouble. With the final banishment of Napoleon, representatives of the great powers who had defeated him met at Vienna to rearrange the boundaries of the European nations. At first they proposed only to re-establish the old order as it had been before the French Revolution. But the victorious nations expected to be rewarded with grants of territory for their aid in the defeat of Napoleon. And, one and all, they were hostile to France. Naturally not everyone could be pleased. The growing spirit of nationalism was completely ignored in the attempt to preserve a balance of power among the great nations.

The decisions which were reached at Vienna gave weary Europe a few years of peace, but they also laid the foundations for much future discord. In later chapters you will read of the effect of the decisions of Vienna on the stories of other nations. As far as France was concerned, all of Napoleon's conquests were lost to her, and her boundaries were fixed nearly the same as they are today.

New ideas and ideals continued to live. The Congress of Vienna had favored the restoration of the old monarchies and the absolute power of the kings over the people. It seemed as though the Third Estate in Europe had made no advance in their struggle for liberty. But this was not entirely true. In France, Napoleon had adopted and confirmed many of the social gains of the Revolution and these remained. Napoleon's soldiers had taken the ideas of the Revolution with them into many lands. Though their leader was an emperor, the soldiers did not forget the motto of the Revolution — " Liberty, Equality, Fraternity." In many countries people cherished a dream of these ideals of justice and equality. The restoration of the old order in Europe was not destined to last for many years.

The French people continued to strive for the right to govern themselves. You will remember that the Englishmen wanted their rights and also their kings. Not so the French after Napoleon's time. About the middle of the 19th Century the people revolted against the monarchy which had been re-established after the defeat of Napoleon. They formed the Second Republic, and elected Louis Napoleon, a nephew of Napoleon I, as president. But Louis Napoleon clearly remembered the career of his uncle, and the presidency seemed only a stepping-stone to him. He tried to revive the glory which France had known under Napoleon Bonaparte. Louis Napoleon was able to change the Second Republic into the Second Empire with himself as emperor. He took the title of Napoleon III. (Napoleon I had a son who would have become Napoleon II if fate had allowed.) But it was too late to attempt to revive the glorious days of the empire. Napoleon III did not have the ability of his great relative and, moreover, the French had become keenly interested in liberty and suspicious of monarchs.

The Franco-Prussian War. In 1870 under Napoleon III France was crushingly defeated by Germany in a short war that had two far-reaching results. It completed the unification of all the German states under one ruler and it increased the bitter feeling between the French and the Germans. To the French, one of the most objectionable features of the peace treaty that concluded this Franco-Prussian War was the loss of a part of her territory called Alsace-Lorraine. The treaty also forced them to pay a huge sum of money as indemnity to the Germans. The bad feeling aroused by this treaty of 1870 was still strong nearly a half century later, so that the

NAPOLEON III AND BISMARCK

The Germans under Bismarck defeated Napoleon III and his army in 1870. Notice the victorious and arrogant posture of the German leader. The carriage in the background is ready to carry Napoleon III as a prisoner into Germany.

Alsace-Lorraine question became one of the crucial issues of World War I.

France under the Third Republic. The National Assembly, which had been elected by the people to make peace with Germany, also reorganized the national government. The Third Republic was formed, and it continued in existence without interruption until World War II. In this republic the French president was elected to the position by the two houses of the legislature for a seven-year term. As the head of the nation, he had much less power than the president of our own country. In fact the premier, who is chosen from the majority party in the French legislature, was the most powerful person in the government. The legislature itself was elected by the peo-

ple, and divided into two houses called the Senate and the Chamber of Deputies, somewhat like the Congress of the United States.

The Third Republic helped France develop as a modern nation. With their new government firmly established, in the latter part of the 19th Century the French turned their attention to other improvements. The army and navy were reorganized and expanded. New laws were passed separating the church and state, and extending the public-school system. A program of public works was also undertaken; the government supported the building and improving of roads, railways, canals, and harbors.

France enlarged her colonial empire. During the middle of the 19th Century

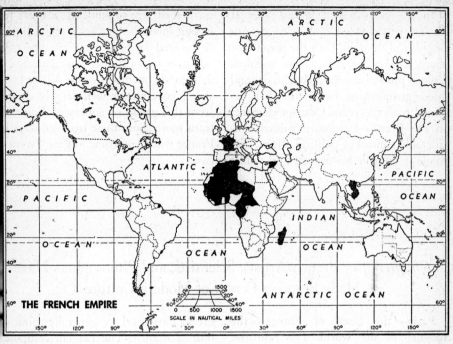

THE FRENCH EMPIRE IN 1939

the French had gained a firm foothold in the African colony of Algeria, but little had been done to develop this territory. In the latter part of the 19th Century, the Third Republic turned its energies toward empire-building on a large scale. Almost all the northwestern part of the North African continent was added to the French possessions. This gave France an African empire many times her own size. The exports and imports of the French African colonies were worth millions of dollars, and trade between the colonies and the homeland helped France to prosper. The French also gained control of a large territory formerly called Indo-China in southern Asia. At the end of World War I France regained Alsace-Lorraine from Germany, and added more territory in Africa to her empire. On the map of the Empire, shown above, notice the French territory in Africa.

The French people in the 20th Century. During most of the history of the Third Republic, the middle class, or bourgeoisie, had the most influence in the government of France. They were democratic and nationalistic in their ideals; but in their desire for national prosperity they paid considerable attention to the wishes of the bankers and capitalists. The foreign policy of France in the 20th Century was influenced by two strong forces — nationalism and imperialism.

After World War I, France, like Belgium, spent a number of years rebuilding her towns, and settling the financial problems that resulted from the war. Since the Germans failed to pay their war debt to France, the cost of reconstruction, added to the French war debt itself, involved the French in serious financial difficulties for a number of years. Riots and political scandals followed.

In the years before World War II France was divided into many groups of political thought, with the result that there was no unified public opinion. French public interest in civil affairs and good government had somewhat declined with the years. Corrupt elements in the French legislature gained considerable control of political affairs, and made it difficult for earnest and public

spirited citizens to guide the country for its best interests. One large political party favored keeping peace at any cost. After the fall of France before the Nazis in 1940, the members of the Vichy [vee' shee'] government were largely chosen from this group of appeasers. You will learn more about these troubled days in France when you come to Part Twenty-two.

Chapter 4 ~ French Artists, Scientists, and Philosophers Have Made France a Center of Modern Culture

Paris — the heart of France — the magnet of the world. For centuries Paris has been unique among the great cities of the world. Not only have its beauty and gaiety charmed thousands of tourists; its theaters, museums, opera houses, and universities have attracted many learned people. Many of the finest art treasures of the world have been brought to the museums of Paris. Her universities have been centers of learning for centuries. For these reasons scientists, musicians, artists, and scholars have come to Paris from many lands. There they have found sympathetic co-workers. Many of these foreigners have regarded France as their intellectual home, and their discoveries and achievements have come to be thought of as French.

In this chapter you will read of Madame Curie [kyoo'ree'], who was born in Poland, but brought glory to France. The great pianist and composer, Frédéric Chopin [fray'day reek' shoh'paɴ], was born in Poland also. But Chopin, like Madame Curie, spent most of his

life in Paris, and we generally think of him as French. The Belgian composer and organist César Franck [say'zahr' frahnk], became so completely identified with France that he is considered the father of modern French music. His compositions are played by orchestras of many countries, particularly his "Symphony in D Minor." Van Gogh [vahn kohk], the modern Dutch painter, did much of his work in France.

Thus France has made many contributions to civilization through the work of her adopted sons and daughters. And of course, French men and women themselves have added to the glory of their country and the good of the world by their work in science, literature, art, and music.

Pasteur, the scientist, discovered how certain diseases may be conquered. One July day about sixty years ago a frantic mother arrived in Paris with her little son, Joseph Meister [mai'st'r]. The lad had been viciously attacked and bitten by a mad dog. In those days, to be bitten by a mad dog meant almost certain death n the convulsions of hydrophobia, or abies. Joseph's mother was urged to ake the boy to Paris, where there was a cientist who had successfully experinented with this disease in animals.

This scientist was Louis Pasteur [pas′ er′], who had discovered that some dis-ases are caused by a tiny germ which annot be seen by the naked eye. He had liscovered also that certain diseases ould be prevented by injections of a erum made from an animal which already had the disease. Such a serum is alled an antitoxin.

The sight of little Joseph Meister tirred Pasteur deeply. Yet with his usual aution and fairness he sought the advice of his fellow-scientists. Although ll of Pasteur's experiments had been vith animals, the scientists agreed that ′asteur's serum treatment was the hild's only chance. Carefully Pasteur ›repared the solutions himself and tried hem out on rabbits to test the strength. Twelve times over a period of ten days oseph was inoculated. All went well vith the boy. Joseph Meister continued o improve, and finally he was able to eturn to his home well and happy. In ′asteur's own words, "one of the great nedical facts of the century" had been stablished. Hydrophobia had been pre-ented in a human being. It had been hown that disease germs could be suc-essfully fought by this new antitoxin.

Pasteur did not confine his experinents to the hydrophobia germ alone. He proved that the souring of milk, vines, and the like was due to germs r bacteria, and that by heating a liquid o the proper temperature these germs vould be killed. This process is known s pasteurization; and most milk commercially sold today is pasteurized. In France Pasteur's discoveries have saved he wine industry from serious losses

LOUIS PASTEUR

Pasteur has been called the Father of Bacteriology. His many successful scientific discoveries have helped to make the world a better and safer place. The Pasteur Institute in Paris, similar to the Rockefeller Institute in the United States, still carries on research work in bacteriology.

and won him the gratitude of his countrymen. He also found a means of preventing the diseases of anthrax and cholera which were destroying the farmer's sheep, cattle, and chickens.

Pasteur's great scientific achievements made his name famous not only in France, but also throughout all Europe and the Americas.

Pierre and Madame Curie became world famous scientists. In an abandoned shed connected with one of the buildings of the Sorbonne [sohr′buhn′], a part of the University of Paris, two scientists set up a chemical laboratory. They were Pierre Curie [pyehr′ kyoo′ ree′] and his wife, Marie Curie. Life for them was not easy. Pierre taught in the

Culver Service

MME CURIE

Marie Curie's scientific achievements made her the world's greatest woman scientist. In 1911 she received the Nobel prize in chemistry. Madame Curie was the only woman ever admitted to the French Academy.

university, and Marie also taught and had the care of home and children as well. But every moment that the couple could find they spent in the dusty old laboratory tending their flasks and fires. Madame would stand for hours stirring a boiling mass with an iron rod. Pierre, with instruments which he had constructed, would make delicate tests.

The work lasted for years, but the Curies had in their hearts the spirit of true scientists. They were on the trail of a secret of nature. Finally two years before the beginning of our century they announced that they had discovered a new chemical element called radium. This substance gave off rays which could penetrate a sheet of metal two and a half inches thick. More striking still, Madame Curie found that radium gave off each hour enough heat to melt its own weight in ice without seeming to change itself in appearance or effective-

ness. It was soon found that radium ray destroyed living tissues when they cam in contact with them, much as burning heat does, but without its accompanying pain. This has led to the wide use of thi strange element in treating such disease as cancer, which is an abnormal an dangerous growth of tissue.

As the Curies well knew from thei difficult laboratory work, radium is rare More than five hundred tons of hig grade radium ore are necessary to pro duce one gram of radium. Its price i therefore high, nearly $25,000 a gram The high price of radium, however, doe not mean that its discoverers becam wealthy. Listen to the words of Madam Curie:

There were no patents. We were work ing in the interests of science. Radium wa not to enrich anyone. Radium is an ele ment. It belongs to all the people.

Soon after the Curies made their dis covery Pierre was run over by a wagon in the streets of Paris and killed. Madam Curie took his place as professor in the Sorbonne and continued the research with radium. Four years later she was able to isolate the pure metal itself. During World War I Madame Curie, with one of her daughters, helped the French hospital service by organizing the X-ray work and training soldiers to handle the apparatus.

Both Pierre and Marie Curie have added true glory to France and given a great gift to the world.

French writers have enriched world literature. In drama, the novel, and the short story, French authors have made lasting contributions to the world's literature. There is La Fontaine [lah fohn' tayn'] whose *Fables* French children know by heart. There are the masters of the short story, Daudet [doh'day'], ind de Maupassant [duh moh'pas'-ahɴ]. Daudet's *The Last Class* and de Maupassant's *The Diamond Necklace* ire both stories you would enjoy read-ng. Victor Hugo, the son of one of Na-ɔoleon's distinguished generals, was also a great novelist and poet, but he was a iery patriot as well. When he strongly lenounced Louis Napoleon and his at-empt to bring back the days of the ·mpire, Hugo was forced to flee from ·rance. While living in exile, he wrote *Les Misérables* [lay mee'zay'rah'b'l], "The Unfortunates," often said to be the greatest novel of all time. To the end of iis eighty-third year Hugo led an active ife of writing, and some of his finest ɔoems were written during his last years. When Hugo died all France mourned iis passing.

Culver Service

VICTOR HUGO

You may have read some of the novels ɔf Alexandre Dumas [a'leks ahnd''r lyoo'mah']. *The Count of Monte Cristo* s the thrilling tale of Edmond Dantès ed'mohɴ' dahn'tehs'], who, after four-een years, escaped from his island prison ɔ inflict vengeance upon those who had vronged him. *The Three Musketeers* ells the story of three rollicking soldier-dventurers whose motto was " All for ne and one for all."

Anatole France is probably the most videly read French novelist of the early oth Century. He attacked the govern-ent, the church, and society in his lever, satirical writings.

Many French writers became out-tanding in the field of drama. The most imous of all French dramatists was Molière [moh'lyehr'], who lived dur-ng the 17th Century. He is noted for is lively comedies that dramatized the anners and weaknesses of the court nd the people. Molière's plays were so opular during his own lifetime that ouis XIV frequently requested him to

This noted French author is one of the great figures in the world of literature. Al-though Hugo died in 1885, his exciting lit-erary characters still live on to bring pleas-ure to present-day readers.

write special ballets and other entertain-ments for the royal festivals. Today, many of Molière's plays are read by high-school students of French. You may already know *Le Bourgeois Gentil-homme,* or *Le Malade Imaginaire.* Mo-lière wrote the latter, a drama of a man who only imagined he was sick, while Molière himself was acutely ill. In fact, he died only a week after the play was first produced.

The 19th Century dramatist, Edmond Rostand [ed'mohɴ' rohs'tahɴ'], cre-ated, among others, two plays that gained wide popularity in the English-speaking world. Both of them have been frequently produced in this country. *L'Aiglon* [lay'glohɴ'], or *The Eaglet,* is the unhappy story of Napoleon's son. Early in the 20th Century the immortal French actress, Sarah Bernhardt, and the

Metropolitan Museum of Art
" THE THINKER "

Rodin so effectively expressed in bronze the pose of a man in deep thought, that this statue has become his best-known work.

great French actor, Coquelin [kohk' laN'], played in *L'Aiglon* in the United States. But Coquelin was even more celebrated as Cyrano in Rostand's *Cyrano de Bergerac* [see'rah'noh' duh ber'jhuh'rak']. This play has been translated into many languages, and the part of Cyrano is one in which many great actors have added to their success.

A modern Frenchman became the greatest sculptor since Michelangelo. As a boy Auguste Rodin [oh'gyoost' roh' daN'] was up at six o'clock in the morning to sketch animals. He was at drawing school from eight to twelve with lunch in his pocket so that he could spend the noon hour in the Louvre [loov'r], that wonderful museum of art in Paris. He clerked all afternoon in the shop of an ornament maker, and drew until late in the evening.

But Rodin worked years without re-

ceiving recognition. Finally, in mid-life he entered a statue in an exhibition in Paris. The French government pur chased his exhibit, and from then on hi fame grew. When Rodin's critics com plained that he too often emphasized ugly features in his figures, Rodin re plied, " Nothing is ugly that has life." At the time of his death, in 1917, Rodin had come to be recognized as the great est sculptor since Michelangelo. A well known example of his work is " The Thinker," which stands in front of the Pantheon in Paris. At the left is a picture of this famous statue. There are other fine examples of his work in the Metro politan Museum of Art in New York City. The Rodin Museum in Philadel phia contains originals or replicas of almost all of Rodin's work.

Millet painted the French peasants and Corot the French landscape. In 181. Jean François Millet [zhaN frahN swah' mee'lay'] was born in Normandy in northwestern France. His parent were humble farmers. As a boy Mille was interested in drawing, and tried t copy the only pictures he had about him — the engravings in the family Bible.

Millet's ambition to study art was soo satisfied, for at the age of eighteen he was on his way to a near-by city to be gin his studies. A few years later he wen to study in Paris. Although he had en rolled in one of the best art schools, he made little progress, for he disliked th set forms and results which were ex pected of him. Disgusted, Millet soo left the art studio and worked alone supporting himself by sign-painting an making copies of great paintings. In all this great artist toiled for twenty year enduring illness and poverty, before hi paintings were finally recognized as th work of a master.

Millet's favorite subjects were peas

"THE ANGELUS"

This work of art by Millet has become one of the best-known pictures in the world.
Millet was a master in portraying peasant life in France.

ants and farm scenes. These he knew well for he had spent much time, as a child, at work in the fields with his parents. From memory, without models or scenes before him, Millet placed the life of the peasants on canvas. He showed them as they sowed and harvested their crops, as they stopped in their work to pay reverent thanks to God. " The Angelus," pictured above, is one of Millet's best-loved pictures. The peasant and his wife stand with bowed heads as the bells of the Angelus from the distant church spire summon them to worship. " The Gleaners " and " The Man with the Hoe" are also fine examples of his work.

Jean Corot [zhaɴ koh'roh'] was a contemporary of Millet. But instead of picturing the sturdy, simple peasants as Millet loved to do, Corot produced poetic, harmonious landscapes. Today Corot's pictures are among the most prized paintings of museums all over the world.

The modern French school of painters brought about a revolution in art. A new school of painters has sprung up in France in the past seventy-five years. The methods, the ideas, and the pictures of these painters are so different from the artists we have just described that they have caused a revolution in art. Not all of the new modern painters were Frenchmen, but most are classified with the modern French school of painting because they got their inspiration in France and did much work there.

THE CARD PLAYERS

The painting above is a fine example of the work of Cézanne, one of the bold experimenters in modern art.

The later artists developed new techniques with the brush, new uses and values of color, and employed line and form in designs which were a new and often a startling departure from the old.

Some of these artists, particularly Monet [moh'nay'], excelled in the painting of light and atmospheric effects. One of Monet's favorite subjects was a pool of water lilies.

Paul Cézanne [pohl say'zahn'] was one of the first of this modern group. Cézanne's work includes a large amount of still life (a piece of fruit, a vase, flowers on a table) and landscapes, as well as portraits. Design and color are used in his work to give life and reality to the figures he painted. One of his best-known paintings is reproduced above.

Paul Gauguin [pohl goh'gaɴ'] also belonged among the first of the new school of painters. Gauguin had been a middle-class banker and family man. He had been a "Sunday-painter." Like many other people, he had spent his week ends in copying the great pictures in the art galleries of Paris. He suddenly changed the pattern of his life from banker to adventurer, quitting his job and leaving his family. The subjects of his paintings were the peoples and landscapes of France and of far-off Tahiti [tah hee'tee] in the South Pacific, where he lived for a time. "I Greet You Maria" is one of his best-known paintings.

There were many others of the modern French school whose pictures are well known. Degas [duh gahs'] is noted for his many drawings and paintings of ballet dancers. Degas liked to produce paintings that were fresh in color and distinguished in design.

In the same school of painters was Renoir [ruh'nwahr'], whose use of color produced glowing flesh tints. As a boy, he painted porcelains at Limoges [lee' mohjh'], where he learned the delicate brush technique which marks his work. His "Mussel Gatherers" is typical. It is reproduced in full color in the *Encyclopædia Britannica*.

Henri Matisse [ahN'ree' ma'tees'], another French modernist, created his own impressions by the use of pure color and the effect of light, and by a perfection in design. Matisse worked in Africa as well as in France. The effect of Oriental art is often noticeable in his paintings.

You should realize that the modern French school of painting is still active, growing and changing. The six men we have mentioned are outstanding examples of revolutionary change in this fine art.

The work of French composers gained wide popularity. French music, like French art, flourished at the turn of the last century. We are indebted to French composers for two of the best-known of modern operas, *Faust* [foust] by Gounod goo'noh'], and *Carmen* by Bizet [bee' zay']. Claude Debussy [klohd duh' byoo'see'] also added to the world's great operas with his *Pelléas et Mélisande* [pel' lay'as' ay may'lee'zahnd'] as did Camille Saint-Saëns [ka'mee'uh saN' sahN'] with *Samson and Delilah*. Debussy, one of the foremost of modern French composers, is especially noted for his orchestral composition, *The Afternoon of a Faun*. The music of Maurice Ravel [moh'rees' ra'vel'] is also widely enjoyed. In America Ravel's "Boléro" is one of the best-known of modern French compositions.

The French People Have Spread the Ideas of Liberty, Equality, and Fraternity

France is located at the crossroads of Western Europe. It is largely protected by natural boundaries, except along the Belgian border, where the coastal plain has been an easy path for invading armies. France has been essentially an agricultural country, but in recent times large-scale manufacturing has been developed. A large percentage of French exports are luxury goods, and "Made in France" has come to be a mark of quality and fine workmanship.

In ancient times France was called Gaul, and was ruled for several hundred years by the Romans. When the Romans withdrew in the Fifth Century, Frankish warriors from northern Europe dominated the country. Gaul came to be called France from the name of these people. Clovis and Charlemagne were the most outstanding of the early rulers. France, like many other nations, suffered from the ruthless pillaging of the Northmen. During feudal times, the kings of France had no more power than many of the feudal lords. At the beginning of the 12th Century large areas of France were held by the English kings as vassals of the French crown. France and England were trade rivals, and disagreed also on fishing rights in the North Sea and the English Channel. The long-standing friction and rivalry between the two nations finally in the 14th Century broke into open war that went on fitfully for about a hundred years. This Hundred Years' War ended in victory for France. The most unusual personality of that period was Joan of Arc, who helped to turn the tide against the English. The fame of Joan of Arc has grown until today she is looked upon as a national heroine.

At first when the Duke of Paris added to his title " King of France," he was king in name only. After the Hundred Years' War, the French kings gradually increased their power until they were considered divine-right rulers. Louis XIV, the Sun King, built the beautiful palace of Versailles, and made French language and fashions the envy of Europe. Successful foreign wars, and the large colonies the French had acquired in the New World, gave France a position of prestige and dominance. But Louis XIV and his successors had been too extravagant. France became nearly bankrupt, and the people's plight looked hopeless. They were overtaxed, and lived as wretchedly as the serfs of feudal times. Voltaire, Rousseau, and other great thinkers championed the cause of justice. In 1789 the mobs stormed the Bastille and the French Revolution broke out. The cry " Liberty, Equality, Fraternity " sounded throughout Paris. The monarchy was overthrown, and for a number of years violence, bloodshed, and confusion were the rule. The government of the Directory which was eventually set up soon proved corrupt and inefficient. It was easily overthrown by Napoleon Bonaparte, the popular military hero of the day. Not only was order restored, but the people soon forgot their insistence upon a republican form of government, and elected this leader of men Emperor. Napoleon attempted not only to improve conditions within France, but to bring the rest of Europe under his rule. The latter proved to be his undoing, and he was defeated by an alliance of European nations at Waterloo in 1815. The Congress of Vienna attempted to reorganize Europe by restoring the old order as it had been before the French Revolution.

The French people continued to strive toward self-government. About the middle of the 19th Century they overthrew the monarchy established after the defeat of Napoleon, and set up a second Republic. Napoleon's nephew, who was president of this Republic, changed it into the Second Empire, with himself as Emperor. During his rule, France was defeated by Prussia in the Franco-Prussian War. At its end, the Third Republic, under which France was governed until World War II, was established. In France the premier was the most powerful person in the government.

France enlarged her colonial empire greatly during the last century by acquiring large territories in Africa. But France suffered great losses in manpower and financial resources as a result of World War I. Financial difficulties helped to bring on political scandals. French politicians disagreed on national policy, and public interest in good government declined. Lack of a national unity of thought, and the presence of corrupt elements in the French legislature paved the way for an easy overthrow of France by the Nazis in World War II.

France has for centuries been a center of culture that has attracted artists, scientists, musicians, and scholars from other lands. These adopted sons and daughters, and French men and women themselves, have brought glory to France by their accomplishments. Pierre and Marie Curie, and Louis Pasteur are among the outstanding French scientists of recent times. Anatole France, Victor Hugo, and Alexandre Dumas rank among the foremost French writers. Molière and Rostand are famous in the field of drama. Auguste Rodin brought distinction to France through his achievements as a sculptor. In modern times many new trends in art have had their origin in France. Millet and Corot have had many followers in other lands. More recently Cézanne and Matisse have been outstanding examples of French artistic genius. French musicians have given us some of our most popular operas, such as *Faust*, by Gounod, and *Carmen*, by Bizet. Ravel and Debussy have also contributed to music with their beautiful compositions.

SELF-TEST

The following kind of test is called an association test because for each item listed you are supposed to associate or recall something important in the story of France directly connected with the item. Two examples are given first to show you what is wanted. Do not write in your book.

	Item	Associations
Examples:	Bartholdi	Statue of Liberty
	1815	Waterloo, or defeat of Napoleon
1.	Pyrenees	21. July 14
2.	Rhone	22. Reign of Terror
3.	Seine	23. the " Marseillaise "
4.	coastal plain	24. the Directory
5.	vineyards	25. Arc de Triomphe
6.	great ports	26. St. Helena
7.	Haviland	27. Congress of Vienna
8.	Cro-Magnons	28. 1870
9.	Gaul	29. North Africa
10.	the Franks	30. rabies
11.	Normandy	31. radium
12.	Hugh Capet	32. Victor Hugo
13.	Black Death	33. *The Three Musketeers*
14.	Rouen	34. Sarah Bernhardt
15.	Versailles	35. Rodin
16.	the Third Estate	36. " The Angelus "
17.	Bastille	37. *Carmen*
18.	La Salle	38. Debussy
19.	Voltaire	39. Cézanne
20.	Monet	40. Vichy

INTERESTING THINGS TO DO
Project for the Chart Maker and Artist

Make a comparison chart similar to the one on pages 582–583 for the French colonial empire. Use headings such as " Location," " Peoples," " Government," " Products." See *Here Is Africa,* by E. M. Gatti and A. Gatti, " Madagascar: Mystery Island," by Paul Alinasy, *National Geographic Magazine,* June, 1942. Look up the individual colonies in an encyclopedia.

Ideas for Your Little Theater

1. With a committee of students, dramatize scenes from the life of Pasteur, Millet, Joan of Arc, Napoleon, or other famous French men and women. For Pasteur, see *Pasteur, Knight of the Laboratory,* by Francis E. Benz; for Millet, see *Fifty Famous Painters,* by Henrietta Gerwig; for Joan of Arc, see *Book of Courage,* by Hermann Hagedorn; for Napoleon, see *Men of Power,* by Albert Carr.

2. Get a phonograph recording of the " Marseillaise " to play for the class. If the song was recorded in French, first read an English translation of the words to the class.

3. With a committee of the class, arrange a display of French art and music. Collect pictures and mount them neatly for display. Plan to have speakers give brief talks about the artists and the pictures displayed. Obtain phonograph records of music by French composers. Similarly, arrange for speakers to tell anecdotes of the life of the composer before playing each record. For biographical information, see *Fifty Famous Painters,* by Henrietta Gerwig, and *Book of Modern Composers,* by David Ewen. See also *Famous Pictures,* by C. L. Barstow, and biographies of painters and composers in an encyclopedia.

Topics for Talks

1. " The fall of France." Within recent years, many books have been written about France and the reasons for her collapse before the Nazis. Consult the list at the end of this section, or your public library, for one of the newer books about France, to read and review for the benefit of the class.

2. " We often meet French phrases." Make a collection of French expressions that are frequently encountered in our English language and literature. You will find help in the foreign words and phrases section of any good dictionary. Some phrases, such as *à la mode,* you already know.

3. " The Dreyfus case made the headlines." Look up the story of the famous Dreyfus scandal that affected not only the French army itself, but influenced the development of political factions in France. See " Dreyfus " in

an encyclopedia. Read also *The Dreyfus Case*, by A. Dreyfus and P. Dreyfus, or *Dreyfus Affair*, by J. Kayser.

4. " The first time I saw Paris." Prepare a talk from the viewpoint of an American soldier entering Paris after it was taken from the Nazis in 1944. See *Life*, Sept. 11, 1944; *Time*, Sept. 4, 1944; *Newsweek*, Sept. 4, 1944.

Adventures for the Amateur Author

1. Prepare an account of an interview you might have had with Napoleon Bonaparte. By looking up some of Napoleon's sayings on war, and related subjects, you will be able to make the account of your interview convincing. See *Napoleon Speaks*, by Albert Carr.

2. Write a few entries which might have appeared in the diary of one of Napoleon's soldiers who took part in the Russian campaign and the disastrous retreat from Moscow. By way of comparison, write a few entries from the diary of a Nazi soldier who served in one of the German armies on the Russian front in World War II. See *Napoleon's Invasion of Russia*, by E. V. Tarle, and *Life*, Jan. 12, 1942. See also *Journey Among Warriors*, pp. 171–182, 249–253, by Eve Curie.

Candidates for Your Album of Famous People

Bizet, Cézanne, Pierre and Marie Curie, Dumas, Joan of Arc, Louis XIV, Millet, Napoleon, Pasteur, Rodin, Rostand, Rousseau, Voltaire. Choose three of the people listed above, or other people mentioned in the story of France for portraits in your Album.

INTERESTING READING ABOUT FRANCE

BERAUD, H. *Twelve Portraits of the French Revolution.* Interesting descriptions of some of the great revolutionary characters and their aims.

Compton's Pictured Encyclopedia. France — A Name That Rings Like a Battle Song.

CURIE, EVE. *Madame Curie.* " She was supported by a will of iron, by a taste for perfection, and by an incredible stubbornness."

DICKENS, C. *A Tale of Two Cities.* " At one of the theater doors, there stood a little girl with her mother, looking far away across the street through the mud."

DUMAS, A. *The Count of Monte Cristo.* " '. . . everyone thinks himself more wretched than another unfortunate who weeps and groans at his side.' "

HAWTHORNE, HILDEGARDE. *Phantom King.* A story of Napoleon's son, the Duke of Reichstadt.

HUGO, V. *Les Misérables.* " He came out of the doorway in which he was concealed."

MacGregory, M. *The Story of France.* " Nobleman and peasants, armed with staves and scythes, set out to chase the royal runaway."

Maurois, André. *I Remember, I Remember.* The autobiography of this French writer pictures men and events since World War I, and a heart-rending account of the fall of France in 1940.

Peck, A. M., and Meras, E. A. *France, Crossroads of Europe.* A simply written and entertaining book about French history, government, literature, social life, and customs.

Riggs, Arthur S. *France from Sea to Sea.* Descriptive sketches of French cities and country scenes highlight this account of a journey across France.

Rugg, H. *Changing Governments and Changing Cultures.* The March toward Democracy in France. " Napoleon over-reached himself and destroyed his own future."

Sabatini, Rafael. *Scaramouche.* A story of the early days of the Revolution.

Tappan, E. M. *Hero Stories of France.* " At ten o'clock cannons were fired, bells were rung. . . ."

Tarbell, Ida M. *Life of Napoleon Bonaparte.* A good biography of the great military hero of the French, and a short sketch of Josephine.

Turner, P. M. *Millet.* " Millet seems particularly to have been impressed with the loneliness of the peasants' labor."

Wilmot-Buxton, E. M. *Jeanne d'Arc.* " Suddenly from the midst of the awful silence her voice rang out. . . ."

The World Book Encyclopedia. " The History of the French Revolution "; " France: The Story of France "; and Index.

PART TWELVE

THE NETHERLANDS AND BELGIUM WERE
. WRESTED FROM RUTHLESS FOES
AND A HUNGRY SEA

THE LOW COUNTRIES

NORTH

SEA

NORTH

FRISIAN ISLANDS

Groningen

NETHERLANDS

GERMANY

Ems R.

Texel

Zuider Zee

Zwolle

Vecht R.

Haarlem Canal   Edam

Haarlem

Amsterdam

Utrecht

Arnhem

Rhine

Leyden

Waal   R.

Nijmegen

Rhine

Duesseldorf

The Hague

Rotterdam

Rhine Delta

Maas R.

Cologne

Maastricht

Aachen
(Aix-la-Chapelle)

Flushing

Antwerp

Louvain

Liége

Moselle R.

Ostend   Bruges

LANDERS   Ypres

Ghent

Scheldt R.

Brussels

Namur

Sambre R.

Spa

Waterloo

Meuse R.

Trier

BELGIUM

LUXEMBOURG

Saar R.

ARDENNE   MTS.

Luxembourg

FRANCE

MILES

0   25   50   100

Sam Brown

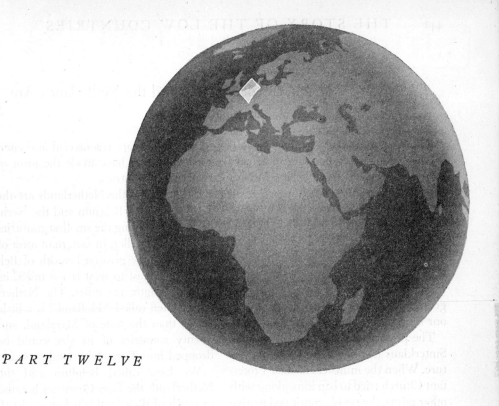

The Garden Spot of Europe

WﾍEN we think of the part the people of the Low Countries have played in the story of nations and of their contributions to civilization, we might well believe that their homelands spread over a large part of Europe. Turn to the map of Europe at the back of the book. How do the Netherlands compare in size with other countries of Europe?

On the map opposite, find Waterloo, where Napoleon's armies met defeat. Notice also Flanders, famous in World War I, and the supply ports of Ostend and Antwerp, which the Allies struggled to seize from Axis control during World War II. Why have so many battles been fought in the Low Countries?

Trace the main rivers which drain these low-lying lands. Would you expect these countries to be well-suited to agriculture? What activities are suggested to you by the number of inland cities and of seaports? The western part of the Netherlands lies below sea level. This land has not only been reclaimed from the waters of the Atlantic, but has been transformed into the garden spot of Europe. Notice the great dike which separates the Zuider Zee from the North Sea. What do these projects tell you of the courage, resourcefulness, and determination of these peoples?

Chapter 1 ~ The Stories of Belgium and the Netherlands Are Closely Interwoven

The Dutch are a determined people. In the Western nations, that imaginary character we call Santa Claus has become an institution. Each year he invades our homes and our stores much to the delight of small children, as well as of grown-ups who have not lost the spirit of Christmas. It was the early Dutch settlers in America who brought that happy tradition with them. They called the old gentleman " Sinterklaus," from which our form of the name comes.

The preservation of their tradition of Sinterklaus is rather typical of their nature. When the ministers of their Protestant Church tried to ban him, along with other saints, the people continued to give toys to their children out of the pack of their Sinterklaus. The 17th Century Dutch painter, Jan Steen [yahn stayn], has left us a charming picture of a Dutch Christmas in his " Eve of St. Nicholas."

The religious intolerance of the 17th Century is gone today, and other great changes have affected the people of the Low Countries. We can be grateful to the peoples of the Netherlands for much more than Santa Claus, as you will discover in Chapter 3. We are accustomed to think of these small countries as the land of windmills and wooden shoes. Children's storybooks have emphasized their quaint customs and picturesque scenes — storks nesting on the roof tops, fields of bright tulips and hyacinths swaying in the breeze, skaters gliding along the frozen canals, windmills with their arms turning briskly in the breeze. But Belgium and the Netherlands are busy and progressive modern nations.

Their peoples are resourceful and energetic, and they have made the most of their small countries.

Belgium and the Netherlands are the Low Countries. Belgium and the Netherlands are among the smallest countries in Europe, smaller, in fact, than most of our states. The greatest breadth of Belgium from east to west is 160 miles, its greatest length, 115 miles. The Netherlands, often called " Holland," is a little larger than the state of Maryland, and twenty countries of its size could be dropped into Texas with land to spare.

We have called Belgium and the Netherlands the Low Countries because so much of their land is below sea level. They are not completely flat, however. The land away from the sea is gently rolling, and there are hills in the southeastern part.

" God made the sea; we made the land." In the early days, the sand dunes along the coast of the Low Countries were frequently cut into by the sea water at high tides. As the sand was washed away, serious floods began to occur. We know that by the year 1000 the people along this coast had already attempted to protect themselves by erecting large banks of earth, called dikes, to keep out the sea water. This campaign against the sea has gone on for many centuries.

In the 17th Century, drainage operations were greatly increased and lakes and swampy areas were reclaimed. The method used then is still followed. A dike was built around the water-covered area, and a canal was cut along the top of the dike. Water was then pumped off the

Orient and Occident

WINDMILLS PROTECT THE HOMES OF THE NETHERLANDERS

The windmills along the dikes are used primarily to pump water from the polderlands reclaimed from the sea. They are also used for grinding grain.

land into the canal by means of windmills. Today, however, the gas engine has largely replaced the windmill, as a means of pumping out the water.

This newly drained land is called a polder [pohl'der]. When a polder has been drained, the canal around it becomes an elevated waterway. Since many of the polders are below sea level, the pumping must be continued daily to keep the land fit for agriculture or pasturage. This makes it necessary to keep an efficient system of canals and ditches in constant operation. Where the canals empty into the sea there are great sluice gates that are opened at low tide to let off the excess water so that the canals will not overflow back into the polders. A section of polderland is shown on page 444.

The Dutch have an appropriate proverb describing their long struggle with the sea: "God made the sea; we made the land." Today there are large stretches of land in the Netherlands, and a smaller area in northern Belgium, that were once covered with water. This land is now fertile and productive because of the energy and ingenuity of the people of the Low Countries.

The greatest reclamation project undertaken by the Dutch in modern times is the drainage of a large bay known as the Zuider Zee [zai'duhr zee']. Here four large polders were to be created. A long dike, wide enough to carry both a motor road and a railroad, was built to cut off the Zuider Zee from the North Sea. The first of these polders was ready for settlement in 1934, and work proceeded on the second polder. The four polders, if completed as they are planned, will increase the area of the

Courtesy Netherlands Information Bureau

PATTERN OF RECLAIMING

This system of dikes has kept the polderland from being covered by the sea. The windmills, like sentry posts, are set in strategic positions.

Netherlands by a half-million acres of rich agricultural land.

Low Country farmers are efficient. Since both the Netherlands and Belgium are among the most densely populated countries in the world, their problem of food supply is an important one. A large percentage of the population in each of these countries is engaged in agriculture.

There are four main reasons for the successful development of farming in the Low Countries. First, the climate is very favorable with its mild winters, adequate rainfall, and long growing season. Second, the land is fertile and, because it is so level, easy to cultivate. Third, rivers, canals, the sea, and the levelness of the land all help to make transportation easy. And fourth, the farmers of the Low Countries have learned how to get the

most out of their land. The farms consist generally of only a few acres, but they are intensively worked. The soil is enriched with large amounts of fertilizer, and the crop yields per acre are among the highest in the world.

Livestock thrives in the Low Countries. The livestock industry is important in the Low Countries. The grassland of the Belgian plain supports dairy cattle and fine draft horses. The grain and grass crops of the Netherlands are grown chiefly for the dairy herds, and the damp coastal meadows make rich pastures. Dairy products, such as milk, butter, and cheese, are among the chief exports of the Netherlands. The Dutch town of Edam near the Zuider Zee has given its name to a famous kind of cheese. Still another well-known cheese is named for the town of Gouda [gou'dah].

Food industries in the Netherlands. The Netherlands imports a number of foods from the Netherlands Indies. These imported foods, as well as the crops and dairy products of the Netherlands themselves, have given rise to an increasingly important food processing industry. The Netherlands has fruit and vegetable canneries, sugar refineries, chocolate factories, and margarine, rice-hulling, and oil mills.

The Netherlands is a land of flowers. The Dutch flower-bulb industry was started on a small scale more than three hundred years ago from the strange seeds and bulbs the Crusaders brought back from their journeys. This industry, centering around Haarlem, is famous all over the world. The setting for Alexandre Dumas' famous novel, *The Black Tulip,* is laid here. Thousands of acres of tulip, hyacinth, and narcissus bulbs are grown for export. The village of Boskoop, with more than six hundred nurseries, is the world's largest center for small fruit and forest trees, as well as ornamental plants.

There are few minerals in the Low Countries. The Netherlands has only small deposits of salt, coal, and clay, but Belgium has limestone, zinc, coal, copper, lead, and iron. The Belgian steel industry, centering around Liége [lyayzh], produces steel products of high quality. Belgium's great coal field provides plentiful fuel for smelting and refining metals. Machinery, railway equipment, firearms, and munitions are produced in sufficient quantities for home use and export as well. The metal industries in the Netherlands depend greatly on imported materials. For example, in normal times much tin ore is imported from the Netherlands Indies; it is partially refined in the Netherlands and re-exported.

Old and new industries flourish in the Low Countries. In spite of their many well-managed little farms, both Belgium and the Netherlands need to import much of their food. They pay for it, in normal times, by exports of manufactured goods. Such goods are of very high quality. The guild system of medieval times, which kept standards of quality high, originated in Flanders, now a part of Belgium. Even during the Middle Ages, Flemish woolen material was known throughout Europe. In contrast to the early importance of manufacturing in the Belgian cities, the large-scale manufacturing in the Netherlands has been a development of the 20th Century.

The old industries of weaving, lace-making, ceramics (pottery-making), and diamond cutting are still important in the Low Countries. Although Belgium has to import all her cotton and much of her flax and wool, her textile industries today rank second only to her iron and steel industry. Also the rugs (Brussels carpet), linens, and laces (Brussels lace) have long been famous. The ceramic industries, begun centuries ago, are still flourishing. Belgium manufactures both pottery and glass. Pottery from the Dutch cities of Delft and Maastricht [mahs'trikt] is widely known. The center of the diamond cutting and polishing industry was, for centuries, the Dutch city of Amsterdam. It has spread in modern times to the Belgian city of Antwerp as well.

Many new industries have developed in the Low Countries in modern times. Both Belgium and the Netherlands have added the manufacture of artificial silk fiber to their other textile skills. Belgium has new chemical and mineral industries, including the extraction of radium from ores imported from the Belgian Congo. Before World War II the Neth-

Courtesy Netherlands Information Bureau

THE PORT OF AMSTERDAM

Can you imagine the clamor of foghorns from so many ships and harbor craft on a foggy day? In peacetime, the shipping of the Netherlands could produce a sizable fraction of the fog signals all over the world.

erlands also developed airplane and radio equipment industries.

Commerce and trade are the life blood of the Low Countries. Foreign trade and commercial activities in the Low Countries have long been highly developed. Geographic position has encouraged commerce, for the Low Countries are surrounded by the leading commercial nations of Europe, and they are located at the crossroads of several of the busiest trade routes in the world. The very waters from which the people took their land serve as highways for trade. The Low Countries have a great many seaports and a great many rivers and canals. The Belgian seaport of Antwerp on the Scheldt [skelt] River is one of the great shipping centers of Europe. Amsterdam and Rotterdam in the Neth-

erlands are both large ports. Amsterdam is connected with both the North Sea and the Rhine River by wide canals. Rotterdam is situated at the mouth of the Rhine. The chief rivers of the Low Countries, the Rhine, the Meuse [myooz], and the Scheldt, are so well connected by a series of canals that all sections of the two countries are within easy reach of the great ports. Belgium, despite its small size, has in addition many miles of railroads.

Education is stressed in the Low Countries. Several of the Dutch universities were established hundreds of years ago. The University of Louvain [lou'vahɴ'], in Belgium, was established in the 15th Century. It was here that Erasmus, one of the outstanding men of the Renaissance, founded the

"College of the Three Tongues" — Latin, Greek, and Hebrew. You will read later of the founding of the University of Leyden [lai'd'n] in the 16th Century. This university was a rallying point for Huguenots and other Protestants during the Reformation, and has been known for the freedom allowed to faculty and students in teaching and writing. In modern times an important development of education in the Netherlands and Belgium has been the spread of vocational schools where special industrial training is given in many varied subjects, such as textiles, navigation, mining, radio, aviation, printing, and agriculture.

The Netherlands has an unusual educational problem in providing instruction for the children and crews of the canal boats engaged in inland shipping. Education for these children has been standardized over the whole country, and instruction is to a large extent individual. A child may go to school on Monday in one town, and perhaps on Tuesday in another, and in each town he visits he can take up his studies where he left off the day before. In some cases the wives of the canal-boat skippers study courses in domestic science in this same way, and the skippers themselves continue their education. The Dutch have been rewarded for their efforts to make learning available to all their people by seeing illiteracy disappear almost entirely from the Netherlands. It is interesting to know, too, that almost all the Dutch people speak one or two other languages in addition to their own.

The Belgians and Dutch have many fine traits. We know of the energy and resourcefulness of the people of the Low Countries in their long battle to safeguard their land from the sea. That constant struggle has called for intelligence and determination. It is understandable that these people are especially home-loving. Probably you have seen pictures of Dutch housewives scrubbing their spotless steps, polishing their copper utensils, or cleaning the colorful tiles that decorate the interiors of their homes. The Dutch are proud of their families and their homes, and greatly enjoy both visiting and entertaining friends at home.

The Belgians are also a sociable people. They like to meet for friendly conversation in the cafes and restaurants. There is a common saying, "When three Belgians come together, they form a club." Many Belgians are fond of music, and almost every Belgian town possesses its own "harmonie" society, or band.

The Walloons and the Flemish live in Belgium. There are two distinct groups of people in Belgium: the Flemish in the north and the Walloons in the south. The Flemish resemble the Dutch people in many ways, and speak a language much like Dutch. The Walloons, on the other hand, have many French characteristics, and their language is a French dialect. Street signs are generally written in both languages. Although these two groups have many different ideas, and disagree sharply with each other, they are alike in their patriotic feeling for their country and become united against outsiders when any danger threatens the security of the Belgian nation.

Chapter 2 ~ The Low Countries Became Separate Nations and Acquired Colonies

Caesar invaded the Low Countries. Little is known about the Low Countries until the time of the Romans. At that time they were not one nation, or two nations, but a number of small, scattered groups of people. Caesar and his Roman warriors subdued a tribe they called Belgae [bel'gai], who lived in the lowlands along the northwestern coast of Europe. We know Caesar thought highly of their bravery, for in describing the various Gallic peoples he wrote, " the fiercest of these are the Belgae." The Romans built military roads along the Rhine and Meuse rivers, and Roman customs began to influence the lowland people in their weapons, coinage, and methods of building. The chief industries among the tribes at that time were fishing, cattle-raising, and weaving.

After Rome was conquered by the barbarian hordes in the Fifth Century, there was very little written history of the Low Countries, and not much is known about them for more than a century. There was no strong governing power to keep the tribes of the lowlands together until the beginning of the Sixth Century.

The Low Countries share the history of the Franks. The Low Countries were the original home of the Franks, about whom you read in the stories of the Middle Ages and France. The kingdom of the Franks expanded until it included almost all of Western Europe. You will recall that Clovis had accepted Christianity; thus the lowlands became Christian. The Low Countries shared the history of the Franks until the break-up of the Frankish Empire at the end of the Ninth Century. Thereafter the northern peoples of the lowlands became part of the German kingdom, and the southern peoples became part of the French kingdom.

The spirit of independence grew strong in towns. Between the 10th and 12th Centuries a number of powerful towns arose as a force for independence. They refused to bow to the obligations and restrictions imposed by the feudal nobles. They were, for those times, unusual examples of attempts at self-government. One of these towns was Bruges [broozh]. It was a junction for trade routes from all directions. Such towns, where merchants from many regions came to trade, encouraged new ideas and furthered the growth of industry and commerce.

Philip of Burgundy. By the year 1300 many of the small feudal regions had become combined under a single overlord. This development continued until, early in the 15th Century, almost all the small states of the lowlands were under the rule of the powerful Duke Philip of Burgundy. The Duke of Burgundy was so powerful that his possessions formed practically an independent state between the countries of France and Germany.

Philip established his court at Brussels, and summoned representatives from the different parts of his land to meet in a states general or legislative assembly. This assembly represented the first move toward real political unity in the Low Countries. Under Philip's rule he coinage was reformed and a uniorm system of justice was adopted.

The Low Countries became a part of he Holy Roman Empire. We have seen n the story of feudalism how land rights vere held by certain lords or overlords .nd were handed down from father to .on. The supreme overlord of a nation vas the king.

Generally the heir to a throne would narry only a member of another royal amily. Since there were not many ruling families in Europe, a number of hem were soon related. A prince might nherit from one or another of his anestors the right to rule over lands far emoved from the place of his birth and >ver peoples for whom he was not natu-ally a national leader.

The Burgundians, the German Hapsurgs, and the royal family of Spain had ill intermarried; so it happened that :arly in the 16th Century a prince, born n the Low Countries, inherited the rights of all these families and became he most powerful ruler of the century: Charles V of the Holy Roman Empire. His territory included the Low Coun-:ries, Austria, the German states, Sicily, :he kingdom of Naples, and the kingdom of Spain, and he had a claim to great territories in the New World as vell.

Charles V persecuted the Protestants. Unfortunately, Charles V did not use his great power and wealth wisely. His loy-alty to the medieval Church led him to :ry to stamp out Luther's teachings. These, you will recall were spread first during the Reformation in the 16th Century. When many people in the northern part of the lowlands were converted to Protestantism, Charles V tried to force them back into the Church. There was a death penalty for discussing the Bible or attending secret religious meet-

ings. Many devout Protestants were tortured and burned at the stake.

Philip II continued the persecution. When Charles V gave up the Burgundian and Spanish parts of his realm to his son, Philip II of Spain, the persecuted Protestants hoped for peace. But Philip carried on a more ruthless war against them than his father had before him. Finally, driven to fury by their persecution, some Protestants broke into a church and destroyed sacred images and priceless works of art. Unfortunately for him, Philip did not realize that the religious feelings of the people were a threat to his rule. He did not understand the liberty-loving people or the fervor of their Protestant beliefs. The people had endured the demands of Charles, for he was a native prince of the Low Countries as well as King of Spain. Philip II, however, ruled from Madrid in Spain. To the people of the lowlands he was a foreigner.

Philip was determined to stamp out Protestantism and to punish the people. He sent one of the most brutal tyrants in history, the Duke of Alva, to rule the Low Countries. With the support of thousands of soldiers brought from Spain, Alva set up his historic Council of Blood. Anyone suspected of taking part in an image-breaking riot was condemned to death without justice or mercy. Thousands fled the Low Countries in fear of their lives.

The siege of Leyden. And here we come upon an exciting story. It is the rebellion of the Low Countries against Spain and the saving of the Dutch city of Leyden from capture by the Spanish. Leyden was located in an area reclaimed from the sea by dikes. For months the Spaniards had surrounded the city. Cut off from the outside world, many of the besieged people died of starvation. But in spite of their hunger the survivors refused to surrender.

William of Orange led the Low Countries in rebellion. In this hour of terror and distress, the Low Countries found a leader — William of Orange. William was a prince whose family had owned lands in the Low Countries for nearly two centuries. He had raised a small army, and he came to the rescue of Leyden. William had the dikes cut so that the water from the sea rolled in over the lowlands. It swept over the camps and battlements of the Spaniards and drowned many of the invaders. The remainder fled for their lives, and Leyden was saved.

William promised to reward the people of Leyden for their bravery. He offered either to have Leyden freed forever from all taxes, or to establish a university there. The decision was left to the people, who chose a university. To this day the University of Leyden stands as a memorial to their courage and patriotism.

Alexander Farnese and the division of the Low Countries. When the Duke of Alva was not able to put down the uprising in the Low Countries, Philip in Spain sent a diplomat and soldier, named Alexander Farnese [fahr nay'say], to take Alva's place as governor. Farnese saw there were sharp disagreements between the various states. He used these differences to stir up trouble between the Catholic provinces in the south and the Protestant provinces in the north. The southern provinces organized into a defensive league and declared their loyalty to Spain. A few years later, in the latter part of the 16th Century, the northern provinces declared themselves independent of Spain, and a new republic, which was called the United Provinces, was formed.

The rebellion against Spain, which had already been going on for more than ten years, was to last eighty years in all. During some of this time the Dutch had the help of the French and English. Finally, in 1648, a treaty of

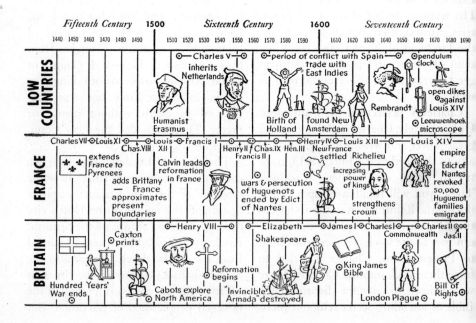

peace was signed, which recognized the Dutch state as an independent nation.

The Golden Age of the Dutch Republic. In spite of the fact that the Dutch were at war during the greater part of the 17th Century, that time is known as the Golden Age of the Republic of the United Provinces. In their struggle for independence the Dutch had developed a sense of tolerance for new ideas and religious freedom. Oppressed Protestants and Jews from other countries found a haven of security in the United Provinces. Several universities were founded, and the achievements of Dutch scholars and scientists were widely known. The arts flourished and many masterpieces in art and architecture were created. This was the time of the great school of Dutch painters, of which Rembrandt and Van Dyck are glowing examples. Of such men and their accomplishments you will learn more in Chapter 3.

This also was a period when Dutch industry and commerce flourished, and the foundations of a colonial empire were laid. Merchants carried on a thriving trade with other parts of Europe and the rest of the world. The city of Amsterdam became a world center of trade and banking, and the Dutch are said to have had more than half the world's cargo ships by the middle of the 17th Century. With this interest in trade and shipping, it was natural that mapmaking was developed early in this country. Almost all the maps from that period still in existence today were published in Amsterdam.

The Dutch East India Company led to colonization. During the 17th Century, exploration increased with the search for new raw materials and better trade routes. And with the Dutch as with other nations, colonization followed commerce. One of the first great corporations in the world, the Dutch East India Company, was organized at the beginning of the 17th Century. This company hired the English captain Henry Hudson to search for a northwest

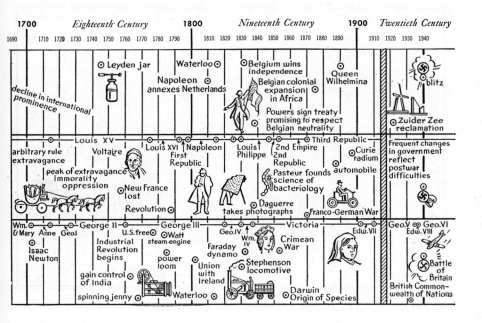

passage to China and the Indies. Hudson's explorations gave the Dutch their claim to territory in North America and led to the establishment of the colony of New Amsterdam (now New York).

The Dutch East India Company was granted generous privileges by the Dutch government, and large amounts of money were invested in it by many people. For twenty years the company carried on constant and relentless war with the Portuguese and the English to secure an unchallenged hold on the East Indies.

Shortly after the East India Company was formed, a Dutch West India Company was organized to take charge of the Netherlands interests in the Americas. Besides the scattered settlements known as New Netherlands in North America, the Dutch also had interests in Brazil and the West Indies.

The Dutch Republic declined. As with so many nations, the power of the Dutch was not to last. In the 18th Century the trade and commerce of the United Provinces began to fall off. Industry had developed rapidly in France, England, and Austria. The Dutch export trade lost many of its markets to these competitors. Wars, unsuccessful for the Dutch, followed. At the same time, the home government was unsettled. The spirit of daring and ambition that had flamed in the 17th Century seemed to have died out. No great statesmen or generals arose to guide the Dutch Republic. Finally, the independent United Provinces lost not only their prestige but their independence as well. Early in the 19th Century, the Dutch Republic fell to France under Napoleon.

The southern provinces during the time of the Dutch Republic. You will remember that the southern provinces of the Low Countries had declared themselves loyal to Spain. For years they were governed successively by Spain, Austria, and France. They, too, had prospered in manufacturing and commerce. But, again like the northern provinces of the Dutch Republic, they found their trade

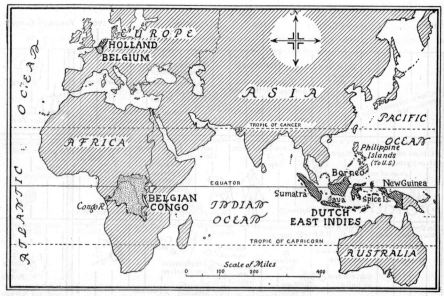

THE EMPIRES OF THE NETHERLANDS AND BELGIUM

uined by competitors from England and other powers.

With the defeat of Napoleon, the Dutch regained their independence from France. A constitution was immediately drawn up, and a member of the House of Orange chosen as king. In the following year the Congress of Vienna united the southern provinces, formerly governed by France, with the new Dutch kingdom. This move was intended to strengthen the new kingdom.

Belgium gained her independence. The union of the Dutch with the southern provinces in the 19th Century was not fated to last many years. Although the southerners and the Dutch were next-door neighbors, they differed in language as well as religion. The Dutch were an agricultural and commercial nation, and favored free trade. The southern provinces were industrial, and they wanted their manufactured goods sold under laws which would keep out the goods of other nations. Within a quarter of a century the southern provinces succeeded in revolting against their union with the Dutch, and they established the kingdom of Belgium.

The Dutch Empire is in Asia and in the Americas. By the end of the 18th Century all colonial affairs managed by the Dutch East India and Dutch West India Companies had been taken over by the government. The modern Dutch Empire is made up of three holdings: the East Indies, a few small islands in the West Indies, and Surinam [soo'ri-nahm'], or Dutch Guiana [gee ah'nuh] in South America. See the map of the world at the back of this book. Surinam is important to us today because it supplies much aluminum ore.

The Dutch East Indies Islands are not to be thought of as small. Java is four times as large as Holland, Sumatra [soo-mah'truh] is larger than California, and Borneo is larger than France. These South Pacific islands produce great quantities of sugar, tin, rubber, coffee, tobacco, cocoa, and many tropical fruits, vegetables, and spices. The extent to which we in America depend upon the Dutch East Indies for these articles was unforgettably demonstrated in World War II when these islands, and many others, were seized by Japan, as you will read in Part Twenty-two, the story of the modern world.

Government of the Dutch Indies aims toward local self-rule. The recent policy of the Dutch government in the East Indies has been aimed toward self-government for the native peoples. Self-government is practiced in the purely local affairs in the villages. As civilization spreads, and education opens the eyes of the native people to their position and responsibilities in the modern world, they are given more voice in their own government. The greatest reform in the rule of the Dutch East Indies came in 1918 with the creation of a People's Council to consult with and advise the governor general, who is appointed by the ruler of the Netherlands.

Belgium developed the African Congo. Toward the end of the 19th Century, Belgium, along with other nations, became interested in the Congo in south central Africa. You can locate the Congo on the map on page 452. See also the map of Africa at the back of the book. Henry M. Stanley's startling adventures through the "Dark Continent" aroused in the king of Belgium an interest in Africa. He formed an association and gained control of the Congo region. A neutral state was organized with the king of Belgium in control. Because the "free" natives were forced to collect rubber from trees in the jungles, to trap ele-

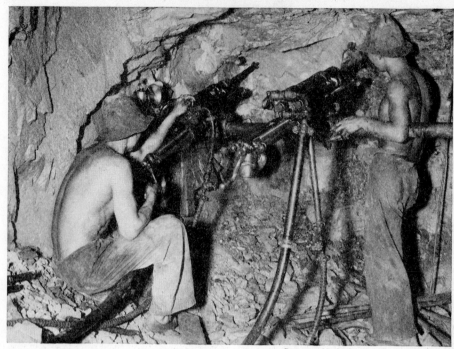

Courtesy Netherlands Information Bureau

LODE MINING OF TIN

Native miners are drilling for tin in a mine in the Netherlands East Indies. In 1941 these islands provided more than a quarter of the tin imported by the United States. The miners in this photograph are using American-made equipment.

phants, to bring in ivory, and to endure many other hardships, control was taken out of the hands of the association and given to the Parliament of Belgium. The Parliament carried out many reforms in administration of the Congo. Careful attention was paid to the needs of the natives and to the expansion of trade. The resources of the Congo have not yet been fully developed. Its chief industry is copper mining. Valuable exports also include diamonds, tin, ivory, rubber, palm-oil, and uranium ore, from which about ninety percent of the world's supply of radium is refined.

The Dutch and Belgians faced modern social problems. Besides being occupied with colonial affairs during the late 19th and the early part of the 20th Centuries, both Belgium and the Nether-lands enjoyed a remarkable growth in manufacturing. That meant factories, and factories meant many workers. There was the need for legislation to protect the rights of the working people. The Netherlands passed its first child-labor law nearly seventy-five years ago. Laws have also been made to safeguard factory workers. Various types of social insurance, such as workmen's compensation, old-age and sickness insurance, have been introduced. Improved housing projects for workers had far-reaching results in the health and happiness of the workers and their families. The Belgians also passed laws governing labor councils, child-labor, and pensions. After World War I, wages and living conditions for the average Belgian workman were greatly improved.

Chapter 3 ~ The People of the Low Countries Have Advanced Civilization

The Belgians have made contributions to music and literature. Belgium is the home of the carillon, a set of bells on which music may be played. The carillons of Bruges, Antwerp, and Ghent have been famous for many years. Belgium has many schools for training carillon players. The Netherlands is a close second to Belgium in the number of its carillons.

The Belgian writer most familiar to us is Maurice Maeterlinck [mah′ter-lingk]. His play, *The Blue Bird,* has been translated into English and is widely known. The Belgians themselves consider Charles De Coster their great national writer. He collected Flemish legends and folklore. His greatest book is his legend of *Till Eulenspiegel* [til oi′lun spee′g′l]. This story of Eulenspiegel and his exaggerated adventures has been compared to the Spanish Don Quixote [dohn kee hoh′tee].

The Dutch made discoveries in science. A professor in the University of Leyden discovered what is known as the Leyden jar, the first electrical condenser. His discovery was the forerunner of later inventions which have made possible the X-ray machine, radio, and other electrical instruments.

Another Dutch scientist who lived at the same time was Anton Van Leeuwenhoek [ahn′tohn vahn lay′wun hook]. He was a student of natural history and a maker of microscopes. Van Leeuwenhoek gave the first complete description of red blood cells and was the first to see protozoa and bacteria.

Dutch scholars and philosophers made their contributions. In the story of the Renaissance you read of the philosopher, Erasmus, who wrote on the social, religious, and educational problems of the time. About a half century later he was followed by Hugo Grotius [groh′shi-uhs], a lawyer for the Dutch East India Company, who became the historian of the early years of the United Provinces. Grotius is remembered today chiefly by

Metropolitan Museum of Art
" THE LAUGHING CAVALIER "
— FRANS HALS

Next to Rembrandt in fame among Dutch painters, Frans Hals is noted for the varying degrees of humor and amusement in his portraits. The so-called Laughing Cavalier is not really laughing. He looks a little ironical.

"SYNDICS OF THE CLOTH HALL OF AMSTERDAM"

This is one of the larger and one of the more noted of the 700 pictures painted by Rembrandt, probably the most famous of the Dutch artists. You will note that the artist has given the same care to detail as if he were painting a single figure, and that this picture is full of life and action.

his writings on law. He was the first to set down clearly the doctrines and practices observed by nations in dealing with one another, making the first clear statement of international law. Another great scholar was Spinoza [spi noh'zuh]. His ideas and philosophy were not appreciated during his lifetime, but they became the basis for the thinking and philosophy of others in more recent times.

The greatest contributions of the Low Countries have been in the field of art. The great progress of the Low Countries in the 15th, 16th, and 17th Centuries was accompanied by great achievements in art. Before this time painters had depended on the Church, monasteries, or court officials for financial support. But then a change began to come about. The wealthy traders and bankers of the rich Flemish cities in the south began to take an interest in painting. They went to a portrait painter as we go today to a portrait photographer. They wanted paintings not only of themselves, but of their own activities and belongings. Later, after the founding of the Dutch Republic, a similar change began to affect painters in the Netherlands. The Netherlands was largely Protestant, as we have learned, and the Dutch art-lover began to lose interest in the old type of religious paintings. Now, he too wanted pictures of his own family, home, and countryside.

You will remember that the Renaissance was the Golden Age in art. It was the period of great artists in the Netherlands as well as in Italy. Early in the 15th Century, the older of the Van Eyck [vahn aik'] brothers found out how to paint with oils on canvas. The Van Eycks painted portraits and religious subjects, one of the greatest of which is "The Virgin and Child."

Peter Paul Rubens [roo'b'nz] was probably the greatest of all Flemish painters. He was a great scholar and could speak eight different languages. He was therefore sent on a number of missions by his government. These journeys gave him an opportunity to study the people and works of art in many countries. He shows an artistic touch that he may have gained from his visits to Venice and other cities in the south. He turned away from formal portraits and religious themes and used subjects drawn from life and nature. "His horses are perfect in kind," says Reynolds. His pictures are studied as much for his method of working out details as for their artistic beauty.

Frans Hals, a friend of Rubens, was one of the foremost painters of portraits. His subjects are all notable for their life-like appearance. His "Laughing Cavalier" is the most widely reproduced and universally liked. Sir Anthony Van Dyck was another extremely gifted Flemish artist. Van Dyck had been a pupil of Rubens, and in his earlier years he spread the influence of his master wherever he went. He painted many religious subjects, but is best known for his portrait of Charles I, which he painted while in London.

The great Dutch painter, Rembrandt, was born in that historic city of Leyden in a house overlooking the Rhine. He was interested in people but cared little for graceful lines and pretty faces. He painted many pictures of his father and his mother and of interesting characters in the town. He also shows great genius in painting groups and religious subjects. One of the most noted of the latter is his picture of "The Holy Family." His group portrait, "Syndics of the Cloth Hall of Amsterdam," shown on page 456, is an interesting character study of the old Dutch merchants.

The Netherlands and Belgium Became Independent Countries

The Netherlands and Belgium are called the Low Countries because much of their land is below sea level. The resourceful, determined peoples of these countries — especially the Netherlanders — have had to wage a campaign against the sea with dikes, canals, and pumping machines such as windmills and, later, gas engines.

Heavily populated, the Low Countries have, as a necessity, developed efficient methods of agriculture and transportation. They have developed industry, too: food and flowers in the Netherlands; the steel industry in Belgium; and in both countries, the older crafts of weaving, lace-making, and ceramics.

The ancestors of the present-day Belgians were the fierce Belgae of Caesar's wars. The ancestors of the Netherlanders were also members of the scattered tribes which became part of the Frankish Empire. Upon the break-up of Charlemagne's empire, the northern Lowlanders became part of the German kingdom, and the southerners remained joined to the French kingdom. By

1500, Philip, Duke of Burgundy, was overlord of the Lowlanders, with his court at Brussels. In the 16th Century, Charles V, Emperor of the Holy Roman Empire, inherited Philip's possessions and thus brought the Lowlanders into his Empire. Under Philip II, who was King of Spain, religious persecution of Protestants in the northern part of the Lowlands was pushed to extremes. Rebellion broke out. Under the leadership of William of Orange the northern provinces detached themselves from Spain, and after long years of revolt, were recognized as an independent Dutch republic, called the United Provinces.

In this nation industry and commerce flourished. The activities of the Dutch East India Company laid the basis for the Dutch empire in the East Indies. But the brilliant period of the Dutch Republic was dimmed in time by unsuccessful wars with its trade rival, England, and by its failure to keep pace with other nations industrially. Early in the 19th Century the nation fell to Napoleon, and became part of his short-lived empire.

Meanwhile the southern provinces of the Lowlands, which had remained loyal to Spain, had been under the rule of Spain, and later of France and of Austria. After the defeat of Napoleon, the Dutch won independence as a kingdom; and to them were joined the peoples of the southern provinces. Differences in religion and in language led to the revolt of the southern provinces and their final establishment as the Kingdom of Belgium.

Both of the Low Countries came to hold wealthy colonial possessions — the Dutch in the East Indies and in South America; the Belgians in Africa.

To the great painting of the world, the artists of the Low Countries have been heavy contributors. Among the greatest of these artists are Rembrandt, Rubens, Frans Hals, and Van Dyck. And the Low Countries have other great names: to the Netherlands belongs the scientist Anton Van Leeuwenhoek; Erasmus, the Renaissance scholar; the philosopher Spinoza; to Belgium belong the writers De Coster and Maeterlinck.

SELF-TEST

I. Make and fill out an information chart comparing the Netherlands and Belgium. List such things as chief cities, rivers, industries, imports, exports, famous people, and so on.

II. Select the phrase that you think best completes each of the statements below.

1. Most of Belgium is (*a*) part of a coastal plain; (*b*) a land of magnificent distances; (*c*) a land of high mountains and deep river valleys.

2. In a sense it is true to say that the Dutch have made their land because (*a*) the Dutch are thrifty; (*b*) William of Orange saved the Dutch; (*c*) much of the land would be flooded except for the dikes the Dutch have built.

3. Belgium has often been called the battleground of nations. A place

name which illustrates this statement is (*a*) Brussels; (*b*) Waterloo; (*c*) Antwerp.

4. Dutch colonies are to be found in (*a*) North America; (*b*) the East Indies; (*c*) East Africa.

III. Match the following correctly by listing on a piece of paper the numbers and letters which mark related items:

(1) Philip II	(*a*)	Maeterlinck
(2) Frans Hals	(*b*)	folklore
(3) home of the carillon	(*c*)	great shipping center
(4) Stanley	(*d*)	reclaimed land
(5) *The Blue Bird*	(*e*)	persecution of Protestants
(6) Louvain	(*f*)	famous battlefield
(7) Antwerp	(*g*)	Belgium
(8) De Coster	(*h*)	African explorer
(9) polder	(*i*)	" The Laughing Cavalier "
(10) Waterloo	(*j*)	famous university

INTERESTING THINGS TO DO

Project for the Chart Maker and Artist

Prepare a rough outline map to show the chief trade routes from the great ports of the Netherlands to her East Indies colonies, and indicate the products exchanged. See *History of Commerce,* by Clive Day. Or look up individual colonies in an encyclopedia.

Assignments for the Roving Reporter

1. The reporter makes a study of one of the common industries of the Low Countries, for example, diamond-cutting, rug-making, tulip culture, or lace-making. He uses his information in preparing an article for a trade paper, like a jewelers' or florists' magazine, or a ladies' fashion journal. See *Belgium,* by Hugh Gibson.

2. The reporter has visited the Dutch East Indies. He writes an article for a popular magazine, describing the larger Dutch colonies and their valuable resources. Before the reporter completes his article, the Japanese have begun to take over the Dutch colonies, and so he hastily adds a paragraph explaining the effect Japanese control of the East Indies will have on the United Nations' war effort. See " Java Assignment," by Dee Bredin in *National Geographic Magazine,* Jan., 1942. See also individual islands in the encyclopedia.

3. Before World War II, the reporter spent a vacation traveling through Belgium. He wrote a travel article describing things that interested him — carillons, architecture, food, Flemish painting, etc. See *Belgium,* by Hugh Gibson, or *Let's Visit Belgium* (a guidebook), by Byron Steel.

Topics for Talks

1. "In darkest Africa." The region of the Belgian Congo was first explored by David Livingstone. Tell the story of Livingstone and also of Belgium's acquisition of the Congo territory. See "Livingstone" and "Belgian Congo" in an encyclopedia. Also, see "Livingstone" in *Book of Discovery,* by Margaret Synge, and in *Book of Courage,* by Hermann Hagedorn.

2. "The Golden Age of art." The Renaissance was the Golden Age of art in the Low Countries as it was in Italy. Prepare a talk about the greatest of the Dutch and Flemish painters of that period. If possible, illustrate your talk with prints of some of their masterpieces. Your school art teacher may be able to help you. See "Painting" in *Encyclopædia Britannica,* and *Famous Pictures,* by Charles L. Barstow.

Candidates for Your Album of Famous People

Duke of Alva, Van Dyck, Erasmus, Grotius, Hals, Van Leeuwenhoek, Maeterlinck, Rembrandt, Rubens, William of Orange. Select two of these people for your Album.

INTERESTING READING ABOUT THE LOW COUNTRIES

BANKS, HELEN W. *The Story of Holland.* "He laid before the King the troubled state of affairs in the Netherlands."

DUMAS, ALEXANDRE. *The Black Tulip.* One of the world's greatest novelists writes of the Dutch hero, William of Orange.

KELLY, E. P. *At the Sign of the Golden Compass.* An exciting story of a boy employed at a great printing house in Antwerp four hundred years ago.

National Geographic Magazine, Sept., 1933. "A New Country Awaits Discovery," by J. C. Krusinga. "Wrecks in a grain field which two years ago was a sea."

——, April, 1938. "Belgium: Europe in Miniature," by Douglas Chandler. "Carillon bells must ring true to the pitch of the tuning fork."

——, Feb., 1940. "Behind Netherlands Sea Ramparts," by McFall Kerbey. ". . . the Dutch had to become good engineers, or drown."

——, Jan., 1942. "Java Assignment," by Dee Bredin. ". . . the most impressive sight is the complete co-operation between the Netherlanders and the natives."

VAN LOON, H. W. *The Golden Book of the Dutch Navigators.* The great Dutch men of the sea in the age of discovery and exploration.

The World Book Encyclopedia. "Netherlands"; and Index: "Belgium"; "Holland."

ZWEIG, STEFAN. *Erasmus of Rotterdam.* The life of the Dutch philosopher who made such a great contribution to the forward-looking thought of his day.

PART THIRTEEN

SPAIN AND PORTUGAL BECAME GREAT POWERS, THEN GAVE WAY TO OTHER NATIONS

SPAIN AND PORTUGAL
Paris
Seine R.
Loire R.
Tours
FRANCE
Garonne R.
ATLANTIC
OCEAN
Bay of Biscay
PASS OF RONCESVALLES
PYRENEES
MTS.
ANDORRA
Santander
Bilbao
Ebro R.
CATALONIA
Barcelona
Coruna
ASTURIAS
Burgos
ARAGON
Santiago
Douro R.
Valladolid
BALEARIC IS.
Majorca
LEON
CASTILE
Madrid
Salamanca
SPAIN
Valencia
Segovia
LA MANCHA
PORTUGAL
Toledo
Tagus R.
Guadiana R.
Lisbon
SIERRA MORENA
Guadalquivir R.
Badajoz
Cordova
Granada
Seville
Malaga
Palos
MEDITERRANEAN SEA
Cadiz
Gibraltar
Ceuta
Tangier
SPANISH MOROCCO
North
NORTH AFRICA
MOROCCO
MILES
5° W.
0°
50° N.
45° N.
40° N.
35° N.

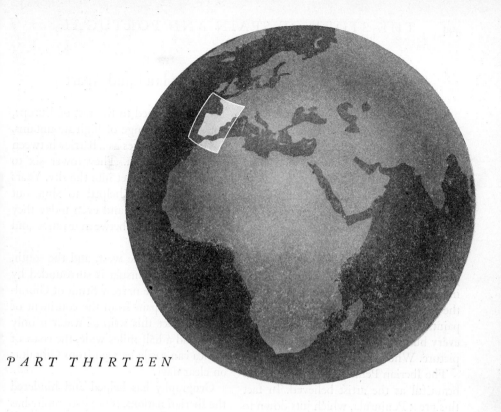

Spain and Portugal — Colonizing Nations

T HE Iberian Peninsula is the home of the Spanish and the Portuguese. It is the westernmost of the three peninsulas which jut out into the Mediterranean Sea, and its western shore is washed by the Atlantic Ocean. From the port of Palos, Columbus sailed west in search of a new route to the Far East and found instead a new world. What other seaport cities do you find in Spain? In Portugal? See how the great Pyrenees Mountains separate the Iberian Peninsula from the rest of Europe. Behind this mountain barrier the Spaniards and the Portuguese developed their own national cultures.

As you can see, the southernmost tip of Spain is separated from Africa only by the narrow Straits of Gibraltar. You have already read how the Moors pushed their way into Spain from the south. Find on the map the city of Cordova, which was the capital of the Mohammedans in Spain. To the east lies Granada, the last stronghold of the Moors. Locate also Madrid, the capital of Spain, and Lisbon, the capital of Portugal. In the story which follows you will read of the rise and fall of these two great nations as colonial powers. You will read also of the Spanish Civil War in the 1930's which proved to be a forerunner of World War II.

Chapter 1 ~ The Iberian Peninsula Is a Land Apart

Spain and Portugal are lands of many contrasts. The story is told of an artist who traveled through southern Spain for the first time. He saw the deep-blue cloudless sky, the faint purple of the rugged mountains standing out clearly in the distance, the dark green of the olive trees, the dainty pink and white blossoms of the almond trees, the green of the orange and lemon trees, the purple of the great bunches of grapes hanging from the vines. He was amazed by the beauty of the scene. "Everything paintable," he murmured, "every tree, every building, every mountain top is a picture. Where shall I begin?"

The Iberian Peninsula is, in places, as beautiful as the artist believed. In fact this great Peninsula, which juts down to separate the Mediterranean Sea from the Atlantic Ocean, is one of the most beautiful lands in all the world. It has great variety and contrasts in scenery.

One sees deep gorges and sunny valleys, high rocky mountains and broad plains, northern lands swept by cold raw winds and southern beaches over which gentle breezes play. Added to these, are extremes of temperature. Inland towns which are rather cold in the winter are hot in summer.

As the traveler goes farther south he finds that southern Spain looks more like Africa than Europe. There are green garden spots alternating with arid stretches of land. There are the same tawny mountains and prickly desert vegetation which are typical of northern Africa.

Mountains, straits, and seas surround the Iberian Peninsula. In some ways the Iberian Peninsula resembles an island.

True, it is joined to the rest of Europe, but a rugged range of high mountains, the Pyrenees, serves as a barrier between France and Spain. They tower six to twelve thousand feet into the sky. Years ago the Pyrenees helped to shut out northern invaders, and even today they make land travel between France and Spain difficult.

On the east, the west, and the south, the Iberian Peninsula is surrounded by water. Only the narrow Strait of Gibraltar divides Spain from the continent of Africa. Since this strip of water is only eight and a half miles wide, the coast of Africa can easily be seen from Gibraltar on clear days.

Geography has helped and hindered the Iberian nations. Since geography has separated Spain from the rest of Europe, we can expect the people of the Iberian Peninsula to be different from the other European peoples. You will see from the map on page 462 that high mountain ranges divide the Peninsula into many sections, as well as isolate it from the rest of the world. In fact, Spain is the highest country in Europe except Switzerland. Railways and roads have been difficult to build. Thus the people in the various parts of the country have been kept apart and have grown to have vastly different customs and traditions.

One might think from looking at the map of Spain and Portugal that boats could travel up and down the long rivers that extend into the heart of the Peninsula. From the high plains in the central part of the Peninsula, the rivers rush down steep mountains and through rocky gorges; but very few of them are deep or safe enough to be useful in bringing products from one part of the country to another. Many are nearly dry in summer. It was therefore natural that Spain and Portugal should develop coastwise shipping and, gradually, an extensive trade by sea with other nations.

In some ways geography has helped to bring Spain and Portugal into contact with the rest of the world. The towering mountains, which were barriers to commerce, have enormous mineral wealth: rich mines of gold, silver, mercury, lead, iron, wolfram, and copper. Time after time fierce invaders have pushed over the mountains, eager to seize the mines. The warm fertile plains on the south and east, covered with olive orchards and vineyards, have been a temptation to less fortunate peoples. The southern tip of the Peninsula — the backdoor of Spain

— lies open to Africa. We shall see how foreigners marched through this open backdoor and could not be forced out of the Iberian Peninsula for almost eight hundred years.

At one time the coffers of Spain and Portugal were overflowing with wealth from their vast colonial possessions in the Americas. Today these countries have lost their colonies, and both are financially poor. Most of their inhabitants depend upon agriculture for a living. In Portugal the chief products are grain, wine, and cork. In Spain the people raise sheep on the great dry tableland in the interior and cultivate orchards and vineyards along the coast. Mining remains important because of the valuable minerals that are to be found in the Iberian Peninsula.

Chapter 2 ~ The Peoples of the Iberian Peninsula Developed Two Separate Nations: Spain and Portugal

Many people were attracted to the Iberian Peninsula. Little is known of the very early inhabitants of the Iberian Peninsula, that is, the men of the early Stone Age. But, as in the rest of Europe, the primitive inhabitants of this region were later followed by the finely formed Cro-Magnons who merged into the modern peoples of Europe. The Cro-Magnons, as you read in Part One, were sturdy hunters and fighters, but they were also artistic, as shown by the graceful drawings of animals found in caves in northern Spain. The first historians who speak of Spain were Greeks, who called the inhabitants Iberians. It is not known exactly where the people came from, however. We still speak of Spain and Portugal as the Iberian Peninsula.

It is known that Phoenicians, from north of Palestine, came to trade in Spain. They founded the city of Cadiz and other colonies about three thousand years ago. At an early date the Greeks also came to trade, in rivalry with the Phoenicians. Both exerted a civilizing influence on the natives, passing on to them some of the knowledge and skill of Mediterranean peoples.

The Celts, somewhat later, followed the Greeks. As you will recall, the Irish and Welsh are also of Celtic origin. The Celts seem to have established themselves most strongly in the west, in the regions now known as Galicia and Portugal. But they mixed with the native inhabitants in many parts of the Peninsula. These were the peoples who lived in the Iberian Peninsula when the Romans entered Spain.

ROMAN AQUEDUCT

This granite aqueduct dates from the time of Augustus Caesar, and is the largest piece of Roman work surviving in Spain today. It brings water to Segovia.

Rome took a rich land south of the Pyrenees. The Romans were among the most important invaders of the Iberian Peninsula. They did not conquer the Peninsula without a long, hard, and bloody struggle, for the descendants of the Celts and Iberians were tough fighters who liked their independence. During the long years while Rome was trying to subdue these people, Carthage attacked Rome by coming up from Africa. You will recall the story of Hannibal's invasion through the Peninsula.

Rome finally completed the conquest of the Iberian Peninsula during the First Century. Spain (which then included what is now Portugal) became one of the richest territories of the far-flung Roman Empire. She also became one of the most Romanized provinces. Julius Caesar, as you may recall, was once governor of Spain. It was on his return from

Spain to Rome that he made his famous remark, " I would rather be first in a small Iberian village than second in Rome."

During the six hundred years that Rome ruled in Spain, she left a lasting mark on her most westerly province. Even today there are in Spain reminders of Roman civilization: strong stone bridges arching over streams, great aqueducts bringing fresh mountain water into the cities and villages, roads so well built that they have stood for almost two thousand years. These bridges, aqueducts, and roads were constructed by the Romans and were used long after the Spanish people had forgotten that the Romans had ever conquered Spain.

Of particular interest are the Roman aqueducts which bring water to the city of Segovia [say goh'vya]. During the Middle Ages, after the power of Rome had disintegrated, the peasants in the vicinity called the aqueduct " el diablo " (the devil). Not knowing who had built it, they decided that only the magic art of the devil was strong enough to place one massive stone on top of the other with such clever design.

Some of the oldest Spanish villages and towns are surrounded by walls, now crumbled, which the Roman soldiers built to keep out their enemies. Others have great triumphal arches through which the victorious troops once marched. Roman colosseums are also to be seen.

The Romans imposed their language, laws, education, customs, and religion on the lands which made up modern Spain and Portugal. The Portuguese language, spoken in the west; Castilian, spoken in the center and south; and Catalan, spoken in the east, are all Romance (Roman-like) languages, derived from Latin. The fundamental laws of Spain and Portugal are based on Roman law. Like Italy, the Iberian Peninsula still has an essentially Roman culture. It was the Romans, too, who brought Spain her religion, first her pagan gods and finally Christianity. It is believed that St. Paul preached in Spain. At any rate, Christianity appeared in Rome in his time, and it soon made its way into Spain. The Roman Catholic faith has been the principal one of Spain and her colonies ever since except during the eight hundred years of Moorish rule. Then the Mohammedan religion was official and predominant.

The northern barbarians swept through Spain. The Romans and Romanized Spaniards, after about six hundred years, seem to have lost much of their early vigor. It was a poor time to become soft, because Germanic barbarians were migrating into Europe. Gothic tribes grew restless. They lived in Roman territory south of the Danube for a time, and even adopted Christianity. But soon they quarreled with the Romans, and, as you have learned, Alaric the Goth captured and sacked Rome.

The Goths also spread to France and Spain, dividing the territory among themselves. One of the barbarian tribes, the Vandals who had entered Spain earlier, took southern Spain. Andalusia, in southern Spain, takes its name from the Vandals. Later attacked by the Visigoths, the Vandals went over to North Africa. The Visigoth monarchy on the Peninsula lasted for nearly three hundred years, until the Mohammedan invasion early in the Eighth Century. The Vandal government was unstable, but it ruled Spain harshly and made slaves of the inhabitants. The Goths, though far less civilized than the people they conquered, at least brought Spain new blood and energy. The Christian Church

helped to unify the inhabitants and the conquerors, and it also helped to keep learning alive.

The Moors marched into Spain. At this point in the story of the Iberian Peninsula, something happened in Spain which brought her culture and learning while the other European countries were still living in ignorance. To understand what occurred we must recall the story of Mohammed, told in Part Seven. At the beginning of the Seventh Century, Mohammed gave a new faith to the Arabs who lived on the great Arabian Desert. His turbaned followers determined to convert the world to Mohammedanism. Mounted on splendid horses, the Arabs raged through northern Africa like a storm, sweeping all opposition before them, and converting the people of North Africa to their faith. Less than one hundred years after Mohammed had given his new religion to the world, his followers stood ready to cross the narrow Strait of Gibraltar and carry their religion and civilization into Europe.

The Goths were weakened by political and religious disturbances, and Spain once again became fair game for invaders. Early in the Eighth Century the Mohammedans from North Africa made what we would now call an amphibious landing at Gibraltar. The Visigoths put up fairly sturdy resistance, but it was useless. Soon nearly all Spain was overrun by the Mohammedans. Here is a description of the Moors which is given by an author who sympathized with the Christian inhabitants of Spain:

. . . the reins of their horses were as fire, their faces black as pitch, their eyes shone like burning candles; their horses were swift as leopards and the riders fiercer than a wolf in a sheepfold at night; . . . the noble Goths were broken in an hour, quicker than tongue can tell. Oh, luckless Spain!

On through Spain marched the victors, over the Pyrenees Mountains and into France. As you read, there they were defeated by Charles Martel at the Battle of Tours in 732, an important date in Europe's history. The map on page 462 shows Gibraltar, where the Moors entered, and Tours, in France, where they were defeated.

The Moors settled and civilized Spain. When the Moors found they could not push their way through France and on into Europe, they returned to settle down on the Spanish Peninsula. Here they built up a Moorish state that lasted almost eight hundred years, or over five times as long as our nation is old. During those eight centuries there was a remarkable civilization in Spain.

While the rest of Europe was in darkness and ignorance, Spain had the benefit of the brilliant learning of the Moors. When London, Paris, and other European cities were mere villages, Cordova [kohr'doh vah], the capital of Spain, was a flourishing city with 200,000 houses and more than a million people. A Moorish writer says that after dark one could walk ten miles through Cordova and never pass through a street not lighted by public lamps. This was at a time when a man venturing out after dark in Paris or London had to take a lantern to light his way and had to wear high boots to wade through the thick mud that often covered the streets. When other Europeans were dressed in skins of animals and in coarse clothing, the Moors were wearing bright silks, cotton cloth, and fine linens. They also took baths in the 900 bathhouses of Cordova. Christian Europe at that time remained relatively unwashed.

The caliph built a comfortable palace. The palace of the caliph, or ruler of the Moors, was far more beautiful and comfortable than any of the castles of the medieval knights. Although rather plain outside, inside it was beautifully finished with highly polished marble. The walls were elaborately carved and the floors covered with colorful mosaics made up of small pieces of colored tile, glass, and stone, carved and fitted together to make patterns. The Moors were masters in mosaic work.

In the palace of the caliph were carved marble columns and fountains. Jets of water played from the fountains. In the winter, soft, handwoven Persian rugs from the East were spread on the floors. Hot and cold water was piped into the bathrooms even at this early date.

The Moorish scholars established schools and libraries. Most of the learning of Greece was unknown in Europe in the Middle Ages. But the Arabs had come into contact with Greek civilization in the parts of the Eastern Roman Empire they had conquered, and they brought it to Spain. There were many noted scholars, both Arabic and Hebrew, in Moorish Andalusia. They helped to transmit Greek culture to the rest of Europe. They made notable contributions to philosophy, medicine, mathematics, chemistry, astronomy, and botany. Numerous schools were established, including hundreds of free schools. The rich could go to private academies and later to universities. There were splendid libraries. In the 10th Century the scholarly caliph of Cordova sent all over the world for books, and finally gathered together a library of four hundred thousand volumes.

The Moors left beautiful monuments in southern Spain, many of which are fortunately preserved: the graceful and lovely Alhambra [ahl ahm'brah] at Granada [grah nah'dah], the thousand-columned Mosque of Cordova, the col-

Gramstorff Bros. Inc., Malden, Mass.

THE MOSQUE OF CORDOVA

This mosque is one of the finest of the Moorish buildings in Spain. It was used as fortress as well as mosque. The interior of the mosque is a forest of pillars. There are over 800 pillars of marble, porphyry, and jasper. Notice the odd striped arches overhead.

orful Alcazar [ahl kah'thahr], or palace, at Seville, and many more. A part of the Mosque of Cordova is shown in the picture on page 469.

Moorish life was based on agriculture and good trade. The Moors introduced rice and cotton and peaches and other fruits into Spain, including the orange and lemon. They also introduced silk culture. They were noted for fine pottery, glazed tiles, silks, brocades, velvet, ornamental leather products, and jewels. Some of the irrigation canals they built are still in use. Moorish civilization, truly a splendid one, had a tremendous effect not only on Spain but on the rest of Europe as well.

The Christians gradually drove the Moors southward. The reconquest of Spain by the Christians took a very long time indeed. Of the several little Chris-

tian kingdoms in the north of the Iberian Peninsula, Castile finally became the most powerful. The Castilian king, Alfonso VI, in the latter part of the 11th Century, extended his power over Toledo; this meant that most of the northern half of Spain was in Christian hands. His most important vassal and best warrior was the Cid [theed] — this Arabic word means "lord" or "master" — Spain's foremost national hero. The Cid was a great soldier, an excellent organizer, and a faithful servant of his sovereign. The Spanish poem *El Cid* tells the story of this most human hero. He conquered the great Moorish city of Valencia, although it could not be held for long. Much later, in the 13th Century, the King of Castile conquered Seville and Cordova. Afterward the Moors were confined to a small area near Granada.

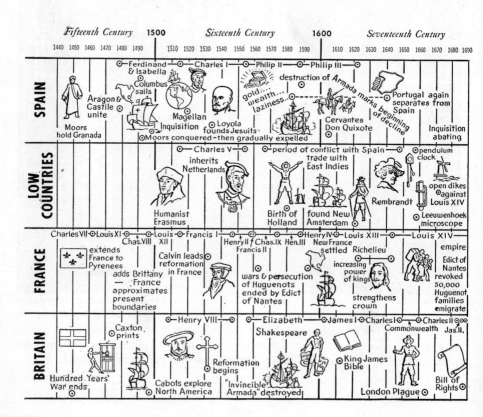

The founding of the Portuguese monarchy. During the early part of the 12th Century the northern part of what is now Portugal was a country ruled by counts who were vassals of the king of León. Pushing south against the Moors, they conquered so much territory that in 1144 Count Alfonso Enriques [ayn ree' kes] took the title of King. Alfonso captured Lisbon. Over the years the Moors were gradually driven southward in Portugal, as they had been in Spain. Portugal remained a separate kingdom for over four hundred years. In 1580, she was taken over by her strong neighbor and, at this time in history, ceased her independent existence and became a part of Spain.

Social conditions in the Peninsula were improving. The history of kings and battles is only part of the story of any nation. The life of the people is of even more importance. And life in the Middle Ages in the Iberian Peninsula was gradually improving. Spain and Portugal had relatively prosperous agriculture; their most important activities were trade and manufacturing. As in the rest of Europe a middle class in the towns rose to prosperity and power, and the lot of the serfs improved considerably.

The kings often sided with the people and the towns against overbearing feudal nobles, and the towns acquired special charters giving them greater privileges. Representatives of the towns were admitted to a national council as early as the 12th Century, probably the first instance of a representative type of government to be seen in Western Europe, not including Rome. The Moors,

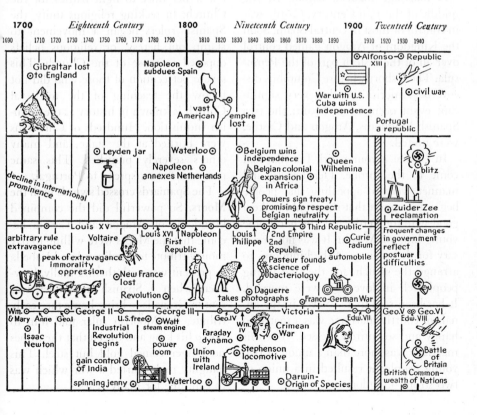

you will recall, were among the best educated peoples of Europe, and education was gradually improved, though still confined to a small select class of people. The great medieval university of Salamanca was founded very early in the 13th Century, and several other universities were founded slightly later. Also the 13th Century rulers encouraged Christian, Hebrew, and Moslem scholars, poets, and musicians. Epic poems and spirited ballads, in which Spain has always been extraordinarily rich, were written. The people could see simple dramas and religious plays. Religion, it should be remembered, was an essential part of life in Spain, and the government and the Church became more and more inseparable. This religious unity made national political unity or growth as a nation easier to accomplish.

A marriage made a nation. By the middle of the 15th Century, Castile was in control of most of central Spain. Soon the Kingdom of Aragon gained control over all of the eastern part of the Peninsula. Then, shortly before Columbus discovered America, another very significant event occurred in Spain; the two Spanish kingdoms, Aragon and Castile, were united.

In Castile a young girl, Isabella, had come to the throne. Her beauty and manner were so appealing that people began to suggest that she would make a good wife for Ferdinand, the handsome young king of Aragon. It was not necessary for the advisers of the kingdoms to arrange the match, for the two young people fell in love and were married. It has been said that " Never in the annals of courtly marriage was a match so happy and so entirely blessed." But this marriage was more than a union of two young people; it resulted in a union of two strong kingdoms.

In governing their kingdoms Ferdinand and Isabella proved positive and determined rulers. Isabella, to force the nobles to recognize her leadership, once had the castles of sixty troublesome barons torn down. Ferdinand was also determined to be complete ruler of his kingdom. " When anything needs to be done," he said, " one head is better than a thousand."

Ferdinand and Isabella tried to unite Spain and to expand their territory abroad as well. This policy was to have a tremendous effect on the rest of the world. Soon Isabella and Ferdinand became the undisputed rulers of all Spain that was not held by the Moors. Ferdinand was glad to extend his kingdom, and Isabella hoped to spread the Roman Catholic faith through southern Spain. She was a devout Roman Catholic and felt it her duty to fight battles for the Church. In seeking religious unity, the Spanish rulers began a movement to stamp out heresy, or religious beliefs opposed to those of the Church. This severe persecution of those who did not follow the teaching of the medieval Church is known in history as the Spanish Inquisition. Hundreds of Christians were burned at the stake, and many others severely punished. This same movement soon spread to Portugal.

The Spaniards crossed swords with the Moors. So powerful did the combined kingdoms of Aragon and Castile become that the Moors were willing to pay money tribute to Ferdinand and Isabella to prevent war with them. Finally, however, when a Spanish messenger was sent to Granada to bring home the yearly tribute, the Moorish ruler told him to say to his king and queen that the mines no longer coined gold but steel. This haughty reply started a war which was to continue for many years.

The desire to expel the Moors from Spain was connected with the idea of religious and political unity. The Moors were foreigners against whom Spaniards had been fighting for nearly eight hundred years, and they were, in the eyes of the Spanish, heathens. As they had not been Christian members of the medieval Church, they were spared the terrible persecution of dissenters in the Spanish Inquisition.

As the years passed success came to the Spanish. Isabella brought into Spain men from England, France, and Germany who knew how to make cannon, which were beginning to be used in Europe. Compared to modern guns, these first cannon were clumsy and inefficient, but they helped to batter down the great walls built around the Moorish cities, and helped the Spanish people to reconquer their land.

One of the last stands of the Moors was made at Granada in the year just preceding that eventful year of 1492. For several months the city was surrounded by the Spanish army with Ferdinand at its head. Seeing that they would be starved into yielding, the Moors finally surrendered. During the next hundred years nearly three million Moors were driven from the country, back into North Africa where Moorish civilization flourished.

The Jews were also expelled from the Peninsula. There was another non-Christian group in Spain: the Jews. They had entered Spain at an early date, and many of them reached prosperity and high positions in the government, during the Middle Ages in Spain. They were, in general, able and industrious. On religious grounds Ferdinand and Isabella decided to expel them from the country unless they accepted immediate conversion to Christianity. The decree of expulsion was carried out, with considerable severity, in 1492. Soon after, the Jews were similarly expelled from Portugal. Here we have another instance of lack of religious freedom and the resulting tyranny over the mind of man.

Chapter 3 ~ Spain and Portugal Exploited New Lands but Lost Power at Home

A united Spain led the Western world. With the Moors conquered, all of Spain was ruled by Spaniards. The kingdom of Isabella and Ferdinand extended from the bleak northern mountains to the warm southern plains. A common purpose, the desire to drive out the Moors, had done much to unite the Spanish people. Spaniards from all parts of the Peninsula had fought side by side and had rejoiced together when the victory was won. With a strong king and queen to head the nation, with the people unified as never before, Spain was to win fame and respect abroad. For a time, she was to have a high place among the nations of the world.

Spaniards searched for gold and glory in the New World. The year 1492 marked the beginning of a new era in Spanish history. Not only was the entire Spanish Peninsula reconquered, but an expedition was sent out which was to bring fame and glory to Spain. It was in this year that Columbus, sailing in ships which had been furnished by Isabella, discovered the New World. The picture on this page shows an important occasion in Columbus' life.

You already know that Spain took the lead in exploring the New World. Hundreds of adventurers sailed in ships that were bought by the king of Spain. Other farsighted men sent out expeditions at their own expense. Some went for gold; some to win glory; some went to carry the name of God into the New World. But Spain's glory came mainly from the explorers who claimed the lands they explored and planted the flag of Spain in all the Americas.

There is not space here to tell again the story of Balboa who discovered the distant Pacific, of Cortés who invaded Mexico, of Ponce de León [pohn'thay day lay ohn'] who searched for the Fountain of Youth, or of De Soto who found the Mississippi. You have learned about the explorers of the 16th Century in your American history. But the map on page 475 will bring back to mind the expeditions of these men and show how much of the New World was explored and claimed by Spain.

During the 16th Century quantities of gold flowed into the treasury of Spain from her colonies in America. Spain became the wealthiest nation in Europe. The nobles of Spain, enriched by plunder, ate their food from gold and silver plates. Ladies wore priceless gems and dresses of gold cloth. Everywhere the flag of Spain was feared and respected.

Portugal also had an eye for exploration. Although many enthusiastic voyagers sailed under the flag of Spain, we

Metropolitan Museum of Art

COLUMBUS PLEADING HIS CAUSE BEFORE ISABELLA

Columbus must have been eloquent and convincing, for Queen Isabella provided the three ships in which he sailed westward and discovered a new world.

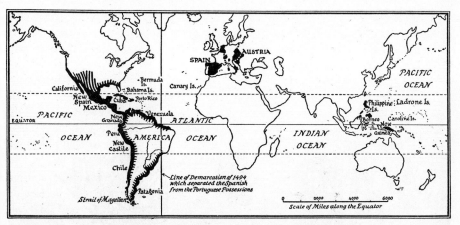

EXTENT OF SPANISH RULE UNDER CHARLES V
The shaded portion of the map shows how much of the Western world was ruled by
Emperor Charles V of Spain. During the 15th and 16th centuries Spain was the wealthi-
est and most powerful nation of Western Europe.

must not forget the exploring spirit of
the Portuguese, who started sailing to
far away places considerably earlier. A
guiding spirit was Prince Henry the
Navigator, who encouraged exploration
in Africa and South America. In the
15th Century Portuguese royalty carried
on his work. Early in the 15th Century,
the Madeiras and the Azores were rediscovered and colonized by Portuguese.
Diaz rounded the African Cape of Good
Hope. In 1498 Vasco da Gama, following the same route, finally anchored in
the harbor of Calicut, in western India.

Many more voyages of discovery were
carried out by the Portuguese. In fact,
during this period of discovery the Pope
conferred on the Portuguese king the
title of "Lord of the navigation, conquest, and commerce of Ethiopia, Persia,
Arabia, and India." The Portuguese also
discovered Java, Siam (now Thailand),
some of the China coast, and Japan.
Magellan, the first man whose ships
sailed round the globe, was a Portuguese,
though he was in the service of Spain.

The Portuguese were seeking trade,
and they did not penetrate far inland in
the countries which they discovered.
Nevertheless they gained an extensive
foreign empire. This included Brazil,
which was visited by Alvares Cabral
[ahl vahr'ays kah brahl']. One day Brazil would be greater than the mother
country, with the largest Portuguese-
speaking city of the world, Rio de Janeiro [ree'oo di zhuh nay'roo].

The Golden Age of Portugal was
brief. The Golden Age of Portugal, like
that of Spain, was in the 16th Century.
The Portuguese were extending their
power abroad, and they were prosperous
at home. They were extremely proud of
their nationality. They were strong in
their religious faith, which they carried
to all lands they touched. As they spread
their trade to other lands, their interest
grew in colonies, and economic expansion abroad. But despite their Golden
Age of trade and expansion the Portuguese were to fall, as you have already
learned, to their powerful neighbor,
Spain, in 1580. Sixty years later Portugal regained independence.

Spain's Golden Age was also brief.
During the first half of the 16th Century,

Culver Service

THE ARMADA

The 131 vessels of the Armada took two months to sail from Lisbon to the English Channel. After a mismanaged voyage and a violent storm and an attack by Drake's forces, only about 50 ships managed to return to Spain.

Spain's ruler was Charles I of Spain, generally called Charles V (of the Holy Roman Empire). He was the most powerful sovereign of his time. He fought, with much success, to extend Spain's political power in Europe. He had inherited the Low Countries, as you read in Part Twelve. Sardinia, southern Italy, and Austria were also inherited. He won most of northern Italy by conquest. As Charles V made Spain the center of his empire, all of these, except Austria, became practically possessions of Spain. As Emperor of the Holy Roman Empire Charles V was also the overlord of Germany. However, Charles was unable to stem the tide of Protestantism in Germany, and he finally gave up his imperial duties and retired to a monastery. His industrious son, Philip II, took over the throne of Spain, and with it all of his father's possessions except Austria and the Holy Roman Empire. These went to Charles's brother, Ferdinand.

Philip II, called by Spaniards " the

Prudent " and by his enemies " the Devil of the South," tried hard to pursue his father's policies. In spite of his best efforts, he also failed.

Spain lost her possessions through neglect and misrule. Under Charles V and later his son Philip II, Spain ruled rich colonies in the New World as well as holding sway over most of the countries of Western Europe. But she governed poorly. Instead of helping her colonies and territories and winning their loyalty and respect, she overtaxed the people and took their gold for herself. Soon parts of the Spanish empire were agitating for independence.

The Netherlands, which at the time were under Spanish rule, were the first to revolt. Then, gradually, the countries of the New World began to fall away. They were tired of the burden of Spanish taxes, of having public offices filled by Spaniards, of having the churches controlled by foreign priests. In 1800 Mexico, Central America, and all of South America except Brazil belonged to Spain. By 1900 she owned not one acre of land in the New World. Neglect, misrule, and selfishness had lost Spain her most valuable possessions.

Another mistake that greatly weakened the Spanish power came through the expulsion of the Moors and the Jews, which we read about in the preceding chapter.

English sea captains gave Spain a great blow. In 1588 a disaster befell Spain from which she was never to recover. In that year, as you will recall from reading the story of the English, Philip II of Spain sent more than a hundred ships and thousands of men to punish England for the part she had played in helping the people of the Netherlands gain their independence from Spain.

From the time the stately Armada sailed from the Spanish harbor of Cadiz until the day a few broken ships straggled back to safety, the men of Spain fared poorly. First, the daring English sea captains threw the Armada into a panic by their defense. Then, as you will recall, a terrible storm in the North Sea sent many of the Spanish galleons to the bottom of the ocean. Only a few of the Spaniards who sailed north to fight the English returned to tell the story. By the destruction of the Spanish Armada, England wrested from Spain her rule of the sea. From that time Spain began to sink into the background, while England ruled the waves and became one of the leading nations of Europe.

The downfall of Spain and Portugal. This eclipse of Spain was to last for three centuries. Not until recent years has Spain again become a significant factor in world affairs. The Spanish monarchy constantly became weaker and Spain declined in every way. Finally she lost not only all her colonies in the New World, but her influence in Europe and her prosperity within her own borders. The course of Portugal, a part of Spain from 1580 to 1640, was similar. We might remember that other empires before Spain and Portugal had risen only to decline and become weak.

The causes of the decline were many and complicated. The Spanish government came to be something closely approaching the 20th Century Fascist totalitarian state, except that in Spain the Church played a very important role. The sovereigns, in furthering the royal power, had suppressed the liberties of which the towns had been so proud. Charles V, for example, vigorously suppressed the towns or cities, like Toledo, which ventured to fight against him for their rights. The national assembly met less and less frequently. Religious liberty was impossible.

Moreover, foreign nations were jealous of Spain's great power and attacked her whenever they could. The foreign wars were so expensive and taxes were so high that it was not profitable to engage in industry or trade. The gold and silver from America seemed to make the Peninsula rich for a time, but the riches brought about high prices and were finally squandered. People found themselves as poverty-stricken as they had been before.

Spain and Portugal had laid no firm foundation for wealth in colonies or trade, or stability at home. Wealth became concentrated in the hands of a few. Court life was extravagant and splendid, much as it was in France at the time previous to the Revolution. The people, of course, became more and more wretched.

In general, Spain and Portugal

GATE OF ALCÁNTARA

This gate is part of a Roman bridge built across the Tagus [tah′guhs] River at Alcántara [ahl kahn′tah rah]. The name of the town means " the bridge " in Arabic.

doomed themselves to disintegration and decay by the 17th Century. They had followed a feudal policy at home with the Church and State combined to gain wealth and suppress economic and religious liberties. That proved to be an outmoded economic and social system for the 17th and 18th Centuries. Their foreign trade had not prospered and their sea power had declined in competition with their great rivals, the British navy, and the British and Dutch merchants. The nations of the Iberian Peninsula were not ready to face the opportunities and effects of the Industrial Revolution which began in the 18th Century. Ceasing to progress and to grow, they had declined.

Three powerful groups determined life in Spain. In the 19th and 20th Centuries, Spain was mainly held in the grip of three powerful groups: the large land-

owners, the clergy, and the army. The land was held by a small number of people, the grandees (Spain's high-ranking noblemen) and wealthy landlords. The peasants did not own the land but farmed it for the landlords, much as the serfs did in the Middle Ages. While the peasants were not bound to the land as their ancestors had been, they were held in such poverty that they seldom escaped. They could not risk other fields of labor. Neither were the large landowners of Spain efficient managers. While the people went hungry they permitted large estates to remain uncultivated, sometimes reserving them merely for hunting or for raising bulls to be killed in the bullfights. Spain's landlord-and-land problem was a tremendous one. Naturally little was done about it under the monarchy, for the king looked to these wealthy landowners for support. Later you will see how the people tried to take things into their own hands, and what happened to them.

The greatest landlord in all Spain was the Church, which had become more than a religious institution. It engaged in many activities, the most important of which were publishing, banking, and government. The Church press was the best equipped and most powerful in the country. Certainly the Church was a powerful economic, social, and political force in the life of the country. It has been said that it was stronger than any man, mightier than any grandee, and more powerful than the monarchy or the army.

A third powerful group in Spain was the army. The Spanish army was unique in many ways. Its size was strangely out of proportion to the needs of the country, and its staff of officers was completely out of proportion to the needs of the army. There was approximately one officer for every six to ten men. Furthermore this officer caste of the army was favored in every way. For years, from two-thirds to three-fourths of the military budget was for officers' salaries. Only a small amount was devoted to armaments and the payroll of the men in the ranks. The Spanish army under Alfonso XIII was noted for being inefficient and ineffective, poorly organized and badly armed. Yet no other army has ever had a greater influence in the rule of a country. Its officer caste resisted change, and used its power to keep Spain from becoming an efficient, modern nation.

The combined power of the wealthy landlords, a very powerful Church, and the army, kept Spain a weak and backward nation. This was the state of affairs at the turn of the century when the last Spanish king came to the throne.

From monarchy to dictatorship. Alfonso XIII, the last king of Spain, had come to the throne at the age of sixteen. He had been brought up by those who thought it was desirable to keep the wealthy landlords, the priests, and the military caste in their traditional roles of power. Alfonso also had been taught, and firmly believed in, the divine right of kings. The histories of England and France furnished him with examples. When his ideas conflicted with the liberal Spanish constitution which had been written in 1912, he always found a way to evade it.

In some ways Alfonso was effective. He realized that Spain needed more industries and better education, and that she should try to catch up with her more prosperous European neighbors. Under his rule factories, mines, and other industries developed; the building of the beautiful University City on the outskirts of Madrid was begun; trade and friendship with South American countries encouraged.

Yet underneath this surface progress, trouble was brewing. A series of incidents occurred with which Alfonso could not cope successfully. World War I burst like a devastating bomb upon the scene, changing life in every European country. Although Alfonso, probably guided by a few intellectuals who warned him against military suicide, managed to keep his country out of the war, he could not escape its consequences. There was a boom in Spanish war industries, but after the war came unemployment, hunger, and unrest. Violent strikes helped to undermine Alfonso's popularity and position. The labor movement was becoming stronger.

Seeking to recover some of his popularity, Alfonso sent a military expedition into Morocco. Seldom has a war proved more disastrous to an aggressor. The inefficient Spanish army proved to be worse than might have been expected. Thousands of Spanish soldiers were killed by the natives of Morocco; and the remainder of the army, together with all of its equipment, was captured. Only when France joined the conflict to protect her colonies in Morocco was the situation saved.

You can imagine the resentment caused in Spain by Alfonso's unsuccessful war. To make matters worse for the king, the Republicans, or liberals, seized this opportune time to insist upon a reform in government. The bewildered, desperate Alfonso knew that he must do something and do it quickly. Observing that Mussolini had been welcomed by the Italian industrialists, he allowed the General Primo de Rivera [pree'moh day ree vay'rah] to take command of the government. And he did not interfere when Primo set aside the constitution.

In Spain as in Italy, dictatorship had become the order of the day.

A bloodless revolution established a republic in Spain. The dictatorship which Alfonso had encouraged lasted until 1931. It had done nothing to help the lot of the impoverished common people. So in 1931 the Republic of Spain was born. Fortunately this came about without fighting and without bloodshed. King Alfonso hurried across the border into France. Seldom has a new government been set up with greater promise. Spain abandoned itself to the gay fiestas for which it is famous, and crowds paraded through the streets of the city, singing, dancing, and carrying banners.

Unlike the Russian revolutionists, who wiped out the royal family, the Spanish liberals treated the terrified queen and her children with the greatest of courtesy. Eyewitnesses say that the gay crowds were so anxious not to embarrass the queen with their liberal rejoicing that they stopped singing and lowered their banners as the queen's car passed. *Buen viaje* [bwen vee ah'hay] (good journey) was shouted after the departing car. The outside world was amazed at the good humor and success of the "bloodless revolution."

Spain as a republic. The men who drew up the new constitution and shaped the course of the nation were professors, writers, doctors, and lawyers. They wrote one of the most liberal and idealistic constitutions ever produced. It provided not only for a representative, democratic government, but for social reforms, such as the care of children, education, and the social and political freedom of women. Manuel Azana [mah nwehl' ah thah'nyah], who was one of the most influential leaders in the early days of the Republic, was such a true liberal that he allowed everyone, even the enemies of the new government, freedom of speech and action.

Azana and the other leaders were not experienced in making their ideas work successfully. By their very liberality they allowed the men who opposed them to gain the strength to overthrow the government. Neither were they sufficiently drastic with the enemies of the Republic who tried to block social reforms by opposing the division of the great estates and refusing to grant better working conditions in the factories.

In 1933 the elections were won by the conservatives, who immediately began to undo the work of the liberals. Money for education was refused; unions for workers were suppressed; the large estates of wealthy landowners were protected; Azana and other liberal leaders were tried and put into prison. When some of the workers' organizations began to resist the new government, there was hard fighting, and Spain entered into a period of terror. Although the liberals regained control of the government in the early 1936 elections, their success was short-lived. Spain's conservative military men began to fear that the liberals would interfere with the army. Therefore a part of the army revolted and, led by General Franco, swept Spain into a bitter civil war.

A clash of ideas became a clash of swords. In this Spanish war of 1936 to 1939 the first conflict was between the organized powerful conservatives, and a duly elected, established liberal government. Clearly opposing each other in the bitter struggle were the forces of liberalism and of Fascism. Representing the powerful interests and Fascism was General Franco, who had on his side most of the army, the monarchists, the landowners, and the more conservative churchmen. These supporters of the rev-

SPANISH LOYALISTS ESCAPING TO FRANCE

Loyalist troops, hard pressed by Franco's Nationalists, are pictured here escaping over the border into France. They are under a French military guard.

lution were called Nationalists because of their nationalistic policies. On the other side were the Spanish liberals ranging from those who hoped to see a really democratic system of government established to those who favored Communism. The liberals were known also as Loyalists because they were loyal to the existing government. Thus Spain became the bloody battleground for the believers in two opposing forms of government and ways of life. An episode from this war is shown above.

The Spanish Civil War was a preview of World War II. In the Spanish Civil War we see the alignment of forces and the methods of all-out brutality which characterized World War II. The Spanish Republican liberals, called the Reds by their enemies, were aided by the planes, guns, and soldiers of Russia.

The Fascist Franco received the support of the German Nazis and the Italian Fascists. Though these powers had not declared war they used the Iberian Peninsula as a proving ground for their arms and methods of warfare. Spain, of course, suffered. Her land was devastated, her university and other modern projects laid in rubble, and her common people stoned, punished with wanton cruelty, and killed.

The democratic nations such as England, as we shall learn, did not feel ready to come to the aid of the liberals in Spain. They were trying to avoid a general war and were pursuing a policy of conciliation. Thus the Fascist forces in Spain won out, the liberals were crushed. Spain now is a Fascist nation, dictated to by a Fascist dictator, Franco. With the varying fortunes of World War II, his position was an uneasy one, for he could not hope to please both the Fascist and the democratic interests. It was probable, however, that the Spanish people would never rest content until they, too, obtained some of the freedoms that are not possible under the Fascist system of government. Spain remained a problem to herself and to the world.

Portugal's course paralleled that of Spain. Portugal ran a course parallel with that of Spain. Her great colony of Brazil declared its independence early in the 19th Century. About one hundred years later, only four years before World War I began, Manoel [mah nwehl'] II, the last King, was forced to abdicate and a republic was proclaimed. The constitution adopted in 1933, and later amended, leans toward a Fascist pattern. Although the virtual dictator, Salazar, seemed in some ways sympathetic with Hitler, Mussolini, and Franco, Portugal remained neutral in World War II.

Chapter 4 ~ Architects, Painters, and Writers of Spain and Portugal Have Added Color to Civilization

The Spanish and Portuguese are music-lovers. The countless artists, writers, and even ordinary tourists who visited Spain and Portugal speak in glowing terms of the beauty, color, and picturesqueness of Spain and Portugal and their people. These peoples have expressed themselves in many forms of art. Their love of beauty shows itself in the so-called minor arts: weaving, ceramics, carving, iron-work, lace-making, as well as in architecture, painting, and literature. Moreover they have brilliantly expressed their joy of life in music and dancing.

The dancing girls of Cadiz were famous in ancient times, and Spanish dances — and every region of Spain has its own variety — are still celebrated everywhere. The fandango and bolero originated in Spain. Spanish folk music is generally considered to be one of the world's richest. It has furnished inspiration to many great composers. Fortunately hundreds of Spanish tunes from the 13th Century onward have been pre-served. The guitar, in the form introduced by the Romans, has been Spain's traditional musical instrument. Those who have heard it only in dance bands may not realize its possibilities when it is played " Spanish style " by a talented Spanish artist. There were many famous guitar players as early as the 16th Century.

Spain has produced great painters. Spain has produced some of the world's great painters. One who is now held in great esteem all over the world was not born in Spain, but on the island of Crete. He lived and painted in Spain for nearly forty years during the last part of the 16th Century. His work portrays the mystic Spanish spirit. His name was Domenico Theotocopuli [doh may'ni-koh thay oh'toh koh poo'lee], but he is better known as El Greco [el gray'koh] (The Greek). Although he also painted portraits, most of his paintings are of religious subjects. They are amazing in structure and balance, and they show El Greco's desire to go far beyond realism into spiritual interpretation. His figures are frequently elongated. His work is remarkable for contrasts of light and shade, and for his use of color and texture. One of his great pictures is "The Burial of the Count of Orgaz."

No artist ever more vividly presented the life of the people about him than did some of the Spanish painters of the 17th Century. Velasquez [vay-lahs′keth], one of Spain's greatest painters, was a man of keen observation. He made his brush picture what he saw. Velasquez painted many portraits of the ugly, lantern-jawed, weak-mouthed King Philip IV, and many court scenes. One of his best-known paintings is the charming and lifelike picture of Don Balthasar [dohn bahl-tah sahr′] cantering over the hills with the snow-capped mountains in the distance. He sits proudly in his saddle and holds a baton in his right hand with almost comic seriousness. This painting is reproduced on this page. Another is of Princess Maria Teresa of Austria. As we see her in her very elaborate court costume, we may wonder if the life of a princess was always happy.

The 18th Century was not a brilliant period in Spain's artistic history, except for one genius in painting: Francisco Goya [frahn thees′koh goh′yah]. He lived lustily and intensely. Fortunately for the world, much of his vitality has been preserved for us on canvas. His range is great, from delicate and tender portraits of children to savage portrayals of the horrors of war, as in his "Shootings of the Second of May," or even in his portraits of the vicious Queen Maria Luisa and the unintelligent King Charles IV. Goya has left us brilliant pictures of bullfights, of popular festivals and games, as well as bitter etchings satirizing human vices.

Courtesy of Brown-Robertson Co. Inc., New York

DON BALTHASAR

The picture of the little prince, Don Balthasar, shows that Velasquez understood children and could make them live in his paintings.

The 20th Century has not produced any El Greco or Goya in Spain, but we can admire the gleaming white and blue seascapes of Sorolla [sohr roh′lyah] or the old Castilian types painted by Zuloaga [thoo′loh ah′gah]. Pablo Picasso [pah′bloh pee kah′soh], who has exerted considerable influence on modern art, is a Spaniard, though most of his work has been done in Paris. Spanish, too, is the eccentric of contemporary art, Salvador Dali [sahl vah dohr′ dah′lee].

Spain has made unique contributions to architecture. Spain's contribution to architecture is as unique as her music and her national dances. The two characteristic features of the Spanish house are the patio, about which the house is built; and the plain walls with small windows on the front or street side. The patio, or open court, may be said to be the living room of the Spanish home. It is surrounded on three or four sides by rooms that open into it and by arcaded

THE INFANTA MARGARITA

The little Infanta [een fahn'tah] or Princess, Margarita, and her lady-in-waiting were painted by Velasquez, who missed no detail of ribbon or flower or smooth silken hair. These figures are part of a larger painting called " The Maids of Honor."

walls and projecting balconies. The artistically designed railings and grills at the windows facing the street are made of wrought iron. The roofs are low and usually covered with red tile.

Spain's architecture may be said to be a mixture of the columns of the Italians, the Gothic arches of France, and the domes and minarets of the Moors.

Medieval architecture in Europe is likely to be thought of as either Romanesque or Gothic. In Spain and Portugal, the Moorish influence is to be seen. The Alhambra, mentioned before, is an ancient palace and fortress built in southern Spain by the Moorish monarchs of Granada. Although much of the old palace was destroyed, the parts that remain and have been restored are enough to give an idea of the richness and the grandeur of this historic structure. The Alhambra is a beautiful building, constructed about numerous courts or patios whose walls are lacelike and whose ceilings suggest a starlit sky. The Court of the Myrtles has a reflecting pool. The fountains and trees in other courtyards give an impression of coolness and freshness. In the Court of Lions is one of the few examples of Moorish sculpture. Lions cut in stone support a heavy basin of white alabaster. Through divided windows one can see white houses with red-tiled roofs and the beautiful valley and mountains in the distance. No wonder the Alhambra, seen by day or on a moonlit night, has always had a strong appeal. Some of the Alhambra's beauty is shown in the picture reproduced on page 485.

THE ALHAMBRA

Brilliant designs in red, blue, black, and gold decorate the stucco and tiled surfaces of the Alhambra. Through the arch at the right in this picture, you can see the Court of the Lions, and the sculptured lions themselves in a ring around the fountain.

Spain and Portugal have great and original literature. Spanish literature has always been close to the Spanish people and represents their life and character. It is individualistic, showing a keen sense of reality, a thirst for adventure, and the vision of an ideal. It may be grave or gay, mild or violent, like Spaniards themselves. We have already read about the poem " The Cid," which reflects grave Castilian character. Another masterpiece, " The Book of Good Love," was written in the 14th Century by the Archpriest of Hita. It is a poem which pretends to be a sermon on the love of God, but it shows its extremely human author in many gay moods. Spain is extremely rich in ballads. The early songs displayed the warlike and adventurous traits of Spaniards with simple vigor and directness. Later ballads are on all sorts of themes, and the ballad form has re-mained highly popular up to the present day. The Spanish novels of chivalry, of which the greatest is *Amadis de Gaula* [ah mah dees' day gou'lah], portray adventures more romantically, much as they are shown in stories of King Arthur and the Knights of the Round Table.

Portugal, too, had her ballads and chivalrous tales. She also had a native lyric poetry, and was the first section of the Peninsula to produce sophisticated troubadour poems. Several thousands of them survive. Portugal produced her masterpiece in the 16th Century: " The Lusiads," an epic poem on the life of the great adventurer Vasco da Gama by the sturdy soldier Luis de Camoens [lwees' day kah maunsch']. It displays the heroic spirit which inspired Portuguese adventurers and conquerors in Portugal's great period, and it is vigorous, dignified, and patriotic.

If you had to pick just one book from all Spain's rich literature, your choice would certainly be the famous novel *Don Quixote* [dohn kee hoh'tay]. Its author, Cervantes [thayr vahn'tays], was a most gifted observer of life. He poured his knowledge of humanity and his vast sympathy into this account of the knight and his faithful, realistic squire, Sancho Panza.

The drama was enormously popular in 17th Century Spain, and it appealed to all classes. Spain's greatest playwright was Lope de Vega [loh'pay day vay' gah], admirable in the quality as well as in the quantity of his production. He composed at least several hundred full-length plays and many miscellaneous volumes. He is a symbol of Spanish life, and also of dramatic skill and lyric grace. Other great Spanish playwrights are the witty Tirso de Molina [teer'soh day moh lee'nah], the social satirist Alarcon [ah lahr kohn'], and the highly poetic religious and philosophical dramatist Calderon [kahl day rohn']. Their equals have not arisen since in Spain, though there have been many good playwrights. In our own days Benavente [bay nah vayn'tay] received the Nobel prize for literature.

Three Spanish philosophers who have been deeply concerned with the problems of Spain and of the world are Miguel de Unamuno [mee gel' day oonah moo'noh], Salvador de Madariaga [sahl vah dohr' day mah dah ryah'gah], and Jose Ortega y Gasset [hoh say' ohr-tay'gah ee gah'sayt].

Ortega y Gasset won fame in the United States, as well as elsewhere, by his book entitled *The Revolt of the Masses,* which develops his preoccupation with the " undisturbed predominance of the masses" and the question, " Can mass man be awakened to personal life?" Ortega's searching inquiry into Spain's decline as a nation has led him to believe that a new type of Spaniard must be created—an awakened Spaniard who will not live the unthinking life of the masses. Other works by Ortega are *Invertebrate Spain* and *Toward a Philosophy of History.*

Spain and Portugal Built Their Nations and Produced Illustrious Men

The Iberian Peninsula, where Spain's twenty-six million inhabitants and Portugal's seven million work on farms, and in vineyards, in cork-oak and olive groves, is a land of strong contrasts in climate and scenery — a land that blends characteristics of Europe and of neighboring Africa. High mountains shut Spain off from Europe and divide the Peninsula into sections.

In the past many strangers were drawn to the Iberian Peninsula. Phoenicians founded colonies there three thousand years ago. Greek traders left traces of their civilization in what is now Spain. Celts settled in the west. The Romans controlled the Peninsula for five centuries. Goths invaded the land in the Fifth Century after Christ. Moors from North Africa followed the Goths, in the Eighth Century. The present peoples of the Peninsula are descended from all these varied invaders, but have been most strongly influenced by the Romans, from whom they derive their religion, the basis of their laws, and their languages. Spanish and Portuguese are called Romance languages because of their Roman origin. The Moors, who built a state in the Peninsula, brought their scientific learning to the Iberian peoples, and left such architectural treasures as the Alhambra.

During the 11th and 12th centuries, Portugal and other Christian kingdoms were being established. In Portugal, the Moors were pushed to the south. In the middle of the 15th Century the kingdoms of Aragon and Castile were united by the marriage of their rulers, King Ferdinand and Queen Isabella, who became undisputed rulers of all Christian Spain and completed the expulsion of the Moors. A united Spain led Europe in exploration and conquest in the New World, through the activities of such men as Columbus, Balboa, Cortés, and De Soto. Portugal, too, sent explorers into the New World, and laid claim to Brazil and to territory in the Orient. But Portugal's period of greatness ended when it was annexed to Spain under the rule of Philip II.

Spain's longer period of grandeur was brought toward a close by the defeat of the Armada by the English and by the gradual loss of Spanish colonies through misrule.

Spain in the 19th and 20th centuries was in the grip of three powerful classes — army, clergy, and landowners — a grip which slowed her development and kept her a weak nation. King Alfonso permitted a dictator to take command of the government. A Republic was established and the king forced to abdicate. The Republic, in turn, was overthrown in the Spanish Civil War by which the dictator, Franco, with the aid of Nazi Germany and Fascist Italy, installed himself in power.

Whatever their political difficulties, Spain and Portugal have made generous contributions to the world's music, art, literature, and philosophy. We have much to thank them for in the paintings of Velasquez and El Greco and Goya, in the literature of de Camoens, Calderon, and Lope de Vega, and in the philosophical writings of Unamuno, Madariaga, and Ortega y Gasset.

SELF-TEST

Review the story of Spain by trying this self-test.

I. Select the best answer or answers:

(*a*) Spain is a land (1) which is easily accessible to Europe; (2) whose inhabitants are descended from one race; (3) which combines traits of Europe and of Africa.

(*b*) The coming of the Moors to Spain improved Spanish and Portuguese civilization because (1) the Moors had superior learning and higher standards of living; (2) the Moors finally had to pay tribute to the Spanish; (3) Spain and Portugal gratefully accepted Moorish rule.

(*c*) The Spanish did not succeed in keeping their conquests in the New World because (1) they were cruel to the peoples they conquered; (2) their main idea was to get as much wealth as they could out of the colonies; (3) Spain was so rich that she did not need to bother with the New World colonies.

II. Tell whether each of the following statements is true or false.

(*a*) The teachings of Mohammed have had little effect on the story of Spain and of Portugal.

(*b*) The year 1588 marks the end of Spanish sea power.

(*c*) For the 16th Century, the Moors were skilled in agriculture.

(*d*) Portugal had no colonies in the New World.

(*e*) The mountains within and on the northern border and the fast-flowing rivers of the country have hindered trade in Spain.

(*f*) Before the existence of railroads and airplanes, it was natural that the Spanish should develop a navy and shipping.

(*g*) In the hundred years between 1800 and 1900, Spain lost her colonies in the New World.

(*h*) For Spain the 18th and 19th centuries were years of great industrial and social progress.

III. Complete the following statements.

(*a*) A few American cities and places the names of which are due to the presence of Spaniards at one time are ——.

(*b*) The narrow waters which divide Spain from Africa are called the ——.

(*c*) Two of the most characteristic examples of Spanish architecture are —— and the ——. Spain's greatest painter is ——, and one of his well-known portraits of a child is ——. A famous Portuguese epic poem is called ——.

IV. Arrange in correct time order the following names of peoples who have played important parts in the story of Spain: (*a*) German barbarians, (*b*) the Romans, (*c*) the Moors, (*d*) the Phoenicians.

V. Here is a test of your acquaintance with Spain and Portugal. Tell what each word stands for or in what connection it was mentioned in the story of Spain and of Portugal.

(*a*) Franco	(*f*) Washington Irving	(*k*) Cervantes
(*b*) Armada	(*g*) patio	(*l*) Lope de Vega
(*c*) Primo de Rivera	(*h*) Salazar	(*m*) Ballads
(*d*) Manoel II	(*i*) Seville	(*n*) Azana
(*e*) glazed mosaics	(*j*) Isabella	(*o*) Bloodless Revolution

VI. Study the map on page 491, and on a separate sheet of paper answer the following questions. (*a*) What two fleets are shown leaving the coast of Spain? (*b*) What do the sketches tell you about the size and sea-worthiness of the ships in these fleets? *c*) What do the sketches show you about how the Spaniards earn a living? (*d*) In what part of Spain is the capital city located? (*e*) What does the map show about the invasion of the Moors? (*f*) What bodies of water touch the coasts of Spain? (*g*) What industry is pictured in southern Portugal?

INTERESTING THINGS TO DO

Project for the Chart Maker and Artist

Make a sketch book or illustrated book of Spanish architecture in which close-ups of the characteristic detail or iron work, windows, roofs, patios, etc., will be shown. See *All the Ways of Building,* by Louise Lamprey, or *Architecture through the Ages,* by T. F. Hamlin.

Topics for Talks

1. " A good book about Spain." Review for the benefit of the class an historical novel or " personal experience " type of book about Spain. Consult the list of books on pages 490 and 492, or ask your librarian for suggestions.

2. " Don Quixote." Prepare a talk on the writer Cervantes, and his book *Don Quixote,* often called the world's greatest novel. See *Story of the World's Literature,* by John A. Macy, or *Soul of Spain,* by Havelock Ellis. Read *Don Quixote de la Mancha,* by Cervantes.

3. " Act I, Scene 1 — World War II." Prepare a talk on the Spanish Civil War, its causes and results. See *Inside Europe,* by John Gunther, pp. 165–186, " Franco " in *Rulers of the World,* by Maurice Crain, and *AP, the Story of the News,* by Oliver Gramling, pp. 441–457.

4. " The next fifty years." Plan a talk in the manner of a radio commentator on world events. Prophesy what you think may happen to Spain in the light of your knowledge of trends in world politics.

5. " A vacation in Spain." Describe and locate the places you would like especially to visit. Tell what characteristics and customs of the people, what features of the landscape, or what occupations or recreations have aroused your interest. See *Discovering Christopher Columbus,* by Charlotte Jordan; *Spanish Towns and People,* by Robert McBride; *Roundabout Europe,* by Anne M. Peck.

6. " Great explorers." Prepare a talk on some of the great explorers of Spain and Portugal. Tell something of their aims in general, their lives and accomplishments in particular. See *Portuguese Pioneers,* by E. Prestage; *Spain in America,* by Edward Bourne.

7. "The Alhambra." Prepare a descriptive talk about the splendid palace of the Moors, and tell the class a few of the legends and stories which have become connected with it. See *The Alhambra,* by Washington Irving.

Ideas for Your Little Theater

1. Prepare a program of Spanish music. You should be able to get records of Spanish folk music, and also of selections from operas such as *Carmen,* and *The Barber of Seville.* Have a master of ceremonies give a translation or explanation preceding each record of song or dance music, and relate the story of each opera before any of its music is played. See *Stories from the Great Metropolitan Operas,* by Helen Dike.

2. Plan a lecture program on Spanish art and artists. Mount prints of Spanish masterpieces for display, and prepare a talk about several of the greatest artists and their work. See *Famous Pictures,* by Thomas Craven; *Fifty Famous Painters,* by Henrietta Gerwig.

Candidates for Your Album of Famous People

Alfonso XIII, Manuel Azana, Cervantes, the Cid, Ferdinand and Isabella, Goya, El Greco, Prince Henry the Navigator, Philip II, Primo de Rivera, Velasquez. Choose three people from the above list or from others mentioned in the text, as representatives of Spain and Portugal in your Album.

INTERESTING READING ABOUT SPAIN AND PORTUGAL

ADAMS, NICHOLSON B. *The Heritage of Spain.* A survey of Spanish literature, art, music, and architecture, sympathetically written and beautifully illustrated.

CERVANTES. *Don Quixote.* " Here," said Don Quixote, ". . . we may hope to dip our hands up to the elbows in adventure."

CRISS, MILDRED. *Isabella, Young Queen of Spain.* The goodness and charm of Isabella stand out in contrast to the splendor and cruelty of the court of Castile.

Compton's Pictured Encyclopedia. " Romantic Spain: Once Mistress of Half the World "; and Index; " Portugal."

ELLIS, HAVELOCK. *Soul of Spain.* A fascinating interpretation of Spanish characteristics and customs.

GALLOP, RODNEY. *Portugal.* " A book of enchantment " about the Portuguese, and their customs and beliefs, their literature and music.

HAMILTON, THOMAS. *Appeasement's Child.* A thorough and honest account of Spain since the Civil War, and of the diplomatic blunders that made the Spanish tragedy the first product of appeasement.

IRVING, WASHINGTON. *Tales from the Alhambra.* ". . . and in a little while he laid open a concealed recess, in which stood two great jars of porcelain."

LINDSLEY, LORNA. *War Is People.* A warm and human narrative of the author's experiences in the Spanish War and on other fronts.

National Geographic Magazine, March, 1936. " A Palette from Spain," by W. Langdon Kihn. " Who has not heard or read of the famous cities of Castile? "

——, Oct., 1936. " Turbulent Spain," by Ruth Q. McBride. " New thinking as well as new machines change the way of Spanish life."

——, Feb., 1938. " Castles and Progress in Portugal," by W. Robert Moore. " Today new foundations have been laid in the Estado Novo, or New State."

PECK, ANNE M., and MERAS, EDMOND A. *Spain in America and Europe.* " The truth is, however, that the great plains and bare mountains . . . are inhabited by a proud, dignified people."

WILSON, C. D. *The Story of the Cid.* " Wherever the Cid went on his gilt saddle, the Moors made a path for him, for he smote them without mercy."

The World Book Encyclopedia. " Spain "; " Portugal "; and Index.

PART FOURTEEN

THE LEADERS OF ITALY SOUGHT THE
GRANDEUR THAT WAS ROME

ITALY
FRANCE
SWITZERLAND
Bern
Munich
AUSTRIA
BRENNER PASS
Graz
HUNGARY
ALPS
LOMBARDY
Trentino
PIEDMONT
Turin
Milan
Verona
Padua
Venice
Trieste
Pavia
Cremona
Po River
Genoa
Parma
ISTRIA
Fiume
Drave R.
Save R.
YUGOSLAVIA
APENNINES
Carrara
Bologna
Florence
Pisa
Leghorn
Nice
Ligurian Sea
Adriatic Sea
ZARA
ELBA
CORSICA
Tiber River
ITALY
Rome
Mt. Vesuvius
Naples
Salerno
Bari
Brindisi
Taranto
Durazzo
Tirana
ALBANIA
SARDINIA
40° N.
Tyrrhenian Sea
North
Palermo
Messina
Mt. Etna
Calabria
SICILY
Mediterranean
10° E.
MILES
0
100
200
Tunis
TUNISIA
Ionian Sea
Pantelleria I.
MALTA
NORTH AFRICA
Sea
Lampedusa I.
35° N.

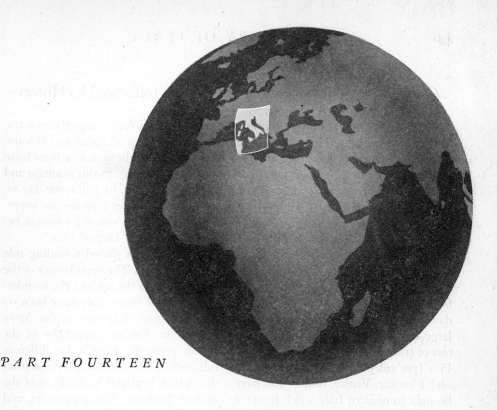

PART FOURTEEN

Ancient Italy Became a Modern Nation

Lᴛᴀʟʏ is a land rich with memories of the past. It has had a long and some-times troubled history. At one time its roads shook with the march of the Roman legions. Later Napoleon invaded the Italian peninsula. In World War II Italy resounded with the thunder of bombing and artillery.

On the map of modern Italy, on the facing page, notice how much of the land is mountainous. Would you expect Italy to produce all the food she needs? Do you see why the Italian government wanted foreign colonies? Notice the position of this boot-shaped country and how nearly it is sur-rounded by water. What neighbors have the Italians to the north and to the south?

Locate Brenner Pass, famous as the scene of fateful meetings between the Fascist dictator, Mussolini, and the Nazi dictator, Adolf Hitler. In the story which follows, you will learn how the Italian city-states of the Renais-sance became welded into a modern nation, how this nation developed for a while along democratic lines, and how, after World War I, Italy was made over into a Fascist state. You will learn, too, of the problems of modern Italy, and of the contributions in science and in music which modern Italians have given to the world.

Chapter 1 ~ The Geography of Italy Has Influenced Its History

The people of modern Italy are proud of their rich heritage. The modern Italians take pride in the fact that they can look back through the golden age of the Renaissance to the days when Rome ruled the Western world. Throughout Italy one may see relics of the Roman Empire and monuments of the later Middle Ages and the Renaissance: awe-inspiring churches or cathedrals, memorial arches, palaces, and museums filled with treasures of the past. In the days of the Renaissance most of the large cities of Italy were thriving centers of trade, art, learning, and religion. Pisa [pee′zuh], Milan, Genoa [jen′oh-uh], Florence, Venice, Rome — all have brought to modern Italy a rich heritage from the past. A scene in Pisa before World War II is shown in the illustration on the next page.

Italy is enjoyed by artists and tourists. Much has been written about the charm and beauty of Italy. Artists from all over the world have painted the matchless sunsets, the green, sloping hillsides, and the towering mountains of northern Italy. This peninsula has also long been a favorite retreat for poets and other writers. Artists and writers are not the only ones who become fond of Italy. In times of peace and plenty, tourists from many countries enjoy the warm evenings, see the sunlight sparkling upon the waters of the beautiful Bay of Naples, and visit Mount Vesuvius, the massive, treacherous volcano at the foot of which cluster rich vineyards. Those who like swimming and sailing enjoy Italy's bathing beaches and fine harbors.

Many people are so enchanted by Italy that they want to stay there. Because the traveler usually leaves regretfully, a tradition has grown up about an old fountain in Rome. If the man who must leave the city will first go to this fountain and toss into it a coin, he will some day return to Rome. Most travelers are superstitious enough to visit the fountain before leaving the " Eternal City."

Geography has played a leading role in modern Italy. The great beauty of the mountains and the sea and the wonderful climate of sunny Italy have been referred to more than once in our *Story of Nations*. But the geography of the Italian peninsula plays a far different role in the lives of modern Italians from that which it played in the lives of the ancient Romans. The mountains and seas gave ancient Rome a protection which they cannot give in modern times. The Romans cultivated a fertile soil, but the Italians today till exhausted lands that must be fertilized. The Romans could depend on their many colonies to provide them with food, raw materials, and even labor. Modern Italy has to depend on the resources of the fields and mines of her home territory or import what she needs from other nations.

A variety of fruits can be grown in Italy. The most important are the grapes from which the Italians make wine and the olives from which they make olive oil. Both of these products are widely used at home, and quantities of them are exported as well. Other fruits grown in Italy are lemons, oranges, and dates. Scientific stock raising is practiced in northern Italy, which is in general more progressive than the south. You may have eaten Parmesan or Gorgonzola cheese from northern Italy. Bologna usage, often made in America also, takes its name from the Italian city of ologna.

Besides fruit, meat, and dairy products, Italy also produces vegetables, at east enough for her own use. Some wheat, corn, and other grains are grown n Italy, but not nearly enough. Italy acks great plains to provide enough rain for her people, and thousands of ons of grain must be imported each ear.

These limitations, however, have been challenge to the Italians of the 20th Century. Marshes have been drained to provide additional fertile land and farm-

ers have begun using improved methods to make their land yield larger crops. The headquarters of the International Institute of Agriculture are in Rome.

Mineral resources that at one time were considered of little value have been developed so that they give work to many men and provide much raw material needed in industry and commerce. One of these new industries is the aluminum industry. The sulphur mines of Sicily gave the Italians for some years almost a monopoly of the sulphur trade in Europe. (American competition caused a great slump in this industry.) The mountains of Italy produce a fair quan-

New York Public Library

PISA

In this photograph of Pisa, taken before World War II, the circular building at the left is the Baptistery. The Cathedral of Pisa is in the center, and the Leaning Tower shows at the right. This tower was begun in the 12th Century. It began to lean after the first three galleries were constructed. At present it slants about fourteen degrees from the perpendicular.

WHEAT FIELD IN SOUTHERN ITALY

How does this field compare with actual wheat fields which you have seen, or with pictures of wheat fields in the United States? Do you think the medieval castle might distract the workers in the field?

tity of lead and zinc. The output of iron ore has been increased, but great quantities of iron and all of the coal she uses still have to be imported. Water power is turned into electricity to be used instead of coal, which Italy does not have. Old factories have been remodeled and new plants built, so that Italy has become one of the industrial nations of Europe. Two of the important newer industries are the silk industry (which depends on the growth of mulberry trees, to feed the silkworms) and the manufacture of rayon. In normal times Italy is one of the greatest rayon-producing countries in the world. In short, Italy has been making great progress toward becoming a more nearly self-sustaining nation, and has also been developing industries which give her many valuable exports.

Italy has long desired foreign territory. Because land is scarce and the population large, many Italians had emigrated to other countries. (At the present time there are more than one and a half million Italian-born people in the United States.) Italy has not been content merely to allow her people to emigrate, but has sought to win colonies as England and France had done, where her people might settle and remain Italian citizens. Much of Italy's progress was offset by her expensive career of foreign conquest, which began in the 19th Century.

Italy had entered the race for colonies somewhat late. The Fascist leaders were not content with the few colonies which she had acquired in the 19th Century, but began to recall the glory of Rome and to dream of a new empire.

Chapter 2 ~ The Italians Formed a Nation but Lost Freedom in
Pursuit of Empire

Ancient Italy ruled the world. From
the Eighth Century, B.C., when Rome
was founded, Roman legend and history
have never lacked tales of bravery and
deeds of daring. Much of the story of
ancient Rome you already know, for it
was told early in this *Story of Nations*.
You will remember how Rome first
brought Italy under her rule and then
sent forth her legions to conquer the
world. By 132 B.C. Rome was the undisputed ruler of the Western world.

After Rome disintegrated from within, in the Fifth Century, an era of darkness and ignorance gradually swept over
Europe. It was centuries before modern
Europeans rediscovered their heritage
from the ancient world and made full
use of it.

Not until almost a thousand years
later did Italy again hold the center of
the stage. The Renaissance, as you will
remember from an earlier story, first
started in Italy.

**Italian city-states led in the Renais-
sance.** Thus from the 13th to the 16th
Century there were many famous Italians. But there was no Italy. Instead of
united Italy we find a group of independent city-states. Genoa, Venice,
Florence, Milan, and other Italian cities
became famous trading and art centers,
yet they were not bound together by a
central government. While in England
and France the foundations for modern
nations were being laid, Italy remained
a group of disunited city-states.

Machiavelli wrote " The Prince." The
leaders and rulers of Renaissance days
were filled with a new sense of power
and often wanted their own way regardless of how they got it. Political intrigue
was common in the Italian city-states of
the Renaissance. About the year 1500, a
Florentine statesman and writer, Machiavelli [mah'kyah vel'ee], was sent on
a diplomatic mission with Cesare Borgia [chay zahr'ay bawr'jah], the son of
a noted Italian family of Spanish origin.
The Borgias were a clever, colorful, powerful family, but many of them were
notorious for their wickedness and
treachery, and Cesare Borgia was perhaps the most so of all. Machiavelli
came to admire Cesare Borgia greatly
and idealized him in a book called *The
Prince*. It is practically a manual of un-
ethical politics, but nevertheless is a remarkable and famous book.

In *The Prince,* Machiavelli set forth
the theory that Italy could be united
only by a prince who was absolutely
unscrupulous in the means he used to
extend his power. Machiavelli went into
this subject quite thoroughly and made
a detailed study of all the tricky and
ruthless means which a prince might
employ. The fact that Cesare Borgia's
double dealing actually made him a
great many enemies and wrecked his
hopes of founding an hereditary kingdom in central Italy, does not seem to
have dampened Machiavelli's enthusiasm at all. Nor did it lessen other people's interest in Machiavelli's book. *The
Prince* was read and talked about by
educated people all over Europe. Machiavelli founded a school of political
thinking which had absolutely no regard for right and wrong. To this day
we speak of an unscrupulous and clever
policy as Machiavellian.

The decline of the Italian city-states.
After the great discoveries and explora-

tions of the Renaissance, the Italian city-states began to lose their power and commercial importance. The center of trade shifted from the Mediterranean to the Atlantic Ocean, and Italy's great seaports were no longer so valuable. As the power of these cities diminished, the people in each state began looking less and less to the city for leadership and for trade. They even began to trade with their Italian neighbors in adjoining states. Some of the barriers between the Italian peoples were thus broken down and the Italians became more conscious of their common needs and interests. The smaller towns were given greater rights of self-government, and the number of Italian states became fewer.

The Hapsburgs and Bourbons. As you will remember from the story of feudalism, much of the Italian peninsula had formed a part of the Holy Roman Empire. Under Charles V in the 16th Century most of the Italian states became little more than dependencies of the Empire of Charles V. The Hapsburgs and their relatives, the Bourbons of France, continued to rule most of Italy without trouble until the latter part of the 18th Century.

The Italians under Napoleon. The French revolutionary ideas of the late 18th Century affected the Italian peoples as well as those in other parts of Europe. Some of the Italians joined in the combination against the French Directorate, but were defeated by the French general, Napoleon. You have read in the story of France how Napoleon, when he became Emperor of France, brought most of Italy under his own rule or that of his brother Joseph. Napoleon also formed an alliance with the Pope.

As things turned out, French domination of Italy actually helped to hasten the day of Italian unity and freedom. This came about in three ways: First, as you have read in the story of France, Napoleon's soldiers spread the revolutionary ideas of liberty, equality, and fraternity wherever they went. Second, the French government did not actually practice these ideals in its dealings with the Italians, but regulated all Italian commerce in the interests of France and treated Italy like a province to be exploited. Under such treatment the Italians began to resent the French intensely and they developed a stronger sense of national unity and solidarity than they had ever had before. Third, Napoleon reduced still further the number of separate states in Italy, and this resulted in blotting out some of the separate customs and loyalties among the Italians.

Revolts against Austria. After the defeat of Napoleon, the Congress of Vienna, of which you have read, in 1815 gave back Austria most of her old rights in Italy. Austria, the Spanish Bourbons, and the Pope were again Italy's masters. The Austrians terrorized the country and tried to wipe out all liberal ideas, but the Italians organized secret societies to work for freedom. In 1848, at the time of a revolution in France, many of the Italians revolted against their governments and gained some new constitutional rights. The liberal-minded Italian king of Sardinia, Charles Albert, even attacked Austria. He was defeated and forced to give up his throne. Then the people all over Italy lost many of their new rights. The Italian states had not worked together sufficiently to gain freedom together on an equal basis with one another.

Three leaders strove for a united Italy. In 1859 Italy was still a house divided against itself — some parts belonging to Austria, some to the Pope, and others to local princes. In 1861 all Italy, except Venice and Rome, was united under the rule of Victor Emmanuel [uh man' yoo'l] II of Sardinia. Even the large western islands of Sicily and Sardinia were included in this union.

How did this happen? What great force in two years cemented together a nation which had crumbled apart more than thirteen centuries before? The "New Italy" came about largely as a result of the labor and patriotism of three men and their brave followers. One was a statesman; one an idealist and philosopher; the other a daring, half-outlaw soldier. Together these three united the small city-states on the Italian peninsula into a single kingdom. The story of their accomplishment is one of the most thrilling bits of history to be found in the story of any nation. In brief, this is what happened.

A statesman planned for the future. After the unsuccessful revolts of 1848, mentioned above, the Italians came to believe that Italy could be united only under the leadership and the rule of one of the stronger Italian states. They began to look to Sardinia to give them this leadership. Victor Emmanuel had become King of Sardinia and part of northern Italy when his father, Charles Albert, had been forced to abdicate. Like his father, Victor Emmanuel was a believer in liberty, but he was a man of only average ability. Fortunately he had a prime minister of unusual brilliance who was supremely devoted to freeing Italy from the grasp of Austria and the Pope. This prime minister was Cavour [ka voor'], who was not seeking a republican form of government. All he desired for Italy was to see her united under Victor Emmanuel with a liberal constitution to insure the rights of the people.

From the time when Cavour became prime minister for Victor Emmanuel until his death in 1861, he showed remarkable statesmanship. Sometimes he used the policy of ruthlessness, but Cavour looked into the future to determine the consequences of his acts. One example will help to illustrate this foresight.

To understand Cavour's actions, it is necessary to keep in mind that two steps had to be taken before all of the Italian states could be organized under one government. The first step was to throw off the Austrian yoke. This he knew could not be done without the help of some strong outside nation. The second step was to get the consent of the city-states to this union. This he felt he could himself handle if Austria were out of the way, even if he had to use force in some instances.

Then the opportunity came to make France his ally. (It may seem a very roundabout way, but the results showed how well Cavour had laid his plans.) Russia had wanted a seaport on the Black Sea, so that she could send her vessels to the ocean by way of the Mediterranean. In order to get them Russia had annexed two provinces of the feeble Turkish Empire. Turkey naturally objected to these annexations. England and France, fearing the growing power of Russia, lent aid to Turkey. The result was the Crimean [krai mee"n] War. This was Cavour's chance. In the midst of the war, troops were sent to support France, England, and Turkey against Russia. Russia was defeated, though it made little difference to Cavour which side won; for by accepting Cavour's help France and England had placed themselves under obligation.

Then came the next step in Cavour's play of power politics. When he thought the right time had come, Cavour managed to get into a war with Austria, and called on France for help. This France gave, in a halfhearted way it is true, but sufficiently to enable Cavour to free the Italian states from Austrian control. England kept out of the war, which was all that Cavour had wished of her. After this success, Cavour turned in earnest to the problem of unifying Italy.

Cavour's methods of unifying Italy were not actually far different from those which had been recommended by Machiavelli. But Cavour's devotion to the cause of a united Italy was so unselfish, his efforts so untiring, and his wily plans

so successful that people have been inclined to forget the means which he used and to remember only his success in freeing and unifying Italy.

A philosopher aroused the desire for Italian independence. In the meantime another force had been at work that made the union of the Italian states a much simpler matter than it might have been. If Cavour was the brains that carefully planned the difficult struggle for freedom from Austria, Mazzini [maht-see'nee] was the philosopher and idealist who aroused the people to fight for their independence. This lawyer and journalist of Genoa was willing to en-

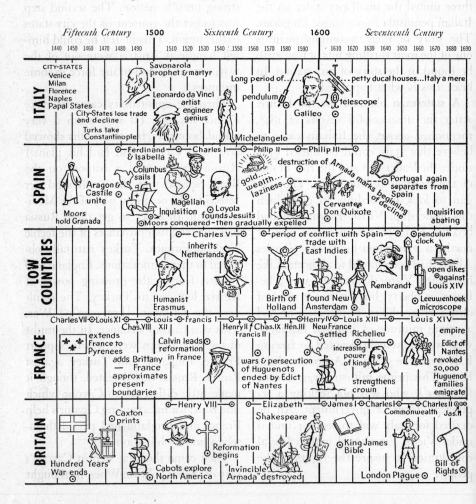

danger his own liberty by writing and talking of freedom to his countrymen.

From the time he was a very young man he placed the interests of Italy before his personal ambitions. This policy soon brought him into trouble with the government and he found himself in jail. When his anxious father inquired why he had been thrown into prison he was told, " Your son has the bad habit of thinking too much." In spite of prison and threats, Mazzini organized a revolutionary society called " Young Italy " which helped to mold the highest patriotic ideals. Mazzini was forced to spend many years in exile but constantly worked and hoped for Italian freedom. Fortunately, he lived (through the stirring years of 1860 and 1861) to see his dream come true.

A soldier subdued Sicily. With Austrian control in Italy limited to Venice, and a willingness on the part of the majority of the people throughout Italy to unite, it remained only for the patriot and soldier, Garibaldi [gah'ree bahl' dee] to get the movement for the unification of Italy well under way. In 1860 he landed in Sicily with only one thousand men. Sicily at that time was part of the Bourbon Kingdom of Naples. Although many of his men carried mus-

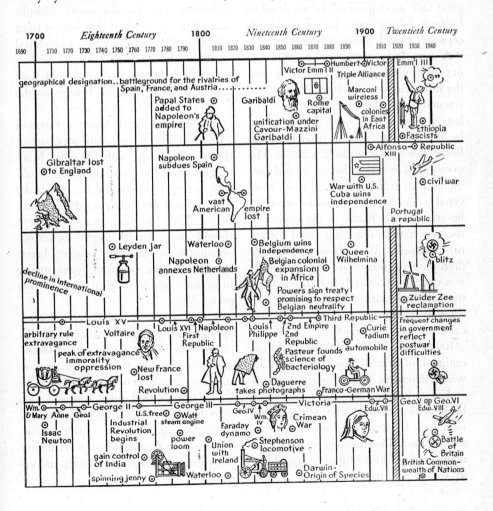

kets that were more fit for the scrap heap than for fighting, Garibaldi, with the aid of the people of Sicily, took the capital of the island from 24,000 regular, well-armed Bourbon troops. Next, he crossed to the mainland and took Naples itself. The king, deserted by his own people, fled from the city, leaving Garibaldi in command of southern Italy.

In November of that same year (1860) Garibaldi resigned his powers over Sicily and Naples and acknowledged Victor Emmanuel II of Sardinia as the monarch of the new Kingdom of Italy. The people of some of the papal provinces also voted to join the new Kingdom. Then, his great task accomplished, he returned to his farm, taking only a large bag of seed-corn and a small handful of money.

A new Italy was born. Within the next few years the rest of Italy joined the new Kingdom of Italy. Venice was wrested from Austria. Rome was the last city in Italy to gain her freedom. In 1870 an Italian army marched into Rome and took it without a battle. The question of whether Rome should join united Italy was left to the people. They voted a hundred to one in favor of annexation. With Rome as the capital of the new nation, one king ruled the entire peninsula. After about fifteen hundred years of discord and disunity, Italy was once more united. But the new nation still had many difficult problems to solve. It was many years before she became a strong power.

Italy's part in World War I. At the outbreak of World War I, in 1914, Italy was in defensive alliance with Germany and Austria-Hungary. After considerable hesitation as to which side she should join, Italy went into the war in 1915 as one of the Allied powers against Germany and Austria-Hungary. By doing so she hoped to gain certain Italian-speaking territories then under Austrian control, which were known as "unredeemed Italy."

Radicals and Fascists clashed in Italy. Italy was successful in getting part of what she wanted, but the end of the war in 1918 found her in a worse economic condition than any other nation in the war except Russia. Unemployment was serious and widespread. There were not enough jobs for the returning soldiers. The government was weakened by inaction and by various shifting political groups.

As conditions grew worse in Italy, socialism and communism gained many followers. The Socialist party thought that all the property of the country from which people made a living, or produced wealth — the land, the mines, the factories, and the railroads — should have common ownership, or belong to the state. The Socialist party could trace its origin back to Karl Marx, a German economist who wrote about socialism in the middle of the 19th Century. Marx taught that the workingmen should seize the government and use it to make the land and the industries the property of all. Then, he said, the government should use its wealth to give better opportunities to all the people: better schools, old-age pensions, government insurance, and free medicine for the poor.

As unrest increased in Italy, industrial, agricultural, and railroad strikes broke out over the country. The port of Genoa was dominated by the Socialist party to such an extent that no ship could be loaded or unloaded unless it was by men who belonged to the Socialist union. Radical groups seized a number of factories and local communist governments came into control in some cities and villages.

Many of these strikes and changes were accompanied by violence. Rioting broke out in some of the large cities. Groups of young men of intense national feeling had banded together and armed in order to oppose the socialists and communists by force. These military-political groups were known as Fascists. They took their name from the fasces, the bundle of sticks bound about an ax, which was the symbol of authority in the days of ancient Rome. (The same symbol appears on the back of the United States dime.)

The man who organized and controlled the Fascist party was Benito Mussolini, the Caesar of modern Italy. This aggressive and ambitious man had been a schoolteacher, a radical journalist, and a soldier in World War I. In his earlier days he had been a member of the Socialist party. But after World War I he quarreled with the socialists, and organized the Fascist party which, as was said, bitterly opposed both the socialists and the communists. Unfortunately, they were also opposed to democracy, and believed in a dictatorial government by force. The Fascist groups at first were composed largely of former soldiers. They were against the internationalism of the socialists and communists. Instead they were intensely nationalistic and had great ambitions for Italy. They also felt that the government had made a mistake in not demanding greater gains at the end of World War I. Armed conflicts broke out between the Fascist and liberal factions. Young men on each side became determined to avenge the killing of their friends. Ordinary citizens had to take to carrying arms in the street in order to protect themselves.

Mussolini brought Italy under the rule of the Fascist party. The Italian government did not succeed in restoring order, and in 1922, the Fascists took control of the country by force. With their leader, Mussolini, they marched on Rome forty-two thousand strong. Each man wore the black shirt of the Fascists. The right of government was turned over to Mussolini and he became one of the most powerful men in Europe. Almost at once Mussolini exercised his power as dictator. He abolished labor unions, forbade strikes and lockouts, and made it a crime for men to be idle.

Many thoughtful Italians looked on the Fascist government with great misgiving. It is true that some acts of the Fascists appealed strongly to the Italian people. Bad slums were cleared. Public works, great buildings, and first-class roads were constructed. Foreigners traveling in Italy brought back reports of the cleanliness, order, and efficiency of the Fascist state. The working people, particularly, and the young people, who had been trained in Fascist schools and youth organizations, were generally enthusiastic.

But behind all this fine-looking front there was trouble in Italy. Both the big industrialists and the middle classes complained that they were being taxed out of existence for the benefit of the working classes. They began to ask what would become of the working classes themselves if the nation became bankrupt.

Naturally people began to wonder how long this would go on. Some observers began to say that an invasion of foreign territory would be necessary to insure that Mussolini's government and the country's economic order would not collapse. But the government built up and equipped the Fascist army. There was endless drilling of the army and the youth groups. It appeared that the Fascists had decided on the next step.

One writer traveling in Italy in 1934 reached these conclusions:

Now Italy had a new Renaissance, and there is a new Caesar there, leader and tyrant to his people, though without foreign victories. He has revived their spirit and pride. He favors youth with its song of " La Giovanezza " [lah joh'vah net'zah]. He is very partial to the multiplication of babies. He has raised his country to the status of a first-class power. His active and subtle mind plays a great part in the diplomatic game behind the scenes. He has real qualities of greatness. But, as my friend in the tobacco shop observed, not even Mussolini can alter the laws of arithmetic. His budget is unbalanced. Business in Italy is strangled by taxation and suffering a loss of markets. The conversations I had did not reveal a sense of prosperity or security. It seemed to me, looking back on all that I had seen and heard, that Italy was expecting some new crisis and was nervous of a new war. Only youth was singing.[1]

The older people, indeed, who remembered a free Italy, and who had been brought up in the traditions of Cavour, had not taken kindly to a dictatorship in which the legislative body had no real power and in which every person was from birth a member of one party — the Fascist party.

Italy was headed straight for war. At times Mussolini talked peace, perhaps to hold the people's good will. At other times he said he absolutely disbelieved in lasting peace, and praised war. His preparations for war and the country's uncertain economic state foretold which of these statements he would act on.

In the disappointment and disorder following World War I, Italy had accepted dictatorship and the rule of force as her solution. She had enjoyed the rapid benefits of rule by a dictator and had boasted of them. But in doing so

[1] From Sir Philip Hamilton Gibbs, *European Journey,* 1934, Doubleday, Doran & Co., Inc.

the Italians had given up their liberties and Italy's historic place among liberal-minded nations. It was natural that many people should feel that Italy had, to borrow Ben Franklin's words, " paid too much for the whistle." But Italy had determined to solve her problems by force. In spite of her past record of liberalism and love of freedom, the world was not too surprised when Italy appeared in her new role — that of an aggressor nation — with the attack on Ethiopia in 1935.

Italian dreams of empire. Behind Italy's Ethiopian aggression lay a rather unhappy history of Italian colonization. To Italy gaining colonies meant becoming a great power. In the 19th Century, after most of Africa had been claimed, the Italians had established colonies on the eastern coast of Africa in a small strip of land called Eritrea [er'ee tray' ah]. Then, Italy had tried to conquer Ethiopia, to add to her colonial holdings, but the Ethiopian army had defeated the Italians.

Early in the 20th Century Italy, by clever diplomacy, had gained the approval of other great powers to certain claims of hers to land between Egypt and Morocco. These lands were held by the Turks. Then Italy made war on the Turks and took this land from them, renaming it Libya. The Italians made great progress in developing Libya, but its development cost more than it proved to be worth. The only value of Italy's African colonies seemed to be the satisfaction the Italians gained from possessing colonies. It became a matter of national pride.

The Fascist road to ruin. After the experience in Africa, one might have thought that the Italians would abandon their desire for colonies. But the old hopes for empire were revived under

MUSSOLINI AND HIS STAFF

The leader of the Fascists and his staff took over the government of Italy in a bloodless revolution. The pose and expression of Mussolini were typical of his early days of power.

he Fascists. In the first place, as we have een, Italy's economic condition at home vas in such a state that a foreign invaion seemed almost necessary. Further-nore, the Fascists, as part of their propaanda, had revived the memory of the ld Roman Empire and had inspired ne modern Italians with a desire to imi-ite its glories.

In 1935, Italy's national debt was great nd the prestige of the League of Na-ons, established after World War I, vas diminished. Italy then picked a uarrel with Ethiopia and undertook an ivasion of " punishment " against her. 'his invasion was a sheer act of aggres-on. Mussolini later boasted that he had lanned it for some time. The Ethiopians vere at a great disadvantage in men and quipment. Gas and planes were used gainst courageous men armed mostly ith primitive weapons. The war soon

ended in complete victory for the Italians. Italy had conquered a new colony and the Italian king, Victor Emmanuel, was made " Emperor of Ethiopia."

Actually there could be little glory in a conquest by the modern Fascist army over the poorly equipped Ethiopian natives. Actually, too, it was an unhappy page in Italian history, yet the conquest of Ethiopia was presented to the Italian people as an exploit worthy of their Roman ancestors.

To the rest of the world the Italian conquest of Ethiopia was one of the first acts of unchecked aggression which ushered in World War II. Another such act, as we shall learn, was Japan's seizure of Manchuria. The League of Nations condemned Italy for this action and some of the great powers cut down their exports to her as an expression of disapproval. But such action was not sufficiently strong or united to stop Italy in her course.

Italy joined the Axis. Nazi Germany, whose doctrines of national and racial superiority were similar to those of the Fascists, gave Italy her economic and moral support throughout the matter.

Only one year after the invasion o Ethiopia, Italy returned this support o Nazi Germany's by joining the Rome Berlin Axis which was to plunge th world into the greatest war of history You will read more about this in Par Twenty-two.

Chapter 3 ~ Modern Italians Have Contributed to Science and Music

Too often we think of Italy and her contributions to civilization in terms of ancient Rome and the works of the great men of the Renaissance. Most of us know that ancient Rome was the organizer, the lawgiver, the builder of roads and aqueducts, the home of noted writers. We have read of her contributions to art during the Renaissance. Not many of us realize that modern Italy also has made rich gifts to science, literature, art, and music.

Galileo was a pioneer in modern science. Galileo [gal′i lay′oh] was born at Pisa at the close of the 16th Century. At eighteen he made a discovery which led to the invention of the modern clock. The story is told that as he sat in the cathedral at Pisa, he saw a lamp swinging rhythmically to and fro and realized — what no one had seemed to think of before — that a pendulum could be used to measure time. The use of the pendulum was only one of Galileo's many remarkable discoveries. By dropping balls of various weights from the leaning tower of Pisa, he proved that all falling bodies, whether heavy or light, fall at the same rate. This experiment is illustrated

on page 509. He also invented the secto that form of compass which students i geometry still use to make various ge metrical figures. He was the first t construct a thermometer. Though h was not the actual inventor of the tel scope, he was the first to make practic use of it. With this type of magnifyin instrument, he swept the starry heaver and opened the way to modern astro omy. He discovered that the moon w marked by valleys and mountains an that the Milky Way was made up o millions of stars. He saw four of the nir satellites of Jupiter.

From the wonders of the sky and h swinging pendulum, Galileo was co vinced that the earth rotates on its ax and revolves around the sun. Galile wrote about these beliefs in *A Dialog Concerning the Two Great Systems the World.*

Galileo was one of the world's mo original thinkers in the field of exper mental science. He was centuries ahea of most men of his period.

Other Italian scientists made valuab discoveries. Soon after Galileo had ma his remarkable investigations, anoth

Italian, Torricelli [tohr'ree chel'lee], discovered how to measure air pressure and how to determine the heights of buildings and mountains by use of this principle. It was a relatively simple procedure. Torricelli took a thirty-six-inch tube of glass, closed at one end, and filled it with mercury. While holding his finger over the open end, he inverted the tube and placed the open end in a cup of mercury. When he removed his finger, he found that the mercury stood at a certain height in the tube. By further experiment, he worked out the relationship between altitude and the height of the mercury column. This simple device was the forerunner of our first barometer.

About a century later an Italian physiologist, Galvani [gahl vahn'ee], observed the effect of electricity on animal muscles. He found that he could make a recently killed frog jump by hanging it by one leg with a copper wire to an iron railing, and then touching the other leg with another wire also connected with the railing. His observations led to the first discoveries in electricity.

It remained for Galvani's fellow countryman, Volta [vawl'tah] a teacher and experimenter in physics, to construct the first electric cell. It is sometimes called the galvanic cell in honor of Galvani, but it is more commonly known as the voltaic cell, after the name of the man first to make it. This wet cell is the ancestor of the dry cell used in the modern flashlight. Volta also made an instrument which measures electric currents. This instrument is called a voltmeter in his honor.

Marconi was the father of the wireless. Guglielmo Marconi [goo lyel'moh mahr koh'nee], an Italian, became one of the most famed inventors of the modern world. As a young man, Marconi at-

GALILEO'S EXPERIMENT

Galileo was professor of mathematics at the University of Pisa at the time he performed the experiment from the Leaning Tower of Pisa. In this picture he is shown about to drop two balls of unequal weight, which he knows will reach the ground simultaneously.

tended the University of Bologna where he became interested in certain experiments with sound which his professor described. Marconi believed that electric impulses produced by sound vibrations could be transmitted to distant points without the aid of wires. In the years that followed he conducted many experiments and made many new discoveries about electric waves. Finally he succeeded in sending a message from one station to another ten miles away. Wireless telegraphy had become a reality. Gradually the distance between stations could be increased. Marconi felt that his invention was an undisputed success when, in 1901, a message was sent across the Atlantic Ocean. This successful cli-

TOSCANINI

Arturo Toscanini is one of the outstanding conductors of all time. He is shown here conducting the NBC Symphony Orchestra.

max came only after years of patient work.

News is now flashed all over the world by wireless telegraph. Today the name of Marconi is honored throughout the world for the invention which has been such a boon to mankind. In 1909 he was awarded the Nobel Prize for his contribution to science. From Marconi's invention the modern radio has developed, which plays such an important role in our present-day world.

Verdi became the greatest Italian composer. One Sunday morning in the early 19th Century, worshipers were gathering for Mass in the chapel of Buseto, a little village at the foot of the Apennine Mountains. At the last moment the organist had announced that he would be unable to attend the services. No one could be found to take his place. Someone mentioned that Giuseppe Verdi [joo sep'ay vayr'dee], a young lad who worked in the warehouse

of the wine merchant, had taken a few music lessons. Perhaps he could play for Mass. Since services were to begin in a few minutes a messenger was sent immediately to find young Giuseppe.

During Mass the priest was much impressed with the unusually beautiful organ music. At the close of the services he sent for the organist to compliment him on his playing. He was amazed when he saw the youthful Verdi.

" Whose music did you play? " he asked. " It was most beautiful."

"Why," answered the boy timidly, " I had no music — I played just as I felt."

So began the career of Verdi as a composer of music. His employer and various members of the church took an interest in helping him develop his talent. An excellent teacher was found. So rapid was his progress that it was felt that Verdi should be sent to Milan to finish his studies.

After he left the conservatory at Milan, Verdi's serious work as a composer began. Like other young musicians he met heartaches and discouragement, but compared to the careers of some of the great composers, Verdi's rise to fame was rapid. When he was only twenty-nine he presented an opera which brought him unhoped-for recognition.

Although many of Verdi's early compositions were excellent, it was his later works that brought him enduring fame. In all, Verdi wrote more than thirty operas, three of which — Rigoletto [ree goh let'toh], Il Trovatore [eel troh'vah tohr'ee], and Aïda [ah ee'dah] — are known the world over. In Rigoletto, Verdi's true power and lyric style are well expressed. But it was Il Trovatore that made Verdi the idol of Rome.

Other Italians won musical fame. Although Verdi is the best known of all Italian composers there are others who ose to great fame. We should remember Rossini [rohs see'nee] for his opera, *William Tell*. Another composer noted for the beauties of his melodies and rich orchestral effects is Puccini [poot che'nee]. His *La Bohème* [lah boh'em'], *La Tosca* [lah tohs'kuh] are well known in America. But his masterpiece and greatest triumph is *Madame Butterfly*.

The Italian love of music has found other outlets besides musical composition. The Italians can interpret as well as create new melodies. The "golden-voiced" Caruso [kah roo'zoh] was called the world's greatest tenor because of the unusual power, quality, and range of his voice. Present-day radio listeners and concertgoers may enjoy the beautiful voices and excellent musicianship of such modern musicians from Italy as Pinza and Martinelli.

American orchestras, concert stages, and opera houses have benefited from the musical contributions of Italian-Americans and of Italians resident or on tour in America.

Perhaps the best-known Italian musician in America is the conductor, Arturo Toscanini [tohs kah nee'nee], who began his musical career many years ago as a cellist. Toscanini had been a famous conductor in Europe for years before he became the conductor of the New York Philharmonic Orchestra. Toscanini is remarkable for his fine sense of tempo and phrasing, his high standards of musicianship, his capacity for endless hard work, and his extraordinary memory. Throughout his life he has conducted without a copy of the music before him.

A devoted Italian, Toscanini has been an opponent of Fascism from its earliest days. When in Italy he has always refused to conduct the party's hymn "La Giovanezza," and was once assaulted in Bologna by Black Shirt ruffians.

After many years as conductor of the New York Philharmonic Orchestra, Toscanini retired briefly to Italy. In 1937 the National Broadcasting Company's Symphony Orchestra was organized, largely for the purpose of bringing Toscanini back to America as its conductor. This plan was successful, and as the conductor of the NBC Symphony Orchestra, Toscanini continues to give pleasure to thousands of radio listeners in this country.

Modern Italy's Greatest Contributions Have Been in the Fields of Science and Music

In some ways modern Italy enjoys the same natural advantages and is faced with the same problems as ancient Rome. But the mountains and sea do not give the same protection in modern times that they gave to the ancient Romans. The soil of Italy has become somewhat exhausted and a growing population has caused her to seek provinces across the Mediterranean. The doctrines of Fascism and the desire to recapture the glory of Rome also made Italy's leaders ambitious to acquire provinces. In the 19th Century, her efforts gave her control of Eritrea and Libya. These provinces have only limited natural resources and have attracted only a few of the people of Italy away from their homeland. Although modern science and inventions help to satisfy her needs, Italy still has the problems of providing adequate land and resources for the support of her people.

The building of Italy into a modern nation was a large and difficult undertaking. For nearly fifteen hundred years Italy was in disorder and made little progress. Three men, Cavour, her brains; Mazzini, her soul; and Garibaldi, her sword, brought about changes that led to the formation of the new Italy. Mussolini did much to change Italy from a weak power into a strong nation. But the acceptance of Fascist doctrines cost the Italians many of their liberties and involved them as an ally of the Nazi aggressors in World War II.

The Italians have made their contributions to civilization in many fields, especially in music and science. Verdi's *Aïda* and *Rigoletto*, Rossini's *William Tell*, and Puccini's *Madame Butterfly*, as well as many other compositions, are among the most beautiful creations known in the musical world. Galileo, whose great work in the field of science during the later Renaissance, and Marconi, a modern inventor who was awarded the Nobel Prize for his contributions to science, have added their fame to their native land by making distinctive contributions to modern civilization.

SELF–TEST

Review the story of Italy by trying this self-test.

I. On a separate sheet of paper, rearrange the items in the following list in correct time order:

(1) Caesar, (2) Ethiopia, (3) Marco Polo, (4) Verdi, (5) Eritrea, (6) Marconi, (7) Cavour, (8) Mussolini, (9) Napoleon, (10) Galileo.

II. Give the names to be inserted in the blanks in the following statements:

1. The man who headed the change in government brought about in 1922 is ——.

2. He is the head of the —— political party.

3. The man who founded a patriotic society called "Young Italy" was ——.

4. The first king of a united Italy was ——.

5. Galileo discovered the use of the ——, which led to the invention of the modern clock.

6. He also was the first to make practical use of the ——.

7. ——, the author of *The Prince,* believed in ruthless, clever politics that disregarded right and wrong.

8. An early Italian who experimented with electric currents was ——.

9. The composer of the opera *Madame Butterfly* was ——.

10. One of the greatest tenors the world has ever known was the Italian ——.

III. Complete each of the following statements:

The Italian peninsula in its shape reminds one of a (1) boot, (2) bell, (3) club. The great central ridge is the (1) Alps, (2) Apennines, (3) Pyrenees Mountains. (1) Venice, (2) Rome, (3) Milan is located on the western side near the coast. New industries which have helped modern Italy to become a leading industrial nation produce ——, and ——. The chief agricultural products in Italy are ——, ——, and ——. The water power of swift mountain streams is being used increasingly to produce —— to run trains and factories. Italy today (1) is, (2) is not, self-sustaining in foodstuffs.

INTERESTING THINGS TO DO

Topics for Talks

1. "High spots of an Italian tour." Many relics of the art and architecture of an earlier time still lend grandeur to modern Italy. Prepare a talk describing some of the treasures of painting, architecture, and sculpture that you would expect to see in a journey through Italy.

2. "A roll call of Renaissance Italians." As a review for yourself, and the class as well, prepare a talk about the great Italians of the Renaissance. Or select a particular type of activity and trace its development in Italy from the Renaissance to the present: for example, music, from Palestrina to Toscanini.

3. "If." Prepare a talk describing what changes you think there would have been in the destiny of modern Italy if Mussolini and his Black Shirts had been quickly and thoroughly suppressed. Give reasons to support your answer.

4. "Mussolini joins the brotherhood of dictators." Compare and contrast Mussolini with some other great dictator, like Napoleon or Frederick the Great, as to his aims, methods, and success. See *Men of Power,* by Albert Carr.

5. "An Italian patriot." Choose one of the men who helped to bring about the unification of modern Italy. Prepare a talk on his life and the service he rendered his country. Ask your librarian to recommend books of collected biography.

Projects for the Chart Maker and Artist

1. Draw a series of sketches, or make a collection of pictures, showing the typical architecture of Italy. Your series may include such famous structures as the Vatican, St. Mark's Cathedral, Milan Cathedral, the Leaning Tower of Pisa, etc. See *All the Ways of Building,* by Louise Lamprey, or *Architecture Through the Ages,* by T. F. Hamlin.

2. Draw a series of sketches which explain Marconi's wireless telegraph. Or draw a sketch showing Torricelli's barometer, and explain its operation. See *Masters of Science and Invention,* by F. L. Darrow.

Ideas for Your "Little Theater"

1. Arrange a concert of Italian operatic selections. You might select a famous song from each of the best-known operas by Italian composers. Or perhaps you might prefer an "all-Verdi," or an "all-Puccini" program. See *Stories from the Great Metropolitan Operas,* by Helen Dike.

2. Dramatize an incident in Italian history, or in the life of a famous Italian. For biographical details, see *Masters of Science and Invention,* by F. L. Darrow; *Book of Courage,* by Hermann Hagedorn.

Candidates for Your Album of Famous People

Caruso, Cavour, Galileo, Garibaldi, Machiavelli, Marconi, Mazzini, Mussolini, Puccini, Rossini, Torricelli, Toscanini, Verdi, Volta.

INTERESTING READING ABOUT ITALY

Compton's Pictured Encyclopedia. "Italy in All Her Glory"; "Beyond the Alps Lies Italy"; and Index.

KYLE, ANNE DEMPSTER. *Red Sky Over Rome.* An American girl in Rome, during the exciting time of Garibaldi and Mazzini, plays a part in the Italian struggle for liberty.

LAGUNA, FREDERICA DE. *The Thousand March.* A story of the adventures of an American boy with Garibaldi.

Life. August 9, 1943. "Modern Italy begins with four patriots and a revolt."

——. August 23, 1943. "The House of Savoy." "At long last the constitution could be thrown . . . to the scrap heap."

MASSOCK, RICHARD G. *Italy from Within.* An honest, readable account of Italy at war, and the Italian people under the heel of the Fascists.

National Geographic Magazine. April, 1924. "Stories and Legends of the Pontine Marshes," by Don G. Cartoni. "Attempts to drain the marshes have extended over twenty-two centuries."

NEWMAN, E. M. *Seeing Italy.* "Luscious grapes above and splendid views below."

TROUTBECK, G. D. *Stories from Italian History.* "When you look at this crown . . . remember the many celebrated people who have been crowned with it."

The Victor Book of the Opera. See Index. The Italian Opera. ". . . attention was paid to melody and vocal display."

WILSTACH, PAUL. *Italian Holiday.* A volume of travel with delightful descriptive details, and sympathetic comments about people and things.

The World Book Encyclopedia. "Italy": The Story of Italy; and Index.

PART FIFTEEN

THE GERMANS BUILT A STRONG NATION
AND TRIED TO CONQUER THE WORLD

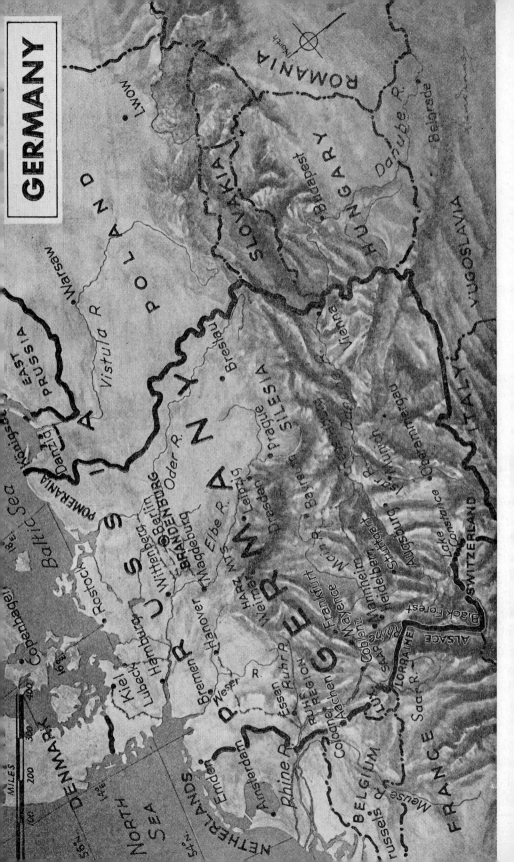

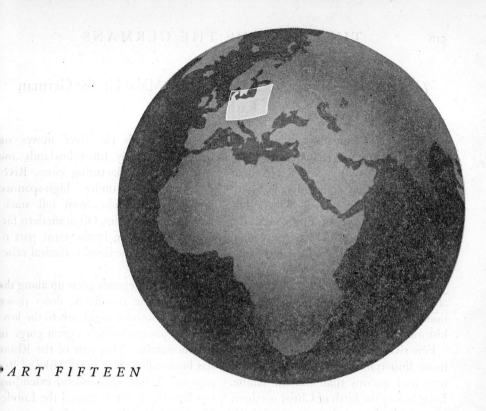

The Homeland of the Germans

BEFORE reading the story of the Germans let us look at the map of their homeland. The boundaries of the land we know as Germany have changed many times since Caesar waged war against the Gallic chiefs. In feudal days there were many states or kingdoms. In time these petty kingdoms became larger states, and the states were united into one large empire. This map shows Germany as it was in September, 1939.

While the boundaries have often changed, the rivers, the mountains, the lowlands, and the highlands have continued through the ages to influence the lives of the German people. Locate the famous River Rhine. In what direction do the rivers of Germany flow? Notice also the many canals. Where is Brandenburg, that one-time little kingdom which, you will learn, led in the building of the German nation? Turn to the map of Europe at the back of the book. Can you see why the Nazi leaders in World War II spoke of Germany as the heartland of Europe and believed they could conquer and control vast territories with Germany as the center? In the story which follows you will learn of German's role in many wars. You will also learn of the contributions which Germans have made to civilization when their energies were not diverted to destruction.

Chapter 1 ~ Highlands and Lowlands Make Up the German Fatherland

The historic Rhine plays an important part in the story of Germany. In Egypt it was the life-giving Nile River about which the ancient civilization grew. In Rome, it was the historic Tiber. The main artery of life in England is the Thames; while in France the capital city of Paris grew up on the banks of the beautiful Seine. In this story of Germany you probably know at once that the river about which German folk tales, traditions, and patriotism have grown is the historic Rhine.

Few rivers in the world have played a more important part in the affairs of men and nations than has the Rhine. Long before the birth of Christ northern Germanic tribes took possession of the Rhineland. Many battles have been waged along the banks of the Rhine, from early times to the present.

Caesar called the Rhine the boundary between the Germans and the Gauls. After Caesar had conquered the Gauls (half a century before the birth of Christ) the Rhine still divided German tribes on the east from Roman civilization on the west. That was before the break-up of the Roman Empire.

From its source in the Swiss Alps, the Rhine winds northward eight hundred miles to the North Sea. As it leaves Switzerland, the river flows rapidly through the highlands in the south of Germany. Continuing north it passes between steep banks on which feudal barons built their castle strongholds. Some of these ancient castles, like the lofty Neuchwanstein Castle, which is pictured on page 519, still overlook the Rhine.

In the north the river moves on through carefully tilled lowlands and past busy manufacturing cities. River steamers pass under high-spanned bridges, and smoke from tall stacks hangs over the cities. Often modern factories can be seen in the same part of a city where a medieval cathedral raises its high spires.

Castles and legends grew up along the Rhine. Where the Rhine flows down from the southern highlands to the lowlands, it passes through a great gorge in the mountains. This part of the Rhine has been called the " Forty Miles of Romance." A jutting headland extending out into the water is named the Lorelei [lawr'uh lai] after one of the stories which have been told about this region. According to the legend, a beautiful maiden used to sit on one of the high rocks there and comb her flax-colored hair. Often fishermen and sailors on the river below became enchanted by the beauty and song of the Lorelei. Neglecting to steer their boats with care through the treacherous waters, they were swept against the rocks and so met their doom.

The Dragon Rock is part of another old story. There, it was said, the hero Siegfried [seeg'freed] killed a dragon in order to bathe in its blood and thereby make himself invulnerable. Later Wagner [vahg'ner], the great German musician, used Siegfried's adventures as the theme of several of his operas.

Besides the old castles and ruins along the Rhine, many of the cities are landmarks. One is the town of Mainz [maintz] which you can locate on the

NEUSCHWANSTEIN CASTLE

On the banks of the Rhine are numerous reminders of the days " when knights were bold and barons held their sway. . . ." This castle was built in what was, in medieval times, an almost impregnable spot. Today, from the air, it looks quite vulnerable.

map on page 516. Here Gutenberg set up his first printing press. You read of him in the story of the Renaissance. Frankfort [frahngk′foort] on the Main [main] River, a branch of the Rhine, is the birthplace of Goethe [gœ′tuh], one of Germany's most famed writers.

The Black Forest is in the German highlands. In the southwestern part of Germany, in a bend of the Rhine, lies the famous Black Forest region. The scenes of many folk tales have been laid in its mysterious depths. In fanciful stories it is the home of dwarfs, elves, and gnomes. You might think that this region got its name from the darkness

under its trees. But the name actually comes from the black fir trees covering the plateaus and rounded mountains. Homes and small hamlets, surrounded by gardens and fruit trees, are to be found in narrow isolated valleys. Cattle graze on the grassy clearings.

The people of the Black Forest still observe many of the manners and customs of earlier times. The forest has so separated them from the life of other parts of Germany that, until World War II, the changes of modern times affected them surprisingly little. For many generations the Black Forest people have been famed for their skill in handicrafts. They are especially noted for their wooden toys, musical instruments, and beautifully carved clocks. These isolated mountain people are proud of their forest, keep it clear of underbrush, and plant young trees to replace those that have been taken out.

The German lowlands are rich farming regions. Not only along the Rhine River but throughout all Germany, the mountains are in the south and the lowlands in the north. Lowlands, as you probably know, are usually warmer than mountain regions. But, since the lowlands in Germany lie farther north than the mountains, the temperature is much the same everywhere throughout Germany. In the higher mountains, of course, it is colder. When German tribes

first took possession of the land south of the Baltic Sea they saw vast forests of oak and pine, and open lands covered with heather, marshes, sandy stretches, and lakes. Through the centuries the cleared away the heather and some of the forests; they drained the marshe and shallow lakes. Originally the land was not fertile, but the Germans, by using the potash from their mines, have made it one of the best agricultural area in Europe.

Rivers and canals connect all parts of Germany. As you will see from the map on page 516, the Rhine is only one of several rivers flowing northward from the highlands and emptying into the Baltic and North seas. The Elbe [el' buh] River is second only to the Rhine

Ewing Galloway

DUISBURG-ON-THE-RHINE

Duisburg, located at the junction of the Rhine and Ruhr, is a busy industrial town. The numerous tugs in the foreground and the docks and railroad yards in the distance offer good evidence of Duisburg's importance as one of the largest inland harbors in the world. Because of its ready access, by two rivers, to the vast system of rivers and canals in Germany, it is a center of inland commerce.

in commercial importance. It is navigable throughout its course in Germany. On its shores are silver and coal mines, pasture lands, and beet fields. The Oder River is the great waterway to the rich mines and manufacturing district of Silesia in southeastern Germany.

Water transportation in Germany has been greatly increased by canals. A canal connects the Rhine and Danube rivers, providing a continuous waterway between the North and the Black seas. The Kiel [keel] Canal is one of the most famous in the world. It connects the Kiel Bay with the North Sea and saves two days for vessels sailing from the Baltic Sea to the Atlantic. The six thousand miles of navigable rivers and fifteen hundred miles of canals have played an important part in the industrial development of Germany.

The Germans make good use of limited natural resources. Compared with many other countries, Germany is not rich in natural resources. The Germans, however, have been resourceful in making the most of what nature has provided. Transportation on their rivers and canals is cheap. They have changed poor soil to productive farm land by drainage and chemical fertilizers, and they have been mining their minerals efficiently. There are still large coal deposits in the basin of the Ruhr [roor], a branch of the Rhine. You can locate the Ruhr Valley on the map on page 516. Coal and the iron of Alsace-Lorraine make the Ruhr and Rhine valleys industrial centers. We have already mentioned the mines along the Elbe River and in Silesia. Copper, silver, lead, and tin are also mined in the mountain regions. Coal is the only natural resource which the Germans have in great quantities. Particularly they lack oil, which is so necessary for industrial growth. The industrial development of Germany has been due more to inventions, highly efficient methods, and frugal management than to abundance of natural resources. German scientists are noted for having found substitutes for many things Germany lacks. These substitutes are called *ersatz*.

Chapter 2 ~ Prussia Forged the German States into a Modern Nation

The early Germans were warring tribes. We first learned about the Germans in the story of Rome. Caesar defeated the barbarian ancestors of modern Germans. He gave us a description of their manners and customs. The German barbarian tribes later swept over the mountain and river barriers and into northern Italy and much of southwestern Europe.

Charles Martel, of whom you have read, was leader of a number of German tribes known as the Franks. In the story of France we learned how the Franks became the leading tribe in what is now northern France, and laid the foundation of the French nation. Early Germanic tribes also crossed the English Channel and had a part in the early development of England. Not all of the long story of the Germans can be told here.

Courtesy McKinley Publishing Co.

A HOMESTEAD OF THE EARLY GERMANS

This illustration gives us a vivid picture of the home life of the early Germans. Notice the weapons of the hunters who have returned home with their kill, and study the costumes and occupations of the other people in the picture.

The earliest Germans seem to have taken possession of the land south of the Baltic Sea very long ago. Later, Caesar and other Roman writers reported that the Germans were strong and rugged, and that they lived more by hunting and fishing than by cultivating the land. Each of their many warlike tribes had a strong chief, and the tribes were often fighting among themselves or attacking others. A picture of some of these warlike early Germans is reproduced above.

The Germans became a separate people. When the Franks became a nation under Clovis, in the Fifth Century, France included much of what is now Germany. Several centuries later the empire of Charlemagne was actually more German than French. It reached as far north and east as the Elbe River, though its boundaries changed through the centuries.

Early in the Ninth Century, as has been described, Charlemagne died and a generation later his empire was divided. The eastern part went to his grandson, Louis. This event marked the real beginning of Germany as a separate nation.

During the Middle Ages the many German states were not often ruled by a strong central government. The people looked to the local nobles for protection. These nobles had constant misunderstandings among themselves. They were still fighting each other as late as the 17th Century.

Long wars held back German progress. The rulers of the German states quarreled over many petty difficulties, but their wars over religion were long and bitter. Early in the 17th Century these conflicts developed into the Thirty Years' War, which in time involved all the leading nations of Europe. It began in a dispute between some of the Protestant princes and the Catholic emperor of Austria. Each side called on allies from the outside, and troops of foreign nations were sent into Germany. It was tragic for the Germans that most of the battles were fought on their soil. Earlier wars had already wiped out many villages and this one also caused widespread destruction. Cities suffered great losses during this time. In Augsburg [ougs'boorg] the people were reduced from about eighty thousand to sixteen thousand. In many places from a third to a half of the inhabitants were killed. As a result of poverty, sickness, and death brought by the Thirty Years' War, people grew up in ignorance. They became, for the most part, cruel and grasping.

In the 16th and 17th Centuries the nations of Europe were taking possession of lands in other parts of the world. They established colonies in America and in the East Indies. The Germans, who were losing people, land, wealth, and security at home, also lost out in the race for colonies. The desire for colonies was one of the reasons why later rulers of the German people led them into the conflicts resulting in World War I and World War II.

Frederick William laid the cornerstone of Prussia. The many small German states were practically in ruin from the religious wars when in 1640 Frederick William became the ruler of one of the larger states, called Brandenburg [brahn'den boorg]. Frederick William was a member of the Hohenzollern [hoh en tsohl'ern] family, which had ruled Brandenburg for more than 200 years. The ruler of Brandenburg was known as the Elector; this title belonged to him as one of the persons chosen to

Press Association

A VIEW OF DANZIG

Danzig, once the capital of West Prussia, was made a free international port at the close of World War I. It is an old city, rich in history, with many relics of medieval times in its art and architecture.

help elect the emperor of the Holy Roman Empire.

When Frederick William came to the throne of Brandenburg he also got the dukedom of Prussia through his family line. This is the state shown on the map on page 516 as East Prussia. You can see that East Prussia was separated from the rest of Frederick William's land by the section called West Prussia, the former capital of which, Danzig, is shown in the photograph on this page. West Prussia belonged to Poland, and was her outlet to the sea. Later, part of it came to be known as the Polish Corridor. Frederick William was not very sure of his authority in East Prussia, however, because the local nobles were strong and because the highest overlord at that time was the king of Poland.

Frederick William saw that little Brandenburg was open to attack from countries such as Sweden, Poland, and Russia. He had only a small, unreliable army and no money at all with which to pay better soldiers. He set out to get aid from the local rulers, taxing their estates and insisting that they help him raise a strong army for the safety of all. He managed to train a better army, and soon the landowners were much more willing to send men for soldiers and money to support the state.

With his new army Frederick William won land in near-by parts of Germany. Some of this he took from Sweden, which had invaded the Continent during the course of several wars. The young Elector continued to strengthen his position.

The rise of Brandenburg-Prussia. When a war broke out between Sweden

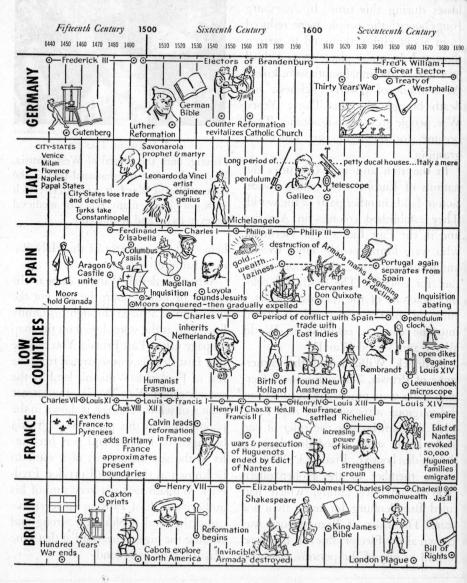

nd Poland it looked very bad for small Brandenburg. The Swedes marched cross some of the Elector's land in the orth. But Frederick William made the most of the situation. He became the ally irst of Sweden, and later of Poland. He managed to make Brandenburg's rising trength recognized by both of these arger states, and through agreement with them he became absolute ruler of ast Prussia.

In spite of Frederick William's doubtful methods of gaining power, as in the Swedish-Polish war, he was always interested in making improvements in his country. As a young man he had studied in Holland and learned how the government was administered in that more advanced country. He encouraged the building of roads and canals. He made improvements in agriculture, schools, and courts of law. Since·there was a

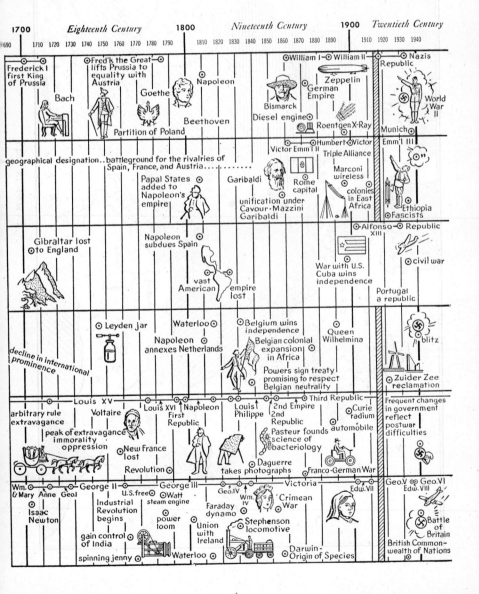

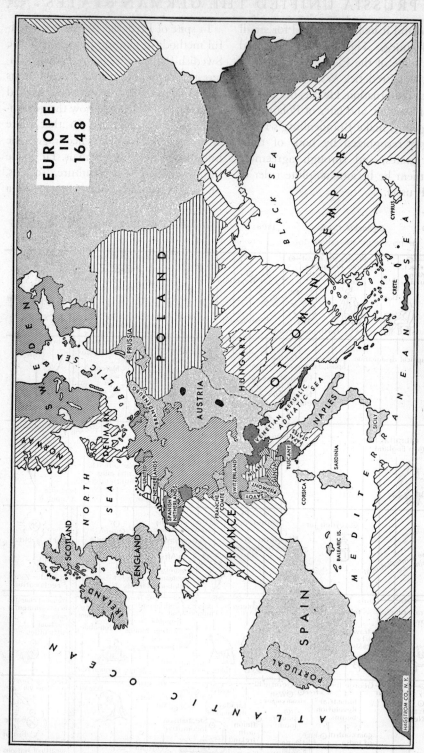

EUROPE IN 1648

hortage of fruit trees he even ruled that no man could marry until he had first planted six new trees.

In the latter part of Frederick William's reign, the Swedes, urged on by France, started to invade Brandenburg. With his strong new army the Elector promptly repelled the invasion. After this time the people, who were pleased because he had not taken the title of King, began to speak of him as the 'Great Elector." He had done much to earn this title. In his time he had changed a war-devastated country into the vigorous young state of Brandenburg-Prussia.

When the Great Elector's son came to power, however, he was not satisfied with the title of Elector and wanted to be made king of Prussia. He enlarged the army, took some more land near by, and in time was able to have himself crowned the first king of Prussia. Thus all the Hohenzollern lands, with Brandenburg as the core, gradually came to be known as Prussia.

A great-grandson of the Great Elector earned the title Frederick the Great. It was the great-grandson of the Great Elector who came to be recognized as a powerful leader in Europe. This later Frederick became known as Frederick the Great. As a youth, he was not interested in the business of kings or in war. He wanted to be a scholar and a writer. He played the flute and wrote French verses. But his father was determined that he should be trained for kingship. His harsh commands led to bitter quarrels. At one time the son ran away. He was thrown into prison and came near being shot as a deserter. Finally young Frederick agreed to follow his father's wishes. First, he had to work long hours as a clerk. Later, he was admitted to the army where he served as a private and then as an officer. When he came to the throne in 1740, just a hundred years after the Great Elector, he had experienced ten years of the most strict kind of discipline. A picture of Frederick the Great is shown on page 528.

Strangely enough, considering his early interests, the young king showed a genius for war. The Prussian army had been made stronger by each succeeding king. But this alone was not enough to account for Frederick's victories; he was a brilliant general. He made a surprise attack on Austria and quickly forced her to give up the rich province of Silesia, shown on the map on page 516.

Frederick the Great won another important slice of land for Prussia. This was West Prussia, that Polish outlet to the sea that had separated East Prussia from the rest of the kingdom. It was Frederick's share of the spoils in the First Partition of Poland. He was glad he had won such a prize, especially since he did not have to fight for it but got it by shrewdness in international politics. In Part Seventeen you will learn more about this ruthless carving up of Poland.

Frederick the Great did not worry about the justness of his claims to new land. Once he said, " I take what I want; there will always be plenty of professors to justify what I do." That attitude has also been true of the rulers of modern Germany.

Frederick the Great was an " enlightened despot." Although Frederick the Great made Prussia important in Europe by his military victories, he liked to think of himself as a builder and a man of peace. He made improvements in farming, trade, and industry. To encourage industry at home he kept foreign goods out of the country. He traveled all over the kingdom to see the needs of

FREDERICK THE GREAT AND VOLTAIRE

Although Frederick was a military genius and an able ruler, his personal tastes wer
those of a poet and a philosopher. He gathered about him many distinguished men o
learning, among them Voltaire, the French writer, shown seated above.

the people and to be sure that everything
was done as he wished. Frederick's attitude toward the people was like that of a
stern parent.

Frederick the Great came to be known
in history as one of the chief of the
"enlightened despots." He did not
claim that he ruled by divine right, but
because he was the one most capable of
ruling. "Chief servant of the state," was
what Frederick called himself. Nevertheless, he was better than such rulers as
Louis XIV of France, who took no interest whatever in the fate of the peo-

ple. Frederick worked hard for the state
and even turned much of his own rev
enues back to the government.

The peasants under Frederick th
Great did not find their lot too intoler
able. There was no revolution as ther
had been in France. This does not mea
that the condition of the peasants i
Prussia was good. They had to toil fo
the state as well as for their landlord.
Frederick took it for granted that th
peasants were, as he said, "the beasts o
burden of society." They were still in
state of serfdom for many years after th

ommon people of England and France ould consider themselves free men.

With the additions Frederick made to Prussia, it was much larger and stronger han it had ever been. But there were no rained statesmen because Frederick had rained the people only to be obedient. The rulers who followed him were weaker and, in a few years, Prussia was o fall an easy prey to Napoleon of France.

Napoleon unwittingly helped in the German states. You learned in the story of France that the French Revolution, which occurred in 1789, soon after the death of Frederick the Great, was not onfined to France. Most of Europe was ffected. A few years later all of Europe became involved when Napoleon made onquests reaching over most of the Continent. But the people of Prussia and the other German states had little understanding of the uprisings in France and were not interested in them. The masses of the people in Germany were till peasant serfs; there was almost no middle class.

At the end of the 18th Century Prussia was ruled by a weak king who was another descendant of Frederick the Great. Other nations fought Napoleon, but for more than ten years Prussia merely looked on. After Napoleon conquered a large part of Western Europe, including other parts of Germany, he finally forced the King of Prussia into war. The Prussian army was quickly defeated, and the country had to give up parts of its territory. This is one of the first incidents that led France and Prussia to look on each other as natural enemies.

Napoleon, in one way, had done the German states, including Prussia, a good turn. He organized the many small states into a few larger ones. By his easy victory, he made the people realize the weakness of their governments, and their need to unite for defense. As the Queen of Prussia said at that time: " We have fallen asleep on the laurels of Frederick the Great, the creator of the new era. . . ." Hoping to improve conditions in Prussia, the Queen used her influence to end serfdom. From that time workers were free to go where they wished. Reforms were made, as well, in the government and in the army. The people were fired with a new determination to throw off the yoke of France. With the rest of the German states, Prussia joined other European nations in bringing about the downfall of Napoleon at Waterloo in 1815.

Austria was Prussia's great rival. Long before the Hohenzollern rulers had begun building up the Kingdom of Prussia, a powerful royal family, the Hapsburgs, had been ruling in Austria. During the Middle Ages, the romantic Danube, which flows through the mountainous country, had formed a part of a great trade route to the Far East. Because of the commerce which resulted, Austria advanced more rapidly than the other German states.

The Hapsburg rulers enlarged Austria and increased its power, sometimes by war and sometimes by marriages with other royal families. Their capital city, Vienna, became one of the centers of culture and politics in Europe. The royal family of Austria came to rule not only over the Germans who lived in Austria itself, but also over many other peoples of Central Europe. As Austria became more powerful, Prussia became jealous of her neighbor.

Metternich played the role of a tyrant. After 1815 Austria's power was made even greater by her prime minister, Prince Metternich [met'er nik]. This man became the power behind the throne. He would not allow Austrians to say or print what they thought, and he put down any revolt with great cruelty. His influence was so great. that kings of neighboring countries had to consider his wishes. For example, just before the middle of the 19th Century the King of Prussia promised his people a constitution. Metternich disapproved; so that promise was broken. For many such acts, he was called " the evil genius of Europe for thirty years."

In 1848, when the common people revolted in most of the countries of Europe, Metternich's power was abruptly broken and he had to flee for his life. There was rejoicing at his downfall throughout the German states. Freed from the suppressive influence of Metternich, they believed that better days could come. But that hope did not last long.

In the German states the movement for greater consideration of the people actually had a setback. The people as a whole were not prepared to rule themselves. At this time, the 1850's, the tide turned against the people and many freedom-loving Germans began to migrate to the United States. In Prussia there followed a time of uncertainty and confusion. It was a perfect condition for the rise of an autocratic government in Prussia.

Bismarck became the strong man of Prussia. The King of Prussia was having trouble with the legislative group in power. He was urged to appoint a new prime minister. The man selected, in 1862, was the shrewd Otto von Bismarck, one of the great landlords of East Prussia. From the time he became prime minister, Bismarck chose to regard himself as an instrument of God. He decided his mission was to help Prussia

create a greater Germany. Being a m. of strong will, he did not hesitate in ca rying out his plans. His supreme co fidence impressed others. One writ said:

Not the least of his qualities was an u usual power of fascinating men, of impre ing them with a sense of his rugg strength and simple honesty. A giant of man he was, calm and deliberate, alwa master of himself, even when pretendi to be angry.

Bismarck conquered by " blood a iron." Bismarck did not consider t wishes of his people. Like Frederick t Great he had no faith in their ability rule themselves. He was ruthless abo the means he used to accomplish l ends. He said, " The great events of o day will not be decided by speeches ar resolutions of majorities . . . but blood and iron." He set about creatin an army that in training and equipme was second to none in Europe.

All the time he was in power, B marck was making conquests for Pru sia by means of politics and war. I said that his purpose was to bring abo the unification of all the German pe ples. This was true, but what Bismar. wanted most was for Prussia, and t Prussian type of government, to be tablished at the head of a united Ge many.

Meanwhile Bismarck was never t busy to keep a watchful eye on affai at home. He constantly worked to ke the government strong and to check a movement toward greater freedom f the people. He provided sickness and cident insurance and pensions for wor ers, to keep them from becoming too i terested in trade unions. Thus he ma aged to forestall the socialists, who we the strongest critics of the governmer As Frederick the Great had done, B

arck looked out for the people to a
rtain extent. He made reforms from
ove in order to prevent revolutionary
forms from below, that is, from the
ople themselves.

Bismarck provoked war with Austria.
ustria had been somewhat less power-
l since the fall of Metternich. Many of
e subject peoples of the Austrian em-
re had revolted in 1848 or later. The
apsburgs put down any uprisings firm-
, but their power had been shaken.
aly seized part of the land which Aus-
ia had held on the Italian peninsula.
here followed revolutions in Italy,
hich later led to a united Italy,
d these helped to weaken Austria's
rength.

Bismarck watched developments and
aited for the best opportunity to strike
ustria, the old rival of Prussia. When
rance — usually an ally of Austria —
as busy trying to set up an empire in
exico, Bismarck provoked Austria in-
war. He had been careful before to
rsuade some of the other German
ates to join him. In a few weeks Aus-
ia was defeated and had to yield some
her territory. But, more important,
e leadership of the German states was
ow taken by Prussia. The Austrian em-
re was at an end; what was left was
e Austro-Hungarian monarchy.

**Bismarck drew France into a disas-
ous war.** With Austria out of the way,
ismarck began to work out his plans
r war with France. He knew that the
rench emperor, Napoleon III, was hav-
g many difficulties and that he might
en regard the war as a way out of some
them. In 1870 Bismarck maneuvered
rance into a position where she would
ve to accept an insult or declare war.
e did the latter.

With his usual foresight Bismarck had
nvinced the other German states that

their safety lay in a union with Prussia,
and in waging war together. The war
lasted only a few months and was
very nearly ruinous for France. As you
learned in the story of France, the monarchy was overthrown; some of France's
land was given up, and a large amount
of money had to be paid. In 1870, France
ceased to be the strongest nation of continental Europe.

By means of war Bismarck had accomplished his ambition to unite all the
German states, except Austria, into an
empire. He had the Prussian king proclaimed Kaiser [kai'zer], or Emperor,
of Germany in the Hall of Mirrors at
Versailles.

The new German Empire became one
of the strongest nations in Europe. It
included the rich provinces of Alsace
and Lorraine, taken from France in
1871. Germany began to consolidate her
gains. She built factories, dug mines, expanded trade, and encouraged her scientists. There was a surprisingly long
interval of peace for Europe. From 1870
until 1914 Germany did not again dis-
turb the peace of Europe as far as actually going to war. We know, too, that
the French recovered quickly, but deep
seeds of rivalry and revenge had been
planted.

**Germany grew strong in forty years
of peace.** From 1871 to the beginning of
World War I in 1914, the people of the
German Empire enjoyed peace and prosperity. More than 67,000,000 people living in a country smaller than Texas
seemed busy and contented. In 1890 the
young emperor, William II, ousted Bismarck from power. But his own policies
were much like those of the man of
"blood and iron." Continuing the plans
of Bismarck, the government made certain provisions for the comfort and security of the people. These benefits seemed

to satisfy the common people. They were passive and not critical, except for certain small radical groups. The Germans were more satisfied than the people of a nation usually are to leave all matters of government and public affairs to their rulers.

German scientists were busy. One of the important factors in the new prosperity of Germany was science. Experts analyzed the soil and prepared nitrates which produced much greater crops. Discoveries in science helped to promote many new industries. The Germans began to produce excellent dyestuffs and drugs with the help of their chemists, and they learned how to make these products cheaply. Moreover they kept the process safeguarded for German use. They applied much patience and skill to such industries as glass manufacturing, and developed camera lenses, telescopes, and other optical glass. The Germans took pride in their work and soon the trademark "Made in Germany" became known throughout the world as a sign of superior workmanship. It was to be seen on chemicals, dishes, tools, and toys, and many other articles sold in America and other countries. Germany became the industrial center of Europe, second only to England.

With a rapidly developing industry and a large population to feed, Germany sought new markets and built new ships to carry her goods. The Germans took colonies and concessions in Africa and the Far East. Their empire now reached to many parts of the world.

Before World War I the Germans had become known as a quiet, hard-working people. Not only their trade but their culture extended far, and they were respected and feared by other nations. The common people were proud of the prestige of the German Empire, in spite of the heavy costs of the military power it was building up. Many of them disliked the arrogance of the military-minded ruling class, but they may have felt that a strong empire required leaders such as these.

When World War I started, the German people were led to believe that their army could not be conquered; that they could win a quick and final victory. Instead, defeat came in 1918, and Germany and Austria both lost much territory and had to pay large indemnities. Austria lost Hungary and the part of her former empire which became Czechoslovakia. You will read about these events when you come to the story of World War I in Part Twenty-two.

Chapter 3 ~ An Ambitious Germany Became Frustrated and Accepted Nazi Doctrines

Germany became a republic. Near the end of World War I, after four years of bitter fighting, revolutionary changes took place in Germany. When the people learned that defeat was at hand, they turned against the groups who were be-

lieved to have brought on the war. The German Kaiser Wilhelm [veel'helm] (William) II was the same emperor who had ousted Bismarck in 1890. He and the local princes of the German states fled. The people established a republic t was called the Weimar [vai'mahr] Republic, because an assembly met in a ity of that name to draw up the constiution. This was the government with vhich the Allies made peace terms at the lose of World War I.

The constitution of the German Reublic appeared to be one of the most lemocratic in the world. It declared that olitical authority is " derived from the eople." All citizens, including women, vere to have equal rights. No titles of nobility were to be granted. The presient of the Republic was to be elected lirectly by the people for a term of seven years. In practice the president did not ake a great part in politics. The chief responsibility of government rested on a chancellor, or prime minister, appointed by the president, and on the Reichstag [raiks'tahg], the parliament, whose members were elected by the people.

The Fatherland was confronted with many difficulties. The new German ship-of-state was launched on a rough sea. In the first place the Republic had been identified with the idea of defeat and humiliation, because this government had made peace settlements after World War I. Soldiers returned home to find that there was no work for them. Industries were disorganized and foreign trade was destroyed. The people were not repaid the money which they had loaned the government for carrying on the war. German money became worthless. Before the war four German marks had equaled one American dollar, but at one time in 1923 an American dollar would buy more than four trillion marks! Germany did not meet the payments imposed by the peace treaty, and as a result the French army occupied the rich valley of the Ruhr.

At various times during the life of the German Republic first one political party and then another tried to seize control. The first president, Ebert [ay' bert], was a member of a party called the Social Democrats. At one time this party had been one of the strongest socialist parties in the world. Even Bismarck had taken extreme measures to break its growing strength. But when it finally came to power this party had grown conservative. It had many great difficulties to face, but it did not face them by making real reforms in government. Throughout the country, moreover, many of the pre-war officials were still in office, and their sympathies were usually with the old, autocratic ruling class rather than with the people as a whole.

The terms of the Treaty of Versailles prevented Germany from having a strong army. Fearful of workers' revolts, the government hired bands of former soldiers to stamp out revolutionary uprisings. These soldier adventurers themselves turned out to be the worst enemies of the state. They looked to the time when the Republic would be overthrown. They were bitter because of Germany's defeat and, in many cases, because they had lost their regular careers in the army. Organized semisecretly on a large scale, they called themselves the Free Corps. These men hid stores of arms which were supposed to be yielded up to the Allies, and they were guilty of secret political murders, some of their victims being men in high government positions.

Hindenburg became head of state. President Ebert died in office in 1925. To succeed him, the people elected General Hindenburg, whom they idolized as a hero of World War I. The choice of Hindenburg was feared by some as a trend back toward monarchy. But the aging general supported the Republic, and

DEM DEUTSCHEN VOLKE

Press Association

VON HINDENBURG LEAVING THE REICHSTAG

This photograph shows von Hindenburg leaving the Reichstag building on the occasion of Germany's national Memorial Day commemorating World War I. The attempted burning of the Reichstag building was one of the big news events of 1933.

did not show favor to any one party. From time to time he had to appoint a new chancellor, as the first president had also done several times, to steer the government's difficult course.

Gradually, after new arrangements with the Allies, which helped to ease the situation for German business, the new Republic found a firmer footing. It organized a new money system, which made it possible to resume foreign trade. Industries were rebuilt and, influenced by the Social Democrats, many businesses were managed by a new co-operation between employers and laborers. Outwardly the Weimar Republic began to look like a stable government.

The situation was ripe for a dictator. The depression which was felt throughout the world in 1929 and 1930 struck Germany a hard blow. There was great turmoil in both business and government similar to that in the worst days just after World War I. The people were ready to follow any political party that could promise better times. President Hindenburg turned to the leaders of first one party and then another. But no party could keep enough support in the Reichstag to carry on the government. As a last resort, in 1933, he called on Adolf Hitler, leader of the National Socialist party, and made him chancellor. It had been in similar times of confusion that Bismarck had come to power seventy years before.

There was little in the early life of Hitler to indicate that he would come to be hailed by the people with an almost religious fervor. There had been many grave danger signals, but many people in Germany had not taken Hitler seriously.

Hitler was an Austrian whose father had held a minor government job. At seventeen, when his father died, Hitler went to Vienna to study art, but with poor success. He lived in poverty. Later he tried his luck in Munich, but although he earned a little money from the sale of postcards or advertising posters, he was no better off.

When World War I broke out, everything changed for Hitler. He joined the German army. Up to this time he had failed at everything, but as a soldier he was more successful; he was even commended for bravery. He did not rise above the rank of corporal, but he took a fanatic joy in the role of soldier. At the close of the war, Hitler was bitter, like most of the German soldiers, because of defeat. But this man seemed bitter, too, because he had simply enjoyed the war more than peace. More confident of his abilities, now, Hitler returned to Munich, where he became one of the soldier adventurers whose services were sometimes hired by the government. He secured a job in Munich, in the information department of the military command of the government of Bavaria. This meant that he was a spy on communists and other radicals.

By 1920, two years after the end of the war, Hitler was spending much of his time in Munich beer halls making fiery speeches, filled with an extreme brand of nationalism. His main group of followers was one known as the German Workers' party. But his speeches were effective with many other discouraged Germans, too. The party was renamed the National Socialist party and Hitler became its head. By his oratory, Hitler attracted to his side strong henchmen from among the soldier adventurers. These men backed up his strength within the party, sometimes by a show of guns. They also recruited new members. The leaders were usually men who were dissatisfied with the government, but, of more importance, most of them had nothing to lose and everything to gain by plotting revolution. This was even more true of the rank and file of the party, who often were simply men out of jobs, who hoped for anything that would improve their condition.

Hitler denounced the Versailles Treaty. Hitler soon showed that he had a genius for stirring the emotions of his followers. His excited speeches had three main themes. First, he fiercely condemned the Versailles peace treaty and its terms which Germany had had to accept after World War I. Second, he declared that Germany had lost the war only because of certain mistakes which should never have been made, and that Germany must now arise stronger than ever, and become the leading nation of the world. Third, he attacked the Jews, many of whom held important positions in Germany, and said that they must give way to persons of pure German extraction. Hitler found it was convenient to blame the Jews for many of the problems of Germany, whether or not there was truth in the charge. This developed into the most intense expression of the " master-race " doctrine. Hitler's determined, fanatical nationalism aroused the pride of his hearers. They were excited by the idea of a greater Germany rising out of their past humiliations.

Wide World Photos

HITLER ADDRESSES GERMAN YOUTH

Chancellor Adolf Hitler as he addressed 60,000 members of the Hitler Youth Association assembled in the Nuremberg Stadium during the National Socialist Congress.

As the party insignia or banner, the National Socialists, who came to be known as the Nazis [nah'tsees], adopted the swastika, a symbol used by ancient peoples all over the world as a good-luck charm or religious token. They bought a newspaper to spread the party's propaganda, and they organized brown-shirted "storm troopers." These troopers used the tactics of terror to promote Nazism. They broke up meetings of other parties, and sometimes beat the opposition leaders. This violence impressed some Germans, who respected their strength, but it frightened others.

Hitler warned the world in "Mein Kampf." In 1923, Hitler, backed by General Ludendorff [loo'd'n dorf] tried to take over the government in Munich. It was a first step in a national revolution, but it failed. At his trial the government authorities, several of whom had conspired with Hitler, were strangely lenient. Many government leaders, like other leaders in the regular army, looked on such movements as Hitler's with sympathy. They themselves wanted to see the Republic overturned. Hitler was sent to prison, but served less than a year of his five-year term.

In prison Hitler began to write the book, *Mein Kampf* [main kahmpf], which means "My Battle." It tells of Hitler's early struggles, his beliefs or philosophy about the German nation, and his plans to make Germany all-powerful. It foretells what other countries Germany must conquer and by what means. It frankly states that to win support at home and seize power among other nations, a leader must lie to his own people and to the world at large. When Hitler came to power he used his book as a blueprint.

After the world depression of 1929 struck, the National Socialists became much stronger. Hitler always won more listeners when the country was in trouble, and he could point to the mistakes of the government. The Nazis now had several thousand storm troopers throughout Germany.

An important part of the party's strength came from Hitler's highly skilled and ruthless aides. Among these were Hermann Goering [gœ'ring], later minister of aviation; Joseph Goebbels [gœ'b'lz], propaganda chief; and Rudolf Hess, Hitler's right-hand man and his secretary at the time he wrote *Mein Kampf.*

Some people believed that it would tame the dangerous Nazi party to let them have some of the responsibilities

f government. In any case Hitler's par-
was the strongest in the country in
933. By making many promises he also
ot enough support from other groups
the Reichstag to give him the major-
y he needed as chancellor, or prime
inister.

Hitler received unlimited power. On
smaller scale, as he built up his party
rough more than ten years, Hitler had
ad much experience in the art of seizing
ower. But what could hardly have been
xpected was that the new chancellor
ould manage to make himself the ab-
lute ruler of Germany within a few
eeks. He used a number of devices to
ake his power complete.

One strong group in the Reichstag,
e Communist party, still opposed Hit-
r. In February, 1933, the Reichstag
uilding burned and the Nazis immedi-
ely insisted that this was the work of
e communists. It is now generally be-
eved, however, that the National So-
alists started the fire, as an excuse for
usting the communists. On this pre-
xt Hitler had these delegates barred
om the parliament. The other mem-
ers were forced to vote to vest all power
the chancellor for a number of years.
When President Hindenburg died in
934, no new president was elected.
here was no longer even a shadow of
ny other power in government than
itler's group of Nazis. Hitler contin-
ed as chancellor, but was now called
e Fuehrer [fyoo'rer], or "leader," of
e nation.

**Germany built a mighty machine un-
er the Nazis.** Very soon after coming
power, Hitler had all possible oppo-
tion crushed. Those who disagreed
ith him quickly lost their posts of in-
uence in schools, courts, and civil serv-
e. The new government did not have
spend any of its energy pleasing its

critics, because its critics lost their jobs if
not their lives.

Germany withdrew from the League
of Nations, and began to make ammunition and rebuild the regular army in
defiance of the peace treaty of World
War I. This created jobs, and many
Germans who had suffered through the
bad times hailed Hitler as the savior of
their country. Wealthy businessmen in
Germany and in other countries began
to back the Nazi government. Some of
these persons must have been shocked a
few years later when they saw how Hitler used Germany's new strength against
her neighbors.

The background of Nazism. You
have by this point in the *Story of Nations* become well aware of the truth
that the affairs of mankind are sometimes vastly complicated, but that there
is always a cause and an effect. It would
be more nearly correct to say that there
is usually a network of causes and effects. Such is the case with the doctrines
of the Nazis. A quick review of the
highlights in the development of the
German state is necessary if we are to
understand the historical background
that made Nazism possible.

It is true that the early German barbarians were warlike, but so were the
barbarians who invaded Gaul (France)
and Rome. The Northmen who settled
in the British Isles and on the Continent
were also a rough and warlike people.
So early ancestors alone cannot explain
the rise of the Nazis.

For a long while the German peoples
were somewhat isolated. The Romans
decided to draw the line of the Empire
in front of them; so the Germans did not
undergo the civilizing power of Rome.
Then, later, the separate little German
states, torn by religious and military conflict, were in a position to fear their

strong neighbors such as France and Russia. Germany could complete the ring of possible enemies by naming Austria to the south and Britain across the Channel. This idea of encirclement seems to have been in the back of the mind of Germans for many years. And there was some truth in it.

By the end of the 18th Century the Germans really began to take pride in being Germans. For instance, they could look back on Frederick the Great. And, later, in the 19th Century the "blood and iron" policy of their great Bismarck had step by step increased the power of Prussia until it was possible to proclaim the German Empire at Versailles in 1871 on the soil of a defeated France. During these many years German writers of literature, history, politics, and philosophy worked diligently to promote German culture and the idea of a strong German state. Some of these writers spoke of the Germans as the *Herrenvolk,* or "master race." Thus by the end of the 19th Century Germany had developed a strong feeling of extreme nationalism. Many of the German people had accepted the doctrines that successful wars strengthen and glorify a nation, that might makes right, and that the state is all-important. It was a case of the individual man or woman existing for the state — so unlike the democratic way of life where the government exists to promote the general welfare of its citizens.

Moreover, since the state was all-important, it could control or forbid any action. Actually " Verboten " (not permitted) signs were in many places. The state dominated. German citizens became accustomed to leaving the business of government to the ruling class of officialdom. This system did not encourage the practice of self-government.

Paternalism in government condition[ed] the Germans to accept being told wh[at] to do and when to do it.

The German leaders told the peop[le] they were a superior race. Their gover[n]ment regulated their lives. They got t[he] habit of obeying, and they accepted [a] fanatical belief in strength through wa[r.] Thus the Germans were quite ready [to] go to war in 1914.

The Germans were defeated and h[u]miliated in 1918. But their military lea[d]ers were still ready and able to pla[n] another war. And with the crack-up [of] their financial and economic affairs [in] the 1930's, the Germans were rea[dy] again to be led into world war. Th[e] Nazis did not miss the opportuni[ty] to furnish that dubious leadership. A[l]though many of the people hated H[it]ler's regime, others plainly were satisfi[ed] to have aggressive, even harsh, leade[r]ship. With strong leaders, they the[m]selves felt strong.

The doctrine of Nazism. The Na[zis] used the arrogant philosophy of the Ge[r]man rulers and thinkers, which ha[d] been developed over a long period, an[d] applied it in an extreme way. Becau[se] conditions were ripe in Germany, t[he] Nazis became all-powerful. They fran[k]ly planned (though at times denying [it] for propaganda reasons) to build [a] Greater Germany that would first ru[le] Europe and then the world.

Briefly, we know, their policies i[n]cluded the doctrine of race superiority. [It] served as an excuse for the persecuti[on] and murder of many thousands of Jew[s.] The Nazis used the Jews as a scapego[at,] blaming them for Germany's trouble[s] and thus calling attention away fro[m] their own mistakes. As a " master race[,"] the Nazis also ordered the ruthless ki[ll]ing of many other men, women, an[d] children in the countries they conquere[d.]

The Nazis overthrew the Republic, and maintained their dictatorship by force. They destroyed all other political parties, and sent anyone who did not approve their acts to a concentration camp. It was their policy to eliminate whoever stood in their way, often in secrecy and in some manner never known to the victim's friends.

The Nazis denounced the democracies as nations of weaklings governed by weaklings. They did not permit freedom of speech, freedom of the press, or freedom of religion. They did not permit freedom of education, but forced schools to teach Nazi beliefs. Some professors and scientists who disagreed managed to flee to other countries before it was too late. This account should help make clear why the United States and our Allies announced that Nazism must be destroyed.

Chapter 4 ~ The Germans Have Furthered Learning and the Arts

German culture is found in many lands. German blood flows in the veins of many peoples. We know from the story of the barbarian invasions that the Germanic tribes found their way to many parts of western and southern Europe. The sturdy Angles and Saxons brought German blood to the English. In modern times we find the adaptable German trader, the thrifty German farmer, and the intelligent German scholar in all parts of the world. In our own country we frequently have neighbors of German extraction and we respect them for their sturdy qualities.

The languages of the Norwegians, Swedes, Danes, and Dutch grew directly out of the language of the early Germans. German is spoken in parts of Switzerland. Many words taken or derived from the German are found in the English language.

City government became a profession. The activities of the German people are very closely regulated by the government, even in times of peace. In a German city many local regulations must be observed. If one changes his place of residence, for instance, he must notify the police. If he hires a servant, he must make a report to the police.

German cities are much governed, but, until recent years at least, many of them have been well governed. The chief business of the city council was to advise and support the mayor or manager, who had to be an expert in city government. Leading citizens were selected as members of the council, and they served from a sense of duty and honor rather than for salary. Members of the council had no jobs to distribute among friends and relatives, so personal or political favors were seldom given. The government of German cities became a science, and a real contribution to progress in this field.

Renaissance painters and modern architects made their contributions to art. The Germans have not had an outburst of art such as Italy experienced during the Renaissance. But like people in all countries, they felt the urge to put on canvas the living pictures they found about them. Unlike the Italians, who portrayed the perfect or ideal, most of the early German painters tried to picture things exactly as they saw them. Sometimes they were so faithful to detail that there was little beauty in their work.

Two of Germany's greatest artists lived during the early part of the 16th Century. These men were Dürer [dyoo'rer] and Holbein [hohl'bain]. Dürer was a master in the use of fine lines to give a lifelike effect, and he knew how to make use of contrasts. As an engraver and woodcutter Dürer was superior to the Italians and equal to the great geniuses of all time. One writer said, " He cut into the copper with the hand of a workman, the heart of a poet, and the brain of a philosopher."

Holbein has been called the greatest of all German painters. In some of his portraits he is as precise as Dürer, and yet he has a greater freedom of touch. His portrait of Erasmus, the Renaissance scholar, is one of his best works.

In modern times one of Germany's chief artistic contributions has been in the field of architecture. During the time of the Weimar Republic, German architects pioneered in modern designs for buildings. In general the aim was to have simple outlines, avoid waste space and materials, and all clumsy, elaborate details, and to use windows so that much more daylight reached the inside. Like the Swedes, Germans began to make simple, strong furniture, built after the same ideas as the modern buildings.

Much of German literature developed from folk tales. With the exception of the long story-poem of the heroic peoples called Nibelungs, the *Nibelungenlied* [nee'buh loong'en leet'], and the works of Martin Luther, the Germans wrote very little of lasting value until the 18th Century. The *Nibelungenlied* is one of the oldest German stories, of which one of the best versions was writ-

ten as late as the 12th Century. It is a heroic tale based on an old myth about the hero Siegfried.

Luther, about whom you read in the story of the Renaissance, lived in the 16th Century. He made a translation of the Bible into German so that his people could read it in their own tongue. This translation is still one of the fine literary works of the German people.

The most famous of all German writers is Goethe. He lived during the latter part of the 18th and the first part of the 19th Centuries. Goethe was a poet, novelist, and philosopher. His greatest work is *Faust* [foust], a drama based on an old legend. The story is about a weary old scholar who sells himself to Mephistopheles [mef'is tohf'ee leez], the devil, that he may taste the joys of youth and of love. Many harrowing and sorrowful experiences are woven into the drama. In Goethe's version, Faust at last finds peace in useful labor and triumphs over the power of darkness. Most of us will become best acquainted with *Faust* through the opera by the French composer, Gounod, which is based on Goethe's dramatic poem.

Another great German writer of the 18th Century was Schiller, who is sometimes called the Shakespeare of Germany. He is best remembered for his drama of *William Tell,* a legendary hero of Switzerland. Like *Faust, William Tell* has also been made into an opera. Perhaps you recall the dramatic incident when William Tell was given his choice of being put to death or of shooting an apple from his son's head. His skill in archery stood him in good stead, so that he won his freedom.

There were, of course, many other noted German writers. One of the best-liked is Heine [hai'ne], author of the *Book of Songs* which includes *Die Lore-*

ei mentioned in the first part of our story. In the realm of fairy tales, German folklore has furnished a rich field for the pens of German authors. Two brothers named Grimm wrote the famous Grimm's fairy tales. You probably remember " The Goose Girl," " Hansel and Gretel," " Snow White," " Tom Thumb," and other stories which have delighted children in many lands.

The Germans have been leaders in education. Have you ever wondered why the school for little children is called the kindergarten? The word *kindergarten* comes from two German words meaning children and garden. It was Froebel [frœ′b′l], a German of the 19th Century, who had the idea of a new type of school for children from four to six years of age. He thought that children should grow in pleasant surroundings and learn by doing things together.

Froebel is only one of many Germans from the time of Martin Luther to the present day who have influenced the schools not only of Germany but of other countries, especially America. Among the leaders was Herbart. He criticized teachers for thinking that memorizing facts was the main work of pupils. He said that school should teach young people how to live well-rounded lives.

The Germans were the first to have medical inspection in the schools, and open-air schoolrooms. The idea that young people should have healthy, strong bodies was carried to an extreme under Hitler's regime. Mass demonstration and military discipline were featured. It was part of the doctrine that the Germans were a race of supermen. In the effort to perfect bodily strength, the Nazis ignored the mind and spirit. All physical weakness was held in contempt, and much cruelty resulted. Phys-

Brown Brothers

DR. ALBERT EINSTEIN

Einstein's theory of relativity, which changes many of our ideas of time and space, has brought him fame and honor. In 1921 he was awarded the Nobel Prize in physics.

ical culture was emphasized for women, too.

The Germans pioneered in trade schools. German boys and girls in their teens who do not go to college must learn a trade. It was because of the example set in Germany that American cities began to offer trade-school courses in part-time and evening high schools.

The Germans have also been leaders in higher education. Many of their distinguished men, especially in the field of science, have been university professors. It has been common for students from many countries to go to Germany for post-graduate work in the sciences and other fields of learning.

Germans have led in science. In Germany it was necessary for science to come to the aid of industry and farming. The government encouraged a large number of scientists to experiment in chemistry, medicine, and physics. The chemists discovered how to make nitrogen from the air. This chemical, like potash, was made into a fertilizer which helped increase the yield of farm lands. Waste gases from coal were turned into dyes and medicines.

One German scientist discovered (with his microscope) that tuberculosis is caused by a germ. Another learned how to make an antitoxin which prevents lockjaw. Roentgen [runt′g′n] won the Nobel Prize for his work which led to the X-ray machine that helps doctors and dentists to diagnose our ills.

Modern ocean liners and battleships are sometimes driven by Diesel [dee′z′l] engines. Rudolph Diesel was the German electrical engineer who invented a motor that could run on cheap crude oil. The Diesel engine can be operated at such low cost that it has revolutionized motor transportation where it is possible to use a heavy engine.

One of the best-known German scientists of today is Dr. Albert Einstein. He has been acclaimed by scientists throughout the world as one of the great minds of this age. He is famous especially for his theory of relativity. It is a theory in the language of mathematics which restates some of our accepted natural laws such as the laws of gravitation. Einstein, however, found it impossible to be a citizen of Germany while the Nazis were in control. He became an American citizen and has been teaching in American universities.

German philosophers have had wide influence. A number of famous German philosophers lived in the 18th and 19th Centuries. Some of their ideas have been real contributions to civilization, but others seem to have hindered more than they have helped the progress of mankind, since some of their theories have been of the kind that promote war.

One of the most famous German philosophers was the professor Kant [kahnt], who lived in the last part of the 18th and early part of the 19th Century. He believed that one's thoughts have a greater influence over his actions than have the people and things about him. He claimed that a person should have the right to determine his own actions, according to his own sense of his duty.

Another philosopher, Hegel [hay′g′l], had great faith in the value of organization, and said that liberty could not be separated from order. The greatest freedom was in doing one's duty to his country. Hegel was in sympathy with the autocratic ideas of government held by the Prussian rulers. Some Germans have used Hegel's ideas as a justification for intense, warlike patriotism. Hegel championed many ideas which Hitler later incorporated into the policies of the Nazi state.

A spokesman for the German "superman" was the philosopher Nietzsche [nee′chuh] who, in denouncing the weaknesses of many persons in history, came to believe that only the strong can survive, and must do so by trampling on the weak. He called Christianity a weak doctrine. Doubtless this philosopher helped to sow the seeds of two world wars, even though he died fourteen years before World War I.

Karl Marx, often called the founder of Socialism, was a German who advocated new ideas for society in general. He urged free public education, a tax on incomes, government ownership of railways and other public utilities, and the abolishment of child labor. He believed that the property of the wealthy at death should be turned over to the state. He claimed that factories and machines, or

From the painting by Beckmann

RICHARD WAGNER AT HOME

The master musician, Wagner, lived in an atmosphere of music. In this picture we see at Wagner's right, his wife Cosima, and at his left is the great musician Liszt, father of Cosima, with his pupil, Moriz Rosenthal.

any other means of production, should be owned by the state and not by private persons or groups of people. With the passing of time many of the followers of Karl Marx have given different interpretations of his teachings. Since 1917 the life of millions of people in Russia has been organized on their interpretation of the philosophy of Karl Marx. His ideas, which are presumed to be the basis of Communism, have been modified to meet changing circumstances.

One of the world's great thinkers of the 20th Century was Sigmund Freud [froid] of Vienna, who was a pioneer in the field of psychoanalysis. This science, still only partially developed, attempts to understand and cure nervous and mental conditions which cause distress and poor adjustment to life.

German composers enriched the world's music. The Germans have always liked to have music when they go to clubs, operas, and beer gardens. From the days of Frederick the Great to the middle of the 19th Century, Germany gave to the world a great many composers who have become world famous. Handel and Bach [bahk] were the first to achieve fame.

The father of George Frederick Handel wanted him to be a lawyer and would not permit him to study music. But the boy could not give up his burning desire to play. He managed to have a clavichord hidden in an attic bedroom and he went there secretly at night to practice. Once his father heard faint music, rushed upstairs, and found his son playing the clavichord. Convinced that the boy was too much interested in music to become a lawyer, the father withdrew his objections to the boy's musical ambitions. Handel wrote more than forty operas before he composed his masterpiece, *The Messiah*. This oratorio tells the story of the birth of Christ. It is probably sung in every Christian country at Christmas time.

There are many stories told about Bach, who was born the same year as Handel. Once, while playing the organ, he became so interested that he forgot the choir he was accompanying, and began to compose new music. Bach is considered one of the greatest musicians who ever lived. His compositions, particularly his fugues [fyoogz], are characterized by a mathematical pattern of great perfection and beauty. His " Toccato and Fugue in D Minor " has been the most widely sold classical recording in America.

Mozart [moh'tsahrt] was a child prodigy. He wrote his own minuets and sonatas at the age of five. He mastered the violin and harpsichord at six. When he was still a child his father, who was also a musician, took him on a tour of England, and the boy was received with enthusiasm when he played in all the larger cities. As an adult, Mozart wrote many compositions which rank with the finest in music. Two of his best known are *The Magic Flute* and *The Requiem*.

One of the greatest composers was Ludwig van Beethoven [loot'vik vahn bay'toh v'n] who, as a child, played

Bach's fugues so well that he became quite widely known. Beethoven studied music under Mozart, and several other well-known musicians. By 1800 he was regarded as an outstanding pianist and composer. He wrote many sonatas and symphonies. Beethoven became deaf when about forty years old. Nevertheless, he continued his career and composed some of his greatest works after his hearing had been completely destroyed. Among these were his Eighth and Ninth symphonies and the " Mass in D." He wrote his famous " Moonlight " Sonata in earlier years. The three short notes followed by the one long note which are the opening notes of his Fifth Symphony form the Morse Code for V ($\cdots$ —), and early in World War II became a symbol of United Nations victory.

Many people think that the most remarkable of all the German masters of music is Wagner. Much of his music can be interpreted as warlike and triumphant in a way that fits in with the " master-race " idea of some Germans. Most music-lovers, however, admire his operas simply for the power and rich harmony of his music, rather than for the stories of the operas. Wherever good music is appreciated, operas such as *Lohengrin, Siegfried,* and *Tristan and Isolde* are enjoyed.

Were there space here it would be possible to tell at length of many other Germans who are famous masters in the field of music. There was Brahms, who composed symphonic music; Schubert, with his *Unfinished Symphony,* and Johann Strauss, called the Waltz King, whose *Blue Danube Waltz* and other compositions you no doubt know. These men make up a galaxy of German musical stars.

The Germans Built a Strong Nation and Tried
to Conquer the World

The River Rhine, flowing from the Alps to the North Sea, with its castled shores and its legendary associations, is the main artery of Germany. The river flows by the Black Forest, through deep gorges, and across wide northern plains. It is linked to the Danube, one of the other great water highways which serve Germany, and make up, to some extent, by cheapness of transportation, for some of her limitations in resources. Germany is not generously supplied with raw materials. She has large coal deposits, but lacks oil and naturally fertile soil. These lacks have led to scientific use of what she has, and to substitution or *ersatz* products.

The early Germans were vigorous warring tribes, who were sometimes defeated by the Roman legions but did not become part of the Roman Empire. They did, later, become part of Charlemagne's Empire but when this organization fell apart, the many small German states were left to their own quarrelsome existence. Their quarrels grew into the bitter, desperate Thirty Years' War between Catholics and Protestants in the 17th Century, a war which destroyed both property and progress among the German states.

Long after other nations of Europe had established strong central governments, Germany was still divided into small warring states. Strong-willed leaders headed the movement that led to the joining of these states into one nation. The Great Elector and his grandson, Frederick the Great, made Prussia second only to Austria in influence among the German people. Later, when Napoleon marched into Germany and defeated Prussia, the Germans saw the need of reshaping and strengthening their union. Metternich, guarding Austria's leadership, opposed the rise of Prussia, but under the influence of Bismarck, prime minister of Prussia, that state managed to weld the other German states together into an empire. At the close of a war in which Germany defeated France, in 1870, the Prussian king was proclaimed Emperor at Versailles.

With the aid of scientists, Germany's imperial leaders made her a great industrial center in Europe. German trade and German ambitions encircled the world. German military power raced forward.

The German people were led by their rulers to expect a swift victory in World War I, but they emerged from that war defeated. They overthrew the Kaiser's government and established a Republic, which tried to deal with the economic troubles besetting the nation. Germany had lost colonies and trade through the war. The period of recovery, difficult and slow, had just got well under way when the world-wide depression crushed it. In a period of turmoil and disagreement, Adolf Hitler and his National Socialist party gained control of the government. The Republic was abolished. Hitler ruthlessly silenced all who opposed him, began to rebuild the army, and moved to carry out his plans for a Greater Germany.

The German genius has not been wholly military; if it had, the world would have had to go without some illustrious painters, writers, scientists, philosophers — and many illustrious musicians. The names of Dürer and Holbein, of Goethe and Schiller, of Roentgen and Diesel, and of Bach, Mozart, Wagner, Beethoven, and Brahms would be unknown to us.

SELF–TEST

Review the story of Germany by testing yourself on these questions.

I. Complete the sentences in the following paragraphs: The historic Rhine has its source in the ⸺ ⸺ and for the upper part of its course forms the natural boundary between ⸺ and Germany. It flows by the wooded mountain region called the ⸺ ⸺, which is noted for its ⸺ stories. In the gorge of the Rhine the river rushes between high cliffs on which may be seen ancient ⸺. This part of the Rhine has been called the ⸺. In the northern part of Germany the river flows more slowly through the (highlands, lowlands), where on its banks may be seen both modern ⸺ with their ⸺ stacks, and medieval ⸺ spires.

II. Tell in a sentence the significance or importance of each of the following in the story of Germany:

(1) Charlemagne, (2) religious wars, (3) Brandenburg, (4) Frederick the Great, (5) Napoleon, (6) Metternich, (7) Bismarck, (8) German scientists, (9) World War I, (10) German Republic, (11) empire building, (12) socialism, (13) dictatorships, (14) education, (15) philosophy.

III. Correct or complete the statements below.

(1) The languages of the ⸺ and ⸺ peoples are said to be Germanic languages because they grew out of the early German language.

(2) By way of the Rhine, connecting canal, and the Danube, it is possible to go from the North Sea to the Black Sea.

(3) After the revolutions of 1848 the people of Germany had a democratic government.

(4) Germany through the centuries has had autocratic rulers.

(5) Hindenburg was president of Germany in the period of the ⸺ Republic.

(6) The Nazis believed in freedom of religion and freedom of education.

(7) The Nazis taught that the Germans were a ⸺ race. They believed the democracies were nations of ⸺ governed by ⸺.

(8) The greatest German painters lived during the —— Century.

(9) The Germans have made distinct contributions in the fields of ——, ——, ——, ——, and ——.

IV. Match the following by writing on a piece of paper the numbers and letters of the items below which belong together or are most directly connected with each other. Do not mark your book.

(1) *William Tell*	(*a*) *Faust*
(2) Holbein	(*b*) *The Lorelei*
(3) Goethe	(*c*) X-ray
(4) Heine	(*d*) Einstein
(5) kindergarten	(*e*) Handel
(6) Roentgen	(*f*) engines
(7) Gutenberg	(*g*) portrait of Erasmus
(8) relativity	(*h*) *The Magic Flute*
(9) *Messiah*	(*i*) Schiller
(10) *Hansel and Gretel*	(*j*) Froebel
(11) *Lohengrin*	(*k*) supermen
(12) Socialism	(*l*) Karl Marx
(13) Mozart	(*m*) revolution
(14) Nietzsche	(*n*) swastika
(15) Diesel	(*o*) Grimm
(16) engraving	(*p*) Kant
(17) 1848	(*q*) Dürer
(18) Hitler	(*r*) printing
	(*s*) Freud
	(*t*) Wagner

INTERESTING THINGS TO DO

Assignment for the Roving Reporter

As a reporter covering German news in the period before World War II, write a story for a paper in this country. Suggested stories: the death of von Hindenburg, the Reichstag fire, the assassination of Dolfuss, the Roehm purge.

Adventures for the Amateur Author

1. Write for a popular magazine an imaginary travel journey about a trip on the historic Rhine. See *National Geographic Magazine*, July, 1925; June, 1936.

2. Prepare a biographical booklet of German scientists. You might use the title, " German Genius and Ingenuity," or use an original title of your own making. The list below includes the names of many of the best-known German scientists: Bunsen, Einstein, Helmholtz, Hertz, Liebig, Ohm, Roentgen, Zeppelin. Books such as *The Advancing Front of Science,* by George W. Gray; *Makers of Science,* by Ivor B. Hart; *Biology and Its Makers,* by William A. Locy; and *Sky High,* by E. Hodgins and F. A. Magoun will be of help to you. Your librarian may be able to suggest other useful sources of information.

Topics for Talks

1. "Germany today." Read, and review for the benefit of the class, one of the recent books of biography or personal experience relating to Germany. Consult the list given in your book, or ask your teacher for suggestions.

2. "As the twig is bent." The Nazis succeeded in establishing their influence more firmly by teaching their doctrines even to children in the schools, and by forming Nazi youth groups. Describe Nazi education and the Nazi youth movement. See *The House That Hitler Built,* by S. H. Roberts.

Idea for Your Little Theater

Prepare a program of phonograph records of typical German music, or of selections from great German composers or famous German operas, and present a concert to the class. Explain the setting or meaning of each selection before it is played.

Candidates for Your Album of Famous People

Bach, Beethoven, Bismarck, Brahms, Diesel, Dürer, Einstein, Frederick the Great, Frederick William, Froebel, Goethe, Heine, Hitler, Holbein, Kant, Mozart, Roentgen, and Wagner stand out in the history of the German people. Make a biographical portrait of at least two of the above famous people for your Album.

INTERESTING READING ABOUT GERMANY

Compton's Pictured Encyclopedia. See "Germany"; "Austria"; and Index.

DODD, W. E. *Ambassador Dodd's Diary.* The private diary of our ambassador to Germany from 1933 to 1937 reveals the frustration and disgust aroused in a democratic diplomat by Nazi ideas and practices.

FRANK, BRUNO. *The Days of the King.* A story of the 18th Century that gives a vivid picture of Frederick the Great.

GUNTHER, JOHN. *Inside Europe.* Mr. Gunther's personality portraits and penetrating comments throw light on conditions in Europe during the critical years leading up to World War II.

MASON, A. E. *Königsmark.* A spirited story of romance in the petty states of 17th Century Germany.

MOWRER, LILIAN. *Rip Tide of Aggression.* A brief, clear review of the significant events in the ambitious Axis dictators' rise to power.

ROBERTS, STEPHEN H. *The House That Hitler Built.* "As soon as the child enters the elementary school (Grundschule) at the age of six, his days are given over to the idealizing of the Nazis."

SHIRER, WILLIAM L. *Berlin Diary.* The personal, uncensored diary of a news correspondent who "covered" Germany while Hitler rose to power.

The World Book Encyclopedia. "Germany"; "Austria"; and Index.

PART SIXTEEN

SCANDINAVIA IS THE HOME OF THREE HARDY NATIONS

SCANDINAVIA

15°W.   0°   15°E.   30°E.

O C E A N

A R C T I C

Hammerfest

Norwegian Sea

Narvik

Torne R.

N.   NORTH

F I N L A N D

Arctic   Circle

Atlantic   *Stream*

O C E A N

Gulf

Trondheim

Lake   Ladoga

Gulf of Bothnia

Leningrad

Helsinki

Sogne Fjord

Gulf of Finland

Bergen

Hardanger Fjord

Stockholm

Tallinn

ESTONIA

Oslo

Lake   Wenner

Riga

LATVIA

Skagerrak

Denmark

Jutland

Kalmar

Baltic Sea

LITHUANIA

Kaunas

Kattegat

Copenhagen

Danzig

Königsberg

EAST PRUSSIA

Berlin

Warsaw

P O L A N D

G E R M A N Y

S O V I E T   R U S S I A

C Z E C H O S L O V A K I A

Miles

0   100   200

Budapest

H U N G A R Y   R O M A N I A

S W E D E N

N O R W A Y

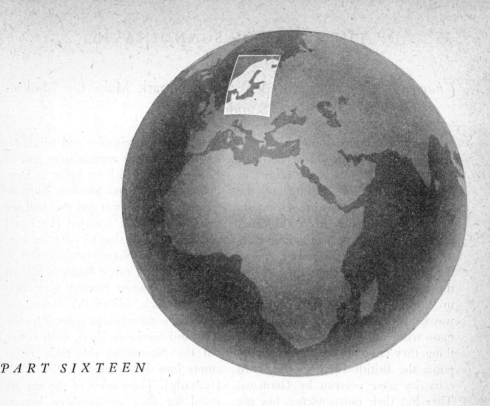

The Land of the Vikings

You will recall that the Northmen, or Vikings, ancestors of the Scandinavians, played important parts in the stories of England and France. In later times, the people of Denmark, Norway, and Sweden have made their contributions to modern civilization. Before looking at the map of the land of the Vikings on the facing page, let us turn to the map of Europe at the back of the book. What part of Western Europe does Scandinavia occupy? How does it compare in size with other European countries?

Now look at the map on the facing page. What natural barriers separate Denmark from Sweden? What barriers separate Sweden from Norway? Why is it that the Scandinavians can carry on fishing and commerce on the western coast of Norway when the Baltic Sea is blocked with ice? Notice the lofty mountains, the deep harbors, and the mountain streams and rivers of Scandinavia. What industries do you think are carried on there? What kind of people would you expect to find living in these rugged northern countries? As you read the story of the Scandinavians you will come to appreciate more and more how the geography of their homelands has helped to shape their manners, their customs, and their institutions.

Chapter 1 ~ Norway, Sweden, and Denmark Make Up Modern Scandinavia

Modern Northmen show their courage. Three small nations of northern Europe today command the respect of liberty-loving people throughout the world. These countries are Denmark, Norway, and Sweden. In World War I fortunately they were able to keep their independence. Then they were among the neutral nations despite the fact that the flames of war raged about them. But in World War II, Denmark and Norway happened to be lands that the Germans wished to invade because, for one thing, they faced on the North Sea, opposite the British Isles. So, these two countries were overrun by Germany. They lost their independence, but not their spirit of independence or their valor in the face of the enemy. It almost seems that a Northman can be captured but seldom conquered.

Sweden, on the other hand, managed to keep her independence. She was stronger in military power, and she did not happen to be directly in the path of conquest. But had it not been for her constant vigilance, she, too, might have known the heavy hand of German invaders and the eclipse of her freedoms.

We know the sort of people these Northmen are. Danes, Norwegians, and Swedes, and their children born in America, live among us. Hardy farmers in our Middle West, thrifty businessmen, doctors, lawyers, teachers, and good mothers and homemakers — all these stem from the Northmen we know as Danes, Norwegians, and Swedes.

Water and mountains divide Scandinavia into three countries. Scandinavia is not the name of any one country. It includes two peninsulas and neighboring islands in the northwestern part of Europe, all of which we know as Denmark, Norway, and Sweden. Turn to the map on page 550 and you will see that the straits of Kattegat [kat'i gat] and Skagerrak [skag'uh rak] separate Denmark from Norway and Sweden. A high mountain range forms a natural boundary between Norway and Sweden. On each side of this range, the tableland is cut across by spurs of mountains and numerous short, swift rivers. On the Norwegian side these rivers empty into deep canyons, called fiords [fyawrdz]. These arms of the sea are noted for their awe-inspiring beauty. They serve as smooth, landlocked, water highways and bring the isolated farmers and small villages closer together. The fiords also make good harbors and provide a coast line of almost twelve thousand miles along which millions of pounds of fish are dried each year.

When looking at the map, you will notice that one-third of the Scandinavian Peninsula lies north of the Arctic Circle. The people of this extreme northern region have continuous daylight during two months of the summer with an equal period of darkness during the winter. In the summer the midnight sun is an unforgettable sight. It looks like a great disk of fire as it rolls across the horizon. The lofty mountains and scenic grandeur of the fiords give this region great charm.

You will notice on the map that the southern parts of the Peninsula and Denmark, across the straits, are less

Norwegian Official Photo

A NORWEGIAN FIORD

The fiords provide good harbors and protected waterways for the people of Norway. Hardanger Fiord, pictured here, penetrates inland for seventy miles, and in places reaches a depth of 355 feet.

rugged. Since these parts of Scandinavia lie as far north as Labrador and Alaska, you would expect them to be cold and bleak. So they would be if it were not for the warm Gulf Stream, which sweeps along the western coast of Scandinavia, raising the temperature and increasing the rainfall. The ports of Norway, even in the far north, are open all winter, although the coast waters of the Baltic are frozen. Nature has given the southern part of Scandinavia a temperate climate.

Nature has supplied Scandinavia with varied resources. Owing to the geography of the country, Scandinavia as a whole is too rocky to be a good agricultural region. This fact partly explains why so many Norwegian and Swedish farmers have emigrated to other places.

Many have come to America, particularly to farms in the Middle Western states. While the people in the southern part of Sweden and in Denmark make their living by farming, the people in northern Scandinavia must depend on other resources.

Sweden's greatest natural resource is her woodland. Sixty percent of her mountains are covered with dense forests of pine, spruce, and fir. The government controls the cutting of the timber. When a tree is cut down, a young tree must be set in its place. During the winter, millions of logs are piled on the ice of the river. When the ice melts in the spring, the water carries the logs to the coast. There great mills make them into lumber, matchwood, and wood pulp for the making of paper.

Swedish Travel Information Bureau

CANAL SCENE IN SWEDEN

A 350-mile water route of lakes, rivers, and canals like this one, connects the Skagerrak with the Baltic coast of Sweden. This scene shows something of the beautiful countryside along the Göta [yo'tah] Canal.

Both Norway and Sweden have iron mines, but Sweden's iron deposits (they are more extensive than those of Norway) are among the richest in the world. Because of its high quality, Swedish iron ore finds a ready market in manufacturing countries like Belgium, Great Britain, and Germany.

As a result of the abundant supply of iron ore, the manufacture of tools and machinery has become an important industry in Sweden. Such steel products as cutlery, cream separators, electrical apparatus, and ball bearings are leading exports.

Norway and Sweden have many swift-flowing streams and rivers that have been harnessed to turn the wheels of electric generating stations. Since both countries lack deposits of coal, the development of hydroelectric power has been a great aid to industry. Also it has made possible the extensive electrification of the railways. Only a small fraction of this power has been utilized, and there are many more possibilities for its future use.

Aided by her abundant electric power, Norway was the first country to manufacture nitrates from the air. Before World War II, both Norway and Sweden were producing large quantities of nitrates for home use and to export to other countries as well.

Electric power made it possible to establish a great aluminum industry in

Norway. Both the aluminum ore and the coal needed to prepare it for the electric furnaces must be imported. In spite of these disadvantages, before World War II Norway ranked among the chief countries of the world in the manufacture of aluminum.

For many centuries the Scandinavian countries have turned to the sea for part of their living. The fishing industry is of considerable importance in each of these nations, and Norway, in particular, exports large quantities of fish to other countries. With many good harbors ice-free the year round, and great forests to furnish lumber for shipbuilding, it is easy to understand how the fishing industry came to be so important to Norway. The coastal waters of the north are excellent fishing grounds for cod, herring, and mackerel. Thousands of men are engaged in the industry. The fish are salted, smoked, or canned for export to other countries. Among the chief markets for dried fish are Spain, Italy, and other countries of southern Europe. Norwegian canned fish products are shipped all over the world. Valuable by-products of the fishing industry are cod-liver oil and fertilizer.

Norwegians lead all other nations in the whaling industry. Whaling vessels today are floating factories. Airplanes spot herds of whales and radio their location to the ship. The whales are killed with modern harpoons shot from a whaling gun. The animal is towed to the factory ship, where bit by bit the carcass is dissected for rendering into a number of valuable products such as oil, fertilizer, and whalebone.

Geography has furthered the development of shipping in Norway and Sweden. The rugged surface of these countries has made railroad construction difficult and expensive. On the other hand, the long coast line and numerous harbors have favored sea-borne trade. Both Norway and Sweden have large merchant marines. In normal times, many Norwegian ships are employed in carrying goods for other countries.

During World War I, a large part of the Norwegian merchant marine was lost through submarine warfare. Within ten years after the war, however, the Norwegians had completed the tremendous task of rebuilding scores of vessels for their merchant fleet. When Norway was occupied by the Germans in World War II, the free Norwegians managed to keep hold of several hundred merchant ships which were of great use to the Allied Nations in the transport of supplies and equipment.

The Danes are a nation of farmers. Denmark and Sweden are completely separated by the Kattegat. See the map, again, on page 550. But in several places the strait narrows to the width of a large river. Trains from Sweden are ferried across to Copenhagen [koh p'n hay'g'n], the Danish capital, in less than an hour. This city is located on one of several hundred islands which, together with the end of the peninsula of Jutland, make up the country of Denmark. This smallest Scandinavian nation has a total area only about half that of our state of Maine.

In many ways Denmark resembles the Netherlands, of which you read in the story of the Low Countries. Both are small and densely populated. Both are lowland countries, forming part of the European coastal plain that widens out like a fan as it spreads eastward into Russia. Both have a moderate climate with about the same amounts of rainfall and with no extremes in temperature in either summer or winter. Like the Dutch, the Danes are a nation of farmers. Since both nations lack water power, extensive forests, and mineral resources, they have for many centuries depended largely on the soil and the sea as a means of earning a living.

Agriculture in Denmark has been scientifically developed. The fertility of Denmark's level, rolling land is practically her only natural asset. Less than a century ago, agriculture in Denmark was confined chiefly to the production of grain. The farmland was divided into large estates, and cultivated for the wealthy landowners by poor tenant farmers. The landlords tried to get as much as possible out of the land, and thus it was not farmed wisely. The sandy soil became worn out, and Denmark, unable to meet the competition offered by cheap grain from the rich plains of the Americas and Russia, lost her European grain markets.

The Danes made a careful study of their unfortunate agricultural situation. They found the soil and climate best suited to the dairy industry. The government aided in a program of breaking up the large estates. Engineers drained the heather-covered wastelands to increase the amount of productive land. Over a period of years the large estates were divided into small tracts and sold to the peasants, until at the time of World War II almost all the farms were owned by small farmers.

Present-day agriculture in Denmark normally produces many crops, mainly those used as food for the livestock. Quantities of grain and oil cake for cattle are imported. The luxuriant Danish pastures support a greater number of animals per square mile of land than do the farm lands of any other country of Europe. The thrifty Danish farmers make sure none of their pasture land goes to waste.

The thrifty Danes learned that co-operation meant prosperity. There is an old saying that if a Danish farmer has only one egg, he can export it and probably will — but not alone. That is simply another way of saying that the Danish farmers have learned to work together in raising their products and selling them. They have formed associations called co-operatives that handle both the purchasing of supplies and the marketing of farm products. By buying in large quantities, these co-operatives can purchase supplies more cheaply. They can also market farm products more profitably than each of the thousands of individual farmers could possibly do by himself.

The farmers have also joined together in employing experts to advise them in raising and feeding their cattle and hogs. Experts run their creameries, meat-packing plants, and butter and cheese factories. Under this excellent supervision, the co-operatives insure a quality product which will bring a good price in foreign markets. Great Britain is normally the greatest market for all Danish farm products, including the rightly famous Danish bacon. The co-operative organizations are not confined to methods of farming, inspection of products, and marketing. The co-operatives serve also as the farmers' stores. There, at cheaper prices, because of the large-scale buying power of the co-operative, the member farmers buy household and personal goods, farm machinery, seeds, and the all-important chemical fertilizers. Thus the members become their own middlemen between the purchaser and the producer, and enjoy the profits in lower purchasing prices. In some instances the co-operatives have been able to raise the standard of goods and improve business practices.

Burton Holmes from Ewing Galloway

FARM SCENE IN DENMARK

Since Denmark is a one-city country, farm scenes like the one pictured here can be seen throughout the land. Cows, pigs, and chickens make up Denmark's chief source of income.

The Scandinavians have improved living and working conditions. The Scandinavians have adopted many progressive measures for social improvement. There are modern housing projects which furnish inexpensive homes for the low-income groups, and other homes for those better off financially. There are no slums such as we see in our larger cities. Electricity is so cheap that most housewives have many electrical appliances in their homes. Stockholm [stok'hohm] and other cities have set aside acres of ground in the suburbs as garden plots for industrial workers. The laborer in the shipyard or factory pays a small sum in produce for the summer rent of his plot. He and his wife and children work in the early morning and late evening raising vegetables and flowers. These garden projects, started during World War I, have been so successful that they are still carried on.

The Scandinavian nations have suffered from few strikes and labor difficulties. Their labor laws and special courts for labor disputes have kept peace in their industrial world. For many years labor and capital in Sweden have settled their disagreements by discussion. Unemployment insurance, workers' compensation, and old-age pensions are the rule. These measures have raised the general standard of living in the Scandinavian countries and made the people more secure. We may correctly say that the peoples of these sturdy little nations have found a middle way in their economic life. Until the onrush of disaster in World War II, this program was providing a way in which all could live in relative economic security, without disastrous clashes between industrial and agricultural interests or serious disagreements between employers and employees.

World War II brought dark days to the Scandinavians. Industry, argiculture, and commerce were, of course, seriously affected throughout Scandinavia during World War II. Under German occupation, the trade of Norway and Denmark was confined to an exchange of products with Germany. But Germany was neither willing nor able to supply these nations with all the things they needed for normal living. Sweden remained neutral, although she was completely surrounded by warring nations. Her land became a haven for refugees. You will read more about Scandinavia and World War II in Part Twenty-two.

Chapter 2 ~ The Land of the Vikings Became Modern Scandinavia

The Scandinavian countries were inhabited before the time of Christ. The early Scandinavian peoples are believed to have spread into the northern peninsulas from the east and the south. Since they were hunters, they may have been attracted northward by the abundance of animals and wildfowl in the Scandinavian region. We call all these Scandinavian tribes *Northmen, Norsemen,* or *Vikings.* For hundreds of years they remained contentedly in their own lands, and were occupied only with local warfare, or peaceful trading with their closest neighbors on the Continent.

The Norsemen developed community life. At the beginning of the Eighth Century the Norsemen were largely farmers and shepherds. They lived in village communities, each with its headman and assembly. A number of these village communities together formed a small tribal state headed by a petty king, who also acted as the leader in religious ceremonies. The king's political power was limited by the village assemblies, for he could perform no important act without their agreement.

Although the Eighth-Century Vikings had no written language, they composed thrilling tales of their own adventures, of the histories of their tribal chiefs, and of their gods. At their feasts and banquets they would recite these well-loved stories, called *sagas* [sah' guhs]. Storytelling, game playing, and drinking quantities of ale were popular as recreation.

The Norsemen developed no feudal aristocracy. For several reasons, no class of feudal aristocrats grew up among the Northmen as it did in the other nations of Europe. The barren soil produced so little that it was not favorable to a system of feudal landholding, as on most of the Continent. The Northmen divided their properties among their descendants, with the result that no large areas of land accumulated under one ownership.

The Norsemen became fishermen, traders, and pirates. The soil of much of Scandinavia was not very productive, as you have learned. As early as the Eighth Century the increased population had forced many Northmen to turn to the sea for their living. They were hardy, adventurous sailors, fishermen, pirates, and traders. Their excellent ships and their skill in navigation made it possible for them to attempt longer and longer voyages. They ventured out into he North Atlantic. They sailed along he northern and western coasts of Europe, and even into the Mediterranean. As these voyages of trade and adventure became more widespread, they resulted in the raids and plundering about which you read in the stories of France and the Low Countries.

About the year A.D. 1000 Eric the Red and his son Leif Ericsson [layf er'ik s'n] reached the shores of Iceland, Greenland, and Labrador. They had come across the open sea in such small oceangoing craft as you see in the picture below. Leif reported that the land they had reached was of no worth, being mostly rocks and ice. It is known that the Norsemen touched the shores of North America, nearly 500 years before Columbus sailed west, and that they may have gone as far south as what is now Rhode Island, where today stands a strange stone tower, possibly of Norse origin. Yet we cannot be sure, since the hardy Vikings, unlike the Greeks, left us no written record.

Norse raids developed into conquests. During the first half of the Ninth Century, the voyages of the Norsemen were summer expeditions. The raiders returned home with their booty in the autumn. However, when the Scandinavian countries became united under a few strong rulers, many tribal chiefs and petty rulers, too proud to accept their defeat, looked to new lands as permanent homes.

There were independent landowners who were unwilling to pay taxes to one ruler. These landholders joined forces with the adventurous seamen. The result was that the Norse raids ceased to be raids only, but became, as well, expeditions looking for land to settle. Thus in the late Ninth and Tenth Centuries, the Norse were colonizing in other lands.

Brown Brothers

THE NORTHMEN ARRIVE IN GREENLAND

The first Viking colony in Greenland was established in the 10th Century by Eric the Red. This picture gives an artist's idea of how these Vikings and their ships looked as they approached the coast of Greenland.

Philip Ainsworth Means

THE NEWPORT TOWER

Many experts believe this old stone tower at Newport, Rhode Island, is a relic of an early Viking colony.

The Norsemen were fearless sailors. The voyages of the Norsemen went on for more than three centuries. Inspired by a love of the sea, the fearless Vikings developed sailing and navigation into a new art. They knew how to tack (sail against the wind); they calculated from the sun and the stars in steering their courses. The sagas show what deep pride the Norsemen took in their ships. They called them by such picturesque names as Elk of the Fiords, and Raven of the Sea. These ships, often assembled in fleets of more than a hundred, were capable of weathering severe storms despite their small size.

Vast areas were influenced by the voyages and settlements of the Norsemen. The Vikings established colonies in Iceland, Greenland, Ireland, England, and France. One group of Norsemen penetrated Russia as far south as the Black Sea, opening a trade route to Constantinople. The Vikings who ventured abroad came to be dreaded by peoples on the coasts of other lands because of their pillaging, plundering, and savagery. When the Norsemen settled down in permanent colonies, however, and intermarried with the earlier inhabitants, they proved an aid in the development of other nations. They added their own skill and resourcefulness to the culture of the earlier inhabitants, much to the benefit of the conquered peoples and of the invaders themselves.

The Scandinavian nations developed their civilization. In the story of the Scandinavian peoples, the three hundred years between the 11th and 14th Centuries are marked by several important changes. The first significant development was the spread of Christianity. For centuries the Norsemen had been devoted to their own gods: Thor, Odin Freya [fray'uh], and many others. They had built temples to them and worshiped them with sacrifices. But in spite of their love for these pagan gods, a number of Norsemen were converted to Christianity during the Ninth and early Tenth Centuries. These first converts were not wholly Christian. Although they acknowledged a Christian god, they continued their lawless raids, and lived by their pagan doctrine of conquest and plunder, cruelty, and revenge.

Finally, during the 11th Century, through the influence of their own Christian kings, nearly all of Denmark, Sweden, and Norway had accepted Christianity. The Swedes also conquered parts of Finland and converted the Finnish people to Christianity. As a result of these missionary activities, Finland became a Swedish province in the early part of the 13th Century.

From the 11th to the 14th Centuries

central governments in the Scandinavian countries were the exception, not the rule. Each of the nations was torn by civil wars at one time or another. At times, by war or by intermarriage of royal families, a single nation might succeed in dominating or subduing one of the others. But such dominance did not generally last long.

The Union of Kalmar joined Norway, Sweden, and Denmark. The Scandinavian nations were united under one ruler at the end of the 14th Century. It was a federation called the Union of Kalmar, so called because it was formed in the Swedish city of that name. The three nations were pledged to eternal peace and equal rights under one king, but each nation was to be governed by its own laws. The joint Scandinavian monarchy created by the Union of Kalmar was at that time the most extensive empire of Europe. It stretched from Finland in the east to the Shetland Islands, Iceland, and as far as Greenland in the west.

Sweden broke the Union and became independent. This Scandinavian union lasted more than a century. Although equal rights for each nation had been agreed upon at Kalmar, from the beginning Denmark had been the dominating nation. This situation had long aroused dissatisfaction in both Sweden and Norway. Finally, at the beginning of the 16th Century, Sweden revolted against the Union. The revolt succeeded completely, and the independent kingdom of Sweden was then established. Norway continued under the domination of Denmark for more than two centuries longer, sinking to the status of a Danish province.

Lutheranism spread through Scandinavia. During the final years of the Kalmar Union in the early 16th Century,

GUSTAVUS ADOLPHUS

Gustavus Adolphus, King of Sweden at sixteen, in later life became the great hero of the Thirty Years' War. In addition to his profitable military campaigns, Gustavus also improved the system of education and encouraged the development of industry in Sweden.

Scandinavian students returning from German universities brought with them the religious ideas of Martin Luther. This new Lutheranism had a strong appeal for the Scandinavians, and many of them left the medieval Church. The doctrines of Luther spread so rapidly in Scandinavia that within a very few years Lutheranism became the state religion. Both Denmark and Sweden took an active part in the Thirty Years' War, the bitter religious conflict between the Protestants and Catholics of which you read in the stories of the Renaissance and of Germany.

Sweden became a world power. Early in the 17th Century, King Gustavus Adolphus [gus tay'vuhs uh dahl'fuhs] came to the throne of Sweden. He helped

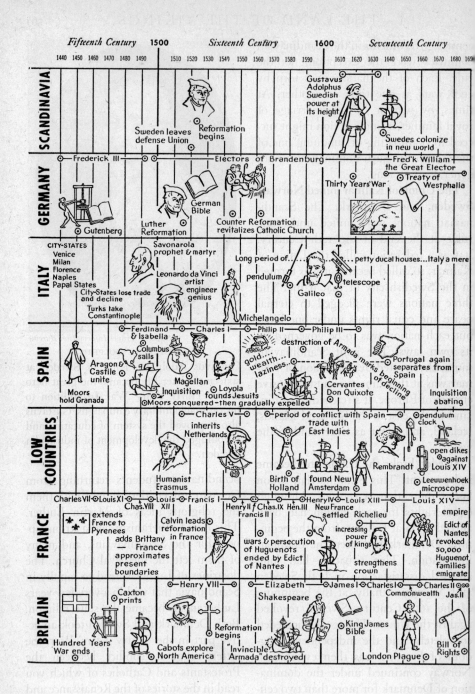

Fifteenth Century **1500** Sixteenth Century **1600** Seventeenth Century

1440 1450 1460 1470 1480 1490 | 1510 1520 1530 1540 1550 1560 1570 1580 1590 | 1610 1620 1630 1640 1650 1660 1670 1680 1690

SCANDINAVIA
Sweden leaves defense Union
Reformation begins
Gustavus Adolphus Swedish power at its height
Swedes colonize in new world

GERMANY
Frederick III — Electors of Brandenburg
Fred'k William the Great Elector
Gutenberg
Luther Reformation
German Bible
Counter Reformation revitalizes Catholic Church
Thirty Years' War
Treaty of Westphalia

ITALY
CITY-STATES
Venice
Milan
Florence
Naples
Papal States
City-States lose trade and decline
Turks take Constantinople
Savonarola prophet & martyr
Leonardo da Vinci artist engineer genius
Michelangelo
Long period of.... petty ducal houses...Italy a mere
pendulum
Galileo
telescope

SPAIN
Moors hold Granada
Aragon & Castile unite
Ferdinand & Isabella — Charles I — Philip II — Philip III
Columbus sails
Magellan
Inquisition
Loyola founds Jesuits
Moors conquered – then gradually expelled
gold... wealth... laziness
destruction of Armada marks beginning of decline
Cervantes Don Quixote
Portugal again separates from Spain
Inquisition abating

LOW COUNTRIES
Charles V inherits Netherlands
Humanist Erasmus
period of conflict with Spain
trade with East Indies
Birth of Holland
found New Amsterdam
Rembrandt
pendulum clock
open dikes against Louis XIV
Leeuwenhoek microscope

FRANCE
Charles VII — Louis XI — Louis — Francis I
Chas.VIII XII
extends France to Pyrenees
adds Brittany — France approximates present boundaries
Calvin leads reformation in France
Henry II — Chas.IX Hen.III
Francis II
Henry IV — Louis XIII
wars & persecution of Huguenots ended by Edict of Nantes
increasing power of kings
strengthens crown
New France settled
Richelieu
Louis XIV
empire
Edict of Nantes revoked 50,000 Huguenot families emigrate

BRITAIN
Hundred Years' War ends
Caxton prints
Cabots explore North America
Henry VIII
Reformation begins
"Invincible Armada" destroyed
Elizabeth
Shakespeare
King James Bible
James I — Charles I
London Plague
Commonwealth
Charles II
Jas.II
Bill of Rights

562

| 1700 | *Eighteenth Century* | 1800 | *Nineteenth Century* | 1900 | *Twentieth Century* |

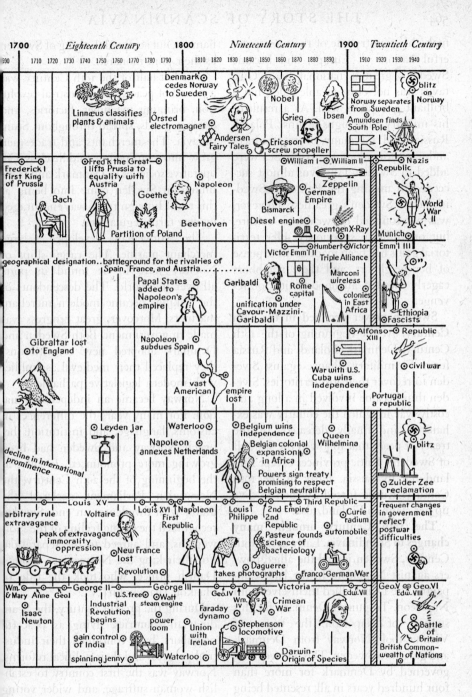

make his country one of the most powerful nations of Europe, and became Sweden's greatest national hero. Gustavus was not only an able ruler, but a brilliant general as well. As a result of his military campaigns against Poland, Russia, and Germany, new provinces and territories along the Baltic Sea were added to Sweden. Gustavus almost succeeded in making the Baltic a " Swedish lake." Sweden's greatness, however, was not founded on wealth or culture, but on military superiority. Her territorial gains had been made at the expense of her neighbors, and these neighbors eagerly awaited an opportunity for revenge.

Swedish power declined in the 18th Century. At the beginning of the 18th Century, Denmark, Poland, and Russia formed a military alliance against Sweden to recover their lost territories. Sweden thus became involved in a long and costly war in which the country was exhausted and finally defeated. In the treaty of peace that followed the war, all of Sweden's Baltic provinces except Finland fell to Russia. Early in the 19th Century, Russia forced Sweden to give up her claim to Finland, also.

The 19th Century brought many changes to Scandinavia. Early in the 19th Century, Sweden joined the allied powers aganist Napoleon. In the later campaigns, the Danes allied themselves with Napoleon. To punish Denmark for this support of Napoleon, the treaty of Vienna took Norway from Denmark and gave it to Sweden. The Norwegians, governed by Denmark for more than four hundred years in all, resented being treated without regard for their own wishes. They were, after all, a high spirited and independent people. They rose in arms, and forced Sweden to recognize a Norwegian constitution and par-

liament, but accepted the king of Sweden as their joint monarch.

The last half of the 19th Century was a period of peace. The industrial revolution, bringing machines, factories, and cheaper goods, spread throughout Scandinavia. The merchants and tradesmen grew into a prosperous middle class. Co-operative societies in Denmark and trade unions in Sweden came into being at this time. Foreign trade was encouraged by new tariff regulations.

The Norwegians developed a large merchant marine. The cargo ships of Norway were to be found in ports all over the world. The descendants of the Vikings became modern merchant mariners. Moreover, great progress was made in government. Both Sweden and Denmark adopted new constitutions; they replaced their medieval assemblies with modern legislative parliaments.

Norway became an independent nation. For many years the differences in customs, language, and institutions between Norway and Sweden had been growing more pronounced. Finally, at the beginning of the 20th Century, the Norwegian Parliament declared the union with Sweden at an end. Sweden recognized the strong feeling of the Norwegians, and agreed to the separation. For their king the Norwegians chose a Danish prince, who took the title of Haakon [haw'kohn] VI.

During the present century, the Scandinavian countries, living as peaceful neighbors, have continued their industrial progress and their political reforms. Norway was the first country to establish woman suffrage, and wider voting privileges were granted soon after in Denmark and Sweden. The modern Scandinavian nations each have their own king and constitution. Norway, with a government much like that of

England, is more democratic in the form of its government than is Denmark or Sweden. In Sweden the king takes an active part in the affairs of government. He still has the power to veto the acts of Parliament. In Denmark, although the people are divided into strong political groups, the king is treated with great respect. The people love and trust their king, and hence he has much power.

Denmark was the only Scandinavian country to own colonies. The Danes long governed Greenland, the world's largest island. Iceland, originally colonized by Norway, was left in the control of Denmark when the union of Norway and Denmark was dissolved by the Treaty of Vienna. Although Iceland and Denmark have had a common king, Iceland has been practically self-governing during much of the 20th Century. In 1944 the Icelanders voted for complete independence. It is interesting to know that in Iceland there is the oldest parliament in the world. The Icelanders call their legislature the Althing [ahl ting'], and in 1930 celebrated its thousandth birthday.

Chapter 3 ~ The Scandinavians Combine Age-old Skills and Modern Thinking

The Scandinavians are leaders in education. The system of adult education in Denmark has attracted the attention of educators in all parts of the world. Nearly one hundred years ago the Danes developed the Peoples' High Schools, rural vocational colleges for adults. These schools make it possible for grown-ups to study special courses during their free time. Many farmers attend school for parts of the winter when the farm work is light. Young girls and farm wives study courses in domestic science. Similar schools for adult education have been established in Norway and Sweden.

We are indebted to Sweden for the idea of manual training, or shopwork, in our schools. Before the Industrial Revolution, the Swedish people produced beautiful handmade articles in their homes. They realized they were losing their appreciation of handicraft with the coming of factory-made goods. A modern arts-and-craft movement was begun, and handicraft clubs were organized for both men and women. These awakened an interest in the creative arts and revived home crafts. Handicraft or manual training was made a part of the work of the Swedish schools. Educators in other countries, including the United States, visited the schools of Sweden and were so impressed that they introduced this new type of work into their own schools.

As a move toward world peace, within recent years the Scandinavian countries have appointed special commissions to make suggestions for the reform of school textbooks. The commissions recommended the removal of all traces of unfairness and national prejudice from the schoolbooks, to prevent old hates and wrongs from being passed on to future generations. The new text-

Swedish Travel Information Bureau

A WEAVING SCHOOL IN SWEDEN

Special schools, like the weaving school pictured here, offer Swedish people an oppor
tunity to develop and increase their skill in a variety of home arts and crafts.

books are to contain a factual reporting of events as they occurred, and a clear statement of different theories and opposing ideas.

Scandinavia is the home of noted scientists and inventors. The roll of distinguished Scandinavian scientists includes botanists, geologists, geographers, physicists, and chemists.

One of the most famous Scandinavian scientists was Alfred Nobel [noh bel'], the great Swedish chemist, whose picture you will see on page 567. He discovered how to make dynamite, smokeless powder, and many other new chemical compounds. Perhaps his knowledge of the destructiveness of the explosives he had developed led him to give his great fortune to the cause of world peace. Nobel is best known throughout the civilized world for the five prizes given annually which bear his name. An award which averages about $40,000

is provided for the most important con tribution made in each of the fields of physics, chemistry, medicine, and literature. The fifth prize is awarded to the person who has done the most to promote world friendship and peace.

Nobel showed his vision of world citizenship when he said, " I declare i to be my express desire that in the award ing of prizes no consideration whatever be paid to the nationality of candidates." Thus many nationalities are represented in the list of the men and women who have been honored by the Nobel prizes

John Ericsson, a Swedish inventor will always have a conspicuous place ir American as well as in Swedish history He invented the marine propeller. H also designed the revolving turret of the historic *Monitor* which defeated the iron-clad *Merrimac* in our War betweer the States. The Swedes in America stil celebrate Ericsson's birthday. Other in

American-Swedish News Exchange

THE NOBEL PRIZE MEDAL

The Nobel prize includes a medal as well as a money award. This particular medal was presented to the English writer, Galsworthy, in 1932, and bears his name on one side.

ventions credited to Scandinavian scientists include the cream separator, the safety match, the nonsinkable lifeboat, and ball bearings.

Scandinavian literature and music are known throughout the world. Many Scandinavian writers have based their stories, poems, and plays on the traditions and the everyday life of the people. Another source of much Scandinavian literature is the folk tale. From the earliest times the people of these northlands spent the long winter evenings around the firesides where stories were told that had been handed down from one generation to another. Mystical peoples, such as those believed in by the Druids in the British Isles — trolls, gnomes, and elves — were believed to dwell in the woods and countryside. Powerful Norse gods made the lightning flash and the thunder roll. Later such stories were written down and finally found their way into print.

Hans Christian Andersen's fairy stories are all folk tales. Henrik Ibsen, the great Norwegian poet and dramatist, wove many of the old folk tales into fanciful stories. The Swedish novelist, Selma Lagerlöf [lah′ger luhf], listened eagerly, as a child, to the tales of the past, and when she became older put them into literary form. Children love her account of *The Wonderful Adventures of Nils,* and older people greatly enjoy *The Story of Gösta Berling*. Books by the Norwegian novelist, Sigrid Undset, who won a Nobel prize in literature, are especially popular in America.

We also find the folk tales in songs and ballads. They are said to have been composed by the people as they sang and danced. They record fairy adventures, tales of love, and historical events. Norwegian musicians have refashioned them into musical compositions which have brought them fame.

The music of the Swedish composer, Edvard Grieg, interprets the spirit of the Scandinavian people. One of his most frequently played compositions is the music he wrote for Ibsen's story of *Peer Gynt.*

More than a century ago the Swedish singer, Jenny Lind, thrilled not only opera-goers but also the great crowds of people that attended the circus of P. T. Barnum, with which she toured America. Her rich soprano voice caused her to be called "The Swedish Nightingale."

In recent times American radio listeners, as well as opera and concert audiences, have enjoyed the voices of great Scandinavian singers. The voices of the Norwegian soprano, Kirsten Flagstad, and the Danish tenor, Lauritz Melchior [mel'kee ohr], are widely admired throughout this country.

Daring Norwegians explored the polar regions. The mystery of the polar regions has been a challenge to the hardy explorers of many nations. Nansen, a Norwegian scholar and explorer, determined, toward the end of the 19th Century, to solve some of the mysteries of these unexplored regions. He sailed north into the Arctic region until the ship became ice-bound. Leaving the ship, Nansen pushed forward on foot until he came within about two hundred miles of the North Pole, far beyond any point previously reached by an explorer. In his later life he became a statesman; he was awarded the Nobel prize for peace in 1922 for his great work in the repatriation of war prisoners and the care of refugees.

Another Norwegian explorer was Amundsen [ah'muhn s'n], who sailed with Nansen on his expedition to the North Pole. Several years later Amundsen made a south-polar expedition, and in 1911 this determined explorer became the first man to reach the South Pole. After his antarctic expedition, Amundsen helped Nobile [noh'bee lay], the Italian explorer, pilot a dirigible from Spitsbergen across the North Pole to Alaska.

Both Ancient and Modern Vikings Have Influenced the Lives of Many People

The independence-loving, hardy Scandinavians live in the three countries of Norway, Sweden, and Denmark, in the northwestern corner of Europe. Their location helped them to remain neutral in World War I. In World War II, Denmark and Norway, although overrun and occupied by Germany, preserved their independent spirit while awaiting liberation.

The three countries are separated by water and mountains, and are supplied with good harbors — particularly Norway, with its picturesque, useful fiords. Scandinavia as a whole is well stocked with natural resources. Sweden has iron ore and forest land and water power for hydroelectric plants. Norway has these same riches in somewhat smaller quantities. Denmark has land suited to agriculture, and has made intelligent, scientific use of it. To all three nations a strong merchant marine has been important.

The Scandinavians are endowed with the ability to work together. In Denmark farmers have formed co-operative organizations for the most efficient purchasing of supplies and marketing of products. Co-operatives in Sweden function in many fields of business. The Scandinavians are progressive; in education, in modern housing, in social legislature, they have set high standards for other nations to follow.

The Norse ancestors of the modern Scandinavians lived on and from the sea, and accordingly did not develop a feudal system based upon agriculture. Some of the seafarers were explorers — Eric the Red, for example, and his son Leif Ericsson, who sailed as far as Labrador. Pirates and colonizers, too, were among the Viking rovers.

At the end of the 14th Century, after centuries of civil wars and wars among the three nations, Norway, Sweden, and Denmark were united in the Union of Kalmar. A century later Sweden broke away from the union, which was dominated by Denmark. Norway, however, remained subordinate to Denmark for two centuries longer.

Lutheranism spread through the three countries and became the accepted form of religion.

In the 17th Century, King Gustavus Adolphus won territory for Sweden by brilliant campaigns against Poland, Germany, and Russia; but these invaded nations recovered their lands in the next century.

In the general European settlement made at the end of the Napoleonic Wars, Norway was annexed to Sweden. The Norwegians forced Sweden to recognize a Norwegian constitution and parliament, under a joint ruler, and later won complete independence by a peaceful settlement. By the 20th Century each of the three Scandinavian nations had its king and its parliament, a peace-loving body of citizens with well-protected civic rights, and an excellent educational system. Nobel, the chemist and advocate of peace; Ericsson, the inventor; the dramatist, Ibsen; the musician, Grieg; and the explorers, Nansen and Amundsen, are a few of the Scandinavians who have contributed to the scientific and artistic development of the world.

SELF–TEST

Review the story of the Scandinavians by testing yourself with these questions.

I. Complete the following statements:

1. Scandinavia is the name given to the three countries ——, ——, and ——.

2. One of the most characteristic geographical features of the Scandinavian coast line is the ——, which is really an arm of the ——.

3. Much of Scandinavia lies north of the Arctic Circle, but the climate is milder than one might expect on account of the influence of ——.

4. —— is a country made up largely of islands.

5. Norway and Sweden are separated from each other by ——, and from Denmark by ——.

6. Denmark and the Netherlands are alike in many respects. Three of the chief similarities between them are ——, ——, and ——.

7. The chief industry of the Danes is ——.

8. Buying and marketing through —— has helped the Danes to prosper.

9. The chief market for Danish goods is the country of ——.

10. Norway and Sweden have several industries in common. Among them are ——, ——, ——, and ——.

11. Norway's most important exports are —— and ——.

12. Sweden exports ——, ——, and ——.

II. On a separate sheet of paper, after the number of each of the following sentences, copy the number of the word or group of words that best completes the sentence.

1. The early Scandinavians or Northmen lived (*a*) as wandering tribes, (*b*) in walled cities, (*c*) in village communities.

2. The voyaging Northmen most often were (*a*) peaceful colonists, (*b*) reckless adventurers and raiders, (*c*) friendly traders with far-off lands.

3. We know the Northmen were hardy, skillful sailors because (*a*) they made many long and successful voyages, (*b*) they had great forests to supply wood for shipbuilding, (*c*) they needed fish for food.

4. The Union of Kalmar was (*a*) a trade agreement between Norway and Sweden, (*b*) a Scandinavian co-operative movement, (*c*) an agreement for the joint rule of the three Scandinavian nations.

5. The Union of Kalmar failed because of (*a*) a lack of financial support, (*b*) long-standing trade rivalries, (*c*) disregard by Denmark of the rights of Sweden and Norway.

6. Gustavus Adolphus, the Swedish national hero, is noted for (*a*) his trade agreements, (*b*) his brilliant military career, (*c*) the invention of the safety match.

7. Sweden lost the supremacy she had maintained in the 17th Century through (*a*) a costly war, (*b*) a great famine, (*c*) a revolution.

8. In the Napoleonic Wars (*a*) the Scandinavian countries were neutral, (*b*) only Sweden fought against Napoleon, (*c*) only Denmark fought against Napoleon.

9. Norway was taken from Denmark and given to Sweden (*a*) to punish the Danes for supporting Napoleon, (*b*) to please the Norwegians themselves, (*c*) to keep Denmark from growing too powerful.

10. The Scandinavian kingdoms are (*a*) absolute monarchies with divine-right kings, (*b*) limited monarchies with many democratic privileges for the people, (*c*) complete democracies with their kings mere figureheads.

III. On a separate sheet of paper, show with what thing of significance you associate or connect each of the following:

(*a*) Newport Tower
(*b*) Hans Andersen
(*c*) John Ericsson
(*d*) *Peer Gynt*

(*e*) Lauritz Melchior
(*f*) The Swedish Nightingale
(*g*) *The Wonderful Adventures of Nils*
(*h*) Peoples' High School
(*i*) Amundsen
(*j*) Alfred Nobel

IV. Look carefully at the pictorial map of Scandinavia on page 572, and turn also to the map of Europe at the back of the book. After studying both maps, answer the following questions on a separate sheet of paper.

(1) What part of Europe does Scandinavia occupy?

(2) How does Scandinavia compare in size with the other European countries?

(3) In times past why has the geography of Norway and Sweden kept these countries free from the influence of affairs in Central Europe?

(4) Why is the northern part of Scandinavia called " Land of the Midnight Sun "?

(5) What natural barriers separate Denmark from Sweden?

(6) What natural boundaries separate Sweden from Norway?

(7) Why are harbors on the west coast of Norway open when those on the Baltic are blocked with ice?

(8) What five industries are pictured in the sketches?

INTERESTING THINGS TO DO

Topics for Talks

1. "There she blows! " A report on the modern whaling industry in which the Norwegians predominate. See " Whaling " in any modern encyclopedia, or see *Whaling in the Antarctic,* by A. G. Bennett.

2. " The grown-ups go to school in Denmark." See *Denmark,* by Agnes Rothery, pp. 33–36.

3. "Gustavus Adolphus — national hero of Sweden." See " Sweden " and " Gustavus II " in *The World Book Encyclopedia* and *Encyclopaedia Britannica.*

Assignments for the Roving Reporter

1. For a farm magazine, write a description of life on a farm in Sweden. Compare various features of farm life in Sweden with those on an American farm. See *National Geographic Magazine,* June 1940.

2. Write about the life and customs of Norwegian or Swedish boys and girls for a young people's magazine. Read *Happy Times in Norway,* by Sigrid Undset, or *Mårbacka,* by Selma Lagerlöf.

3. Write an article for a popular national magazine on " What Happened When the Nazi Totalitarians Moved In." See " Denmark " and " Norway " in *Encyclopaedia Britannica.*

ARCTIC CIRCLE

Reykjavik   Mt. Hekla

Miles
0   50   100

ICELAND
The Land of the Sagas

ARCTIC
OCEAN

The Land of the Midnight Sun

ATLANTIC OCEAN

Hammerfest   North Cape
The northernmost Port

L A P L A N D   KOLA PEN.

Tromso

Narvik

Kiruna

Torne

ARCTIC   CIRCLE   White
Sea

Here the
Ancient Vikings
made their Home

FINLAND
For Centuries part
of Sweden

RUSSIA

GULF OF BOTHNIA

DOVRE
FJELD

NORWAY   SWEDEN

Lake
Ladoga

Sogne Fiord
Hardanger
Fiord
SCANDINAVIAN
Bergen   OSLO
(Formerly Christiania)

PEN.   Gävle

Uppsala
Old University

Åland
Is.

St. Petersburg
Founded 1703 by Peter
the Great to secure his
conquests from Sweden

Neva R.

STOCKHOLM

Gulf of Finland

Reval

L. Wenner

ESTONIA

RUSSIA

Göta
Canal

NORTH
SEA

Göteborg

BALTIC

Gotland

S E A

L A T V I A   Riga

Kalmar

COPENHAGEN

LITHUANIA   Vilna

Memel

DEN-MARK

Rügen

Danzig

EAST
PRUSSIA

Kiel
Canal

Hamburg   POMERANIA
Stettin

Berlin

G E R M A N Y   P O L A N D

Lützen
Gustav Adolph's last Battleground

SCANDINAVIA

Miles   100   300

4. Write an article on co-operatives for such a magazine as *Reader's Digest*. Denmark has for many years been an outstanding example of the success of the co-operative movement, but many of the other nations you have studied also have successful co-operatives of one kind or another. See *Denmark* and *Sweden*, by Agnes Rothery; *France to Scandinavia*, by Frank George Carpenter; and " Co-operation " in *Encyclopaedia Britannica* and *The World Book Encyclopedia*.

Projects for the Chart Maker

1. Draw a map of the polar regions on which you trace the routes of the arctic explorers, Amundsen and Nansen. See *Heroes of the Farthest North and Farthest South*, by J. K. Maclean and C. C. Fraser.

2. Draw an outline map of Europe, and trace on it the routes of the Northmen in their voyages of plunder. Mark also the most important countries where they established colonies. Write a legend under your map explaining why it is correct to say the Northmen had an Empire of the Sea.

Adventures for the Amateur Author

1. Write an essay on " The Contributions of Scandinavians to American Life."

2. Write a short history of the ski. Illustrate it with your own sketches or cartoons, or pictures from newspapers and magazines.

3. Write a poem about the robust, daring Northmen. You might draw a comparison between these sailors of the North and those great trading sea-rovers of earlier times, the Phoenicians.

Candidates for Your Album of Famous People

Gustavus Adolphus, Amundsen, Andersen, Grieg, Ibsen, Lagerlöf, Nansen, Nobel, Undset. Write a biographical portrait of one person from the above list for your Album of Famous People.

Ideas for Your Little Theater

1. Put on a short scene from one of Henrik Ibsen's plays. You might have members of the class learn the parts, if there is time. Or they can merely read the parts from books or scripts. In giving a short scene in this way, you should first give a summary of the play for the benefit of the members of the class who have not read or seen the whole play. Be sure to select a scene that has meaning when given by itself.

2. Choose a number of phonograph recordings from Grieg's *Peer Gynt Suite* to play for the class. You can make the music more interesting if you interpret it by reading first from Ibsen's poetic drama, *Peer Gynt*, the part of the story put to music.

INTERESTING READING ABOUT SCANDINAVIA

Compton's Pictured Encyclopedia. Denmark: Sturdy Little Denmark and Its Progressive People; Norway: The Rugged Land of the Midnight Sun; Sweden: Frosty Land and Sturdy People.

FRANCK, H. A. *A Scandinavian Summer.* " At the Ford and General Motors' factories in Denmark, only . . . heads of the establishment came in cars. All other employees arrived on bicycles."

GULBRANSSEN, T. *Wind from the Mountain.* A story of Scandinavia in the time following the Napoleonic Wars.

LAGERLÖF, SELMA. *Mårbacka.* " Sweden's great national writer tells of her childhood at her ancestral home, and the traditions of her family and neighborhood.

MEDILL, R. *Norwegian Towns and Peoples.* " In Norway the hay is dried on racks which are seen everywhere as a picturesque feature of the landscape."

National Geographic Magazine, Feb., 1932. " Royal Copenhagen, Capital of a Farming Kingdom," by J. R. Hildebrand. " King Christian walks briskly through the streets unattended, greeting this and that citizen."

——, Jan., 1940. " On Danish By-Lanes," by Willis Lindquist. ". . . man is still rolling back the heaths and swamplands. . . ."

——, June, 1940. " Under Swedish Roofs and Skies," by Elizabeth W. Wilson. " The kitchen is the most important room, and a very busy place, too."

——, March, 1943. " Norway, an active Ally," by Wilhelm Morgenstierne. ". . . parts of Norway . . . eluded Hitler's grasping fingers."

OLSON, ALMA LUISE. *Scandinavia.* " Hereafter a war between Scandinavian kinsmen is impossible."

ROTHERY, AGNES. *Denmark.* " The normal ambition of man to achieve independence is encouraged by state and school."

——. *Norway.* A travel book, with anecdotes of people and places, written with words " as exciting as those used by sports writers to describe a football scrimmage."

——. *Sweden.* " When the layman thinks about co-operation it is usually in relation to the consumer."

SMITH, C. M. *Northmen of Adventure.* A splendid account of some of the greatest of the adventurous Vikings.

The World Book Encyclopedia. " Denmark "; " Norway "; " Sweden "; and Index.

PART SEVENTEEN

A SHIFTING BELT OF BUFFER STATES EXTENDS FROM THE BALTIC TO THE MEDITERRANEAN

THE BUFFER STATES

ARCTIC OCEAN

North

NORWAY

SWEDEN

Lapland

FINLAND

KARELIAN ISTHMUS

Gulf of Bothnia

Oslo

Stockholm

Helsinki Kotka

Hangö Gulf of Finland Leningrad

SOVIET

Tallinn

ESTONIA

DENMARK

Copenhagen

Baltic Sea

Gulf of Riga

Riga

LATVIA

RUSSIA

Moscow

Volga River

Memel

LITHUANIA

Kaunas

Wilno

Gdynia Danzig

Polish Corridor

EAST PRUSSIA

Elbe R.

Berlin

Vistula R.

Warsaw

GERMANY

POLAND

Kiev

UPPER SILESIA

Prague

Moravian Gate

Cracow

Lwow

UKRAINE

Danube River

CZECHOSLOVAKIA

Carpathian Mts.

Dnieper R.

SWITZERLAND

AUSTRIA

Vienna

Budapest

Tokay region

HUNGARY

Transylvania

ROMANIA

CRIMEA

Sevastopol

Belgrade

BOSNIA

YUGOSLAVIA

HERZEGOVINA

Ploesti

Bucharest

Danube River

BLACK SEA

CORSICA

Rome

ITALY

Adriatic Sea

Sofia

BULGARIA

Durazzo

Tirana

ALBANIA

Gallipoli

Istanbul

Bosporus

SARDINIA

40°N.

Dardanelles

Ankara

TURKEY

GREECE

Piraeus

Lepanto

Athens

ANATOLIA

Asia

Minor

SICILY

Aegean Sea

TUNISIA

MEDITER

CRETE

CYPRUS

Miles
0   100   200

PART SEVENTEEN

A Belt of Buffer States

THIRTEEN little nations are shown on the map on the facing page. Why do you suppose these little countries are frequently called Buffer States? The Buffer States in the north are important, because like the Scandinavian countries, they are located on the Baltic. Notice that the southernmost Buffer States are on the Mediterranean. On the map locate the Dardanelles. Which nation controls this entrance to the Black Sea? Notice the mountain ranges which break up the central and southern part of this belt of little countries. Do many of the Buffer States have strong natural boundaries? Why have their boundaries changed so many times, as you will read in the story which follows? The boundaries are shown here as they existed in 1939 before the outbreak of World War II. Rivers as well as seas are important in the trade and defense of the Buffer States. Trace the course of the historic Danube. What great capitals are located on this river? What military or trade advantage do you see in their location?

In the story which follows you will learn of the many different peoples who occupy this troubled area. Their history is important to the welfare and peace of the modern world.

Chapter 1 ~ Frequent Political Change Keeps the Buffer States in Turmoil

What do we mean by Buffer States? You would not knowingly move into a house between two quarreling neighbors. But East Central Europe is made up of thirteen little nations who live in this position much of the time. On the map on page 576 you will see these small countries, located between two straight lines drawn roughly from north to south. The eastern line has been drawn from the North Sea down to the Bosporus, the narrow strait between European Turkey and Asia Minor. The western line runs from the North Sea to the Adriatic. To the east of this belt of little nations lies Eastern Europe, occupied by the European part of Russia; to the west lies Western Europe in which Germany, in particular, has been a troublemaker for years. The thirteen little nations which make up this belt between powerful neighbors are called Buffer States. A buffer is anything which deadens the impact or collision of two bodies. As you have already seen in this *Story of Nations,* impact or collision has occurred more than once between the powerful nations of Eastern and Western Europe. Particularly in more recent years, the states of East Central Europe have acted as buffers between them. They have been, from time to time, easy prey for their more powerful neighbors, and so they are always a possible center of international quarrels. We need to know about them if we are to understand the difficulties of keeping peace in Europe and, therefore, in the world.

The boundaries of the Buffer States have changed frequently. All the Buffer States together occupy a territory only three-fifths the size of Western Europe and have only half as great a population. You may well wonder how such a small territory happens to be broken up into so many little countries. It has not always been so. Russia, two hundred years ago, had only three neighbors on her west — Sweden, Poland, and Turkey (the Ottoman Empire), much as they are shown on the old map on page 526. More than half the countries of East Central Europe were created at the end of World War I. And the others are fairly young; the only one much more than a hundred years old is Turkey.

Why have there been so many changes in the Buffer States? In this *Story of Nations* you have watched the formation of a number of modern countries. You have seen how the people of Germany, France, the Netherlands, and Belgium, for examples, each became a united separate group of people and established an independent nation.

Usually, as you have seen, nations have come into being within natural boundaries of mountains, seas, or rivers, which enabled the citizens to protect themselves against invaders and maintain themselves as independent peoples. Usually, too, the people of a given nation are bound together by a common national language. Frequently they share common history, traditions, and customs; and sometimes they are also bound together by a common religious faith.

None of these conditions which favor the rise of clear-cut national states have been present in East Central Europe. That is why the boundaries and govern-

CENTRAL EUROPE
1939

Key to language groups

	Norwegian
	Swedish
	Finnish
	Lettish and Lithuanian
	Danish
	German
	Polish
	Czech and Moravian
	Slovakian
	Hungarian
	Romanian
	Slovene
	Serbo-Croatian
	Bulgarian
	Turkish
	Albanian
	Bulgarian and Turkish
	Greek
	Italian

NORWAY

SWEDEN

FINLAND

DENMARK

Baltic Sea

ESTONIA

LATVIA

LITHUANIA

RUSSIA

Great Russian

White Russian

EAST PRUSSIA

GERMANY

POLAND

Little Russian

UKRAINE

CZECHO-

SLOVAKIA

HUNGARY

ROMANIA

CRIMEA

ITALY

Adriatic Sea

YUGOSLAVIA

ALBANIA

BULGARIA

Black Sea

GREECE

TURKEY

SICILY

CRETE

Mediterranean   Sea

CYPRUS

ments of the Buffer States have changed so frequently. In the first place, geography has not provided defensible natural boundaries in this region. Many different peoples migrated into these lands in both ancient and medieval times; and they have brought their various customs, faiths, and loyalties with them. These different peoples have not settled in well-defined areas, but are intermingled geographically. Then, too, since strong well-defined nations have not grown up in East Central Europe, its lands have been ruled over by various conquering peoples in the past, and such rule has given rise to conflicting claims and loyalties. Finally, in modern times various world powers have sought to control the Buffer States for reasons of trade or military advantage. In some instances they have even taken the land of these people in order to exploit its natural resources.

In general, the Buffer States fall into three groups: those on the Baltic; the inland countries; and the nations of the Balkan Peninsula. By glancing briefly at each of these groups, we can more readily understand some of the changes in East Central Europe.

The Baltic is the Mediterranean of the north. You have seen what an important place the Mediterranean Sea has held in the history of southern Europe. In more modern times the Baltic Sea has held a similar position in the trade life of northern Europe. It forms the water highway for all the nations surrounding it. Struggle for control of this inland sea has often changed the boundaries and fortunes of the Baltic nations. You have already read about two of the Baltic nations — Sweden and Denmark — in the story of Scandinavia. Russia, as you will read in Part 18, struggled for centuries for an outlet on the Baltic Sea. The Baltic members of the Buffer States are

Finland, Estonia, Latvia, and Lithuania. None of these nations is rich in any natural resource except forests, and their livelihood depends upon access to the sea. All of them are geographically part of Eastern Europe. But much of their culture and the religious faith of many of their citizens have come from Western Europe. Therefore they are culturally a part of Western Europe. Finland has had to resist the political domination of both Germany and Russia. Estonia, Latvia, and Lithuania are important chiefly because their seaports are trade outlets for the vast resources of their great eastern neighbor, Russia. But in outlook they are outposts of Western Europe. And they are made up of different peoples with different origins and histories. All these things help explain their uncertain position in the modern world.

As it became apparent that World War II was about to break out in Europe, Russia brought pressure to bear on her smaller Baltic neighbors. She demanded territory, ports, and airplane and railroad bases to aid her in her defense against Germany. Finland resisted some of Russia's demands, as you will see further in the next chapter, and war between the two countries followed. Estonia, Latvia, and Lithuania yielded. Before long, Russia annexed these three little countries as members of the Soviet Union. Once again, conflict among the great powers had resulted in wiping out some of the Buffer States.

Poland, Czechoslovakia, and Hungary. In the heart of East Central Europe, lie Poland, Czechoslovakia [chek' oh sloh vah'ki uh], and Hungary. See the map on page 576. These nations lack defensible natural boundaries and strong military power, and have been a prey to their more powerful neighbors.

Poland has shared the troubles of the

Baltic nations. One of her problems has been to have access to the Baltic. But like the other Buffer States in the heart of East Central Europe, her lands have been coveted chiefly for their minerals, forests, and farms. Her territory has been divided and redivided.

These nations have not, in general, kept pace with changes in Western Europe. Varying hostile groups within the nations, and the habit of clinging to the ways and memories of the past have in some instances prevented effective co-operation and made the problems of these three nations more difficult. Czechoslovakia and Poland were the first victims of Nazi aggression which heralded World War II. Hungary, on the other hand, joined with the Axis against her neighbors.

The Balkans are the "Powder Keg" of Europe. The southernmost Buffer States are called the Balkans, from a word meaning "mountains." These states — Romania, Bulgaria, Yugoslavia, Turkey, Greece, and Albania — occupy the mountainous region between the Black Sea and the Adriatic, which juts out as a peninsula into the Mediterranean Sea. So many European wars have started in this region that it has been called the "Powder Keg" of Europe. You will see these six nations on the map on page 576.

The modern nations of the Balkan Peninsula, like those of ancient times, are important because of their position on the Black Sea and the Mediterranean. They are strategically valuable for both trade and military purposes. Besides, more powerful nations desire the resources of these little countries. The Balkans are still largely backward, and most of the people make their living by agriculture. Their resources of oil, coal, and water power are still largely undeveloped. This makes them attractive prey to any aggressor nations.

In the six Balkan States there are fifteen groups of peoples of distinctly different nationality. There are also six different major religious groups that tend to separate these peoples. In fact, none of the Buffer States from the Baltic to the Adriatic have more complex problems than the Balkans.

From earliest historic times all the great empires of Eastern Europe have included the Balkan Peninsula. From the map on page 162, you can see how much of this territory was included in the empire of Alexander the Great. Later, the Balkans were a part of the Roman Empire. In the Fifth Century, when the western part of the Roman Empire crumbled away, the eastern part lived on as the Eastern or Byzantine Empire. Its capital was at Byzantium, then called Constantinople and now Istanbul [ee'stahn bool']. About the end of the Fifth Century, Slavic tribes were seeking admittance into the Eastern Empire, much as the Goths had sought admittance into the Western Empire. Various Slavic tribes — Serbs, Croats [kroh'atz], and Slovenes [sloh veenz'] — settled in different parts of the Balkans. Then, in the Ninth Century, the Magyars [mag'yahrz], from the Ural [yoo'r'l] Mountains of Russia, invaded Europe. These people, of partly Mongolian blood, took possession of the Danube Valley and settled there.

The division of the Roman Empire into an eastern part and a western part resulted in a division of government control in the Balkans. The northwest portion of the Balkans, for example, was under the control of the western part of the Roman Empire. Consequently the Slavs and Magyars who had settled in the Balkans found part of the Peninsula

CHART OF EUROPEAN BUFFER STATES

ITEM	FINLAND	ESTONIA	LATVIA	LITHUANIA	POLAND	YUGOSLAVIA
Population (1940 estimate) and main geographical features	3,887,000; about 134,600 square miles; many lakes, rivers, marshes; heavily forested areas	1,134,000; about 18,400 square miles; long coastline on Baltic	1,951,000; about 25,400 square miles; several good ports on the Baltic	2,879,000; about 23,000 square miles; no harbors on Baltic, only access to sea the German city Memel	34,776,000; about 150,500 square miles; plains to the north; extensive marshlands on Russian border; Carpathian Mts. to the south	16,200,000; about 95,600 square miles; rugged mountains; inland plains; navigation on Danube and Sava rivers
Resources	Timber, gold, nickel, copper, lead, zinc	Timber, few minerals	Timber, few minerals	Timber	Coal, timber, zinc, petroleum, salt	Copper, iron, bauxite, coal, lead, salt, timber
Products	Flax, sugar beets, rye, potatoes; main exports: wood pulp; woolen goods; finished lumber; dairy products	Cattle, dairy products, flax, rye, potatoes, sugar beets, wheat, oats, barley, timber	Dairy products, flax, rye, potatoes, sugar beets	Dairy products, flax, rye, potatoes, sugar beets	Rye, potatoes, wheat, barley, sugar beets, cattle, hogs	Copper, lead, iron, bauxite, wheat, corn, hops, cattle, lumber
Major cities	Helsinki, capital	Tallinn, capital	Riga, capital and main port	Wilno, capital; Kaunas, former capital	Warsaw, capital; Gydnia, Baltic port; Posen, Lodz	Belgrade, capital; Split, Adriatic port
History	Moved to Finland from Volga Valley about A.D. 500; ruled by Sweden 1154-1809; by Russia 1809-1917; became republic 1920; fought Russia in World War II; made peace 1944	From 13th Century, controlled in turn by Danes, Germans, Swedes; 16th Century became part of Russia; made independent 1918; absorbed by Russia 1940	Letts appeared in ancient times; conquered by Teutons in Middle Ages; ruled in turn by Sweden, Denmark, Poland, Russia; made independent 1918; absorbed by Russia 1940	Lithuanians appeared in ancient times; independent from 13th Century; was partitioned but regained independence 1918; absorbed by Russia 1940	Kingdom in 10th Century; strong power 1300-1600; partitioned 18th Century by Prussia, Austria, Russia; republic 1918; held by Germany during most of World War II	Kingdom established 1918; formed of old Serbian kingdom, portions of Austria-Hungary, and kingdom of Montenegro; conquered by Axis in World War II
Language	Resembles speech of Estonians and Hungarians; of Asiatic origin	Resembles speech of Finns and Hungarians; of Asiatic origin	Indo-European	Indo-European	Slavic	Slavic
Religion	Lutheran church the state church, but there is complete religious freedom	No state church; most are Lutherans; about one-fifth are Greek Catholics	No state church; more than half are Lutherans	No state church; most are Roman Catholics	No state church; most are Roman Catholics; some Greek Catholics; about one-tenth Jews; few Protestants	No state church; most are Serbian Catholics; many Roman Catholics; some Mohammedans
Minority groups	Swedes, Lapps	Russians	Russian, Jews, Germans	Germans	Jews, Russians, Germans	Croats, Slovenes, Serbs, Mohammedans, Albanians
Important figures	Risto Ryti; Field Marshal Mannerheim; Jean Sibelius				Boleslav the Mighty; John III, Kosciusko; Pilsudski, Paderewski; Chopin, Mme Curie	King Peter II, Slobodau Jovanovitch, Marshal Tito

ITEM	BULGARIA	ALBANIA	CZECHOSLOVAKIA	HUNGARY	RUMANIA	GREECE	TURKEY
Population (1940 estimate) and main geographical features	6,550,000; about 42,800 square miles; eastern border on Black Sea; northern border Danube River; mountains in center	1,003,000; about 10,500 square miles; mountainous country bordering on Adriatic Sea	15,247,000; about 54,200 square miles; rimmed by Carpathian Mts.; well forested	14,733,000; about 66,400 square miles; large fertile plains; few mountainous areas	13,201,000; about 74,200 square miles; hilly east to west; east fertile plains extend to Black Sea	7,109,000; about 50,300 square miles; long, irregular coastline on Aegean and Mediterranean; mountainous	17,870,000; about 294,400 square miles (figures include European and Asiatic Turkey). Little territory in Europe
Resources	Coal, timber	Timber and minerals	Coal, iron, copper, lead, silver deposits	Coal, bauxite, oil	Extensive petroleum deposits; iron; copper; low-grade coal	Iron, lignite, salt, zinc	Chrome, zinc, manganese, copper, antimony, and other minerals undeveloped
Products	Tobacco, wheat, rye, corn, potatoes, fruit, dairy products, coal, attar of roses	Tobacco, timber, cattle, sheep, wool, dairy products, bitumen	Corn, hops, oats, wheat, rye, munitions, textiles, glass products, chemicals, leather goods, wood pulp	Coal, bauxite, oil, cereals, potatoes, sugar beets, wines, flax, cattle, hogs	Oil, wheat, corn, barley, oats, rye, lumber, fruits	Wheat, corn, barley, oats, olives, fruits; some iron, zinc, and low-grade coal; wines	Olive oil, figs, raisins, mohair, rugs
Major cities	Sofia, capital; seaports, Burgas and Varna on Black Sea	Tirana, capital; Durazzo, seaport on Adriatic	Prague, capital; Bratislava, industrial center	Budapest, capital	Bucharest, capital; Ploesti, oil center; Constanta, port	Athens, capital; Thessaloniki, the Piraeus, ports	Ankara (Anatolia in Asia Minor), capital; Istanbul, Constantinople
History	Settled by Bulgars about A.D. 500; ruled by Turks 1500-1878; 1878 semi-independent; independent kingdom 1908; joined Central Powers World War I; joined Axis World War II; made peace 1944	Settled by Slavic tribes about A.D. 500; ruled by Turks from about 1500; became independent 1912; a republic 1924-1928; kingdom 1928-1939; 1939 seized by Italy	Settled by Slavs; kingdom of Bohemia established in Middle Ages; later part of Hapsburg empire; later part of Austria-Hungary; independent republic 1918; conquered by Axis in World War II	Settled by Huns and Magyars about A.D. 400; later by Slavs; kingdom of Hungary recreated after World War I; joined Axis in World War II	Part of Roman Empire; Slav immigrants intermarried with Roman settlers; ruled by Turks from 1500 to 1877 when became independent; joined Allies World War I; joined Axis but made peace 1944	In ancient times center of culture; made part of Roman Empire; held by Turks 1453-1829; 1829 independent kingdom; joined Allies in World War I; war with Turkey 1920-1923; conquered by Axis in World War II	Remains of the once great Ottoman Empire that extended to east central Europe from western Asia. Reached its height during 15th and 16th Centuries; then declined. Turkey was greatly modernized after World War I
Language	Slavic	Slavic	Slavic	Resembles speech of Finns and Estonians; of Asiatic origin	Romance language based on ancient Latin	Basically ancient Greek but modified by Slavic and Turkish speech	Turkish — an Asiatic language
Religion	Greek Catholic Church, official religious belief	No state church	No state church; most are Roman Catholics; large Protestant minority	No state church; two-thirds Roman Catholics; many Protestants; small minority Greek Catholics and Jews	Greek Catholic but religious freedom is guaranteed	Greek Catholic is official church	No state church but most Turks are Mohammedans
Minority groups	Turks	Mohammedan Turks in south; Roman Catholic Ghegs in north; some Greek Catholics	Germans	Jews, Czechs, Romanians, Slovenes	Germans, Hungarians, Jews	Albanians, Turks	Armenians, Greeks
Important figures	King Boris II; King Simeon II; Dobri Boshiloff	King Zog fled in 1939 when Italy invaded Albania	John Huss, Comenius, Masaryk, Smetana, Dvořák, Eduard Beneš	Admiral Horthy, Ferenc Szalasy	Ex-King Carol; King Michael; Ion Antonescu	John Metaxas; King George	Mustapha Kemal Atatürk; Inonu; Saracoglu; Menemencioglu

ruled from the city of Rome, part from the city of Constantinople.

The division of the Church into the Roman Catholic Church, ruled from Rome, and the Greek Catholic Church further split the interests and loyalties of the Balkan peoples.

From the 11th Century on, the Turks attacked the Byzantine Empire and seized parts of it. Finally, in 1453, they took Constantinople, the capital of the Empire, and then for three centuries it was the Turks who ruled the Balkans.

You will recall that the Hapsburg line of emperors had made Austria a major power in Europe by about the middle of the 17th Century. The Hapsburgs feared the presence of the Turks in Europe; so they organized the people of the Balkans and drove the Turks out of much of the Peninsula. In this way the Balkans came under what was called the protection of the Hapsburg emperors. But these rulers used harsh measures. They tried to force the Balkan people to speak only German. They attempted to make the Roman Catholic faith the sole church for all, even for those who were members of the Greek Catholic Church. Moreover, one of the Hapsburg rulers settled a number of German colonists in the part of the Balkans on the Danube in an effort to Germanize the people.

In the meantime, Russia had become a great power, and Peter the Great, whom you will read more about in the next Part, decided that taking the Bosporus and the Dardanelles from Turkey was the " historic mission " of Russia. For two hundred years the Russians fought the Turks in their efforts to take the Dardanelles.

The Balkans had long had too many national groups living in a small area. In the modern world they found they also had too many " protectors."

Albania was the first of the Balkan countries to suffer from the Axis aggression which led up to World War II. This little country was seized by Italy in 1939 and ceased to have a separate existence. Yugoslavia and Greece were overrun by Axis armies during the war. Romania and Bulgaria became allies of the Axis. Only Turkey maintained an uneasy neutrality.

In this Part, we survey quickly many nations. Up to this point in our Story of Nations, most Parts have told the story of only one people or one nation. In this Part Seventeen, we need to survey thirteen states. We do not have the space in this book to tell you about each of the Buffer States in detail and you do not have the time in a one-year course to study each of them thoroughly. So we have given you here a brief survey of their general problems and history. If you wish to look up specific facts about any particular Buffer State you can turn to the reference chart on pages 582 and 583. In the next chapters we shall tell you more about four typical Buffer States: Finland in the Baltic region, Poland and Czechoslovakia among the inland countries, and Turkey in the Balkans. As you read about these countries, notice how four factors — geography, migrations, conquests, and the conflicting claims of greater powers — have affected their troubled history.

Chapter 2 ~ Finland Puts Independence First

Finland is the republic farthest north. Conquering the northernmost regions of the world has called for great ruggedness and intelligence and determination. The republic which lies farthest north is Finland, and the Finnish people are noted for their strength, determination, endurance, and resourcefulness. They have made the most of the limited resources of their native land and are a highly cultured people. On the map on page 576 you can find their country, a lake-scattered country which is about three times the size of New York State. There too you may find the Karelian [kah ree'li'n] Isthmus. Notice how Fin-

land lies between Sweden and Russia on the Baltic Sea, which serves all the nations surrounding it as a water highway into the rest of the world.

Who are the Finns? The Finns are not Scandinavians like the Swedish, or Slavs like the Russians. Early in the history of Europe, tribes were migrating to more favorable regions. During those years a group of tribes whose language was of Asiatic origin, moved, probably from the Volga River Basin, to the shores of the Baltic Sea, and from there into what is now Finland. These people drove the Lapps whom they found there into the northern part of

Wide World Photos

VIEW NEAR HELSINKI

The aerial view above shows one of the interesting forest and water patterns that one sees constantly throughout Finland. This scene is near the capital, Helsinki [hel seen'kee].

A SHEPHERD BOY AND HIS DOG

A Lapp shepherd tends large herds of reindeer, for it is this animal that provides the Lapps with most of their food — reindeer meat, cheese, and reindeer milk. Notice the boy's costume and his skis.

the country and settled down to a period of tribal warfare. After the Finns emerged from this tribal period, they drew their religion and culture from Sweden and Germany. Missionaries and traders came from these countries by way of the Baltic to Finland.

By the 13th Century Sweden had brought the Finnish people under her rule, but her conquest did not subdue the independent spirit of these people. By the 14th Century, the Finns had united and established their own nation, which they called Finland, or land of the fens, or swamps.

Finland is a highway for war. Living between two large, hostile neighbors, Finland became a highway for wars between Sweden and Russia. It remained under Swedish rule until 1809 when Sweden was made to give Finland to Russia. As a Grand Duchy of Russia, or a semi-independent state ruled over by a grand duke, Finland for some time managed to keep a certain amount of self-governing power. Even when the Finns were subject to other nations — as they were for about seven centuries — they kept alive their national spirit and struggled to preserve at least a degree of self-government. As a people, they were not easily daunted. Of their two rulers, they preferred Sweden; and they resisted Russian influence staunchly and steadily.

Toward the end of the 19th Century, Russia took away most of Finland's power of self-government. But in 1917, when Russia was upset by revolution, Finland declared her independence. Helped by German intervention, she had established herself as a free republic in 1920.

The Kalevala. The Finnish language is related to the language of the Magyars and belongs to the same language family as Turkish. *Kalevala* [kah'lay-vah'lah] means *land of heroes*. It is the name of Finland's epic poem, which tells stories of Finnish folklore — of pine forests and dark rivers and wild swans and the hero and his quest for the maiden in Lapland. Many legends from the *Kalevala* have been put to music in tone poems by Jean Sibelius, Finland's great composer. In *Finlandia,* for example, Sibelius has expressed the moving spirit of the heroes who have held to the Finnish ideals of ruggedness, dependability, and faith in the destiny of their forest-shadowed country.

What are the Finns like? In the war for liberation from Russia in 1917, when the men were away fighting, the schoolboys in a little country town decided that they too should go to war. At a signal during their morning classes, they got up, left the school, and managed to reach the front, more in fear of punishment from their fathers than of the Russian soldiers. But the fathers, instead of punishing their sons, put them to work at such jobs as observing the enemy from treetops. These were Finnish boys; the ones who survived the war grew into Finnish men determined to uphold the traditions of Finland.

The Finnish citizens have been strongly nationalistic but not aggressive. They have been orderly in domestic affairs, and have shown foresight, a progressive spirit, and sound planning. Public education is widespread in Finland. In 1940 more than 99 percent of the Finnish population could read and write. The Finns have conserved their forests, the products of which have formed most of their exports and a good part of the world's supply of wooden products. In the 1930's for example, Finland was producing about eighty percent of the spools used in the world. The Finns have balanced their national budget. They kept up the interest payments on debts of World War I when other, larger, nations were defaulting. Finland was the first nation in Europe to give women the right to vote.

The Finns hold cleanliness next to godliness, making almost a ritual of the sauna [sow'nuh], or steam bath. The sauna is a bathhouse with a fireplace or pile of stones over a firebox, and a platform at the opposite end. When the stones in the fireplace are heated, water is thrown on them. The bather sits on the platform in the steamy atmosphere and switches himself, preferably with birch twigs, to stimulate circulation. In earlier days the sauna was used as a place for prayer, but now in Lutheran Finland, the purpose of the sauna is physical cleanliness. A Finn has said, " A smoking bathhouse, a barking hound, a crowing cock, and a mewing cat — these are the signs of a good farm."

To many Americans the position of Finland as an ally of the Axis in World War II was a cause for regret. Finland and the United States had been friendly in the recent past and the Finnish interest payments on her debts had impressed Americans with the honesty and trustworthiness of the Finnish people. The Germans had helped the Finns gain freedom from Russia. Even after Finland had established itself as an independent republic it remained under the watchful eye of Germany. On the other hand, when war began to threaten between Germany and Russia, Russia was determined to have what aid she could from Finland. In 1938 Russia had made demands on all the smaller Baltic states for concessions to aid in her defense against Germany. Estonia, Latvia, and Lithuania yielded. From Finland Russia demanded fortified territory along her eastern coast and the right to lease the port of Hangö. Finland refused; so war with Russia began in the fall of 1939. Finland's white-clad troops moved into the snow-covered forest lands in defense of their national integrity. This brief war came to a close in March, 1940. Hangö was leased to the Russians.

But it soon became apparent that Russia was still not satisfied. War broke out again in 1941 and continued, to the distress of the democratic nations, who by now were fighting side by side with the Russians against the Axis. Finland claimed that she was not an Axis ally but was fighting a separate war with Russia. The Allies claimed that Finland was aiding the Axis, whatever her motives were. The Germans of course brought pressure on Finland to continue fighting the Russians and sent troops into Finland. The Allies urged Finland to make peace with Russia, and Finland said that Russia's terms were not acceptable. Finally, and reluctantly, the United States broke off diplomatic relations with Finland. Early in the fall of 1944, however, Finland accepted Russia's peace terms. Russia was granted the right to have a naval base in Finland, and was given some other ports for commercial use. Finland agreed to pay Russia an indemnity of $300,000,000, and to clear Finland of all the German forces stationed there.

Chapter 3 ~ Poland Lives in the Hearts of Her People

Poland is an old country. If you have seen a great nation collapse — and anyone living in 1940 saw that tragic thing happen to France — you can imagine what happened toward the end of the 18th Century when three of Poland's neighbors partitioned her into three pieces, each of them seizing a piece for itself.

Poland has a strong national history. Boleslav [boh'luh slahv] the Mighty was King of Poland in the year 1000. Cracow [kray'koh], the early capital, founded in A.D. 700, was the birthplace of a university in the second half of the 14th Century — over a hundred years before Columbus discovered America. This ancient capital holds castles and cathedrals — for Poland early in her history became a Roman Catholic nation. Warsaw became the capital of Poland early in the 14th Century. By the middle of the 16th Century Poland was at the height of her power and glory. Polish territory reached across central Europe from the Danube River to the Baltic Sea. Its western boundary was only ninety miles from Berlin. Among the countries making up Poland was the modern nation of Lithuania.

The decline of a great kingdom. Many things contributed to the decline of the once powerful Polish nation. For one thing, the Polish assembly, or Diet, had an old-fashioned rule which required unanimous consent to any action which the government took. You can imagine how hard it would be for the United States to defend itself if every action taken by our Congress had to be unanimously agreed upon.

Poland was further weakened for a long time by the lack of a powerful middle class of merchants, businessmen, or tradesmen. Poor peasants there were, who lived miserably, and a class of rich and extremely powerful nobles. These nobles became more powerful than the king himself. They discouraged the rise of a middle class, which would actually have made Poland a stronger nation; and they themselves sometimes neglected to provide for the national defense.

In the latter part of the 17th Century the Turks pressed into central Europe, burning, killing, and pillaging. The most famous Polish king of all time, John Sobieski [soh byes'kee], or John III, was then reigning. He found it necessary to defend the nation with the Polish army, with practically no help from the nobility. A great military leader, John III was made commander-in-chief of the Polish, Austrian, and other Christian armies which joined together to drive out the Turks. In 1673 under Sobieski's command, these armies rescued the Austrian capital of Vienna, which had been besieged by the Turks for fifty-eight days.

In spite of his great military success, and the acclaim of the Polish people, John III was unable to curb the power of the nobility, or bring about needed reforms within Poland itself. He died a disappointed man. No leader of like brilliance succeeded him. And the Austrians soon forgot their debt of gratitude to Poland's king, and were willing to take what they could from the weakening Polish kingdom.

Poland was culturally tied to France. In the 17th and 18th Centuries Poland was close to France in literature, music, and in art. Many nobles, who as a class had risen early in the history of Poland, modeled their castles after those of the French. Here is a description, by a Polish writer, of a typical palace of this time.

The palace of Grudno stood in the depths of an old park. It was built toward the end of the 17th Century by one of the Princes Gintult, who established his residence here, modeling it upon the French courts of the day. In the course of years the growth of the trees destroyed the former symmetry of the garden; here and there, even, groves of young hazel trees stole into the avenues once so carefully trimmed and pruned. The palace, built upon the groundwork of an old castle, was surrounded by reservoirs of mildewed water. Its walls were several cubits thick, especially around the base, which still contained vaulted, dungeon-like rooms, with grated windows. Thick, slanting abutments, like monstrous feet, sank in the insidious waters of the old, deep, stone-girt moat.[1]

[1] From *Ashes* by Stefan Zeromski. Alfred A. Knopf, Inc., New York, 1928.

The Polish nobles lived on their estates and hunted in forests where a legendary stag " carrying the wood of the True Cross between his antlers " was believed to appear once in a hundred years. Not all the nobles were wealthy or had large estates. There is a saying that the dog of a poor nobleman, even if he sat down in the middle of the estate, would have his tail in a neighboring estate.

Poland's neighbors were not good neighbors. Like Finland, Poland was the victim of a bad-neighbor policy. Austria, Prussia, and Russia made their first partition of Poland in 1772, and extinguished the nation's independence in 1795. One of Poland's heroes, Kosciusko [kahs′i us′koh], who had helped Washington fight for independence in North America, led a Polish insurrection but was crushed by the partitioning powers. From 1795 until 1920, Poland existed only in the memories and hopes of the Polish people.

In 1830, encouraged by the French, the Poles revolted against Russian rule in Warsaw, but were again subdued. At this time many Polish men of intellect and learning took refuge in Paris, thus bringing closer the sympathies of France and Poland.

Poland came back to life. The land of the Poles was a battleground during World War I and again during World War II, which you will read about in Part Twenty-two.

The Poles themselves were determined to gain their freedom. They took World War I as an occasion to fight for it. Unfortunately, they were not agreed as to which of the ruling powers — Germany and Austria or Russia — should be defeated first, or which might be trusted to keep her promises of greater freedom for the Poles in return for Polish military support. The result was that a Polish legion fought under German command, not for love of the Germans, but to free Poland from Russia. Other Poles enlisted in the Russian army and fought against the Germans, and their own brothers, in order to free Poland from Germany. Still other Poles made their way to France and fought with the Allies under France.

The situation was cleared up somewhat in 1917 when the United States came into the war and President Wilson declared in favor of an independent nation to be made up of all land occupied by "indisputably Polish" people. In that year also the Russian Revolution took Russia out of the war and resulted in somewhat more acceptable Russian terms for Poland.

President Wilson's plan did not mean the end of Poland's trouble after the closing of World War I. It was 1920 before Poland was actually free of warfare. First the Ukrainians, in western Russia, tried to set themselves up as an independent nation with Lwów [lvoof] in eastern Poland as their capital. The Polish soldiers were still scattered over Europe. But Lwów was defended by its own civilians, including the women and children, and the Ukranians' plans came to nothing.

Poland, still quarreling with Russia over boundaries, was invaded by the Russian Red Army. With French aid, Poland forced Russia to yield territory on the east. Finally in 1920 Poland, though still surrounded by unfriendly neighbors, was at last a live free nation. Her territory then included the province of Wilno, taken from Lithuania. Poland, however, needed a port on the Baltic Sea. Therefore, at the Paris Peace Conference in 1919, a strip of land called the Polish Corridor was granted to Poland. The Corridor cut across East Prussia

from Poland to the seaport of Danzig. This port was made a free city controlled by the League of Nations. A part of Upper Silesia also was given to Poland. Its choice of nationality had been determined by vote of the people. You may compare the extent of the new Poland with that of the earlier Poland by using the maps on pages 526 and 576.

Poland's leader in its return to national life was Marshal Pilsudski [pil soot´ skee], sometimes called the Washington of Poland. Unlike our own revolutionary hero, Pilsudski was of peasant origin. As a boy he was sent to a school in Wilno which was taught by Russians. There he learned to resent the Russians' attitude of superiority toward the Polish people. Pilsudski was a military genius, and a deeply determined man. Shrewd and skeptical, he knew how and when to play the great European powers against each other for the liberation of Poland, without actually trusting any of them. Opposition, even among the Poles, only made him more determined. When Poland's independence was won, Pilsudski quietly organized her government. He proved to have unusual grasp of European affairs and to be a gifted diplomat, among the most able in Europe.

Poland was coveted by Germany. In Part Twenty-two you will see how a group of German people revived the old idea of national or race superiority which had already caused so many conflicts among peoples. You will see, too, how they seized territories in the Buffer States, and planned to make those peoples the permanent vassals of a Greater Germany. Perhaps no nation suffered more severely under German occupation than the Poles. Warsaw, the capital city, was bombed. The Polish people, particularly those of Jewish birth, suffered terribly under German rule. Thou-

Wide World Photos

POLAND UNDER THE NAZI HEEL

The German occupation of Poland brought suffering and death to hundreds of thousands of Polish people. Many were forced to work at the direction of the Nazis inside Poland, and others were sent to labor or fight in Germany.

sands died of starvation and disease, or were murdered ruthlessly by their Nazi overlords.

But like other conquered peoples the Poles looked forward to liberation and freedom. It was certain that victory of the Allies would liberate the Poles. It was by no means certain that Russia, which had contributed so much to conquering the Nazis, and which appeared to have designs herself on certain of the Buffer States, would leave Poland's boundaries exactly as she had found them. The exact nature of Poland's future remained uncertain, but her spirit of resistance was very much alive.

We all know Polish people. Even if you do not personally know any Polish men and women — and there are many in the United States — or if you have not seen the sleek Polish vessels that during peacetime brought Polish passengers and Polish farm products to this country, you will know some Polish names. You will know of Paderewski [pad'uh-rehf'skee], the world-famous pianist and composer and valiant worker for Polish interests, who at one time was President of Poland. And you have read of Madame Curie in the story of France. You will probably also know of Chopin [shoh'paN'], the Polish-French composer. And you may have read stories of the sea written in English by Joseph Conrad, who was a Pole. The name of Sikorski [see kor'skee], aviator and designer of aircraft, is familiar to many of us.

Chapter 4 ~ The Czechoslovakians Are a People with a Will

The name *Czech* comes from an old Slavic word meaning *to will* or *to begin*. For almost a thousand years the Czechs have willed to uphold their own national interests despite the efforts of the Germans to overcome them. The conflict began when Charlemagne, the leader of the Germanic tribes about A.D. 800, looked with distrust at certain Slavic groups. Later these particular peoples came to be known as Czechs and Poles. They lived on the eastern boundaries of Charlemagne's empire. The Czechs at that time were known as Bohemians. This home was surrounded by mountains, as you can see by the map on page 576. In Charlemagne's time this land was heavily forested.

In this mountain-ringed forest land the Czechs developed early the spirit of independence and Czech unity with which they were to resist their Germanic neighbors for centuries. Charlemagne forced them to pay tribute to him, but that did not mean that the Kingdom of Bohemia was ever willing to acknowledge German superiority. Through the following centuries until their creation as an independent nation after World War I Bohemia repeatedly challenged the authority of German emperors of the Holy Roman Empire and the supremacy of the Roman Catholic Church.

Bohemia was an ancient nation. Early in the 10th Century there ruled in Bohemia " good King Wenceslaus " [wen' ses laws] whose name is familiar to us from the well-known English Christmas carol which tells a beautiful medieval legend about this Christian king.

Bohemia, which you have read about in Part Eight, was a member of the Holy Roman Empire. The Empire was a loose confederation of nations, chiefly Germanic. From this confederation the Austro-Hungarian Empire and modern Germany were to emerge.

Even before the middle of the 14th Century, however, the Emperor Rudolph of the Hapsburgs — that famous family which furnished many rulers of the Holy Roman Empire — had reduced the size of the Bohemian kingdom and taken away some of its possessions.

Meanwhile, Bohemia and England had been brought into contact by the marriage of King Richard II to a Bohemian princess. This was the time when the English dissenter, John Wycliffe, was preaching the reformation of the Catholic Church, as you have read in

Wide World Photos
A SCENE IN PRAGUE

Prague, the capital of Czechoslovakia, is an interesting old city built on the banks of the Moldau River. The steps in this photograph lead to an old castle that has long been a famous landmark in Prague.

Part Ten. His writings had impressed the Bohemian priest named John Huss, who was connected with the University of Prague [prahg]. Huss, as you have read, was a loyal Bohemian and a spirited advocate of church reform. When a Church Council was to be held in Germany, Huss secured a promise of safety from the German emperor, and journeyed there to make a bold plea for reform. Despite the emperor's promise of safety, Huss was arrested and burned as a heretic.

The tragedy of Huss's martyrdom deepened the hatred between Czech and German. In the religious war which followed, Bohemia defended Protestantism and her own national independence against German attacks, but was finally forced to yield to a Hapsburg emperor, who was also ruler of Austria. Later Bohemia was to be included in the Austro-Hungarian Empire.

A great Czech became a world citizen. When the Hapsburg rulers took their vengeance on Protestants in Bohemia, after the religious wars, they forced into exile a Czech who was to become famous. This man was Johann Comenius, a teacher and philosopher. When he was forced to escape from Bohemia, Comenius gave England, Sweden, and Holland the benefit of his work and ideas. You have already read of the works of Johann Comenius in the story of the Renaissance. He reorganized school systems and developed the theory of education upon which a large part of our modern teaching is based.

The Czechs put their will power to work. The Czechs have been described as a devout people who became commercial and industrial as a matter of necessity — in order to keep their national and religious ideals alive.

Quite soon after the religious wars Czech Protestants were despoiled of their possessions and treated somewhat as aliens in Bohemia. Driven out of cities, they went to live in the hills and mountains. They became miners, woodworkers, and weavers. They laid the foundation for Bohemia's industrial prosperity. Also they kept their convictions about religion and nationalism.

The Czechs held their own in the Austro-Hungarian Empire. As a subject group in the Austro-Hungarian Empire, still under Hapsburg rule, the Czechs continued their remarkable industrial development, and also kept on working and agitating for their independence.

During the outbreak of World War I, Czech fighters made a difficult and roundabout journey to Western Europe by way of the East, in order to fight with the Allies.

Czechoslovakia — born 1918. The nation of Czechoslovakia takes its name from the Czechs and from the Slovaks — another Slavic people, who are also a large part of its population. When World War I was drawing to a close and Austria was crumbling, Czechs seized the government at Prague and declared their independence. Thomas Masaryk [mah' suh reek], a friend of President Wilson, became first President of the Republic of Czechoslovakia. The boundaries of the new republic were established by the Peace Conference after the war. The Czechs had won their long struggle.

Part of their success they owed to the inspiration and practical efforts of Masaryk, a patriot of peasant family, half Czech and half Slovak. Masaryk was a lifelong educator and liberal, with a down-to-earth practical realization of the needs of his people. He had worked tirelessly for their freedom, education, and advancement. Patriot that he was, Masaryk represents an enlightened de-

WENCESLAS SQUARE, PRAGUE

When Hitler occupied Czechoslovakia in 1939, his forces marched down this wide boulevard. Czech patriots, many of them in tears, defiantly sang their national anthem, and hissed the procession of German soldiers.

votion to his country. This was in contrast to the fanatic nationalism which is sometimes too common among patriotic leaders. Masaryk himself wrote of his younger days in Prague:

I based nationality and statehood on morality, and for that reason I came in conflict with the narrow circle of well-known men who regarded it as the motive force of all individual and social life.

It was a great satisfaction to Masaryk, years later, to be able to assume the responsibilities of the presidency for the nation he had helped bring into being.

Czechoslovakia's days of security were brief. In 1938 the Germans began to whittle away at the borders of this long, narrow country, by threat and bluff, as you will learn in Part 22. The democratic nations were not prepared to come to the defense of the little republic they had helped create after World War I. Czechoslovakia, like the other Buffer States, was occupied by the Nazi conquerors. A part of the country, Croatia, fought beside the Nazis. But Czechoslovak patriots continued to hope and work for the liberation and restoration of their country.

The imprint of Czechoslovakia. Toys and pottery, delicate glassware, textiles, shoes, munitions — these products of Czechoslovakia are exported all over the world and are known in many lands. But the musical compositions of Dvořák [dvawr'zhahk] and of Smetana [smeh' tah nah] bear the imprint of Czechoslovakia even more strongly than the Czech handicrafts. In a series of symphonic poems entitled "My Fatherland," Smetana has described his native land in music. If you have not heard these musical works, try to hear them — especially the tone picture of the River Moldau [mawl'dou], flowing through woods and past castles and fortresses.

Chapter 5 ~ Turkey Is the Gatekeeper of the Black Sea

The Turks crossed into Europe and established an empire. We have already seen in Chapter 1 that the Turks came into Europe in the 15th Century, overthrew the Byzantine Empire, and for three hundred years ruled all the Balkan Peninsula.

This great conquest had not come about suddenly. Originally, the Turks had migrated from their home in Iran, to Asia Minor. On the way they had become converted to the Mohammedan faith, and they came into Asia Minor as devout Moslems, or Mohammedans. You have already read in this *Story of Nations* how the Moslem peoples spread throughout North Africa and part of Europe and how the medieval Christian world feared their advance. The Turks' first attack on the Byzantine Empire came in the 11th Century. They wrested control of Asia Minor from the weakening Byzantine Empire and took it for themselves.

At this time the Turks in Asia Minor were still living in scattered clans or groups. Then in the 13th Century a brilliant leader named Osman, or Ottoman, welded them into a strong religious and military unit. From the name of Osman, the Conqueror, the Turks called themselves Osmanlis, and the empire which they later established in Europe and Asia Minor was known for centuries as the Ottoman Empire.

It was natural that this warlike Turkish state on the Asiatic side of the Bosporus should eye with interest the key city of Constantinople across the straits. Constantinople was on the highway for trade between the East and the West. It commanded the Dardanelles, part of the waterway between the Mediterranean and the Black Sea, as you can see by the map on page 576.

Across the Bosporus, Constantinople, capital of the unsteady Eastern Roman Empire, was being approached from the west by the expanding Serbian nation — that nation which was to play a dramatic part in the conflict of which you will read in Part 22. But before the Serbs could take Constantinople, the Turks (some forty years before Columbus discovered America) had crossed the Bosporus and begun their conquests in Europe. The Turks conquered from Constantinople through the Balkan Peninsula, and into Hungary. They penetrated into parts of Poland, in Austria to the gates of Vienna, and briefly even into Italy. This Asiatic intruder was also to conquer Egypt, Tripoli (or Libya), Syria, Palestine, Arabia, and Mesopotamia.

In the 16th Century the Ottoman Empire, ruled by Sultan Suleiman [soo′lay-mahn′] the Magnificent, had reached its greatest size and power.

What the Turks did to Europe. The Turks brought the superior culture and learning of the Mohammedans to the more primitive peoples of the Balkans. On the other hand they completely crushed all the medieval aristocracy of the little Balkan states. Nobles were required to become Mohammedans or surrender their lands to the Turks. The old aristocracies continued only in Hungary and, to some extent, in Romania. And any attempts at rebellion were put down with fearful cruelty. The peasants, themselves, however, were generally better off under Turkish overlords than they

St. Sophia at Constantinople

St. Sophia, the largest Mohammedan mosque in the world, was originally a Christian church more than 1400 years ago. Beautiful marbles, fine mosaics, and precious ornaments of many kinds make its interior one of the architectural wonders of the world.

had been under the Christian overlords. Taxes were in general less oppressive. Religious liberty was allowed to most groups as long as they submitted to Mohammedan rule. But only the Mohammedan people were allowed any political rights. And the Balkan peoples never became resigned to the rule of the Turks.

The scars of the Turkish wars were twofold. First there were those inflicted in the original Turkish conquests. In addition there were the scars of conflict inflicted during the struggle for freedom from Turkish dominion and in the conflicts among the powers engaged against the Turks. In the Mediterranean a league of Austrians and Venetians and Spaniards checked the Turks at the Battle of Lepanto [lay pahn'toh]. By 1600 the Turks on land had been driven out of Hungary. Then Russia was to emerge as

the champion of the subject Balkan peoples, and so arouse all her old enemies who feared a great union of the Slavic peoples. As one historian has said, " The decline of Turkey proved quite as painful to European peace as was its [Turkey's] advance."

The painful break-up. Serbia was the first of the subject nations to break away from Turkey and to win partial independence. The revolt of Greece followed. On both sides it was a bitter, brutal war. Then came the Crimean War. It began in the middle of the 19th Century with Russia's attempt to establish a protectorate over the Christians in the Ottoman Empire. This move on Russia's part was regarded suspiciously by other powers. They believed that Russia would use the protectorate as a means to get control of the ports of the Ottoman Empire. This possibility alarmed Britain and France when war broke out between Russia and Turkey in 1853. The next year Britain and France joined forces with Turkey. Russia was defeated in a decisive action at Sevastopol [see vas'toh pohl] in the Crimea.

A little more than twenty years later Russia was again at war with Turkey in the Russo-Turkish War. Although Russia was the victor in this war, her jealous European enemies forced her to settle it by means of a general European conference. The Congress of Berlin was made up of delegates from many European nations. It made changes in the map of Europe that frequently set aside the national interests of smaller nations. Later, in Part Twenty-two, you will read about a peace conference that made its new European map as far as possible along the lines of national groupings of peoples. Yet in the Balkans it was difficult to draw such boundary lines. There, as we have seen, the peoples are intermingled geographically. It is almost certain that there will be some minority groups within any state established there. Such proved to be the case in 1919. The Congress of Berlin in the previous century had not even attempted to follow the wishes of the different national groups involved. Among the questionable results of this Congress was the granting to Austria-Hungary of the administration of the Serbian provinces of Bosnia [boz'ni uh] and Herzegovina [her'tseh goh vee'nah] which the Turks had formerly held.

The independence of Serbia, Romania, and Montenegro, and the partial independence of Bulgaria were established by the Congress of Berlin. Bulgaria declared her complete independence in 1908. Turkey was occupied with her own internal problems at that time, because a party known as the Young Turks was trying to secure a constitution for Turkey.

But the Balkan wars were not over. Italy went to war on Turkey, taking Libya under partial control. Greeks, Serbs, Bulgars, and Montenegrins — another group of strongly nationalistic Slavic peoples — fought against Turkey and among themselves. And between Russia and Austria-Hungary jealousy and distrust had been deepened by the whole series of wars with Turkey.

Turkey stays in Europe. Turkey itself had come to be called "the sick man of Europe." The Turks had seen their European possessions, their African territory, their Asiatic holdings, dwindle until all that was left was a small area around Constantinople in Europe and the province of Anatolia in Asia Minor.

Turkey, however, held Constantinople. She still controlled the Dardanelles, the bottleneck to Russia from Western Europe, and she was still important enough to be courted by the Germans in World War I. In this war, the Turks and Germans together defended the Dardanelles and defeated the British at Gallipoli. "The sick man of Europe" had been able to throw considerable weight into the war.

The new Turkey. The sick man revived even further under the new nationalistic, Westernizing work of Kemal Atatürk [kuh mahl' ah'tuh tyoork'] and his followers. When the Allied nations who were making the peace settlements would have taken away even more Turkish territory and awarded it to Greece, Kemal took charge of Turkey, setting up a republic with the Asia Minor city of Ankara [ahng'kuh ruh] as its capital, and led his troops against the Greeks. He won recognition of his right to keep what was left of Turkey.

TURKEY'S NATURAL DEFENSES

The wild, mountainous terrain pictured here, characteristic of a good deal of Turkey, can serve as a strong barrier to any invading force. Roads are few and sharply winding.

Installed as president of his small nation of sheepherders, farmers, producers of attar of roses, and rugmakers, Kemal began to revolutionize the life of Mohammedan Turkey. He decreed that Mohammedanism was no longer the state religion. Schools were to be free from Mohammedan control. Women were not to veil their faces and live in seclusion but were to take part in business and professions. Polygamy was to be abolished. The Roman alphabet was to replace the Turkish alphabet. Kemal even attempted a language reform, which would substitute Turkish words for the large number of Persian and Arabic words in the language. This leader of modern Turkey died in 1938 and was succeeded by General Ismet Inonu [is met′ ee′noh nyoo].

With the passing of Mohammedan control over all aspects of life in Turkey went the ban on representing the human figure in any form of art. This restriction had caused artists and craftsmen to concentrate on abstract designs such as those you have seen in Oriental rugs. One of the first statues of human beings — possibly the very first statue — in Turkey was a figure of Kemal himself.

One modern writer has said of Turkey, "The destiny of the Turks is strange: they were Asiatics in Turkey for six centuries and only began to be Europeanized after 1913 when they were definitely pushed back to Asia."

Except for some rebellious tribes known as Kurds [koordz] in Anatolia, most of the people now ruled over by the Turks are actually of Turkish blood. Modern Turkey is a small, rather intensely nationalistic state which is patterning its development after Western nations. Kemal's government is doing all in its power to make Turkey a self-sufficient modern nation.

The government is encouraging more efficient and modern methods of farming, in order to increase the productivity of the land. High tariffs protect Turkish manufactures from foreign competition. Turkey badly needs capital to finance the construction of railroads and factories. But rather than place herself under the business domination of larger nations who could supply such capital, Turkey prefers to develop her own resources, more slowly, perhaps, but independently.

From being a mighty empire, ruling over the Buffer States of the Balkans, where East meets West, Turkey herself has now become a Buffer State. She is striving to maintain her national integrity amidst the conflicting claims of greater powers. And she clings stubbornly to her age-old strategical right to close the gate of the Dardanelles in time of war — a gate of the utmost importance to her giant landlocked neighbor, Russia — and also to the great seapower Britain, which has vital interest in the Near East and Middle East.

Change Is Characteristic of the Buffer States

Thirteen little nations of East Central Europe are called Buffer States because they lie between powerful and often hostile large nations. The Buffer States have complicated problems. They have undergone many changes, lying as they do in regions without defensible natural boundaries. Many of them were established by the treaty that ended World War I.

The Buffer States fall into three groups. Finland, Estonia, Latvia, and Lithuania are important because of their position on the Baltic Sea. Poland, Czechoslovakia, and Hungary, in the heart of East Central Europe, have been coveted for their minerals, forests, and farm lands. Romania, Bulgaria, Yugoslavia, Turkey, Albania, and Greece, which make up the Balkan States, are important for their location on the Black Sea and the Mediterranean. They also have undeveloped resources of oil, coal, and water power which make them attractive to more powerful nations.

Finland is a hardy, independent nation which preserved national identity through centuries of rule by Swedish and then Russian overlords. In 1917 Finland won independence from Russia, and established a republic. The popularity of the music of Sibelius and the substantiality of Finnish immigrants to America were factors in the friendship of Finland and the United States.

Poland, once a great kingdom which had defended Europe against Turkish invasions, later suffered from the aggression of her neighbors which had grown powerful: Austria, Prussia, and Russia. At the end of the 18th Century Poland was divided among these three nations. Not until 1920, after World War I, did Poland gain her freedom. Her leader, Marshal Pilsudski, led her in wars for the recovery of Polish territory. The French assisted her; and her independence was confirmed by the Treaty of Versailles, which gave Poland a corridor to the Baltic Sea.

Germany coveted Poland, and resented the fact that the Polish Corridor separated East Prussia from the rest of Germany. In 1939 Germany invaded Poland. Despite her centuries of subjection to other powers, Poland made many contributions to civilization. Madame Curie, the scientist, and Paderewski, the pianist, are two of the great Polish world-citizens.

The Czechoslovaks inherited a history of conflict with Germanic oppressors. Part of this struggle was religious. In the martyrdom of John Huss, the Bohemian Protestant leader, the Bohemian people suffered one of the tragedies in their history. Alienated and deprived of their property after the religious wars, the Bohemian Protestants developed their own trades and industries and thus made a basis for their survival, and for the survival of their faith. They kept their identity even as a subject group in the Austrian Empire. The work of the patriot-statesman Masaryk, supported by the Peace Conference after World War I, brought into existence the independent Czechoslovak republic. The new republic's sound economic and national life was cut short by the Munich Agreement and the German occupation shortly before the beginning of World War II.

The Turks, moving west from Asia, built an Empire in Europe, Africa, and Asia, with Constantinople as its capital. For three centuries the Turks ruled over the Balkan Peninsula. One by one, the European nations broke away. Turkey lost her African holdings, too, but kept a European foothold in Constantinople, at the strategic gate to the Black Sea. In World War I, Turkey fought on the side of Germany. At the end of the war, Turkish nationalists set up a republic with Kemal Atatürk as president and a new capital at Ankara in Asia Minor. Kemal Atatürk entered upon a Westernizing program which brought tremendous changes into the lives of the Turkish people. Mohammedanism ceased to be the state religion; women were encouraged to play a part in business and the professions; and the Roman alphabet replaced the Turkish alphabet.

SELF–TEST

Look back at the story of the Buffer States by trying this self-test. On a separate sheet of paper write the words that will make each of the following statements complete.

1. Thirteen small nations in East Central Europe are called —— —— because they have acted as —— among more powerful nations. The boundaries and the —— of the Buffer States have frequently changed. The Baltic group of Buffer States are ——, ——, ——, and ——. The three states in the heart of East Central Europe are ——, ——, and ——. In the Balkan peninsula are the states of ——, ——, ——, ——, ——, and ——.

2. The republic farthest north in the world is peopled by the hardy, independent ——. These people lived under —— rule until the 19th Century, and then under —— rule until 1917, when they won their independence. In their struggle for freedom they have lived up to the traditions of the heroes in their epic poem, —— ——.

3. In Poland's long history, a great chapter was supplied by the exploits of the king and military leader ——, who rescued Vienna from the invading ——. Poland's development as a nation was hindered by the absence of a powerful —— class. Her neighbors ——, ——, and —— partititioned Poland. From 1795 until the end of —— —— ——, Poland had ceased to be an independent nation. After quarrels with —— over boundaries, Poland was at last free and at peace. She was given a corridor to the —— Sea. Her leader in these triumphs was —— ——. But the troubles of the Poles were not over. Like many other European nations, Poland was to be overrun by the —— in World War II.

4. Czechoslovakia's people have used their —— —— to keep their national and religious ideals alive. Through their —— development, they laid a solid foundation for independent national life. After long years of subjection to the rule of the —— family, Czechoslovakia won independence in ——, through the efforts of ——, and with the aid of President ——.

5. Turkey brought the culture of the —— to Europe, but involved the European nations in wars. Turkish conquests were checked by the naval battle of ——, and one by one the conquered nations broke away. The loss of so

much territory caused Turkey to be called the —— —— —— ——. But Turkey retained the city of —— at the gate to the —— ——, and was able to help the —— —— in World War I. Under the progressive leadership of —— —— Turkey adopted many of the customs of Western nations.

INTERESTING THINGS TO DO

Projects for the Chart Maker and Artist

1. Draw an outline map of the Buffer States, and show pictorially the location and distribution of natural resources. See *Goode's School Atlas,* by John P. Goode, or textbooks of economic geography.

2. Draw a map of the Buffer States, and show with different colors their changing boundaries. See *Atlas of Current Affairs,* by James F. Horrabin, and *Historical Atlas,* by William R. Shepherd.

Topics for Talks

1. "Portrait of a Buffer State." Choose one of the Buffer States for special study, and read more about the land and people, their history and their problems. Condense your information into a brief, informal talk about the particular state you have studied. See the book list on pages 603–604, or ask your librarian for suggestions.

2. "Rivers and peoples." Prepare a talk comparing the Danube with some other great river you know about, such as the Mississippi, or the Nile. Explain the influence of a great river on the life of the people. See *The Danube,* by Emil Lengyel.

3. "The bad-neighbor policy." Explain in a brief talk how the Buffer States have been the victims of a bad-neighbor policy. Give definite examples in support of this viewpoint.

4. "In the news today." Choose one or two of the Buffer States, and, for at least a week, cut out from current magazines and newspapers any articles which refer to the countries you have chosen. At the end of the week, prepare a digest of the present state of affairs in these countries, and present your findings to the class in an oral report.

5. "Little Paris." Prepare a travelogue on Bucharest, the capital of Romania, explaining why it is called "Little Paris." Or you may prefer to present a travelogue on Belgrade, the "White Castle" of Yugoslavia, or some other capital of the Buffer States. Tell something of the geographical location of the capital you choose, and how its location has affected its history.

6. "A colorful personality." Read about one of the colorful leaders of the Buffer States, perhaps St. Stephen, the 10th Century King of Hungary, whose holy crown is still enshrined in Budapest; or John Metaxas, 20th Century

Greek dictator; or Marshal Tito, leader of the resistance movement in Yugoslavia in World War II.

7. " Summarizing the Buffer States." Members of the class might report on the topic " Major Problems of the Buffer States Today." One pupil should discuss Albania; another, Bulgaria; a third, Czechoslovakia; and so on through the thirteen states taken up in Part Seventeen. For guidance consult the table of the Buffer States on pages 582–583. For more information consult the current *World Almanac* (see index, " Albania," " Bulgaria," etc.), and any up-to-date encyclopedia.

Ideas for Your Little Theater

1. Make a list of names of places, people, and events in the story of the Buffer States. Use your list as the basis for an " Information, Please " program with a committee of " experts " chosen from the class.

2. Prepare a musical program using recordings of compositions by Sibelius, Smetana, Dvořák, and Paderewski. Precede the playing of the compositions of each composer with a brief summary of his life and work.

3. Plan a group of readings from recent tributes to Czechoslovakia under the Nazi heel, such as Edna St. Vincent Millay's poem, *The Murder of Lidice,* and the radio play " The Long Name None Could Spell," by Norman Corwin, from *More by Corwin.* Or you may prefer to play a phonograph recording of *The Murder of Lidice.* (Columbia record N536.)

4. With a committee of the class, plan a program about the Slavs in the United States. You might assign a different national group, as Czechs, Slovaks, or Poles, to each speaker for a report. For information, see *We Who Built America,* by Carl F. Wittke, or *Our Foreigners,* by Samuel P. Orth. You may obtain the recordings: *The Slavs in the United States* in *Americans All — Immigrants All Series* from the United States Office of Education, Federal Radio Education Committee, Federal Security Agency, Washington, D. C.

Candidates for Your Album of Famous People

Dvořák, Ismet Inonu, Kosciusko, Masaryk, Osman the Conqueror, Paderewski, Marshal Pilsudski, Kemal Atatürk, Jean Sibelius, Sikorski, Smetana, John III. Write short biographies of at least five of the people listed above for your Album.

INTERESTING READING ABOUT THE BUFFER STATES

ADAMIC, LOUIS. *The Native's Return.* A delightful portrait of a land and people seen through the eyes of a native son who returns after nineteen years in America.

CALDWELL, E. *North of the Danube.* A book of dramatic photographs and sympathetic description of Czechoslovakia and her people.

DAVIS, W. S. *A Short History of the Near East, from the Founding of Constantinople*. A readable survey of Turkey's history and her influence on the Balkan countries.

EKREM, S. *Unveiled*. An autobiography of a Turkish girl that gives a charming picture of family life and social customs in Turkey.

HASTINGS HOUSE. *This Is Greece*. ". . . a beautiful pictorial representation of the common life as well as the scenery and antiquities of Greece."

KELLY, E. P. *Trumpeter of Krakow*. A story of mystery and adventure in early Poland.

LENGYEL, EMIL. *The Danube*. An excellent book about the lands along the great Danube.

LINKE, LILO. *Allah Dethroned*. The fascinating story of a journey through modern Turkey, with its many contrasts between the old and new.

National Geographic Magazine, December, 1929. "Danube, Highway of Races," by Melville Chater.

——, December, 1930. "New Greece, the Centenarian, Forges Ahead," by Maynard O. Williams.

——, February, 1931. "Europe's Newest Kingdom" (Albania), by Melville Chater.

——, April, 1932. "Looking in on the Everyday Life of New Turkey," by H. H. Kreider, M. O. Williams, and G. Courtellemont.

——, April, 1932. "Poland, Land of the White Eagle," by Melville B. Grosvenor.

——, June, 1932. "Budapest, Twin City of the Danube," by J. R. Hildebrand.

——, August, 1932. "Bulgaria, Farm Land without a Farmhouse," by Maynard O. Williams.

——, January, 1933. "When Czechoslovakia Puts a Falcon Feather in Its Cap," by Maynard O. Williams.

PETROV, B. G. *Son of the Danube*. A story of a Bulgarian boy, picturing life along the Danube.

ROTHERY, AGNES. *Finland, the New Nation*. A comprehensive story of Finland, her history, geography, industries, schools, and her famous sons.

SAPHIEHA, V. P. *Polish Profile*. The biography of an American girl who became a Polish princess, and through her patience and humor came to understand the age-old customs and nationalistic feelings of her adopted land.

SEREDY, KATE. *White Stag*. The heroic story of the legendary founding of Hungary.

STRODE, HUDSON. *Finland Forever*. An enjoyable book about a brave and hardy people.

THE PEOPLES OF RUSSIA AWAKENED TO THE POSSIBILITIES OF THEIR VAST LAND

NORTH POLE
Permanent ice cap
Limit of floating pack ice
Ocean
105°
120°
135°
150°
165°
180°
165°
150°
135°
120°
ALASKA
Lena R.
Arctic Circle
60° N.
BERING SEA
SOCIALIST REPUBLICS
KAMCHATKA
SEA OF OKHOTSK
50° N.
LAKE BAIKAL
Amur R.
Irkutsk
MANCHURIA
Vladivostok
40° N.
SEA OF JAPAN
Mukden
CHOSEN (KOREA)
Port Arthur
Tokyo
JAPAN
Yellow R.
Yellow
CHINA

The Lands of the Russian Bear

THE Union of Soviet Socialist Republics includes the country which we used to call Russia and new lands which have been added to it by the Soviet. All Soviet territories are now often called Russia. Turn to the map of the world at the end of the book and compare the size of the Soviet Union with that of other countries. Notice also the globe above. Then study the map on the two pages preceding this one. What extremes of climate would you expect to find in this vast land? What variety of natural products? Do you think that all Russians are alike, from one end of the Soviet Union to the other? Why would you expect Russia to be somewhat like the countries of Western Europe and somewhat like the countries of the Orient?

Notice the great mountain ranges of Russia, and the rivers which water her plains and help furnish inland transportation. Through what seas can Russia carry on shipping with the rest of the world? Which countries control the outlets of these seas? Locate the important Russian port of Vladivostok, on the Sea of Japan. What neighbors does Russia have to the West? To the East? Consult this map as you read the colorful story of Russia which follows.

Chapter 1 ~ Landlocked and Icebound Russia Has Her Resources Spread Across Europe and Asia

The Russian bear has changed masters. Just as the American eagle and the British lion are symbols of nations, the bear is sometimes used as a symbol of Russia. When the czar [zahr] held the glorious royal title "Emperor of All the Russias," we may imagine that the Russian bear was closely chained, and winced when that autocratic monarch cracked the whip. So did the Russian people suffer when ruled by the czar. But today we see a new master in Russia. The working class now puts the Russian bear through its tricks. Instead of picturing the Russian bear as wearing a gold collar and chain, we may imagine the powerful brute driving a tractor or tending a clanking machine in a state factory. The Russian bear has a new master. Under the control of the powerful Communist party, Russia has become an industrialized state. Extreme class distinctions have been swept away and the people, many of whom were formerly ignorant, are being educated so that they can govern themselves.

Russia is a kaleidoscope of shifting patterns. As striking as this change has been, of particular interest because it has happened within the last thirty or forty years, it is not surprising for Russia. Immense Russia is a land of contradictions. She is hard for the outsider to understand because she is so many things at the same time, and because conditions in Russia have been changing so rapidly.

Before the Revolution in 1917 the majority of the Russians could not read or write; there was little manufacturing. Within thirty years this picture has changed completely. Today many Russian communities have excellent schools and libraries; manufacturing has increased by leaps and bounds. Russia has become one of the most vigorous and powerful nations in the world. As you know, Russia, Great Britain, China, and the United States were the four most powerful members of the United Nations in World War II.

Attempting to get a true picture of Russia is much like looking into that childhood plaything, the kaleidoscope; we turn the barrel and the bits of glass fall into ever-new patterns.

The returned traveler from such Russian centers as Moscow and Leningrad [len'in grad] tell us of the workers' apartments, of the theaters, or of the Soviet [soh'vyet'] museums — and there is one picture of Russia. Earlier travelers have told us about two million peasants who were starved because of a man-made famine in 1932 — and that, perhaps, is another Russia. An American engineer tells us of the great dam built across the Dnieper [d'nyeh'p'r] River, the state farms where the overseer uses an airplane to visit the fields, or the complete industrial center at Magnitogorsk in the Ural Mountains. We see a motion picture that shows the great heroism of the Russian people, their kindliness and simplicity, their loyalty to the ideals of their state, and their belief in the Russian way of life. Then we hear of the engineers of a wrecked train being "liquidated" or the manager of a collective farm sentenced to twenty years of imprisonment because a number of

Sovfoto

IRON AND STEEL WORKS AT MAGNITOGORSK

Magnitogorsk is a new industrial city built on the formerly barren steppes in the Ural region. Many similar large-scale projects were part of the Soviet plan for modernizing and expanding industry. As a defensive measure, the Soviets broke up the concentration of industry in Western Russia, and planned new industrial centers closer to raw material resources.

cattle had died on his farm — and is that Russia?

It is not easy to become acquainted with Russia. One difficulty in understanding Russia comes from the fact that most present-day writers seem biased, or prejudiced, either against or for the government which has been set up there. To one, everything seems bad; to another, the good things about a great experiment in social control far outweigh the evils. It is no wonder that the fair-minded citizen, reading both sides of the story of modern Russia, constantly has to ask himself, " What am I to believe? "

Little wonder that it is difficult to get a true picture of Russia. For one thing, language is a barrier, and it is said that few languages are as difficult to master as the Russian. Size is a difficulty, for modern Russia's 8,800,000 square miles make her the largest of all countries, except for the combined lands of the British Empire. Russian territory stretches across the Northern Hemisphere from Scandinavia, the Land of the Midnight Sun, to the islands of Japan. In the north some of the Russians live within the Arctic Circle, while in the south Russian boats sail the Black Sea. A non-stop flight at 250 miles per hour from Leningrad on an arm of the Baltic to Vladivostok [vlah′di vos tok′] on the Sea of Japan would take about sixteen and a half hours. On the trip you would cover a distance almost twice that from New York to San Francisco.

CHIRCHIK ELECTRO-CHEMICAL PLANT

The canal being filled with water in this photograph is part of a large electro-chemical plant developed in Kirghiz, one of the Soviet republics in Central Asia.

For the size of the country the population of Russia is not great. But its 190,000,000 people present still another obstacle to understanding. In Russia the East and West have met and sometimes intermingled. Fair skin and blue eyes mark the Nordic peoples; slant eyes and high cheekbones mark the Mongols. Often one sees the traits of both in the face of some Russians. Many of the Russians are largely Slavic in origin. These three peoples are not all, however. There are many other national types in Russia: in all, 182 different nationalities, which speak 149 different tongues. Under such circumstances the difficulty of forming a clear picture of Russia does not seem strange. One traveler told of a mountain colony which was discovered in the 1920's by members of the Russian Academy of Science. The people had heard rumors of the crowning of Czar Nicho-

las II, but had had no news since. That ruler, the last of the czars, came to the throne in the year 1894. Some thirty years later the news had reached the colony.

It seems that the only keys to even a partial appreciation of what has taken place and is still taking place in huge Russia are two: The nature of the land — Russia's geography; and the long suffering of a large portion of the Russian people — Russia's history. Let us see first what hope the resources of Russia's storehouse offer, and what characteristics of land and climate play an intimate part in the story of the Russian peoples.

The Russians have faced the task of developing vast resources. No country has a richer storehouse of natural resources than Russia. She has practically every resource a modern nation could need. Much of her wealth lies underground. Her great coal deposits are believed to be three times those of Germany. She also has mountains of iron ore. These give Russia that combination of coal and iron which is so necessary if a nation is to develop its resources. There are beds of manganese, the element so important in the production of high-grade steel. There are mines of rock salt, of mercury, of asbestos, and of that rare metal, platinum. Oil stands in huge pools under the surface of the earth. Mighty rivers make possible the development of electricity from water power. Before World War II Russia had harnessed some of her great rivers by building huge dams and power stations. The electricity generated was used to light new cities, run new factories, and operate new railroads. Russia is also fortunate in possessing vast timberlands. Timber is so abundant that the dense forests of northern Russia could supply all the world with lumber for many years.

Russia has the resources to become a first-class industrial nation, and is making tremendous progress in this direction. The Soviet government owns and controls all large-scale industry, and each industry produces according to specific plans in which its output is geared to the needs of the country. Even before World War II there were nearly six hundred thousand industrial plants in Russia, employing more than twenty-five million workers. Even so, Russia has been throughout her history an agricultural country, a nation of farmers, and primarily she still is. Most of her people live not in cities but on farms on Russia's great plains or steppes [steps], as they are called. For the most part, the soil of the steppe region is fertile and has encouraged the Russian to farm. Unlike our own farms, which usually are owned and operated by individuals, most Russian farms now belong to the state and are worked by many farmers under government supervision. Before the Revolution, Russian farmers used crude primitive methods of production which would have yielded only small crops had it not been for the fertility of the soil. Now the government has introduced modern machinery and the state-controlled farms are run on a large scale by modern scientific methods.

Russia has a difficult problem of transportation and communication. Russia has one of the longest main railroad lines in the world. It is the famed Trans-Siberian Railway which stretches for 5,400 miles across the Soviet Union, connecting European Russia with the Asiatic part of Russia which borders on the Orient. In the years between World War I and World War II, Russia made many improvements in her means of transportation and communication. More engines and cars were built and more men and women were taught to operate the railroads. For a time accidents and breakdowns were frequent, but as the state became strong and the inefficient workers were liquidated, railroad transportation became better. But it would be a mistake to think that Russia's railway system is now fully developed and sufficient for her needs. Because of the country's immense size, even those railroads which she now has are inadequate. Russia has relatively few main-line railroads compared with our much smaller country.

Russia, in the old days under the czars and later under the Union of the Socialist Soviet Republics, has never had a fine system of motor highways such as we have in so many parts of our union. In fact, there have been almost no improved main highways. As to the side, or feeder, roads of the farming regions, these were commonly little more than wagon tracks of dust or mud striking straight across the flat lands.

Today, throughout great parts of Russia, people must still depend very largely upon the kind of transportation that their ancestors used hundreds of years ago. Since the earliest days of their history, the people have relied upon their many rivers to carry the skins, grain, vegetables, and other produce from one part of the country to another. Within recent years these rivers have been made even more useful by the construction of a system of canals. Barges, loaded with products from farm and forest, ply up and down the broad, winding rivers and canals. The greatest rivers are the Don, the Dnieper, and the Volga [vawl'gah]. Years ago the peasants who toiled along the banks of the Volga, dragging the heavily loaded barges upstream, sang as they worked to lighten the labor. " The Song of the Volga Boatman " is famous.

Even though Russia has greatly enlarged her railway system, built more roads, improved her rivers, and constructed canals, the problems of quick communication and transportation to all parts of the Soviet Union still remain to be solved. The radio and the airplane, however, seem to be tailor-made answers to the problem. Powerful state-owned and controlled broadcasting stations now reach the remote settlements of the Union. Not only has radio made quick communication possible, but also the state has been able to use the radio as a means of education and state propaganda. The airplane, too, has, in effect, conquered the vast distances in Russia. As in our country it is used both for quick travel and fast transportation of cargoes. There is no doubt that radio and the airplane will continue to speed up greatly the advance of the Soviet Union and help to bind her widely separated peoples together.

Russia is landlocked and icebound. Russia faces an even more difficult problem of transportation in keeping in touch with foreign markets. But here, again, the airplane may become a partial solution, and bring her into closer relations with other countries. Look at the map on pages 606–607; you will see the position of Russia in relation to the markets of the world. Barriers of land and sea and cold have kept her from reaching out and selling her products to the world. For more than four centuries Russia has desired a good warm-water seaport. What seaports does she have today? To the north, on the White Sea, is Archangel [ahrk ayn'j'l], but this is icebound almost the entire year. Murmansk, on the Arctic Ocean, is ice free. To the west, on the Baltic, is Leningrad, but for five months of the year this port is icebound. Furthermore, Norway, Sweden, and Denmark control the outlet to the ocean, and Finland always stands in the path westward. To the south, on the Black Sea, are several seaports; but Turkey, controlling the Bosporus and the Dardanelles, could effectively block passage from the Black Sea to the Mediterranean. England in turn controls the outlets of the Mediterranean, so that, in time of war, Russia could be effectually blocked by these two powers from any attempt to take to the sea in this direction. To the east, on the Asiatic coast, is Vladivostok, which, though it is the terminal of the Trans-Siberian Railway, is thousands of miles from the richest grain-producing regions of Russia. Besides, this port can be kept open in winter only by ice-breaking ships.

Thus the full use of Russia's assets — her rivers, her forests, her wheat-growing plains, her great mineral wealth —

has been checked by her lack of seaports. The desire of Russia for an all-year seaport has influenced her foreign policy for hundreds of years. She has always hoped to overcome this lack, and because of it has fought wars, but up to World War II she was still somewhat remote from the rest of Europe.

Chapter 2 ~ The Russians Struggled for a New Political, Social, and Industrial Order

Northmen organized the Slavic tribes. Slavic forest tribes had settled along the Dnieper, Don, and Vistula [vis'chuh-lah] rivers several centuries before the birth of Christ. They had banded together for protection against foes. In the Ninth Century, however, they were overcome by invading Northmen. These Vikings were of the same people who were then plundering and terrifying the coasts of Western Europe. The Northmen were so attracted by the land which was to become Russia that they settled down and effectively organized the Slavic tribes. From their descendants came many of the early Russian princes. They established towns, one of which was Kiev [kee'yev] on the Dnieper River. For hundreds of years Kiev was one of the great trading centers of this part of Europe.

The name " Russia " is thought to have come from the word *Rous,* meaning " rowers " or " seafarers," which was the name that the near-by Finns gave to the Northmen. Very gradually these people who were living in the valleys of the Russian rivers began to spread eastward to claim the fertile plains of Russia. Through trade they then came into contact with Constantinople, which was still the center of Greek civilization in the East. You will remember that the Roman emperor, Constantine, had made

this city his capital, and that later, in A.D. 395, it had become the capital of the Byzantine, or Eastern, Empire.

From Constantinople the Russians acquired Christianity. For centuries the state religion of Russia remained that of the Greek Orthodox, or Russian Orthodox, Church, becoming more national in character as the years passed. The beginnings of Russian civilization also were taken from the Greek, or Hellenistic, civilization of this Eastern Empire. Throughout all these changes in Russia, the Russians kept the practice of local town meetings which they had carried over from the early tribal days of the Slavs. Then the Northmen had invaded the land and set themselves up as a ruling class of almost feudal princes or dukes. There also grew up in Russia a class of wealthy landowners, or lesser nobles. These people were to rule Russia and guide its history for centuries.

The " Golden Horde " swept through Russia. In the 13th Century a race of fierce warriors called the Mongols or Tartars [tahr'tarz] invaded Russia. A Chinese author wrote the following description of these Mongolian tribes who lived east of Russia in Mongolia:

They are ignorant of the nature of a town or a wall. They are ignorant of writing and books. . . . The strongest among them have the largest and fattest morsels at feasts; the old men are put off with the fragments that are left. They respect nothing but strength and courage; age and weakness are condemned. . . . They move on horseback; when they wish to capture a town they fall on the suburban villages. No place [can] resist them. After a siege the entire population is massacred without distinction of old or young, rich or poor, beautiful or ugly.

United and led by their famous leader, Genghis Khan [jen'ges kahn], about the 13th Century, the "Golden Horde," as they were called, swept through Russia. "Russian heads fell beneath the sword of the Tartars as grass beneath the scythes." Within a few years all Russia was in the possession of the Orientals.

Russia groaned under the Mongol yoke. The Mongols demanded a heavy tax from the Russian people. Officers were sent out from house to house to collect this tax in either money or fur. Those who would not or could not pay the taxes were sold into slavery. For nearly three hundred years the Russians had to pay tribute to the Tartar Khans. But the various Russian dukes or princes were becoming more powerful. Particularly powerful was the Duke of Moscow. The city of Moscow was an important center of river trade. The dukes of Moscow became ambitious to unite all Russian territory into one state. For this plan, they secured the blessing and approval of the Greek Church. (You may recall from the story of France, how Pippin, the father of Charlemagne, secured the consent of the Pope to his plan to sweep away the old line of Frankish rulers and establish a new one.) With the approval of the Church, these dukes of Moscow became influential beyond their own lands and began to call themselves grand dukes of all Russia. Late in the 14th Century one of these grand dukes led most of the national armies in

a brief victory over the Mongol hordes. Though this victory was short-lived it did lessen the power of the Mongol conquerors, and further served to give the Russians a feeling of unity. Then, finally, in the last years of the 15th Century, another grand duke of all Russia, Ivan III, led in throwing off the Mongolian yoke and actually united most of Russia.

Russia was freed at last from control by the Far East. But the Orient had left many traces. The Slavic and Mongolian peoples had mixed to some extent. The Russian court showed oriental traces in dress and manner right up to its fall in 1917. The desire for extreme show of wealth and power, such as the Great Khans displayed, can be seen today in the astounding architecture of imperial Russia. The magnificent eight-towered cathedral of St. Basil the Blessed, shown on page 619, is a striking example of this Oriental influence.

The grand dukes became czars, or caesars. In the meantime, as you know, Constantinople, which had been the last remaining capital of the old Roman Empire, had fallen to the Turks. The Greek Church now regarded the grand duke of Russia as the rightful heir of the Christian empire, and looked upon Moscow as the "Third Rome." When the son of Ivan III succeeded to his father's throne, he was crowned czar. He was Ivan IV, and the first Russian ruler to take the title of czar. The word *czar* or *tsar* comes from the Roman name, *Caesar.* Roman emperors had claimed they were descended from Julius Caesar, and his name had become a sort of royal title. Ivan IV, who was to go down in history as "Ivan the Terrible," followed the careers of the Caesars from whom his title was taken. He reformed and organized the army in order to keep out

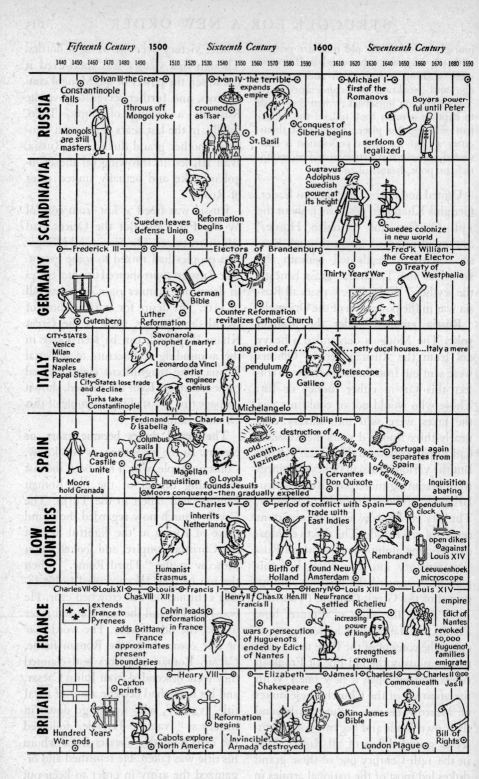

Fifteenth Century **1500** Sixteenth Century **1600** Seventeenth Century

1440 1450 1460 1470 1480 1490   1510 1520 1530 1540 1550 1560 1570 1580 1590   1610 1620 1630 1640 1650 1660 1670 1680 1690

RUSSIA
⊙─Ivan III–the Great─⊙   ⊙─Ivan IV–the terrible─⊙   ⊙─Michael I–⊙
Constantinople falls
throws off Mongol yoke
expands empire
crowned as Tsar
first of the Romanovs
Mongols are still masters
St. Basil
⊙Conquest of Siberia begins
Boyars powerful until Peter
serfdom ⊙ legalized

SCANDINAVIA
Gustavus Adolphus Swedish power at its height
Sweden leaves defense Union
Reformation begins
Swedes colonize in new world

GERMANY
⊙─Frederick III─⊙   Electors of Brandenburg
Fred'k William the Great Elector
⊙Gutenberg
German Bible
Luther Reformation
Counter Reformation revitalizes Catholic Church
Thirty Years' War
⊙ Treaty of Westphalia

ITALY
CITY-STATES
Venice
Milan
Florence
Naples
Papal States
Savonarola prophet & martyr
Leonardo da Vinci artist engineer genius
Long period of.....petty ducal houses...Italy a mere
pendulum
telescope
City-States lose trade and decline
Turks take Constantinople
Michelangelo
Galileo

SPAIN
⊙─Ferdinand & Isabella─⊙   ⊙─Charles I─⊙   ⊙─Philip II─⊙   ⊙─Philip III─
Columbus sails
destruction of Armada marks beginning of decline
gold...wealth...laziness
Aragon & Castile unite
Magellan
Inquisition
Loyola founds Jesuits
Cervantes Don Quixote
Portugal again separates from Spain
Moors hold Granada
⊙Moors conquered–then gradually expelled
Inquisition abating

LOW COUNTRIES
⊙─Charles V─⊙   ⊙period of conflict with Spain─⊙   ⊙pendulum clock
inherits Netherlands
trade with East Indies
Humanist Erasmus
Birth of Holland
found New Amsterdam
Rembrandt
open dikes ⊙against Louis XIV
⊙ Leeuwenhoek microscope

FRANCE
Charles VII ⊙ Louis XI ⊙   ⊙ Louis ⊙ ─Francis I─ ⊙   Henry II Chas.IX Hen.III   ⊙Henry IV─Louis XIII   ⊙ Louis XIV
Chas.VIII   XII   Francis II   New France
extends France to Pyrenees
Calvin leads reformation in France
settled
Richelieu
empire
adds Brittany — France approximates present boundaries
wars & persecution of Huguenots ended by Edict of Nantes
increasing power of kings
strengthens crown
Edict of Nantes revoked 50,000 Huguenot families emigrate

BRITAIN
⊙─Henry VIII─⊙   ⊙─Elizabeth─⊙   ⊙James I⊙ ⊙Charles I⊙   ⊙Charles II⊙
Caxton prints
Shakespeare
Commonwealth   Jas.II
Reformation begins
King James Bible
Hundred Years' War ends
Cabots explore North America
"Invincible Armada" destroyed
London Plague
Bill of Rights

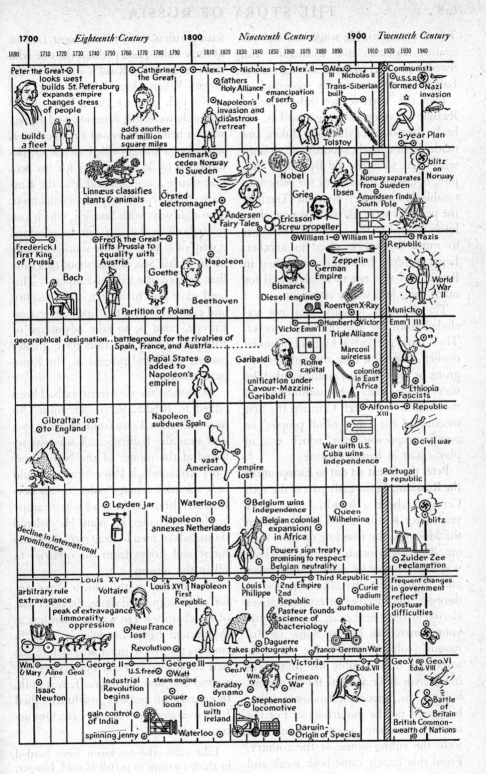

Tartar invasions. He waged a long war against Poland and Lithuania and Sweden in order to break through to the Baltic Sea and was finally successful.

Ivan the Terrible not only enlarged Russia; he vigorously organized it. He broke the power of the lesser dukes, and made them entirely subordinate to himself. Then, from the old Byzantine Empire, he adopted a system for recording taxable land. Under Ivan the Terrible, the peasants were for the first time absolutely bound to the land and forbidden to move from one place to another. Legal serfdom had been established in Russia and was not to be abolished for many long and weary centuries.

The Russian nobility was not excluded from the government, however. They took part in a kind of national council, and for a time through a small group or kind of privy council, ruled the state. It was they who summoned, in the middle of the 16th Century, the first meeting of the " men of all people," or popular representatives, which was to play a part in Russia's future.

Peter the Great set out to Europeanize the Russians. In the early part of the 17th Century, about a hundred and thirty years after Russia had been freed from the Mongols, the first line of czars died out. Russia was torn by civil strife, which was made worse by wars with Sweden and Poland. Finally, after a period of disorder, the meeting of representatives elected as their new czar, an aristocratic young merchant by the name of Romanov [roh'mah nawf]. He was only seventeen, and possibly his youth was in his favor as a candidate for the throne, because the important landowners felt he would not be too arrogant. For the next three hundred years the Romanovs were the ruling house of the country. From this family came both weak and strong rulers. One of the most famous of these rulers, and perhaps the one who did the most for Russia, was Peter the Great. When Peter became czar, late in the 17th Century, the customs of the Mongols were still common and Russia was far behind the rest of Europe. Peter, who was a strong-willed character, determined to do two things for his people: secure a seaport; and lead the Russians to accept European civilization. Through wars with Sweden, which you read about in Part Sixteen, he obtained a strip of land along the southern shore of the Baltic Sea. It was about this time that he took the title of Emperor. This land gave him his first wish, a seaport, and enabled Russia to " open one eye on Europe," that is, to take advantage of European trade, and thus have greater contact with, and interest in, the European world.

As soon as the new territory had been added to Russia, Peter determined to move his capital city from Moscow to a spot near the Baltic Sea. A site was selected at the mouth of the Neva [nee' vah] River, which Peter foresaw would be a splendid vantage point for his new Russia. Although the land was swampy he did not change his plan. He ordered thousands of men to drag trees from the forest and stones from the quarries to fill in the swamp.

The cruelty with which Peter enforced his command shows the other side of his character. He was as relentless as the ancient Egyptian pharaohs were in constructing their pyramids. Before the new city, called St. Petersburg (later Petrograd and now Leningrad), was built, thousands of peasant workmen died from overwork and lack of care. One account says:

Like cattle the workmen were herded in these swamps to perish of cold, hunger,

THE CATHEDRAL OF ST. BASIL ON RED SQUARE, MOSCOW

This magnificent cathedral, built in 1554 under Ivan the Terrible, shows the Oriental influence in its architecture. Eight towers, each of a different design, are built around a main chapel that is crowned by a bulb-shaped dome.

CATHERINE THE GREAT

Catherine the Great, a German princess by
birth, became Empress of Russia after the
murder of her husband, Czar Peter III.
Through war with Turkey, she gained for
Russia an opening to the Black Sea.

and scurvy. As fast as they were swallowed
up, more serfs were driven in. They dug
the soil with hands and sticks, carrying it
off in caps and aprons. With thudding
hammers, cracking whips, and groans of
the dying, St. Petersburg rose like the pyramids — in the tears and the anguish of the
slaves.

Peter was no less determined about
introducing European customs than he
had been about securing a seaport and
building a new capital. He himself had
made a first-hand study of the civilization of Western Europe by visiting foreign countries. He was determined that
Russia should learn Western ways and
forget those of the Mongols. He opened
new highways, introduced the study of
the sciences, built schools, and founded
academies in which he invited European
scholars to teach. His reforms extended
even to dress and personal appearance.
He ordered all men to abandon their
long-skirted robes and to shave their
faces in European fashion.

Although Peter did much to Westernize Russia, he was not altogether successful. One writer of the period recorded that

Forty years have passed, yet only the
summits have caught the western light;
the vast valleys still lie plunged in the
shadow of the past.

The Russian serf lived in slavery.
Most of the czars and czarinas [zahr ee'
nuhz] who followed Peter the Great
were ambitious for the greatness of Russia. Outstanding among them was Catherine the Great. This strong-willed empress, who reigned in the 18th Century,
took advantage of the discord between
Austria and Germany to gain more territory for Russia. By taking part in two
Turkish wars, first on the side of Prussia
and then on the side of Austria, she
managed to be given a share in the two
partitions of Poland and to gain other
territories along the southwest border of
Russia. Though new territories were
added to " all the Russias " throughout
the centuries, the later rulers had very
little concern for the health and happiness of the Russian peasant. While the
czars and the nobles looked on with
seeming indifference, the great mass of
the Russian people lived in poverty,
ignorance, and squalor. Great palaces
and churches were built. Millions were
spent by the czars and nobility which
came from the taxes that were collected
from the poor Russian peasants.

Few stories of human wretchedness
equal that of the Russian serf. A Russian
poet has given this description, entitled,
" A Night in a Village ":

Sultry air, the smoke of shavings,
    Dirt spread over all,
Feet and benches dirty; cobwebs
    To adorn the wall;

Smoke-begrimed each cottage chamber,
  Bread and water stale;
Spinners coughing, children crying —
  Want and woe prevail.
Hand to mouth lifelong they labor,
  Then a pauper's grave —
Oh! what need to learn the lesson —
  "Trust, my soul, be brave!"

Years after the serfs of other European countries had gained their freedom, the Russian serf was still bought and sold with the soil. At the beginning of the 18th Century, the wealth of a Russian nobleman was counted not by his money or his land alone, but by the number of "souls" on his property. The owner of the serf could sell his servants as he desired. This advertisement was taken from the Moscow *Gazette* of 1810:

To be sold: Two coachmen, well trained and handsome, the one eighteen and the other fifteen years of age, both of them good-looking and well acquainted with various kinds of handwork. . . . In the same house are sold pianos and organs.

Before the law no serf had any right to legal protection from his master. A royal decree during the 18th Century provided that —

If any serf shall dare to petition against his master he shall be punished with the knout [a kind of whip] and transported for life to the mines.

Napoleon influenced the story of Russia. You have read in the story of France that Russia joined the other nations of Europe in the wars to defeat Napoleon Bonaparte. Napoleon with his Grand Army invaded Russia in the winter of 1812–1813 and burned the city of Moscow. Many of Napoleon's troops were annihilated during their long retreat across the snow-covered wastes to their homeland. But though Napoleon was defeated, his invasion and the burning of Moscow had important effects on the life of the czar, Alexander I, and on the future of Russia. In the earlier years of his reign Alexander I had shown some liberal tendencies; he had been interested in public education; three universities had been founded; he had even arranged for the freeing of a few serfs.

After defeating the French in Russia, Alexander I, as might be expected, took part with other European nations in the continued wars against Napoleon in the next two years. Then the Czar played an important part in the Congress of Vienna, which, you will remember, rearranged the states of Europe. Alexander I had not altogether abandoned liberal ideas, but as a result of the French invasion he had become something of a religious mystic and felt he had a divine mission to help keep order in Europe. He proposed the formation of a "Holy Alliance" of monarchs to preserve the peace. The wily Austrian diplomat Metternich, who controlled the Congress, appeared to agree with Alexander. Actually, Metternich used Alexander's idea of the Holy Alliance as a means of crushing all attempts at liberal reforms in Europe.

In the meantime the young Russian officers who had taken part in the wars against Napoleon had absorbed some of the French revolutionary ideas of liberty, equality, and fraternity. They had observed Western representative assemblies in action, and had read French books about philosophy and politics. It may seem strange to us that the Russian officers should adopt the ideas of the people that they had been fighting against. But under absolute monarchs, the soldiers and even the officers often felt that wars were fought largely to satisfy the ambitions of their rulers above them. They themselves sometimes felt little concern in the quarrel beyond doing their professional duty. Further-

THE CORONATION OF CZAR ALEXANDER II

At the moment shown in this engraving Alexander II is being crowned Czar of Russia.
A high official of the Orthodox Catholic Church is in charge of the ceremony.

more, the French Revolution, as the monarchs feared, was somewhat international in character. The ideas of the French revolutionists lived on, even under Napoleon. The French people believed in these ideas, were proud of them, and were eager to pass them on to others. It was impossible that Russian soldiers and officers, occupying conquered French territory, should not be affected by such ideas.

When these Russian soldiers, and particularly the officers, returned to Russia, they found themselves quite impatient with its autocratic and inefficient government, the conditions of the serfs, and the lack of public education. At the same time, as we have seen, the government itself had become more reactionary. There was a widening gap between what the Russian people had and what they were determined to win for themselves.

Czar Alexander II freed the serfs.
About the time of our War between the States the conditions of the serfs were somewhat improved. Alexander II, one of the most humane of the Russian czars, in 1861 issued his famous decree freeing all the white serfs in Russia. By Alexander's decree the peasants were not only made free but the plots of ground upon which they had worked were given to them at a fixed rental charge with the privilege of purchase. The government often paid the landlord for the lands and collected the rent and taxes directly from the peasants. But the life of the peasants was not much improved. The serfs had to pay such heavy charges for the land that in some districts they found it difficult to buy food for their families. The peasant still had little or no opportunity to improve his lot. He was often illiterate. He remained doomed to constant toil and taxes. But he was legally free.

Besides freeing the serfs, Alexander reformed the law courts and established county and town councils in a number of districts. The members of these councils were elected by the people and were responsible to them. In districts where these were established they helped somewhat to improve the living conditions of the people. They were responsible for public health, welfare, and education. They provided more assistance for the poor and dependent and made better medical care available. The laws were also reformed in the reign of Alexander II, and a system of trial by jury was set up. His reign likewise saw increased industrialization in Russia, the building of railways, and the extension of the banking system.

But Russia's social and economic problems were too vast to be taken care of by the slow reforms of the unwieldy imperial government. The radical Russian press became more and more extreme in its demands for reform. To the influence of French liberal and radical thinkers there had been added the socialistic doctrines of Karl Marx, which you have read about in the story of Germany. Some of Marx's followers deny that he approved the use of violence to bring about control by the working classes. But many of the Russian radicals felt that if an extreme change of government was to come about they could well hasten it by revolutions. It so happened that on the very day Alexander II had signed his approval to a project to bring about further governmental and financial reforms in Russia, he was assassinated by a group of revolutionaries.

Reaction, war, and unsuccessful popular uprisings followed the reign of Alexander II. The ill-organized attempt at revolution which had resulted in the death of Alexander II was easily put down and his son succeeded to the throne without difficulty. Alexander III was a reactionary ruler. He spent his life trying to keep the old autocracy unchanged and living in constant fear of the revolutionists. He in turn was followed on the throne late in the 19th Century by his son, Nicholas II.

The new ruler had much the same ideas of absolute autocracy that his father had had. The people were still discontented. Nicholas II chanced to deepen and sharpen this discontent by a most unsuccessful foreign war. This came about in the following way. The rulers of Russia had always been eager for more land, particularly if it would provide them with seaports. The German Kaiser, Wilhelm II, who was a cousin of Czar Nicholas II, cleverly suggested to Czar Nicholas II that the Russians might expand eastward into Asia instead of westward into Europe. The Czar adopted this plan and the Trans-Siberian Railway was extended by the East China Railway to run through Manchuria. Then the Czar obtained the permission of the Chinese to construct a branch through Mukden (later famous in World War II) to Port Arthur on the Yellow Sea. Here the Russians became involved in a quarrel with the Japanese, who controlled near-by Chosen, and went to war with them.

The Russians soon found that Japan was much better prepared for war than the Russian government had realized. A number of Russian military defeats gave the revolutionists further grounds for agitation and complaint. They increased their demands for a parliamentary government in which everyone had a right to vote. After Russia had been defeated by Japan, there was an uprising and general strike among the workingmen. This uprising accomplished little. Although the Czar promised the people more power in the government, it was not given.

Conditions in Russia proved ripe for revolution. There are differences of opinion about the conditions in Russia early in the 20th Century. Some claim that Russia was making rapid progress in industry and education, that its courts were functioning well, and that the people had many civil rights. The czarist government has been pictured as more incompetent than despotic. An intelligent and sympathetic finance minister had done much to give the peasants increased prosperity. Co-operative farming was encouraged. Peasants who wished to sell their land and go into trade in the towns might do so. Both the peasants and the towns often benefited by this greater freedom.

Most of the Czar's ministers, unfortunately, were not so helpful as the minister of finance. In general, the ministry was reactionary and it came into conflict with the people's national assembly, or *duma*. The Czar himself was an able man, but rather weak. He was greatly influenced by a small circle of noble advisers, who formed many of his decisions. All in all, changes in Russia were not keeping pace with popular demands.

In 1917, during World War I, a series of events occurred which drastically changed conditions in Russia. After fighting bravely on the side of the Allies for two and a half years, the Russian army began to crumple from within, its morale weakened by the inefficiency, corruption, and mismanagement of the czarist government. Moreover, on the home front there developed a shortage of fuel, clothing, and food; the gaunt specter of famine stalked through the great cities. As their suffering grew more acute, crowds of starving, freezing workingmen stormed the breadshops.

Revolt flamed into revolution. At first people did not realize that the great Revolution which was to change the face of Russia had actually begun. Various radical parties with different beliefs and plans had been active throughout the country for years. The revolutionists were not well organized and had no over-all plan for revolution at this time. To the casual observer there was little to distinguish the early stages of the Revolution of 1917 from any of the unsuccessful little revolutionary uprisings which had been occurring from time to time for decades. But conditions now proved to be ripe for a general uprising. For one thing, the Russian soldiers who had returned from World War I were demanding to be given land of their own. And discontent with the czarist government had spread among various classes of people. When Czar Nicholas II called out his mounted dragoons to put down the bread riots, they refused to fire upon the hungry people. Soon strikes and open rebellion flared from Moscow to Leningrad (then Petrograd) and flamed throughout the land. When 300,000 of the Czar's best soldiers went over to the support of the people, that unhappy ruler knew that his fate was sealed. It was the end of the house of Romanov, the royal family which had ruled Russia for three centuries.

The Communists seized power in a time of chaos and bloodshed. For Russia, the fall of the Czar marked the beginning of a period of chaos. As with the French Revolution, the days and years which followed were filled with bloodshed and disorder. Hundreds of the old aristocracy, including the Czar and his family, met death; thousands were killed or starved to death. Some saved their lives by fleeing from the country. For centuries the Russian peasants had been trampled upon by the ruling class; now they mercilessly destroyed the people who had kept them in bondage, and a good part of Russia's small middle class as well. In the violence of the Revolution most of the old Russia was swept away. Wendell Willkie, who made a trip to Russia in 1942, wrote —

The true story of that period will probably never be told in detail. For except for those who escaped to other lands, and they were relatively few, practically the whole upper and middle classes of Russia have been completely exterminated. . . . it is ruled by and composed almost entirely of people whose parents had no property, no education, and only a folk heritage.[1]

In this time of bloodshed a group of aggressive, radical socialists called Communists, who believed in the use of violence to attain their ends, seized the government. After much trouble among conflicting parties the present Union of Soviet Socialist Republics (U.S.S.R.) was established in Russia. From the beginning the Communists urged that the state should seize the large estates of the nobles and should gain control of all industry. To eliminate the " parasites of the Russian society " they emphasized that everyone should work.

Lenin and Trotsky worked through the Soviets. Two of the most conspicuous leaders of the Communists were Lenin [leh′nin] and Trotsky [trawt′ skee]. Lenin, who came from a well-to-do family, had been a lawyer and writer. He was a revolutionist to the very core and so radical in his political sympathies and activities that the czarist govern-

[1] From Wendell Willkie, *One World*, 1943. Simon and Schuster, Inc.

Press Association

LENIN

The memory of Lenin is still revered by the Soviets. His body has been carefully preserved inside a sealed glass case in an imposing tomb facing Red Square in Moscow. Every day in peacetime patriotic Russians stream slowly past his coffin to gaze at the face of their former leader.

ment had exiled him from Russia. Shrewd and brilliant, Lenin returned to take part in the Revolution of 1917. Trotsky, an eloquent and forceful Jew of the middle class, also had spent most of his life in exile. When the Czar was overthrown, Trotsky likewise returned to Russia, and became an active coworker of Lenin. Lenin and Trotsky not only believed in the Communist revolution in Russia, they preached a doctrine of worldwide revolution and encouraged their followers to try to bring about the overthrow of government in other lands in order to establish communism throughout the world. This policy was to have a serious effect on Russia's foreign relations until later leaders announced its abandonment.

At the time of the Russian Revolution, committees called soviets, which were made up of workingmen, soldiers, and peasants, had already been established by the Communist party. These served as local governments. Lenin used these soviets and made them the basis of the organization of the Russian government. The local soviet became the smallest unit of government; above it stood the district, provincial, and state soviets. This organization may appear somewhat similar to our own local, state, and national government. However, in practice it worked quite differently. In the United States we have had two strong political parties, which continually check each other. In Russia there is only one legalized party, the Communist party. Russia's one-party system threw the power into the hands of the party managers. Lenin, as the most influential and respected party manager, really became the "boss" or dictator of Russia.

Stalin built industry and raised the standard of living: the two Five-Year Plans. When Lenin died in 1924 it seemed for a time that the Russian dictatorship might be concentrated in the hands of a group of Communist party managers. However, within a few years another strong dictator, Joseph Stalin [stah'lin], began to draw the reins of government into his own hands. Stalin, who was the son of a peasant shoemaker, first planned to be a religious teacher and then joined the communist movement as a follower of Lenin. He was a forceful leader, realistic in his thinking and often severe, even ruthless, in his actions. Of Stalin, Wendell Willkie wrote, "Stalin is a hard man, perhaps even a cruel man, but a very able one." [1] On the personal side, he added that

[1] From Wendell Willkie, *One World*, 1943. Simon and Schuster, Inc.

Stalin was without affectations or poses, a simple man with a robust sense of humor.

Under Stalin's leadership Russia embarked upon two "Five-Year Plans." In the first Five-Year Plan (1928–1933) Russia built up her heavy industries such as steelmills and railways, and turned the small individual farms into big collective farms on which the people of a whole village worked together. Results were all-important to the Communist government; so they did not hesitate to allow several million peasants to die of famine or to exile them to Siberia when they refused to turn their small farms into collectives. The famine itself was aggravated by the fact that the government was exporting grain at the time in order to buy armaments, and not leaving enough to provide for the needier districts. When officials failed to reach the output the government demanded of them, they were liquidated. In the second Five-Year Plan Stalin tried to raise the low living standard of the Russian people by making more goods for the Russians, giving them better food, clothing, and homes.

The small Communist party controls a vast land. The 190,000,000 people of Russia are now ruled by the Communist party, which has a membership of only about 4,000,000 people. But under its direction there is a junior party, the Comsomol, which trains its members in duties and discipline, and there is also a still younger group, "The Young Pioneers." For this youngest group the government supplies after-school educational projects in crafts and arts, and other activities. On page 627 you will see a picture of young people taking part in a Youth Sport Day celebration in Red Square. All these groups together make up about 20 percent of the total popu-

Sovfoto

A SPORTS PARADE IN RED SQUARE

In czarist days only the wealthy had an opportunity to take part in sports. Since the establishment of the Soviet Union, physical training has been included in the modern compulsory school program for all Russian young people.

lation, and there are millions more of nonparty believers in communist ideas. Nonparty members may be elected to public office, but generally speaking, it is the members of the Communist party who make up the aggressive leadership in any Russian community.

Seven years of elementary education are now compulsory for all children in Russia. Then they may go on to a higher school or a trade school. Government funds are available for gifted students who wish to study in the universities. Compulsory military training for boys begins at the age of twelve. Men and boys between the ages of sixteen and fifty are liable to compulsory military service.

Contrary to popular belief, Stalin is not the head of the Soviet government.

It is true that Stalin is Premier of Russia, and Defense Commissar, and occupies other important government posts. Perhaps more important, he is General Secretary of the Communist party. The party affects the Russian government in the following way:

The party members elect a directive body called the Central Committee. The Committee selects the Political Bureau. It is this Bureau which makes party decisions. And the party decisions are acted upon by the Soviet government. All government radio and other facilities are available to the Communist party and are used for its propaganda.

The governing body of the Soviet Union is the Supreme Soviet of the U.S. S.R., but in practice it does not meet so often or have so much power as our

Acme

STALIN

Since the beginning of the 20th Century Stalin has worked determinedly to further communist ideas. He escaped from exile in Siberia on five different occasions before the Revolution. Since 1917 he has continued to justify his name, which means "man of steel."

Congress. Like Congress, it is made up of two chambers. One of these is the Soviet of the Union, in which there is one deputy for each 300,000 of the population. The other chamber is the Council of Nationalities, which is made up of a number of delegates from each of the various republics and provinces of the Union. These two chambers elect a smaller governing body, the Presidium. Between sessions of the Supreme Soviet, the Presidium rules Russia and has vast powers. It even has the right to ratify treaties and declare war. The President of the Presidium (during World War II, Kalinin [kah lee'nin]) is the theoretical head of the Soviet government.

This exact method of governing Rus-

sia has been in effect only since 1936, when the Soviet adopted a new constitution. Not until then did all the Russian people obtain the right to vote for which they had been clamoring even before the Revolution. Under the first years of the Soviet rule only a limited number of people were allowed to vote. Non-Russian peoples in Central Asia, the Caucasus, and other outlying districts, which had been absorbed by the Russians in earlier centuries, had not enjoyed equal rights with the Russian Soviet Socialist Federated Republic (Soviet Russia proper). The voting rights of agricultural workers as compared with those of the city workers had also been greatly restricted. The new constitution of 1936 changed the basis of all this, at least in principle. As the constitution becomes fully operative it will give all Russian citizens the right to vote. The secret ballot is to be used throughout Russia. At the same time that this constitution was being prepared and adopted, an extensive campaign of Communist party propaganda was carried on to make sure that the people voted to maintain the Communists in power.

The Russian experiment is not absolute communism. It would be a mistake to believe that the Russian government is following absolute communist principles and practices. They have not been able to put into practice the standard communist doctrine, "From each according to his ability; to each according to his needs." In order to get results they have found it worth while to reward greater efforts with greater pay. A factory manager is paid more than a routine worker; he usually buys a house in the country as soon as he can. Workers who produce more than their quotas are grouped as Stakhanovites [stak hahn' oh vaits] and paid higher wages. Joseph

E. Davies, when he was ambassador to Russia wrote, " There are reports of sabotage by labor in many instances as a resentment against the piecework and the speeding-up system of the Stakhanovites." The classless society which the Communists preached has not come into being. Whether it ever will in the future, as the Communists believe, remains to be seen. Great wealth, and hereditary wealth, have of course been abolished. But distinctions based on the output and quality of work or service to the state remain. So far the Soviet has found these distinctions necessary.

Neither should you think that all the small luxuries of daily life have been ruled out of Russia. Up to the time of World War II the state itself ran florist shops, where you could buy as expensive flowers as you might wish, or could pay for. And Mme Molotov [mah'lah tawv], the wife of Russia's Commissar for Foreign Affairs during World War II, was herself Commissar for Cosmetics.

The Soviet government feared foreign invasion. From the beginning the relations of the Soviet government with other nations were somewhat difficult. It was some time before other nations recognized the new Soviet government. Other peoples disliked the violent measures which had brought the Soviet into being, and they also resented the fact that the Soviet government long refused to pay the debts of a short-lived Russian government which had ruled for a time between the Revolution and the rise of the Soviet Union.

It was 1933 before the United States recognized the Soviet government and renewed diplomatic relations with Russia. The 1930's were troubled years for the whole world. The Nazis were threatening the peace of Europe. Fear and distrust reigned on the Continent. The Russians in particular feared invasion from both Germany and Japan. The American minister to Moscow, Joseph Davies, reported as follows to the American Secretary of State in 1937, about a talk with Maxim Litvinov, the People's Commissar for Foreign Affairs.

. . . he thought they ought to let him [Hitler] " stew in his own juice "; that Hitler's policy had not changed from that which he had announced in his book *Mein Kampf;* that he was dominated by a lust for conquest and for the domination of Europe; that he could not understand why Great Britain could not see that once Hitler dominated Europe he would swallow the British Isles also.[1]

However, Russia did not succeed in persuading Britain and France to form a firm policy for opposing Hitler. Russia then sought her own means of defense. In 1937 and 1938 the world was startled by a series of treason trials and executions in Russia. In these bloody purges a number of high-placed military and governmental leaders were convicted of treason and shot. Some had confessed to almost unbelievable connivance with officials of both Japan and Germany and to betraying to these foreign powers information important to the defense of the Russian state. Apparently the conspirators had intended to give over the western Soviet lands to Germany, the eastern to Japan, and to take over the government of the central districts themselves as a " pure " soviet state.

American public opinion was shocked by these trials, because under Soviet law the accused men were compelled to testify against themselves and had practically none of the protection against their accusers which American law gives to us. Nonetheless, the detailed nature

[1] From Joseph E. Davies, *Mission to Moscow,* 1941. Simon and Schuster, Inc.

Sovfoto

A FIELD NEWSPAPER

These women, who work on a collective farm, have paused briefly to read a newspaper set up in the field. The Soviet economic and educational program has greatly improved conditions for workers such as these.

of the evidence appears to indicate that some of the men were guilty.

These trials strengthened the Russian state and kept the administration firmly in power. But they made other nations feel less sure of the Russian government's strength and perhaps less inclined to join her in taking a firm stand against Germany's demands on Czechoslovakia.

Having failed to secure a combination of powers against Germany, the Russian government, in 1939, suddenly startled the world by signing a non-aggression pact with the Germans. In view of the Russians' complete awareness of Hitler's aims and intentions, this pact seems to have been a play for time until Russia could completely prepare for war and withstand a German attack. Later, in 1940, Russia attacked one of her small neighbors, Finland. This at-

tack met with considerable disapproval throughout the world, and Russia was barred from the League of Nations. Likewise in 1940 Russia absorbed into the Soviet Union as new Soviet Republics, Estonia, Latvia, and Lithuania. The United States government did not recognize the addition of this territory. All these moves the Russians defended on the grounds that they were necessary for Russian security.

Russia did not come into World War II until the summer of 1941, a year after the fall of France. Then the Germans invaded Russia in defiance of their non-aggression pact and Russia became an ally of the United Nations. In Part Twenty-two you will read more of Russia's part in the war.

Russia today and tomorrow. No matter what one may think of the ruthlessness of Soviet methods, in Russia they did achieve remarkable results. Only thirty or forty years ago the Russian peasants were an illiterate lower class who had no hope of changing their lot. Today these people, whose parents had a narrow life of toil with few opportunities, have a different lot. Today almost every Russian has more than his fathers and grandfathers had before him — an education, a library in his village, a chance to improve his position, care if he is ill, a knowledge that he will be cared for in his old age. The Russians do not have the freedom which we consider a part of our heritage — they do not have freedom to disagree with the government leaders, freedom to change their jobs when they wish, or freedom to build a business of their own. They do not have the protection from the courts to which we are accustomed. They are not free from the constant presence of the government's secret police. The present-day Russians have never had this freedom; so perhaps they do not miss it or are not certain such freedom is a good thing. Generally, conditions are so much better for the common people than ever before in the history of Russia that they are grateful to their leaders and loyal to the ideas and ideals of the Communist party. We must see Russia in the light of her history rather than attempt to make comparisons with ourselves; it has been many years since our own European or English ancestors were serfs. Russians, just as we do, think that their kind of government and way of life is the best in the world.

Many people have been bitterly opposed to Russia for fear the Communists would encourage world revolution and overthrow other governments. The idea of world revolution, as you know, was supported by Lenin and Trotsky,

but has been dropped by the present Soviet government, according to an announcement by Stalin. He has said that the Russians should give all their energies to the development of Russia itself. During World War II Americans began to learn more about the Russian people, what they stood for, and what an heroic struggle they have been making to improve their conditions. They admired the courage and endurance which enabled the Russians finally to sweep out of their country the mechanized German armies which had invaded Russia in the summer of 1941 expecting a quick victory.

The United States and Russia were favorably impressed with each other's accomplishments in war production. Common interest in production and in development of their countries seemed to lay a foundation for further co-operation in peacetime through export and import trade. Eric A. Johnston, President of the United States Chamber of Commerce, who visited Russia in 1944, spoke as follows at an official reception in his honor in Moscow:

Some of you, I know, thought our private enterprise system, which you think is too chaotic, could not produce the necessary volume of goods for this war. Some of us, I know, thought that your state-enterprise system, which we think is too rigid, would utterly fail to produce the necessary volume of goods for this war. We were both mistaken. . . . I like your manganese. There is one frightfully nice thing about it. It does not know that it is socialist. It would just as soon go into a furnace in Pittsburgh as in Stalingrad. And you like our machine tools. They do not know they are capitalistic. They would just as soon chip pieces out of metal in Kharkov as in Detroit.

It became apparent that the Russian experiment in a new type of government had welded its people into a loyal, effective society. Russia had emerged from her years of strife and struggle as one of the world's most powerful nations. Today Russia stands forth as a vigorous country, a dynamic force which cannot be ignored or brushed aside. She is one of the great nations of the world that the United States must work with and co-operate with in the future if we are to do our part in maintaining world economic welfare and a lasting peace on the earth.

Chapter 3 ~ Russian Writers, Musicians, and Scientists Have Marked the Path of Progress

Russia has contributed to the knowledge and culture of the world. The average American probably will frankly admit that he is not sure which of the conflicting stories about modern Russia he should believe, or whether the truth lies somewhere between them. But he probably appreciates the fact that Russian authors, musicians, and scientists have made outstanding contributions to civilization. In our public libraries he sees volumes written by Russian poets and novelists. Over the radio he hears deeply stirring music composed by Russian masters. Or he may know some of the popular Russian folk songs, such as "Dark Eyes" or "Two Guitars." On the stage he may see the native dress and the dances of Russia. He may have read of the remarkable achievements of Russian doctors during World War II. There are so many evidences of Russian culture in the United States that we cannot be unaware of Russia's gifts to civilization. In this story of Russia, as in the stories of other nations, we shall mention only a few of the greatest men of literature, music, and science, who represent the genius of their native land.

Tolstoy wrote of the social evils of his day. Of the Russian writers, none stands above Count Leo Tolstoy [tahl' stoi], who died in 1910 at the age of eighty-two. His life extended through the troubled years of the 19th Century and almost to the end of czardom. When Tolstoy was only a boy, he wrote this sentence in his journal, "There is something in me which makes me think I was not born to be just like everybody else." Tolstoy was right. Even in his youth his friends realized that he had outstanding ability.

It was not mere ability that made Tolstoy different from others. He had a deep love of truth — a desire to seek the truth and to tell it in his novels. On every side he saw the distress and poverty of the Russian peasants. He longed to help set them free by revealing their plight to the world. Not even the government's displeasure and the threat of exile could turn him from his purpose.

As a young man just out of school, Tolstoy entered the army, but he was never satisfied with his work there. His extremely serious point of view caused him to disapprove of the gay, careless life he

J. Jay Hirz

TOLSTOY

Although Tolstoy opposed all violence and revolution, his memory is nonetheless revered by the Soviets. His family estate is now a museum. During World War II invading German army officers used the building and attempted to destroy it when they retreated, but the watchful caretakers foiled the attempt.

and the other young men led. Gradually he turned to writing. Soon he abandoned his military career altogether. He believed in a simple, pure life and by his example tried to persuade others to accept his own high ideals. His great novel, *War and Peace,* showed his belief in the futility of war and the danger of worshiping military heroes. *Anna Karenina* [ah'nah kah reh'nyee nah] and *Resurrection,* two other novels, strikingly portrayed the social conditions, common in Russia during the 19th Century, which badly needed reform.

At sixty-three Tolstoy wrote that man could reach happiness if he would be perfectly pure and perfectly free. He felt that man should never use violence to protect himself or others, but should always do good to his enemies. Tolstoy

also believed that man should not live by the labor of others but should earn his own bread. He himself, though of the nobility, put this belief into practice by renouncing a life of ease and by laboring in the field at the side of a peasant. One night he horrified his family by telling them that he intended to divide his property among the poor. Only after hours of pleading was he persuaded to turn it over to his wife instead. From that night Tolstoy made his living by cobbling and writing. Never again did he have a penny he himself had not earned.

When Tolstoy died, he was mourned by the world. Though people did not always agree with his ideas, he was respected for his honesty and ability. During part of his life he was acknowledged as the greatest living writer. His works were translated into forty-five different languages. In everything he wrote, Tolstoy was fearless in making plain the evils of the day. Had it not been for the love of the people and the fact that he himself was a noble, he would probably have been arrested and exiled from Russia, for his criticisms were feared by the government because he wrote with such power and strength that he influenced many people. Even with the threat of banishment hanging over his head, Tolstoy wrote honestly and without timidity.

Other Russian writers revealed life in Russia. Tolstoy is not the only well-known Russian writer. Dostoevski [daw'stoh yef'ski], the author of the novel, *Crime and Punishment,* is famous for his descriptions of the agonies of the human mind. Pushkin [poosh'kin] has been called the " Uncrowned Czar of Russian Poetry." Gorki [gawr'ki] is famous as the preacher of revolt and the voice of the worker. The short stories of Chekhov [che'khawv] are known throughout the world. Chekhov, the son of a freed peasant, seemed to have an unlimited knowledge of human nature, which he used in his fast-moving stories. The novels of Turgenev [toor ghe'nyev] reveal a master in painting with words the realities of life. His book, *A Sportsman's Sketches,* dealt with the life of Russian serfs so vividly that it played a large part in the abolishment of serfdom.

As in France before the Revolution, the literature of Russia reflects the social history of the country. Through the writings of most Russian poets and novelists runs the crimson thread of revolt. The poets and novelists were daring enough to tell of the suffering of the people, to criticize the government, and to preach freedom. Usually their writings were bitter, grim, but sincere. " No nation boasts writers who make one see more vividly or feel more deeply."

A Russian composer won the appreciation of American people. On a night in May, 1891, the music lovers of New York City crowded into Carnegie Hall to hear the composer, Peter Tchaikovsky [chai kawv'ski], conduct his own compositions at his first concert in America. A hush fell over the group as the master walked across the stage to stand straight and distinguished before the orchestra. After a quick formal bow, Tchaikovsky turned to his orchestra and held aloft his baton. All eyes were focused upon him as he led the first crashing chords of his composition. As the music continued, the audience began to fall under its spell. At times there was a savage gaiety; strange varied rhythms followed each other; strong, vigorous life coursed through the music; then came heartbreaking despair and tragedy. The audience, which sat awestruck, followed each change of mood and felt itself carried into another world. When the last throbbing notes died away, there was a moment of silence. Then long applause brought the great composer again and again to the center of the stage. The American people had heard Tchaikovsky, the Russian master of music.

This musician who won the appreciation of his listeners is perhaps the greatest of all Russian composers, and probably one of the most versatile composers in the world. His works range from simple waltzes and delightful suites, such as the gay *Nutcracker Suite,* so popular with young people, to his major works — piano concertos and magnificent symphonies. The *Symphonie Pathétique* [saɴ'foh'nee' pa'tay'teek'] is the most famous of all his works. In this symphony the melancholy and tragic despair which are found in many of his finest compositions rise to a new intensity. One cannot listen to the strange, passionate melody without catching the composer's spirit.

Other Russians won fame as musicians. Although Tchaikovsky probably is the most famous, he is by no means the only great Russian musician. Anton Rubinstein holds a place scarcely less exalted. The musical compositions of Sergei Rachmaninoff [sehr'ghey rahk-mah'ni nawv] are appreciated wherever they are known. His *Prelude in C Sharp Minor* is particularly well liked. Another composer, Nicholas Rimski-Korsakov [rim'ski kawr'sah kawv] through his music has interpreted oriental influences in Russia and the Far East. You may know his *Song of India,* and will enjoy *The Young Prince and the Young Princess* or the *Festival at Bagdad.* Two great names among living Russian composers are Sergei Prokofieff [pro kaw'fyev] and Dmitri Shostakovich [dmee'tree shah-stah kah'vich]. Prokofieff's work is often satirical or humorous. His *Scythian Suite* for orchestra is well known in America. His ballets and a number of his concertos for piano and violin have also been performed here. As a child, you may have enjoyed his *Peter and the Wolf,* which relates in music the adventurous fairy tale of a small boy's encounter with a beast of the forest.

Dmitri Shostakovich had written six symphonies before the outbreak of World War II. The Sixth in particular was well known in America. Then during the siege of Leningrad in 1941, he wrote his Seventh Symphony, which was received with great acclaim in America as well as in Russia. Shostakovich himself divided his time that year between working as a firefighter in defense of the city and composing this great work, which is, as he said, " an interpretation of the war." It meant a great deal to the Russian people that the composition of this work had gone on even while the enemy was at their gates. Shostakovich's Eighth Symphony, performed in 1943 and rousingly received, was likewise based directly on Russia's part in the war.

Russian scientists have advanced the world's knowledge. In the first half of the 19th Century there was born in a small town in the Ural district of Siberia a boy who was to become one of the leading chemists of the world. After attending school in his own home town of Tobolsk, Dmitri Mendeléyev [men'dyeh lyah'yehf] continued his study of science at St. Petersburg. There he became an instructor and finally a professor of chemistry.

Mendeléyev is best known for his arrangement of chemical elements in a periodic table, according to their weights and properties. By means of this table Mendeléyev was able to predict the existence of some elements before they had been discovered, and even to tell what their properties are. Mendeléyev also investigated the effect of heat on the expansion of liquids and gases, and studied the nature and origin of petroleum. His work was known throughout the world. His lecture room was thronged with students, and his best-known book, *The Principles of Chemistry,* was translated into many languages.

Another great Russian scientist of the 19th Century was the biologist, Ilya Metchnikoff [il'yah mech'ni kawv]. Metchnikoff was born in Kharkov and studied at the university there, and in France. Like his contemporary, Mendeléyev, he became an instructor and then a professor. He was particularly interested in the nature and behavior of microbes. In order to study them further, he journeyed to Messina, then went to Paris to study with Pasteur, the French chemist, whom you have read about in the story of France. It was Metchnikoff who discovered and explained to the world the fact that white blood corpuscles keep up a constant warfare against bacteria and devour them in the body. His chief work is *Immunity in Infectious Diseases,* which was translated into English. In recognition of his discoveries, Metchnikoff, early in the 20th Century, was awarded the Nobel Prize for medicine.

Another Russian scientist honored by the Nobel Prize was the physician, Ivan Pavlov [ee vahn′ pah′vlawv]. Pavlov was one of a number of Russian physiologists who were interested in the behavior of animals. From his experiments with the behavior of dogs, Pavlov was able to learn the nature of conditioned reflexes in human beings, as well as animals, and to understand how they come about. This was a real contribution to psychology. It has enabled modern psychologists to understand many things about human behavior which would otherwise have been difficult to explain.

World War II offered grim occasion for the exercise of the skill of Russian doctors and other men of science. Although Russia does not yet have nearly all the doctors she needs, the courage and accomplishment of those she does have offer good hope for her continued contributions to the welfare and knowledge of mankind.

The Russian Bear Changes Masters

The revolution of 1917 transformed czarist Russia, with its rigid class distinctions, its illiterate masses, and its autocratic government, into the Soviet Union of today. In the Soviet Union there are only minor class distinctions; education is not only available to everyone, but is also compulsory; and the people have a certain amount of representation in the government. Industry has increased. Russia has become one of the most powerful nations in the world. It is difficult to understand Russia today. For one reason, the rebirth of this immense nation has been sudden; furthermore, many people distrust the Communist theory of government. Apparent contradictions in recent Russian history are puzzling at long range. What we can be sure of is that this great nation of Slavic and Nordic and Mongol peoples, with its rich supplies of natural resources, is making powerful industrial progress, has raised the educational level of its people, and is on the way toward overcoming its problems of communication and transportation.

Early in the history of Russia, Slavic tribes living in the western river valleys, were overcome and organized by Northmen. Gradually, as the communities grew, they spread eastward. From their contacts with Constantinople, the Russians acquired Christianity. The original Slavic peoples, the Norse feudal barons, or dukes, and a class of landowners, or lesser nobles, formed the three groups that were to exist through centuries of Russia's history. In the 13th Century the Mongols swept through Russia. They kept the Russians under subjection for two centuries, and left oriental influences upon the character of the Russian people.

Grand Duke Ivan III became the first Russian czar. Later rulers included Ivan the Terrible; Peter the Great, who tried to Westernize Russia; and Catherine the Great, who extended Russia's territories but took no more care of the wretched serfs than her predecessors had done. Czar Alexander I, who was on the throne when Napoleon invaded Russia, played an important part in the Congress of Vienna. Under Alexander II the serfs were freed, but were given scant opportunity of making a living or securing education.

Meanwhile a group of revolutionaries against the misery and injustice in Russia had been growing stronger. These men were influenced by the French Revolution and later by the theories of the socialist Karl Marx. An attempted uprising resulted in the assassination of Czar Alexander II; but the revolt was crushed. Nicholas II reigned as Czar through a fateful period of Russian history — a period which included the Russo-Japanese war and World War I and the Revolution of 1917, in which the Czar and his family were executed.

The revolutionary leaders, Lenin and Trotsky, and their supporters established the Soviet Union on the socialistic principles of Karl Marx. Stalin succeeded Lenin as the most powerful member of the Communist party — Russia's one political party. Under Stalin's direction, heavy industry was built up; farms were organized into large collective units; and attempts were made to raise the standard of living.

The Communist party includes only a small fraction of the Russian people. It may be said to shape the policies of the nation. The Central Committee of the party selects the Political Bureau, which makes daily decisions concerning policy. The Supreme Soviet of the U.S.S.R. is the representative body of the government. Between sessions of the Supreme Soviet, the Presidium carries on the work of governing. The new Russian constitution of 1936 provides for extension of the right to vote. Communism in Russia is not absolute. Differences in wages and salaries exist; but the vast inequalities of the Czarist period have been removed.

During the years immediately preceding World War II, Russia was somewhat isolated from other powerful nations because many people in these nations distrusted Communist policies — especially the idea of World Revolution. Recently this part of Communist theory has been officially abandoned by the Soviet government. Russia's agreement with Germany in 1939 startled the rest of the world. But the rest of the world was startled again by the magnificent offensives with which Russia turned back the attacks of the Nazis when Hitler broke the Russian agreement and invaded Russia.

With the British, the Chinese, and the United States, Russia was a member of the United Nations.

Russian contributions to the world's literature and music and science have been impressive. The novels of Tolstoy and Doestoevski and Turgenev, and the poetry of Pushkin, are part of the indispensable literature of the world. Tchaikovsky, Rachmaninoff, Rimski-Korsakov, Prokofieff, and Shostakovich are known to lovers of music the world over. In science, Mendeléyev, Metchnikoff, and Pavlov have made distinguished contributions.

SELF-TEST

In this story of Russia, do whatever the statements call for.

I. Russia's vast territory stretches from —— in the northwest to —— in the east. In the north, Russians live near the —— Circle, and in the south they sail on the —— Sea. Many Russians show by their features and coloring that they are of ——, ——, or —— origin. Russia is well supplied with natural ——, but the size of the country has created problems of —— and ——.

II. In ancient times Slavic peoples settled along such rivers as the ——, the ——, and the ——. Then in the Ninth Century came the —— who organized the natives into self-protecting communities. Hundreds of years later in the 13th Century, Russia was overrun by the —— who added their racial characteristics to those of the —— and the Slavs, who had mixed together. Finally, after about (100, 300, 500) years, the Russian princes became stronger and one of them, the Grand Duke of ——, freed Russia from the yoke of the (western, eastern, northern) peoples. From the time of the first Romanov until the year (1918, 1776, 1917, 1789) Russia was ruled over by a series of extremely despotic autocrats. One of these rulers, who was called ——, tried to Europeanize Russia. The Russian Revolution in the year —— swept away most of the old imperial Russia. Now the nation goes by the name of U.S.S.R. These letters mean —— —— —— ——. The government is in the control of the —— party.

III. Russia's gifts to civilization in the field of the fine arts include such names as ——, who wrote, as a converted aristocrat, of the social evils of his day. Some of the other Russian writers are ——, ——, ——, ——, and ——. The grimness of much of Russian literature, tinged as it is with the spirit of ——, is due to the social conditions which existed under the imperial rulers. The greatest name in Russian music is that of ——. Other well-known names of Russian musicians are ——, who wrote the *Song of India;* —— whose *Prelude in C Sharp Minor* is a familiar number on the concert platform; and ——, whose Seventh Symphony is well-liked in the United States. Three well-known Russian scientists are ——, ——, and ——.

IV. Study the map of Russia on page 640, keeping always in mind what you have already learned in the story of Russia. Then answer the following questions on a separate sheet of paper.

(1) Why would you expect Russia to be somewhat like the countries of Western Europe and somewhat like the countries of the Orient?

(2) What is the significance of the hammer and sickle in the upper right-hand corner of the map?

(3) Russia has long been handicapped by lack of seaports. Name and locate the seaports on which the Russians chiefly depend for access to the trade routes of the world.

(4) What changes in Russia are symbolized by the tools and machines in the sketches?

(5) Which of the many rivers shown on the map have been most important in the story of Russia?

(6) What would you assume about the climate of Russia after a study of the map?

(7) Where is Russia's most fertile agricultural region?

(8) Where is the best grazing land?

INTERESTING THINGS TO DO

Projects for the Chart Maker and Artist

1. Draw a large outline map of Russia, and indicate on it the variety and location of her many natural resources. See *Atlas of Global Geography* by Erwin Raisz; *New World Horizons*, by Chester Lawrence; or other modern atlases and books of economic geography.

2. Draw a cartoon that catches the meaning of some interesting incident or aspect of the story of Russia. For example: "The Russian Bear Takes Strides"; "The Airplane Conquers Russia's Vast Distances"; "The Union of 149 Languages."

3. Make a comparison chart in parallel columns for the United States, Russia, and another nation that you have studied. Use headings such as "Area," "Kind of Government," "Natural Resources," "Recreation," "Schools," "Industries."

Topics for Talks

1. "In the time of the Czars." Prepare a talk on life in Russia during the years preceding World War I. See *Green Worlds*, by Maurice Hindus; *The Education of a Princess*, by Grand Duchess Marie.

2. "Siberia —— vast and unknown." To most Americans, the name Siberia brings to mind immense distances of barren, frozen land. Prepare a talk about Siberia that describes its present conditions and future possibilities. Make your discussion a lively blend of history, geography, and description. See Emil Lengyel's *Siberia*.

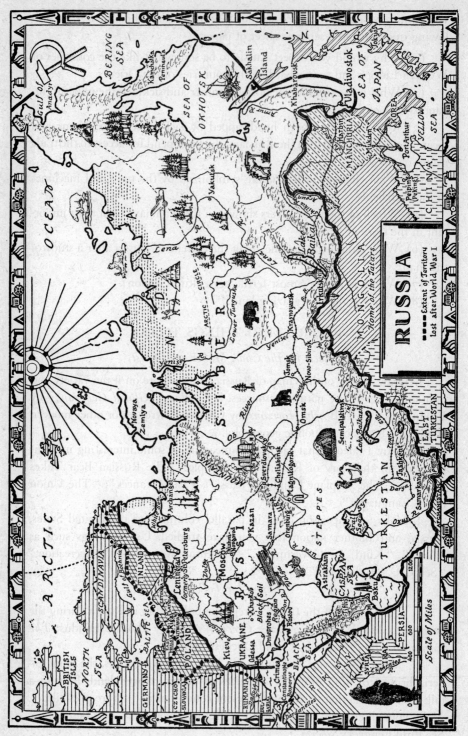

RUSSIA

---- Extent of Territory
░░░ lost after World War I

3. "Many families under one roof." Prepare a talk about the many peoples of different customs and language that work together in the Soviet State. See *Life*, March 29, 1943. See also *Land of the Soviets*, by Nikolas Mikhailov, or *Peoples of the USSR*, by Anna Louise Strong.

Assignments for the Roving Reporter

1. After visiting one of the new industrial centers, the reporter writes an article about Russian industry under the Soviets. See "Valiant Russia's Industrial Might," by John Scott, *National Geographic Magazine*, November, 1943. See also *Made in Russia*, by William Chapman White.

2. The reporter, writing about the outbreak of the Russo-Japanese War, sends a dispatch to his paper that describes some of the causes of disagreement and explains the issues involved. See *AP, the Story of the News*, by Oliver Gremling.

3. The reporter writes a biographical article about Stalin for a popular magazine. See "Stalin" in *Men of Power*, by Albert Carr; or in *Rulers of the World*, by Maurice Crain.

Ideas for Your Little Theater

1. Arrange a program of Russian music. Try to secure phonograph records of at least one composition by each of the Russian composers mentioned in your test.

2. Write a short play that dramatizes an incident from the life of Peter the Great, or Tchaikovsky. For information about Peter the Great, see *Famous Men of Modern Times*, by John Haaren and Addison Poland; or *Van Loon's Lives*, by W. H. Van Loon. For information about Tchaikovsky, see *Stormy Victory*, by Claire Lee Purdy; or *Complete Book of the Great Musicians*, by Percy Scholes and Will Earhart.

Candidates for Your Album of Famous People

Alexander I, Alexander II, Catherine the Great, Ivan the Terrible, Lenin, Mendeleyev, Nicholas II, Peter the Great, Rachmaninoff, Stalin, Tolstoy, Trotsky, Tchaikovsky. Select at least three of the people listed above, or mentioned elsewhere in the story of Russia, for biographical portraits in your Album.

INTERESTING READING ABOUT RUSSIA

Compton's Pictured Encyclopedia. "Russia"; and Index.

HINDUS, MAURICE. *Humanity Uprooted.* An interpretation of the methods and results of the Soviets.

——, *Mother Russia.* How the average Russian man and woman lives and works in wartime to make possible the military miracles achieved by the Russian army.

HINDUS, MAURICE. *Green Worlds*. The author writes of his boyhood in Russia, his life as an immigrant to America, and the changes in the two countries during his lifetime.

LENGYEL, EMIL. *Siberia*. " Soviet Asia controls key positions in relation to all the strategical fronts of the world, the only country having such an advantage."

Life Magazine, March 29, 1943. " Special Issue U.S.S.R." " 100,000,000 have learned to read and write."

MARIE, GRAND DUCHESS OF RUSSIA. *The Education of a Princess*. An enthralling autobiography that tells of the childhood, education, and training of a Russian princess, and of her thrilling experiences as a young woman in escaping the Bolsheviks during the Revolution.

MIKHAILOV, NIKOLAS. *Land of the Soviets*. An excellent book of geography that describes the vast country of the U.S.S.R., and the many and varied peoples that live and work together under the new Russian state.

National Geographic Magazine, July, 1942. " Roaming Russia's Caucasus," by Rolf Singer. " The Caucasus is a plant hunter's paradise."

——, December, 1942. " Mother Volga Defends Her Own," by Maynard O. Williams. " There she flows, Russia's Mississippi, which unites the land from snowy pine forest to hot salt desert."

——, May, 1943. " Valiant Russia's Industrial Might," by John Scott. " I saw a city spring from nothing."

——, November, 1943. " I Learn About the Russians," by Eddy Gilmore. " The Russians like to enjoy themselves in a large way."

NEWMAN, E. M. *Seeing Russia*. " Books in abundance but only those which the censor allows."

RUGG, HAROLD. *Changing Civilizations in the Modern World*. Russia; and the Russian people. " Not a village but has ways of its own."

——, *Changing Governments and Changing Cultures*. Russia: New Experiments in Government. " Slowly throughout the huge land, from cities to villages, the spirit of revolt spread."

SKARIATINA, IRINA. *First to Go Back*. A member of the Russian nobility finds strong contrasts between the Russia she knew and the Russia of today.

The Survey Graphic. February, 1944. " American-Russian Frontiers." An analysis of different aspects of Russian life to aid Americans in understanding Russia and the Russian viewpoint.

WHITE, WILLIAM CHAPMAN. *Made in Russia*. The arts, handicrafts, customs, and social life of the Russian people.

WILLIAMS, A. R. *The Soviets*. Eighty-eight questions and answers cover almost all phases of Russian life and government, and make this book a very readable source of information.

The World Book Encyclopedia. " The Story of Russia "; and Index.

PART NINETEEN

ANCIENT CHINA IS STRUGGLING TO BECOME A MODERN NATION

RIA
SAKHALIN
Amur R.
MANCHURIA
MONGOLIA
Vladivostok
Mukden
Sea of Japan
JAPAN
Peiping
Tientsin
HOPEI
CHOSEN (KOREA)
Tokyo
Yellow R. (Hwang Ho)
Yellow Sea
Tsingtao
Suchow
HONAN
NA
Nanking
Shanghai
East China Sea
Hankow
Changsha
KIANGSI
Hengyang
FORMOSA
Canton
Hong Kong
Macao
PACIFIC OCEAN
South China Sea
LUZON
PHILIPPINE ISLANDS
Miles
0 100 200 300 400 500
45°
35°
30°
25°
20°
15°
10°N.
130°E.

China Looks Forward

AND here is the East before you! In the center of the map on the two pages preceding this one you see China Proper, a land of river valleys and mountain ranges. The two greatest river valleys of China are those of the Yellow River in the north and the Yangtze to the south. The Yellow River winds eastward across the dusty rich plain of northern China. In the story which follows you will learn why it has been called " China's Sorrow." In the south-central part trace the Yangtze. It is the waterway to the interior of China.

The southern part of China reaches to the jungle lands of Indo-China. The back door of China is the " roof of the world," the Himalaya Mountains, and the high, bleak plateau of Tibet. On the north are the wind-swept Gobi Desert of Mongolia and the rich lands of Manchuria, from whence came the conquerors who ruled China for centuries.

The long coastline of China is washed by the mighty Pacific. Not far to the East and Northeast lie the islands of the Japanese Empire. You will read in the story which follows of great changes which are taking place in China as it becomes a modern nation. You will read too of the Japanese aggression in China which was one of the first steps toward World War II.

Chapter 1 ~ The Modern World Looks at Ancient China

The history of China reveals an ancient civilization. The story of China begins at the time when ancient civilizations flourished on the banks of the Nile and in the land "between the rivers." But unlike the early civilizations of Egypt and Mesopotamia, China's lives on today. Between two and three thousand years before the birth of Christ, the Chinese nation came into being. Thus China is now about four thousand years old.

For years we people of the Western world — Europe and the Americas — looked upon China as the unchanging giant of the Orient.

It is true that China long remained industrially undeveloped compared to countries of the Western world. But the Chinese have good reason to take profound pride in their ancient civilization. At the time when Caesar landed on the shores of the British Isles and found priests who worshiped under the sacred oaks, the Chinese had already existed as a nation for some two thousand years. They had an organized government, an emperor who believed that the gods expected him to serve his people, a royal library of hundreds of volumes, and many other evidences of a high degree of culture.

When the great Venetian traveler, Marco Polo, returned from China to Italy, in the 13th Century, China had a much higher civilization than any country of Europe. People ate from porcelain dishes instead of wooden platters as in Europe; almost everyone, except the very poorest, had at least one silk gown. In Europe many wealthy people had never seen silk.

China is taking her place among modern nations. China's future may prove to be even more interesting than her glorious past. China is a large country, much larger than the United States. The Chinese people, about 450,000,000 in number, make up one-fifth of the population of the world. China also has vast natural resources, a great part of which are still undeveloped.

You probably know something of the vital part played by China in the world-wide struggle against the Axis in World War II. The war brought the end of certain treaties which had given the Western powers unusual rights in China. They are commonly referred to as extraterritorial rights and gave Western peoples commercial and legal privileges at the expense of China. With the end of these treaties China has been rapidly becoming an independent country, free from Western interference. The Chinese government has also been interested in modernizing China, as well as making her completely independent. Even during the progress of the war China continued to lay large-scale plans for the industrial development of the country. As China does become industrialized and her resources are more fully developed, she will certainly play a major role in Oriental politics, as well as among the nations of the world.

America's interest in China. To Americans the story of China is of particular interest. Though we look more frequently across the Atlantic, from where our heritage of culture has come, our country faces also on the Pacific. The United States has over 1,300 miles of coastline on the Pacific Ocean. Our Ter-

OROC

THE OLDEST ASTRONOMICAL OBSERVATORY IN THE WORLD

This ancient observatory was built on the walls of Peiping by Kublai Khan in the 13th Century. It was looted by the Germans during the Boxer Rebellion, and some of the instruments were later replaced by models.

ritory of Alaska faces the Orient along a combined Arctic and Pacific coastline over 6,000 miles long. And our most important island possessions are in the Pacific. In the past we have bought much from China and, in turn, sold her many things. As China develops industrially and as transpolar flying across the "top of the world" becomes more practical, this trade is likely to expand.

In the past there have been certain barriers to our understanding of China. We can appreciate the history of Europe, for

our forefathers came from "the old country." But the story of China for most of us has been a closed book. The language of the Chinese is strange to us and difficult to learn, their social customs are different from ours, and their land — until the coming of the airplane — has seemed far away. But now that China is taking her place as a modern nation and the world is, in effect, shrinking in size, we are learning more about our great neighbor in the Eastern Hemisphere.

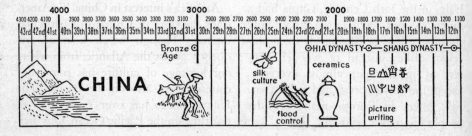

Unfortunately, some Western businessmen in the Orient have in the past been less enlightened or well informed than others, and have shown an attitude of superiority toward Chinese people. Also they have sometimes ruthlessly exploited China's resources. Naturally the cultivated Chinese were quick to resent such treatment, particularly because it was in their own land. Certain of the well-educated and aristocratic Chinese, in their turn, have taken the attitude that the Westerners are a young and barbarous people with nothing to offer the Orient except mechanical skills and industrial and scientific methods. Yet the great bulk of people in China and America have shown considerable good will toward each other, for, as the Chinese philosopher, Confucius, wrote, "Between the four seas all men are brothers."

In order to understand the Chinese better, we shall need to become acquainted with their ancient civilization, to know a few of their major problems, and to understand some of the tremendous trials and changes which China has been going through in becoming a modern nation.

Chapter 2 ~ Geography Set the Stage for the Story of China

Greater China is an immense territory. Greater China is an immense country of over four million square miles which occupies about one-fourth of the continent of Asia. It is larger in area than the United States, Mexico, and Central America together. These statements refer to Greater China. In order not to become confused we must understand the difference between Greater China and the territory within it which is called China Proper.

Five parts make up Greater China. The map on pages 644–645 shows us that Greater China is really made up of five parts or five separate countries, each of which is linked to the others, in various degrees, in history, in culture, and in politics. Foremost is China Proper, which is on the south and east with its long eastern coastline on the Pacific Ocean. To the west of China Proper is the high tableland and mountainous region called Tibet. North of Tibet is China's back door to Europe, the parched desert stretches of a dominion which the Chinese call Sinkiang [sin'kyahng']. East of Sinkiang and north of China Proper is Mongolia with its famous Gobi [goh'bee] Desert and its bleak, windy plains. To the northeast is Manchuria, bordering on the peninsula of Korea, and

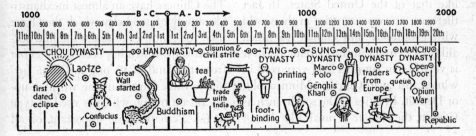

thus bringing China into contact with the Empire of Japan. Manchuria, Mongolia, Tibet, and Sinkiang have served as buffer states, separating China from nations to the west, north, and south.

China Proper is protected by ocean, mountains, and a great wall. It is necessary only that we understand that Greater China is made up of these five main regions. The story which we tell here has to do mainly with that part known as China Proper. The major part of the population of Greater China is found here. Here the great drama of Chinese history has been played and her art and culture developed.

The map on pages 644–645 shows us that the main part of China Proper forms a triangular-shaped land whose curving outer edge is washed by the waters of the Pacific Ocean. On the northeast a chain of mountains and highlands separates China from Mongolia. On the south and west the mighty Himalaya Mountains form a great natural wall separating China from Burma, India, and Tibet. A glance at the map will show that the Great Wall which the Chinese built to keep out the Mongolians on the north is actually a continuation of another wall of mountains. These are the Kun Lun, whose branches stem north and east from the Tibetan plateau, and divide North China from South China. You can see a picture of the Great Wall on page 669.

China is like the United States. The geography of China (Proper) is much like that of the United States. In fact there are no two countries in the world with geography and climate so much alike. In Peiping in the extreme north it is very hot in summer and very cold in winter, just as in Chicago, Minneapolis, or Detroit. In cities of the south, such as Canton, the climate is much like that of Florida. It is never really cold in Canton, though there may be days in February when the evenings are chilly. Western China is much like California, not only in its climate but also in the great variety of its products.

But there is one characteristic of the climate of China which is peculiar and which has had great influence on the country. In all parts of China the winters are very short. This means that the seasons when crops can be planted, cultivated, and harvested are unusually long. That is the reason why in most parts of the country two or more crops per field are grown each year.

China has many natural resources. Much of the forest land of China has been cleared so that the land could be farmed and the wood used for fuel. The unrelenting search for fuel with which to cook is one of the most difficult problems facing the average Chinese.

Many different plants grow in China. From China peaches and oranges were first brought into the Western world, and so were many of our common flowers — azaleas, rhododendrons, and chrysanthemums. The poppy, from which opium is made, has been a social curse as well as a medical blessing to China and to the world. Perhaps the most versatile Chinese plant is the bamboo. Young bamboo shoots can be eaten, and many things can be made from the grown plants: paper, furniture, boats, and even houses.

China's mineral resources are great. The Chinese have an almost inexhaustible supply of good clay which they have used for centuries to make the fine porcelain ware which has been called *china* from the land of its origin. China furnishes three-fourths of the world's supply of antimony, which is used in type metal. Perhaps most important of all

OROC

A Chinese Farmhouse

The life of a Chinese farmer is simple and frugal. The walls of this typical Chinese farmhouse are made of dried mud and the roof is covered with straw. The door of a Chinese house is usually in the longer side of the building, as shown here.

for her industrial future, China has great supplies of coal and iron. And her great rivers, when properly channeled and harnessed, can furnish an abundant supply of water power for the making of cheap electricity.

Besides her farming land, China has another source of food: the waters of China provide large quantities of fish, more than a billion pounds a year. Fishing is important in all parts of China except in the west.

China is an agricultural nation. China is a fertile country and the chief occupation of the Chinese people is farming. About eight-tenths of the Chinese make their living on farms, and every Chinese is very close to the soil in his daily life. Notice the typical Chinese farmhouse pictured above.

Chinese farming is quite different from farming in America. In the first place, a Chinese farm is small. One acre is ample, and it has been estimated that the average Chinese farmer can support himself and his family on two-thirds of an acre. Farming in China is intensive, rather than extensive; it is *subsistence* farming, or farming designed mainly to provide a livelihood for the owner and his family, not to produce quantities of produce for the market.

There are few cattle or large draft animals on Chinese farms. Most of the Chinese eat only vegetables; so they do not depend on animals for food. The livestock of the average Chinese farmer is largely made up of chickens, ducks, geese, and, most important of all, pigs. Pork is the only meat except fowl that millions of Chinese have ever tasted. They say that while cows, horses, donkeys, camels, and mules all have other uses, a pig is fit only for food. Furthermore, many devout Buddhists who would not think of eating beef have no qualms about eating pork. Also, of course, a pig can root for itself or live on scraps and does not require expensive feed. Since the Chinese farms are small, draft animals are not needed. Comparatively few Chinese use animals to haul and carry as do the farmers of Western nations. The cheapest thing in China is human labor. Hence man is the chief carrier of burdens; he can be kept alive with a smaller plot of ground, with a smaller quantity of food, than can horses or cattle. He may toil long, hard hours on his few acres, or he and his son may plod many miles to market with heavy packs strapped to their backs.

China has not had many large industries, and the symbol of wealth in China has been land. If a man had money to invest there was little for him to invest it in except land. For this reason, perhaps, some 30 percent of Chinese farmers are tenants and pay rent in produce to the owners of the land they farm. Other Chinese farmers are owners or part-owners of their land.

North and South China. The two best known parts of China Proper are North China and South China, which are separated by the rugged Ts'in-ling [jee'ling'] Mountains, a branch of the Kun Lun range. Until recent days they have been much more important than the lesser known Western China. North and South China present two entirely different pictures.

North China is a great plain, practically unbroken. The land is fertile, but some of it does not have enough water. The southern part of China is broken up by numerous mountain ranges, some large, some small. Between these mountain ranges are green and fertile valleys which are well watered by many rivers and streams. Much of the mountainside land has been terraced by the Chinese farmer so that it can be cultivated.

The geography of North China and of

J. Jay Hirz

COOLIE LABOR IN SHANGHAI

Coolie labor is the cheapest kind of labor in China. It costs much less to hire a coolie than to feed a horse or to buy fuel for an automobile. Coolie draymen such as these earn only a few cents a day.

South China is so different that the people in these two parts of the country live differently, have unlike problems to meet, and often have different ideas and customs. On the other hand, in many ways they are surprisingly alike. Though they speak different dialects they have the same written language. They know many of the same poems and stories, have the same historical heroes, and have in a general way the same standard of conduct.

Rice eaters are in the South and noodle eaters in the North. The climate as well as the topography of a country causes great differences in the food habits of the people. It is customary to think of Chinese as rice eaters, but there are millions of Chinese who have never seen a grain of rice. The numerous waterways of southern China make possible the growing of rice on the thousands of little terraced fields which are built on the lower slopes of hills surrounding the valleys. Except in a few places rice is not grown north of the Yangtze [yahng'tseh'] River.

The great northern plains are more suited to the growing of wheat, maize, and barley. The result is that while rice is the staple article of diet in the South, it is practically unknown in the North. Barley is eaten there but the most popular food comes from wheat flour. This is eaten in the form of noodles or macaroni. In fact, it is generally believed that the world first heard about noodles and similar dishes from China, when Marco Polo introduced Chinese dishes into Italy.

The Yellow River winds its way through North China. Passengers on ships approaching the coast of China notice that the blue waters of the Pacific have changed their color, becoming a yellowish muddy blue. The change is due to the silt-bearing waters of one of China's great rivers, the Hwang Ho [whahng' hoh'], which finds its way into the Yellow Sea. As the Chinese word for yellow is *hwang,* and for river, *ho,* the name means Yellow River.

This mighty river, with its source in northwestern China, meanders in great bends, first north and then south, through the great plain of North China, until it sweeps eastward to deposit its load of silt in the ocean. The Hwang Ho is like our Mississippi River in some respects. Sometimes it changes its course by miles. Often it breaks through the levees and floods the low farmlands. Then the cruel hand of famine strikes North China and thousands die because crops have been washed away. For this reason the Hwang Ho is sometimes spoken of as "China's Sorrow." Although the Yellow River brings sorrow, it also, like our Mississippi and the Nile of Egypt, brings life to the land through which it flows. It provides water for irrigation and deposits the silt which, after the floods have receded, leaves a deposit of fertile soil. Also in the long history of China, the Yellow River has often been the principal barrier against invaders from the northwest.

You may wonder where this fine yellow soil comes from. The whole plain of North China is covered with it as with a mantle. It is known as loess [loh'es]. The loess gives its yellow hue to all the scenery in North China. During windstorms the air is filled with the fine yellow dust. Buildings, the little mounds marking ancestral graves which dot the fields, the leaves of what few trees there are — all are tinged with the yellow dust of the loess. It is thought that many thousands of years ago, long before the Chinese lived in the land, this peculiar soil was deposited in North

China by great windstorms. These storms, it is said, swept out of Mongolia carrying with them the fine dust-soil, leaving the plains of Mongolia barren and desert-like and covering the plains of North China with a cape of loess. As a traveler who visited this region says —

. . . the most striking difference . . . between Northern and Southern China . . . is the great boundless stretch of yellow loess in the north which blankets every natural feature and which penetrates everything; it forms the soil from which everything grows, it is used to build houses and walls, and when the wind is blowing from the north it fills the air with a yellow fog so dense that one can hardly see.

Wheat, soybeans, and other crops feed the people of North China. The basin of the Hwang Ho, or Yellow River, is crowded with millions of people who live there and who must find food. Signs of the struggle for food are to be seen everywhere. The plains have been cleared of all natural vegetation so that there may be more land for the most common crops — wheat, maize, barley, millet, soybeans, and kaolang or sorghum, a plant which furnishes grain, syrup, and forage. There are no fences to waste useful strips of land and the few roads are likely to be mere paths or deep muddy ruts.

One does not see cows grazing or lambs scampering over green pastures as in our Mississippi Valley. There are mainly chickens, ducks, geese, and pigs. It is true that here in North China there are hardy little horses which carry their riders over the plains. Also there are oxen which pull the heaviest loads and the camels which transport goods into the desert regions. But here as elsewhere in China, human labor is cheap. Men carry packs on their backs or often use a large single-wheeled wheelbarrow up-

on which the load to be carried is skillfully balanced. When the wind is favorable a sail may be hoisted on a makeshift mast and the force of the wind helps push the heavy vehicle. The single wheel of these barrows cuts deep tracks in the soft, dusty loess of the North China plain. The loess is so soft that some old roads in China are worn down to as much as six feet below the surface of the land. You may have seen roads wearing down below the surface of the earth in parts of our Middle West which also have loess soil. The roads in China have been used much longer.

A rough silk is made in North China. Besides food crops, North China, particularly Shantung Province, produces a great deal of silk, though of an inferior quality. The best silk comes from South China, where the mulberry tree is grown. The mulberry tree will not grow in North China, but the silkworms there feed on oak leaves, producing a coarser grade of silk.

The people of North China feared famine and respected government. Even though the flat loess lands in the basin of the Hwang Ho are fertile, the population is so dense here, and the floods so destructive, that the Chinese must work hard in order to avert famine.

North China, as you can see by the map on pages 644–645, touches Mongolia and Manchuria on the north. Vast hordes of conquerors have more than once swept into China from these regions. Because of the geographic location of North China, the people have feared invasions. They have, unlike their southern countrymen, paid a great deal of attention to the art of war. All of the great military leaders of China, up to the present century, came from the north. In fact, Generalissimo Chiang Kai-shek [chyahng′ kai′shek′] was the first Chiese born south of the Yangtze River to become an outstanding military figure.

The peasant farmers of North China throughout the centuries became used to a strong central government. During the centuries that the government of China was in Peking (now Peiping) it held a very firm control on North China but exerted less authority in the southern and western parts of the country. The result was that revolutionary societies flourished in South China and in Western China, but they were rigidly suppressed in the North.

Foreign ideas of all kinds found a less ready acceptance in the North than in the South, for it was far away from such foreign centers as Shanghai and Hong Kong. Chinese from South China are to be found all over the world, but northern Chinese have seldom gone to any foreign countries. The result of this is that North China is much more conservative than South China, and has made less progress.

The Yangtze is one of the world's greatest rivers. Imagine a river valley about three times as large as the state of Texas containing approximately two hundred million people, 50 percent more than live in the United States. Such is the wide valley of the Yangtze-kiang. This mighty river weaves its way for thirty-two hundred miles across southern and central China until it empties into the ocean at the farthest outer curve of the coast of China. Although part of this river is located in South China it marks the division between the civilizations of North and South China.

The Yangtze is the great inland water highway of China. What the Great Lakes, and the Ohio and Mississippi rivers are to the interior of our country, the Yangtze is to China. In fact, the Yangtze is even more important, because

China is not so well supplied with roads and railroads. Ocean-going ships can steam six hundred miles up its course, and the smaller craft can carry their passengers and goods fourteen hundred miles from the sea. Unlike the meandering Yellow River, the Yangtze does not flow on a plain, but along a hard river bed between secure banks and often high bluffs.

Many of China's most important cities are located on the Yangtze. About six hundred miles inland is the busy commercial city of Hankow. It has a population of over one and a half million people. Because of its central location and because it is an important trading center, we may think of Hankow as the Chicago of China. Nanking, less than two hundred miles from the coast, was an important center of government before World War II, and may again become a great administrative center. At the mouth of the Yangtze is the seaport of Shanghai. It is the New York of China and the country's busiest center of trade. Each day, in normal times, dozens of ships from foreign lands arrive at this port with cargoes of Western-made goods, many tons of which are sent into the interior of China by the way of the Yangtze River. Down the Yangtze come vessels laden with the products of China, which are loaded into the steamers at Shanghai and sent to many ports of the world. The amount of tonnage carried by vessels entering and clearing the port of Shanghai is normally about the same as that in New York.

The fertile valleys of southern China are well watered. In North China we found a flat yellow plain upon which winds the Hwang Ho. In South China there are mountains and many valleys, but a total absence of the loess soil which covers the north. The fertile valleys of the South are well watered by many rivers, the greatest of which, we have learned, is the mighty Yangtze, which has several important tributaries. The climate, too, is different from that of North China. The sun is warm, the rains are frequent, and there are no bleak winters to discourage the farmer.

Rice is king in South China. In many shallow swamplike fields the green shoots of the rice plant may be seen. Awkward, fierce-looking water buffaloes slosh along, dragging the farmers' crude cultivators. This useful beast takes the place of the ox, the occasional horse, and the camel of the North. There are few carts or wheelbarrows in South China, for in the South rivers and canals are the roads, and boats are the means of transportation. It is probable that China has more small boats than are to be found in all the rest of the world together. Anyone who travels about the country can readily believe that this is true for he is seldom out of sight of a sail. Of course many of these boats are the flat-bottomed craft which the farmer poles through creeks and canals. Besides boats which are used for transportation, there are many thousands of houseboats which provide dwelling places for the very poor. The boat population of Canton alone is said to number one hundred thousand.

South China has tropical fruits and tea. In this well-watered southern land, famines are not so frequent as on the plains of the Hwang Ho. When famines do occur in the South they are caused by the flooding of a river valley which destroys crops. Transportation in China is still poor and there is great difficulty in sending food from one section to another in order to relieve such a famine when it does occur. In addition to the abundant crops of rice grown in South China, many other products are raised. Tropical fruits are common. Tea plants flourish on the hillsides, furnishing the Chinese with their most cherished drink.

South China produces fine silk. South China is a great silk producing country. The best silk is made from the cocoons of silkworms which have fed on mulberry leaves. The mulberry tree flourishes in South China. So it is South China which has produced the shimmering silks which have made China famous throughout history.

The people of South China have an independent spirit. Just as the geography in the South is different from that of North China, so too are the people and their manner of living. The people of the South are darker than those of the North and have broader noses, perhaps because of their mixture with the neighboring peoples of Malaya and Indo-China.

The southern Chinese have not learned to respect a strong central government as much as the northern Chinese do, although we should realize that the Chinese do not feel about central government as we do. Independent local governments in the villages and cities of the South were long the rule. Hence the southern Chinese developed a spirit of independence which still exists. Often the government in North China, with the capital at Peiping (formerly Peking), tried to control the southern provinces, but such attempts usually failed. Thus the South became more open than the North to new political ideas.

Western China, a little known region. It has been seen that the northern and southern parts of China Proper are separated into two natural divisions by rug-

CNS *Photos*

MING SUNG SHIPYARD

This shipyard is on the Yangtze River at Chungking, capital of the Chinese Republic. At this port the large junks that bring cargoes up the river are unloaded into smaller vessels that can navigate the upper reaches of the river. Land transportation through this mountainous region of Western China is extremely difficult.

ged mountains. A glance at the map will show that a third natural division is found in the West, where high mountain ranges form a barrier, the fringe of a shelf which is marked farther west by the Himalayas. It was over this mountainous country that airplanes operated in World War II, carrying vital cargoes from India into Western China. This is the least known part of China, a part that was formerly looked on by the Chinese the way Russians once looked on Siberia. In the old days of Manchu rule (before the Chinese Republic was founded) an official who was transferred to this area felt that he had been given a death sentence. Western China was a place full of mystery and real or imagined dangers. Some of the dangers were real enough, for on the Burma border there was, and still is, one of the most

dangerous malaria sections in the whole world.

The barrier of mountains, which isolated this part of China from the rest of the country, was to prove of immeasurable benefit to the country in World War II when the Japanese armies began moving westward along the Yangtze. The Chinese government moved to Chungking and established its main armies there. Industries, factories, and even the Chinese universities were transferred there, sometimes piecemeal. Millions of refugees from other parts of the country also moved into this area which in a few months was changed from one of the least important to the most important part of China.

West of the forbidding mountain ranges and east of the higher Himalayas there are several great upland plains, the most famous one being the Red Basin. (See the map, pages 644–645.) It is one of the most fertile spots on earth and is densely populated. The climate is mild and great areas are irrigated by a system of reservoirs and canals built by a famous Chinese engineer more than two thousand years ago. There are no sharp distinctions between the seasons on these upland plains, and several crops a year are grown. It is said that every day in the year seeds are being planted in the Red Basin and crops are being harvested. This plain is about one thousand feet above sea level. Farther to the south is the loftier Yünnan plain, six thousand feet above sea level. It was across Yünnan that the famous Burma Road, China's "life line," wound in World War II.

Western China produces practically everything that is produced in either North or South China: cotton, wool, silk, hemp, ramie (from which grass cloth is made), rice, wheat, corn, sugar cane, oranges, apples, peaches. Fishing is not important here as it is in other parts of China, but the district is famous for its own breed of pigs. An abundant supply of food is produced in normal times.

Largely because they could not find a market for their surplus crops the farmers of this area many years ago turned to the growing of opium, for that drug sells for a very high price and is easily transported. The Chinese government has made a successful attempt to stamp out the opium traffic with the result that the growth of the opium poppy had practically ceased until the Japanese, during World War II, attempted to spread the opium habit more widely.

With the establishment of the Chinese government in Chungking, a great deal of attention has been paid to the development of this hitherto neglected area. Highways over which it is possible to drive a car have been built, crude airfields have been laid out, and a start has been made in the building of railways. As Japanese forces threatened the coast a great many factories were moved to the vicinity of Chungking and other new factories constructed. From being the most backward and isolated section of the country, Western China is very gradually becoming somewhat modernized.

Workmen, tradespeople, and merchants live in the Chinese cities. Many of the centers of population in China are walled cities. In recent years the walls of some cities have been torn down to make room for motor roads. Although the cities differ in some respects, each is typically Chinese. In the coastal or river cities there is usually a water front with its mass of boats. Small shops where whole families live, work, and trade, and large business houses owned by wealthy merchants and filled with the art and wealth of China may be seen in all cities. In a few are located foreign sections in which people from the Occident live and carry on their official and business affairs much as they would in their own countries.

Chapter 3 ~ The Chinese Have Sought Security from Foreign Exploitation and Civil Strife

Changing China. In relating the story of many of the nations, such as England or France, we have traced the main thread from earliest times down to the present. We shall not attempt to present the story of China in this way. The account of four thousand years of changing rulers with ideas and names strange to us of the Western world would be unnecessarily confusing. But modern China is being built on the foundations of ancient Chinese civilization. Thus we should know something about the last of the Chinese dynasties and the way in which it came to be overthrown.

Manchu invaders founded a dynasty. The natives of Mongolia and Manchuria are not settled farmers like the Chinese, but are nomadic and make their living by herding sheep and cattle. They have more than once invaded China, in spite of the Great Wall which the Chinese built about 200 B.C. to keep them out. (See map, pages 644–645.) The Manchurians, or Manchus, conquered China in the 17th Century and ruled it until they were overthrown by revolution in 1911. Throughout all these years the Manchus remained separate from the Chinese people they ruled. They had their own laws and special privileges. The Manchu government was naturally not popular with the people. By the middle of the 19th Century it had grown corrupt and indifferent. There were numerous revolts against it. In the greatest of these, the Tai-ping Rebellion, millions of people on both sides of the conflict were killed by violence and butchery.

The Western world made demands on China. The Chinese had had little contact with the Western world except through the Dutch, Spanish, and Portuguese seamen, who had first gone to China to trade in the 16th Century. Then in the 19th Century, when China was going through these disturbances at home, the West again knocked at her gates. She found herself faced by the demands of the great Western powers who wanted territory or greater trading privileges in China. Twice in the latter half of the 19th Century China found herself at war with Great Britain over trade rights. For one thing, British merchants insisted on trading in opium in China, although the Chinese wished to forbid such trade. In both these wars China was defeated and forced to yield to Britain's demands. Other nations did not wish to be left behind in the race to secure advantages in China Proper or in Greater China. The French established an empire in Indo-China. In the 20th Century Russia was given land in Manchuria which she wanted for the ice-free port of Vladivostok [vlah'di vos tok']. To Russia, France, Germany, and the United States China granted the right to trade in certain ports called "treaty ports." Some ports were leased to the foreigners. Foreigners even controlled Chinese tariffs, or tax payments on imports, in order to guarantee payment of loans which they had made to the Chinese.

China itself began to be divided into "spheres of influence." One of the great powers, such as France, Britain, or Ger-

Philip D. Gendreau, N. Y.

THE BUND — SHANGHAI

Shanghai is the principal port of central China. It became an open treaty port in the middle of the 19th Century, and British, French, and American foreign settlements were established there. This photograph shows the famous Bund, or embanked thoroughfare which runs along the river frontage of the foreign settlements.

many, would ask for all the commercial concessions such as railroads, mines, and so on, in a given province.

Japan took Korea. China was also faced by the demands of her Oriental neighbor, Japan. For hundreds of years the Japanese had been coming as pirates to the coast of China. They had first invaded Korea, or Chosen, in the 16th Century. In 1894 they waged war on China and took Korea for themselves. As a result of this war the Chinese were also forced to give up the island of Formosa to Japan.

The Boxer Rebellion was put down by Western nations. Naturally all these foreign inroads were resented by the Chinese. Some of the Chinese leaders thought that the country should be modernized so that China could hold her own with foreign nations. Others wanted to cling to old ways, strengthen the army, and drive the foreigners out. Some of the latter group formed a secret society called "Boxers," which mobbed and looted and killed the foreigners. The Boxer Rebellion (1900) was put down only by the combined forces of the Western nations in China.

The United States insisted on an "Open-Door" Policy. After the Boxer Rebellion the United States objected to China's granting any further rights or privileges to foreign powers. The United

States insisted that, except for privileges already given, all foreign nations were from then on to receive the same treatment in China. Partly because the great powers could not come to any other agreement with one another about their different claims in China, they agreed to this policy of the United States, which was called the "Open-Door" policy.

The Manchu dynasty came to an end. In 1911 a revolution broke out which changed the whole course of Chinese history. It brought the Manchu dynasty (the last of the many dynasties in China) to an end. Then a Chinese republican government was set up. Sun Yat-sen, who was called the "father of the revolution," was chosen as its first president. The republican government did not succeed in winning control over the whole country, however, and in about a year it collapsed.

Japan interfered in China's government. For about fifteen years after the collapse of this short-lived republican government, China was ruled by so-called warlords, men who kept up their own private armies and controlled various parts of the country while they contended with each other for more power. Although the world was not aware of it at the time, the Japanese had long been laying plans to gain complete control of China, and they helped to keep China weak and disorganized by lending money to the warlords and supplying them with arms.

In 1915 World War I was being bitterly fought on various battlefronts in Europe, and Japan saw this would be a strategic time for her to act in China. She believed that the great powers were so occupied with the European war that they would not dare risk further trouble by interfering with her. As a result, she presented to the Chinese govern-

Thomas Kwang, Chungking
Paul Guillumette, Inc. Agents

SUN YAT-SEN

Sun Yat-sen was an ardent worker for the establishment of the Chinese Republic. In private life he was a doctor, with a practice in Canton. After an unsuccessful attempt at revolution he was exiled, but returned to China and became first provisional president of the Chinese Republic founded after the revolution of 1911.

ment a list of Twenty-one Demands. Acceptance of these demands would have given Japan complete control of China's finances, customs service, and foreign policy. The huge country of China would have become a mere colony under complete domination by Japan. The United States and Great Britain brought pressure on Japan and some of the Japanese demands were withdrawn. But Japan continued to plot and wait for a favorable opportunity to seize control of all or a part of China's territory.

The "People's Party" set up the Nationalist Government. Sun Yat-sen had organized the first genuine political party in China, the Kuomintang [kwoh-min tahng] or "People's Party." In 1925 this party had established a provisional or temporary government in Canton. This government was in control of several southern provinces, while various warlords controlled different sections of the North and West. The chief aim of the Kuomintang was to unify the country under its one Chinese government.

With that object in view the party started a military expedition commanded by General Chiang Kai-shek. The expedition marched against the northern warlords with remarkable success. This success was largely owing to the fact that the Kuomintang had popular support. The armies of the warlords had been fairly well disrupted by Kuomintang political propaganda. During 1927 the power of the warlords was crushed in a large part of the country. But north of the Yangtze-kiang, the progress of the Nationalist troops was delayed by Japanese armies. Some provinces of North China the troops could not bring under the control of the Kuomintang. To do so would have meant all-out war with Japan. The Kuomintang decided to pause for awhile, with its present gains, and strengthen its position. It set up in Nanking a government called the Nationalist Government. It controlled the most important provinces in the country. This government was immediately recognized by most of the great powers. It is a government of one party, the Kuomintang. You will recall that Russia also has a one-party government.

Sun Yat-sen, the founder of the Nationalist movement had died in 1925, and the leadership of the party passed to Generalissimo Chiang Kai-shek. Chiang's power was based partly on the army, but he managed to hold together many different types of people in sup-port of the Nationalist Government. This government got under way an ambitious program for the economic development of China, and began to build highways, railways, and bridges, and to improve the waterways. During the Manchu rule the officials had stolen the public funds. Later the warlords had done the same thing. Now for the first time the Chinese people saw their money being spent for the public benefit.

The "Mukden Incident" was Japan's excuse for the seizure of Manchuria. You will recall that Japanese interference had kept the Chinese Nationalist armies from entering northeastern China and bringing that territory under the Kuomintang. But some of the people in northeastern China wanted union with the Nationalist Government. The Japanese, who did not want a strong and united China, forbade the Chinese warlord who ruled northeastern China to bring about such a union with the rest of his country. In 1929 this warlord defied the Japanese by coming to an agreement with the Kuomintang, acknowledging its authority, and raising the Nationalist flag. For two years the Japanese debated among themselves as to whether they were prepared for war. The time seemed opportune. A great financial depression which began in 1929 had seriously affected the Western nations. They were hardly in a position to try to stop Japan's aggression in China; perhaps they would look the other way. So in 1931 the Japanese sent troops into northeast China. Then by a manufactured incident they provoked an open war.

On the excuse that Chinese troops stationed in Mukden had mutinied and attempted to derail a Japanese railway train which ran through northeastern China, Japanese troops occupied that city and in a few days were in complete possession of Manchuria. This was in clear violation of a number of treaties in which Japan had pledged herself to respect the sovereignty and territorial integrity of China. The Chinese government laid the case before the League of Nations and an international commission found Japan guilty of aggression. Japan refused to accept the decision and withdrew from the League.

Japan set up a puppet government in Manchuria. Japan's next step was to set up a puppet government in Manchuria. It was a pretext or front, behind which the Japanese could conveniently control. Manchuria was renamed Manchukuo [mahn'joh'kwoh']. The Japanese placed a figurehead on the throne: Pu Yi, the last Manchu emperor, who had been forced to give up the throne of China by the revolution of 1911. Manchukuo was governed by the Japanese army, which used it as a sort of cat's-paw to take more territory from China. Japanese troops, wearing the uniforms of Manchukuo, entered the Chinese province of Jehol [reh'hoh'] and attached it to Manchukuo. Officials of the Chinese government were fully aware of Japan's plans to conquer their country, if possible. But at this time they did not dare carry on an all-out war with Japan. It was impossible to send troops to back up those in northeastern China without leaving the whole coastline of China undefended and open to Japanese attack. So from 1931 on, the Chinese and Japanese carried on a limited war on Chinese territory. During the course of this limited war the Japanese seized other lands in North China. Furthermore, the Chinese were forced into a number of humiliating agreements. Popular anger against Japan was rising, and the government continued to make preparations

for defense. Japan, on her side, continued to pile up stocks of scrap iron and other war materials, much of which she purchased from Western nations. Also, Japan interfered in every possible way with the economic development of China. By 1935 all-out war in the Far East appeared to be inevitable.

China suffered from disunity at home. In the meantime China was not yet completely united. The Nationalist party itself was divided into two factions, conservative and radical. Besides, some thousands of Chinese Communists refused to recognize the Nanking government and set up the Chinese Soviet Republic in the province of Kiangsi [jyahng'see']. There was conflict between the Chinese Red Armies and the Nationalist Government from the time the Nanking Government was founded until 1937. Then all parties made all-out war against the Japanese invader.

Great problems face modern China. Great problems face China in the future. One of them is the achievement of real political unity and national solidarity after the Japanese invaders have been driven from her country. The present government of China is only a provisional or temporary one. Had it not been for the war, a constitutional convention, representing all the different parties of China, would have met in 1939 to set up a constitutional government. Other great problems are those relating to raising the living standard of the country, and to developing China's resources by the use of modern industry.

China faces a severe problem in providing food for her people. You have doubtless heard of the great famines which from time to time have taken the lives of thousands or millions of the Chinese. Even in ordinary times the vast majority of the people in China have barely enough to live on. Hunger is common and starvation the lot of thousands.

You may wonder how such conditions have come about in a country which has such vast resources as China. In the first place, a great part of China's cultivable land, like her other resources, has not been fully developed and used. Some 75 percent of China's 450,000,000 people are crowded into 15 percent of the land surface of China. Farming families have tended to concentrate in five fertile areas in eastern China. A single great river flood can wipe out the crops and means of livelihood of hundreds of thousands of people. If this does happen, transportation in China is still so inadequate that food cannot be brought in in sufficient quantities to relieve the situation. Surplus food might, for instance, be spared for some districts in northern China from the tableland of Western China, which has an abundance. But the mountains form an impassable barrier. Food cannot be brought in easily.

People have congregated in the lowlands partly because the Chinese rulers in the past have not protected their people from civil war and brigandage. People have abandoned upland villages because they did not feel safe in them. Animal husbandry has been neglected, partly because the farmers did not care to live in outlying districts with sufficient grazing land around them to support sheep or cattle. It was safer to cling together. Then, China's government in the past has also discouraged animal husbandry by placing heavy taxes on movable property. All in all, the people have preferred to crowd together and run the risk of recurring famine.

Stable government, law and order, freedom from foreign invasion and interference, an improved transportation system, and education in new methods of living and working are necessary if the great resources of China are to be used as they should be to support her people properly.

The Chinese leaders are naturally anxious to solve these problems. The Chinese government has been working on a plan of reconstruction that will give the people more food and raise the standard of living. Great progress has been made and the work has been continued in spite of the war, which has disrupted transportation and in every way tended to make the food problem more severe. The farmers have been made more prosperous by the building of crude but passable highways over which their surplus products can be carried to market by motor trucks. Many thousands of acres of land have been irrigated. Other thousands of acres have been protected from the ravages of floods. Swamplands have been drained. Farmers are being taught better methods of cultivating the soil and supplied with better seeds. In some places the production has been increased as much as 15 percent. If that could be done all over the country, it would give China a huge food surplus. Besides these plans to increase farm production the Chinese government is planning to establish a great many industries which will give employment to the laborers who are not necessary on the farms. China's problems are vast and complicated and we cannot expect all of them to be solved overnight. Only a beginning has been made, and much remains to be done if great suffering and unrest are to be avoided in postwar China. But if the plans of the government can be carried out, even in part, China will be able to support her population and raise the standard of living.

Industry demands capital. Since China has not been an industrialized country, her private citizens do not have money to finance large industries. Therefore most of the heavy industries such as steel-making, and the railroads, and public utilities, such as electricity and tele-phones, have been owned by the govern-ment. The so-called "light" industries are left to private capital to finance.

In the future when China carries to completion the tremendous construction projects she now has under way, she will need to look to foreign countries for the capital to finance them.

It is important, however, that China's resources and industries be developed to the best interest of the Chinese them-selves. An independent, stable China, with an opportunity to develop her gov-ernment along more democratic lines, is important to the peace and welfare of the world. Thus the interest of Western nations in China will continue to be active. Moreover, China's postion in the Orient and in the world is of utmost im-portance to other nations as well as to herself.

Chapter 4 ~ China, the Nation of Long Life, Has Built a Remarkable Civilization

A Chinese sees himself as a link in an unbroken family chain. In China, the family is considered all-important. If we can come to understand the feeling that the Chinese have for their families, we can begin to appreciate many of their customs and attitudes. A Chinese father thinks of himself as but another link in an endless chain. Before him have lived his honorable ancestors. It is his duty, while they are alive, to respect and obey them, and when they are dead he reveres their memory. After him, if fortune smiles by bringing sons into the family, the unbroken family chain will continue forever. When he has finished his days on earth, the Chinese father believes that he will join the host of ancestors.

It is common to refer to this feeling of the Chinese as "ancestor worship," but many missionaries say that such an expression is wrong. A few Chinese may believe that the ghosts of dead ancestors exert a powerful influence on the lives and fortunes of the living descendants.

But for many others the simple rites which they observe at the ancestral shrine might be compared to our ob-servance of Memorial Day when we place flowers on the graves of the dead.

Duties toward the living family. The duties toward the living are clearly stated in the classics of Master Kung, or Confucius, the Sixth-Century Chinese sage whom you read about in the story of religions. First there was the emperor, to whom the highest respect was due. Next came one's parents, particularly the father, or, if living, the grandfather. Next in order came the elder brother; then the wife; and finally, one's friend. This strict order of duties became firmly fixed in Chinese thinking, even in the customs of the lowest and most ignorant classes of people. Centuries have passed; China has seen rulers come and go, but, owing to the deep respect of the Chinese for their obligations to family and friends, they have remained one people, even when disunited politically.

New York Times

A MODERN CHINESE GIRL

This Chinese girl guerrilla fighter typifies the spirit of young China in its heroic resistance against the Japanese invaders.

We in the Western world also respect our parents and friends, but in China the customs which result are different from ours. If there were a famine, we should first care for the children. In China, the old grandfather is given his grain or rice, even though the younger members of the family go hungry.

The Chinese family does not consist, as does the American family, of a father and mother and children. It includes brothers, sisters, nephews, nieces, uncles, and aunts — in fact everyone of the same blood. According to a code which has prevailed for many centuries these relatives share their prosperity and their misfortunes. The code has been expressed in a single phrase: " Contribute all you can, take only what you must." In almost every community in America we know of families which have poor members and prosperous ones. A situation like that is rarely found in China, where a man who is prosperous considers it his duty to take care of his less fortunate relatives.

The family is more important than the individual to the Chinese. China's solidarity of family life has contributed to her strength and prepared her for the united front that she has shown in her long and bitter resistance to Japanese aggression.

The place of women in the Chinese family. If the first-born is a male child, there is great rejoicing, for it means that the family name is being carried forward into another generation. From her birth a girl is looked upon as only a temporary member of her family, since she will marry and become a member of her husband's family, and will train her sons to revere their father's ancestors.

Chinese girls are taught to be good cooks, housekeepers, and seamstresses, to be thrifty, obedient, diplomatic, and good-natured. When a girl is old enough to be married her family provides her with a dowry and arranges a suitable match for her. (Two persons with the same family names never marry because they are presumed to be related.) The bride then enters the home of her husband's parents to do her part in the work of the household along with their other daughters-in-law and perhaps some young daughters, too. With so many young women working together in a household it is probably just as well that tradition decrees that the mother, or the grandmother in the household, if she is living, shall do the directing and give the orders.

All business problems concerning any member of a Chinese family are discussed in the traditional Chinese household. Until recent years women did not take direct part in business, but they did take part in family discussions and decisions. And there have always been old grandmothers who were the real rulers of the family.

Women are winning new places in Chinese life. When Chinese women, under the influence of the Western ways, finally began to go into business, their acceptance was rapid. China is one of the few countries in the world today which has women bankers. There are also many women doctors and lawyers. The more able and educated Chinese women have, in the past few years, been able to follow careers. When constitutional government is established the women of China expect to be allowed to vote.

Training in tolerance. The average Chinese is peace-loving and friendly. With wife, father, elder brothers, sisters, sisters-in-law, and numerous other relatives to satisfy, the Chinese man has learned the art of keeping peace. It has been only by tolerance that big families have been able to live together in peace. So tolerance has become an outstanding national characteristic.

The Chinese value personal dignity. Every Chinese places a great deal of importance on what is called "face," that is, his appearance before the world. This attitude is really quite easily understood. A Chinese is keenly conscious of his own personal dignity as a man. He dislikes above everything else to be publicly humiliated. In other words, a Chinese has a supreme desire to maintain his own self-respect and the esteem of his associates. This applies to all ages and all classes. Thus a teacher will seldom reprimand a scholar before others. When it is necessary to replace an official he is usually sent on a vacation. He takes the hint and does not return.

Ancient superstitions are now passing away. The Chinese have been a very superstitious people, but with education, the influence of Christian missionaries, and contact with Western science, many of the old superstitions are fast disappearing. They are still preserved in architecture, however. On the eaves of roofs will be seen sharp barbs, placed there to ward off evil spirits who might otherwise get into the building. Screens are often erected before temple doors and the doors of homes, so that the spirits, which are believed to travel only in straight lines, cannot enter. For the same reason bridges across streams in ornamental gardens are often built in a zigzag fashion.

The Chinese look forward to their festival days. Of all their festivals, the Chinese New Year's Day is most enthusiastically celebrated. Then long, wriggling dragons are carried through the streets, and firecrackers are set off. The Chinese invented these noisemakers to use on their festival days. Colored paper lanterns, feasts, and processions mark the occasion. There are many other festival days, such as the Feast of the Lanterns, Dragon Festival, Moon Festival, and the celebrations marking the seasons of the year. Even the birth of a son or the funeral of a relative who has joined his honored ancestors is celebrated in a way which is difficult for a Westerner to appreciate. Yet it is not hard to understand how a people who must toil so long and hard should look forward to their festival days. Christmas is widely observed in China although there are only perhaps twelve million Christians there, very few compared to the total population. Many non-Christian Chinese join in the celebration of Christmas because it gives them another holiday to celebrate.

SOME ANCIENT GEMS OF CHINESE WISDOM

If you love your son, give him plenty of the cudgel; if you hate your son, cram him with dainties.

The best cure for drunkenness is, whilst sober, to observe a drunken man.

Modesty is attended with profit; arrogance brings on destruction.

Let every man sweep the snow from before his own doors, and not trouble himself about the frost on his neighbor's tiles.

Learning without thinking is labor lost; thinking without learning is perilous.

He who overcomes others is strong; he who overcomes himself is mightier still.

A gem is not polished without rubbing nor a man perfected without trials.

Rewards and punishments are the lowest form of education.

A nation of joiners. The Chinese are ardent joiners. Guilds, tongs, chambers of commerce, and societies of many kinds abound. Many of these groups probably had their beginning in the strong family ties of ancient China. But in modern times these family groups have broadened their membership. Now it is the labor unions and the merchants' chambers of commerce that are most common. And we have described the Kuomintang, one of the most important of present-day organizations.

China has been opening public schools. The great majority of the Chinese people cannot read or write. The Manchu dynasty, which ruled the country until 1911, did not provide any public-school system, and only the well-to-do could afford to send their children to private schools.

The present Chinese government has ambitious plans for a school system which will provide an education for everyone. Even during the struggle with the Japanese invaders in World War II, the government made great progress in educating the people and in reducing the number of those who could not read or write.

The scholar is honored in China. Many of the Chinese have not been able to have an education, but there is no country where scholarship is more highly honored. The Chinese divide society into five classes: the scholars, the farmers, the skilled craftsmen, the merchants and businessmen, and the soldiers. The introduction of factories and industrial managers has somewhat changed this classification. Yet the scholar is still looked upon with utmost respect. For generations in China the scholar has held important governmental positions. It was he who preserved the ancient learning.

To become a scholar was a serious undertaking. Any who could qualify, no matter of how lowly birth, might make the attempt. Many Chinese families

OROC

THE GREAT WALL OF CHINA

The Great Wall of China winds over mountains and across valleys for more than fifteen hundred miles. It was built over two thousand years ago to protect China against the warlike Mongolians.

early selected their most promising son. He was excused from manual labor and given every advantage in the home. By long, intensive study the young man prepared himself for the government examinations. He had to become master, not of the sciences and mathematics, but of the ancient classics of Confucius and other great Chinese writers. Then came the grueling five-day examination. To prevent dishonesty, each student was assigned a cell-like room where he must work alone. The successful candidates found government positions awaiting them.

Since China has taken the form of a republic, the old-fashioned examinations have been abolished. A more modern civil service examination is being developed, in which less attention will be paid to classical literature and more to modern sciences. The scholar, however, whether he be a master of the ancient

classics or a returned student from a foreign university, is still highly respected. Students, as future scholars, share this public respect.

Chinese literature is filled with the wisdom of the ages. In the story of religions, you were told about the Chinese sage, Confucius. That story will not be retold here. Even before the time of Confucius (about 500 B.C.) there were great Chinese thinkers who, by their teachings and writings, tried to explain the life of man and nature. Unlike the ancient Greeks, the Chinese did not care to speculate about philosophy or science. They have always been more concerned with practical ethics and the problems of everyday life. They delight in short sayings or proverbs. These bits of wisdom, drawn from the classic literature, are often heard in conversation. Read the quotations given on page 668. Some of them may seem familiar to you.

OROC

PAVILION NEAR PEIPING

This massive pavilion stands in the gardens of the Summer Palace near Peiping. Note that the roof with ornate eaves is the most outstanding feature of the building.

In China, architecture begins with a wall. We have learned that many of China's cities are surrounded by walls. In fact, the same Chinese word is used for *city* and *city wall*. In some cities, as in Peiping (formerly Peking), there are walls within walls. Sometimes these walls are mere mounds of dried mud built about a small village. Sometimes they are massive structures which tower far above the single-story Chinese houses which they shelter. Ornamental gates allow passage into the city at well-guarded points. The most famous structure in all China is the Great Wall of China. The Great Wall is like a continuous massive fort, about fifteen hundred miles in length. Straightened out, it would reach from Washington, D.C., to Denver, Colorado. The wall is from twenty to thirty feet high in most places

and wide enough to allow for a roadway along its top. It is really two walls made of huge bricks, filled in between with earth and broken stone. The top was paved with bricks. Every few hundred yards a tall, square tower rises. On the top, signal fires were kept ready. Soldiers used to be stationed in these towers to pass on an alarm from one tower to another and to defend the wall when attacked. On page 669 you will see a photograph of the enormous handmade fortification, which runs like a ribbon across mountains and valleys in North China.

Temples, public buildings, and bridges. The temples and public buildings are usually single-story structures, rectangular in shape. They are often set well back on a terrace. A beautiful marble stairway with a carved stone balustrade on each side may lead up the terrace to the temple. The roofs of Chinese buildings are their most noticeable feature. These roofs are sometimes double or triple, and are made of bright-colored, glazed tiles. Often the sides of the roofs curve upward. It is said that these curving roofs may have developed from the curve of the tents in which early Chinese tribes probably lived. A fine example of these graceful roof styles may be seen in the illustration above.

Clay and wood are the most widely used building materials. For this reason, there are few buildings in China more than a hundred years old. But the style of architecture is old, for when a new building is put up or an old one rebuilt it is usual to copy the old designs.

A black-and-white photograph cannot give the brilliant coloring which a Chinese building presents to the eye. The pagodas, or towerlike temples, also show upturned roofs and lavish ornaments. A pagoda is either six- or eight-sided and always of an odd number of stories.

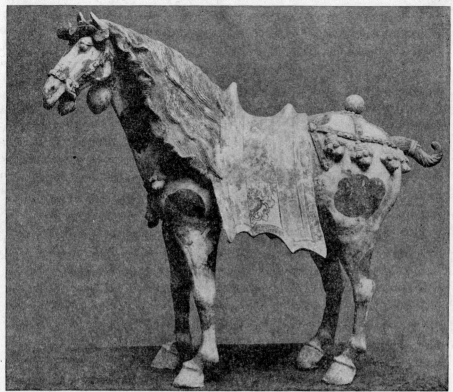

Metropolitan Museum of Art

A T'ANG HORSE

This statue of a horse was fashioned during the T'ang Dynasty, which ruled in China through the years A.D. 618–906. Sculpture of the early T'ang period is considered the most perfect kind of Buddhist sculpture in China.

The arts and crafts of China are varied. The artists and craftsmen of China work with many materials. A beautiful hard stone, called jade, is brought from the mountains of Western China. With long, painstaking labor and the crudest of tools, it is fashioned into a vase, earrings, or perhaps a squat Buddha. The velvety softness and smoothness to the touch of finished jade is said to please the Chinese as much as beautiful line or color. Chinese place a higher value on a rare piece of jade than on a diamond.

The Chinese are skilled in embroidery and other needlework. Chinese cabinetmakers have produced beautiful cabinets with a highly polished lacquer finish. This lacquer may be of brilliant red or glossy black and gold. Rich Chinese rugs of shimmering colors; green and bronze bowls, bells, or statues; and gracefully formed vases in brilliant blues or deep reds can now be bought in practically any large city in the world.

Chinese sculpture. Among the early forms of Chinese sculpture were little figures constructed of clay. These were placed in tombs, in much the same way that the Egyptians buried little figures with their dead. Later, sculptors worked in wood or stone. Figures of priests and Buddhas, animals or goddesses, were favorite subjects. Some of the stone statues were huge in size. A few of the large stone statues made in the Seventh Century had human bodies but the heads of beasts. Such statues were symbols of strength, like the human-animal statues of Mesopotamia. The Chinese also made portrait statues, as fine as those of the Romans, and little statues of spirited horses, which you may have seen in a museum or shop window.

Chinese painting. In the Sixth Century before Christ, at the time of Confucius, Lao-tze, and other great Chinese philosophers, temple walls in Western China were being decorated with animated wall paintings. The subjects and styles of Chinese painting varied greatly through the changing centuries. Religious subjects, flowers, birds, bamboo plants, monkeys, horses, and dragons, beautiful women, scenes of family and household life, and landscapes, all inspired the paintings of Chinese artists. The Chinese word for landscape means mountain and water. The lofty mountains and tumbling waterfalls are featured in many Chinese landscapes. The landscape painting of South China, from the 10th to the 13th Centuries, is thought by many people to be the most remarkable Chinese painting of all. Such paintings place China among the most accomplished nations of the world in the fine arts.

China, the Undying Nation, Built a Remarkable Culture

China is almost four thousand years old. In the 13th Century her civilization was far ahead of European civilization. But while younger nations were developing from feudalism toward the modern industrialism, China remained unchanged and unmodern, except as she was exploited by Westerners. The United States has strong interest in this enormous, ancient nation because both nations have a Pacific coastline.

China Proper is somewhat like the United States in geography and in climate, and has many natural resources awaiting development. Most of the 450,000,000 Chinese make their living on small farms. North China is a fertile plain; South China is divided by mountains into valleys, where rice is grown in terraced fields. The inhabitants of the two regions differ in dialect and in customs. Through North China flows the famous — and infamous — Yellow River, which is helpful for irrigation and for depositing fertile soil, but which overflows and washes away crops. The yellow soil of the loess region is another characteristic of North China. Rough silk is produced in the north; in South China the finer silk is made. The division between the two sections is formed by mountains and by the Yangtze River, the great inland waterway on which the cities of Hangkow, Nanking, and Shanghai are located.

Mountain ranges shut off the western region of China. Its remoteness from Japan has made it a refuge for the seat of the government. Chungking replaced Peiping as capital of China in the war with Japan which began in 1937. Universities and industrial plants also have been moved into this region.

The Dutch, Portuguese, and Spaniards were the first to open up trade with China in the 16th Century. The Western world again knocked at the gates of China in the middle of the 19th Century. At that time the Chinese were engaged in revolts against the corrupt and indifferent Manchu dynasty, which did not put up a strong resistance against the foreigners. The Western powers obtained leases, treaty ports, and important trading concessions within China and tended to divide it into spheres of influence. For hundreds of years the Japanese had been coming as pirates to the coast of China. In 1894, Japan fought China and took Korea.

The Boxer Rebellion of 1900 was an unsuccessful attempt by the Chinese to drive out the foreigners and return to the old ways. After the Boxer Rebellion the United States proclaimed the Open-Door Policy in China. In 1911 the Manchu dynasty was overthrown by revolution and a short-lived republican government set up. It soon fell, however, before the quarrels of contending warlords. During World War I Japan presented Twenty-One Demands on China which would have reduced her to a huge colony of Japan's. Only through the insistence of Great Britain and the United States were these demands modified.

In 1925 Dr. Sun Yat-sen's People's Party, or the Kuomintang, which was the first political party in China, set up a provisional government. In 1927 this Nationalist government was recognized by most of the great powers. It did not have the support of all China, however. The Nationalist government and the Chinese Red Army fought with each other until they were forced to unite against the Japanese. In 1931 Japan seized Manchuria from China, set up a puppet government there, and used Manchuria as a pretext to seize other Chinese territory. The Nationalist government built up its defenses. Finally the Nationalist Army and the Chinese Red Army fought the Japanese invaders. The outbreak of World War II made China a partner with the other nations united against the Axis.

Even during China's bitter, long struggle with Japan the Nationalist government under the leadership of Chiang Kai-shek, carried on its extensive plans and projects for industrializing China, building roads, improving agriculture, raising the living standard of the people, and providing public education. Two other great problems faced China for the future: that of uniting her conflicting parties in a unified constitutional government, and that of obtaining the needed foreign capital for the building of industry.

Respect for family, present and past, rather than for the individual marks the Chinese civilization. Women, traditionally confined to a narrow domestic life, have only recently been permitted to enter business and professional pursuits. As a whole, the Chinese are a tolerant people. Traditional festivals fill their calendar. Scholars are honored; but before the period of the present Republic, little was done to decrease the widespread illiteracy of the masses.

Confucius is one of the great men of China, — a philosopher whose teachings have been a force in Chinese life since 500 B.C. Walls, pagodas, and bridges figure prominently in Chinese architecture. Chinese craftsmen and artists work with jade, make exquisite silk embroidery, and weave brilliantly colored rugs. Among the favorite subjects of Chinese sculptors are figures of the Buddha, goddesses, and spirited horses and other animals. Chinese paintings — particularly the water colors of Chinese waterfalls and woods — create an unforgettable impression of beauty even in a Westerner's senses.

SELF–TEST

Complete the following statements. Look back upon the story of China's ancient civilization by trying this self-test.

I. Chang was born in Northern China, that part of China covered with the fertile yellow soils known as ——. His father was a ——, like most of his fellow countrymen. The waters of Northern China's greatest river, the ——, furnished the irrigation for the crops of ——, ——, or ——. But that was long ago in Chang's youth, for a great —— of the mighty —— River had washed away his father's crops and brought famine and death to his family. Chang, with his sister and mother, had escaped to Southern China. There he, too, had become a farmer raising —— in —— fields. The great river of Southern China, the ——, served as a water highway into China for hundreds of miles inland from the broad Pacific. At its mouth was the port of Shanghai and along its course were important cities such as —— and ——. Chang was proud of his country. The foreigners whom he saw in the river cities dressed so peculiarly and acted so strangely that he wanted to laugh. But many of these foreigners also respected China because they knew her civilization extended back for about —— years. Although Chang was not well educated, he knew many bits of wisdom that he had learned from his parents. Chang, of course, could not read the classic writings of the great philosopher, ——.

II. The last of the changing groups of rulers or —— in China were the —— who conquered China in the 17th Century. Under these unpopular rulers, there were numerous ——. At this time the great —— powers demanded special privileges in China, and were granted the right to trade in certain ports. These were known as —— ports. The Chinese who objected to these concessions started the —— ——, which was crushed in 1900. The United States insisted on the —— —— policy in China. In 1911 the Manchu dynasty was overthrown, and a republic founded, with —— —— —— as its first president. The first political party in China was called —— —— ——, or ——. Japanese aggressions began in 1931 with the seizure of ——, which Japan renamed ——. The Chinese Republic was not unified. There was friction between the conservative Nationalists and the ——. When Japan invaded China in 1937, the Chinese president was —— —— ——, who had tried to unify the factions in China.

INTERESTING THINGS TO DO

Topics for Talks

1. "Silk — the most beautiful and romantic textile." Prepare to tell the story of silk, from the legend of the Empress Si Ling-Shi to modern silkworm culture. What nations today rival or surpass China in silk production? Why has this industry not been successfully developed in the United States? See "Silk" in *The World Book Encyclopedia*. See also *Made in China,* by Cornelia Spencer.

2. "The scene is laid in China." A special list of books of fiction is included in "Interesting Reading about China." Read and review one of these books for the class. Keep in mind that the scenes and customs described in the book may apply to only a particular part of China, and locate carefully the scene of the story you read.

3. "Chinese art." Prepare a talk about some branch of art or architecture in China. See *Made in China,* by Cornelia Spencer; *My Country and My People,* by Lin Yutang.

4. "Chinese-Americans." Prepare a talk on the Chinese in this country. For information on Chinese-Americans in New York's Chinatown, see *Shake Hands with the Dragon,* by Carl Glick.

Projects for the Chart-Maker and Artist

1. Make a series of pen sketches such as might be used to illustrate a travel pamphlet on China, for example, a Chinese fishing boat, a temple, a Chinese bridge, a statue of the Buddha, a Chinese kite.

2. Draw an outline map of China that shows the distribution of China's resources, and any items of interest that you can discover concerning her population, transportation, industries, and climate. Consult any modern atlas, and notice particularly the special maps of geopolitics and world problems. See *Atlas of Far Eastern Politics,* by G. F. Hudson and M. Rajchman.

Questions for Round-Table Discussion

1. Will a strong and united China be a source of trouble in the Far East?

2. What are the propects for permanent unity in China following World War II?

3. Will the future China tend toward self-development, or welcome the help of foreign investors and businessmen?

Candidates for Your Album of Famous People

Write biographical sketches of Chiang Kai-shek and Sun Yat-sen for your Album.

INTERESTING READING ABOUT CHINA

AYSCOUGH, F. W. *Firecracker Land.* A book of travel and description that gives "fascinating glimpses of both old and new China."

CLARK, E. T. *The Chiangs of China.* The saga of the famous Soong family and its connections.

COOPER, ELIZABETH. *My Lady of the Chinese Courtyard.* The great contrasts between old and new China are revealed in this interesting book of letters.

Compton's Pictured Encyclopedia. "China: Ancient China, Vast and Strange"; and Index.

CROW, CARL. *China Takes Her Place.* This exciting eye-witness account of the last thirty years in China's development gives us a background for understanding the China of tomorrow.

——. *Chinese Are Like That.* "The Chinese child . . . is the central figure of a whole series of festivals and ceremonial observances."

——. *Four Hundred Million Customers.* Economic and social conditions among the "interesting, exasperating, puzzling, and almost always lovable Chinese people."

KUO, HELENA. *Giants of China.* A pageant of twelve of the greatest men in China's long history.

LIN YUTANG. *My Country and My People.* A brilliant interpretation of the characteristics of the Chinese, relating China's present to the centuries-old culture of her past.

National Geographic Magazine, February, 1942. "Taming Flood Dragons Along China's Hwang Ho," by Oliver J. Todd. "We saw how the Yellow River produces a spirit of fatalism among the people. . . ."

——, March, 1944. "6000 Miles Over the Roads of Free China," by Josephine A. Brown. "These men had made of their bodies the New Great Wall to turn back the invader."

WALN, NORA. *House of Exile.* An entrancing account of Chinese family life and some history of the recent years of war and confusion.

WEBSTER, H. *Historical Selections.* China. "The nobler sort of man is proficient in the knowledge of his duty."

The World Book Encyclopedia. "The Story of China"; and Index.

Books of Fiction About China

BUCK, PEARL S. *The Good Earth; The Patriot; The Young Revolutionist.*

CRONIN, A. J. *The Keys of the Kingdom.*

HOBART, ALICE TISDALE. *Oil for the Lamps of China; Yang and Yin.*

LEWIS, ELIZABETH. *China Quest; Ho-ming, Girl of New China; Young Fu of the Upper Yangtze.*

LIN YUTANG. *Moment in Peking.*

JAPAN BECAME A WORLD POWER AND SET OUT TO DOMINATE THE ORIENT

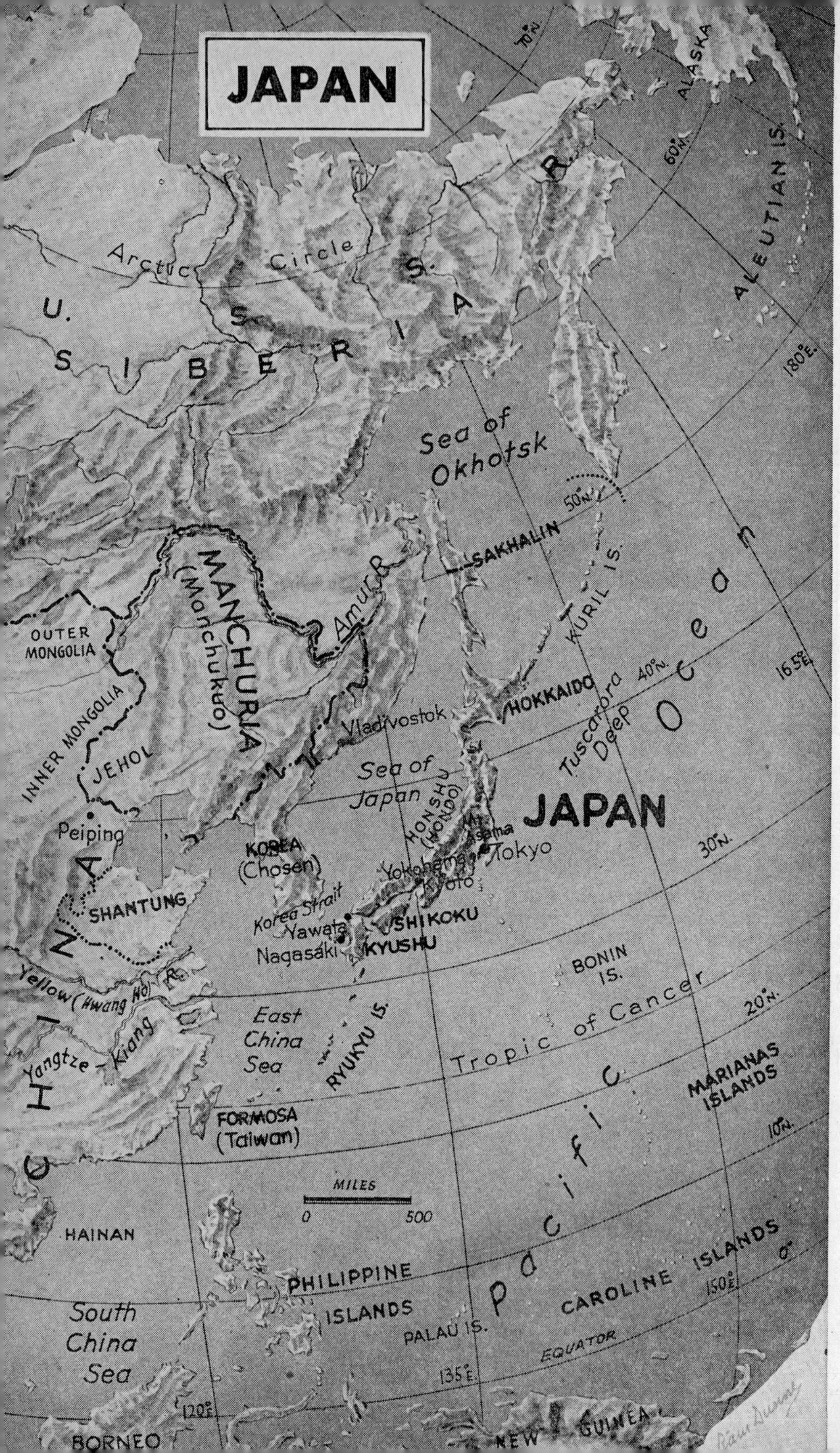

JAPAN

U. S. S. R.

Arctic Circle

S I B E R I A

Sea of Okhotsk

OUTER MONGOLIA

MANCHURIA
(Manchukuo)

Amur R.

SAKHALIN

KURIL IS.

INNER MONGOLIA

JEHOL

Vladivostok

HOKKAIDO

Tuscarora Deep

Sea of Japan

Peiping

KOREA
(Chosen)

HONSHU
(HONDO)

Mt.
Asama

JAPAN

SHANTUNG

Korea Strait

Yokohama
Kyoto

Tokyo

C H I N A

Yellow (Hwang Ho) R.

Yawata

Nagasaki

SHIKOKU

KYUSHU

BONIN
IS.

Yangtze - Kiang

East
China
Sea

RYUKYU IS.

Tropic of Cancer

MARIANAS
ISLANDS

FORMOSA
(Taiwan)

P a c i f i c

O c e a n

ALEUTIAN IS.

ALASKA

HAINAN

MILES

0   500

PHILIPPINE
ISLANDS

CAROLINE ISLANDS

South
China
Sea

PALAU IS.

EQUATOR

BORNEO

NEW GUINEA

Japan, Empire of the Orient

SCAN this map of Japan and the eastern coast of Asia. You may wonder why two large territories on the mainland have two names apiece. Chosen is the Japanese name for Korea, a territory which the Japanese acquired from the Chinese who formerly dominated it. Manchukuo is the name the Japanese gave to the puppet state they set up in Manchuria, after they had conquered it by surprise attack in 1931. For centuries Japan had lived as an isolated feudal nation. Can you see from the map any reasons why the Japanese wished to control possessions on the Asiatic mainland?

You may be surprised at the great length of Japan. You will see that Japan's chain of islands extends from the warm latitudes not far from the Philippines, well north to the cold of the Arctic. Across the shallow Sea of Japan is that part of the continent of Asia which is of such great interest to the Japanese. From Korea, you will learn, came Buddhism on which much of the Japanese civilization is based. You will read in the following story of Japan the startling tale of how that nation became a modern and aggressive world power in the lifetime of persons living today. You will read also of her attack on China, which was one of the first steps toward World War II,

Chapter 1 ~ Japan: Island Empire of the Orient

Japan's empire began as a strip of islands. Across the pathway of the morning sun as it sweeps west to the continent of Asia sprawls Japan, a chain of islands 2500 miles long. Most early peoples at some time worshiped the sun. To the Japanese, who live where sunrise begins for Asia, the sun has always had an especially deep significance, for they identify the sun with their own land. Their name for their country is Nippon, " the place where the sun rises " or " the source of the sun," and they commonly refer to their country as " the land of the rising sun." The red circle on a field of white, which forms the design for the national flag, represents the rising sun.

The climate of Japan is varied but moderate. The islands of Japan have about the same area as the state of California. There are over 4000 of them, but most of the people live on the three central islands, Hondo [hon'doh], Shikoku [shee'koh'koo], and Kyushu [kyoo' shoo]. Except for the island possession of Formosa, Japan lies in about the same latitude as the United States. But the climate varies greatly, from semiarctic in the northern islands to tropical in the south. A warm current which comes up along the east shores of the main islands makes Japan warmer than the near-by mainland of Asia in the same latitude. Because of a very heavy rainfall, the crops grow well; but during the height of summer Japan is hot and humid.

A long coastline encourages fishing. Until after the middle of the 19th Century, when the Japanese first began to trade with foreign nations on a large scale, the main occupations were always agriculture and fishing. The Japanese have a coastline as long as half the distance around the world, and no spot in the islands is more than a hundred miles from the sea. Because of the importance of fish as food, it was natural that thousands of the people should become skilled fishermen. Even today, one out of every forty Japanese — a total of more than two million — is a fisherman, and usually he works on a very small boat. The waters around Japan furnish many varieties of fish which may be caught all the year around. Whale meat, for example, is always on sale in the butcher shops. And schools of migratory fish visit Japan at different seasons. Fish is not the only food provided by the sea. Japanese eat large quantities of an edible seaweed, a kind of sea spinach.

Only a small part of the land can be cultivated. The mountain ranges, which help to give Japan much of its dramatic beauty, cover so much of the land that only about one-seventh of it has been successfully cultivated. There is some wasteland which can still be made productive, but most of it is too hilly. Although Japan is no larger than California, the native population is about 72,-000,000, or nearly three-fourths as large as that of the whole United States. Thus land is at a premium. The average size of a Japanese farm is barely two acres. The moderate climate, heavy rainfall, and intense cultivation make it possible to grow heavy crops of rice and other products. But an increased population has made it difficult for Japan to feed all her people. It has been estimated that the population of Japan increased one

Ewing Galloway

A TEA PLANTATION

These Japanese girls are working among well-ordered rows of tea bushes. Central Japan is one of the greatest tea-producing regions in the world.

million a year from 1930 to 1938. Japanese agriculture was not able to provide for this increase in population.

The Japanese farmers have learned to make the most of what nature provides. In the southern districts, by irrigating the rice fields, they are able to grow two crops of rice each year. The rice fields are separated from each other by small ridges, and on these are planted mulberry trees to provide food for silkworms. Strangely, the mulberry leaves eaten by the worms just about equal in weight the rice eaten by the people. Tea shrubs are planted on hilly land which is not level enough for irrigation and so cannot be used for growing rice. The picture above shows how the Japanese grow tea shrubs on terraced hillsides.

Geography and religion determine the Japanese diet. There are few wild animals in Japan, and even domestic animals are rare. Most Japanese do not eat meat, for one of their main religions, Buddhism, frowns on the eating of the flesh of animals. The great supplies of fish in the seas so near them, and the crops of rice, beans, radishes, and potatoes from their own soil as well as eggs and poultry, offer a natural selection for the Japanese diet. Perhaps from generations of habit, most Japanese still prefer fish to pork or beef, and rice is always their mainstay. Rice has been so important to the Japanese that it has often served in the place of money, especially in medieval times. It is also used to make the yellowish-white wine called sake [sah′kee], of which the people are fond.

A great many of the poorer people cannot afford rice and eat barley instead. Very fine sweet potatoes are grown in Japan, but they are considered such a lowly food that Japanese will eat them only in private. Of recent years, however, there has been a growing demand for "foreign-style food," that is, beef and bread.

The Japanese are an island people.
The early Japanese lived apart from the
rest of Asia for a long period of time.
The food supply helped to make this
possible, but it was not the only reason.
If you refer to the map on page 678,
you will see that the Sea of Japan
separates the islands from the mainland.
In some places the sea is only fifty miles
wide, as at Korea Strait, but in others it
is about five hundred miles wide. In the
days before modern navies these distances seemed greater, and in early times
it was not often that ships sailed from
one shore to the other. Moreover, since
the Sea of Japan is shallow, it proved
rough and treacherous in storms.

In the 13th Century the sea saved
Japan from being invaded by an enemy.
At this time the Great Khan of the
Mongols sailed with an armada of nine
hundred vessels to conquer the Japanese,
but a severe storm came up and destroyed many of the ships. He turned
back and made no other attempt to invade Japan.

**The origins of the Japanese are un-
known.** Little is actually known about
the early history of the slight, dark-
haired, slant-eyed natives of Japan. Scientists believe that the two main strains
are Mongol and Malay. The yellow-
skinned Mongols came from the mainland of Asia — from Mongolia, China,
and Korea (now called Chosen). The
brown-skinned Malays probably found
their way north from the islands of the
South Seas.

Ewing Galloway

THRESHING RICE

Rice is one of the principal foods of the Japanese. Rice threshing in Japan is either done
by hand or with the aid of very simple machinery like that shown here. But labor is
cheap in Japan. Farmers have large families, and men, women, and children work in
the fields.

Ewing Galloway

A TORII GATE

Shinto gateways like these usually stand at the entrance to a sacred place, but those shown here are at either end of a commercial street in Kobe. Such gateways are sometimes constructed in Japanese harbors. There is a superstition among Japanese sailors that they will have fair weather and success if their craft passes through a Torii gate.

In Hokkaido [hohk′kai′doh], the large northern island of Japan, there still live primitive tribes of a light-skinned and once fierce race, known as the hairy Ainu [ai′noo]. It is thought that the Ainu may have been the earliest inhabitants of Japan, and that they were driven north by invaders hundreds of years ago. There is a picture of an Ainu on page 22.

The patriotism of the Japanese is fanatical. Their geographical location, on islands off the mainland, and the local food supply have allowed the Japanese to live apart from other peoples. But these two things do not fully explain their long separation from the rest of the world. The Japanese have a fierce love of their homeland which approaches a fanatical degree. They not only worship their emperors and the

founders of the race, whom they believe to be of divine origin, but they also worship the land itself. In their mythology the land is called " a brother to man, for it, too, was born of divine parents." Through most of their history the Japanese have preferred to stay apart from other peoples. They have considered themselves a definitely superior race.

Even in the 20th Century there is a sense of " long ago and far away" in Japan, where thousands of shrines honor many deities of nature. You may see a statue or a shrine erected to a man of earlier days; but the next shrine you see may be dedicated to an animal god such as a fox, and the one after that may honor a beautiful tree. The most splendid object of worship in nature is snow-capped Fujiyama [foo′jee yah′muh], more than twelve thousand feet high. It is not very far from the capital city, Tokyo [toh'kyoh], near the east and central part of the largest island, Hondo; but it can be seen from almost anywhere on the island, and is the one sight most familiar to Westerners.

Earthquakes have brought disasters to the Japanese. Japan is in a zone of severe earthquakes and volcanic action. Many of the Japanese mountains are volcanoes. Some, like Fujiyama, are extinct, but others are active. One of these erupted at the close of the last century, and killed hundreds of people living along its slopes. Another, Asama [ah'suh muh], lies northwest of Tokyo; its rumblings can be heard for miles around, and every so often glowing lava bursts from its tip.

The earthquakes of Japan are even more destructive than the volcanoes. The center of such disturbances seems to be in the Tuscarora Deep, a depression in the Pacific Ocean bed on the east side of Japan. (It is named after the American battleship *Tuscarora* which made the first soundings.) The water there is almost 28,000 feet deep. It is one of the deepest places in the world.

The Japanese have as many as two thousand quakes per year. When the tremors are mild, the people hardly think about them. Some quakes, of course, are too slight to be detected except by delicate scientific instruments. Yet anyone who lives in Japan can expect at least one bad earthquake in his lifetime. During a great earthquake, in 1923, the port city of Yokohama [yoh'koh hah'muh] was almost completely destroyed. A third of Tokyo was also laid in ruins. In all, about ninety thousand people were killed and a half million homes were wiped away. American aid and relief work were generous; our contributions amounted to more than twelve million dollars.

Typhoons cause great destruction. Each year in spring, and more frequently in the early autumn, Japan is visited by the cyclonic storms called *typhoons* (from the Japanese word, *tai-fu,* meaning " great wind "). The rains and winds beat down, flooding rivers, destroying land, and often causing great loss of life. Yearly more than a thousand people are killed, many houses are destroyed, and crops are ruined.

The Japanese have grown accustomed to these fierce storms, and prepare for them in a surprisingly matter-of-fact way. The people who live in valleys which are subject to flood, often build their houses so that the bamboo walls of the lower floor can be rolled up when the flood waters rise. The whole family goes up into the loft, and waits while the flood rises and then subsides. If they have time, the mother and grandmother first prepare many rice balls to be eaten while the family is marooned on the top floor. Other families, whose houses are not so adaptable, go to temples or other buildings on higher ground.

When a severe typhoon is expected, Japanese fishermen seek a safe haven or harbor and observe a peculiar religious service. To an accompaniment of flutes and drums they push out to sea a papier-mâché devil-god, made in the shape of an octopus. This is supposed to earn the good will of the sea-god and keep him from sending a typhoon. The Japanese have many such rituals, but when disaster does strike they accept it with impassive courage. That is the nature of these people.

Chapter 2 ~ The Japanese Developed a Feudal Nation

The Japanese borrowed a religion, and word-signs for writing. Until the middle of the Sixth Century after Christ, the Japanese had no alphabet and no written language. Therefore we have no authentic history of Japan before that time. The only information that we have about the early Japanese is in the stories and legends which were handed down by word of mouth. The earliest known mention of the Japanese is found in Chinese records of the Third Century. These sources also mention that for a time, about the Fourth Century, warriors from the islands conquered parts of the mainland.

About A.D. 550, Buddhist missionaries came to the islands of Japan from Korea. With them they brought a message about Buddhism from the Korean king: " This doctrine is hard to understand, but marvelously excellent. It furnishes men with treasure to their heart's content. Every prayer may be fulfilled and every wish granted."

The Japanese welcomed the Buddhist missionaries and their teachings, for they had heard stories of the learning and the arts which had flourished in China for many centuries, and which had also spread into Korea. Many of the Japanese became Buddhists, and in doing so became acquainted with other forms of wisdom and culture brought from the older civilizations of China and India. The first important result was that they learned the Chinese language. Once they had mastered the Chinese characters, they adapted them to their own spoken words.

One of the famous men of Japan, Prince Shotoku [shoh'toh koo], was at the head of the government near the end of the Sixth Century. He acted as a skillful go-between or popularizer, bringing the written language and other new learning to the people. He wrote in a simplified form the principles of Buddhism, and he also drew up a code of laws. Japan began to advance out of a state of barbarism.

At first it might seem surprising that the Japanese adopted Buddhism, a religion that was new to them, almost as soon as it reached their shores. The reason was that they had no religion except a collection of myths and superstitions, in which a fear of demons and witchcraft played a large part. These beliefs were the background of Shinto, or " The Way of the Gods," about which you read in the story of religions. Shinto, you may remember, cannot be called a religion in the usual sense, but a kind of religious patriotism. It is a worship of the homeland and the ancestors, who, like the emperor, are revered as gods. It has no creed or sacred book, only the stories of the ancestors.

Japan's emperor comes of a long line of rulers. Japan's line of emperors goes back in an unbroken line to a time before Prince Shotoku and the first written history. It is surprising that one family of rulers should manage to remain on a throne so long, even though royal families in Japan adopt new members and adoption means more there than elsewhere. The person taken into a family is considered part of the direct line of descendants.

According to the teachings of Shinto, the Japanese religion, the present line of emperors goes back even much further than the written language — back to 660 B.C., when the empire was founded by Jimmu [jim′moo], a descendant of the Sun Goddess. Every year the Japanese celebrate February 11 as the date on which Jimmu ascended the throne.

Since the Japanese are taught that their emperor is the descendant of the Sun Goddess, they call him the "Son of Heaven." The Japanese believe that he rules not merely by "divine right" but because he is a living god, the supreme god who should rule both heaven and earth. That is why they call their wars of conquest "holy wars." He is so sacred to the people that they prefer not to speak his name aloud, and they will not look directly upon him on the rare occasions when they have the opportunity to do so.

The shoguns became the real rulers of Japan. Japan has always had a military form of society. Not long after the Japanese learned how to write their language, great feudal lords began to compete for power. Many bloody civil wars were fought in which the victor always killed all of the defeated clan — men, women, and children — so that none would be left to plot against him.

Between the Eighth and the Twelfth Centuries, a feudal baron frequently wrested the real power from the emperor, forcing him into the background. Near the end of the Twelfth Century, the emperor who was then on the throne accepted the changed situation. He appointed one of these powerful lords to be his military dictator, or *shogun* [shoh′goon], which title is equivalent to "Barbarian-Subduing-Great-General." From that date the shoguns, rather than the emperors, were the real rulers of the nation for centuries.

The rule of the shoguns was militaristic. The shoguns had under them other lesser lords called *daimyos* [dai′myohs], who controlled large areas of land and had authority in their own districts. This loosely centralized military government also gave rise to a special warrior class, the *samurai* [sah′moo rai]. They were the knights who served the daimyos. The samurai were highly skilled in the use of the sword, and they made war their only business. They looked with scorn on merchants, farmers, and laborers. They were taught that the noblest thing they could do would be to die for their lord, that is, for the particular daimyo under whom they served.

Japanese history has glorified this professional warrior and has recorded many

4000										3000										2000									
4300	4200	4100	3900	3800	3700	3600	3500	3400	3300	3200	3100	2900	2800	2700	2600	2500	2400	2300	2200	2100	1900	1800	1700	1600	1500	1400	1300	1200	1100
43rd	42nd	41st	40th	39th	38th	37th	36th	35th	34th	33rd	32nd	31st	30th	29th	28th	27th	26th	25th	24th	23rd	22nd	21st	20th	19th	18th	17th	16th	15th	14th	13th	12th

Bronze Age

silk culture

ceramics

HIA DYNASTY — SHANG DYNASTY

CHINA

flood control

picture writing

interesting stories of his exploits and his skill with his sword. But according to American standards of conduct, he was bloodthirsty and criminal, more like our gangsters than any other class that has ever lived in this country. The samurai was above the law and had the right to kill with his sword any common man who offended him. The young samurai who had not yet " sheathed his sword in blood " was looked down on by his elders, and as a result was always looking for an opportunity to use his sword. The picture on page 688 shows the armor and swords worn by these bloodthirsty warriors.

The samurai has been compared to the knights of medieval Europe. However, the European knight had a code of chivalry which made him the protector of the weak and the defenseless. He fought only with his equals. The life of the samurai was also regulated by a code — Bushido [boo'shee doh'], or " the code of the warrior." This differed greatly from the code of chivalry. It prescribed a rigorous life of exercise and training, all pointed to making the samurai an effective, though ruthless, fighting man. There was no chivalry in the samurai. He often killed defenseless farmers for no other reason than that he thought they had not shown him the proper respect. It was a common practice for the samurai to "bathe his sword " in the blood of a beggar. They did this without any feeling of shame or guilt. It was their code.

By their heroes you shall know them. The founder of the samurai tradition was Yamato Dake [1] [yah mah'toh dah' keh], greatest hero of the country and a man whose story is known to every Japanese schoolboy. No similar character ever figured in American history. Yamato Dake was the son of one of the early emperors. The act which first brought him into fame was the murder of his twin brother. He not only killed his brother with his sword but cut his body into four pieces and threw them north, south, east, and west. He said he had killed his brother because he had been disobedient to the emperor. To be sure, with his brother out of the way Yamato Dake was certain to succeed to the throne.

The office of shogun became hereditary. After their rise to power in the 12th Century, the shoguns continued to rule in Japan for nearly seven hundred

[1] *Yamato* was the ancient name of Japan and the name *Yamato Dake* really means " bravest in Japan."

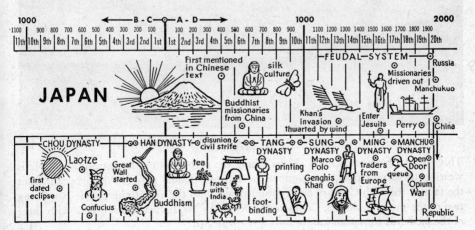

A JAPANESE ACTOR

This modern Japanese actor is shown taking the part of an old Japanese general. He is wearing the armor that was worn in the Japanese feudal period, which began about the first of the 17th Century and continued well into the 19th Century. He is wearing two of the samurai swords. Compare the armor and equipment shown here with those of the medieval European knight shown on page 262.

years, until after the time of our War between the States. Several generations of shoguns from the same important family and even the same line would rule uninterruptedly for years. Then they and their families would lose control and representatives of another great family would come into power, as the result of civil war.

None of the shoguns ever made an attempt to become emperor, for it was more convenient to control the emperor and to rule in his name. We may be sure that these shoguns who told the emperor what he could do, did not believe very thoroughly in his divine origin, but they talked a great deal about it because that was the easiest way to secure the obedience of the people.

The actual position of the emperor fluctuated greatly from time to time. Some shoguns provided for the emperors very generously and even consulted with them on governmental affairs. At other times the emperor was neglected and ignored. One of them was reduced to such poverty that he had to make a living by sitting at the palace gate and selling his autographs.

"The dream of Hideyoshi." Some of the shoguns of Japan were ignored by powerful daimyos, who took authority completely into their own hands as semi-independent chieftains. Near the end of the 16th Century, however, Hideyoshi [hee'deh oh'shee], a remarkable military leader, completely subdued the rebellious daimyos and brought about a more unified nation. He became the most powerful man in the state, but, because of his low birth, he was not given the title of shogun. Hideyoshi had been a peasant. He had risen to power through military politics. Soon after subduing the daimyos, he sent armies to Korea in an attempt to conquer the part of Asia

which, the Japanese believed, comprised the rest of the world.

Hideyoshi, who was the dictator of that period in Japanese history, was completely confident of success. Even before he sent a single soldier overseas he divided up certain parts of China and India among the most powerful families of Japan. He invited the king of Korea to join him in his attack on China, but the Korean ruler indignantly refused to join in a treacherous assault on a friendly power. Hideyoshi then attacked Korea, but although he killed many thousands and destroyed many cities, he did not conquer the country; and furthermore his soldiers never set foot on the soil of China. The Japanese troops finally withdrew from Korea in 1600, bringing back with them, however, many thousands of slaves.

Japanese boys have been taught to remember "the dream of Hideyoshi," which was to conquer the world and make all nations subject to Japan. This dream has been cherished for nearly four hundred years.

Japan sealed itself against the outside world. The ruling classes of Japan — the shogun, the daimyos, and their samurai — hated and feared foreigners and looked on them as barbarians. They were afraid of new religions and political ideas, and dreaded the thought of other nations getting a foothold in their country.

A little less than half a century after Magellan's trip around the world, St. Xavier [zav'i uhr], with a few other Jesuit priests, arrived in Japan. There they made some converts to Christianity. As time went by there was a strong reaction against these priests and other foreigners; Hideyoshi himself felt that they were trying to obtain power, and he began their persecution. Early in the 17th

Century all foreign priests were banished from Japan. Some years later many of the Christian converts were massacred. Japanese Christians continued to meet secretly, however, and when Christian missionaries were allowed to return many years later, they found many Christians in Japan.

In 1637 the ruling shogun issued an edict which barred all foreigners from Japan. The only exceptions were some Dutch traders who were allowed to send one trading ship a year to a small port on a lesser island. It was even made a crime for the Japanese to leave their own land or to send a letter abroad. When other nations tried to deal with the Japanese they replied curtly, "Speak to the Dutch. They will carry any message it is necessary for us to know." This policy of isolation was maintained for more than two hundred years.

Chapter 3 ~ The Doors of Japan Were Opened to the Influence of the Western World

Commodore Perry delivered a letter. The closed-door policy of Japan did not please other nations. They wanted to trade with the Japanese, and they did not see why their ships should not be allowed to enter Japan's ports — at least for supplies. American interest was also aroused because when American whaling ships were wrecked on the Japanese coast the Japanese treated the shipwrecked seamen cruelly.

President Fillmore of the United States determined to make a treaty with Japan. He wrote a letter to the emperor, and asked Commodore Perry to deliver it. Perry, with four ships of the navy, arrived in the Bay of Tokyo, then called Yedo [yeh'doh], in July, 1853.

The Japanese were very much disturbed when they saw four strange "black" warships in the bay just ten miles from their capital. They gazed in curiosity and anger at the powerful-looking fleet of "foreign barbarians." Never having seen a steamship, they could not understand how a ship could move without sails. They sent messengers to persuade Perry to leave, but he insisted that his letter must be taken to the emperor. At last, the Japanese agreed to deliver the letter. They received the Commodore on the beach, where he landed with three hundred soldiers and sailors. When they had accepted the President's letter, the Japanese handed Perry a note which read, "The letter being received, you will leave." Perry informed them that he would return in a few months for an answer to the letter.

The people were excited, and the ruling shogun considered whether he ought not to make a treaty with the foreigners. He sent copies of the President's message to all the daimyos, and asked for their advice. The daimyos protested. The Japanese began to arm themselves for the return visit. They cast bells into cannon, and built mud forts. They drilled the samurai in the use of guns.

Perry returned with strange gifts. In February of 1854, Commodore Perry re-

OROC

PERRY PRESENTING GIFTS TO THE JAPANESE

Although the Japanese at first resented the landing of Perry and his men upon their shores they later made a treaty with the United States allowing trading privileges. This illustration appears in Perry's official report.

turned with a fleet of ten ships and two thousand men. He brought the Japanese a number of presents, among them a telegraph line with a mile of wire, and a model steam railroad, complete with engine, car, and circular track. There were also rifles, clocks, and a sewing machine. Perry had these curiosities set up on the beach and demonstrated them to the people. This dramatic occasion is pictured above.

The Japanese saw that they could never hope to resist the foreigners until they, too, had learned to handle Western machines. It was clear to them that the West had much to teach them.

Japan agreed to a treaty of navigation with the United States, giving us the privilege of calling at certain ports for fuel and water and promising humane treatment for shipwrecked sailors. The American consul-general, after great effort, made a trade treaty. The medieval nation of Japan suddenly opened its eyes to a modern world of steam and humming factories.

The emperors were returned to power. Some of the daimyos and samurai rebelled when the shogun signed a trade treaty with the United States. A movement to restore the emperors to their original power became the battle cry of these groups, and in time they forced the shoguns out of office. The last shogun resigned in 1868, at the same time that a new emperor, Mutsuhito [moot' soo hee toh], came to the throne.

The Restoration of the Emperors, as this occasion was called, caused a new wave of patriotism and unity. Some of the daimyos gave up their powers and land of their own free will, and others were persuaded to do the same. The samurai class was abolished at the same time. But in most cases the daimyos were given land, and the samurai were granted government pensions.

Japan learned from many people. The new emperor was an alert man, and anxious to see his nation advance in every way. All groups united behind him and Japan began to make itself over according to Western models. Soon afterward, a delegation of Japanese went around the world to learn of any new ideas that might be used to advantage at home. Unusually capable students were sent to foreign universities. The Japanese started a public-school system, copied from that of the United States, although girls were educated only through the primary grades. You will read more about it in the next chapter. Japan also built a modern navy and, in 1889, even adopted a constitution. The principal purpose of the constitution, however, is to uphold the supreme authority of the ruling clique and it contains no bill of rights for the people.

Marquis Ito [ee'toh], who was one of the greatest Japanese statesmen, purposely chose the constitution of Germany as a model for Japan. A Diet with a House of Peers and a House of Representatives was set up. New titles for the peerage, such as prince, count, and baron, were borrowed from Europe. These titles helped to console some of the former samurai, who had lost all of their earlier honors. The vote was granted to a limited number of men, depending on their tax payments. The women were not allowed to vote at all. In the meantime the army was reorganized on the model of the French army, with German officers to drill it.

The expanding nation began building factories and railroads, and by 1890 had two hundred factories and four thousand miles of railway lines. With new industrial growth, a few Japanese families, later called the " Big Families," began to get control of business and to have a strong voice in government. Often the " Big Families " were in opposition to military groups, but at times the latter had an even stronger influence. Japan has been described as a dictatorship of groups. The prestige of the emperor has prevented the rise of a single dictator like Hitler or Mussolini. But various groups have governed Japan in a dictatorial fashion. The new army of soldiers from all classes has showed as much fighting skill and spirit as the samurai, and the same eagerness to serve the emperor. Japanese soldiers, like all the Japanese, conform to the strictest discipline. Japan has a two-party government. Both parties are supported by the wealthier people, one party largely by the wealthy landowners, who support the military group, and the other by wealthy industrialists, who have tended to be more moderate in their foreign policy.

Japan combined Western ideas and machinery with feudal traditions. No nation ever moved out of feudalism into modern Western ways of life so swiftly as Japan. The very speed with which she learned methods and techniques of the Western world seems to be the source of some difficulties which the nation has suffered since that time. Since Japan had ready-made models to follow, she skipped centuries of the " trial-and-error " processes through which Europe had passed. It was a case of " adopt, adapt, and adept." She efficiently adapted models from other civilizations to her own uses, without the same thorough experience. In absorbing so much in a hurry, it was as if Japan sprang out of childhood into maturity all at one jump, without really having time to grow up. She has mastered the machines of the West — but has retained the attitudes of her medieval feudalism.

Japanese military power grew rapidly. In 1894 Japan made war on China, and the next year won a decisive victory. Her chief gains were Korea and the luxuriant island of Formosa. In 1902 Japan formed a defensive military alliance with Great Britain, the greatest imperial nation of the time. In 1904–1905 Japan again waged successful war, this time with Russia, as you have already read in the story of Russia. Japan wanted to curb the growth of Russian power in Korea and in the three northeastern provinces of Greater China known as Manchuria. At that time Russia seemed the principal obstacle to Japan's " dream of Hideyoshi."

A peace settlement was made at Portsmouth, New Hampshire, in 1905, with President Theodore Roosevelt as the arbitrator. Japan was given Port Arthur and the southern part of the island of Sakhalin [sak hah leen'] and she won a free hand in Korea. Russia also gave up railroad and mining rights in Manchuria. A few years later, in 1910, Japan annexed Korea outright, and renamed it Chosen.

In the space of a few years Japan had brought about an industrial revolution in her own country, and had fought two successful wars. The world was astonished at this sudden rise of a medieval nation. Japan was proving what no one had suspected: that a nation of the Orient could keep up with the West. She was the dominant nation of the East, and was fast becoming a world power. The " dream of Hideyoshi " was taking a new form. Japan was the first country of the Orient to become a powerful industrial nation. She saw herself as the

rising imperial power which would control the lives and supply the needs of the one billion people living in the Orient.

Japan moved into China in World War I. World War I gave Japan a remarkable opportunity to strengthen her position in China and the Pacific. She had a trade and mutual-assistance alliance with Great Britain, made early in the 20th Century. On the basis of this agreement, Japan entered World War I on the side of the Allies in the summer of 1914. The Germans had a colony in Tsingtao [ching'dou'], a territory on the near-by province of Shantung. The Japanese moved against it, and soon captured it. As for the Chinese owners, they were not sure that they were not rid of one master only to acquire another.

Chinese suspicions were well founded, for several months later Japan suddenly presented to China a list of Twenty-one Demands. Of these we spoke in the story of China. In them the Japanese insisted upon strong privileges and authority in China. The Western world was too busy with the war to pay much attention, but the United States and Great Britain did enter a protest. Probably as a result of their protest, Japan's demands were greatly modified. In their milder form, however, China was forced to agree to them.

War encouraged Japanese commerce and industry. When the peace settlement was made, Japan — in spite of eloquent protests from China — was given all Germany's former possessions in Shantung province and a mandate, or a commission to rule, over the islands in the Pacific which had formerly been in Germany's hands. These islands, the Marshalls, the Carolines, and the Marianas, were of great military importance to Japan. From one of these islands, the Japanese are believed to have launched their surprise air attack on Pearl Harbor before declaring war on the United States in World War II.

In the course of World War I Japan had also improved her wealth and credit by selling munitions to other countries. She manufactured and sold war materials on such a scale that by the end of the war her business was five times what it had been in 1914. When peace came, Japan suffered the abrupt loss of these markets.

In 1919 China found a way to retaliate against Japan's continued expansion and the Twenty-one Demands. The greatest part of Japan's foreign business and property were in China. Led by Chinese students, the people organized a thorough boycott of Japanese goods and business. This boycott had such a serious effect that Japan began to doubt the wisdom of her aggressive policies toward China. A new spirit of nationalism had sprung up in China as was described in the story of that land, Part Nineteen.

Japan shifted between policies of peace and aggression. During the 1920's Japan's foreign policy was cautious. Some Japanese statesmen favored peace and tried to keep the army groups from influencing the government into waging aggressive wars. The "Big Families" of Japanese business are said to have favored nonaggressive policies, and to have wished to keep the friendship of the West. Peace with the West was good for business. At least the "Big Families" did not wish to attack until they were quite sure Japan's chances were good.

Some of the army men, however, had come to feel that other factions were richer and more privileged than themselves. Army pay was small, soldiers did not have anything very important to do, and they remembered the honors and

the code of the samurai. They also believed Japan had a great destiny and must pursue it. There was constant shifting of power in Japan between those groups who wanted war and those who did not.

Japan invaded Manchuria. Suddenly, in 1931, Japan invaded and seized Manchuria, the vast northern province of China, which is as large as France and pre-war Germany combined. The Japanese set up a puppet government in the territory, and renamed it Manchukuo, as you have read. Two years later the invaders swung west into the province of Jehol, just past Manchuria in inner Mongolia, which is noted for its production of opium.

Most of the Western nations were disturbed by the taking of Manchuria, but did not unite in taking firm measures against Japan. A commission sent by the League of Nations found that Japan had violated various treaties in which she had promised to support the territorial integrity of China. Hoping to avoid measures of disapproval by the League, Japan called Manchukuo an "independent" state. But the League disapproved, and the representatives of Japan dramatically left the League of Nations.

Japan moved into Shanghai and began the war with the Chinese. Less than six months after the conquest of Manchuria, fighting broke out in China in the Shanghai district. As you have read in the story of China, Chiang Kai-shek [chyahng'kai'shek'] did not have the support of all the Chinese people, but was engaged in a civil war with the Chinese Communists. Thus there was no united resistance against Japan at Shanghai. Furthermore the Chinese could not send great armies to northeast China without leaving the whole Chinese coastline exposed to Japanese attack. A truce was agreed upon and Japan's troops were withdrawn. There was not any widespread or continuous fighting again for four years. During that period, Japan tried to separate five North China provinces from the rest of China through machiavellian politics, but this was not successful. In the meantime, the Japanese found Manchuria valuable as a source of soybeans. The new lands seized by the Japanese also stimulated Japanese heavy industry. Thousands of miles of railroads had to be built. And of course Japan restricted the trade of her seized lands to dealings for her own benefit.

By never actually declaring war on China, Japan hoped to escape being outlawed for taking Manchuria. This strategy of not being at war, at least officially, was successful for a while. During the early 1930's most of the world was intensely peace-minded, and no other nation was ready to act. Though Japan was condemned by the League, the practical result was not much worse than a scolding. Feeling was growing, though, and many people in other nations joined China's boycott of Japanese goods.

The military class again became strong. Between 1932 and 1936 the more war-minded military leaders in Japan gained complete control of the government, partly by a policy of having their opponents in the government murdered. Thus any Japanese leaders who opposed the Japanese policy of conquest and expansion were liquidated, much as the anti-Nazis had been done away with in Germany.

Japanese business was geared to the needs of war. There were other ways in which Japan prepared for war in the 1930's. Business in Japan is not run as we are used to seeing it run in the United States. The Japanese government closely controls all Japanese business firms. Great monopolies are the rule, particularly in the export trade, and no business is allowed to become very great without government approval. During the 1920's Japan's most important manufactured products — and her most important exports — had been silk and other textiles. During the 1930's the nature of Japan's manufacturing changed. She manufactured fewer textiles, and she began to manufacture more iron, steel, machines, chemicals, and electrical equipment.

One reason for this change was that the worldwide financial depression, beginning in 1929, had made it hard for Japan to sell textiles abroad. People could not afford to buy much silk, for instance. By manufacturing cheap machines, such as bicycles and typewriters, the Japanese were able to undersell the British in Asia and Africa. African natives, for example, bought bicycles from the Japanese for five dollars apiece. But the Japanese saw another advantage to themselves, besides trade, in making this change in their type of manufacturing. Iron, steel, machines, chemicals, and electrical equipment are essential to modern warfare. Plants which are producing one kind of machines can be converted, or made over, to produce another kind of machine, if war demands. By 1938, 60 percent of Japan's manufacturing was for war needs. Japan herself imported scrap-iron for manufacture. Germany sold to her because she felt that Japan would be an ally in the coming world war. Other nations sold because their governments were afraid that refusing to do so would bring on a war before they were prepared for it. The result was that Japan was excellently equipped.

Ewing Galloway

ELECTRICAL TRANSFORMERS

These huge machines are part of an electric power plant which belongs to the Kiso River development, near Nagoya. They give some idea of the extent to which modern Japan has been industrialized. The Kiso River development includes the largest dam in Japan.

Japan's army and navy were prepared for world-wide war. We have seen that the Japanese military class is powerful in modern Japan, even as it was in the Japan of feudal days. All men in Japan between the ages of seventeen and forty are liable to compulsory military service in either the army or the navy. Active service usually begins at the age of twenty and continues for sixteen months. Additional periods of service in the reserve forces may follow later. The Japanese soldiers are trained in military tactics, group action, and blind obedience.

Their equipment and training are modern; but their beliefs are feudal. They have been taught that Japan's rule of Asia is " the will of Heaven," and they have accepted this ready-made belief with a blindness and fanaticism which is hard for the civilized world to understand. The Japanese soldier has had great confidence, perhaps because — up to 1942 — the Japanese army had never been defeated or even suffered any severe setbacks. The Japanese have been accustomed to fighting mostly against the Chinese, who have often been ill-equipped.

Part of Japan's program of modernization was to build up a great merchant navy. Before World War II all of Japan's exports were carried in her own ships. Of course a merchant navy is immensely useful in time of war for carrying supplies to troops, particularly over such widely separated lands and islands as those of the Japanese Empire. Also, from the time she became a modern nation, Japan has been ambitious to become a great sea power. She built the third greatest navy in the world. Her navy was only slightly smaller than that of Great Britain, which itself was only slightly smaller than that of the United States.

In order to increase her sea power still further, Japan also fortified the Marshall, Caroline, and Marianas islands, which, as we have seen, had been given to her to rule as mandates after World War I. This action was in direct violation of a treaty which Japan had signed in 1922 together with Great Britain and the United States.

In every way Japan was preparing for a great military and naval contest. In Part Twenty-two you will read how all-out war came again when Japan began a new invasion of China in 1937.

Chapter 4 ~ Life in Japan Is a Strange Mixture of Old and New

A new education. Perhaps the most thorough of all the changes of the new Japan was in education. Public-school education is compulsory for all children to the age of thirteen. Nearly all Japanese can read and write, which is in great contrast to conditions in the rest of the Orient. Education, however, has been controlled by the army and has been used to build up and strengthen the military machine. Much time is taken up in all boys' schools with military drill and war games. Courses called " moral instruction " teach the superiority of the Japanese race, and the divinity of the emperor and the glory of dying in battle for him.

The schools provide a training for craftsmanship. When the schoolchild in Japan is learning to write, he is automatically learning a basis for handicrafts. The student must learn at least three thousand characters to have a fair knowledge of the difficult Japanese language, and he must draw the characters with a writing brush instead of a pen. He must patiently construct fine lines and beautiful curves. In Japanese the one word *kaku* means writing, drawing, and painting.

Most girls do not attend school except for the primary grades, but there are a few high schools for girls. The girls' schools teach the language, the stories of the gods, arithmetic, ethics, and a little European history. Geography tells chiefly of the national shrines, where the nation's gods are especially honored. For girls the emphasis is on the domestic courses: cooking, laundering, and sewing. There are also special courses which adults can attend in flower arrangement, ethics, and the tea ceremony.

Japanese literature is restricted by rules. Japan has no great literature. No one has dared to write anything that might offend the upper classes. The literature of Japan has always followed fixed forms, just as the lives of the people themselves have been regulated by their rulers.

The poetry of the Japanese shows their rigid observance of rules and patterns, as well as the love of making small, dainty things. The forms came originally from China and have been much the same for a thousand years. Almost the only poems are the tanka, a five-line poem of only thirty-one syllables, and an even smaller poem, the hokku [hok'koo], in three lines with only seventeen syllables. Often the poet describes only a small detail of a scene or a mood, but if he is accomplished he may suggest much more by these details. Japanese women excel in these small poems, in which each word is the " leaf of an idea " which is supposed to suggest more than the word itself.

The theater reflects the Japanese idea of loyalty. The Japanese are very fond of going to the theater. Their plays are quite formal, but they are violent in their plots. The favorite drama of the Japanese is " The Forty-Seven Ronin." It is based on the experience of a mighty lord

in the 18th Century. The lord was at court where an enemy insulted him, forcing him to draw his sword. For this crime against the court he had to commit hara-kiri [hah'rah kee'ri] (a suicide by a prescribed ritual); his house and wealth were abolished and his retainers disbanded. For two years the retainers concealed themselves by many disguises and devices until they found the hour to strike. They finally brought the head of their lord's enemy to the temple where he was buried. Their faithfulness proved, the forty-seven ronin then proudly committed hara-kiri on the spot. The people are familiar with all the details of this story. It reflects a special idea of loyalty and courage that seems peculiar to our Western minds. But the Japanese believe and will act upon it.

The exports of Japan. You have probably heard that Japanese farmers raise silkworms to help eke out their poor living. The most important export material of Japan after she became industrialized was silk. (Japan finally surpassed even China in the silk trade.) The Japanese themselves use a great deal of cotton cloth in the kimonos which most of the people wear. Few can afford costumes of silk. Textiles, usually silk or cotton, form more than half the foreign trade business of Japan. Japanese factories have also manufactured porcelain, glass, cheap hardware, and electrical goods. We have seen in the last chapter how the Japanese swung to the manufacture of machinery and other " Western " goods in the 1930's.

The home workshops are part of industrial Japan. Japan has some large factories. Although she has a number of heavy industries, there are hardly any industrial centers. This is because so many (more than 60 percent) of the things manufactured come out of the small home workshops. All day long, father, mother, children, and perhaps one apprentice, work incessantly in their one-room home, making paper lanterns, toys, pottery, tops for canvas sneakers, machine parts, or a thousand and one other items. The materials are from a large corporation, and are furnished by a middleman. The millions of small articles — many of them of a flimsy nature — which have been produced under these conditions have made it possible for the Japanese to undersell most other markets.

Industrial progress has benefited only a few Japanese. Usually a Japanese working family earns barely more than enough to pay for rent and food. Most of the people are poor, and they do not live very differently from the way their ancestors lived in medieval times. Even in the large cities, where there are signs of Westernization in the downtown districts, few of the small homes have gas or even cold running water. Most of the cooking is still done over charcoal braziers. Not the people, but the war machine and a few " Big Families," have benefited from Japan's industrial progress.

The place of Japanese women. One reason that factory work can be maintained on small wages and sold for low prices is that a great part of it is done by women. Nearly 85 percent of all the women in Japan (between the ages of fifteen and sixty) do industrial work. Their wages are even lower than those paid to men. Japanese women do not question this status. They are not expected to have ideas of their own. Japanese women do not take part in business and they do not vote. They are accustomed to obeying their fathers and husbands, as the people all owe unquestioning obedience to the emperor in the larger family of the nation. It is *shukan,* " it is so done," and so the best way.

The idea of loyalty rules the Japanese. The idea of loyalty to the family, the clan, and the nation is all-important to the Japanese. The dread of tarnishing the family name is the greatest fear that a Japanese can have. Even hara-kiri, although it is not common in the everyday lives of the people, does not seem strange or difficult or wrong to them, as it does to Western minds. A father instructs his children in the ritual, so that if the time comes they will know what to do. A Japanese is not supposed to hesitate to commit hara-kiri if it is a question of honor. The people believe it is glorious to join one's ancestors, and that the present life is only an interval between lives in the more godlike world where the ancestors live.

Life follows a set pattern in Japan. All the people in Japan live completely by rules and observances, although men have more authority and freedom in their families than do women. The people accept teaching like that of Buddhism, which schools them to fatalism and self-control. It is not *shukan* to show grief or anger or joy. Where there is so much restraint, natural emotions will sometimes break through in some direction, and perhaps more violently than if they had not been repressed. This is thought to be one of the reasons why the Japanese have committed such uncivilized acts in the treatment of conquered peoples. But most of the time the people seem to accept their lot calmly and with grace. With fanciful and poetic ideas of the gods which guard their land, with their peculiar literature and art, with colorful ceremonies, and with the set pattern of their lives, they seem to escape from harsh realities into a world of make-believe.

Japan Comes Out of Isolation to Become a World Power

The Japanese built their empire on a fringe of volcanic islands stretching far along the eastern coast of Asia. In many ways geography has powerfully affected the growth of their civilization. The resources of land and sea have furnished them the means for unusual independence. The beauty of their mountainous islands helped to give them an almost fanatic love of country, as expressed in their patriotic religion of Shinto. Natural calamities, storm and earthquake, have only strengthened their love for the home of their emperor and their ancestors.

From an almost unknown country Japan has suddenly developed into a power in the modern world. But in many ways Japan still lives like a medieval nation. Before the coming of Commodore Perry in the middle of the 19th Century, Japan had a feudal system made up of fighting samurai who loyally served the daimyos. The chief lord, the shogun, really held the ruling power. When Japan had to abandon her "closed-door" policy, she decided to learn all that she could from Western advances in science and industry. The emperor came to the fore, with all groups united behind him. Japan began to make industrial progress. The Japanese navy came into being. The army was reorganized. A constitution was adopted, and a Diet and House of Representatives were established.

Japan's military power grew rapidly. Victory in wars with China and with Russia confirmed Japan's aggressive policies. During World War I, in which Japan was one of the Allies, she attempted to force a list of Twenty-one Demands upon China, but was prevented by the United States and Great Britain. Japan's gains from World War I gave her new strength to enter into the next phase of aggression, invasion of Manchuria in 1931.

Japanese civilization is based upon the learning and skill of the Chinese which reached Japan through Korea. Their language, their arts, and their Buddhist religion came originally from the Chinese. But the Japanese have adapted what they have learned from other nations to shape their own civilization. They have applied much of their knowledge to a policy of aggressive nationalism.

SELF-TEST

Look back upon the story of Japan by trying this self-test. For each item listed you are supposed to associate or recall something important in the story of Japan directly connected with the item. An example is given first to show you what is wanted. Write your answers on scratch paper or in your notebook.

Item	Associations
Nippon	Name for Japan — the place where the sun rises

1. Kyushu	12. samurai
2. sake	13. Yamato Dake
3. Sea of Japan	14. daimyo
4. Ainu	15. "the dream of Hideyoshi"
5. Fujiyama	16. closed-door policy
6. Tokyo	17. Commodore Perry
7. Prince Shotoku	18. "Big Families"
8. Shinto	19. Chosen
9. Jimmu	20. Manchukuo
10. Son of Heaven	21. "The Forty-Seven Ronin"
11. shogun	22. hara-kiri

INTERESTING THINGS TO DO

Projects for the Chart Maker and Artist

1. Draw an outline map of Japan and near-by islands of the Pacific, and indicate relative distances from Japan to Alaska and the Aleutians, to Hawaii, the Philippines, and Midway. Indicate also the lands on the east coast of Asia. See *Atlas of Global Geography,* by Erwin Raisz; *New World Horizons,* by Chester Lawrence; or any modern atlas your librarian recommends.

2. Make sketches of houses and shrines that are typical of Japanese architecture before Westernization. Be prepared to explain how this type of building suits the Japanese climate and the available resources. See "Japanese Architecture" in *Encyclopaedia Britannica.*

3. Draw a cartoon that dramatizes the rise of Japan to world prominence, and her change in attitude in foreign relations.

Topics for Talks

1. "The earthquake of 1923." See *Life,* Aug. 16, 1943. See also *An Outline History of Japan,* by Herbert Gowen, or "Earthquake" in *Encyclopaedia Britannica.*

2. "The Forty-Seven Ronin." What characteristics and customs set forth in this play still apply to the modern Japanese? See *An Outline History of Japan,* by Herbert Gowen.

3. "Japanese art." Choose a type of handiwork in which Japanese artisans are skilled, such as lacquer ware, embroideries, hammered brass. Prepare a talk on the methods of the Japanese artisans. See "Japanese Art" in *Encyclopaedia Britannica.* See also *Japan, Korea, and Formosa,* by Eunice Tietjens.

4. "No wonder the Japanese undersold us." Prepare a talk explaining how many Japanese manufactures can be produced so cheaply. Contrast the living standards of Japanese and American workmen. Contrast home industries in Japan and in the Scandinavian countries.

Candidates for Your Album of Famous People

Yamato Dake, Hideyoshi, Marquis Ito. Write brief biographical summaries of the three candidates listed above. Explain the significance of these men in the development of Japan.

INTERESTING READING ABOUT JAPAN

BYAS, HUGH. *Government by Assassination*. A superb and amazing account of Japan's drift toward war through the rise of the militarists and the increasingly close relationship between crime and patriotism.

Compton's Pictured Encyclopedia. " Japan: the Land of the Rising Sun "; and Index.

DILTS, MARION. *Pageant of Japanese History*. A brief, readable history of the Japanese and their culture from the Stone Age to recent times.

ISHIMOTO, BARONESS SHIDUÉ. *East Way, West Way*. An autobiography of a modern Japanese girl.

KIYOOKA, CHIYONO. *Chiyo's Return*. Ten years in the United States have made this author sensitive to the wide contrasts between the two countries.

LATOURETTE, K. S. *History of Japan*. This short but complete history of Japan from early times to the present tells in a simple, interesting manner what makes the people of Japan think and act as they do.

MEARS, HELEN. *Year of the Wild Boar*. ". . . . a nation living in the age of nature gods, with a nature god for its Head of State; a nation that taught this mythology in school and called it history."

National Geographic Magazine, March, 1933. " Japan: The Child of the World's Old Age," by W. E. Griffis. " Tokyo's architecture goes modernistic."

——, November, 1942. " Japan Faces Russia in Manchuria," by Willard Price. " Japan considers Manchuria the first essential in her ambitious plan to rule the earth."

——, April, 1944. " Japan and the Pacific," by Joseph C. Grew. " ' Victory or death ' is no mere slogan for these soldiers."

PRICE, WILLARD. *Children of the Rising Sun*. " The process of Japanizing China . . . has been proceeding for four decades."

SUGIMOTO, E. I. *A Daughter of the Samurai*. " It is never wise . . . to say too much on any subject."

TIETJENS, EUNICE. *Japan, Korea, and Formosa*. Personal observations and remarkable photographs are combined in this informative and detailed account of the everyday life, customs, scenery, art, and industry of Japan, Korea, and Formosa.

The World Book Encyclopedia, " The Story of Japan "; and Index.

PART TWENTY-ONE

THE AMERICAN NATIONS, THEIR WEL-
FARE, AND THEIR DESTINIES ARE
CLOSELY INTERWOVEN

THE AMERICAS

GREENLAND

DOMINION OF CANADA

NEWFOUNDLAND

QUEBEC

NOVA SCOTIA

NEW BRUNSWICK

ME.

Quebec

Montreal

St. Lawrence R.

Boston

Plymouth

New York

Philadelphia

N.J.

ONTARIO

MICH.

N.Y.

PA.

Jamestown

VA.

N.C.

S.C.

UNITED STATES

NORTH AMERICA

Savannah

St. Augustine

FLA.

Miami

BAHAMA IS.

SANTO DOMINGO

HAITI

Chicago

Indian-apolis

OHIO

IND.

ILL.

Ohio R.

KY.

TENN.

GA.

ALA.

Havana

CUBA

WIS.

MINN.

IOWA

Kansas City

St. Louis

MO.

MISS.

New Orleans

Gulf of Mexico

BR. HONDURAS

N. DAK.

S. DAK.

NEB.

KAN.

ARK.

LA.

Guatemala City

GUATE. HONDURAS

MONT.

WYO.

COLO.

Denver

Santa Fe

N. MEX.

OKLA.

TEXAS

San Antonio

Nuevo Laredo

MEXICO

VeraCruz

YUCATAN

PAN-AMERICAN HIGHWAY

Portland

Seattle

WASH.

IDAHO

ORE.

NEV.

UTAH

ARIZ.

Dolores

Guadalajara

Mexico City

San Francisco

Los Angeles

San Diego

CALIF.

Atlantic Ocean

Pacific

120°W.

105°W.

90°W.

75°W.

60°W.

45°W.

30°W.

20°W.

30°N.

40°N.

50°N.

60°N.

70°N.

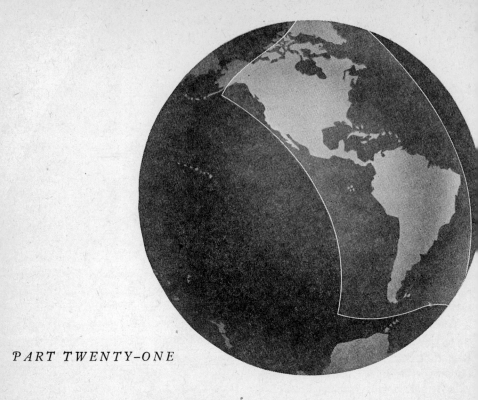

Our American Neighbors

Take a rapid overview of the map on the two pages preceding this one. North of the United States lies Canada, a member of the British Commonwealth of Nations, which you have already read about in Part Ten. To the south lies the homeland of our Latin-American neighbors. Notice how much of it lies east, as well as south, of our country. On the map of the world in the back of the book, see how close Natal, in Brazil, is to Dakar, in French West Africa.

If we could fly over the Western Hemisphere by airplane we would see many different types of scenery. In northernmost Canada we would find a barren wilderness. Southern Canada is much like the northern part of the United States. Flying southward over Latin America we would find moderate climates as well as tropical ones, plains, forests, and mountains. And Tierra del Fuego, in southernmost Argentina, is as bleak as the northern parts of Canada. We would find small primitive villages and great modern cities. There would be mile after mile where no one lives. Although Latin America covers an area almost three times as large as the United States, its population is smaller than ours. The products of Latin America are as varied as its lands and climates.

Chapter 1 ~ The Old World and the New World Have Merged in the Americas

Who is an American? That is a fair question to ask. The answer becomes clear when we look at a map of the Western Hemisphere. Canadians live in the Americas; so do the people of Argentina, Brazil, Costa Rica, Mexico, and Cuba. We of the United States and the people of many other nations live in the Americas. What is more, the people who came to the New World explored and settled two vast continents.

You have learned how geography set the stage for life in what is now the United States. Our coastal plains, mountainous areas, forest lands, wide river valleys, and broad prairies became the home of the people of the United States. This is likewise so of the people of Canada, of Mexico, of Central America, and of South America. You will learn that these nations have histories much like that of the United States.

The Mayan civilization was brilliant and barbaric. Long before the Spaniards and Portuguese, of whom you have learned in your earlier study of American history, arrived on American shores, the Indians had developed at least three great centers of civilization. The earliest, that of the mysterious Mayas of Guatemala and Yucatán (see the map on pages 704-705), was dead, but many of its characteristics had been taken over by other tribes.

The Mayan civilization had been in the jungles of Central America and Mexican Yucatán. About the First Century these people began to build stately pyramid temples, astronomical observatories, and the tall stone columns on which their history is carved. Their artists produced wonderful sculpturing and brilliantly colored frescoes. Their scientists developed an extremely accurate calendar, based on observations of the stars. They invented a hieroglyphic alphabet, and a system of numbers almost as advanced as that of Europe. They also knew the use of rubber many hundreds of years before it was utilized by the white man.

Mayan society was greatly influenced by a number of Mayan religious ideas. Priests were the real Mayan rulers, their most learned men, their greatest artists. Beautifully wrought plumed serpents decorated the columns of many of the temples, which stood on great pyramids high above the surrounding plains. One of the principal Mayan deities was the God of the Plumed Serpent. All the Mayan carvings and architecture have a religious character. Religion played a large part in Mayan history and in the hieroglyphics.

Some of the ancient Mayan religious centers in the jungles of Central America have only recently been excavated and studied. Only three Mayan manuscripts have come down to us. The writing on the fiber pages (made of the century plant) is exquisitely formed and colored. These manuscripts have not yet been translated, and, therefore, archaeologists have much to learn about Mayan civilization.

We do know, however, that the civilization of the Mayas had two periods of great height: the first was during the Sixth Century after Christ and the other, and last, reached its peak around the year 1000. At this time feudal life and customs were spread through most of northern Europe, and William the Conqueror had not yet invaded England. About 1200 the Mayas were overcome by the fierce Indian warriors from the Mexican plateau, and not long after that their civilization passed into decay. This was only a century or two before the Renaissance brought a re-awakening of civilization to the people of Europe.

The Incas organized a highly co-operative society. The second great American civilization was that of the Incas. Their capital, Cuzco [koos'koh] was in the Peruvian Andes. The Incas were not the first civilized Indians of the Andean region. There are many fine examples of ancient stonework constructed by their predecessors. However, the Incas took over the civilization of these earlier peoples of Peru, which you see on the map on pages 704–705.

The Incas were the first Indians of South America to organize a strong government to hold their civilization together. All their lands were divided into three parts, one for the Inca, or ruler, one for the Sun God, and one for the people themselves.

Inca architects constructed many miles of aqueducts, temples, fortresses, and palaces, all of beautifully cut stonework. Much of the land was on mountain slopes, but the workers erected stone terraces and filled these in with good topsoil so that even this land could be cultivated as farmers in upland China do to this day. In the days of the Incas, many parts of the Andes resembled gigantic staircases covered with green. Some of the stones which the Incas employed in their construction weighed thousands of pounds. How they were cut and put into place still remains a mystery. Since none of the Indian peoples had discovered the use of the wheel, it seems that the stones must have been dragged by sheer man power, sometimes over a distance of many miles, as were the stone blocks for the pyramids and temples of early Egypt.

The Incas did not evolve a system of writing, as did the Mayas. They depended on rudely knotted strings for their records. Strings of different colors had different meanings. For example, a yellow string signified gold, and a red one referred to war. The number of knots in a string told the reader the year or the quantity involved. There were many official "keepers of the strings." Each keeper was responsible for being able to read his own records. Consequently, while yellow would mean gold in a gold-producing district, it might refer to corn in a corn-producing district. This method of record-keeping was primitive, and provided inadequate means of recording abstract ideas, descriptive stories, or scientific facts.

The Inca social organization was very strict. Every worker had a job, sufficient clothes to wear, and enough to eat, for the government took care of these things. But he had to remain at the job to which he was assigned until his death. He was not even allowed to move freely from one place to another.

Inca society was closely tied together. When the central knot was broken or cut, the whole structure quickly fell apart. This was exactly what happened when Pizarro, the ruthless Spanish soldier of fortune, in 1531 captured the Inca emperor by inviting him to his camp and imprisoning him, and later executing him. You learned this story of Pizarro's conquests in American history. After the execution of this Inca emperor, the conquest of the Incas was easy, for without leadership they were lost. Pizarro and

Press Association

EARLY AMERICAN ART

The terra cotta vase, water vessel, and singing tea kettle pictured here are relics of a people who existed before the Incas. Notice how closely they followed natural forms in the making of everyday objects.

his soldiers took many millions of dollars' worth of gold from the Incas.

The third great early American civilization was that of the Aztecs, in Mexico. Cortés, as you learned in American history, conquered the Aztecs and took from them a great treasure in silver and gold. The Aztecs had taken over many of the discoveries of the Mayas. Their traditions, their architecture, and even their writing showed this debt to their predecessors. They were an extremely warlike people. Their religious ceremonies called for thousands of human sacrifices yearly. Like the Incas, they divided their lands among their people who worked them together. Private ownership of the land, such as we have today, was not known in ancient America. In Chapter 3, about Mexico, you will learn more about the Aztecs and Cortés.

The Indians had great influence on Colonial society. When the Spaniards came to the Americas, they encountered and conquered two primitive civilizations, that of the Incas in Peru and that of the Aztecs in Mexico. In all the other regions their conquest was over more savage Indians who lived in small scattered tribes. The natives in the Portuguese territory in Brazil also fall into this group. These less civilized Indians were much like those who lived in North America. As a result of these two types of conquest we find that two different kinds of Colonial society began to develop after the Spaniards and Portuguese took over. In Mexico and Peru the white men had a large number of well-organized Indians to work for them. Here the new society became strongly class-conscious. Rich mines of gold and silver in these countries made it increasingly so, because a small group of Spaniards in Mexico City and Lima [lee'mah], Peru, ruled millions of half-civilized Indians.

Where there were no great organized

groups of Indians, the conquest moved along slowly. The scattered Indian tribes did not come out in a single great army to seek victory. They fought a warfare of guerrilla tactics, attacking here, burning there, always a menace in some quarter, and kept the invaders constantly on the alert. Consequently, Colonial society in the countries of Chile, Argentina, Uruguay [yoo'roo gway], and Brazil advanced more slowly than that of Mexico or Peru. But it also advanced more surely, for it was on a surer base. The Spaniards and Portuguese in those countries could not at once become idle aristocrats; they had no great mines of gold or silver, and their constant fight against the Indians held them together in strong, alert, and progressive unity.

Colonial Latin America was poorly governed. By 1600, Central and South America were fairly well explored by the Spanish and Portuguese. The people were living under well-organized Colonial governments. There were about 250 towns in Latin America at that time, occupied by about two hundred thousand settlers from the Spanish Peninsula. The Spanish and Portuguese systems divided both the lands and the Indians among the early conquerors; this meant that about five thousand men controlled the greater portion of the territory and its inhabitants. This ownership or control of the land was passed down from father to son, and the custom has survived today in Latin America's many huge estates.

The government of these colonies was in the hands of governors and viceroys who represented the king. They did not hold office for long and many of them made the best of their brief time in office to amass all the wealth they possibly could, just as many a Roman governor used his position to enrich himself at the expense of the province he ruled.

A general disregard for the central government began to creep into the minds of the people all over Latin America. The extreme distances from the mother country, and the ignorance of the conditions displayed by the law-makers back home, probably did more than anything else, however, to build up this disregard.

Spain and Portugal exploited their New World colonies. While Latin America was undergoing the first centuries of its development, Spain and Portugal attempted to hold a monopoly on their commerce. They prohibited the colonies from trading with any except the mother countries. In order to enforce this rule, all merchandise which was sent to the New World had to be shipped in convoyed fleets which sailed from the ports of Seville, Cadiz, and Lisbon. Merchant ships were not allowed to sail from any other place. On reaching America the Spanish ships were allowed to unload at only four ports.

The settlement of Canada and the United States. While these things were going on in the southern countries of the New World, the lands which are

Fifteenth Century **1500** *Sixteenth Century* **1600** *Seventeenth Century*

1440 1450 1460 1470 1480 1490 | 1510 1520 1530 1540 1550 1560 1570 1580 1590 | 1610 1620 1630 1640 1650 1660 1670 1680 1690

THE AMERICAS

Amerigo Vespucci - America his namesake

Balboa finds Pacific
Negro slavery
Pizarro despoils Incas
Cortés in Mexico

first press in new world
Mexico City

Portuguese colonized Brazil

Inquisition brought to America

first English Colony in West Indies

Jamaica acquired by England

now the United States and Canada were without a single permanent colony. When one was finally established, it was founded by Spain at St. Augustine, in what is now Florida, in 1565. Spanish explorers pushed ahead through the territory which now makes up Florida, Georgia, Alabama, Mississippi, Texas, New Mexico, Arizona, and California. De Soto, about twenty years earlier, penetrated overland from Florida to the Mississippi River. Another Spanish explorer spent years searching throughout the Southwest for a fabled city of gold. Church missionaries later established missions in these regions, especially in the Southwest.

The first permanent English colony was at Jamestown, Virginia, in 1607. The Pilgrims who came over in the Mayflower landed on Plymouth Rock in 1620. In the meantime the Dutch, in 1614, had established themselves in what is now New York, and the first permanent French colony had been founded by Samuel de Champlain where the old city of Quebec stands above the broad St. Lawrence River in Canada. Canada was called New France; the northeast section of the United States was known as New England; New York was New Amsterdam; and Mexico was New Spain. Everyone who came to the New World had some reason for wanting to leave the old, but the most important reason of all was the desire to begin a new life.

This urge for new opportunity and new life did not express itself the same way in all of the colonies. A majority of the early Spaniards came to America hoping to find gold. Cortés and Pizarro had opened the way, and from then on the dream of El Dorado, a land of gold and easy living, drew thousands across the ocean. Many others came for adventure or for glory, for in their warfare against the Moors the Spaniards and Portuguese had become accustomed to fighting and conquest. Still others came to convert the savage Indians to the Christian faith. The three main reasons for the conquest and colonization of Latin America, then, were gold, glory, and the desire to spread Christianity.

The explorers who came to what is now the United States had other ideas. These people never found any great mines of gold or silver. They never encountered any great native civilizations. They did not come to America primarily for gold, or for glory, or even to spread the gospel. They came mainly for political, religious, and economic freedom. They dreamed of a " life in which a man could think as he would and develop as he willed."

One of the acts of each group of Colonists in the British colonies was to organize a vigorous self-government. Just before the Pilgrims landed they drew up the famous Mayflower Compact, which was a sort of constitution for those early days. For many years the settlements founded by the different groups of Colonists had to fight in order to survive.

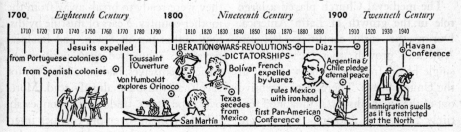

That fight made them strong, and the practice of self-government, among many Colonists, from the very day of their landing made them rather democratic-minded. Their town meetings and Colonial assemblies were representative of the people, though the right to vote in some communities depended upon holding property or belonging to a given church. There was no strongly centralized government over these settlements. Aristocratic classes were not so firmly entrenched as those of the Spanish and Portuguese colonies or of the Old World. The land was usually owned by many people, and not by a selected few.

The colonization of Canada was more like that in the primitive regions of Latin America. The settlements there were few and far between even compared with those in the British colonies. Most of them were missions founded by the Jesuit or Franciscan fathers about whom you read earlier in *Story of Nations,* or were mere trading posts on the Indian frontier. However, the French moved down the Mississippi, founded New Orleans, and established a series of forts along the Mississippi, Ohio, and St. Lawrence rivers, in order to block the expansion of the English. (See the map on pages 704–705.) As you know, they were not successful in this venture. Just a few years before the United States declared its independence, Wolfe had defeated Montcalm at Quebec and Canada had become an English colony.

The medieval Church played a large role in the growth of Latin America. During the early centuries of Latin America's growth, there was never a single broad frontier such as existed in the United States. There were extensive out-of-the way districts inhabited entirely by savage Indians. These were overcome and added to the colonies of Spain and Portugal by the work of the missions. and soldiers. In many places, missionaries of the Church, unaccompanied by soldiers, plunged into the wilderness among the savage tribes. Here they founded mission settlements in which the natives were given some elementary education, instruction in the arts and crafts, and perhaps some mechanical or manual training. The cities of San Antonio, Santa Fe, San Diego, Los Angeles, and San Francisco were all originally Spanish mission settlements.

There was another side to this church influence in Latin-American life. Some church groups gradually came to control as much as half the land and half the total wealth in some of the southern countries. Especially in large cities, some priests grew rich and powerful and frequently used their religious standing to interfere with politics. Their influence did not always encourage the development of the Latin-American colonies. Political ambitions often interfered with the desire of other churchmen to further education.

Spanish America rebelled against Old-World dominion. As England became stronger, Spain lost her position as a great world power. As you learned in the story of Spain, the defeat of her Armada in 1588 was the beginning of her decline. Constant warfare hastened that decline and sent her into bankruptcy.

The American colonies of Spain had by this time reached the point where they were ready to break away from the mother-country. Years of misrule by distant authorities in Spain, and by local governors who used their positions to enrich themselves, had paved the way for revolt, as you have already read. Moreover, the strict trade regulation established by Spain over the colonies interfered with their agricultural and industrial growth. During the wars of Napoleon, about which you learned earlier, Spain had been unable to keep a firm grip on her colonies. They seized this opportunity and, with no home government left to supervise them, began a rebellion. Simón Bolívar [see mohn' bohlee'vahr] was the leader in Venezuela [ven'ee zwee'luh]. San Martín [sahn mahr teen'] was the leader in Argentina. Many years previously Bolívar had pledged his life and his fortune to the liberty of his people. During the first thirty years of the 19th Century he worked increasingly to redeem that pledge. He talked, wrote, and persuaded. He organized soldiers, and planned and directed campaigns.

His forces were constantly outnumbered, but in a series of battles he defeated the Spaniards and advanced as far south as Peru. In the meantime, San Martín had formed a small army in Argentina; he led it across the hazardous Andes and defeated the Spaniards in Chile. Then with the help of an exiled Englishman, Lord Cochrane, he collected a fleet, mostly of Spanish ships, and carried his soldiers to Lima. The Spaniards there fled into the hills.

Bolívar and San Martín met in Ecuador [ek'wuh dawr] to plan. But as a result of Bolívar's dictatorial manner, San Martín left the conference and sailed back to Argentina and then on to France. Knowing that with Bolívar's temperament there was not room in Peru for two generals, San Martín deliberately withdrew, facing ridicule, hatred, and exile, in order that South America might really obtain her freedom. Bolívar and his able general Sucre [soo'kray] met the Spaniards in battle

again, and defeated them soundly. The entire continent was free at last. You will learn more about these leaders in a later chapter.

The results of Colonial errors began to show themselves. At this time the Spanish colonies faced a situation somewhat similar to that which had confronted the United States after their own war of independence. Each state wanted to govern itself, and in the Spanish colonies' case, the states did prevail. South America now contains ten republics; Central America has six; Mexico, Cuba, Santo Domingo, and Haiti [hay'ti] are also independent republics. This makes a total of twenty individual Latin-American republics.

After freedom was won, each general and each region rebelled against all central authority. Bolívar fought steadfastly for one great nation or one great confederation, but his fight was hopeless. Division was followed by general strife. As they had had little experience in self-government, the Spanish American nations were faced with near-chaos. Laws could not be enforced. Battles between generals continued. Slowly this period of military strife gave way to a period of military dictatorships. Each nation had its *caudillo* [kau dee'lyoh] or dictator, and for some years tyranny and economic oppression continued. But one by one these military despots gave way to a more normal civil government. Many of the nations of Spanish America developed comparatively democratic systems of government, as you will learn in later chapters. Others unfortunately still continue under dictatorships. These dictatorships, however, are very mild compared to the despotisms of the early *caudillos*.

Chapter 2 ～ Nature Has Endowed the Americas with Great Resources

Latin America has great differences in geography and climate. You can see by looking at the map on pages 704–705 that the greater part of South America lies east of the eastern coast of the United States. That is one reason why important air routes to Europe cross the Atlantic Ocean between South America and Africa.

Mexico, the nations of Central America, and those of South America spread over an area nearly three times as large as the United States. It may seem difficult to believe, but one of the Latin-American countries, Brazil, is considerably larger than is the United States. Moreover, we should remember that a very considerable portion of Latin America lies in the temperate zone of the Southern Hemisphere. Therefore in this area the temperature and climate are much like those in the United States. But if you plan to travel in Chile or Argentina in July or August you will encounter cold weather, just as you would in the northern part of the United States in our winter months.

Another glance at the map on pages 704–705 will show that the equator passes through the northern parts of Brazil and Ecuador. But do not think that Ecuador is entirely tropical because it is on the equator. The high mountains of this smaller nation give portions of Ecuador a cool, bracing climate. Furthermore, the climate of lowland Venezuela, the Guianas [ghee ah'nuhz], and the Central American states is generally hot and humid, except in mountainous or plateau areas. This is likewise so in many parts of Mexico. In other words, in the countries of Latin America we find great variety in climate and geography.

Except for Canada, the republics of Latin America are our nearest neighbors. Mexico is just south of our own border. Furthermore, two of the most distant countries of Latin America, Argentina and Chile, are only twenty-four hours by air from New York.

When we speak of the " good-neighbor policy " we must bear all of these things in mind. The republics of Latin America, along with the United States and Canada, make up this Western Hemisphere in which we Americans all live. It is the duty and responsibility of every " good neighbor " to know something about the history, the language, the traditions, and the way of life of the peoples who live next door to him if we are to develop greater trade and cultural relations with one another.

Latin America's undeveloped resources are extensive. There are many and important reasons why Latin America is of primary importance to the citizens of the United States. In the first place, the nations south of us are not, in general, so highly developed economically and industrially as we are. One of the principal reasons for this difference is that the Latin-American nations are more thinly populated than the United States. In fact, the population of the entire region comprising the twenty republics is approximately the same as the population of our own country. As a result of this and other reasons which we shall take up later, Latin America is

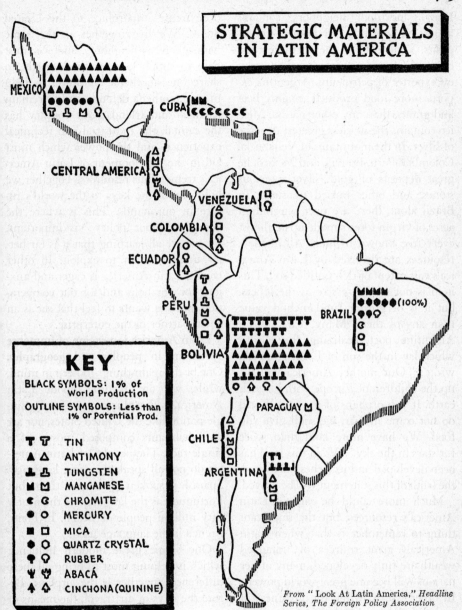

STRATEGIC MATERIALS IN LATIN AMERICA

KEY

BLACK SYMBOLS: 1% of World Production

OUTLINE SYMBOLS: Less than 1% or Potential Prod.

T T	TIN
▲ △	ANTIMONY
⚒ ⚒	TUNGSTEN
M M	MANGANESE
C C	CHROMITE
● ○	MERCURY
■ □	MICA
◆ ◇	QUARTZ CRYSTAL
♥ ♡	RUBBER
♣ ♧	ABACÁ
♠ ♤	CINCHONA (QUININE)

From "Look At Latin America," Headline Series, The Foreign Policy Association

in a very real sense like a last frontier. You will remember the frontier in United States history. The frontier of unexplored, unknown lands of course no longer exists in the United States, but it does exist in Latin America, where there are still millions of square miles uninhabited and undeveloped.

The wealth of some of these regions is so great that it seems overwhelming. For example, in Brazil there is a single great mountain of iron ore which contains approximately one-fourth of the total world's supply of iron. Brazil also produces about 70 percent of the world's coffee. The country of Bolivia, one of

Brazil's nextdoor neighbors, contains about one-fourth of all known tin deposits. Venezuela on the northern coast of South America is the world's greatest exporter of petroleum. Argentina exports more food products, mainly beef and grains, than any other nation. Mexico contains the world's greatest deposits of silver. In the mountains of Venezuela, Colombia, Peru, Bolivia, and Mexico, lie great deposits of gold, silver, precious stones, and other buried treasures. In Brazil alone there are over one billion acres of virgin forests made up of almost every tree known to man. All of these resources are dwarfed by Latin America's vast extent of rich untilled soil. This item is not so impressive as the others, but it is of greater fundamental value than any of them. Many years ago an Argentine poet, realizing the wealth which lay in the soil of Latin America, wrote: "Our mother America will lift up the children of Europe with her rich earth. If you orphans of the Old World do not come in war, we shall give you food. We have more land than space for stars in the sky." When this land has been developed and its riches uncovered, the truth of this statement will be proved.

Much more could be said of Latin America's resources, but the important thing to remember is that when Latin America's great sources of untapped wealth are fully developed, many of her nations will become great world powers. In other words, while the greatness of some of the world civilizations which we have already studied belongs to the past, the greatness of Latin America lies in the future, and that future is just across the threshold from us *now*.

The good-neighbor policy means being friends and partners in the New World. For all of these reasons the twenty republics of Latin America are of extreme importance to the United States. We live together in the same hemisphere as neighbors, and we must help to supply one another's needs, to share one another's literature, to help in one another's defense, and to remain partners and friends. Our country has the capital, the industrial and technical experience, and the power which must aid in the development of Latin America's tremendous resources. Together we hold one of the keys to the world's future in our hands. This is where the "good-neighbor policy" is important, for we are all learning that it is far better to share than to exploit. In other words, Latin America is eager and anxious for our help and for our co-operation, but she wants to feel that she is an equal partner in the enterprise.

Latin America is a region of immense variations in peoples and geography. One of the main things to keep in mind, while we are reading about Latin America, is that this region is not a single nation like the United States, nor are its inhabitants composed mostly of a single race. The peoples of Latin America do not all speak the same language. Spanish is spoken by most of them, but Portuguese is the language of the nearly fifty million people of Brazil. In Haiti, French is the language used.

One single great modern influence which is helping most to bring all these differences together is the airplane. Before the days of air travel, the means of communication inside Latin America were scant. It was too expensive to lay out railways or roads across miles of towering mountains or through endless forests or swamps. But the airplane has changed those conditions almost overnight. During the 19th Century, railroad building in the United States laid the foundations for our country's great-

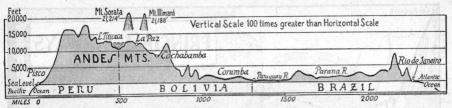

Feet
-20000-   Mt.Sorata   Mt.Illimani
          21,214'   21,188'
-15000-   L.Titicaca   La Paz   Vertical Scale 100 times greater than Horizontal Scale
-10000-   ANDE MTS.   Cochabamba
- 5000-   Pisco   Corumba   Paraguay R.   Parana R.   Rio de Janeiro
SeaLevel   Atlantic
Pacific Ocean   PERU | B O L I V I A | B R A Z I L   Ocean
MILES 0   500   1000   1500   2000

A CROSS SECTION OF SOUTH AMERICA

This map shows a cross-section view of the surface of South America between Rio de Janeiro, Brazil, on the east coast, and Pisco, Peru, on the west coast.

ness. Some of our southern neighbors will not have a similar period of railroad building. They will pass directly into the stage of air communication where geographic barriers no longer exist. American airlines are already helping to develop air transportation among the Latin-American nations.

In order to get a quick bird's-eye view of all our southern neighbors, let us imagine that we are taking a trip by air over the entire region. Glance at the map on page 718 and follow our trip as we go from Miami, Florida, all the way around South America.

We leave Miami in the early morning and within only an hour or so we are over the island of Cuba, which Columbus said was the "most beautiful land that human eyes had ever seen." Below us is the metropolis of Havana, with its wide palm-lined avenues and its shining new houses, which contrast with the narrow streets and tightly packed dwellings of the old quarter of town. Then we fly over vivid green fields in which Cuba's two most important products are grown: sugar cane and tobacco. Since tropical rains fall frequently every month in the year in Cuba, the vegetation is always lush and rich in appearance. Sugar-cane plantations cover miles and miles of land, and are dotted with huge palm trees and crossed with roads leading to the large refineries. These are the Cuban plantations that in a single

year send to the United States four billion pounds of sugar, that is, about thirty pounds for every man, woman, and child in this country.

Colombian cities are separated by great swamps, jungles, and towering mountains. After leaving the lovely green fields of Cuba, we fly over the Gulf of Mexico for several hours until we reach the city of Barranquilla [bahr' rahn kee'lyah], Colombia, an enterprising and modern town on the mouth of a great river. We notice many small settlements along the tropical coast of Colombia. The entire Gulf of Mexico region has a large proportion of Negro and Mulatto inhabitants.

The moment we leave Barranquilla, we understand why railway transportation has been so backward in some parts of Latin America. Swamps and jungles extend in every direction. If a track were laid in this swampy region, the cost of its upkeep would be excessively great.

After a few moments in the air, we circle over the ancient city of Cartagena [kahr'tuh jee'nuh] with its huge reddish walls. These were erected in order to keep out the English pirates who frequently attacked the Colonial city to sack and destroy. From Cartagena we head over more swamps and jungles and flooded fields until we reach the highlands near the capital city of Bogotá [boh goh tah'].

As we enter the mountainous region,

PRINCIPAL AIRWAYS

U.S. LINES
GERMAN LINES
SYNDICATO CONDOR (BRAZ.)
VARIG (BRAZ.)
VASP (BRAZ.)
AERO POSTA (ARG.)
LLOYD AEREO BOL. (BOL.)
LUFTHANSA PERU (PERU)
SEDTA (ECUADOR)
ITALIAN LINE
DUTCH LINE
LOCAL LINES
Controlled or operated by Germans

From "Look At Latin America," Headline Series, The Foreign Policy Association

we see in valleys below us stone ranch houses and fields of coffee. In Colombia alone there are nearly five hundred million coffee trees. Suddenly we cross a high mountain barrier and there very near beneath us is the fertile savannah of Bogotá with the great city itself situated under the protection of towering peaks. We are in one of the agricultural districts of Colombia; the land is level and fertile, and the air is cool in contrast to that of the tropical coast lands. We are now at an altitude of nearly nine thousand feet, where the weather is never hot. Yet we are so near the equator that it never becomes really cold. The people

A STREET IN QUITO

Rows of low adobe houses like these are typical of Quito, the capital of Ecuador. Quito was formerly the site of an old Indian nation and is one of the oldest cities in South America. It is located in a ravine on the side of a volcano.

who live here have a large proportion of Indian blood in their veins. One of the largest and most beautiful university campuses in Latin America is located in Bogotá, and that city also has one of the finest libraries in this hemisphere.

As we leave Bogotá, we pass over even more extensive mountain barriers and then come out upon the beautiful fertile Cauca [kau′kah] River Valley. We are amazed, however, at how few cultivated fields the long river valley contains. The population is not great enough yet to call for the cultivation of more than a very small part of the nation's soil. We pass over several lovely cities in the Cauca Valley, which is just high enough above sea level for the climate to be comfortably warm throughout the year, and

for the growth to be tropical with myriads of brilliant vines and flowers.

As we near the southern border of Colombia, we enter the mountains again. This is our first glimpse of the great ridge of the Andes which extends all the way down the continent to southernmost Patagonia. See the map on pages 704–705.

In this mountain region, and on the great plateaus and valleys between the ranges, we find a population that is mostly Indian and *mestizo* [mes tee′ zoh], that is, mixed Indian and white. From Bogotá southward, in mountainous Colombia, Ecuador, Peru, and Bolivia, these descendants of the ancient Andean Indians still make up the vast majority of the inhabitants. Some of them in the more remote districts do not even speak the Spanish language but cling to their native dialects and their primitive way of life. In many of the small villages and cities of the Andean highlands such modern conveniences as good drinking water, sewage disposal, well-paved and well-lighted streets, and good schools, are completely unknown.

Ecuador is a picturesque country of mountains with a large Indian population. The thickly populated part of Ecuador falls almost entirely in this mountainous region, except for its narrow tropical coast. Quito [kee'toh], the capital city, is almost on the equator but it is cool the year round because of its altitude of about nine thousand feet. The mountains of Ecuador are a beautiful green and every valley contains its primitive but picturesque settlement of Indians and *mestizos*. Many of them gather coffee beans, and cacao beans from which we make chocolate. Ecuador owns the Galapagos Islands, which are 600 miles off the coast along the equator. These islands were once a refuge for pirates and buccaneers.

Peru is a land of gigantic contrasts. After leaving the mountains of Ecuador we find ourselves suddenly flying over a desert of rocks and sand. All along the coast of Peru this great desert extends. In a few spots petroleum has been found, but outside of a few drab oil towns and one or two fertile valleys this coastal strip of Peru is deserted. It is not very wide, however, and just a few miles back from the coast rise the Andes. The Peruvians say that their country is really geographically divided into three Perus, the narrow but long coastal desert, the huge range of the Andes, and on the other side of these mountains, the low jungle regions which reach down to the Amazon. The climates of these three regions are completely different. Rain

rarely falls on the coast and the land is arid; in the Andean valleys, the weather is cool, and the region is inhabited mostly by Indians who cultivate the fertile valleys. The tropical jungle region on the other side of the mountains is wet and hot, and so full of insects and disease that it has not yet been greatly populated. You can find these three regions on the map on pages 704-705.

About halfway down the coastal strip of Peru we see the capital city of Lima. It is situated in a valley partly surrounded by barren gray peaks, and is only a few miles from the Pacific Ocean. Fresh breezes from the Humboldt sea current keep it cool all the year round, but during our summer and fall the sky is almost constantly overcast with a heavy pall of wet gray clouds which rarely break into rain. Lima is a modern capital, but its atmosphere is like that of a city in old Spain. Nearly all the wealth of Peru is funneled into Lima, the only large city in Peru.

Peruvians are made up of two classes, Indians who live mostly in the highlands, and *mestizos* and whites who live along the coast. The country is ruled mainly by the aristocratic whites, who, under the Spanish regime, used to be the government officials and large landowners, and who have kept this power even since Peruvian independence. Consequently there is distrust and even hatred between them and the more primitive Indians. However, the ruling white class, in realization of its responsibility, is building schools, hospitals, roads, and airfields throughout the country. Workers are assured of minimum wages, and the government is making a sincere attempt to better their lot in life.

Chile is a progressive democracy with fewer inhabitants than the state of Ohio. South of Peru is another coastal desert which covers the northern part of Chile and extends for several hundred miles down to the central valley of Santiago [sahn'tee ah'goh]. When you refer to the map on pages 704–705, notice that Chile is a coastal country; behind it lie the towering Andes. Beyond these mountains is Argentina. The Chilean desert is barren, but it is far from being worthless land. It is the center of the world's greatest nitrate deposits, from which commercial fertilizer is made.

The region of the nitrate deposits is desolate. For over a thousand miles this great desert reaches southward. At its end we come to the rich central valleys of Chile, where the greater portion of the population lives. Here there are well-kept vineyards, fruit orchards, cattle ranches, and cultivated fields of all descriptions. The capital city of Santiago is in one of these valleys surrounded by mountain peaks. The city is modern, its inhabitants are democratic and progressive. The women in Chile enjoy more freedom than those in any other nation of Latin America, for many English, French, and German settlers have established themselves in Chile, and have broken down the Spanish custom of keeping the women isolated from business and even to a large extent from social life. In either Peru or Colombia, " dates " between young girls and boys would generally not be allowed unless some older person were present as chaperon. This is not true in Chile where the women enjoy much freedom, and hundreds of them work in offices and factories. We are informed that the population of Chile is mostly white. The strong Indian element which predominates in the central Andean region has disappeared, or rather has been absorbed into the white group, for many Chileans are partly Indian.

When we leave Santiago, we head directly through the towering crest of the Andes in order to cross the southern part of the continent and reach Argentina. The air becomes cold as we gain height. Jagged peaks of rock covered with snow float by on each side of us. As we fly on, the pilot rings an electric gong in the cabin to call our attention to the massive statue of the Christ of the Andes on a ledge down below us. Many years ago the governments of Chile and Argentina erected this monument as a constant reminder of their pledge never again to wage war against each other. The statue bears these words: " Sooner shall these mountains crumble to dust than the people of Argentina and Chile break the peace which they have sworn to maintain at the feet of Christ, the Redeemer."

Argentina is Latin America's furthest developed nation. Within half an hour we have made our way through the Andes and find ourselves out above the Argentine foothills. These gradually level off and eventually become the flowing pampas, the greatest and richest prairie on earth, larger than our Texas plains, with deep fertile soil like that in our Mississippi Valley. The land is like a wide sea of grass. Cattle and agricultural crops raised here are the country's great products. This great plain extends for hundreds of miles in every direction. Through the pampas there are many lovely country estates or *estancias* [es tahn'see ahs]. Travel is easy across the pampas, and road and rail lines cover it thoroughly. The climate is good. The inhabitants are mostly European immigrants of Spanish and Italian stock who tend to their ranches and farms much as we do in the United States. You can see on the map on pages 704–705 that much of Argentina consists of this plain. On the eastern edge of the pampas,

THE CHRIST OF THE ANDES

This statue was erected by the peoples of Chile and the Argentine to remind them that quarrels between nations can be settled without war and bloodshed.

spread out along the southern banks of the River Plata, is Latin America's largest city, Buenos Aires [buay'nohs ai'rays]. Its lovely homes, huge stores, magnificent avenues, and cosmopolitan and progressive air make it by far the most impressive Latin American city, and the most wealthy. Under its streets run subways. A single parking lot underneath one of the buildings has space for over a thousand automobiles. Its university is among the finest in the world. Into the port along the river bank come ships from all the seven seas, and from its railway stations moves South America's greatest system of land transportation. The entire pampas empty their wealth into Buenos Aires which occupies the position of a hand holding a great fan. The hand is Buenos Aires, the fan which seems to flow out from it is the Argentine pampas.

The map on pages 704–705 shows that to fly from Buenos Aires to Brazil, we first cross the wide River Plata, and then come to Montevideo [mohn'ti vi day' oh], capital of Uruguay, which is not far away. It is a much poorer city than Buenos Aires, and its people have had to work much harder to earn a living. The land itself is much like the Argentine prairie, but is on a smaller scale. Uruguay is also a great cattle country. Its social legislation (minimum wages, hours, unemployment compensation) is among the most advanced and democratic in the world. North and west of Uruguay is land-locked Paraguay [par' uh gway] — a comparatively backward country. Even further north and west the map shows us another land-locked nation, Bolivia. A bitter three-year war between Paraguay and Bolivia over disputed territory was ended in 1935, and the two nations settled their differences by arbitration.

Gigantic Brazil is a nation of promise. Before long we reach Brazil, which is about the size of the United States plus an additional territory as large as France. Only the coastal strip of Brazil is thickly populated, and behind that the forests and Amazon jungles seem to extend indefinitely. In contrast to the population of Uruguay, Argentina, and Chile, which is mostly white, a large proportion of the inhabitants of Brazil contain some Negro blood. They are descendants of slaves who formerly worked on Brazilian plantations, much as they did in our old South. Rio de Janeiro is a beautiful capital city situated on the Atlantic and rimmed by green mountain peaks. Its twin city São Paulo [sauɴ pau'loo] (meaning St. Paul) is an industrial metropolis of a million and a half people. The real wealth of Brazil, however, lies in the interior, and its development has scarcely begun. When more adequate transportation is provided, Brazil's great resources can be utilized. When you look at the map on pages 704–705 you see that Brazil is also much larger than any other Latin-American country.

Venezuela is the world's greatest exporter of petroleum. From Rio we fly northward across tangled Brazilian jungles where orchids grow wild and thousands of brilliant butterflies fly among the trees and creepers. The flooding waters of the Amazon pass slowly under us like an octopus with all Brazil in its grasp. The distance seems limitless, but at last we cross the Guianas and enter Venezuela, a petroleum and cattle country, where United States' oil companies have invested millions of dollars. We see their neat settlements and derricks along the coast of the Caribbean Sea. These coastal regions of Venezuela are hot and humid, but among the mountains or on the plateau of the interior the weather is mild the year round. Like Brazil, Venezuela is developed only along the seacoast. In the interior, village life has remained primitive. Venezuela is the birthplace of Simón Bolívar, the liberator of a great part of South America, of whose colorful career you have already read. The country also gave birth to the last of the old-line tyrants, the bloody and dictatorial Juan Vicente Gómez [wahn vee sayn'tay goh'mes], who ruled Venezuela rigidly between 1908 and 1935, imprisoning or exiling all those who dared hold an opinion different from his own. He built himself a private fortune of over $200,-000,000, while his people continued barely to subsist.

The six countries of Central America present many variations. On leaving Venezuela we again cross a part of Colombia and then turn northward into Central America. The map on pages 704–705 reveals to us a region made up of six small republics. Panama is the one we know best, because of the canal. What we have accomplished in Panama in blotting out tropical diseases and in bringing sanitation and more pleasant living will no doubt be copied in other hot regions of Latin America. Among the five other Central American republics we find a great similarity so far as the mountainous landscape is concerned, but there are great differences among the people. Costa Rica, of an almost entirely white population, is a country of small farmers. It is one of the most democratic and forward-looking nations in all Latin America. Education is provided for all. Guatemala is almost entirely Indian. It has been under a nearly perpetual dictatorship. In Nicaragua, Honduras, and Salvador, the Indian and *mestizo* population is large. There also

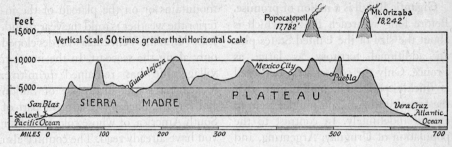

A CROSS SECTION OF MEXICO

This map shows a cross-section view of Mexico between Vera Cruz on the east coast and San Blas on the west coast.

the tendency has been toward dictatorial government. Economically, these small countries are all dependent on the United States. North American companies own vast banana plantations there, and nearly all Middle America's coffee comes to this country.

Mexico is a forward-looking country ruled by its mestizo population. The last country we fly to is Mexico, our next-door southern neighbor. The map shows it to be somewhat like South America on a small scale. Mountains ridge its interior and lift up to a high central plateau, while the coast regions are tropical. The people are predominantly *mestizos* and Indians. In direct contrast to Peru, where the white aristocracy is the ruling caste, in Mexico the Indians and *mestizos* themselves run the government. All the Andean countries of South America are watching the Mexican experiment closely. Perhaps with the lesson of Mexico before them they will be able to avoid a violent civil war such as the Mexican Revolution of 1910–1917.

Mexico ranks as the second most populous nation of Latin America, and has about twenty million inhabitants. Most of them earn only a few cents a day, and the average income is less than a hun-

dred dollars a year. However, Mexico continues to move forward, and looks to the United States for co-operation. Her magnificent landscape, hospitable people, and picturesque cities have already drawn thousands of American tourists across her borders, and now that the Pan-American Highway is paved all the way to Mexico City, in normal times more people will make the trip yearly.

Latin America differs in people, geography, and politics. When we leave the Mexican capital, we swing out over the rich agricultural district around Mexico's second largest city, Guadalajara [gwah-thah lah hah'rah], and then fly northwest across the barren wastelands to Los Angeles. As we take leave of Latin America, several general impressions will stand out in our minds. First of all, Latin America is a geographical region of the greatest possible variations. In the second place, Latin America is a region of several widely differing peoples. In the third place, the regions differ in their governments, their products, their society, their degree of advancement, and their outlook on life. In the fourth place, even those countries which are inhabited by similar peoples, such as Mexico and Peru, are in many ways utterly distinct.

Chapter 3 ~ Mexico Is a Changing Nation with a Great Cultural Heritage

The Spaniards under Cortés conquered Mexico. The greatest of the Spanish conquerors was Hernando Cortés, who overcame the empire of the Aztecs under Montezuma and thus gave Spain her wealthiest and most populous colony. This Spanish hero of the early 16th Century has already been mentioned. The governor of Cuba said he was not to head the expedition to Mexico. Cortés, however, prepared his men and ships during the night and slipped away at dawn. On reaching the Mexican coast his small force of about 550 men, 16 of them mounted, met and defeated a much larger army of Indians. The natives had never before seen a horse and thought that the rider and animal were one. Nor had they ever before seen firearms or cannon, and the noise and destruction of these weapons, and the great courage of the Spaniards, soon overcame them.

Cortés immediately had them all baptized as Christians, and tore down their idols to which they had formerly made human sacrifices. He then made ready to march into the interior where he had been told there was a famous city. The emperor of the Aztecs, Montezuma, had already heard of the arrival of these strange white men who sailed on the sea in " thunderbirds," and he was not at all anxious to meet them face to face.

Montezuma sent gifts to the Spaniards. There was an Aztec legend that someday blond warriors would come from beyond the ocean and conquer the Mexican nation, and Montezuma believed that perhaps this prophecy was about to be fulfilled. The God of the Plumed Serpent at that time was believed to have taught both the Mayans and Aztecs the arts of civilization. Many centuries before, he had taken leave of his people and sailed away across the waters toward the east on a raft formed by coiled serpents. When the god departed he had said the white warriors would come. With this legend in his mind, Montezuma sent Cortés gifts and urged him not to come to the Mexican capital, saying that it was entirely too far and the journey too difficult. Among the presents of the Aztec emperor were two plates, one of gold and the other of silver, both of them " as large as carriage-wheels " and decorated with carved plants and animals. The gold plate alone was valued at more than $200,000. There were also other gifts of fine cloths, cloaks of exquisite featherwork in brilliant colors, and a helmet filled with gold dust.

These things made Cortés more eager than ever to march on into the interior. So that there could be no possible turning back he destroyed all but one ship. He told his men that if any of them wanted to leave they could board that vessel, for it was going to return for supplies. Not a man accepted his offer, and soon they were all on their long journey over the difficult mountainous territory which lay between the coast and Mexico City. On their way they came upon several hundred Indians, who resented being ruled by the Aztecs. These Indians were willing to join with Cortés against Montezuma. One fierce tribe challenged the Spaniards' passage, but after being defeated on the field of battle, they, too,

THE POWER OF CORTÉS

In their search for treasure Cortés and his followers used torture to subdue the Aztec leaders. This picture is from a painting in the national Museum, Mexico City.

joined the white men in the march on the capital.

The Spaniards saw the wild splendor of Mexico's capital. Montezuma had decided to receive Cortés courteously. When his little band of soldiers, which had now dwindled to about 400 (not counting the Indian allies), came into Mexico City, the entire populace had turned out to greet them. The Spaniards were amazed at the sight. The city was surrounded by enormous trees and was in the center of a valley. The houses of the chiefs were of red stone, and were decorated with flowers. In the center of the capital was a pyramid on top of which stood three temples to the Aztec gods. The Aztec chiefs who had come out to receive Cortés were dressed in feather cloaks and were adorned with pieces of gold. Even the common people wore brilliant cotton clothing. It was a colorful spectacle such as had never been seen by a European.

The Spanish soldiers overcame Montezuma's empire. Cortés had not come to Mexico as a friend but to make the Aztecs subjects of his emperor Charles V, and to convert its people to Christianity. He was also eager to lay hands on some of that Aztec gold. Consequently, when he saw that things were not proceeding to his liking he made Montezuma a prisoner, and later when the natives rebelled he attacked them. He was driven from the city and more than half of his men were slain, but as soon as reinforcements were received he went back again, laid siege to the place, and after destroying it block by block, eventually captured what remained of it. Most of the population had by that time already died of starvation, and Montezuma had met his death.

The Spaniards as rulers. Cortés then had an opportunity to show what kind of administrator he was, and he soon proved his capacity beyond any doubt.

A wise policy of conciliation and stern justice was put into effect, and the country was quickly reorganized and order restored. Mexico City was rebuilt and almost immediately became one of the largest centers of the New World. Spanish viceroys soon took the place of Aztec chiefs or emperors, and life went on much as before except that the Indians were now forced to work for the Spaniards instead of for themselves. As a matter of fact, when a Spaniard was assigned a large plot of land by right of his part in the conquest, a certain number of Indians went along with it in much the same way as did the serfs during feudal times in Europe. Some of them became his domestic servants, others tilled the fields. The Spaniards themselves did not have to do any hard labor, for the natives had been used to working for their own chiefs, and it was merely a matter of accustoming them to new and harder masters.

Consequently, Mexico became a colony in which there was a small wealthy class of Spaniards, and a large poor class of Indians and *mestizos*. Life was so easy for the small upper class that little was done to educate or raise the standard of living of the masses. What little was done for the lower class was carried out by the Church, which had charge of the schools and of the missions. Here the Indians were taught the arts and crafts, and many types of work in wood, iron, and leather which were new to them. Very few, however, learned how to read or write.

Mexico continued in much this same way until the 19th Century. A constant stream of wealth flowed out of the country to Spain, and a comparatively small group of government officials and large landowners continued to rule the country. Many beautiful churches and cathe- drals were built, and in the capital a great university was founded. But Mexican life, as you see, was like that of the Middle Ages, with a great lord at the top and hundreds of servants and workers under him. Many priests became wealthy also, and by the year 1800 the Church owned approximately half the land in Mexico. Some of these priests identified themselves with the wealthy ruling class, but others gave their lives trying to help and to educate the poor people. Meanwhile both the white and the Indian classes were gradually becoming smaller and smaller, and were forming the large *mestizo* population which makes up most of Mexico today. These people are often called peons [pee'ahnz], and the great majority of them are agricultural workers.

Mexico won her independence from Spain. At the beginning of the 19th Century there arose a strong movement for independence. The United States had just won its freedom from England, and France had thrown off the yoke of the aristocrats. Spain, overrun by Napoleon's forces at that time, could do little to govern her colony properly. With all of these things before them, the Mexican people were ready for independence.

One morning in the year 1810 the priest of a little church in Dolores, Mexico, called his congregation together and urged them to follow him in the fight for freedom. The priest was Miguel Hidalgo [mee gwel' ee dal'goh], and his call to liberty is known as " the cry from Dolores." Thousands of people gathered under his banners, and they marched on Mexico City. For a time their campaign was successful, but Hidalgo knew nothing of military tactics and he was finally captured and executed. Another priest named Morelos [moh rayl'ohs] immediately took up the battle. He also was killed. The aristocrats and some of the more powerful churchmen were afraid of this " poor rabble " which might endanger their own positions, and so fought on the side of Spain. In the long run, however, the masses were successful and independence was finally won.

But Mexico now learned what a mistake it had been not to educate all classes of its people. The poor Indians and *mestizos* had had no experience in self-government; most of them could not even read or write. And so the old ruling caste continued to hold the power to govern. Mexico found herself as badly off as she had been under the government of Spain. One dictator succeeded another, the schools were neglected, the standard of living remained low. Finally while the War between the States was going on in the United States, and when we could not take action, several thousand French troops came to Mexico and made the Austrian archduke, Maximilian, Emperor of Mexico.

The Mexican Lincoln, Benito Juarez [bay nee'toh hwah'res], gathered a rebel army around him and continued to challenge Maximilian's power. Juarez was a full-blooded Indian and was worshiped by the masses. Finally, when his forces were strong enough to meet the emperor in battle, Maximilian was defeated. Mexico again had a chance for freedom, but again she was thwarted, for another, sterner, dictator slipped into the saddle.

This time it was Porfirio Diaz [pohr-fee'ree oh dee'ahth]. He ruled for over thirty years. Diaz urged Americans to invest money, built railroads and factories, established an orderly police force, made Mexico an apparently progressive nation. But most of her progress was on the surface. The old rulers still exerted their power, and the people in general were little better off than they had been before.

The violent Mexican Revolution finally upset the ruling aristocrats. Not until 1910 was the undemocratic state of things changed. By that time conditions had become so bad and oppression so widespread that the masses arose in spontaneous groups all over the country. Diaz was overthrown, and the famous Mexican Revolution was under way. The poor peons who made up most of the rebels were still illiterate, but four centuries of oppression had taught them at least one simple truth, which became the battlecry of their revolt: Land and Liberty! They wanted the land which had been taken away from them, and they wanted freedom to work that land. The guerrilla bands began to flow over the land like a swarm of locusts fighting, burning, killing, destroying everything in their path which even remotely suggested the old way of life. It was the first time that the Mexicans had ever had a real revolution of the oppressed, the first time that these uneducated masses had been able to put their accumulated violence into effect, the first time that the people of a backward Indian and *mestizo* country had found their voice and had spoken. For seven years a state of chaos reigned in Mexico, until finally in 1917 some measure of discipline was restored and the country gradually became orderly again. The masses had won their revolution. What would they do with the victory?

The results of the Mexican Revolution were widespread. The first thing the Mexican people insisted upon was that the great estates be broken up and the lands divided among them. This was begun soon after the Revolution, and more than fifty million acres of this land were returned to the people during the succeeding years. This land did not become their private property, however, but belonged to the village people in common just as it did in the days of the Aztecs. Holders could retain their land for life, and even pass it on to their heirs, but failure to work it for two years in succession would cause them to lose their rights.

Other things which the people of Mexico wanted were more schools, more health centers, more public works, more roads, more modern sanitation in their towns and cities, and more up-to-date houses to live in. Little by little all of these things began to be accomplished. The standard of living is still low if compared with that in the United States, but it is now far better than it was during the years of the dictator Porfirio Diaz. Thousands of little white schoolhouses have already been constructed all over the country, and medical centers are being established. The people of Mexico are on the move forward.

Out of the social unrest of their Revolution the Mexicans created a great art and a great literature. Perhaps when their souls and their bodies were so sorely tried they came to see the realities of life in a clearer light than ever before. This new insight was the basis of their new cultural development. At any rate the paintings of Diego Rivera [dyay'goh ree vay'rah], of José Orozco [hoh say' oh rohz'koh], and of many other Mexican artists are among the first in the world. And their school of painting, deeply rooted in the soil of Indian Mexico, has inspired artists all over Latin America and in the United States. Their use of brilliant native colors combined with human figures which express all the pathos of poverty and oppression, have raised mural art to its highest level since the days of the Renaissance.

Acme

DIEGO RIVERA

The Mexican painter, Rivera, is working on one of his mural paintings.

The mural that Diego Rivera painted on the walls of the Detroit Institute of Art is a splendid example of Mexico's new art. Rivera wanted to paint a mural that would be symbolic of the industrial life of the "city of automobiles." Therefore he made a thorough study of the city and its people before he began to paint. He made hundreds of preliminary sketches of factories, machines, and workers.

When Diego finished his mural, he had given a vivid picture of Detroit. He showed mass production of automobiles, workers at their machines, and the sources of the power that operates the factories. Rivera's mural so influenced this type of art that in many of our public buildings you may see other murals designed to catch the life and spirit of the town or city in which the building stands.

In Mexican literature a parallel development has taken place. The greatest novel of the Mexican Revolution is entitled *The Underdogs*. This novel and similar books which have followed it express the violent strivings of the submerged Mexican masses to attain a new state of liberty and democracy such as they have not known before. The novels of the Mexican Revolution are filled with ugly and bloody scenes, but these are always counteracted by a thread of poetry which comes out at unexpected moments to suggest man's aspiration for a better, a fuller, and a richer life. However, these novels do not make any attempt to draw a moral. They merely paint the scenes which unroll before the eyes of the author. One age is dying and another is being born, and it is that change which offers us hope in the future of Mexico.

Along with these new developments in art and literature came other advances. The Mexican people have found new interest in music and folk dances and the native arts and crafts such as pottery making, silver work, weaving, woodcarving, and featherwork, are all very much alive today. This folk voice of ancient Mexico, which has changed its harmony and enriched its tones since the coming of the Spaniards, is a thing of unique beauty in our modern world. It shows us that Mexico is a nation which is fusing or blending Spanish and Indian cultures into one, and that this development has already accomplished much in the stimulating of literature and music and painting.

Chapter 4 ~ Chile Is a Progressive Nation Gifted with Natural Resources

The Chileans have always been a hardy and progressive people. Chile lies along the west coast of South America, as you have learned. It begins at the southern border of Peru and extends southward for nearly three thousand miles. At its broadest point the country is only about two hundred miles wide. The geography of Chile, together with the hardy and warlike Indians who lived there at the coming of the Spaniards, have combined to make the Chilean people alert and forward-looking from the earliest Colonial times. As a result, Chileans today enjoy a greater degree of personal freedom than the citizens of almost any other Latin-American nation.

When the little band of Spaniards which was to begin the conquest of Chile left Peru under the leadership of Pedro de Valdivia [pay′dro day vahl-dee′vee ah], it took them a full year to cross the northern desert of this new country where no green thing grows. It was one of the difficult expeditions in the history of Latin America. When the Spaniards finally entered the central valley, they founded the first Chilean city, Santiago, in 1541. There was little gold in this wild land, and the Indians were organized into small independent tribes. They could never be met in a single great battle and defeated. They harried the Spaniards at every turn, and once completely destroyed the city of Santiago. The Indians who were captured made poor workers, for they were not used to tilling the fields or mining gold. After nearly half a century of constant warfare, the Spaniards managed to push the natives down into the southern part of the country, and there along the banks of a river the colonists established a series of forts and garrisons to protect themselves from Indian raids. This frontier had to be maintained for nearly 250 years, and it was not until 1882, in fact, that a final peace treaty was signed between the whites and the Araucanian [ar oh kayn'i'n] Indians.

The frontier spirit has done much to form the character of the people who settled Chile. The constant danger in which they lived not only made them alert, but gave them a feeling of unity which molded them into a great nation. Very few Spanish soldiers brought their wives or families to live with them in this dangerous territory, but many of them married Indian women. From these families the Chilean *mestizos* descended. This mixing of the races proceeded much more rapidly in Chile than it did in Mexico or Peru. Before many centuries the full-blooded Indians had become a small minority of the population of Chile.

All the colonists in the Spanish part of the country from the beginning were forced to work hard for a living. They owned few slaves and little gold had been found. Although there were many large landowners, nothing comparable to the old aristocratic classes of Mexico or Peru existed in Chile. The spirit was much more democratic from the beginning, and the Chilean masses of today, made up mostly of *mestizos* in whom white blood predominates, are hardy and independent in spirit.

The great number of European immigrants who entered the country during the last century have also added greatly to Chilean progress and democracy.

The map shows there are three Chiles just as there are three Perus. First, there is the great northern desert of nitrate deposits. Then there is the fertile central valley where nearly 90 percent of the people live. Finally there is the "Chilean Switzerland" in the southern part of the country, which is covered by high green mountains, beautiful lakes, and magnificent forests. In this part of the country there are vast sheep and cattle ranches, and also tremendous deposits of coal and iron. Many thousands of Germans have settled in these southern regions and their neat farms and cities have added much to the national wealth. The center of this area is the trim little city of Valdivia. The scenery of "the Chilean Lake District" is as imposing as anything in the world and attracts thousands of tourists every year.

The Araucanians were South America's fiercest warriors. Who were these natives whose primitive warriors challenged the Spaniards for 250 years? Their blood has mingled with that of the white settlers to form the Chilean masses of today. But their brave struggle against the white invader helped to make the country into a unified, hard-working, hard-striking nation. This struggle, moreover, provided the theme for early Chilean literature.

Compared with the Incas of Peru or the Aztecs of Mexico, the Araucanians were a primitive people. They had no central city or organization, they were poor, and they lived a half-nomadic agricultural life. Their small settlements were usually on the banks of streams or in valleys, and their houses consisted of a few poles stuck in the ground to form a rectangle or a circle, and then covered with a roof of other poles, on top of which was placed straw or cattails. Their beds were heaps of straw. In the center of their huts a fire was kept burning almost constantly. When they had hunted or fished one district out, they moved on to another. In many ways they resembled our North American Indians, but the Araucanians were relatively more numerous. Living as they did in the mountains and forests, they were able to hold the Spaniards at bay for many years.

The struggle of these Araucanians against the invaders gave Chile her greatest poem, the famous epic entitled *La Araucana*. The author of this poem was a Spanish soldier who took part in the wars against the Araucanians under one of the first Spanish governors. This soldier, named Alonso de Ercilla [ah-lohn'soh day ayr see'lyah], was so impressed by the bravery of the natives that he began to write about some of the events he had witnessed while he was still actively taking part in the campaign. Often at night around the campfire he would compose heroic stanzas commemorating the deeds of his enemies. For want of sufficient paper he often wrote on small strips of leather and even on leaves. When the poem was completed, it gave a detailed picture of the early Araucanian wars, of the customs of the natives, and the manner in which the Spaniards treated them.

One of the most interesting parts of the poem describes how an Indian hero named Lautaro [lau tah'roh] met and defeated Valdivia, the founder of Santiago.

Lautaro became such a national hero that he greatly inspired the Indians, and when Chile fought for her own independence from Spain, a group of *mes-tizos* and whites organized themselves into the " Sons of Lautaro " and were in the forefront of the struggle. The first warship of the Chilean Navy was also named " Lautaro."

Chile became an independent nation. The man who was to be " the father of his country " in Chile was the son of an Irish trader named O'Higgins. The elder O'Higgins had come to Peru from Ireland and had tried to earn a living in Lima by running a small shop near the great cathedral. He was not able to compete with the big merchants of that wealthy center, however, and soon went down to Chile and joined the forces along the southern frontier. Here he distinguished himself quickly with his abilities as a surveyor and engineer. For fourteen years he was head of the frontier posts and public works maintained in southern Chile. He built roads, surveyed and worked mines, constructed even irrigation ditches, and fortified several cities. He insisted on blotting out Indian serfdom, and thus became deeply loved by the natives as well as highly respected by his white companions. The king of Spain finally recognized his merit, a rather unusual thing in those days when the government officials were mostly persons who had influence in court, and O'Higgins became governor of Chile. Later on, he was raised in rank and appointed as viceroy of Peru.

His son, Bernardo O'Higgins, had an almost completely Chilean background. His mother was a woman of Spanish descent, and Bernardo himself grew up in the midst of Spanish custom. From his father he had inherited a keen mind and a great capacity for leadership, and when the struggle for independence began, he was one of the principal leaders. With the help of San Martín, Argen-

Courtesy Grace Line

SANTIAGO, CHILE

Santiago, which was founded in the middle of the 16th Century, is one of the oldest cities in the New World, and one of the most beautiful. This picture shows the flower market. Santiago is located in an arid region, but beautiful trees and flowers are grown there by irrigation.

tina's great liberator, he freed his country. Bernardo and San Martín built up the mixed Chilean and Argentine army which sailed for Lima and drove the Spaniards into the hills. There Bolívar defeated the Spaniards. This liberated the entire continent. The army led by the young O'Higgins and San Martín was escorted on its way by the Admiral Lord Cochrane, an Englishman who had recently come to Chile to live because of ill-treatment in his home country. His ships ranged up and down the western coast of South America and cleared it of Spanish vessels. It is characteristic of Chile that such a cosmopolitan group should have won its independence: the "Sons of Lautaro"; San Martín of Argentina; Bernardo O'Higgins, son of an Irish immigrant and a Spanish lady; Lord Cochrane, a self-exiled English

gentleman; and thousands of white and *mestizo* troops. Although always outnumbered, they consistently outfought and outmaneuvered their Spanish adversaries.

O'Higgins was elected the first president of Chile, and became virtual dictator of the country. It was not long, however, before some of his enemies were crying out that he was following a strong anti-church policy, and that he was never willing to compromise. O'Higgins, seeing that his popularity was on the wane, and that his leadership was no longer effective, resigned. He left the country, and went to Peru, where he spent the remainder of his life. Without a leader, Chile's fortunes suffered for several years before order was brought out of chaos and a new government emerged.

Chile today is one of Latin America's most advanced nations. Chile is not a large country, and she will probably never be able to support a large population. Much of her land is a desert, and although this desert contains great wealth, it will not grow food. The present population of the country is around five million. But even if Chile is not a large nation, she makes up for it in her spirit of progress, her excellent school system, her fine universities, her aggressive democracy, and her general social advancement. Santiago, her capital, is a city of nearly a million people, and is one of the show places of Latin America. It enjoys a climate much like that of Los Angeles, California. The large central valley in which Santiago is located is one of the most fertile and beautiful agricultural regions in the world. Even this rich valley, however, could not produce enough food to support a greatly enlarged population.

Among Chile's disadvantages is her long coastline, which is very vulnerable to attack. Another is her small population, which makes the development of many large-scale industries impossible. Moreover, terrible earthquakes sometimes take hundreds of lives and destroy cities and towns.

A great proportion of the good land which she does contain is in the hands of relatively few owners. The small farmer, who is the mainstay of agriculture in the United States, is in an extremely small minority in Chile. Instead there are several enormous estates called *fundos* on which most of the agriculture is carried on.

The great nitrate deposits found in the northern wastelands brought in over a billion dollars in taxes between 1880 and 1940. This gave the people a mistaken notion of wealth which was very similar to that found in the United States before the great depression of 1929. When the prices of her nitrates and her copper sank very low, Chile underwent a depression much like our own, and was considerably longer in recovering from it. Her nitrates are used to make fertilizer. Explosives also are made from nitrates. Moreover, an important byproduct of nitrates is iodine. The value of these nitrate deposits is not so great as formerly because scientists have recently learned how synthetic nitrates may be manufactured. The country now depends primarily on its agriculture, its cattle and sheep raising, its mining, and its small industries.

The general feeling of life in Chile is more closely akin to that in our Mid-West than is that of any other Latin American nation, and as a consequence the citizen of our country feels at home there almost immediately upon his arrival. There is also a close economic relationship between our two nations because North American companies have large investments in Chilean copper and nitrates. In our ideas, and interests, we have come closer together in recent years and have carried on an extensive exchange of artists, writers, students, and teachers. Chile has always been, and is likely to remain, among the leaders of Latin-American democracy, culture, thought, social progress, and general advancement. She is a relatively small nation but a most significant country in South America.

Chapter 5 ~ Argentina, Land of the Pampas, Is a Highly Developed Nation

Argentina's wealth is the fertile pampas. The heart of Argentina is its great level pampas, one of the richest agricultural and cattle districts on earth. The pampas lie in a temperate region extending for five hundred miles from north to south and from east to west as you will see by consulting the map on pages 704–705. Much of the pampas are like our Great Plains. Where the pampas are not under cultivation they are covered with a rich growth of grass.

On their north side the pampas face towering tropical forests in which grows the ax-breaker tree, quebracho [kay-brah′choh] whose wood is so heavy that it will sink in water. On the south the pampas meet the cool southern Argentine Lake District, where green mountains, blue lakes, and lofty snow-capped peaks remind the traveler of Switzerland. Because of this region, Argentina exports a vast quantity of foodstuffs. Yet the pampas have thus far only reached the primary stage in their development. Because Argentina is capable of such tremendous food production she is now, and is likely to remain, of great importance in the family of nations.

The two foundings of Buenos Aires. In the first third of the 16th Century the first large Spanish expedition sailed west from Spain to settle in the mouth of the La Plata River, which is the water highway across Argentina. There were eleven ships, twelve hundred men and women, and about one hundred horses. It was the largest fleet to sail from Spain in many years. The colonists sailed up the wide La Plata and estab-lished themselves on the southern bank. As one of their men landed, according to the legend, he remarked: "How fine are the airs of this land! " So the colony became known as the city of " good airs," or Buenos Aires.

The early life of these settlers was difficult. Savage Indians attacked them again and again. There was little food. The wandering tribes had not developed much agriculture. Soon famine and pestilence broke out within the mud walls of the city, and after a few years had gone by, a great part of the inhabitants were dead. The remainder sailed up the river and founded the city of Asunción [ah soon′syohn′] in Paraguay. Years later, the mouth of the great river was still uninhabited. Paraguay progressed rapidly, however, and the colonists there gradually moved back down the river. They founded cities as they went. Then in 1580, nearly forty years after Buenos Aires had been deserted, they refounded their new capital on the ashes of the old.

In the meantime, something had happened which affected the entire history of the country. When the starved and weary colonists had left Buenos Aires to move on to Asunción, they had abandoned many horses. These had escaped to the open pampas, and living on the succulent grasses there had multiplied. Cattle had also escaped from Asunción and other settlements, and they too were roaming the pampas in great wild herds. They became the wealth of the new Argentina.

During the Colonial days Buenos Aires was a wide-awake commercial center,

Evans from Three Lions

AN ARGENTINE GAUCHO

The *Gauchos* are the cowboys of Argentina. The *Gaucho* pictured above has dressed in his holiday suit to attend a country festival in the province of Buenos Aires.

but Lima and Mexico City surpassed it in wealth and easy living. It was a town of merchants, of cowmen, of traders, and of smugglers. As we have seen, the Colonial trade policy of Spain did not permit ships to enter the harbor of Buenos Aires; so all imported goods were supposed to be shipped by way of Panama and Bolivia, over a long round-about sea and land voyage until they finally reached Buenos Aires. Prices were exorbitant. A yard of imported cloth cost

$25, a quart of imported olive oil was worth $30, and other prices were similarly ridiculous. Of course, the colonists would not endure this situation long. Whether the central government liked it or not, they imported many items directly from Europe and let smuggling vessels enter their port of Buenos Aires.

The Gaucho was Argentina's frontiersman and pioneer. While these things were happening, wild cattle and horses on the pampas continued to increase. In some years nearly a million and a half hides were exported to Spain. The life of the trader was hard, for a whole hide was worth only a dollar or two and a horse purchased for the price of a couple of needles was a good horse.

Indian warfare had never ceased; the central parts of Argentina were still dangerous for the white man. The frontier between white civilization on the coast and Indian savagery in the interior was a sort of no-man's-land over which were spread a series of small forts as a security against Indian raids. The territory for many miles around these forts was occupied by *Gauchos* [gau'chohz].

The *Gaucho* has been called the Argentine cowboy, but he was far more than that. He was the Argentine frontiersman, pioneer, and border soldier; and in his veins ran the blood of both whites and Indians. His father as a rule was white, his mother Indian, and he himself always identified himself with his father's race. His language was Spanish; his songs, ballads, traditions were mostly of southern Spain; his horse was his pride and the saddle was his castle, for he dwelt in no home for a very long period of time. With his wife and family he constructed a rude hut in the midst of the pampas, and lived by the wild cattle whose hides he sold to traders from the coast. He would frequently follow the herds about from place to place, and as soon as they had been cleared out in one district, he would move on to another. He was both a protection against the Indians of the interior, and a racial link with them. He was himself the frontier of Argentina.

Argentina became an independent nation. Gradually the large Argentine landowner extended his fences over the wild pampas. He turned the Gaucho into a soldier, and took over the wild herds. The landowner participated in politics against the Spanish-born officials who were still trying to rule his country. By 1816 when Argentina declared her independence, there were several large fortunes in Argentina, all based on cattle. Buenos Aires was still a relatively small city of perhaps twenty-five thousand, and the population of the whole nation was only half a million.

But the basis of a vigorous and wealthy independent nation was there. The people had fought hard and suffered much to build up their country, and now they were ready to try to govern it by themselves. The clergy too were strongly in favor of independence, and in the Congress in 1816, when freedom from Spain was declared, there were sixteen priests present.

However, the Argentines made one fatal error. Each district was jealous of each other district, and all were unwilling to submit to a central authority, which would have meant the dominance of Buenos Aires. It was more or less the same situation which faced the fathers of our country at the time our Constitution was adopted. The people of Argentina chose the other course from that of our Constitution. They put states' rights first, and made the states more powerful than the national government. Civil war and chaos broke out on a large

scale. One petty tyrant clashed with another, and all of them clashed with Buenos Aires, which they regarded as a center of a more European than South American way of life.

After some years one tyrant, stronger than the rest, came out on top. This was the bloodthirsty dictator Rosas [roh' zahs]. His secret police were busy for many years ferreting out and killing all who dared disagree with the chief tyrant. He ruled Argentina with an iron hand from 1829 to 1852 when his forces were defeated and he fled to England in order to save his skin. The country then entered a period of democratic government under a series of excellent presidents.

Sarmiento was elected president. The greatest of all Argentine presidents, Sarmiento [sahr myayn'toh], who occupied office from 1868 to 1874, was also one of the closest friends which the United States has ever had in Latin America. Sarmiento not only was a great admirer of this country, but also did everything in his power to make Argentina develop along the same general lines. He was an intimate friend of the American Horace Mann, founder of our public-school system. Sarmiento visited his home during an extended visit in the United States. Mrs. Mann translated into English one of his books, *Life in the Argentine in the Days of the Tyrants.* It is a clear picture of Argentine life under the tyrant Rosas, and Sarmiento's central purpose in the book was to explain the conflict between " civilization and barbarism " or " unity versus chaos " in his country. He knew what he was writing about at first hand, for he himself had been forced to flee for his life when Rosas came to power.

Sarmiento was only a young man then, and the story goes that when he

Philip D. Gendreau

A SCENE ON THE PAMPAS

The pampas in central Argentina — great stretches of almost treeless land — are used for pasturing and for haying.

crossed the mountains leading to Chile and safety, he carried along a heavy bundle which attracted much comment. This bundle contained neither food nor clothes, but books. Ever since that day, Sarmiento had applied his mind and his pen to combat the loose thinking which may lead to intolerance, dictatorship, and barbarism.

Sarmiento was elected to the Argentine presidency while he was in the United States, and on his return he arranged to have sixty-three normal-school teachers from this country sent down to Argentina to help found a national school system there. A Protestant missionary was asked to recommend the teachers who were to go. This tolerant gesture toward Protestantism in a Catholic country produced good results in the establishment of educational systems in Argentina.

While Sarmiento was president, the stability and progressiveness of Argentina attracted European immigrants in increasing numbers. The number rose from thirty-four thousand in 1868 to eighty thousand in 1873. The country was at last fulfilling the prophecy of one of its famous thinkers who had said: " to govern is to populate." This statement suggests an interesting comparison with the United States whose population gradually extended westward from the thirteen original colonies *after* we had gained our independence. In Latin America there was no such movement as this, for nearly all of that vast territory had already been occupied by the early Spaniards and Portuguese *before* the struggle for independence. But the territories were so great and the population so small and so thinly spread that a closely knit and efficient government was impossible. However, in the United States where the territory occupied was relatively small, it was possible to establish a strong democratic government soon after independence was won.

Argentina's main problem was to populate her great pampas with new blood, and this she began to do on a vast scale. Several millions of Italians and Spaniards entered the country and became fine citizens and workers. There were also many thousands of English and Irish immigrants and nearly one hundred thousand Germans. Argentina became a modern nation, railroads were built, cities expanded, and wealth increased. The great natural wealth of the pampas underlay the progress and prosperity of the entire country.

Buenos Aires became a giant among cities. The wealth of Argentina flowed toward Buenos Aires as liquids flow through a funnel. From the pampas this great city received many goods, and its growth was phenomenal. In 1855 it had a population of only ninety thousand; by 1895 this was increased to six hundred and sixty-three thousand; and by 1940 it was three million. In other words nearly one-fourth of all Argentines now live in their capital city. If a similar situation prevailed in the United States, our largest city would have a population of about thirty-three million. Buenos Aires really rules the country. Some people who made their wealth out of the rich soil have left that soil and its traditions for easier living in the great capital. They have tended to become indifferent to world problems, self-satisfied in their wealth. They are nationalistic, and intensely proud of their own leadership in that part of Latin America, and resentful of the influence of the United States. They have been Latin America's number-one isolationists.

Argentina and the United States. Consequently when World War II came, Argentina refused for over four years to break with the Axis Powers. Long after all other Latin-American nations, she finally declared war in April, 1945. The influence of the United States in Argentina was never at a lower ebb than in the later years of World War II. This is indeed a far cry from the days when President Sarmiento did so much to develop his country in harmony with ours.

Where does the difficulty lie? Not only the Argentines were at fault. There are three reasons for the Argentine attitude during World War II: first, the psychological reason of national pride given above; second, the United States, by taking the Panama Canal Zone through force and by intervening violently in the affairs of some Latin-American countries, aroused the anger and distrust of the Argentines as well as other Latin Americans. Third, the United States and Argentina do not have favorable trade relations with each other because such Argentine products as beef, wheat, corn, we also produce and do not need to buy. Therefore, when Argentina wants machinery or industrial equipment there has been a marked tendency to buy it from the European countries which buy from her. This has always been the primary rule of international commerce. Argentina, then, during the past several years has leaned more toward Europe than she has toward the United States. She has spent many millions of dollars in this country because our machines, automobiles, and industrial equipment are excellent, but she has resented these purchases because ordinarily we buy so little from her.

This is a rather difficult situation but it does not mean that friendship between our two great nations is impossible. It is not only possible but imperative. We have always been friends with Canada, many of whose products compete with our own, and we can also be friendly with Argentina. Our part in drawing the great southern nation toward us is to continue the Good-Neighbor Policy. We must cease further interventions in Latin-American internal affairs. We must make a special effort toward friendly relations with Argentina, especially by studying her language, her history, her culture and her people; and to improve economic relations. Friendship between the United States and Argentina is essential for solidarity in the Western Hemisphere in which both of our nations live, Argentina in the south, the United States in the north. As a famous Argentine writer recently said: "We can and *must* understand each other." We must begin by being cultural friends and customers for each other's exports.

Chapter 6 ~ Brazil, a Land with a Future, Is Latin America's Largest Nation

Latin America's largest and most populous nation was founded by the Portuguese. It was in the year 1500 that the Portuguese took possession of the land we know as Brazil. There were no legends of gold in this immense territory, and there were no great Indian civilizations to overcome. Consequently, the king of Portugal had the greatest difficulty in persuading colonists to settle there. Many minor crimes were made punishable by exile to Brazil, and large numbers of persecuted Portuguese Jews were also shipped to the new colony. Small settlements were established in the north and in the south. Soon the colonists had the good fortune of meeting shipwrecked Portuguese sailors in each locality who had already been living among the natives for many years. These sailors and their families and friends helped the new settlers to adjust themselves to their strange surroundings.

The principal product in these early days was brazilwood, a native tree. This produced a much prized red dye known in Europe as *brazil*. This dye gave its name to both the native tree and to the land in which it thrived.

Fifty years passed before Portugal undertook the colonization of Brazil on a large scale. By that time conditions had become so bad among the settlers, who were fighting both with the Indians and among themselves, that a governor was sent to take charge and restore order. He established his large colony at the city of Bahia [bah ee'ah] in 1549. Accompanying him were the first Jesuit priests to enter the new territory.

These Jesuit fathers immediately left the relative safety and comforts of life in the coastal settlements and plunged into the interior to work among the natives. It was not long before they were known as the Indians' best protectors, for the colonists along the coasts, especially the *mestizos,* called *mamelucos* [mam'uh loo'kohz] in Brazil, wanted slaves to sell or to work for them. Sugar plantations had already been laid out and as sugar at that time was almost worth its weight in gold, this desire for slaves to till the land became extremely great. The Jesuits did everything in their

Philip D. Gendreau

RIO DE JANEIRO

The capital of Brazil combines the advantages of a fine modern city with the charm and beauty of the old world. Its harbor is said to be the most beautiful in the world and is large enough to hold the navies of all the nations of the world. This picture shows the Copacabana Beach from Sugar Loaf Mountain.

power to restrain the slave-gatherers, and time and again their missions were attacked, pillaged, and destroyed. The poor Indians who survived were forcibly dragged back to the coastal plantations to be sold as slaves.

This struggle between the Jesuits and the slave traders continued for nearly a century and a half, until about 1760. It was centered around the city of São Paulo. The *mameluco* inhabitants of that city organized themselves into huge bands, sometimes numbering two or three thousand, and with a banner to lead the way tramped miles into the interior in search of Indian slaves. The Portuguese word for banner is *bandeira* [bahn day′rah], so these slave traders became known as *bandeirantes* [bahn-day′rahn′tayz], or followers of the banner. They usually went on foot, and frequently would cover many hundreds of miles before returning to their homes.

Sometimes the expeditions would last for several years, and the *bandeirantes* would take time to plant and gather crops before taking up the march again. Their groups were literally traveling communities. Nothing seemed to be able to hold them back, neither disease, nor famine, nor fatigue, nor constant fighting, nor the most difficult mountains, forests, or precipices. Although their primary purpose was to capture Indian slaves, they were similar to our early pioneers and explored the new country back into the farthest reaches of the Amazon basin. The Jesuits drew away from these *bandeirantes* if they possibly could, but many of the Jesuits were forced out of their missions altogether. Still the struggle continued until finally the king of Portugal, goaded by the majority of the colonists, expelled all Jesuits from Portuguese territory. The king of Spain did the same thing.

Negro slavery was introduced into Brazil. The use of Indian slaves had not been very successful. The supply was inadequate, and those who had been forced into slave labor did not prove to be good workers. But the large sugar and tobacco plantations demanded a supply of cheap labor. This was especially true in northern Brazil, close to the equator, the hottest part of the country. As in the United States, Negro slavery seemed, to the plantation owners, to be the only solution. Therefore hundreds of thousands of Negroes were brought into Brazil during the 17th and 18th Centuries by slave traders who obtained them in Africa.

The plantations of northern Brazil were similar in some ways to those of the old South in our country. There was the " great house " of the master, with its thick walls, its dozens of rooms, its school, hospital, and its rich furnishings. And there were the slave quarters, much poorer and more crowded buildings where the Negroes lived. There was one great difference between this plantation life of Brazil and that of the United States. Some of the Brazilian masters made a point of selecting well-educated Mohammedan Negro slaves who knew how to read and write in Arabic. It was not long before there was considerable intermarriage between the two groups. A large Mulatto class grew up in the central region of Brazil.

About the year 1700 gold and diamonds were discovered in the southwestern part of the country, and suddenly new interest was given to colonial life. There was a great rush toward the gold and diamond regions from all quarters of Brazil, with two groups predominating: the *mamelucos* of São Paulo, and the plantation owners and their slaves from the north central regions. Sometimes there were battles royal between the two groups. Prices went sky high just as they did in California and in Alaska during the gold rushes there. Some hard-to-get items increased as much as twenty or more times in value. For example, a loaf of bread cost in the neighborhood of two dollars!

The Indians and *mamelucos* made poor miners, and the Negroes were soon doing most of the work, without of course getting much of the profit, which went to their masters. The discovery of these mines changed Brazilian life almost overnight, for the huge plantations were poorly taken care of or not taken care of at all while the hunt for gold was carried on.

Brazil, as we have learned, has suffered a series of such sudden changes in her economic life, each of which seemed to promise great wealth at the beginning, and each of which proved a deception in the end. First it was brazilwood, then it was sugar cane, next it became gold and diamonds, around 1900 it was wild rubber which brought fabulous prices, and now it is coffee. The result of these changes was that Brazil has always been largely a " one-crop " country. She has not produced a variety of products. This has not only kept her much poorer than she would otherwise have been, but it has meant that her extremes of poverty and wealth were intense and almost constant.

During the past few years, however, Brazil has made a prolonged attempt to develop her vastly rich resources by a carefully planned program of economic expansion. The United States government has aided her greatly in this by lending millions of dollars for the purchase of machinery, for the building of factories, foundries, railways, public works, and for the expansion of education.

Brazil became an empire in her own right. In the year 1807 when the forces of Napoleon advanced on Lisbon, the Portuguese king had to choose between capture by the French or flight to Brazil. He took the latter course, and his great fleet of vessels carried many hundreds of the finest families of Portugal to Rio de Janeiro. They brought along all their worldly possessions, objects of art, books, and customs. Rio now became a much more cosmopolitan city. A few years later, in 1821, after Napoleon had been defeated, the Portuguese king was called back to his old country, but he left his son Pedro to rule in Brazil. Before leaving he is said to have told Pedro: "If the time comes when Brazil wants to be independent of Portugal, make yourself her ruler."

This was wise advice, and not much more than a year had passed before Pedro I became emperor of an independent Brazil. The revolution, if it may be called that, was not at all a violent one like those experienced by most Latin-American countries. Pedro I, however, was not an able ruler. He had been born in Portugal and his interests were in Europe. After a stormy nine-year period he was forced to abdicate in favor of his son, Pedro II, who at that time was only a child of six. For a few years the real ruler of the country was an extremely able priest. But in the meantime, however, Pedro II was given a careful and thorough education and when he came to the throne, he made an excellent emperor. One famous Latin-American historian wrote that the greatest

"democracy" in South America during the past century was the Empire of Pedro II. He was liberal-minded, progressive, and a great patron of the arts. His rule lasted from 1831 to 1889, one of the longest in history. During this time European immigrants came in by the thousands, and Brazil was welded into a modern nation. In 1888 Brazilian slaves were freed by decree. Liberal-minded Brazilian slaveowners had made this step possible by willingly freeing their own slaves, and the final decree of abolition was the natural result of their efforts.

Brazil became a republic. The Empire of Brazil could not last forever surrounded, as you can see on the map, by Latin-American republics. The Brazilians began to feel that their empire was outdated. Finally, in 1889, after a reign of nearly sixty years, Pedro II was asked to leave the country so that a republican form of government might be established. He did so, and again the nation went through a great national change without a violent conflict. The modern development of Brazil began in the last years of the past century. Millions of dollars were spent in building ports and railways, in modernizing the cities, in carrying out sanitation projects which entirely did away with yellow fever, and in establishing banks, commercial firms, and new industries.

It was at this time also that one of the most famous of all Brazilians, Santos-Dumont, came to be well known. He was born on a large coffee plantation in the state of São Paulo. As a boy he spent many hours daily reading the fantastic novels of Jules Verne, and in driving the locomotive which his father used on his huge estate. After graduating in mechanical engineering from the University in Rio, Santos-Dumont went to Paris for further study. Four years later he built his first "aerial automobile," which was a dirigible with a motor attached. It was the first airship in the world to fly under its own power. From this time on Santos-Dumont dedicated his life to building airplanes, and in 1906, two years before the Wright brothers gave a public exhibition of their own flying machine in action, Santos-Dumont flew his own crude bamboo airplane before a great crowd in Paris.

Santos-Dumont thought that the airship would make war so terrible that people would never fight again, but when World War I broke out and he saw that this was not the case, but that on the contrary his beloved machine had made destruction even more terrible, he returned to Brazil in a state of deepest melancholy, and from that time on could not be persuaded to take any part in either scientific or social affairs. The beautiful modern airport in present-day Rio de Janeiro is named for this man, Santos-Dumont. An even greater tribute to his memory is the fact that Brazilian airlines cover more miles of territory than those of any other Latin-American nation. These lines which know no obstacles of geography or distance will be a prime factor in the swift development of Brazil's vast uninhabited interior regions. Without them that development would be delayed at least a century.

Brazil found new wealth in her "black gold." Rubber was known to the Mayans and the Aztecs, but it was not introduced into Europe until the 19th Century. Its first use was in the form of flexible tubes which performed many functions in hospitals; then in 1852 a sea captain of Boston imported five hundred pairs of rubber overshoes made by the natives of Brazil and sold them in the United States for $5.00 a pair. These rubbers were not of a good quality, but they were absolutely waterproof. Years after this the automobile was invented and the demand for rubber to be used in tires suddenly became very great. Brazil was the largest known source of natural rubber, for in her vast jungles were an estimated three hundred million wild rubber trees. The price of the new commodity rose to over $3.00 a pound and at that price Brazilians were glad to abandon their easy life in the cities to seek their fortunes in the jungles. Most of them did indeed earn tremendous sums of money, but the big rubber companies which directed their labor got nearly all of it by charging workers outrageous prices for everything they wore or ate. Finally, some shoots of rubber trees were smuggled out of the country and planted in the Dutch East Indies, mainly Java and Sumatra. Production there on the carefully supervised plantations soon displaced Brazil's "black gold." The price went down to about twenty cents a pound. Another of Brazil's economic bubbles exploded.

Brazil's coffee still floods the world's markets. In the year 1754 a Franciscan monk carried some coffee seeds to Rio de Janeiro. He planted them in the garden of his monastery. This was the beginning of an immense new coffee industry. The plant seemed to thrive easily in the country's mild climate, and before many years had passed the Arabian coffee plantations had been displaced by those of Brazil. At present nearly 70 percent of the world's supply of coffee comes from this one country. We in the United States purchase a major portion of it, for we consume approximately two billion pounds of coffee each year. This has made Brazil's economic life strongly dependent on our buying, and has been one of the reasons for the close relationship between our two countries during the past several decades. Another reason for this friendship is that Brazil is the only Portuguese-speaking country in Latin America. Feeling the difference from the nations around her she has sought her closest friend in the great democracy of the north. During World War I she was the only South American country to join her hands with the Allies. During World War II, Brazilian troops fought in Italy along with British and American forces. You will read about this war in Part Twenty-two.

Brazil stands on the threshold of a great future. Even today the immense territory of Brazil is only sparsely inhabited. The narrow strip along the Atlantic coast is the only highly developed region, as you will see by the map on pages 704–705. In that strip lies the great Amazon Basin which is destined someday to become one of the world's most productive centers. Even that coastal territory is not inhabited by a single people with a strong feeling of unity. In the hot regions above Rio de Janeiro dwells a large Negro and Mulatto population. In the city itself there are many Negroes, but Rio de Janeiro is essentially Portuguese. Also, Rio de Janeiro is a very modern, well developed city. It is somewhat like Paris in its social and cultural life. Many travelers have said that it is the most beautiful city in the world. About three hundred miles south of it, as you may see by the map, lies the city of São Paulo, a great industrial center. Most of the factories

of Brazil are situated here. The state of São Paulo produces half the entire industrial output of the country, and pays more than half the federal taxes. It is by far the wealthiest state in the country. The city itself, which contains more than a million and a half people, seems to be in a constant building boom. Everything is new and bustling in São Paulo. A great rivalry sometimes bordering on violence exists between industrious São Paulo and polished easy-moving Rio de Janeiro.

South of bustling São Paulo is the great agricultural and cattle region of the country. About half a million German immigrants and their descendants live here. Perhaps three times that number of Italians are also settled in this southern region. The climate of these provinces is much like that of the southern United States, and the land is extremely fertile. It is the most promising section of the entire country. See the map on pages 704–705.

Brazil is a land of gigantic contrasts. At present she is greatly concerned with the development of her resources. She covers an area far larger than our own, and will someday become one of the great world powers. Her size and her population approximately equal the other nine South American nations put together. European immigrants may make her more populous and more wealthy still. Her future and that of the United States are linked together inseparably, for we are not only near neighbors in this hemisphere, but have always been good friends.

Neighbors in the Western Hemisphere

Three ancient civilizations flourished in what we now know as Latin America. The brilliant society of the Mayans with its temples and its calendar had died by the time Cortés had conquered Mexico, but had left influences on the civilization of the warlike Aztecs, whom he made subject to Spain. In Peru, Pizarro and his followers came into contact with the civilization of the Incas.

In other parts of Latin America the Spaniards and Portuguese extended their conquests over scattered Indian tribes. By 1600 the people in Mexico and in Central America were organized under Spanish and Portuguese colonial government, which was exercised for the benefit of the conqueror. Here colonization was carried on largely for the purpose of enriching the colonizers, not, as in the British colonies, for the sake of starting a new life in a new world.

The desire to spread the power of the Roman Catholic Church was another motive in the colonization of Latin America. The exploitation by Spain and Portugal led to insurrection among the Latin-American colonies. Simón Bolívar led the revolt in Venezuela. In Argentina San Martín formed an army; he defeated the Spaniards in Chile. When the continent of South America had been freed from the Spaniards, a period of separate military dictatorship followed, instead of the federation for which Bolívar had hoped. Gradually the dictatorship tended to give way to more democratic forms of government, but there was no union among the separate nations.

Today the Latin-American republics are important neighbors of the United States. Although their culture had an earlier start than ours, their enormous resources have been far less developed economically and industrially than have those of the United States.

The good-neighbor policy is important for economic reasons. It has been a valuable policy in helping to unite the peoples of the Western Hemisphere in World War II.

A good way to become acquainted with our neighbors to the south would be to take an airplane trip from Florida to Cuba, then on to Colombia, with its coffee fields and jungles. From Cuba we would pass over the mountains of Ecuador and Peru and Bolivia; then over the deserts and rich central valley of Chile, and across the Andes to the pampas of Argentina; north to the jungles and great plantations of Brazil; from Brazil to the oil and cattle country of Venezuela; farther north over the countries of Central America to Mexico.

Mexico was brought into the Spanish Empire by Cortés, who overcame Montezuma, the Aztec ruler. Three centuries later, Mexico won independence from Spain. Later when the Emperor Maximilian had assumed control of the nation, Mexico's great patriot Juarez led a revolution which unseated the emperor. Dictatorship followed; and in 1910 another revolution, which resulted in the break-up of great estates. Mexican painting, music, and literature are firmly rooted in the deep permanent elements of Mexican life: the traditions of the original Indian inhabitants and the blending of Indian and Spaniard in their long common history.

Chile is another nation which has particular interest to us. The Chileans have loved liberty. Today Chile is one of the most advanced nations in South America. An excellent educational system marks her progress.

The most highly developed South American nation is Argentina, whose pampas are one of the richest agricultural and cattle districts in the world, and whose capital, Buenos Aires, holds about a fourth of the nation's people. In World War II the wealthy Argentine has wavered toward friendship with the Axis, and has been the least friendly of the neighbors of the United States.

Brazil is the only Portuguese-speaking nation in Latin America. At one time an Empire under Pedro II, Brazil became a republic, without violence. With her tremendous size and her wonderful natural wealth, Brazil is destined to be one of the major powers of the future.

SELF–TEST

Review the story of the Americas by trying this self-test.

I. For each item listed below, recall something important in the story of the Americas directly connected with the item. Study the examples given below, and then write your answers in your notebook or on a separate sheet of paper.

Example: Venezuela Cattle and petroleum producing country

(1) Cuzco (8) Cuba
(2) "Keeper of the strings" (9) *mestizos*
(3) Aztecs (10) Christ of the Andes
(4) Vera Cruz (11) pampas
(5) Jamestown, Virginia (12) good-neighbor policy
(6) Mayflower compact (13) Bogotá
(7) Mission settlements (14) quinine

II. On a separate sheet of paper write whatever words or phrases are necessary to complete each of the following statements.

(1) The Aztecs and their emperor, ——, were conquered by Spaniards under ——.

(2) Under the Spaniards, Mexico was largely ruled by a small group of ——

(3) Little was done to improve conditions for the common people except by the ——.

(4) Early in the 19th Century, a country priest named —— began a movement for the liberation of Mexico.

(5) But freedom from Spain made little change in the condition of the people, for one dictator followed another. One of the sternest dictators was ——, who ruled for over thirty years.

(6) Not until —— did the oppressed Mexican peons finally upset the ruling aristocrats.

(7) One of the first results of the Mexican Revolution was the —— of the large estates.

(8) In recent times, improvements have also been made in —— and ——.

(9) The foremost Mexican artists are —— and ——.

III.

(1) Chile lies along the —— coast of South America.

(2) The first Chilean city, ——, was founded by the Spaniards in 1541.

(3) Geographically Chile is divided into three parts: ——, ——, and ——.

(4) The Chilean Indians, South America's fiercest warriors, were called ——.

(5) The bravery of these natives so impressed a Spanish soldier named —— that he recorded many events of their heroic struggle in an epic poem known as ——.

(6) The Indian hero of this poem was ——.

(7) The liberation of Chile from Spain was finally brought about by ——, son of an Irish trader, and ——, the liberator of Argentina.

(8) The chief natural resource of Chile is ——.

(9) The country depends also on industries such as ——, ——, and ——.

IV.

(1) One of the richest agricultural and cattle districts in the world is the level grassy —— of Argentina.

(2) Early in the 16th Century a large group of Spanish colonists founded the city of —— at the mouth of the —— River.

(3) Argentina's pioneer and frontiersman was called a ——.

(4) Among Argentine presidents, perhaps the greatest was ——.

(5) He established a —— system in Argentina.

(6) There are three chief reasons for the friction between Argentina and the United States in recent times: first, —— ——; second, —— ——; and third, —— ——.

V.

(1) Brazil was founded by the ——.

(2) The country took its name from a —— which produced a dye highly prized in Europe.

(3) At first —— plantations were Brazil's source of wealth.

(4) The discovery of —— and —— suddenly changed Brazilian life.

(5) In the present century, —— and —— have become more important in Brazil's economy.

(6) Brazil gained her independence in the —— Century.

INTERESTING THINGS TO DO

Project for the Chart Maker

Make a comparison chart similar to the one on pages 582–583 for Latin-American countries. Use headings such as " Present Head of Government," "Capital City," "Seaports," "Natural Resources," "Exports," "Imports," and " National Heroes." See the names of individual countries in *The World Book Encyclopedia*. Consult also *Goode's School Atlas*, by John P. Goode; *Latin America in Maps*, by Alva C. Wilgus; or recent textbooks of economic geography.

Topics for Talks

1. "Early Americans." Look up more information about one of the early Indian civilizations, Inca, Aztec, or Mayan. Organize your information in the form of an interesting oral report. See *Indians of the Americas*, by Edwin R. Embree; or *Story of the American Indian*, by Paul Radin. Consult also the *National Geographic Magazine Index*.

2. "What will the new air age do for our southern neighbors? " Explain the effect that air transport systems have already had, and are likely to have in the future, on the position of Latin America in world affairs. See *Wings Over the Americas*, by Alice Hager.

Assignments for the Roving Reporter

1. The reporter writes an article for a travel magazine about the islands of the West Indies. He tells something of their history, their natural beauty, and of life there today. See *Islands on Guard*, by Helen Follett.

2. The reporter writes a descriptive article about the Pan-American highway for the magazine section of his paper. He tells of some of the tremendous problems of construction that had to be faced, and gives interesting details of the lands and peoples affected by this great project. See *Pan-American Highway*, by H. A. Franck and H. C. Lanks. See also " Pan-American Highway " in *Encyclopedia Britannica*.

Candidates for Your Album of Famous People

Bolívar, Cortés, Dom Pedro II, Porfirio Díaz, Juan Vincente Gómez, Hidalgo, Benito Juarez, O'Higgins, Pizarro, San Martín, Sarmiento, de Valdivia. Prepare biographical portraits for your Album of at least four of the people listed above or mentioned elsewhere in the story of the Americas.

INTERESTING READING ABOUT THE AMERICAS

ALEGRIA, FERNANDO. *Lautaro.* A stirring biography of the Indian hero, Lautaro, who led the Chileans against the Spanish conquerors.

Compton's Pictured Encyclopedia. See the names of the individual nations.

GUNTHER, JOHN. *Inside Latin America.* A companion book to the well-known *Inside Europe* and *Inside Asia,* analyzing the political situation and the essential problems of our southern neighbors.

HAGER, ALICE R. *Brazil: Giant to the South.* The dramatic story in pictures of Brazil's history and geography, her people and resources.

HUDSON, WILLIAM H. *Far Away and Long Ago.* "The house where I was born on the South American pampas was quaintly named *Los Veinte-cinco Ombues,* which means ' The Twenty-five Ombu Trees.' "

KUMMER, FREDERICK A. *Courage Over the Andes.* "If you are a friend of the Chilean people, my house and all I have are yours."

LA VARRE, WILLIAM. *Up the Mazaruni for Diamonds.* "I need a partner in a diamond mining venture. Are you game to try it out with me? "

National Geographic Magazine, March 1943. "Bolivia — Tin Roof of the Andes," by Henry A. Phillips. "Bolivia's tin has become more precious than her silver ever was."

PECK, ANNE M. *Roundabout South America.* "Once in the main river, the banks recede to the distance and the steamer sails over a yellow flood so wide it is like the sea."

——. *Young Mexico.* "Satisfied as they are with simple homes, food, and clothes, provided they have music and fiestas. . . ."

VAN LOON, H. W. *Life and Times of Simón Bolívar.* "This is the story of Simón Bolívar, liberator of Venezuela, the man who first of all had the vision of a united states for the whole of the American continent."

VERRILL, A. H. *Before the Conquerors.* "As the last of the cotton padding fell away I uttered a cry of delight as I saw the beautiful robe beneath."

WILDER, THORNTON. *The Bridge of San Luis Rey.* "And on that instant Brother Juniper made the resolve to inquire into the secret lives of those five persons, that moment falling through the air, and to surprise the reason of their taking off."

The World Book Encyclopedia. See the names of the individual nations.

PART TWENTY-TWO

DEVASTATING WARS HAVE MADE IT NECESSARY TO FACE WORLD PROBLEMS REALISTICALLY

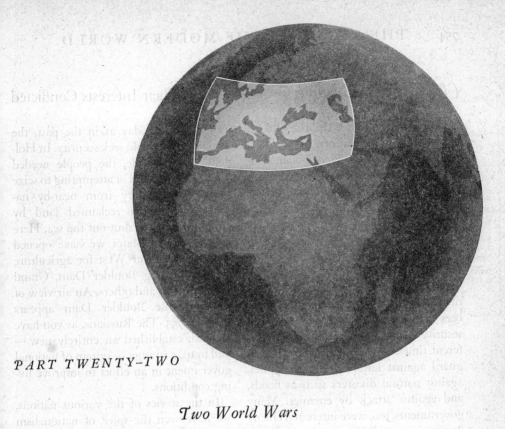

Two World Wars

Here we have a map of Europe as it appeared in 1914, before World War I. Notice the size of the German Empire and of Austria-Hungary. Compare the boundaries shown here with those of the old Holy Roman Empire (page 248). Can you find Poland on this map? Czechoslovakia? Where are they? What important natural boundaries do you find? Do you believe that if all nations had strong natural boundaries their quarrels in the past would have been avoided or greatly reduced? Will natural boundaries continue to be so important as air power increases and more powerful robots and rocket bombs are built?

The various peoples of Western Europe have developed a strong sense of nationalism and maintain large armies and navies to protect themselves from attack by their neighbors. Twice within twenty-five years not only Europe but the world has been plunged into war. The story which follows tells us something of these two world wars and their causes. On this map notice the wide plain which stretches from eastern Germany across Russia and on into the East. For centuries this open plain was a highway for armies from the East which invaded Western Europe. We shall see how the Germans, in World War II, tried to reverse this process of invasion by advancing eastward to attack Russia.

Chapter 1 ~ As Nations Grew Powerful, Their Interests Conflicted

Many changes mark the rise and fall of nations. In early times, as you have read in *Story of Nations,* wandering tribesmen spent most of their time and energy in getting food, clothing, and shelter. A council of warriors, or of elder tribesmen, provided all the government that was needed.

As the way of life became more complex, so did methods of government. Then, as now, the purpose of government was to make it possible for members of the group to live in security. But security means different things at different times. Governments have had to guard against failure of food supplies, against natural disasters such as floods, and against attack by enemies. Many governments, too, were interested chiefly in security—or luxury—of a small ruling class. Then, as in more recent years, governments sometimes were taken over by autocratic rulers. Some of these rulers were chiefly concerned with the happiness and well-being of their people, but others thought only of their own glory and pleasure. Sometimes, as you have read, ambitious rulers led their people into disastrous wars. You know, too, that sometimes nations were swept aside by more powerful, less cultured people such as the German barbarian tribes and Norsemen.

So the story of nations continued. Struggle followed struggle. But these earlier peoples always were striving for security. Have the needs of men changed greatly as the centuries passed? The answer is no, the problems today are basically the same as they were thousands of years ago. Men are still searching for freedom from fear and from want. In other words, today as in the past, the people of the world seek security. In Holland, for example, the people needed more land. Instead of attempting to seize additional territory from near-by nations, the Dutch reclaimed land by building dikes to shut out the sea. Here in the United States we have opened large areas in our West for agriculture by constructing Boulder Dam, Grand Coulee Dam, and others. An air view of the immense Boulder Dam appears on page 755. The Russians, as you have learned, established an entirely new — and to us, a strange — system of national government in an effort to improve living conditions.

In the stories of the various nations, we have seen the spirit of nationalism grow. Likewise we have seen people struggle to secure their rights. The causes, such as geographical conditions, types of peoples, desire for security, and other factors, have been studied. You have seen how the Industrial Revolution stirred nations where the factory system had spread, and changed the daily life of the people, and how nations turned to other countries in search of raw materials and markets for manufactured goods. The struggle for colonies, and "spheres of influence"—foreign areas controlled indirectly by the more powerful nations—was renewed. The manufacturing nations, in their search for security, set aside the interests of weaker countries. This attitude displayed by the more powerful nations toward weaker or more backward peoples is known as imperialism. It brought with it a race among the great powers for control of foreign territories.

Courtesy Union Pacific Railroad

BOULDER DAM

The airview from the face, or upstream side, of the dam shows the giant intake towers. Compare their size with that of the automobiles on the highway along the top of the dam. On the left of the dam is Arizona, and on the right, Nevada.

National patriotism has developed through the centuries. The national spirit and pride of the citizens of modern nations did not develop in a short period of time. In ancient days, nationalism was strong among the people in such city-states as Athens. The Romans, too, were intensely patriotic and proud of their republic. In feudal times, though, there was no strong love of country or feeling of national patriotism. Royal or national governments, such as that provided by the emperor of the Holy Roman Empire, were so weak that people were scarcely aware of their existence.

Toward the end of the Middle Ages, late in the 15th Century, national governments grew stronger, while the in-dependent power of the feudal lords declined. People became accustomed to looking to the king or prince for such things as protection, leadership, administration of justice, and control of trade and commerce. And as they did so, they became more conscious of the fact that they belonged to a larger group than that ruled by a feudal lord. War has always helped to fix men's loyalties. In the Middle Ages most wars were between feudal lords and so developed feudal loyalty. By the 14th Century national governments were strong enough to carry on international wars, which tended to create national patriotism.

Another factor in creating patriotism is a common language. People who speak the same language tend to unite against foreigners whom they cannot understand. With the increase of wealth toward the end of the Middle Ages more people learned to read and write and books were written in the national languages, rather than in Latin. After printing was invented in 1450, these books circulated more freely. They were read by many people in the nation. It thus became necessary to standardize the national language.

Still another factor in creating national consciousness is common economic interest. In the Middle Ages each city controlled its own trade and industry and the citizens stood together against all outsiders. But as business developed on a larger scale, and as national governments became stronger, the state took over control. Thus the whole national group became an economic unit.

The Reformation during the 16th Century, and the religious wars that followed, also promoted the growth of nationalism in many countries of Western Europe. Religious wars divided people into units, each group struggling to establish its own religious beliefs. These struggles encouraged nationalism.

It was not until well into the 19th Century that the search for foreign markets, stimulated by the Industrial Revolution, brought modern imperialism and the renewed search for colonies that had marked the 16th, 17th, and 18th Centuries. This desire for colonies, " a place in the sun " as some people described it, has strongly influenced the revival of nationalism as countries have strived to insure their economic security during the past hundred-odd years.

The Industrial Revolution strengthened the power of the middle class. After the Industrial Revolution was well under way, the middle class became a power in the social and political life of Western Europe.

The growing power and wealth of the rising class of merchants, bankers, and manufacturers contributed indirectly to the growth of nationalism. This middle class wanted more wealth and believed that extensive foreign markets would promote prosperity. Because there was little chance for increasing their trade with other manufacturing nations, business interests turned to Africa, Latin America, the Far East, and other parts of the world to which the factory system had not spread.

In some cases the urge for foreign markets resulted in colonies controlled by the manufacturing nations. In other cases, the industrial states made agreements with the rulers of the " backward " countries and obtained what are called spheres of influence. This gave the European nations some control over parts of such countries as China. In still other cases, large corporations built up great trading organizations in other nations and sometimes controlled the economic life, and indirectly the government, of these little countries.

Unfortunately, colonies and spheres of influence caused jealousies to grow between nations and strengthened old rivalries. England and France nearly went to war over territorial rights in Egypt and the Suez Canal in the latter part of the 19th Century. France and Germany disputed bitterly over Morocco in 1905 and again in 1911. Russia and Japan fought a war over territory Japan had taken from China. In other words, imperialism, encouraged by the Industrial Revolution, became a rallying point for nationalism in the 19th and 20th Centuries.

Nationalism grew strong in Europe. There was ample cause, too, right in Europe itself, for international rivalry. In the Balkan Peninsula, as you read in Part Seventeen, are a number of states with large Slavic populations. These people are racially akin to the Russians. But these people in the Balkans were under the rule of the Turks — old enemies of Russia. Because of their racial kinship, among other reasons, Russia cast an envious eye on the Balkans. This alarmed Austria-Hungary because there were many Slavs in her hodge-podge empire. If Russia gained control in the Balkans, would she next attempt to weaken Austria-Hungary's control of the Slavic peoples in the Austro-Hungarian Empire? Austria's rulers had good reason to fear such a possibility. The Slavs in the empire were discontented, and some wanted to break away to join the near-by Balkan kingdom of Serbia, a Slavic nation. Austria, however, managed to hold on to her Slav minorities. But tension mounted between the Austro-Hungarian Empire and Serbia, which was backed by Russia, during the late 19th and early 20th Centuries.

Regardless of the causes, 19th Century imperialism reopened the old struggle for security. Keen competition developed among European nations for raw materials not produced at home, such as cotton, silk, copper, iron, tin, coal, nickel, zinc, rubber, and oil. The "have-not" nations, such as Germany, that had few or no colonies and "spheres of influence," eyed jealously the "have" nations, such as England and France, that had large colonial empires. The race was on. Fear of one another led the "have" nations and the "have not" nations to increase the size of their armies and their navies.

International fears led to rivalry in armaments and to alliances. The nations of Europe did not trust their security to their armies and navies alone. Diplomacy, or the coming to agreements by official discussions, treaties, and alliances, was resorted to as never before. The German chancellor, Bismarck, of whom you read in Part Fifteen, made a Triple Alliance with Austria-Hungary and Italy. This agreement stated that if one of the member nations should be attacked, the others would aid or remain neutral. France, too, acted to protect her interests. She arranged an alliance with Russia in which England, who feared the growing power of Germany, joined later. This Alliance was known as the Triple Entente [ahɴ'tahɴt'], and it established a concentration of power that, with a number of other international agreements, maintained peace in Europe for a few short years.

The stage was set for the tragedy of nations. During the hundred years following the downfall of Napoleon and the reconstruction of Europe by the Congress of Vienna, developments in Europe may be likened to the building of a huge stage and the casting of parts for the great drama of war. Many materials or forces entered into the setting. Germany, playing the leading role, had a united and blindly patriotic people. Most Germans were willing to follow their ambitious leaders without question. Austria, and presumably Italy, stood by to support Germany. The Germans were in a mood for action. Many thought themselves and their culture superior to the people and cultures of other nations. Germany, as was described in Part Fifteen, believed that she was surrounded by an "iron ring" of possible enemy nations. She planned to be ready to strike the first blows in the war she foresaw.

Elsewhere in the world in the 19th and early 20th Centuries, imperialism began to shape the interests and attitudes of other nations. The United States had developed a strong sphere of influence among the Latin-American nations that bordered on the Caribbean Sea. You learned about such nations in Part Twenty-one. In 1898 war broke out between the United States and Spain over Cuba. As a result of this war Cuba received her freedom and the rich island became a republic. Cuba, however, was not completely free. She had to promise not to make international agreements without the consent of the United States. Moreover, many of Cuba's great sugar and tobacco plantations were controlled by business organizations in the United States. In 1934 Cuba gained complete political independence.

As the 19th Century drew to a close, the United States entered into the race for colonies in the Pacific Ocean and in the Far East. We annexed the Hawaiian Islands. The plantations on these islands were already controlled by American businessmen. Furthermore, the United States purchased the Philippine Islands from Spain at this time. Some Americans believed that possession of the Philippines would provide a key to open the door to the markets and raw materials on the mainland of Asia.

Japan, during the last years of the 19th Century, had, as you read in Part Twenty, reached the continent of Asia. You may recall that she defeated China in 1894 and secured a part of Korea and all of the island of Formosa. Between 1900 and 1911 Japan made further gains in Korea, and checked Russia's efforts to expand in Manchuria. It was evident, even then, that Japan intended to develop the resources and markets of the Far East for herself.

In the background were nations in many parts of the world which were destined to play a part in the impending drama that opened in Europe. On which side would they play? Would they assume important or only minor roles? The stage being set, when and how was the signal for the raising of the curtain on the tragedy of nations to be given?

Chapter 2 ~ International Rivalry and Tension Burst Forth Into World War I

The murder of Archduke Francis Ferdinand became an excuse for war. In the summer of 1914 the nations of Europe were at peace. Most of the people were living the normal lives of peacetime. But there were statesmen and military leaders who knew that this peace was an uncertain one. The Balkan Wars of 1912 and 1913 had weakened Turkey's influence over the Slavic nations of the Balkans. On the other hand, the wars had strengthened indirectly the power of Germany and Austria-Hungary in the Balkan Peninsula.

Nationalism among the Slavs in the Balkan states had grown as an outcome of the Balkan War. This was true particularly in Serbia and Montenegro. The Serbs felt they had earlier been cheated out of Bosnia, a part of Austria-Hungary on the Adriatic seacoast. See the map on page 752. The people of Bosnia were mostly Slavs who wanted to join the neighboring Slavic kingdom of Serbia. Possession of Bosnia, moreover, would have given Serbia ports on the Adriatic Sea. But Austria-Hungary retained Bosnia. The feeling mounted in Serbia against the Austro-Hungarian Empire and Germany, Austria-Hungary's ally.

In June, 1914, Archduke Francis Ferdinand, heir to the throne of Austria, went to Sarajevo [sah′rah′yeh′voh], a city in Bosnia not far from the border of Serbia, as you may see by referring to the map on page 752. He went to review Austrian army maneuvers. Crowds lined the streets as the Archduke and his wife rode by in an open carriage. Suddenly a man broke through the lines and shot them both.

The whole world was shocked to hear of these assassinations. Great excitement prevailed in both Austria-Hungary and Serbia. The captured assassin turned out to be an Austrian subject, and it was hoped that Serbia would not be accused by Austria of plotting Ferdinand's murder. Austrian officials took no action for almost a month. Then, backed by Germany, they sent Serbia a harsh note, or ultimatum, declaring that the Slavic kingdom must purge itself of all anti-Austrian influence. The ultimatum also demanded that Austrian officials be permitted to enter Serbia to run down those who plotted the assassination of the heir to the Austrian throne. Serbia had just forty-eight hours to accept or reject these harsh terms. She agreed to all except the one permitting Austrian officials to carry on their investigation in Serbia. Would the crisis pass? The world thought so, but Austria-Hungary, encouraged by Germany, already had determined upon her course of action and set her troops in motion. She had decided to crush Serbia and put an end to the political

troubles that the Slavs had been making for her. This, of course, aroused Russia, who was on friendly terms with Serbia.

The European powder box exploded. One event followed another with lightning speed, as you will see by a glance at the timetable of World War I on page 804. Within twelve days all Europe was rushing to arms, led by Germany and Austria-Hungary on the one hand, and by the members of the Triple Entente on the other. The German Kaiser's greygreen clad troops poured into Belgium. This was in absolute disregard of a nonaggression treaty between the two countries in which Germany had promised not to invade Belgium. The Germans were applying their plan to strike first and fast. Germany's disregard of the treaty to respect the neutrality of Belgium led England to declare war on Germany. In the course of the next few days, one declaration of war followed another, as you can see by the timetable on page 804. On one side were Germany, Austria, Bulgaria, and Turkey. On the other were Belgium, France, the British Empire, Japan, Russia, Serbia, and later Italy. Later events brought the United States, China, and many other nations to declare war against the powers of Central Europe.

1914. The roots of World War I lie deep in the past. It should be clear that the assassination of the Austrian archduke was not the cause of World War I. The event, as was described, was used as a pretext by Austria and Germany to begin the conflict that would break, they hoped, the " iron ring " of powers surrounding them. That Great Britain, France, and Russia were unfriendly to the imperialistic ambitions of Germany is also certain. Those nations had imperialistic ambitions of their own, as we know. To that degree both the Central

AN ISLAND IN THE SEA OF MARMARA

This island is one of the Princes Islands in the Sea of Marmara, close to Istanbul and the Dardanelles Straits. The Sea of Marmara is one link in the much-desired waterway which can be shut or opened by the nation holding the narrow Dardanelles.

European Powers and the Allies, as they came to be called, were responsible for World War I.

Germany and Austria wanted war. England, France, and Russia did not. These countries had what they wanted in the way of colonies and resources. They wanted to keep conditions as they were. Germany, on the other hand, had undergone the Industrial Revolution somewhat later than had some other countries. Germany wanted colonies, and power in the Balkan Peninsula. Moreover, the long struggle to achieve national unity in Germany, about which you read in Part Fifteen, developed war-like ideas among the German people. They believed it was all right to use force to seize what they wanted. It is

clear that the aggressor nations in 1914 were Germany and her ally, Austria-Hungary. It was these partners that other European nations feared.

The formation of international alliances such as the Triple Alliance of Germany, Austria-Hungary, and Italy, and the Triple Entente, of England, France, and Russia, had heightened international fears. Such pacts were made to maintain power and security, but often secret side-agreements were reached between nations so that uncertainty and international distrust were increased.

The rush for foreign markets, which was the reason for the imperialism of the preceding hundred years, was, as you know, an underlying cause of ill-feeling among nations. Germany had started

too late in the race for colonies to secure any really profitable territories, except those in Africa and in the Pacific.
Thus other European nations suspected
Germany might try to gain colonies by
wresting them from their European protectors. It was feared, also, that Germany
might try to expand her influence in
central and southeastern Europe at the
expense of weaker nations. Austria, as
has been pointed out, held Bosnia, with
the seaports coveted by Serbia. Neither
was willing that the other should have
Bosnia. Russia's northern ports were icebound in the winter. The value of her
ports on the Black Sea was lessened because Turkey, Russia's old enemy, controlled the Dardanelles through which
ships must sail to reach the Mediterranean. You can see these places on the
map on page 752. The picture opposite
shows part of the strategic waterway
connecting the Black Sea and the Mediterranean Ocean. These factors help to
explain why Russia wanted to further
the interests of the Slavic states in the
Balkans. Such support would help to
weaken Turkey and bring the Russian
and Balkan Slavs more closely together.
These conditions had helped to encourage extreme nationalism.

The profits to be made by supplying
warring nations with munitions also appear to have been a cause of war. Corporations that manufactured supplies
needed for war created trouble and discouraged peaceful settlement of disputes
between nations.

**World War I became a stalemate in
the trenches on the Western Front.**
When World War I began in July, 1914,
many people on both sides thought it
could last only a few months. Few expected that the conflict would go on for
more than four years. Germany was far
better prepared for war than were her

opponents. The Germans expected to
subdue France before the Russian Czar's
forces could be mobilized to threaten
Germany's backdoor to the east. With
France defeated, Germany's leaders
thought, they could readily dispose of
England's small army.

But this plan called for speed that
would catch the Allies unprepared and
paralyze them before they could strike
a counterblow. So German troops struck
into Belgium. The little Belgian army,
by heroic resistance, set back Germany's
schedule. This delay gave England time
to send reinforcements to France, and
enabled Russia to assemble her forces for
attack in East Prussia. The Germans
were finally halted at the first battle of
the Marne [mahrn], only 35 miles from
Paris. See the Timetable of World War I
on page 804.

The war on the Western Front settled
down to four long, exhausting years of
trench warfare. We shall not relate the
long story of the many campaigns of
World War I. The Allies in the west
seemed able to do little more than hold
the German war machine at bay for
three years.

Control of the sea was in Allied hands.
While the Allies were unable to break
the German lines on the Western Front,
they did much to weaken the German
war machine. The British, French, Italian, and later, United States navies prevented the Central Powers from import-
ing raw materials and other goods. The
German navy, except for submarines, or
U-boats, was bottled up for most of the
war.

Russian armies collapsed in the east.
On the Eastern Front the Germans were
able to defeat the vast, but poorly
equipped, forces of the Russian Czar.
As you have read in the story of Russia,
the Russian people revolted in 1917 and

set up a new government that made peace with Germany. This of course helped the Germans greatly. They could now transfer their armies from the Eastern Front to France, and renew their efforts to defeat the Allied forces on the Western Front.

The entry of the United States into World War I threw the balance in favor of the Allies. When the German war lords made their careful plans for World War I, they made at least one mistake. They decided it was unlikely that the United States would join the Allies. America's armed might and her great industries, added to those of our Allies, proved to be more than the Germans could match. Early in 1917 the United States declared war on Germany.

Why did the United States enter the war? There were many reasons. The immediate cause was the savage, unrestricted submarine warfare that Germany waged. Over a hundred American lives were lost in the U-boat attacks. Our government protested, but Germany's promises to respect our rights, as neutrals, to freedom of the seas were of no value. Besides, some of our citizens believed that German spies were stirring up labor troubles and destroying munitions factories to prevent the United States from selling war material to the Allies. Still others believed that Germany was not only responsible for opening the attack but also for bringing the war about. These people thought Germany was an aggressor who should be halted and punished. The well-planned propaganda sent out by the Allies, however, should not be overlooked. This helped to bring America into the war, as well as the fact that American business interests had more money invested in the Allied countries than in Germany. Furthermore, England and France were democracies. Americans wanted to see the autocratic, militaristic government of the Kaiser defeated and crushed.

In any case, it is true that most Americans believed that their country was entering the war for unselfish reasons. This ideal was well expressed by President Wilson in his address to Congress asking for a declaration of war. He said that we were going to war because —

The world must be made safe for democracy. Its peace must be planted upon the tested foundations of political liberty. We have no selfish ends to serve. We desire no conquest, no dominion. We seek no indemnities for ourselves, no compensation for the sacrifices we shall freely make. We are but one of the champions of the rights of mankind. We shall be satisfied when those rights have been made as secure as the faith and freedom of nations can make them.

Americans " did their bit." When Congress declared war on Germany in 1917, the people of the United States wholeheartedly supported this declaration. America put forth every effort to bring the war to a speedy and successful end. Our factories worked overtime to produce ammunition, clothing, shoes, and other supplies for the French and British armies as well as for our own. Our farmers raised wheat, corn, and sugar to feed our Allies, whose normal food supplies had been reduced greatly.

At the time the United States entered the war she had only a small army. Although military experts said it would take two years to raise and train an army of a million men, the United States had two million men in training within a year. By the fall of 1918 there were about two million " Yanks " in France, many of them on the firing line. Moreover, another million men were in training camps in the United States.

TRENCH WARFARE MARKED WORLD WAR I

This picture shows some of the equipment used by the trench fighters of World War I.
Notice the shallow helmets which were worn at that time.

The climax of World War I came in the summer of 1918. The efforts of the Allies to drive the Germans back from their lines, extending from the borders of Switzerland northward through France and Belgium to the North Sea, were of little avail. On the map on page 752 find the territory through which this long battle line ran. Bitter, costly attacks, when troops went "over the top" at "zero hour" after the artillery barrages were lifted, usually accomplished little more than to straighten a portion of the line here and there.

It was evident that a united command was necessary if Germany was to be defeated. Accordingly, Marshal Ferdinand Foch [fohsh], of the French army, was selected in the spring of 1918 to weld the forces of the Allies, including the growing American forces, into a single war machine. Marshal Foch was a general who knew how to put his theories into practice. He was noted for his bulldog tenacity and courage. On one occasion he said, "My right has been rolled up, my left has been driven back, my center has been smashed. I have ordered an advance from all directions." He stands out as one of the great heroes of French military history.

New weapons changed the tactics of warfare. Here we interrupt the story of the progress of the war to describe the new weapons which made this war so different from any that had been fought before. Mechanized warfare had been practically unknown until World War I. Until that time wars were often a succession of battles fought by the same troops in many widely separated areas. Such wars have been described as "wars of movement." The machine gun was one reason why the first World War became one of trench warfare. Until an effective means to combat the machine gun was developed, armies had to stay in their trenches — zig-zag rows of opposing ditches, lined with sandbags and equipped with dug-outs for shelter.

Large-scale attacks usually were preceded by barrages of heavy artillery fire that continued sometimes for hours in an effort to knock out all opposition. The French "75," a three-inch field gun; heavy guns called howitzers that lobbed sixteen-inch shells; long-range rifles mounted on railway carriages; and many others were used widely. The range of some field guns was increased to six miles. Heavier guns had much longer ranges. The projectiles fired were highly developed during the course of the war. Armor-piercing shells, smoke shells, gas shells, and shrapnel were used.

Airplanes were used for scouting purposes quite early in the war. Later, some planes were equipped as bombers. Other lighter planes became the ancestors of the fighter planes of World War II. But large-scale bombing, such as became common in World War II, was not developed. Even more decisive than the machine gun or the airplane, was the tank. This was a cumbersome affair only generally resembling the modern tank. Designed to overcome the effectiveness of the machine gun, the tank was introduced by the British. These first tanks were slow and their gasoline engines often broke down. The tanks, nevertheless, helped the Allies greatly.

Germany, realizing that she could not challenge British seapower on the surface, planned to cut off the Allies' shipping line from abroad by sinking the merchant vessels carrying the goods. For a time the German U-boats, or submarines, appeared to be succeeding as the rate of sinkings increased. Eventually, however, the convoy system was worked out by the British and American navies.

The depth charge, and listening devices by which surface vessels could detect moving submerged submarines, came into use. By 1918 Germany's U-boat campaign had been greatly checked.

Poison gas was used widely in World War I. It was introduced by the Germans in 1915 at Ypres [eep'r]. Many forms of poison gas were used, but mustard gas, which inflicted serious external and internal burns, and often caused agonizing death, was the most common.

American troops played a decisive part in World War I. In the spring of 1918, the American forces began to play a decisive part in the Allied offensive. American troops went into action with other Allied troops at Cantigny [kahɴ'tee'nyee']. At Château-Thierry [sha'toh' tyeh'ree'] they checked a determined German advance. Then in September, 1918, General John J. Pershing's troops were ready for action on a large scale. They took over the southern portion of the front, while French, British, and Canadian forces farther north prepared for what were to be the final drives.

American troops drove the Germans back at St. Mihiel [saɴ mee'ee'el'] to open the concluding Allied offensive. While other Allied forces attacked farther north, the American Expeditionary Force on the south and French troops on the north thrust into the Argonne [ahr'gahn'] Forest.

These repeated blows of the unified Allied armies under Marshal Foch were too much for the Germans. In the fall of 1918 the military machine of the Central Powers showed signs of breaking. High German military leaders warned the German government that there was no hope of victory. An Italian offensive defeated the Austrian forces. Shortly afterward Austria sued for an armistice. Everywhere German armies were meeting

A SUMMARY OF PRESIDENT WILSON'S FOURTEEN POINTS

Wilson's Suggestions:

1. There should be no more secret treaties between nations. All treaties should be "open covenants openly arrived at."
2. There should be "freedom of the seas." International laws should clearly define the rights of neutrals and warring nations on the seas.
3. Tariffs which create economic barriers between nations should be removed.
4. There should be a reduction of armaments.
5. There should be an adjustment of all colonial claims, on the principle that the interests of the colonies should be considered first.
6. Russia should be allowed to develop her future without dictation from other nations.

7. All armies should be withdrawn and damages should be paid to Belgium.
8. The rich territory of Alsace-Lorraine should be returned to France, its original owner.
9. The Italian frontiers should be adjusted along lines of nationality.

10. Austria-Hungary should be broken up into a number of separate nations, giving freedom to the subject races.
11. The boundaries of Serbia, Montenegro, and Romania should be adjusted along lines of nationality.
12. Subject nations under Turkish rule should be freed.
13. An independent Polish state with a free and secure outlet to the sea should be established.
14. A League guaranteeing security to both large and small states should be organized.

What Actually Happened:

1. The League of Nations required that copies of all treaties made by League members should be filed with the League secretariat.
2. Some attempts were made to limit naval armaments and to bring about definite understandings between nations with great navies.
3. Very little was accomplished toward removing economic barriers, for no nation would allow others to interfere with its tariff laws.
4. After 1918 there were a number of disarmament conferences aiming at this problem.
5. The colonies of Germany were seized and divided among Britain, France, and Japan.

6. European nations sent armies into Russia when she refused to pay the debts of the Czar's government. However, the Russians expelled these invaders.
7. This was accomplished.

8. This was accomplished.

9. This was partially accomplished. Unfortunately, however, Italy also secured some territory inhabited by Austrians and Slavs.
10. Czechoslovakia, Yugoslavia, Austria, and Hungary were formed out of the old Austro-Hungarian Empire.
11. This was largely accomplished.

12. Although a few Arab states were formed, little was accomplished.
13. This was accomplished.

14. A League of Nations was established.

EUROPE BEFORE WORLD WAR I

Compare the size of Austria-Hungary and of Germany before World War I. Notice also the nations of the Balkan Peninsula. What nations familiar to you today do not appear on this map?

disaster. Their soldiers were discontented; revolution broke out among the German people. The Kaiser fled to Holland in fear of his life, and the new German government asked for peace. The Armistice was signed on November 11, 1918.

The Allies dictated terms of peace to the Germans. As you are well aware from what you have read earlier in *Story of Nations,* wars often breed the hates and fears that give rise to later armed conflicts among nations. President Wilson was determined that such was not to be the case after this "war to end wars." Accordingly, in January, 1918, he set forth his famous "Fourteen Points," the basis upon which he believed a just and lasting peace could be

made. It was upon these Fourteen Points that the Germans had relied when they asked for the armistice eleven months later. What were these Fourteen Points? Were they carried out by the terms of the Treaty of Versailles [vehr′sai′ee]? Let us examine Woodrow Wilson's platform for world peace, and see what happened to it when the statesmen of the world gathered to make what they said was to be an enduring peace.

A few months after the armistice was signed, delegates from the Allied powers met in Paris to make the treaty of peace, signed later at Versailles. The world waited breathlessly to see the terms of this treaty. Many people believed with President Wilson that the war had ushered in a new era of inter-

THE MAP THAT THE STATESMEN DREW IN 1918

What nations do you find here which did not appear on the map of Europe in 1914? What nations have grown much smaller or disappeared? Which is the largest of the new or reborn nations?

national affairs and that the new treaty would prevent future wars. Idealists were to be sadly disappointed.

Although Wilson fought determinedly for the principles of justice which he had outlined in his Fourteen Points, only a few of them were realized. The summary on page 765 will show what Wilson suggested and what actually happened in determining the Treaty of Versailles.

Statesmen rearranged the map of Europe. A comparison of the maps on pages 766 and 767 shows how World War I altered the map of Europe. Notice that Germany lost Alsace-Lorraine to France, who also obtained control for fifteen years of the rich German coal mines in the Saar Valley. Later the people of the Saar were allowed to decide to which country, France or Germany, they should belong. They voted to return to Germany.

Finland, Estonia, Latvia, Lithuania, Poland, Yugoslavia, and Czechoslovakia, about which you read in Part Seventeen, were created at this time. Can you tell from which nations these new states were carved?

In addition to her other losses, Germany was asked to pay reparation, a huge amount of money, to repair the damage caused by the war. The exact amount of this sum was not fixed at the time.

Wilson objected to some terms of the treaty, which he believed were too severe. The Germans sent in a written pro-

Wide World Photos

THE "BIG FOUR"

Orlando of Italy, Lloyd George of Britain, Clemenceau of France, and Wilson of the United States were the "Big Four" of the Paris Peace Conference.

test, and the German cabinet resigned rather than submit to what they considered such an unfair settlement. But in spite of the storm of disapproval, the treaty was finally signed by the German National Assembly.

President Wilson bargained for a just peace. Were Woodrow Wilson's ideas for a lasting peace adopted by the peacemakers at the close of World War I? The answer is no. Nationalism, the old fears that had haunted Europe, selfish interest, and secret treaties between other Allied nations came first in the minds of Europe's statesmen. Woodrow Wilson had to be content with the acceptance of only a part of his program, as you see by looking at the summary of the Fourteen Points on page 765. Who were these other leaders at the Paris Peace Conference with whom Wilson argued and fought?

The British Empire was represented by Prime Minister David Lloyd George, a fiery little Welshman, and head of the English government, as was Winston Churchill in World War II. Premier Georges Clemenceau [jhohrjh kluh′ mahɴ′soh′], the "Tiger of France," had been a bitter enemy of Germany all his life. Clemenceau remembered how Germany had humiliated France in 1870 and he was determined that Germany must be so crushed that she never again could threaten France. Lloyd George, Clemenceau, and Wilson were the "Big Three" at the Paris Peace Conference. Italy, which had joined the Allies in 1915, was represented by the head of its government, Premier Orlando. These leaders became known as the "Big Four." A picture of the "Big Four" is shown above. The other three leaders forced Wilson to give way on many of his

Fourteen Points. This he agreed to do but only when they promised to back his proposal for the League of Nations.

The aftermath of war brought suffering to both the victors and the vanquished. At the time peace was made with the Germans, the Allies believed that they had won the war. But as the years rolled by, they became less certain. Germany was unable to pay the war debt. Trade markets were destroyed. Nations found that taxes must be increased to meet the war expenses which remained unpaid. Old national jealousies and rivalries continued. In fact, as people were to see even more clearly with the outbreak of World War II, the war settled nothing and all nations lost as a result of it.

The great powers created a League of Nations. When President Wilson finally agreed to a treaty of peace which both he and his supporters considered unfair in some respects, he did so because it was necessary to grant concessions in exchange for votes for a League of Nations. Like many other world-minded leaders, he believed that some kind of international organization, which would promote co-operation between nations and settle their disputes, was necessary for the welfare of the world. Consequently he was forced into compromise. But just what was this League of Nations for which Wilson was willing to sacrifice so much?

Like the Congress of the United States, the League of Nations was made up of two houses, the Assembly and the Council. Also, there was a Secretariat, or permanent body of officers in charge of such work as keeping records, publishing information, registering treaties, and directing the work of the various international bureaus. They made their headquarters in Geneva, Switzerland.

The Covenant, or agreement signed by the members of the League, provided that the Assembly should consist of from one to three representatives from each member nation, and that the Council should consist of five permanent members and ten nonpermanent members, the latter to be elected by the Assembly. These permanent members were, at different times, France, Great Britain, Italy, Japan, Germany, and Russia. Germany and Japan, as you know, withdrew from the League, and in December, 1939, Russia was expelled from the League.

Another body provided for in the Covenant of the League, although independent of it, was the World Court. The World Court had fifteen judges and four deputy judges, elected by the Council and the Assembly. Its function was to settle international legal problems, which were to be voluntarily submitted by nations in disagreement. No way was provided for forcing nations to submit their disputes to this body. Nevertheless, the decisions made by the Court helped to strengthen the system of international law. The World Court grew steadily in prestige and usefulness until another war broke out.

The United States refused to enter the League of Nations and the World Court. Although President Wilson had been one of the leaders in the establishment of the League of Nations, the League fared worse in the United States than elsewhere. There were many reasons why the American people opposed it, but perhaps the chief one was their fear of being drawn into European politics. Many people believed that America had gained nothing — indeed, that it had lost a great deal — by entering World War I. They felt that by joining the League of Nations the United States would constantly be forced into positions contrary to her best interests. Then, too, many citizens were advocates of the old policy of aloofness and isolation from the affairs of Europe—a policy which had worked successfully in the days of Washington and Monroe.

Finally, entry into the League became a political issue. One group of United States Senators resented the rather high-handed way in which Wilson handled affairs at the Peace Conference, and put forth every effort to defeat his proposals. When Wilson asked Congress to approve the entry of the United States into the League of Nations, the Senate refused to ratify the treaty.

Although every American President from Wilson to Franklin D. Roosevelt urged the United States to enter the World Court, with certain reservations, to protect her interests, these efforts fared little better than Wilson's attempt to make the United States a member of the League of Nations.

The League of Nations attempted to maintain world peace. The League was founded for the promotion of international co-operation and good will. During the earlier days of the activity of the League of Nations, it seemed to grow in power and influence, and gave some promise of accomplishing the purposes for which it was organized. It provided an opportunity for the representatives of many nations to gather at a council table, talk over their difficulties, and arrive at acceptable agreements. It aided a number of countries, especially Austria and Hungary, to recover from the devastating results of World War I. It awakened the nations to the dangers of the international traffic in drugs, and encouraged them to co-operate in their efforts to control it. It gave consideration to many other humanitarian problems, such as child labor and the conditions of women, especially those without means of support. At all times it tried to extend the principle of arbitration and the limitation of armament.

The League was successful in settling disputes between small nations, but failed to settle disputes between the larger ones, as you will read in the next chapter. There are many reasons that account for the League's failure to meet the expectations Woodrow Wilson held for it. Chief among these reasons was the unwillingness of more powerful members of the League to co-operate effectively. The refusal of the United States to join the League of Nations also weakened the organization greatly.

Chapter 3 ~ The Nations Fumbled the Peace and Continued the Struggle for Security

The nations looked for permanent security. On November 11, 1918, the warring nations laid down their arms in relief after four years of bitter struggle.

New hope dawned. Peace and security at last seemed possible. Farmers went back to their fields. Industrialists, who had been making munitions, reorganized their factories and built new ones to replenish the badly depleted stock of peacetime goods. Men found work. Merchants filled their shelves in anticipation of profitable sales.

International co-operation appeared to be the goal during the 1920's. At the Paris Peace Conference the statesmen had tried to satisfy the victors, discipline the defeated, and unsnarl tangled international problems. The League of Nations and the World Court seemed to have taken long steps toward the peaceful settlement of disputes between nations.

At Washington in 1922 representatives of the leading world powers, including Japan, agreed to limit their naval armaments. They promised to respect the rights of China, as well as those of other nations in the Far East and the Pacific islands.

At Locarno [loh kahr′noh], in 1925, the diplomats of some of the leading European nations signed a pact in which they agreed to respect national boundaries. And at Paris in 1928 the major world powers signed the Kellogg Pact renouncing war as a means of settling disputes between nations.

The great depression began in 1929. Within a decade after the Treaty of Versailles, the dark cloud of a world-wide depression cast its gloom over the family of nations. Some countries, particularly Germany, had experienced the pinch and pressure of hard times immediately after World War I and had not shared in the prosperity of the 1920's. In the wake of world depression came a train of severe problems. Some of them were due to the discontent and the unsettled issues that were the aftermath of World War I. Others had their roots deep in the difficulties of nationalism and imperialism which, as you have

learned, grew so important in the 19th and the early 20th Centuries.

Other problems of the depression seem entirely new and hard to account for unless we remember that the Industrial Revolution was and is still going on. After World War I, men made new uses of machinery and new applications of science. The markets of the world were flooded with goods. Factories turned out more products than people could buy. Therefore factory production was cut, and large-scale unemployment resulted. Farmers suffered because they could not sell their products. Merchants closed their shops because neither farmers nor people in cities and towns had money to buy what they had to sell. Security of livelihood and, in some countries, security of life became increasingly uncertain.

Nationalism flared up again, fanned by dictators. Politicians and statesmen busied themselves searching for the road back to security and prosperity for their nations. In some countries these leaders followed the path of selfish nationalism in their search for security.

Many governments were taken over by dictators who suppressed the rights of citizens. Some countries with teeming populations looked covetously at convenient lands and territories where they might find more land and resources.

We face the world as it is. Frequently in these pages, we have used the term "security" to describe what men and nations have strived for over countless centuries. Fundamentally, this means economic security, the opportunity and the resources to produce goods and to maintain the standard of living the people want. Italy, for example, has very little fertile soil, and scarcely any coal and iron. France, on the other hand, has all three and many other natural advan-

THE SHIFTING PATTERN

(Note: This chart is presented as a scheme of constant comparison. The continually shifting pattern of national and inter 1945 — a time when most of the problems of nations were connected with war and the problems of effecting a lasting peace

ITEM	GREAT BRITAIN	CHINA	FRANCE	GERMANY
1. Area (square miles)	103,000 (not including Irish Free State)	2,279,100 (China proper)	212,700	225,300 (Including Austria and Sudetenland)
2. Population	47,886,000 (not including Irish Free State)	422,708,000 (estimated) (China proper)	38,000,000	79,375,000
3. Population (per sq. mi.)	465 (not including Irish Free State)	141	179	352
4. Natural Resources	Little surplus; British Isles lack much; British Empire has everything	Most essential raw materials	Relatively little surplus. Lacks oil and rubber	Relatively little surplus. Lacks oil, rubber, copper
5. What People Do for a Living	Farming; fishing; manufacturing; merchandising; shipping; mining	Farming; industry; fishing	Farming; manufacturing; fishing; shipping; mining	Farming; manufacturing; shipping; mining
6. What They Want to Sell	Manufactured goods; ship transportation	Tea, silk, hides, skins, wool, coal, iron ore, vegetable oil	Wines, perfumes, silk textiles, cotton textiles, machinery	Manufactured goods
7. What They Need to Buy	Food; raw materials; armaments	Manufactured goods, armaments	Coal, coke, vegetable oils, wool, foods, lumber, oil, rubber	Food and raw materials, especially rubber, oil, aluminum, copper
8. Form of Government (in theory)	Limited constitutional monarchy	Republic	Republic	
9. Form of Government (actually)	Representative democracy	Military dictatorship	Temporary military government	Temporary military government
10. Head of Government (in theory)	King	President	President	
11. Head of Government (in practice)	Prime Minister (Churchill)	President (Chiang Kai-shek)	General Charles De Gaulle	
12. Political Leaders	Churchill Beaverbrook Eden Halifax Hoare Ernest Bevin	Chiang Kai-shek Mme. Chiang Kai-shek H. H. Kung Mao Tse-Tung T. V. Soong Chen Li-fu Chou En-lai Chen Chang	De Gaulle Thorez Leclerc Koenig	
13. Political Friends	China Denmark Norway France The Netherlands Belgium Portugal Russia United States	United States Great Britain Russia	Denmark and Norway Great Britain The Netherlands Belgium Russia United States	
14. Major Problems: Economic, Social, Political, International	In May, 1945, the problems of all nations — economic, social, political, and international — were bound			

OF NATIONS

national relations makes weekly revision necessary. The information given describes conditions as they were in May
In the chart these problems have not been listed in order of importance.)

ITALY	JAPAN	RUSSIA	UNITED STATES
119,800	148,800 (proper)	8,819,800	2,977,100 (continental)
45,801,000	72,875,000 (proper)	192,696,000	131,669,000
382	490	22	44
Lacks most raw materials — iron, rubber, coal, oil, copper	Lacks many raw materials	All essential resources but rubber	All essential resources but rubber and the less common metals
Manufacturing; farming; shipping	Farming; fishing; manufacturing; shipping; merchandising	Farming; manufacturing; mining	Manufacturing; farming; merchandising; mining; fishing
Manufactured goods	Manufactured goods, raw silk	Agricultural products, manganese	Industrial and agricultural products
Raw materials, especially food, coal, oil	Raw materials, especially cotton, oil, iron, lead, aluminum, rubber	Machinery, technical labor	Some rubber, some metals
Limited constitutional monarchy	Monarchy	Soviet Republic	Republic
Temporary military government	Military dictatorship	Communist dictatorship	Representative Democracy (Republic)
King	Emperor	President of the Presidium	President
Lieutenant-General of the Realm (Prince Umberto) and AMG	Military clique	Chairman of Council of People's Commissars of U.S.S.R. and Field Marshal (Stalin)	President (Truman)
Prince Umberto Bonomi Croce Sforza	Suzuki Yonai Nomura Oikawa Toyoda	Stalin Molotov Dimitroff Bulganin	Truman Dewey Hull Stettinius Byrnes Hopkins Wallace Winant
		Great Britain China United States France	France Great Britain Latin America Russia China Norway Denmark Portugal The Netherlands Belgium

up with World War II and its outcomes.

tages. Yet both countries have millions of patriotic citizens who are in want of economic security.

Few areas of the globe are so well stored with a variety of natural resources as to be self-sufficient. Probably the United States and Russia come closer to being self-sustaining than any other large nations of the world, yet both nations find it necessary to import certain commodities. Great Britain and Japan, on the other hand, have relatively few natural resources. Both, even in peace-time, imported vast quantities of iron and oil, essentials of industry today. Great Britain and Germany cannot grow enough food on their own soil to supply their populations.

Thus it is perfectly clear that nations must depend upon one another for the goods that the modern world needs. This raises the question of how much of such goods nations must import. The answer to that depends partly upon how many people there are in each nation and what standard of living this population wants.

The chart of "The Shifting Pattern of Nations" on pages 772–773 will enable you to make a number of interesting comparisons between the leading nations, or world powers. Notice the first three items in the left-hand column. They are, respectively, area, total population, and population per square mile. You will notice that the pressure of population is most severe in Japan and in Great Britain (the British Isles, not the whole British Empire, which is quite a different story). Russia and the United States, on the contrary, have the lowest number of inhabitants per square mile. Glance down the left-hand column to the items dealing with natural resources and what the nations want. You will see the relations between the concentration of population, the abundance or scarcity of natural resources, and the things which the nations need the most.

Still another example of the pressure of population on the resources of a country is seen in the condition of Germany. Germany's position can well be compared with that of Japan. The chart will show you that Germany has about the same population and about the same area as Japan. German farm lands are not fertile as compared with farm land in some other countries, but she does have coal and iron. Germany lacks oil, rubber, and several other raw materials needed in manufacturing. She must have markets for the many products of her factories. If she cannot sell her goods abroad, she cannot buy the additional foodstuffs which she must have. Without markets for her goods neither can Germany pay for the imported oil, cotton, copper, and other materials needed for the manufacture of the goods turned out by her factories.

So in Germany we have a large population per square mile who have come to feel that in some way they must expand. The cycle is complete. To live, the Germans must manufacture. To manufacture, they need additional raw materials. To buy these necessities, they must sell in foreign markets. To have those markets, they must have access to areas not already controlled directly or indirectly solely by other manufacturing nations. We shall see how such a situation has brought war into the picture.

Japan's situation in this respect was not unlike that of Germany. Consequently the Japanese planned to control much of the mainland of Asia and many of the Pacific islands. They planned also to build up a prosperous trade with Latin America, where they could send their manufactured goods in return for raw materials.

. MACHINES ADD TO A NATION'S RESOURCES

This machine, which harvests and threshes at the same time, has greatly increased the amount of wheat that one farmer can raise. Mechanized agriculture thus multiplies a nation's resources.

Nations belong to two camps: those who have and those who have not. On the chart referred to, read across the horizontal column of Item 4, which deals with the natural resources of each of the nations whose story you have read. The nations which are best supplied with natural resources, either at home or in their colonies, belong to the camp of the " haves." Though these nations may be interested in new territories or new trade advantages, their main interest is in keeping what they have, that is, in keeping things between nations about as they have been.

Many nations have established trade regulations such as tariffs. In many cases, these regulations have prevented the free flow of goods between countries.

During the years between World War I and World War II there grew up a tension between the nations that preferred a democratic way of life and those that followed a totalitarian system. It became increasingly clear during the 1930's that, sooner or later, these conflicting ideas would clash. The totalitarian nations feared the democracies and these, in turn, watched anxiously the growing power of the dictatorships.

Fundamentally, the reasons for these fears are easy to understand because Italy, Germany, and Japan, all totalitarian countries, were among the " have-not " nations. Would they attempt to obtain the foreign markets that provided outlets for the surplus goods of other industrial nations? Would they use their growing military might in their search for security to seize territory from other nations? As you know, Germany, Italy, and Japan did each of these things and

CARGOES FOR OTHER COUNTRIES

The free movement of goods between nations, many people think, is one of the guarantees of peace. Another guarantee is the free exchange of services, such as carrying cargoes in a ship.

therefore the national security of other nations was threatened.

So, in a simplified statement, this is the problem of economic nationalism. Americans, British, French, Italians, Germans, Japanese, Greeks, Russians, and other nationalities want to have prosperous home markets and at the same time sell their surplus goods in foreign markets. It is a hard problem which leads one around in a circle, and a problem for which the proper solution is uncertain. But you should be aware that the problem does exist, even though only the elements of the difficulty can be presented here.

Two things appear certain: (1) the country that will not buy foreign goods cannot expect to sell abroad; and (2) somehow there must come a much greater degree of co-operation between nations if we are all to live happily in a world of nations. The day may come when the desire for national security will not lead nations to shut out one another's goods. The lesson of a fair exchange of goods and services needs to be learned. The first steps in that lesson have been learned within nations by both farmers and merchants. Perhaps some day a similar plan of fair trade will be worked out among the various nations. Unfortunately, economic nationalism during the years from 1919 to 1939 heightened ill-feeling between the nations.

Fear led to increased armaments and alliances. As the nations attempted to make their economic position more secure, they likewise began to strengthen their armies and navies. The "have" nations feared the "have-not" nations, and the "have-not" nations feared the "have" nations. Put wants and fears together and you have the practical reasons for marching men and ships into battle line. The same underlying elements that brought on World War I were present, in increasing force, perhaps, during the years that led up to the second global conflict. There was the search for security supported by economic nationalism, and its companion, imperialism. There was militarism encouraged by fear, and by those who hoped to profit personally by the sale of armaments.

Events of the later 1930's pointed toward World War II. The history of Europe in the 1930's is a record of repeated war scares and of crisis after crisis. In 1936 came Italy's conquest of Ethiopia, in spite of the disapproval of Great Britain, France, and the League of Nations. In 1937 Japan began a new invasion of China. Two years later Austria fell into the hands of the Germans. So it was that the rising tide of dictatorships during the 1930's drowned the rights and interests of other nations. Why were the aggressor nations not checked before they plunged the world into global war? Let us see how dictators set about obtaining their demands. As we do so, we may see why little was done to check them.

The techniques of aggressor nations led to World War II. Dictators, as you have learned from what you have read in earlier chapters, created an inflated nationalism in their countries by fervent campaigns of propaganda in the press, over the air, and in the schools — all un-

der their control. And propaganda, we were told by the ministry of propaganda in Nazi Germany, "knows neither right nor wrong, neither truth nor falsehood, but only what it wants." These same dictators armed their nations to the teeth, sacrificing bread and butter for swords and submarines. They staged grand military and naval reviews and thus made their people thrill with a new sense of power. At the same time, they ridiculed with disdain what they said were the weaknesses of those countries that were reluctant to sacrifice democratic ideals in order to make the state strong enough to resist aggression. In short, these "have-not" nations made themselves so strong that they believed they could take what they wanted. Thus we came to speak of the "have-not" nations as "aggressors."

The aggressor nations found a formula for gaining what they believed to be their needs. The first step was to disregard any treaty or international agreement that stood in their way. You have read how Hitler defied the Versailles Treaty and how Italy, when she decided upon her conquest of Ethiopia, withdrew from the League and defied the member nations to stop her. You know how Japan ignored her treaties concerning China and the Pacific islands. Sometimes aggressor nations did not ignore treaties. Instead they interpreted the treaties to suit their own interests and aims. Japan had agreed to the Kellogg Peace Pact "to renounce war as an instrument of national policy," but she invaded China just the same. Japan argued that China was a menace to the security of Japan and a threat to the peace of the Orient.

Once the aggressor nations renounced an international agreement or twisted its meaning, they turned to the next step in

Press Association, Inc.

AXIS LEADERS

In this group in a reviewing stand, notice the different methods of saluting. Mussolini is giving the Fascist salute and King Victor Emmanuel is saluting in the old style. Hitler is not saluting by any method.

their formula. This was to bluff concessions from the "have" nations. The plan followed was to make loud, threatening demands for a new piece of territory, for favored treatment, or some other concession — accompanied by threats of war. And this scheme worked for a time, because Great Britain and France believed that it was better to appease the aggressors by granting concessions than to have war. The United States remained aloof. Apparently our attitude was that what went on in Europe and the Far East was of little concern to us. In short, none of the great democracies took adequate steps to check the aggressor nations. England and France adopted a policy of appeasement. Apparently they believed that the aggressor nations would cease their demands after a time; so the best way to preserve peace was to grant their demands.

Unfortunately, the dictators were in a position to make very strong threats. Hitler, for example, in the late 1930's had the world's most powerful air force, and British and French statesmen dared not refuse his demands because they realized London and Paris could readily be bombed. Thus the dictator nations were able to enlarge their territories at the expense of other nations.

The third step used by the aggressor nations was to mark time for a while after they obtained their immediate wants. They held conferences, made treaties, and in other ways went through the motions of showing respect for international agreements. Through this procedure, however, the conceding, appeasing, nations officially approved what the dictators had done and gave a flavor of respectability to the gains these international gangsters had made. The picture on page 778 shows one of the public appearances of the leaders of these gangsters.

Hitler's demands for Czechoslovakia were met. These steps were used in the crisis that led up to the dismemberment of Czechoslovakia. Hitler wanted this republic. It stood between him and his plan for Germany's eastward expansion, as you can see from the map on page 767. Hitler began by demanding that Czechoslovakia turn over to Germany a portion of territory in which many Germans lived. When Czechoslovakia refused to give up this part of its land and, instead, guaranteed the safety and rights of the Germans who lived there, Hitler was not satisfied. German agents in Czechoslovakia trumped up stories of atrocities, and Hitler's propaganda machine went to work. British and French statesmen feared that war between Nazi Germany and the Czechoslovak Republic would begin. They therefore persuaded Czechoslovakia to turn over to Hitler some of its land.

Hitler, however, was still not satisfied and said he would send his armies into the little country by October 1, 1938. His threat worked. At a conference in Munich three days before his deadline, Hitler, Mussolini, and the leaders of the British and French governments met. The Republic of Czechoslovakia was carved up to suit the Nazi leader. But this policy of appeasement did not bring an end to Hitler's demands. A few months later, in the spring of 1939, Hitler took over what was left of Czechoslovakia and began to make demands upon Poland.

Meanwhile, the peace-desiring nations increased their armaments, in the hope that adequate defense would heighten their ability to bargain with the dictatorships by decreasing the possibilities of attack. The show-down came when Hitler tried his formula to seize territory in Poland, as we shall see in the next chapter.

Chapter 4 ~ World War II Engulfed the Nations

Germany's aggressive action toward Poland precipitated the outbreak of World War II. Matters came to a head in the summer of 1939. Trouble between Germany and Poland had been brewing. In the spring of that year Hitler had demanded that Poland turn over the city of Danzig and a strip of territory across the Polish Corridor to connect East Prussia to Germany. (See the map of Europe at the back of the book.) Poland refused these demands; Germans could cross the Polish Corridor; and Danzig had been a free, self-governing city since 1919. The Nazis then cancelled the nonaggression agreement made by Germany and Poland in 1934, and made preparations for war. The German propaganda ministry's accounts of Polish "atrocities" upon Germans were spread by means of the Nazi-controlled newspapers and radio.

WAR SHRINKAGE OF EUROPEAN NATIONS

This map shows the territorial losses by Germany and other nations in Europe as a result of the World War of 1914–1918. What nations suffered the severest reduction in size?

Poland, too, made ready for war. Britain and France, mindful of their agreements with Poland to aid her should she be attacked, warned Hitler that they would not stand idly by if he made war on Poland. They tried to find means to bring about a peaceful settlement between Germany and Poland. Then on August 29 Hitler demanded that a Polish representative with full power to act appear by midnight of August 30. This was impossible, of course, and Hitler had insisted upon it knowing it was im-

possible. Apparently he was looking for an excuse to declare that his peaceful intentions had been ignored.

By dawn of September 1, 1939, the troops Hitler had massed on the Polish border poured across the boundary line. Overhead the planes of the German air force roared to blast Polish airfields, railroads, and cities. Within forty-eight hours Great Britain and France declared war on Germany, but Poland collapsed under the blows of Hitler's mechanized ground forces before Britain and

Used by permission of Emil Herlin and " The New York Times "

EUROPE AT THE END OF 1939

Compare the extent of Germany shown in this map with the extent shown in the map on page 780. What nations were swallowed up to form the new Germany?

France were ready to act. As German forces swept into Poland from the west, Russian troops crossed her boundaries in the east. The Poles were unable to protect their nation from this dual invasion. Poland was once again partitioned as she had been divided three times before.

The first year of World War II ended triumphantly for the Axis. When Hitler's " Panzer," or mechanized, divisions raced across the plains of Poland under cover of the German Air Force, they overcame Polish resistance in less than

a month's time. Meanwhile, French troops had been stationed along the Maginot [mah'zhee'noh'] Line. This was a chain of fortresses on the border between France and Germany. It faced Hitler's troops in the pill boxes and tank traps, and other fortifications of the German Siegfried Line. British forces were landed in France and the armies of Belgium and Holland were held in readiness.

Meanwhile, the United States had announced its neutrality. Our neutrality

THE ARMISTICE CAR

The French delegates are shown arriving to sign an armistice with the Nazis in the old railway car in the Forest of Compiègne. Twenty-two years before, the Germans had been the ones to sue for an armistice. The historic railway car had been kept in the forest as a monument to Allied victory in World War I.

laws that had been passed earlier in the 1930's forbade American manufacturers to sell goods to warring nations. These neutrality laws, however, were revised so that supplies could be sent to England and France, provided the goods were paid for in advance and shipped in vessels not owned by Americans. The Selective Service Act was passed to build up an American army. Fifty old destroyers were turned over to the British in return for the right to use British territory for naval bases in the Western Hemisphere.

Russia warred on Finland and won certain possessions which she considered necessary for defense. Japan became a partner in the Axis. So the war went through the fall and winter of 1939–40. Then suddenly, the Nazi Blitzkrieg, or

lightning war, struck. German troops surged into Denmark and Norway, which had been neutral nations. By May of 1940 Hitler had a strong grip on these two nations. From them his air force could patrol the North Sea and his raiders could menace Allied vessels.

Later in the spring of 1940, the splendidly co-ordinated German military machine whirled across Holland and Belgium, two more nations that had remained neutrals until this sudden, merciless German attack. Nothing could stop it. Allied forces and civilians alike were mowed down by swarms of airplanes. Holland surrendered, but British, French, and Belgian forces retreated stubbornly in Belgium. French forces fell back from Luxembourg. Then, by order of its king, who thought resistance hopeless, the Belgian army laid down its arms. This exposed British and some French forces to renewed attack, and they retreated to Dunkirk. Here the British, backed up against the Channel, were saved from annihilation by one of the most heroic actions in history. Under relentless bombing by the Germans, ships and even small craft of the British fleet stood offshore, took on board thousands of trapped, harassed soldiers, and carried them across the Channel to England. The name of Dunkirk promised to bear something of the sense of deathless courage that the name of Thermopylae holds. But at Dunkirk rescue brightened destruction.

Then, on June 17, came the end of the first "Battle of France." The swift-moving mechanized divisions of the German army, paced by Hitler's efficient, ruthless airplanes, were too much for the dazed and battered French armies. The Germans had swung north of the Maginot Line and these huge fortifications, on which the French nation had pinned its faith, were proved useless. France's urgent pleas to America, during those short days of her conquest, for "clouds of airplanes" could not be met. The United States did not then have the planes to send. Mussolini seized this opportunity to declare war on France. He hoped to obtain a part of the French Mediterranean coast adjoining Italy, and to get Tunisia, a French possession in North Africa opposite Sicily, which may be seen on the map on page 752. Hitler and his staff dictated armistice terms to France in the old railway car where Marshal Foch had announced terms for the armistice in World War I.

Thus it was that by the summer of 1940 England faced the Axis alone. Doubtless Hitler expected the British people to surrender. But Prime Minister Churchill spoke for his nation, saying, "We shall fight on the beaches, we shall fight on the landing grounds, we shall fight in the fields and in the streets, we shall fight in the hills, we shall never surrender. . . ." Churchill promised victory but only after a long trial of "blood, sweat, and tears." The concerted attacks upon Britain began when German bombing planes battered London, Plymouth, Coventry, and other British cities. Britain's Royal Air Force, however, with its fighter planes of superior firing power, counter-attacked Hitler's aircraft. German losses were so great that the effort to knock England out of the war by bombings was abandoned. "Never in the field of human conflict," said the British Prime Minister, of the members of the victorious Royal Air Force, "was so much owed by so many to so few."

Apart from their defeat in the "Battle of Britain" the Germans everywhere else continued their successes. The fall of France gave them seaports on the Atlantic Ocean from which they sent out their U-boat packs to destroy shipping. They fortified the coasts to prevent the landing of opposing forces. Hundreds of thousands of the people of these conquered nations were put to work in their fields and factories for the Germans. Thousands more were sent as forced labor to Germany. Conquered countries were systematically looted of food by German officials who left the helpless civilians at the point of starvation. The British fleet, aided by other Allied vessels, blockaded coastal areas under German control, and little or no food reached the occupied countries.

During the spring of 1941 German troops conquered Yugoslavia and Greece. Next the great island of Crete fell. Then Hitler, despite his treaty of friendship with Stalin about which you read in

A SUMMARY OF THE ATLANTIC CHARTER

1. No territorial or other gains should result.
2. No territorial changes should be made without " the freely expressed wishes of the people concerned."
3. All peoples should have the right to choose the form of government under which they will live, and self-government should be restored to those deprived of it.
4. All nations should have " access on equal terms, to the trade and to the raw materials of the world. . . ."
5. Improved labor conditions, economic advancement, and social security should be provided.
6. The Nazi tyranny should be destroyed so that a peace may be established, permitting peoples and nations to live in safety, and freedom from want and fear.
7. Freedom of the seas should be provided for all nations.
8. Aggressor nations should be disarmed, and provisions made for the organization of a wider, more permanent system of general security. Armaments should be reduced.

Part Eighteen, treacherously hurled his forces into Russia. Romania and Finland joined with the Axis, whose war machine rolled relentlessly eastward across the plains of Russia. These smaller nations hoped to get a portion of Russian territory. Japan, too, was again on the move in her program to get control of the Far East. Her troops occupied French Indo-China. This gave her bases for her later conquests of Burma, Singapore, and the East Indies. (See the map of the world at the back of the book.)

The United States became the " arsenal of democracy." Long before the outbreak of World War II, it was evident that the great majority of the American people hoped to see an end put to the onward march of the aggressor nations. Therefore, as the war progressed, Americans wondered how they might help the nations opposing Germany, Italy, and Japan. Just before the fall of France, President Roosevelt said, ". . . we will pursue two obvious and simultaneous courses; we will extend to the opponents of force the material resources of this nation, and . . . we will harness and speed up those resources in order that we ourselves in the Americas may have equipment and training equal to the task of any emergency and every defense."

During, and shortly after, the first battle of France in 1940, Congress had voted money to purchase 50,000 airplanes, and had authorized construction of a two-ocean navy. Seven billion dollars was appropriated for military purposes. Moreover, with the passage of the Selective Service Act, the creation of an American army of over 7,000,000 was planned. Some of the nations of North and South America prepared themselves for the defense of the Western Hemisphere.

In what other ways, short of war, could the United States help? Congress answered by passing the Lend-Lease Act in the spring of 1941. This meant that the United States would furnish supplies of all kinds to England, Russia, China, and the other nations at war with the aggressor nations, and would not expect a cash settlement for these goods. Instead, these nations would repay the United States with still other goods and services. Lend-Lease, in short, enabled the United States to provide the Allies with the armaments and other supplies necessary to continue their war against the Axis nations. By mid-summer of 1944, Lend-Lease shipments had mounted to twenty-seven billion dollars' worth.

The Atlantic Charter announced a broad program for international security. In the summer of 1941, while Hitler's armies thrust deeper into Russia, Prime Minister Churchill and President Roosevelt and their military, naval, and diplomatic advisers met aboard a British warship in the Atlantic Ocean. A list of general principles, known as the Atlantic Charter, was drawn up. These principles, these leaders believed, would serve as a basis for making peace. In many respects the Atlantic Charter resembled Woodrow Wilson's Fourteen Points, summarized on page 765. Compare these two programs for peace.

The Atlantic Charter influenced the thinking of many people about the peace, and the problems of the postwar world. During World War II, moreover, the Atlantic Charter helped to bring the nations battling the dictator states more closely together. Within a few months after its terms were announced, came the Declaration of the United Nations. This agreement bound together twenty-six countries in a pledge not to make a separate peace with the aggressor states. The twenty-six nations also approved the Atlantic Charter. Other nations joined this group as the war continued.

Japan's "sneak attack" on Pearl Harbor brought the United States into World War II. On Sunday morning, December 7, 1941, Japanese planes swept down on Pearl Harbor, the great naval

Press Association, Inc.

FIREFIGHTING AT PEARL HARBOR

Set afire during the Japanese assault at Pearl Harbor, the battleship *West Virginia* was saved from destruction. United States sailors manned the fireboats by which the fire was brought under control.

base of the United States in Hawaii. Small submarines also took part in the raid. The Japanese hoped to destroy our Pacific fleet with this blow, and they very nearly succeeded. Five battleships were sunk or badly damaged, as were three destroyers. One hundred and fifty American airplanes were wrecked, most of them on the ground. Over 3000 officers and men of the Navy and Marine Corps were killed. Japanese losses were light.

The next day, in his war message to Congress, President Roosevelt said:

Yesterday, December 7, 1941 — a date which will live in infamy — the United States of America was suddenly and deliberately attacked by naval and air forces of the Empire of Japan. The United States was at peace with that Nation and . . . was still in conversation with its Government and its Emperor looking toward the maintenance of peace in the Pacific. Indeed, one hour after Japanese air squadrons had commenced bombing in Oahu [the island on which Pearl Harbor is situated], the Japanese Ambassador to the United States and his colleague delivered to the Secretary of State a formal reply to a recent American message. While this reply stated that it seemed useless to continue the existing diplomatic negotiations, it contained no threat or hint of war or armed attack. It will be recorded that the distance of Hawaii from Japan makes it obvious that the attack was deliberately planned days or even weeks ago. During the intervening time the Japanese government has deliberately sought to deceive the United States by false statements and expression . . . for continued peace. . . . I ask that the Congress declare that since the unprovoked and dastardly attack by Japan, on Sunday, December seventh, a state of war has existed between the United States and the Japanese Empire.

Three days later came our declarations of war on Germany and Italy, following the declarations of war by these nations on the United States right after the attack on Pearl Harbor.

When war broke out in Europe in September, 1939, Japan decided the time had come to reach farther, and to take what she wanted in the Far East. Japanese troops poured into French Indo-China after the fall of France in 1940. At this time the United States and Britain decided it was time to check Japan's expansion. All efforts at negotiation failed, however, when Japan refused to co-operate with the United States to insure peace in Asia.

It was while these fruitless talks between American and Japanese statesmen were going on in Washington that Japanese warships were steaming toward Pearl Harbor. At the moment that bombs were pouring down on Pearl Harbor, two representatives of the Japanese government were seated in the office of Cordell Hull, the American Secretary of State, in Washington, D.C. They had come bearing a written message stating that further negotiation between the two countries would be useless. This message was filled with falsehood and purposely twisted the account of the American attempts at peaceful settlement. Japan apparently had used these days of negotiation as a screen while she made ready for her attack on Pearl Harbor. In other words, the attack on Pearl Harbor and the events leading to it were typical of the acts which the aggressor nations had been using for some years to gain their ends.

Therefore, as the year 1941 drew to a close, World War II had engulfed both hemispheres. If you will look at the table on page 788 you will see how the nations of the world were lined up in January, 1942. It was clear that there were to be two major areas where the war would be fought, Europe and the Pacific. The main aim of the United Nations did not change either at this time or later. This

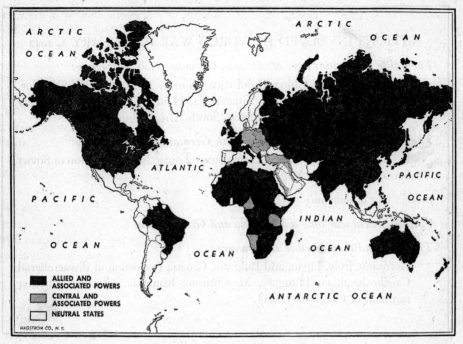

LINE-UP OF POWERS FOR WORLD WAR I

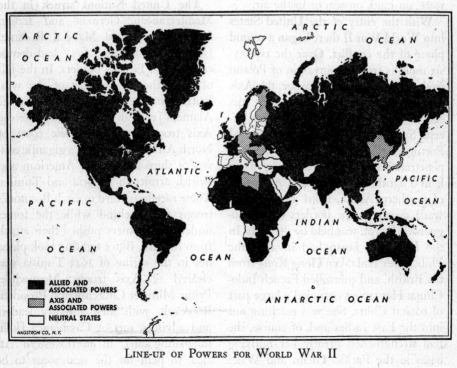

LINE-UP OF POWERS FOR WORLD WAR II

NATIONS INVOLVED IN WORLD WAR II, JANUARY 1, 1942

The following nations were at war with Germany, Italy, and Japan:

Australia, Canada, China, Costa Rica, Dominican Republic, El Salvador, Free France, Great Britain, Guatemala, Haiti, Netherlands, New Zealand, Nicaragua, Poland, Panama, South Africa, United States.

The following nations were at war with Germany and Italy alone:

Belgium, Czechoslovakia, Greece, Luxembourg, Norway, Union of Soviet Socialist Republics, Yugoslavia.

Bolivia was *at war only with Japan*

Finland was *at war only with Russia and Great Britain*

The Axis and their satellite states were:

Germany, Italy, Japan, and Bulgaria, Croatia (a portion of dismembered Czechoslovakia), Hungary, Manchukuo, Romania, Slovakia (another remnant of Czechoslovakia).

---

objective was to crush the aggressor nations completely wherever their forces were, on land, on sea, or in the air.

With the entry of the United States into World War II there began a second phase of the conflict. Over the twenty-six months from the invasion of Poland to the attack on Pearl Harbor, the Axis nations seemed to have been very successful. Western continental Europe, except Sweden, Switzerland, Spain, and Portugal, was in their hands. They had penetrated halfway into Russia. They held Yugoslavia and Greece. A portion of northern Africa, from Tunisia eastward nearly to the borders of British-guarded Egypt, was held by the Axis. In the Far East, Japan had invaded the Philippines, had taken Hong Kong from the British, and controlled French Indo-China. Her troops occupied a large part of coastal China. She was reaching out into the East Indies and, of course, she had strengthened greatly her outlying bases in the Pacific. Guam and Wake Island had been seized from the United States' forces.

The United Nations struck in the Mediterranean. German and Italian forces under Field Marshal Rommel [rahm'l], " the desert fox," had driven eastward to Egypt's borders. In the fall of 1942, the fourth year of the war, British and Australians attacked at El Alamein [el al uh mayn'] and drove the Axis troops back along the coast of North Africa. Meanwhile a gigantic convoy of ships had landed American and British armies in Algeria and Tunisia. These raced eastward to catch Rommel's troops from behind while the forces under Montgomery pushed their attack from the east. Bitter fighting took place, but in the spring of 1943 Tunisia was cleared of Axis troops. Meanwhile, Prime Minister Churchill and President Roosevelt, with their military leaders and advisers, met at Casablanca [kah-sah blahng'kah], in northwestern Africa, to plan for the next steps to be taken. A picture of the two leaders at the time of the Casablanca conference is shown below.

The destruction of German and Italian forces in northern Africa cleared the way for an assault on Italy. In the summer of 1943 Sicily was conquered by British and American armies. Mussolini fled and Italy surrendered. Next, the United Nations' armies moved into Italy itself. German forces retreated slowly northward in Italy. The American Fifth Army took Naples. British troops, aided by Polish soldiers, drove up the east side of the Italian peninsula. Six months later, after severe fighting at Salerno [sah lehr′noh], Anzio [ahn′zyoh], and

in the mountainous country to the south in and around Cassino, Rome was occupied by United Nations troops. The drive continued as the Germans fell back into northern Italy.

Conquest of Italy helped to clear the Mediterranean of danger to Allied shipping. Thereafter, United Nations supply lines to the Far East were much safer from attack by sea and air raiders. In midsummer of 1944 American and Free French forces drove into southern France. They joined forces with British, Canadian, American and other United Nations forces who, as you will learn later, had landed in northern France on " D-day," June 6 of that year.

Press Association, Inc.

ROOSEVELT AND CHURCHILL

At Casablanca Roosevelt and Churchill met in one of their historic conferences. After this meeting, notice was served upon the enemy that the United Nations would accept only unconditional surrender as the basis for ending the war.

CONVOY OF WORLD WAR II

The rows of gray merchant ships moved steadily toward their ports. Their work was to supply the forces of the United Nations. Convoys such as this one carried the trucks and the other sorely needed material for the Russian Armies. A United States Navy blimp is watching for submarines that might attack this convoy.

Moreover, Greece and Yugoslavia were within reach. Furthermore, Allied bombing planes, based in Italy and North Africa, could strike telling blows into southern Germany and Austria.

The mighty Red Army struck back. You will remember that Germany and Russia had signed an agreement not to attack one another. But in June, 1941, Hitler treacherously sent his armies into Russia. Apparently he believed he could quickly crush the Russians. The German armies pushed rapidly into Russia. It was not until the winter of 1941-42 that Russian troops began a counter-offensive. This checked Hitler's forces temporarily but in the spring of 1942 they resumed their drive across Russia. They reached Stalingrad on the great bend of the Volga River. (See the map of Europe at the back of the book.) Meanwhile, Lend-Lease supplies had been flowing into Russia by way of Murmansk in the north and through Iran to the south.

The great supply of Lend-Lease weapons, trucks, clothing, food, and countless other items was carried from the United States to other United Nations in merchant vessels. Many of these were built in the United States expressly for this purpose, and were called Liberty Ships. The vessels sailed in convoys, protected by escort ships. Some convoys were accompanied by small aircraft carriers. Part of a convoy is shown above.

Without these vital supplies from the United States other United Nations would have fought at great disadvantage. In an effort to check the flow of goods from the United States, German submarines hunted in packs for the convoys as they steamed slowly across the Atlantic Ocean. For a time it seemed that the U-boats might win the Battle of the Atlantic. This grave threat to United

Nations victory, however, was overcome. The convoy system, which you will recall was successful in World War I, was greatly improved. And, as you will learn later, improved electrical devices efficiently detected the presence of enemy submarine, surface, and air raiders.

With the coming of winter, Russian troops opened a second attempt to drive the Germans back. Russian forces fought heroically at Stalingrad. Early in 1943 Hitler's troops retreated from Stalingrad while other German forces were being defeated in North Africa. This was the turning point in the Battle of Russia. The Russian drive continued and Axis troops gave ground.

Late in 1943 at Tehran [teh hrahn′], in Iran, Roosevelt, Churchill, and Joseph Stalin met to make plans for an attack upon Hitler in the west, while the Russians continued their blows from the east. By January, 1944, the Russian armies had forced the Germans back into Poland and by early spring had reached Romania. By the summer of 1944 Romania suddenly left the Axis side and joined the Allies, and Bulgaria dropped out of the war. Meanwhile the Russian troops had reached the borders of East Prussia and were driving Germany's forces back into central Poland. Hitler's scheme to crush Stalin's armies and seize the rich wheat fields and oil wells in southern Russia had failed. His ally, Italy, had surrendered, and German troops were in retreat through northern Italy.

The United Nations opened a Western Front. Preparations for a Western Front in France began in 1942 with the first of the large-scale air raids on German industrial centers. The first detachments of American troops arrived in England during that year. By January of 1943, American bombers appeared in ever-increasing numbers. Together with the bombing planes of the Royal Air Force, they kept up a continuous battering of Germany's aircraft and munitions centers. Railroads and bridges were blasted. These heavy raids continued for months. One German city after another was subjected to searing blows that slowed down Germany's industrial production.

Then, on Christmas Eve, 1943, came the announcement of General Eisenhower's appointment as supreme commander of the United Nations in Western Europe. Eisenhower and his staff went to London. Did this mean the opening of the long awaited attack by ground troops in Western Europe? If so, where would these forces land?

Through the anxious spring months of 1944 the aerial blows at Germany increased. Efforts of Hitler's air force to stop them became weaker. It was obvious that now the tables were turned. The United Nations ruled the skies over Europe.

In France itself there was a secret organization, later called the French Forces of the Interior. The *Maquis* [mah′kee′], as they were named, had been organized by General Charles de Gaulle [duh gohl] and his aides. General de Gaulle had his headquarters in London. He was the leader of the French people who had not submitted to German rule after the fall of France early in the war. The Maquis destroyed railroad lines and bridges behind the German lines. They provided the Allies with information about German troop movements.

Then suddenly, on June 6, 1944, immediately after Allied troops had taken Rome, came "D-day." American, British, Canadian, and some Free French soldiers landed in northern France. American troops broke through the Ger-

LOADING FOR THE INVASION

At an English port these landing craft are being loaded in preparation for D-day, June 6, 1944. What signs do you see of protection for this vast loading operation?

man defenses at St. Lô while the British and Canadian armies pinned down German forces farther to the north and east. The Germans were driven back and northwestern France became a great base for further blows at Hitler. By the early fall United Nations troops reached the borders of Germany and were attacking the Siegfried Line.

The United States took the lead in the war in the Pacific. When the Japanese raiders flew away from the smoking shambles of Pearl Harbor on December 7, 1941, they believed that they had destroyed the United States fleet. For a few weeks Japan's conquests in Malaya and the East Indies continued. Then Japan's navy received its first jolts. Off Java, United Nations warships clashed suc-

cessfully with Japan early in 1942, only about three months after the American fleet had been "destroyed." In the late spring in the Coral Sea, and again near Midway Island, Japan's warships were defeated. These victories helped clear the sea approaches to Australia and opened the way toward the southernmost islands then in Japanese hands.

Japan had taken over the Philippines despite the heroic defense made by the small United States and Filipino forces on the Bataan [ba tan'] peninsula and the islands of Corregidor [ko reg'i-dawr]. These outnumbered troops finally surrendered in the spring of 1942.

Land forces began to seize islands as steppingstones to Tokyo. In the summer of 1942 American marines landed on

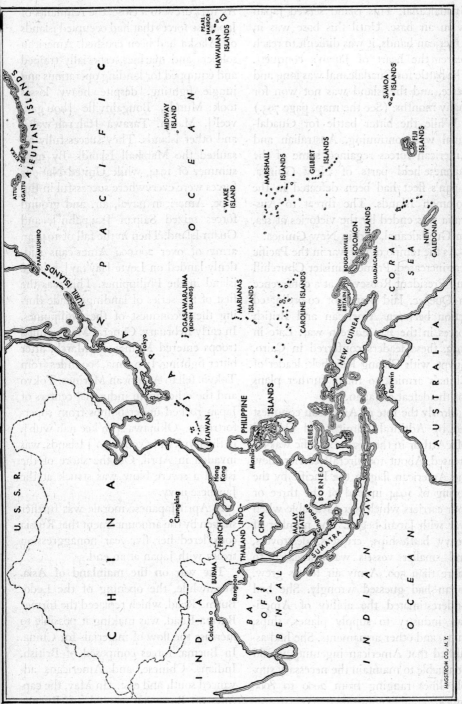

WORLD WAR II IN THE FAR EAST

Guadalcanal. This island served Japan as an air base. Until this base was in American hands, it was difficult to reach nearer the heart of Japan's conquest. The battle for Guadalcanal was long and fierce, and the island was not won for many months. (See the map, page 793.)

While the bitter battle for Guadalcanal was continuing, Australian and American forces regained some of the Japanese-held parts of New Guinea. Japan's fleet had been defeated in the Solomon Islands. The threat to Australia was ended by the victories at sea, on Guadalcanal, and in New Guinea.

As the tempo of the war in the Pacific was increased, Prime Minister Churchill and President Roosevelt, at a conference in Quebec, laid plans for co-ordinated action between American and British forces in the Far Eastern war. Late in 1943, these leaders conferred in Cairo, Egypt, with Chiang Kai-shek, leader of China's armies, to make further plans for the defeat of Japan.

Slowly the rate of American conquest led by Admiral Nimitz and General MacArthur in the distant Pacific was increased. About 100 aircraft carriers flew the American flag in the Pacific by the spring of 1944 instead of the three or four carriers which were available when war with Japan began. The number of heavy battleships, cruisers, destroyers, and smaller vessels was increased to more than 500. Army air forces grew. Japan had guessed wrongly. She had underestimated the ability of American industry to supply planes, ships, guns, and other armaments. She had assumed that American ingenuity would be unable to maintain the necessary supply lines ranging from 2000 to 8000 miles.

During 1943 and 1944 one Pacific island after another was taken from Japan.

As 1943 drew to a close, the remnants of Japanese forces that had occupied islands off Alaska had been crushed. American soldiers and marines, especially trained and equipped for landing operations and jungle fighting, despite heavy losses took Munda, Bougainville [bou'gan' veel'], Makin, Tarawa [tah rah'wah], and other islands. They successfully assaulted the Marshall Islands. By midsummer of 1944, while United Nations forces were everywhere successful in Europe, American naval, air, and ground forces seized Saipan [sai pahn'], and Guam Island. Then in the fall of 1944 an army of over 200,000 Americans suddenly landed on Leyte [lay'tay], a large island in the Philippines. This was the first of the series of landings made during the reconquest of the Philippines. In early February, General MacArthur's troops entered Manila. In March, after bitter fighting, Iwo Jima, 800 miles from Tokyo, fell to American Marines. Tokyo and the other main industrial centers of Japan rocked under bombs from superfortresses. Okinawa [oh'kee nah'wuh], in the Ryukyu [r'yoo'kyoo'] Islands, was invaded in April. Off the shore of the island a severe blow was struck at the Japanese navy.

In April Japanese morale was further shaken by the announcement that Russia considered her five-year nonaggression treaty with Japan at an end.

The war on the mainland of Asia. Meanwhile, the opening of the Ledo-Burma Road, which replaced the former Burma Road, was making it possible to increase the flow of materials for China. In Burma, forces composed of British, Indians, Chinese, and Americans advanced south and east. In May, the capture of Rangoon, capital of Burma, marked the fast approaching end of any Japanese survival in Burma.

WATER TEST

Four of the United States Army's General Lee M4 A 1 tanks are being tested in water. They are being driven across a river at the testing grounds of a tank factory in the Pacific Northwest. The motors of the tanks are well covered, and the wiring is waterproofed.

The Western Front. In November, General Eisenhower set in motion the British, American, and French armies under his command. The offensive started well. Just before Christmas, however, the Germans drove a powerful thrust into Allied lines between the Ruhr and the Saar valleys, forcing them back in a dangerous bulge. At the cost of heavy fighting and severe losses, the Allied armies hammered at the bulge. Not until almost two months later had they regained the ground lost to the Germans in December.

The Eastern Front. Meanwhile in Eastern Europe the Russian armies continued their campaign in the Balkans, and in January captured Budapest. In the same month they broke into a series of tremendous drives through East Prussia; through Poland into Germany; and

on from Budapest toward Vienna. By the time the Western Allied armies were ready for the final effort of the war, the Russian armies were at the Oder River, at one place only about 30 miles from Berlin.

Teamwork. In February, 1945, while Russian armies threatened Berlin from the East, and the armies of the Western Allies were preparing to move from the West, the leaders of three great Allies — Churchill, Stalin, and Roosevelt — with their foreign ministers, met in the Russian city of Yalta on the Black Sea. At the conference the Big Three planned for the final stages of the war against Germany. They considered also problems arising in liberated countries, in particular the conflicting claims of the Polish Government in Exile and the Lublin Government. And — of major importance — the three leaders planned for a conference of representatives of the United Nations to prepare the charter of a world security organization. The conference was scheduled to be held at San Francisco, on April 25, 1945.

In Mexico City in February, 1945, a movement toward postwar co-operation among the nations of the Western Hemisphere brought about the "Conference of American Republics on Problems of War and Peace." At the conference the representatives of the republics discussed such questions as their relations to Argentina — which alone of the American nations had not declared war on the Axis. Other problems involved economic and political relations in the Western Hemisphere after the war. The harmonious end of the conference, expressed in the Act of Chapultepec [chahpool'tay pek'], promised well for the participation of American nations in the San Francisco Conference. And finally, in April, Argentina joined the rest of the Western Hemisphere in declaring war against the Axis.

The conference at Yalta was the last meeting of the three great leaders of the United Nations. On April 12, 1945, Franklin Delano Roosevelt died at Warm Springs, Georgia. The loss of his leadership in war and toward peace was mourned throughout the United Nations. In London Parliament adjourned; over the Kremlin the Soviet flag was bordered with black.

Harry S. Truman, who succeeded Roosevelt as president, reassured his nation and its allies as to his intention to follow Roosevelt's policies.

The final thrust. All that was needed to end the war in Europe, Churchill said in the winter of 1945, was one "strong heave" on the part of the Allies. That strong thrust began on the Western Front at the end of February. This tremendous movement of armored divisions, infantry, airborne troops, and artillery, supported by air armadas, carried nine armies — Canadian, British, American, and French — across the Rhine, through the Netherlands to the North Sea, and through the Ruhr and Saar valleys toward Berlin. Trapping German armies and capturing great cities — Cologne, Bremen, Frankfurt, Hanover — Allied armies penetrated deep into Germany.

The Russians meanwhile were approaching Berlin from the east; in the south they had captured Vienna and were moving toward the Alpine fortress where the Nazis were expected to attempt a desperate final defense.

In Italy, where the Germans had been crowded north into the mountains, the Allied armies stepped up their offensive, capturing Bologna and moving into the Po Valley.

Unconditional surrender. During March and April the Western and Eastern Fronts had been moving rapidly toward each other. But swift as their advance had been, it was suddenly accelerated at the end of April. In the first eight days of May, the machinery of the German war effort broke down. In these eight days Mussolini was shot by Italian Partisans in Northern Italy; Berlin fell to the Russians; the death of Hitler was announced; German armies in Italy, Austria, the Netherlands, Denmark, and Northern Germany surrendered; and finally, Hitler's successor, Admiral Doenitz, delivered the remaining fragments of German power to the Western and Eastern Allies in unconditional surrender. On May 8, 1945, in the sixty-eighth month of the war, V–E Day — the day of victory in Europe — was a reality.

THE U.S.S. LEXINGTON

The intensive use of aircraft based on carriers was an important development of World War II. The carrier shown here is the *U.S.S. Lexington*. After valiant service, the *Lexington* was sunk, in the Battle of the Coral Sea.

Modern science brought many changes in the technique of war. You will recall that World War I brought widespread use of the machine gun and the submarine, that tanks were invented, and airplanes came into use. Cannon became far more destructive, and poison gas was introduced. World War II, however, not only made wider use of such weapons, but improved their efficiency. New devices and techniques were used.

World War II was featured by the rapid movement of ground troops traveling in various kinds of armored vehicles. These mechanized forces were supported by convoys of specially designed motor trucks, carrying equipment and supplies. Columns of these fast-moving units sometimes traveled 30 or more miles in a day.

The fire power of the individual soldier was greatly increased. "Tommy-guns" were carried by many. Americans were equipped with the rapid-firing Garand, a weapon that outmoded the rifle of World War I.

Battles between opposing squadrons of tanks became common. These tanks varied in size and fire power. There were small tanks that could be carried in planes or gliders. Others weighed as much as 60 tons; they could travel at 25 miles an hour and were equipped with the powerful "75 mm" guns and, in some cases, with even larger cannon. Tank destroyers were developed, too. These were heavily armored vehicles carrying heavier cannon. Some American tank destroyers could travel at a speed of 55 miles an hour.

The cannon of both tanks and destroyers were equipped with stabilizers and other electrically operated controls. These enabled a high degree of accuracy of aim even if the vehicle were traveling over rough ground at high speed. Rocket guns came into use, too. These became very effective against tanks. Planes were equipped with rocket-firing devices. Rockets were also fired by ground troops. The famed American "bazooka," readily handled by two men, came into wide use.

Even more spectacular than tanks were the air fleets. Planes were used for many purposes. Low-flying ships supported ground troops, flying immediately ahead of the advancing troops, to bomb and machine-gun opposing forces. Control of the air became essential. Without it, ground troops became almost helpless targets. Huge fleets of armed bombers, guarded by long-range fighter planes, raided enemy airfields, shipyards, munitions dumps, and industrial centers. Raids by a thousand or more planes were frequent, beginning in 1942. Such cities as Hamburg, Bremen, and Berlin received poundings far greater than those given to London by the German air force earlier in the war. Antiaircraft guns and ammunition were greatly improved. Electronic devices automatically plotted the aiming and the firing of the guns.

By means of an intricate electrical device that sends out radio waves, it became possible to figure exactly the position of invisible aircraft and ships, and to determine their speed and direction. Use of this refinement of radio, called radar [ray'dahr], was well illustrated when shells apparently from nowhere fell on a Japanese warship. This vessel was steaming on the opposite side of an island from an American warship. The radar device on the American ship indicated the exact position, direction, and speed of the Japanese vessel. The American gun crews simply loaded and fired at the proper point, beyond the forest and hills of the island. The shells destroyed the Japanese ship. Radar likewise played an important part in helping to detect the presence of Hitler's "wolf-packs" of submarines. This, together with greatly improved depth-bombs, ship-based airplanes, land-based blimps, and sturdy escort vessels, protected the convoys crossing the seas.

As the war went on, the range and speed of fighter and bombing planes increased. Bomb capacity, to say nothing of the size and destructive force of the bomb itself, more than doubled. The bombsights gave astonishing accuracy. The American air forces, in particular, developed precision bombing.

Jet-propulsion airplanes were developed, too. Instead of being pulled through the air by propellers, these "jet" planes were pushed by a column of air forced out of the tail by means of a compression engine. Then there were the "robot-planes," or "robombs," sent against London in 1944 by the Nazis. These were something like rockets. They were launched from apparatus on the French coast. The robot planes were actually flying bombs. Although they were very inaccurate, they did much damage and took many lives in and near London in 1944. The United States also developed robot bombs for use on the Pacific front.

Airplanes in World War II were also used to transport large bodies of carefully trained "paratroops." These landed behind enemy lines. They seized key airports and communications centers, and added immeasurably to the striking power of ground troops. By mid-1944, a fully equipped army of United Nations paratroops played its part in the war in Western Europe.

To put troops ashore in France or in

the Pacific areas required special equipment and training. Therefore, types of landing craft hitherto undreamed of were built. These were able to approach close to shore. Watertight, hinged doorways were dropped to provide ramps or bridges to the shore for troops and mechanized equipment.

Let us now consider briefly some of the advances in medical and other sciences that were intended to preserve, not to destroy. In World War II, the proportion of wounded men who recovered was amazingly high, as compared to earlier wars. There were many reasons for this record. Sulfa drugs and penicillin [pen′i sil′n] checked infection. The speed, wherein transport planes played a part, with which the wounded were transported made early treatment possible. Surgeons often operated in flight.

The wide use of whole blood and blood plasma for transfusions saved the lives of thousands of wounded men. Plasma, the dried remainder after the red and white corpuscles have been removed, "performed miracles," according to an outstanding authority. "Ninety-seven per cent of the men who received it on the battlefields are kept alive until they reach some hospital behind the lines."

Other drugs also were developed or improved to meet the needs of war. Plastic surgery, which had been improved during World War I, was greatly advanced. It was particularly necessary in treating those suffering from burns and saved many from permanent, disfiguring scars.

Civilian life was greatly affected by World War II. In the occupied countries of Europe, particularly in Poland and in Greece, millions of people suffered terribly from starvation and disease, the partners of war. In England,

German air raids and robot bombs destroyed thousands of homes. Many families lost all of their possessions. Thousands of people were killed or wounded by bomb fragments, by the terrific air blast of the exploding bomb, or by fragments of flying debris. Others were killed or injured by fires set by incendiary bombs. Moreover, the "blackouts" contributed to accidents.

As was described, in the occupied countries many able-bodied men, women, and sometimes children, were obliged to leave their homes and work in Germany producing supplies for Hitler's war machine. Such slave-like workers totaled several million people. This forced labor scattered families. Many parents were separated from their children and never saw them again.

Governments in many of the nations at war set up what amounted to dictatorships if they were not already ruled by dictators. In many countries, men and women were drafted to work in the fields or factories just as men were drafted to fight. Rigid restrictions were placed upon the amounts of food, fuel, clothing, shelter, and many other items that a person might want. Rationing became common on such things even in the United States, where the effects of the war were felt far less than in England and in Europe. Taxes soared. "Ceilings" were placed on almost all kinds of civilian goods in an effort to keep living costs down. These costs, however, tended to rise in the United States. There were many volunteer civilian organizations. Older men and younger women organized civilian defense units. They served as auxiliary firemen, air-raid wardens, Red Cross workers, hospital attendants, and in many other necessary jobs for which they got no pay. In short, civilians played their part in World War II.

Chapter 5 ~ The Problem of Permanent Peace

Whither civilization? Much has been said earlier in these pages about the past. The great question before us now is, " Whither civilization? " In other words, after the aggressor nations have been checked, will ways and means be found so that ". . . all men in all the lands may live out their lives in freedom from fear and want. . . ."? You will remember that the world asked this same question as the peacemakers gathered in Paris at the close of World War I. You will remember how badly they failed in making a peace that was to last. The Allies " won the war but lost the peace." Between 1919 and 1939, as you have learned, England, France, and the United States adopted comparatively feeble and conflicting policies toward Italy, Germany, and Japan. England, France, and the United States could not seem to present a firm, united front when the aggressor nations first adopted their program of force. What can be done to prevent the United Nations from losing the peace at the close of World War II? What can be done on the one hand to check the forces of selfish nationalism and imperialism, and to promote international good will and co-operation?

Misunderstanding and fear create rivalries between peoples. When war destroys the peaceful relations between two nations, their people often believe each other to be cruel and inhuman. Unfortunately some nations, or at least some of the people in them, have demonstrated great cruelty and barbarity. Probably the people of one country rarely understand or appreciate its neighbors. They are too ready to believe the worst. Means must be found to overcome the notion that some nations and some peoples are superior and therefore should rule all others. World friendship, however, cannot be brought about unless the conditions that cause insecurity and fear among nations are removed. This is more than a matter of providing economic security for all people. World friendship also requires that all people be educated to understand the problems of one another. Steps toward such an educational program had already been taken by a group of United Nations educators in 1943.

United Nations statesmen outlined a program for international security. If you will turn to the table containing a list of eight points of the Atlantic Charter, on page 784, you will find there a broad program for international security. Thirty-three nations have given the Atlantic Charter their approval as their peace aims. The United Nations, moreover, have taken further steps designed to help solve many of the world's postwar problems. In 1943, for example, the United Nations Relief and Rehabilitation Administration was set up with the approval of forty-four nations. This organization was to find means to provide food, clothing, and new homes for the suffering peoples of war-torn areas. In 1944, a conference of bankers and other financial authorities was held to plan for the making of loans between nations, and for adjusting the flow of gold in international trade. The United States and Britain drew up an agreement to assure a fair distribution of petroleum resources after the war. The agreement stated that

Ewing Galloway

THE CONGRESS OF THE UNITED STATES

The President is delivering a message at a joint session of Congress. All the lawmakers whom you see here have been elected by the citizens of the United States. Although Congress represents sharply different beliefs and points of view, it functions within this nation. Might it be used as a model for an international representative body?

other nations could participate in this plan and obtain a fair share of oil.

Late in October, 1943, England, the United States, and Russia, the "big three" of the United Nations, took steps to put teeth into the last point of the Atlantic Charter. These three powers agreed to co-operate for the " maintenance of peace and security after the war." What kind of organization they would create for this purpose remained to be seen. One thing, at least, was apparent. The aggressor nations would be disarmed and the victors would see to it that powerful forces would be kept ready to preserve world peace. Maintenance of peace by armed might alone, however, would

not be the answer to the problems confronting the world after World War II was ended. Ways to assure security for all nations, victor and vanquished alike, must be found. These problems were discussed by representatives of the United States, Great Britain, Russia, and China at the Dumbarton Oaks conferences in Washington, D. C., in the summer of 1944. The representatives of these countries, however, had no power to take official action for their governments. Instead, the representatives reported the recommendations to their governments for such action as the governments wished to take. At San Francisco on April 25, 1945, representatives of 46 of the 47 United Nations met to carry further the proposals made at Dumbarton Oaks and to do the actual work of forming a world security organization. That the United States must take a lead in the settlement of these vast and complicated problems was clear. As Sumner Welles, well-known American statesman, wrote in the summer of 1944, " The people of the United States are once more afforded the chance to offer their co-operation and their leadership to other nations. . . . The decision they make now will determine their destiny."

A man who has endured the hardships of the battlefield, has seen his comrades maimed and killed, and has experienced the miseries that result from war can fully understand the folly of war. The same thing should be true of a nation. It has been said that modern civilization is a race between education and catastrophe. This race is a challenge to the youth of every land. A world peace will be won only when men have learned to understand and respect the rights of others and to co-operate with others in achieving the greatest good for mankind. Meanwhile, peacefully inclined nations must realize their mutual need for organizing to suppress those that are unwilling to respect the rights of others.

The time has come when we must have a new patriotism, an international as well as a national patriotism. We must look toward a true peace. It is to the interest of all nations to advance civilization. As one philosopher has said:

Inventions and discoveries bring benefit to all. The progress of science is a matter of equal concern to the whole civilized world. Whether a man of science is an Englishman, a Frenchman, or a German is a matter of no real importance. His discoveries are open to all, and nothing but intelligence is required in order to profit by them. The whole world of art and literature and learning is international; what is done in one country is not done for that country, but for mankind.

The international spirit will be something added to love of country, not something taken away. True patriotism does not prevent a man from loving his family. The international spirit ought not prevent a man from loving his own country. But perhaps it will change his attitude. He will no longer desire for his own country the things which can be acquired only at the expense of others. He will wish for other things which will be an advantage to all the world.

If civilization is to advance, the world must rid itself of war. Peace and good will must become the new patriotism of mankind. People in all nations must strive for understanding. World friendship is the hope of mankind!

In a few years' time you and your generation will be responsible for the conduct of world affairs. You will inherit our world with all its institutions, its greatness, and its problems. You will inherit with it such international machinery for preserving the peace as has been devised. By keeping informed about current affairs, by joining with others in striving persistently to solve the problems of peace, you may live to see a new era in history. By learning from the achievements and mistakes of those who have preceded you, you may build a new world in which international co-operation replaces destruction. You will face obstacles — tradition, ignorance, greed, intolerance, and narrow sectionalism.

Complete victory over these barriers to international understanding may not be achieved next year, possibly not even in the next century. But you must not give up the struggle for peace, for the world depends upon its achievement. It is up to you to make the kind of world in which you, and those who follow you, can live in freedom.

WORDS OF THE WISE ON WAR AND PEACE

Peace hath her victories no less renowned than war.
— *John Milton, 17th Century English poet*

The vastness of the expenditure on armament is a satire on modern civilization, and if continued it must lead Europe into bankruptcy.
— *Sir Edward Grey, English statesman*

As long as mankind shall continue to bestow more liberal applause on their destroyers than on their benefactors, the thirst of military glory will ever be the vice of exalted characters.
— *Edward Gibbon, 18th Century English historian*

The real conquerors of the world are not generals, but thinkers.
— *Sir John Lubbock, English scientist, archeologist, and author*

I hold that mankind is approaching an era in which peace treaties will not only be recorded on paper, but also become inscribed in the hearts of men.
— *Albert Einstein, American scientist*

Whether we wish it or no, the hour has come when we must be citizens of the world or see civilization perish.
— *Anatole France, French author and critic*

Coöperation is not a sentiment — it is an economic necessity.
— *Charles P. Steinmetz, American scientist*

We are participants whether we would or not in the life of the world. The interests of all nations are ours also. We are partners with the rest. What affects mankind is inevitably our affair as well as the affair of the nations of the rest of the world.
— *Woodrow Wilson, twenty-eighth President of the United States*

Give man time and he will yet learn to handle the new relationships for fraternity and not for war.
— *Harry Emerson Fosdick, American clergyman*

Not only must people have access to what other peoples produce, but their own products must in turn have some chance of reaching men all over the world.
— *Wendell L. Willkie, American businessman*

The only thing we have to fear is fear itself.
— *Franklin D. Roosevelt, thirty-first President of the United States*

By collaborating with the rest of the world to put productive resources fully to work, we shall raise our own standard of living and help to raise the standard of living of others.
— *Henry A. Wallace, former Vice-President of the United States*

Timetable of World War I

(This Timetable and the one for World War II are not intended to be learned.)

1914	June 23.	Archduke Ferdinand assassinated at Sarajevo, Serbia
	July 28.	Austria-Hungary declared war on Serbia
	August 1.	Germany declared war on Russia
	August 3.	Germany declared war on France; German troops entered Belgium
	August 4.	Britain declared war on Germany
	August 23.	Japan declared war on Germany
	September 26.	Germans stopped at first battle of the Marne
1915	April 22.	Canadians checked German drive at Ypres
	May 7.	Lusitania sunk by submarine
	September 25.	Allies launched offensives on Western Front
1916	February 21.	German attack on Verdun began
	May 31.	Naval battle of Jutland won by British fleet
	July 1.	The battle of the Somme began
1917	April 6.	The United States declared war on Germany
	April 9.	Allies opened attacks on the Hindenburg Line
	December 15.	Russians accepted German armistice terms
1918	March 21.	Germans began large-scale offensive on Western Front
	July 18.	Allied offensive began with second battle of the Marne
	September 26.	French and American troops attacked in the Argonne Forest
	November 11.	Germany accepted the terms of the Allied Armistice

Timetable of World War II

1939	September 1.	German invasion of Poland began
	September 3.	Britain and France declared war on Germany
1940	April 9.	Germany invaded Denmark and Norway
	May 10.	Germany invaded Holland, Belgium, and France
	June 10.	Italy declared war on France and Britain
	June 17.	End of the Battle of France: France surrendered
1941	April 6.	German invasion of Yugoslavia and Greece
	June 22.	German invasion of Russia
	December 7.	Japanese attacked Pearl Harbor and Philippine Islands
	December 8.	United States declared war on Japan
	December 11.	Germany and Italy declared war on the United States
1942	January 2.	Declaration of the United Nations signed
	May 13.	Japanese forces took Corregidor
	June 7.	Japanese fleet defeated in the battle of Midway
	August 7.	Battle of Solomons began on Guadalcanal
	November 2.	Axis forces defeated at El Alamein
	November 8.	American and British forces landed in North Africa
1943	February 2.	German retreat from Stalingrad began
	May 13.	United Nations conquest of North Africa completed
	July 10.	United Nations invaded Sicily
	September 3.	Italy surrendered
1944	January 29.	United States forces invaded the Marshall Islands
	June 6.	D-Day: United Nations forces landed in northern France
	August 15.	United Nations forces landed in southern France
	August 25.	Paris freed of German forces
	September 2.	United Nations forces reached the German border
	September 15.	United States forces landed on the Marianas Islands
1945	February 5.	American forces entered Manila
	April 12.	Roosevelt died; Truman became President of United States
	April 25.	San Francisco Conference of United Nations began
	May 2.	Berlin fell to Russians
	May 8.	Nazis surrendered unconditionally

From World War I to World War II

Over the past eight hundred years many factors have promoted nationalism among the peoples of the world. The struggles of early people for security; religious beliefs; wars; the growth of the middle class; the search for foreign markets stimulated by the Industrial Revolution — these were some of the main nationalistic forces. The search for foreign markets led to imperialism, which caused tensions and mistrust among the great imperialistic powers.

In 1914 the tensions in Europe culminated in World War I. Austria's attempt to punish Serbia for the assassination of the Grand Duke and his wife was the immediate cause of the conflict in which Germany, Austria, Bulgaria, and Turkey fought against Britain, Belgium, France, Serbia, Japan, Russia, Italy, and the United States. This war dragged through four grim years of trench warfare and submarine warfare, of sea blockade by Britain's navy. The weight of the United States, thrown into the war after 1917, compensated for the withdrawal of Russia and the separate peace made with Germany by Russia's revolutionary government. In 1918, after a revolutionary movement in Germany, the war ended.

Hope for a lasting peace settlement was buoyed by President Wilson's fight for the League of Nations. The League was established; a period of prosperity seemed on the way. But there was little international co-operation. Difficulties in foreign trade often caused by high tariffs led to monetary troubles within the nations. Two hostile new theories of government grew in Europe — Fascism, or Nazism, and Communism. The economic depression of 1929 strengthened the side of the dictators in chaotic countries in Europe. International agreements lost their force. Hitler as ruler of Nazi Germany was able to break the terms of the Peace Treaty. Germany was rearmed. No nation or group of nations opposed Hitler's annexation of Austria, or his dismemberment of Czechoslovakia. In 1939 Hitler made new demands upon Poland. Poland, backed by France and England, fought rather than yield; but was crushed. Before World War II was a year old, the Nazis, reinforced by the Italians, had put out of the war all their opponents except Britain. Britain's air force alone held off the enemy. Lend-Lease aid from the United States began to reinforce Great Britain. The use of radar devices aided the British aerial and submarine warfare. In 1941 Russia and the United States were drawn into the war. The Pacific had become the second main area of war. Japan's early victories mounted.

The Nazis fought a devastating submarine war against supply lines in the Atlantic, the Mediterranean, and the northern seas, and at last overran the Balkans. But Russian counterattacks and sustained offensives; the United Nations victories in North Africa and Italy; the United States victories against Japan in the Pacific; and Allied bombing of Nazi industrial centers finally led to " D-day " and to the promise of victory for the United Nations in both hemispheres. The Atlantic Charter and policies reached at conferences at Tehran and at Dumbarton Oaks gave promise at least, that the United Nations might remain united, and, by their union, keep another peace from being fumbled.

SELF–TEST

Review the Story of the Modern World by completing the following statements:

I. As a result of the Industrial Revolution modern nations searched for foreign —— for their manufactures, and foreign —— as sources of raw materials. The two forces of nationalism and —— led to rivalries and to an increase in the manufacture of ——.

II. The immediate cause of World War I was the —— of the Austrian —— ——. The national ambition of the —— peoples in the Balkans was an underlying cause. The early years of this war were marked by fighting in the —— of the Western Front, and by the British —— at sea. Submarine warfare was one of the causes for the entrance of the —— into the war in 1917. In the same year, —— was forced out of the war. The next year —— signed an ——, which ended the war. The Treaty of —— brought new —— into existence in Europe. Some of them had been part of the —— Empire. The Treaty also provided for the establishment of a ——.

III. In the years following World War I many nations established trade regulations, or ——, to protect their own ——. In addition to trade barriers between nations, sharp differences in forms of government emerged. Government took the form of —— in Italy, of —— in Germany, and of —— in Russia. Aggressor nations began a series of conquests. Italy conquered ——; Japan began a new invasion of ——; Hitler annexed —— and gained control of ——. The final aggression which started World War II was Hitler's invasion of ——.

IV. By the summer of 1940, Hitler had beaten down all his opponents except —— ——. The war spread into the Pacific when the —— attacked the —— —— at —— ——. Meanwhile, the Battle of —— was being waged in eastern Europe. And at sea the Battle of the —— was fought against the German ——. After the United Nations had cleared the enemy from North Africa, they invaded Sicily and ——. Finally, on ——, the Allied invasion of France began. In the Pacific the United States had captured strategic islands from Japan; in the fall of 1944 she was ready to begin a campaign to retake the —— Islands. Leaders of the United Nations had held important conferences at ——, ——, and ——. And at —— ——, near Washington, D. C., representatives of the —— ——, —— ——, ——, and —— discussed the problem of winning a lasting peace.

INTERESTING THINGS TO DO

Projects for the Chart Maker and Artist

1. Draw a time line showing the main events in the growth of the spirit of intense nationalism in the 19th and 20th Centuries. Use dates, and names of men and events.

2. Construct a tree chart showing that the roots of either World War I or World War II extend back many years. Label the fruits of the tree with some of the many miseries and losses brought to the world by war.

3. Draw an original cartoon that dramatizes the cost of war.

Topics for Talks

1. "Empire builders." Prepare a talk about some of the well-known men who have helped to build empires, for example, Cecil Rhodes, Disraeli, Bismarck. For "Rhodes," consult "Rhodesia, Hobby and Hope of Cecil Rhodes," *National Geographic Magazine,* September, 1944. See *Disraeli,* by Andre Maurois; or "Bismarck" in *Men of Power,* by Albert Carr.

2. "The awkward peace." The Peace of Versailles has frequently been blamed for much of the tension and controversy that troubled the world in the years following World War I. Prepare a talk about the most disturbing tensions and inequalities left unsolved by the Versailles peace. See *Windows on the World,* by Kenneth Gould; *The Peace That Failed* (Headline Books), by the Foreign Policy Association.

3. "The world of tomorrow." Prepare a talk about the effect of wartime inventions and improvements on life in the postwar period. Consult *Miracles Ahead,* by N. V. Carlisle and F. B. Latham. See also Public Affairs Pamphlets, p. 78, "The Airplane and Tomorrow's World," Public Affairs Committee, Inc., 30 Rockefeller Plaza, New York 20, New York, 10 cents.

4. "Animals go to war." Prepare a report on the use of animals in modern war. See *Animal Reveille,* by Richard Dempewolff.

5. "The Atlantic Charter." Prepare a talk about the Atlantic Charter. Is it a workable and just foundation for peace? Would you add any other provisions to the charter? What changes would the provisions of the Charter bring about in the totalitarian states? Compare the Atlantic Charter and the Fourteen Points as workable platforms for world peace.

6. "The minority problem." Plan a discussion of the minority problem which has given rise to so many disputes in central and eastern Europe. Did the Peace of Versailles help to lay the foundation for some of these disputes? To what extent was the minority problem a cause of World War II? How do you think this problem can be most justly handled? See *Human Dynamite* (Headline Books), published by the Foreign Policy Association.

7. "An exciting book about life in wartime." Read and review for the class one of the books of fiction or personal experience listed on page 809.

Questions for Round-Table Discussion

1. What ten inventions or advances in science, government, or the fine arts have been the most influential for the good of mankind?

2. What five forces or inventions have been most influential in preventing mankind from achieving a world of security and equal opportunity?

3. Are the people of all countries fundamentally the same, and do they all strive toward the same goal?

4. What were the chief drawbacks to effective action by the League of Nations?

5. Does the Atlantic Charter provide a more workable basis for world peace than did Wilson's Fourteen Points?

6. Is free trade the best preventive against war?

7. Should all munitions and armaments manufacturers be controlled by a world organization for the prevention of war?

Candidates for Your Album of Famous People

Winston Churchill, Premier Clemenceau, General de Gaulle, General Eisenhower, David Lloyd George, General MacArthur, General Pershing, Admiral Nimitz, Field Marshal Rommel, President Roosevelt, Joseph Stalin, President Wilson.

Assignments for the Roving Reporter

1. The reporter writes an article for a popular magazine about the Big Four at the Versailles Peace Conference. See *Modern Short Biographies and Autobiographies,* by Marston Balch.

2. The reporter interviews one of the Allied leaders of World War II, and writes an article giving his impressions of the leader, and descriptive and biographical details about him. See *Inside Europe,* by John Gunther; *One World,* by Wendell Willkie.

3. The reporter sends his paper a dispatch about one of the most exciting events of the war years: the armistice, 1918; Pearl Harbor, 1941; the fall of Mussolini, 1944; "D-Day," 1944; attempted assassination of Hitler, 1944.

4. The reporter writes an article for a popular magazine contrasting the varied nationalities that live peacefully and constructively in the United States, with the discontented minority groups in European countries. See *Our Foreign-Born Citizens,* by Annie Beard; *Human Dynamite* (Headline Books), by the Foreign Policy Association.

5. The reporter investigates some of the great advances in medicine and surgery; blood plasma, " sulfa " drugs, penicillin, plastic surgery, artificial limbs, atabrine, chemical therapy. See *Miracles Ahead,* by N. V. Carlisle and F. B. Latham.

INTERESTING READING ABOUT WORLD WAR I
AND WORLD WAR II

Compton's Pictured Encyclopedia. See names of nations, and Index.

CURIE, EVE. *Journey Among Warriors.* " Nobody, *nobody* I had seen on the battlefields wanted to go back to the past."

GOULD, KENNETH. *Windows on the World.* The problems and controversies of modern times — communism, imperialism, industrial control and organization, cooperation, socialism, corporations, fascism — all are simply explained as a background for understanding the modern world.

GUNTHER, JOHN. *Inside Europe.* A vigorous and vivid political guide to Europe through personality portraits of the dictators, and analysis of social movements and political intrigues.

—— *Inside Asia.* This comprehensive story of Asia pictures outstanding persons, and the new forces and movements that are stirring Oriental peoples.

HOOVER, HERBERT C., and GIBSON, HUGH. *Problems of Lasting Peace.* Two famous men write of the forces that make for peace and war, and of some of the attempts at peace throughout history.

HORRABIN, JAMES F. *Atlas of Current Affairs.* Helpful, simple sketch maps show changes in frontiers, areas of conflicting interests, and the expansion of empire.

LIDDELL HART, BASIL. *The War in Outline.* A condensed, but clear and readable account of World War I.

LIPPMANN, WALTER. *United States War Aims.* The United States must accept its responsibilities as the center of the Western world if we are to secure a lasting peace.

MILLIS, WALTER. *Why Europe Fights.* An interpretation of events and forces which led from one great war in Europe to another.

STALLINGS, LAURENCE. *The First World War.* A fascinating photographic history of the drama, destruction, and futility of World War I.

WALLACE, HENRY A. *The Century of the Common Man.* " We of the United States who now have the greatest opportunity that ever came to any people do not wish to impose on any other race or to thrust our money or technical experts or ways of thought on those who do not desire them."

WELLES, SUMNER. *The Time for Decision.* " Our policy should aim to prevent, by means of international agreements, the recurrence of the monopolistic practices which existed in the period between the wars."

WILLKIE, WENDELL. *One World.* " Perhaps the most significant fact in the world today is the awakening that is going in in the East."

The World Book Encyclopedia. Articles on World War, and the names of individual nations.

Books of Fiction and Personal Narrative

HALL, JAMES NORMAN. *High Adventure.*

HEIDE, DIRK VAN DER. *My Sister and I.*

KANTOR, MACKINLAY. *Happy Land.*

MACINNES, HELEN. *Assignment in Brittany.*

NORDHOFF and HALL. *Falcons of France.*

PYLE, ERNIE. *Here Is Your War.*

—— *Brave Men.*

REMARQUE, ERICH MARIA. *All Quiet on the Western Front.*

RONALD, JAMES. *Old Soldiers Never Die.*

SHIBER, ETTA. *Paris-Underground.*

SHUTE, NEVIL. *Pied Piper.*

TREGASKIS, RICHARD. *Guadalcanal Diary.*

See also recent files or current issues of such magazines as *Scholastic, Time, American Observer;* and the *Public Affairs Pamphlets,* published by the Public Affairs Committee; *Headline Books,* published by the Foreign Policy Association and distributed by Silver Burdett Company; *World Affairs Pamphlets,* published by the Foreign Policy Association.

Appendix

What Maps Tell You

The first maps made by man were probably rude drawings scratched in the earth with a stick, in order to show a hunter or traveler how to get from one place to another. The earliest maps that have come down to us are charts of sections of Mediterranean coastline, showing harbors, inlets, rivers, and a few important trading towns. These charts were cut on small pieces of flat stone which could be carried easily.

As civilized men began to travel over more of the earth's surface, it became impossible for them to make a map of the known world which would be reasonably accurate in every way, even though their skill in map making had increased. The reason for their difficulty is: The earth is a sphere, and therefore it cannot be accurately represented *in every respect* on a flat map.

If you want to see just what kind of problem the map maker faces when he tries to make a flat map of the world, you can take a globe, a tangerine, a small paring knife, and a fountain pen and find out for yourself. First draw the outlines of the continents on the tangerine with your fountain pen, using the globe as a guide. (You can do this easily with a tangerine because the peeling of the tangerine is fairly dry. The peeling of an orange is too oily. You need not try to draw the continents too carefully.) Then cut a strip down one side of the tangerine and remove the fruit through this opening, section by section. From each end of the hollow tangerine peel, at the place corresponding to a pole, cut out a small piece of peeling, about the size of a dime. Then beginning at the place where you cut out the first strip, unroll the peeling and try to flatten it out against the table. You will find that in order to do so, you would have to stretch the top and bottom parts of it a great deal, so much so that the edges split. Something of this sort always happens in the making of a flat world map. Parts of the earth are drawn as if stretched out in comparison with other parts. Such a departure from the truth is called *distortion*.

There are different kinds of distortion. Noticeable distortion *of one kind or another* is present in all flat maps of the earth's surface or of any large portion of it. On a map of a small area, the distortion is so slight that it cannot be noticed.

We have said that a flat map of the world cannot represent the earth accurately *in every respect.* Different kinds of flat maps may be drawn that are distorted in different ways, while telling the truth in other ways. Some flat maps tell the truth in some respects, and some in others. Only a globe shows countries and oceans in their correct *areas* and *shapes,* and all places in their true *directions* and *distances* from one another. Any map can show some of these things correctly, but it can never show all four of them correctly at the same time — simply because it is a flat map. The different methods of representing the surface of the global earth on a flat piece of paper are known as different kinds of *projections*. In using any map, you should understand what kind of map it is so that you know what it tells you the truth about. It isn't possible to say that one projection is better than all others, because the choice of projection depends upon what you want your map to tell you the truth about; it depends upon the purpose for which you wish to use your map.

You may be wondering why men continue to make flat maps if they must all be inaccurate in one way or another. One or two reasons will occur to you right away. A flat map is easier to carry around than a globe. A flat map lets us see the whole world at one time, while on a globe, we can see only a little less than half the world at a time. Also, a map of a small part of the world can show more detail than the average globe can show. But there is still another reason for using flat maps. Strange as it may seem, although they will always tell some untruths, some of them can be more useful in certain ways than the globe itself. Let us study a few of the more common types.

Sailors like the mercator map. The world map that is probably most familiar to you is the kind shown on page 425. On such a map the countries in the extreme north and south latitudes, near the poles, are represented as much larger than they really are in proportion to other lands. Notice how large Greenland appears, as compared to the United States on a mercator map. If you look at a globe you will see that Greenland is actually much smaller than the United States. Are distances shown correctly on such a map? Obviously they cannot be. Distances are shown correctly at only one place — on the equator. The scale on this map warns you of that fact. Study this scale, notice its shape and see how, as the latitude increases, a greater and greater distance on the map is used to represent a fixed number of miles on the earth's surface.

We can see that the mercator is not a true-distance or a true-area map. What does it tell the truth about? It is sometimes called a *true-shape* map. This means that the shape *of a small area* anywhere on a mercator is the same as the shape of that area on the earth itself. The shape of a large land mass such as North America is somewhat distorted, of course, because the land is increasingly blown up as it extends northward from the equator. But generally, the mercator map gives a fair idea of the shape of the continents, as you can tell by comparing it with the globe.

Look again at our mercator map on page 425. You will see that the meridians are shown as *parallel* to one another. On the globe, as you know, the meridians meet at the poles. Can you tell from your study of geometry why the poles themselves can never be shown on a mercator map? You may remember that parallel lines never meet.

Notice, also, the spacing of horizontal parallels on the mercator map. You will find that the parallels are spaced *irregularly farther apart* as the eye moves from the equator toward one of the poles. This spacing has been carefully worked out by mathematics so that at any point on the map *the relation between a degree of latitude and a degree of longitude is just the same as it is on the earth's surface.* In other words a mercator map is a *true-direction* map, or a *true-angle* map. Sailors can set a constant (unaltering) course and chart it on such a map *by a straight line.* For this reason the mercator map has been used for years in navigation, and is sometimes called the sailors' map.

This type of map takes its name from Gerhard Kremer, a 17th Century map maker, who came to be called *mercator,* which is the Latin for merchant or trader. You may be curious to know that such a map is made by wrapping a cylinder of paper around a globe, *tangent* to the equator, and *projecting* the parallels, or carrying them forward, upon it like this:

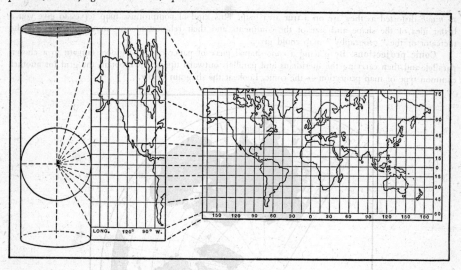

FIG. 1

The map is then modified so that the exaggeration of size near the poles will not be too great. The pattern of parallels and meridians upon which a map is drawn is called a *grid*. Get in the habit of noticing the grid on a map.

Equal-area maps or geography maps. We have said that different kinds of maps may be drawn so as to show different things correctly. A map which shows *areas* correctly can be drawn on a grid which is arranged on an *ellipse* that is twice as long as it is wide. (See Fig. 2, page 812.)

Any square inch anywhere on such a map corresponds to a fixed number of square miles on the earth's surface. Such maps are used to show the areas of different lands accurately. You have probably seen such maps, or variations of them, in your geography books. They are often used to show the distribution of populations or of different material resources throughout the world. Notice that the central meridian of such a map is straight and that those on either side of it curve outward, more and more sharply as they near the edge of the ellipse. *Shapes* are distorted on such a map. The lands near the center are shown almost correctly. Distortion of shape increases toward the edge of the map.

A compromise map. The reference map of the world at the back of your *Story of Nations* is a compromise between the sailors' map and a " geography " map. This map is not a true-angle map like the mercator, or a true-area map like a " geography " map. But since you will not be using it for navigating or for comparing distribution of resources or people, these things will not matter. The lands near the poles on this map are not *so greatly* enlarged as they are on the mercator map. And shapes are not

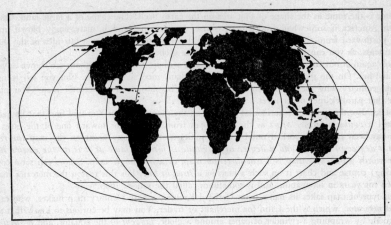

FIG. 2

so much distorted as they are on a true-area map. This kind of compromise map serves to give you a better idea of the shape and size of the continents and their relation to one another than either the mercator or the "geography" map could give.

Conic projections. By placing a cone-shaped piece of paper over the globe, tangent to a chosen parallel, and then carrying the meridians and parallels outward upon it, we obtain the grid for another common type of map projection — the conic. Look at the diagram below.

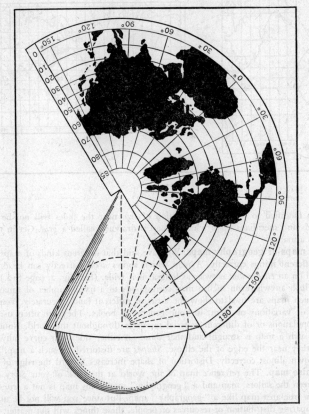

FIG. 3

Notice that the parallels are shown as arcs which have the same center, and that the meridians are evenly spaced radii of the pole. This kind of map will show accurately the regions near the chosen parallel. Both shape and size will be increasingly distorted north and south of this parallel. A more accurate map can be made by projecting the grid outward upon an interrupted cone, which is tangent to two chosen parallels, as shown in Fig. 4.

Such maps are practically true-angle and true-shape maps, and for small sections of territory make good aeronautical charts. ·

The maps on pages 220 and 644–645 were made on a variation of the conic projection.

"Equal-distance" global maps. One of the new polar-centered "airplane" maps, which is probably familiar to you, is shown here. (Fig. 5.) The projection on which this map is drawn is not new at all, but has been known for over three hundred years. It is more widely used now in the Air Age, when transpolar travel is becoming more practicable. This map shows vividly the air-route relations of the great nations of the world. The North Pole rather than the South Pole is usually chosen as its center because three-quarters of the earth's land surface lies in the northern hemisphere.

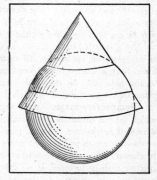

FIG. 4

Notice the grid of this map. Be sure to notice the scale also. It warns you that distances are shown correctly *only along the meridians*. Such a map is called *azimuthal equidistant*. *Azimuthal* is merely another term for direction. All places on this map are shown in their correct *direction from the central point of*

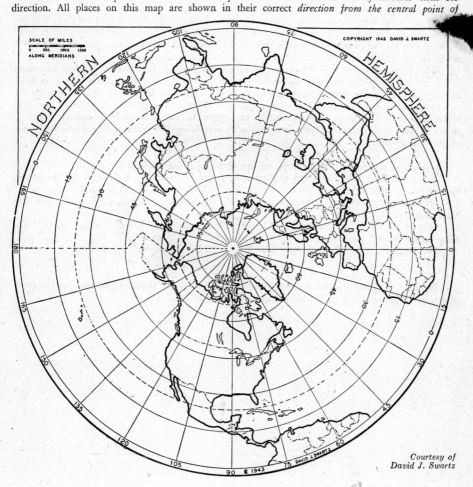

Courtesy of
David J. Swartz

FIG. 5

the map. In this limited sense it is a true-direction map. All *distances* from the center of the map are shown correctly too. This map has a particular advantage for aviators. Any straight line *passing through the pole* represents a great circle on the globe, and a *great-circle route* is the shortest distance between two points on the earth. The distortion is least near the center of the map, and greatest near its edges. Beyond the equator the distortion of shape and size becomes very great. That is why it is customary to show only the northern hemisphere on such a map. A similar map, centered on the South Pole, may be used to show the southern hemisphere.

An azimuthal equidistant map does not have to be centered on one of the poles. It may be centered at any place on the world. All distances and directions can then be shown correctly from that chosen place. Such a map could be centered on your home town. Then a straight line from your home town to any place else on the map would be part of a great-circle route, or the shortest distance to that place. Of course the grid on such a map looks entirely different when it is not centered on a pole.

Perspective maps. At the beginning of most of the Parts in *Story of Nations* you will find maps which give a distinctly global effect. These maps are not made on any projection whatever, but are *drawn in perspective.* That is, they are like a photograph of a part of a true sphere. It is not possible to show as much as half the earth's surface, or a hemisphere, on a perspective map. The most that can be shown on a perspective map at one time is a little less than a hemisphere. Like all flat maps, the perspective map is distorted. If we consider it *purely as a map,* the distortion of shapes and sizes of continents is fairly obvious. As the eye approaches the horizon line of the map, less and less space is used to represent a fixed number of miles. But this distortion will not mislead us, for the appearance of the map reminds us that it is drawn in perspective, that it is a *picture* of a part of the globe. We feel instinctively that the lands shown on the farthermost part of the map would appear larger if we could turn the globe and get a closer view of them.

cause these maps are drawn in perspective, the scale shown for them can be only approximate. not be absolutely accurate for every part of the map. But it will be close enough to accuracy to be useful to you, for these maps show only a rather small part of the earth's surface, and the distortion is not great.

Relief is not shown in scale. On Part-opening maps throughout your *Story of Nations* (see pages 2, 32, 50, for examples), the map maker has drawn mountain chains, plains, and valleys in relief in order to help you picture the countries which you are going to be reading about. Naturally the mountains are not drawn to scale. They would not show so distinctly if they were. The map maker has drawn in these features merely to suggest to you the kind of country which is shown in each map and to aid your imagination in visualizing the scenes among which the stories of the various nations unfold.

If you wish to read more about maps, see one of the following publications:

Airways to Peace: An Exhibition of Geography for the Future. The Bulletin of the Museum of Modern Art, 11 West 53rd Street, New York, 19, New York. 7 Volume XI, August, 1943. 25 cents.

Globes, Maps, and Skyways (Air-Age Education Series), by Hubert A. Bauer. New York. 1942. The Macmillan Company. 40 cents.

Look at the World, by Richard Edes Harrison. New York. 1944. Alfred A. Knopf. $3.50. "The Geographical Sense," page 10.

Life, August 3, 1942. "Maps: Global War Teaches Global Geography," pages 57–65.

Figures 1, 2, 3, and 4 in this Appendix were taken from *Globes, Maps, and Skyways,* by Hubert A. Bauer, with the permission of The Macmillan Company, publishers.

FIVE CENTURIES IN EUROPE AND AMERICA

Fifteenth Century — 1500 — Sixteenth Century — 1600 — Seventeenth Century — 1700 — Eighteenth Century — 1800 — Nineteenth Century — 1900 — Twentieth

1440 1450 1460 1470 1480 1490 1500 1510 1520 1530 1540 1550 1560 1570 1580 1590 1600 1610 1620 1630 1640 1650 1660 1670 1680 1690 1700 1710 1720 1730 1740 1750 1760 1770 1780 1790 1800 1810 1820 1830 1840 1850 1860 1870 1880 1890 1900 1910 1920 1930 1940

BRITAIN
Henry VI — Edward IV — Edw.V — Richard III — Henry VII — Henry VIII — Edw.VI — Mary — Elizabeth — James I — Charles I — Commonwealth — Charles II — Jas.II — Wm. & Mary — Anne — George I — George II — George III — Geo.IV — Wm.IV — Victoria — Edw.VII — George V — Edw.VIII

Hundred Years' War ends — Caxton's prints — Cabots explore North America — Reformation begins — "Invincible Armada" destroyed — Shakespeare — King James Bible — Harvey discovers circulation of blood — London Plague — Bill of Rights — Union England & Scotland — Isaac Newton — Industrial Revolution begins — gain control of India — U.S. free — Watt steam engine — power loom — spinning jenny — Union with Ireland — Waterloo — Stephenson locomotive — Faraday dynamo — Crimean War — from captured guns the Victoria Cross — Darwin Origin of Species — Irish Free State

FRANCE
Charles VII — Louis XI — Chas.VIII — Louis XII — Francis I — Henry II — Chas.IX — Henry III — Francis II — Henry IV — Louis XIII — Louis XIV — Louis XV — Louis XVI — Napoleon — Louis XVIII — Chas.X — Louis Philippe — 2nd Republic — 2nd Empire — Third Republic

extends France to Pyrenees — adds Brittany — France approximates present boundaries — Calvin leads Reformation in France — wars & persecution of Huguenots ended by Edict of Nantes — increasing power of kings — Richelieu strengthens crown — New France settled — empire arbitrary rule extravagance — peasants severely oppressed — Edict of Nantes revoked 50,000 Huguenot families emigrate — peak of extravagance immorality oppression — New France lost — Voltaire — balloon ascension by Montgolfier — First Republic — Revolution — Curie radium — Pasteur founds science of bacteriology — Daguerre takes photographs — Franco-German War — automobile — frequent changes in government reflect postwar difficulties

GERMANY
Frederick III — Electors of Brandenburg — Frederick William the Great Elector raises Prussia to greatness — Fred'k I first King of Prussia — Frederick William I — Frederick the Great lifts Prussia to equality with Austria — Fred'k Wm.II — Frederick William III — Fred'k Wm.IV — William I — William II — Republic — Nazi

Gutenberg — Luther Reformation — German Bible — Counter Reformation revitalizes Catholic Church — Thirty Years' War devastates Germany — Treaty of Westphalia — Bach — Partition of Poland — Goethe — Beethoven — Napoleon annexes coastlands — Bismarck — German Empire founded — Zeppelin — Diesel engine — Roentgen X ray — Munich

RUSSIA
Vasily II — Ivan III the Great — Vasily III — Ivan IV the terrible — Feodor I last of the line of Rurik — troublous times Polish rule — Michael I first of the Romanovs — Alexis — Peter the Great — Anne — Elizabeth — Catherine the Great — Alexander I — Nicholas I — Alexander II — Alex.III — Nicholas II — Communists

Constantinople falls Seat of Orthodoxy goes to Moscow — Mongols are still masters — throws off Mongol yoke — adopts crest of Byzantium — crowned as Tsar — St. Basil — expands empire — first Russian book printed — conquest of Siberia begins — serfdom legalized — Boyars powerful until Peter — looks west builds St. Petersburg expands empire changes dress of people — builds a fleet — adds another half million square miles — fathers "Holy Alliance" — Napoleon's invasion and disastrous retreat — Crimean War — emancipation of serfs—a hollow formality — Tolstoy — Trans-Siberian built — U.S.S.R. formed — 5-year Plan

SPAIN
Ferdinand & Isabella — Charles I — Philip II — Philip III — Napoleon subdues Spain — Alfonso XIII — Republic

Moors hold Granada — Aragon & Castile unite — Columbus sails — Inquisition — Moors conquered—then gradually expelled — Magellan — Loyola founds Jesuits — gold wealth laziness — Cervantes Don Quixote — destruction of Armada marks beginning of decline — Portugal separates from Spain 59 years after annexation — rigors of Inquisition abating — Gibraltar lost to England — vast American empire lost — War with U.S. — Cuba wins independence — civil war — Portugal a Republic

ITALY
CITY-STATES: Venice, Milan, Florence, Naples, Papal States — Long period of .... petty ducal houses ...... Italy a mere geographical designation ...... battleground for the rivalries of Spain, France, and Austria ...... Victor Emml.II — Humbert — Victor Emmanuel III

Turks take Constantinople — City-States lose trade and decline — Byzantine scholars flee to Italy — Savonarola prophet & martyr — Leonardo da Vinci artist engineer genius — Michelangelo — Galileo pendulum telescope — Papal States added to Napoleon's empire — unification under Cavour Mazzini Garibaldi — Garibaldi freedom from Austria — Rome capital — Triple Alliance with Austria & Germany — Marconi wireless — colonies in East Africa — Ethiopia — Fascists

LOW COUNTRIES
Charles V inherits Netherlands — period of conflict with Spain — Birth of Holland — trade with East Indies — found New Amsterdam — pendulum clock — decline in international prominence — Napoleon annexes Netherlands — Waterloo — Belgium wins independence — Queen Wilhelmina

Humanist Erasmus — Council of Blood — Rembrandt — Cape Colony — Leeuwenhoek microscope — open dikes against Louis XIV — Leyden jar — Cape Colony lost to British — Powers sign treaty promising to respect Belgian neutrality — Belgian colonial expansion in Africa — Zuider Zee reclamation

SCANDINAVIA
Reformation begins — Sweden leaves defense union — Gustavus Adolphus Swedish power at its height — Swedes colonize in New World — Linnaeus classifies plants & animals — Denmark cedes Norway to Sweden — Ørsted electromagnet — Andersen Fairy Tales — Ericsson screw propeller — Nobel — Ibsen — Grieg — Norway separates from Sweden — Amundsen finds South Pole

THE AMERICAS
Americo Vespucci America his namesake — Balboa finds Pacific — first press in New World—Mexico City — Portuguese colonized Brazil — first English colony in West Indies — Jamaica acquired by England — Jesuits expelled from Portuguese colonies from Spanish colonies — LIBERATION WARS REVOLUTIONS DICTATORSHIPS — Diaz rules Mexico with iron hand

Negro slavery — Cortés in Mexico — Pizarro despoils Incas — Inquisition brought to America — Toussaint l'Ouverture its heroes — von Humboldt explores Orinoco — San Martín — Bolivar — Texas secedes from Mexico — first Pan American Conference — Argentina & Chile pledge eternal peace — Immigration swells as it is restricted at the North

UNITED STATES
Columbus — Cabots come from England — Coronado brings the horse — St. Augustine oldest permanent settlement — Jamestown — Plymouth — Pennsylvania — Franklin lightning electricity — Independence Constitution — Monroe Doctrine — steamboat — cotton gin — telegraph — Confederacy — Edison incandescent lamp — Bell telephone — Wrights fly — Peary North Pole — Pacific cable — Panama Canal opened — Economic problems challenge people & government

WORLD WAR — WORLD WAR II

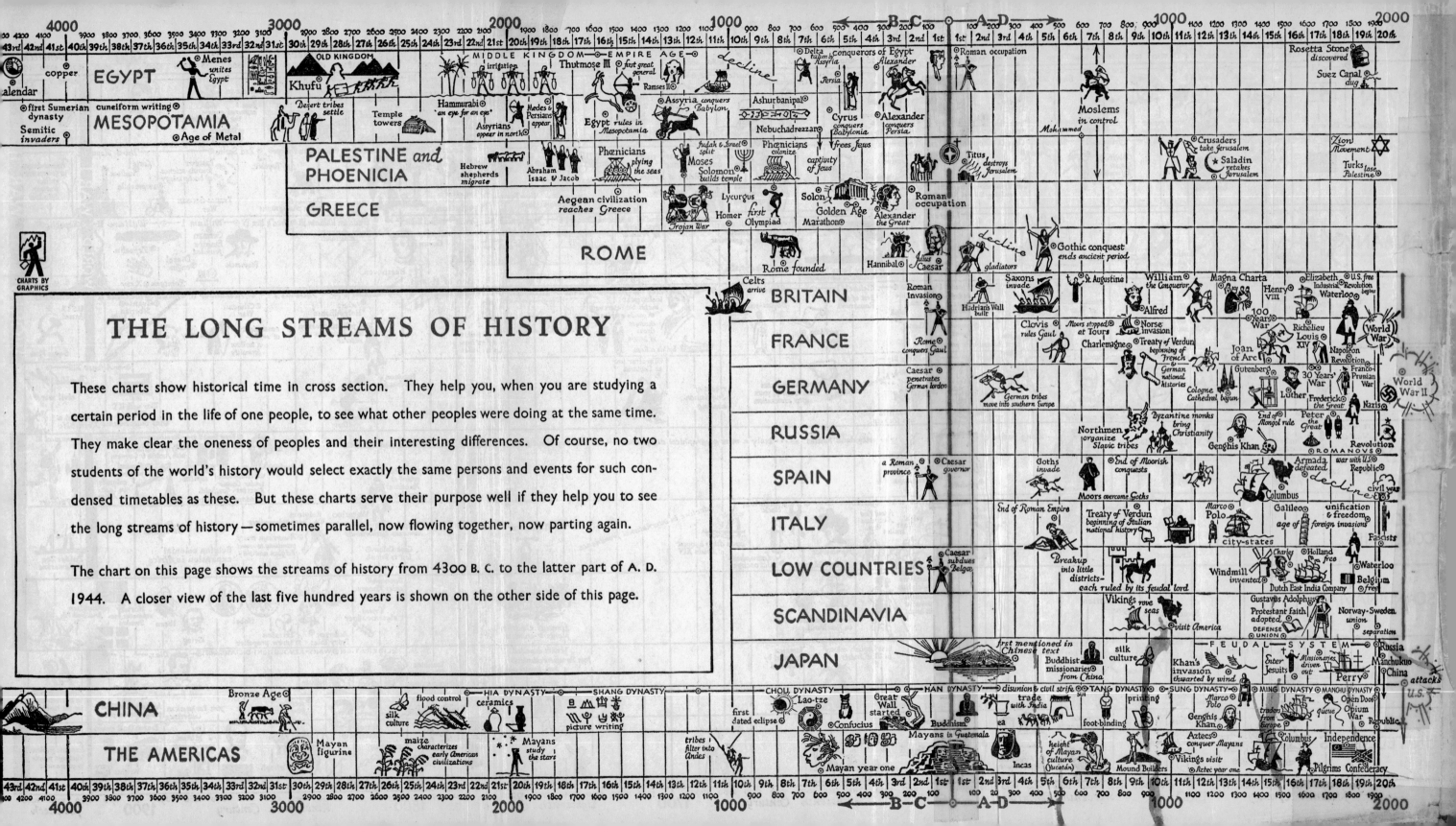

THE LONG STREAMS OF HISTORY

These charts show historical time in cross section. They help you, when you are studying a certain period in the life of one people, to see what other peoples were doing at the same time. They make clear the oneness of peoples and their interesting differences. Of course, no two students of the world's history would select exactly the same persons and events for such condensed timetables as these. But these charts serve their purpose well if they help you to see the long streams of history — sometimes parallel, now flowing together, now parting again.

The chart on this page shows the streams of history from 4300 B. C. to the latter part of A. D. 1944. A closer view of the last five hundred years is shown on the other side of this page.

CHARTS BY GRAPHICS

EGYPT

MESOPOTAMIA

PALESTINE and PHOENICIA

GREECE

ROME

BRITAIN

FRANCE

GERMANY

RUSSIA

SPAIN

ITALY

LOW COUNTRIES

SCANDINAVIA

JAPAN

CHINA

THE AMERICAS

Index

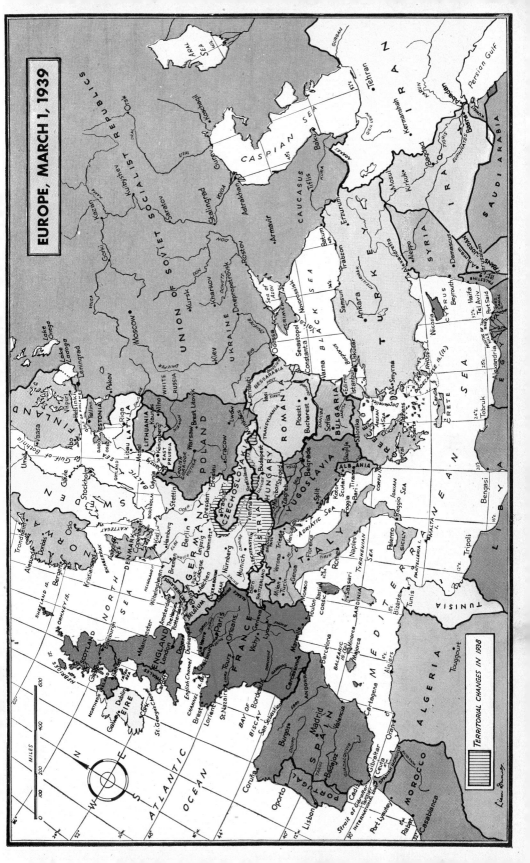

EUROPE, MARCH 1, 1939

TERRITORIAL CHANGES IN 1938

ARCTIC

GREENLAND

SEA

BARENTS SEA

SPITZBERGEN

FRANZ JOSEF LAND

NOVAYA ZEMLYA

80°

Baffin
Bay

DOMINION OF CANADA

60°

Hudson
Bay

LABRADOR

NEWFOUNDLAND

NOVA SCOTIA

ICELAND

FAEROE IS.

NORWEGIAN SEA

NORWAY

SWEDEN

FINLAND

UNION OF SOVI

SCOTLAND

BRITISH ISLES

NORTHERN IRELAND

EIRE

NORTH SEA

DENMARK

ESTONIA

LATVIA

LITHUANIA

NETH.

BEL.

GERMANY

POLAND

FRANCE

LUXEMBOURG

SWITZ.

AUSTRIA

CZECHOSLOVAKIA

HUNGARY

ROMANIA

YUGOSLAVIA

BULGARIA

Black Sea

Caspian
Sea

SINKIANG

TIBET

CHO

UNITED
STATES

NORTH ATLANTIC

OCEAN

PORTUGAL

SPAIN

ITALY

ALBANIA

GREECE

TURKEY

SYRIA

IRAQ

IRAN

AFGHANISTAN

INDIA

AZORES IS.

BERMUDA I.

SP. MOROCCO

Mediterranean
Sea

MADEIRA IS.

CANARY IS.

TUNISIA

EGYPT

SAUDI
ARABIA

Red Sea

Arabian
Sea

Bay
of
Benga

Gulf
of
Mexico

BAHAMA IS.

RIO
DE
ORO

ALGERIA

LIBYA

20°

MEXICO

CUBA

BR. HONDURAS

GUATEMALA

HONDURAS

NICARAGUA

COSTA RICA

PANAMA

JAMAICA

Caribbean Sea

PUERTO RICO

DOMINICAN REP.

Martinique I.

CAPE VERDE IS.

Dakar

PORT. GUINEA

GAMBIA

FRENCH WEST AFRICA

SIERRA LEONE

LIBERIA

GOLD COAST

NIGERIA

FRENCH EQUATORIAL AFRICA

RIO MUNI

ANGLO
EGYPTIAN
SUDAN

ITALIAN
EAST AFRICA

FR. SOMALILAND

BR. SOMALILAND

ADEN

LACCADIVE IS.

ANDAMAN
IS.

NICOBAR
IS.

CEYLON

MALDIVE IS.

VENEZUELA

BR. GUIANA

DUTCH GUIANA (SURINAM)

FRENCH GUIANA

COLOMBIA

ECUADOR

Natal

Ascension I.

BELGIAN
CONGO

KENYA

SEYCHELLE IS.

INDIAN

OCEAN

PERU

BRAZIL

BOLIVIA

St. Helena I.

ANGOLA

RHODESIA

MOZAMBIQUE

MADAGASCAR

20°

PARAGUAY

SOUTH
WEST
AFRICA

CHILE

ARGENTINA

URUGUAY

SOUTH ATLANTIC

OCEAN

UNION OF SOUTH
AFRICA

Cape of Good Hope

40°

Kerguelen I.

0° Panama Canal

Strait of Magellan

FALKLAND IS.

TIERRA
DEL FUEGO

Cape Horn

SOUTH GEORGIA

40°

20°

0°

20°

40°

60°

80°

60°

80°

SO. SHETLAND IS.

NORTH
GRAHAM
ISLAND

ANTAR

SCALE OF MILES ALONG THE EQUATOR

0   500   1000

THE WORLD, MARCH 1, 1939

AFRICA, MARCH 1, 1939

Liam Dunne

Legend:
- British
- French
- Italian
- Spanish
- Portuguese

EUROPE

ASIA

TURKEY

SYRIA · IRAQ · IRAN

SPANISH MOROCCO · Tetuan · Algiers · Tunis · TUNISIA
Casablanca · Oran · Tripoli · Bengasi · Alexandria · Cairo · SAUDI ARABIA · TRUCIAL OMAN

MADEIRA Is. (Port.)
CANARY Is. (Sp.)

MOROCCO · Colomb-Béchar · ALGERIA · LIBYA · EGYPT · Suez Canal · Persian Gulf

RIO DE ORO · SAHARA · YEMEN · ADEN PROTECTORATE · Gulf of Aden · SOCOTR (Br.)

CAPE VERDE Is. (Port.)
FRENCH WEST AFRICA · SENEGAL R. · NIGER R. · LAKE CHAD · ANGLO-EGYPTIAN SUDAN · Khartoum · Asmara · FRENCH SOMALILA

Dakar · GAMBIA · Bathurst · PORT. GUINEA · SIERRA LEONE · Freetown · Monrovia · LIBERIA · GOLD COAST · Accra · Kano · NIGERIA · Lagos · CAMEROUN · Yaounde · Addis Ababa · SOMALILAND · ITALIAN EAST AFRICA

Takoradi · Gulf of Guinea · RIO MUNI · FRENCH EQUATORIAL AFRICA · UBANGI R. · CONGO R. · LAKE ALBERT · UGANDA · KENYA · Nairobi · Mogadiscio · EQUATO

Brazzaville · Stanleyville · BELGIAN CONGO · LAKE VICTORIA · Mombasa · ZANZIBAR · TANGANYIKA · Dar es Salaam

Léopoldville · LAKE TANGANYIKA · LAKE NYASA

ASCENSION I. (Br)

ANGOLA · Nova Lisboa · ZAMBEZI R. · NO. RHODESIA · MOZAMBIQUE · MADAGASCAR · Tananarive

ST. HELENA I. (Br.)

Livingstone · SO. RHODESIA · ZAMBEZI R. · MAURITIUS · RÉUNION I.

ATLANTIC

SOUTH-WEST AFRICA · BECHUANA-LAND · LIMPOPO · Pretoria · Lourenço Marques

OCEAN · Johannesburg · ORANGE R. · VAAL R. · MOLOPO · Durban · BASUTOLAND · SOUTH AFRICA

Capetown · Port Elizabeth · Cape of Good Hope

INDIAN OCEAN

MILES
0 · 500 · 1000 · 1500 · 2000